A HISTORY OF
THE ENGLISH CORN LAWS
1660-1846

A HISTORY OF
THE ENGLISH CORN LAWS

FROM
1660-1846

By

DONALD GROVE BARNES, Ph. D.

REPRINTS OF ECONOMIC CLASSICS

Augustus M Kelley
New York 1961

Original Edition, *1930*
Reprinted, *1961*, by arrangement with Donald G. Barnes

TO
MY WIFE

CONTENTS

vii

CONTENTS

PREFACE

THE principal object in writing this book is to give a continuous narrative of the English Corn Laws from the Restoration in 1660 to the repeal of these laws in 1846. The history of the activities of the Anti-Corn Law League and of the repeal has been written often and well; but that of the Corn Laws before 1838, and even more before 1813, has been comparatively neglected. As far as I have been able to discover, only two works have been written which have attempted to cover the entire field. J. S. Nicholson, in his excellent little work *The History of the English Corn Laws*, has sketched the history of these laws from the fifteenth to nineteenth century from the point of view of the consumers, the producers, and the interests of public policy. Mary A. M. Marks, in *The Corn Laws: A Popular History*, has subjected these regulations to an extremely hostile criticism. Unfortunately this book is out of print, and very few copies are available. The comparative neglect of the earlier phases of this subject is noteworthy because several outstanding works have appeared in recent years on the Chartist movement, which paralleled the final years of the agitation against the Corn Laws.

The emphasis in this study is placed upon public opinion. An attempt is made in the case of each law passed and of each measure agitated to determine what social forces and classes favoured or opposed the proposal. The operation of the different laws, or groups of laws which made up a system, is also studied both from the point of view of contemporary opinion and from such statistics as are available for each period. But this is a history of the Corn Laws and not of the corn trade, and hence no attempt is made to describe either the internal or external grain trade. Both aspects have been treated for certain periods of the years from 1660 to 1846 in able monographs: the internal by Westerfield in *Middlemen in English Business, Particularly Between 1660 and 1760*; and the external by Galpin in *The Grain Supply of England during the Napoleonic Period*. Since the expression of opinion is emphasized, the sources of which the widest use is made are Parliamentary debates, reports of select committees of Parliament, pamphlets, periodicals, newspapers, and even the preambles of laws. The great majority of the several hundred pamphlets examined are in the British Museum, the Goldsmith Library in London, and in my own collection.

It may occasion some surprise in the course of the narrative that greater use is not made of the published memoirs and private papers of the prominent statesmen, and of the Home Office Papers. The memoirs and correspondence are valuable principally for the light they throw on the attitude of the various ministers, at the time when different corn bills were considered by the government, and on the reasons for certain minor points being introduced in the resolutions upon which a bill was to be based. There is seldom anything in the correspondence of these statesmen, except compromises on details between two or more members of the ministry, which cannot be found at greater length elsewhere. Since the size of this volume does not permit a lengthy account, in most instances, of the drafting of the numerous corn bills, this source of information has been of comparatively little value. The Home Office Papers are useful in this study principally for the light which they throw on the food riots in periods of scarcity; but in most cases these riots are described at greater length in pamphlets, newspapers, and periodicals. In general these disturbances were more or less alike and hence nothing is gained by giving a detailed account of each one. Further, the Home Office was interested in affairs of this sort chiefly from the point of view of law and order; whereas, in this study, the interest lies in the causes for the scarcity which produced the riots, and in the remedies suggested and carried out for alleviating these conditions.

A brief summary at this point of the principal phases and chief chronological divisions of the history of the Corn Laws from 1660 to 1846 may be of some assistance to the reader in finding his way through the detailed chapters.

The laws governing the corn trade, both before and after 1660, fall naturally into three divisions: those regulating the internal trade; those regulating exportation; and those regulating importation. Before 1660 the laws covering all three of these phases were, in the main, administered in the interests of the consumers: the activities of the corn dealers were closely checked; exportation was forbidden when prices of grain rose above fixed levels; and importation was seldom restricted. After 1660 the producer received fully as much consideration as the consumer. Practically all restrictions on the activities of the internal corn trader were removed by the law of 1663, although the menace of indictment under the common law was not removed until 1800. But much more important changes were also made in the laws governing importation and exportation. By the law of 1670 importation was regulated by a sliding scale of duties which varied according to the price of the different kinds of grain; and by the law of 1689 exportation was facilitated through the payment of a bounty when the price of the various sorts of corn fell below certain levels. These two laws, and subsidiary ones, made up a system which was based on the principle of helping the producer to dispose of his surplus when the price of grain was low and of keeping out foreign imports until the price was high. Before 1660 the regulation of the internal grain trade and of exportation was important, and that of importation relatively insignificant. After 1660 (1663 to be exact) the regulation of the internal trade sank into the background; that of importation became of greater but not of first-rate importance; and that of exportation, particularly in the seventy-five years following the passing of the bounty act of 1689, was easily the most significant phase of the corn trade.

These three phases of the regulation of the corn trade when considered chronologically may be divided into three periods in which different ideas of social justice prevailed. Numerous minor exceptions can be made to all three of these divisions, but that does not seriously impair the value of the generalization. Down to 1660 the interests of the consumer were primary; from 1660 to 1814–15 a price fair to both producer and consumer was most important ; and from 1814–15 to 1846 the interests of the producer were given first consideration.

All three phases, however, do not receive equal emphasis in the periods following 1660. From 1663 to 1800 the regulation of the internal corn trade receives only occasional consideration, and after that date none at all. From 1689 to 1765 exportation is most important, from then until 1814 it shares this position with importation, and after that date it is of no further interest. Importation from 1814 to 1846 is the only phase that is treated. A few words on the arrangement by chapters of these principal phases and divisions may also be useful to the reader. Chapter I is a brief sketch of the Corn Laws to 1660, and is based almost entirely upon secondary works. Chapters II to V, inclusive, take up the formulation of the policy of a sliding scale of duties on imports and of a bounty on exports from 1660 to 1689 ; and the history of this policy down to abolition of the bounty in 1814 and of the sliding scale of duties in 1815. Chapter VI gives a short account of the enclosure movement, particularly from 1765 to 1815. Like Chapter I, it is based on secondary authorities. The only contribution made is in showing the relation of this movement to the later history of the Corn Laws. Chapters VII to X, inclusive, deal with the attempt of the landed interest to maintain, first, an exorbitant rate of protection until after the law of 1822, and then a more reasonable one, especially after 1828. Chapters XI and XII take up the familiar story of the activities of the League and the actual repeal in 1846. Chapter XIII gives a summary of the volume on a larger scale than the brief outline in this preface, a review of my own opinions on all important aspects of the Corn Laws, and an estimate of the results of free trade in grain since 1846.

I have received assistance and advice from many sources. First and foremost I am indebted to Harvard University for granting me travelling fellowships for the years 1920 to 1922, which enabled me to gather the material for this volume. Professor Harold J. Laski suggested the subject to me in 1920. Mr. R. H. Tawney, during the year 1920–21 when I was a student in the London School of Economics, and Professor J. H. Clapham, during the year 1922, when I was a student in King's College, Cambridge University, made many valuable suggestions. Sir William Beveridge courteously permitted me to make use of his unpublished researches dealing with the price of grain in England for the years 1660 to 1770. Miss Bertha Putnam and my sister, Miss Viola Barnes, both of Mt. Holyoke College, gave the first draft of my manuscript a thorough criticism. My colleagues at the University of Oregon read the manuscript at different stages and offered many helpful suggestions. Dean H. D. Sheldon, Professor Dan E. Clark, and Mr. Pat Morrissette read every chapter ; and Professors C. V. Boyer and Andrew Fish, chapters one, three, six, seven, nine and thirteen. The Research Committee of the University of Oregon generously granted me money to have source material copied and the manuscript typed. My wife spent a great deal of time in reading proofs and checking quotations.

A HISTORY OF THE ENGLISH CORN LAWS FROM 1660 TO 1846

CHAPTER I

THE CORN LAWS BEFORE 1660

Corn Laws regulate the internal trade, exportation and importation—Market development from the twelfth to the eighteenth centuries—Interests of the consumer considered primary—History of the regulation of the internal trade —Governmental regulation of exportation—Of importation—Underlying causes for the policies of the government in all three phases—Status of the three kinds of Corn Laws in 1660.

THE English[1] Corn Laws[2] had a long and intricate history before 1660 which can be understood only as a part of the general economic policy of the country. These laws regulated three distinct phases of the grain traffic :[3] the internal trade, exportation and importation. The ones best known are those governing importation during the first part of the nineteenth century, yet in the period down to 1660 importation was of less significance than the internal trade and exportation. All of these laws, naturally, were influenced by economic and political conditions, and by ideas of social justice prevalent at the time that they were promulgated. It is possible to treat these acts for the entire period from the point of view of consumer, producer and government ;[4] or to take up separately the three phases listed above, as will be done in this chapter, and attempt to show the underlying causes that will explain the different policies.

Perhaps nothing furnishes a better background for considering the internal trade, exportation and importation than the market development down to the eighteenth century.[5] In the manorial marketing system, during the period following the Norman Conquest, one manor would supply the deficiencies of another, and in years of exceptionally good crops the surplus would be exported. As towns of importance grew up within the kingdom, the local market system gradually evolved. With the decline of the inter-manorial marketing system, came the development of a local system and corn policy which were adapted to the necessities of the growing industrial and commercial communities.[6] After 1500 the development of the metropolitan or London market was the decisive factor. During the sixteenth century corn went to London for consumption only, but after 1600 it was sent for export as well.[7]

Under the manorial marketing system, and even under the local, it was inevitable that the regulation of the internal trade should be more

B   I

important than either exportation or importation. Long before the national government intervened action was taken by localities to prevent persons from monopolizing or cornering the food supply. The means of transportation were so primitive that each manor, or group of manors, or borough, relied upon what was produced in the locality, and hence competition from the outside was difficult. In addition to, and perhaps partly because of, this condition, it was believed in the mediæval period that commodities should be sold at " just " or reasonable prices. The just price varied according to circumstances, but anyone who charged more than was deemed reasonable was violating moral law. In case the expressed disapproval of religious teachings and the force of public opinion proved inadequate, local municipal regulations, and later national laws, were passed to prevent anyone from cornering the market or charging high prices.

The practices which aroused the most complaint were known as forestalling, engrossing and regrating. According to the act of 1552, which merely reproduced earlier acts and even local regulations, a forestaller was one who bought, or caused to be bought, any merchandise or food-stuffs or any other thing whatsoever, coming by land or water toward any market, fair, city, port, haven, creek, or road of England or Wales, or from beyond the sea ; or contracted for, or in any way by motion or word, enhanced the price, or dissuaded anyone from bringing any of the above mentioned to market. A regrator was a person who bought provisions in a fair or market and resold any part of them in any fair or market within a distance of four miles. An engrosser was one who obtained possession of grain or other food by buying or contracting for them before harvest, with the intention of selling again. The penalties were, for the first offence, two months' imprisonment and forfeiture of the value of the goods ; for the second, six months' imprisonment and forfeiture of double the value of the goods ; and for the third, forfeiture of all property, punishment in the pillory, and imprisonment during the King's pleasure. [8]

In the municipal regulations and in the statutes it is clear, first, that the interests of the consumers rather than the producers were being protected ; and second, that corn was merely one of the commodities that was jealously guarded against the monopolists. Furthermore, laws against forestalling, regrating and engrossing were not the only ones favouring the consumers. The assize of bread, which fixed the weight or size of the loaf according to the price of corn, and laws compelling landowners to convert sheep farms into arable land, are additional evidences of this same concern for the consumers on the part of the government.

The regulation of the exportation of grain, if not as significant as that of the internal grain trade under the manorial and local marketing system down to about 1500, became equally important after that date. The policy as a whole shows no consistent purpose during the three hundred years before 1660. At one time exportation would be forbidden in order to ensure cheapness and plenty for the consumer ; and at another time it would be permitted in order to help the producer to dispose of a surplus. Again this phase is interesting because of the light that it throws on the constitutional struggle between the Crown and Parliament. The King claimed the right of granting licences to export, but Parliament attempted to restrain this practice. The relative power of the two, during the three centuries before 1660, is shown, roughly, by the variations in the licensing power. Edward III. resisted the attempts of the Commons to prevent him from issuing licences, but with the increase in the power of Parliament at the end of the fourteenth, and during the greater part of the fifteenth centuries, the export trade came to be regulated more and more by statute. Under the Tudors the growing power of the Crown led to an increase in the use of licences and to the restricting of exportation by order in council. Charles I. attempted to use the royal power in this direction, as well as in many others, and thus helped to bring on the Civil War.[9]

In the law of 1437, an important innovation was introduced which permitted the exportation of wheat without a licence, if the price did not exceed 6s. 8d. a quarter.[10] This principle was adhered to in practically every act dealing with exportation down to 1814. As late as 1555 these terms of the law of 1437 were renewed;[11] but eight years later the price level, below which exportation of wheat was permitted without a licence, was raised to 10s.[12] This marks the recognition by the government of the rapid rise in prices after about 1550. Successive acts advanced this price level higher and higher: in 1593 it was fixed at 20s.;[13] in 1604 at 26s. 8d.;[14] in 1624 at 32s.;[15] and in 1656, during the interregnum, and again in 1660, at 40s.[16]

The laws of 1563 and of 1571 were strongly mercantilistic. The navy was to be strengthened by the merchant marine, which was to be increased in order to carry corn from England to other nations. For this reason exportation was to take place only in vessels belonging entirely to English-born subjects. The preamble to the act of 1571 stated that its purpose was " For the better encrease of Tyllage and for mainteinance and encrease of the Navye and Marioners of this Realme."[17]

Clearly no fixed principles or policy characterize the laws regulating exportation from the fourteenth century to 1660. The laws passed during this period are too numerous and contradictory to make possible any sweeping generalizations. Nevertheless, " it is evident that there were three changes of policy, alternating between prohibitions and permission of exportation. Corn export was prohibited either almost completely, as by the law of 1361, or only partially as in that of 1534. Or exportation was permitted (a) by general licence as by the law of 1394, (b) under certain price maxima as by the laws of 1437, 1555, 1559, 1563, 1593, 1604, 1624, 1627, 1656, 1660 and 1663, (c) by the provision that prices were to be reasonable before export might take place, as by the law of 1571 . . . "[18]

Before the Restoration the regulation of the importation of foreign grain was less important than that of the internal grain trade and of exportation. This, doubtless, was due to the fact that during most of the period the country produced more than enough grain for her own needs. The only act of real significance dealing with importation

before 1660 was that of 1463. The preamble stated that " the
Labourers and Occupiers of Husbandry within this Realm (of
England) be daily grievously endamaged by bringing of Corn out of
other Lands and Parts into this Realm (of England) when Corn of the
growing of this Realm is at a low Price."[19]   In order to protect the
producer it was forbidden to import wheat, rye, or barley, unless the
prices were above 6s. 8d., 4s., and 3s. a quarter respectively at the
place of purchase.[20] This act was not repealed until 1624 ; but it was
of no real importance after 1550 because of the rise of prices, and
because even before that time its influence was questionable.   Perhaps
nothing gives a fairer index of the comparative indifference to the
question of the importation of foreign grain than this paucity of
legislation.

For this apparently contradictory and unrelated legislation on the
internal trade, exportation, and importation it seems, at first sight,
as though no satisfactory explanation of the underlying causes could
be offered.   Sometimes it is assumed that all three were the result of
mere opportunist policies on the part of the government.   But it
is not impossible to reconcile underlying causes with opportunist
actions.   To those who emphasize the constitutional development,
the government policies on all three phases fit in the struggle between
Crown and Parliament.   Faber expresses this point of view in the
following summary : " Up to 1394 the crown managed the corn trade
for its fiscal advantage ; thenceforth parliament, gaining the upper
hand, introduced a mercantile policy ; the early Tudors, victorious
over parliament, reverted to the fourteenth century policy, while
Elizabeth beneficently re-introduced the mercantile policy ; Charles I.
rode rough-shod over this policy, substituting one of restraint, the
licensing system ; the Civil War, however, brought the mercantile
system to the front again, a system which the Restoration parliaments
carried to its fullest developments."[21]

Gras, however, believes that such an explanation fails to show the
relation that these changes bore to the actual corn trade, which, he
holds, are to be found in the market development described earlier
in this chapter.   As long as the manorial marketing system was
functioning satisfactorily, no national corn policy was necessary.
The King, like other feudal lords, collected toll on the internal corn
trade in his territories, and later seized upon the export trade as a
source of revenue.   When the growth of towns caused the development of the local market, it brought in a new interest, the consuming
area along with the manorial producers and the Crown.   The policies
of these three interests had little in common, and it was the work of
Parliament to reconcile them.   The Corn Laws of the fourteenth and
fifteenth centuries represent the compromise of the three.   At the end
of the period the policy was, in normal years, to allow exportation on
the payment of a duty as long as prices were at a moderate level, and
when above, to permit importation.   In an emergency the regulation
of the trade was left to the Crown.[22]   The enormous growth of London
in the sixteenth century, caused partly by the enclosure movement,
marks the third stage in market development—that from a local to a
metropolitan market.   The demand for grain was so great in London

that the officials used every precaution to prevent any being sent abroad. A long series of petitions to the government and an almost equally long series of proclamations in favour of stopping exportation show to what a considerable extent London dictated the Tudor corn policy.[23] Thus the statutory policy of the government is of little significance in the sixteenth century. It represented on the one hand the mercantilist aims of the government, and on the other, the views of the corn-producing area. Yet it was not followed, because the price levels of the laws regulating exportation were too low, and because the Crown constantly overrode the laws by proclamations and orders in council.[24] From 1600 to 1660 London was not so importunate in pressing its export policy on the government, partly due to the fact that the government had already adopted it, and partly that the available corn supply was greater. Thus the country had adjusted itself to the metropolitan market, and London now found it possible to export part of the corn which was poured in from the grain producing districts.[25]

In conclusion, what was the status of the regulations governing the internal grain trade, exportation and importation in 1660 ; and what was the status of the corn policy as a whole ? The laws governing the internal trade were extremely significant in both the local and metropolitan market periods. They were passed largely in the interests of the consumers, and were only one phase of a series of regulations passed for that purpose. Those concerned with forestalling, engrossing and regrating were revived about 1550, when the influx of American gold and silver brought about a rise in prices, and whenever a temporary scarcity caused an advance in the cost of grain. But on the whole, by 1660 the day of internal regulations was over. The elaborate paternal bureaucracy of the Tudors with the Privy Council and the local Justices of the Peace had aroused the resentment of the English people when it was continued by the Stuarts. In 1641 this elaborate machinery, which might have served to enforce such regulations as those on the internal corn trade, was abolished and was not restored in 1660. Even if it had been restored, it is unlikely that these regulations would have survived. The coming economic thought was based upon mercantilism and not upon internal restrictions.

The laws regulating the exportation of corn were originally passed to secure cheapness and plenty for the consumers ; but in the fourteenth and fifteenth centuries, when the price levels permitted, they often enabled the producer to get rid of a surplus. From about 1500 to 1660 the laws are not significant, because during the greater part of the period, particularly after 1550, the rise in prices made exportation under the price levels of the acts in operation practically impossible ; and because the real governmental policy is to be found in the acts of the Privy Council and not in the statutes. With the breakdown of the conciliar government in 1641, and with the increased importance of the landowners in both national and local government after the Restoration in 1660, this statutory system of restricting exportation in the interests of the consumers had no future.

The laws regulating importation had almost no past in 1660, but they were to have a wonderful future. The only act of any significance—that of 1463—was obsolete because of the rise in prices long before it was repealed in 1624. This slight regulation of the import trade was certainly advantageous to the consumer from the fourteenth to the seventeenth century, for in 1660 there was no real statutory restriction to importation. On the other hand, it must be remembered that England produced more than enough grain for her own needs.

Down to 1660 the Corn Law policy—internal, export and import—was largely in the interests of the consumer and public policy. The consumer profited by the elaborate regulation of the internal trade, by the restrictions on exportation, and by the slight regulation of importation. Public policy included questions of morality such as the attempt to enforce a " just " price, the right of the Crown to issue licences and thus abrogate the law, revenue, and questions of national power such as the mercantile system. The producer was given much less consideration. Freedom to export and protection against imports when the price was below certain levels, and the right of purchasing a licence to export at other times, were small concessions in comparison with those given consumers, especially when the rise in the price level is taken into consideration.

In 1660 the real history of the elaborate regulation of the internal corn trade, the shadowy statutory regulation of exportation during the previous century and a half, and the strange neglect of the regulation of importation, were all drawing to a close. Within a few years after 1660, epoch-making changes were made in all three of these phases.

CHAPTER I

NOTES

[1] After 1707 these laws should, to be strictly correct, be called *British* Corn Laws instead of *English* Corn Laws ; but the latter term has become so well established by usage that any attempt to change it would only result in confusion.

[2] Corn is used in the English sense of grain. It includes wheat, oats, rye, barley, malt, peas, beans and maize ; and should not be confused with American corn or maize.

[3] Laws regulating the measures to be used in grain and ordering pasture lands to be put in corn again will not be treated under Corn Laws.

[4] Nicholson, in *The History of the English Corn Laws*, 1904, has followed this plan.

[5] See Gras, *The Evolution of the English Corn Market*, 1915.

[6] *Ibid.*, pp. 212–13.   [7] *Ibid.*, p. 242.

[8] 5th and 6th Edward VI., c. 14.

[9] Nicholson, *op. cit.*, pp. 107–8.

[10] 15th Henry VI., c. 2.

[11] 1st and 2nd Phillip and Mary, c. 5.

[12] 5th Elizabeth, c. 5, sect. 17.

[13] 35th Elizabeth, c. 7, sect. 5.

[14] 1st James I., c. 25, sect. 203.

[15] 21st James I., c. 28, sect. 384.

[16] 12th Charles II., c. 4, sect. 11.

[17] 13th Elizabeth, c. 13.

[18] Gras, *op. cit.*, pp. 146–7. The acts of 1670, 1673 and 1689 were omitted at the end of this quotation because they cover a period beyond the limits of this chapter. Gras points out that the laws regulating exportation from 1361 to 1689 may be arranged in nine groups. The seven included in the limits of this chapter are as follows : " The first consists of the law of 1361 prohibiting export. The second is the law of 1394 permitting export. The third is the law of 1437 establishing machinery for regular uninterrupted export. The fourth is the statute of 1534 which prohibited unlicensed export. The fifth contains the three acts of 1555, 1559 and 1563 which restored the Lancastrian maximum price clause of the law of 1437. The sixth is the law of 1571 allowing export when prices were reasonable. The seventh group is the largest of all. Beginning with the act of 1594 and ending with that of 1663, it restored the price provision of the third and fifth groups." (p. 146).

[19] 3rd Edward IV., c. 2.   [20] *Ibid.*

[21] Gras, *op. cit.*, p. 210.   [22] *Ibid.*, pp. 210–17.   [23] *Ibid.*, p. 225.   [24] *Ibid.*, pp. 229–30.   [25] *Ibid.*, p. 244.

CHAPTER II

THE RESTORATION CORN LAWS

Revolutionary changes in all three kinds of Corn Laws after 1660—Government now favours the producer—Act of 1663—Act of 1670—Bounty acts of 1673 and 1689—English agriculture from 1689 to 1750—Influence of good and bad crops, wars, value of money, improvements in agriculture, and the Corn Laws of 1670 and 1689 upon the price of grain and the size of the exports—Statistics on exportation—Lack of general interest in the Corn Laws—Failure of the government to provide machinery to administer these laws—Crude system of administration.

In the years following the Restoration, the policy of the government in dealing with the importation and exportation of grain, and with corn dealers, underwent a decided change. Until this period the government was chiefly concerned about the consumer, and restricted exportation, and allowed importation to prevent scarcity. After 1660 the exportation of grain was encouraged instead of discouraged, and importation was permitted only when a certain price was reached. This price was changed from time to time, and was intended to represent a point above which the producer no longer required protection. Thus the laws passed now favoured the producer by keeping out imports and encouraging exports. However, those who favoured this policy argued that the consumer was also benefited, since he was assured of a steady supply at a reasonable price. The preambles of Tudor statutes expressed the same eagerness " for the better encrease of Tyllage " as did those of the Restoration period; but the statutes themselves did not give the producer either a monopoly of the home market or a bounty to aid him in exporting the surplus.

There is no explanation for this change which meets with general agreement among the writers on the period. Gras ascribes it to the fact that Restoration Parliaments appreciated, as the preceding governments had not, the great developments in the first half of the seventeenth century and framed the national policy in accordance with the new market conditions.[1] Cunningham believes that it was due to the initiative of the new blood injected into the landowning class as a result of changes in ownership during the period of the Civil Wars and Protectorate.[2] The destruction of the power of the Privy Council in 1641 and the failure to revive it after 1660 gave the Cavalier Parliament (1661–79), in which the gentry predominated, the chance to inaugurate a policy favourable to their own interests. This same Parliament passed the Navigation acts in the interests of the commercial rather than the agricultural class; but later Parliaments also cheerfully passed laws for the benefit of the trading class, provided these measures did not infringe upon the interests of the landowners.

The first step in the policy of encouraging the producer came with

the act of 1663.   The preamble stated the desirability of such a policy
on the grounds that the encouragement of tillage was the surest means
of promoting trade ; and that great quantities of land, which might
be improved if sufficient encouragement were given, were at the time
lying idle.   The sentiment expressed is practically the same as that
of the Tudor statutes, but the steps taken to put it into operation
show a decided change.   The Tudor method, as we have seen, was to
encourage production by permitting the exportation of grain unless
the price exceed a limit fixed by law.   This plan was retained in the
act of 1663 and the price level fixed—48s. for wheat, 32s. for rye, peas
and beans, 28s. for barley, malt and buck-wheat, and 13s. 4d. for
oats—was merely the highest point reached in a long series of acts
passed since 1555.   The section of this act dealing with importation
is of much greater significance.   A duty was placed on all grain
imported when the prices mentioned above were not exceeded.   In
the case of wheat this duty amounted to 5s. 4d.[3] The principle of
excluding foreign grain when the price in England was below a certain
level had been applied in the act of 1463, and violation of this provision was punishable by forfeiture of the cargo so imported ; whereas
the law of 1663 merely placed a duty on imported corn.

A third part of this act represents a reaction against the earlier
restrictions on the activities of corn dealers, since it made lawful
the buying of grain in the open market to store and sell again, on
condition that the prices did not exceed the level given in the earlier
provisions of the act, and that the person so buying did not sell the
grain again in the same market within three months' time.   Adam
Smith holds that this law " with all its imperfections has perhaps
contributed more both to the plentiful supply of the home market,
and to the increase of tillage, than any other law in the statute book.
It is from this law that the inland corn trade has derived all the liberty
and protection which it has ever enjoyed ; and both the supply of
the home market, and the interest of tillage, are much more effectually
promoted by the inland than either by importation or exportation
trade."[4]   This statement is undoubtedly an exaggeration, as both
contemporary and modern writers have shown, and was due, perhaps,
to his desire to prove the harmfulness of the bounty given by the
act of 1689.   Even the liberty extended to the corn dealers was not
an innovation, since the same concession was granted by the act of
1552 when the price of wheat did not exceed 6s. 8d. a quarter.[5]
These terms were continued by temporary acts and made permanent
by the law of 1571 ; but it is very questionable whether they afforded
any relief to the corn dealers because the rise in prices in the sixteenth
and early seventeenth century kept the value of wheat well above
6s. 8d.[6]

Even greater encouragement to the producer of grain was given by
the act of 1670, which, the preamble stated, was " for the further
Encouragement of Tillage for the common good and welfare of this
Kingdom."   Exportation was now to be permitted at all times on
condition that the export duty be paid.   The section dealing with
importation was of greater significance.   For the fixed duty of the
act of 1663 a sliding scale of duties varying with the price of grain was

substituted. In the case of wheat, when the price did not exceed 53s. 4d. a quarter, the duty was 16s. ; when it was above 53s. 4d. and below 80s., the duty was 8s. ; and when above 80s., the duty was 4d. as fixed by the act of 1660.[7] Thus the producer was practically guaranteed a monopoly of the home market when the price was below 53s. 4d. ; and he was protected by a substantial duty above that price.

To the concessions already made to corn growers of exporting grain without restriction, provided that the export duty was paid, and of cutting down importation by heavy duties, a third was now added. By an act passed in 1673[8] a bounty was granted on grain exported, and export duties were remitted, when the price did not exceed a certain level. These provisions are to be found in a statute entitled, " An act for Raising the Sum of 1,238,750 pounds for the Supply of His Majesties Extraordinary Occasions." The bounty sections of this act were known and evidences of its workings cited in the great controversy waged in the last half of the eighteenth century over the effects of the bounty on the production of grain ; but after that time knowledge even of its existence was, apparently, lost until its re-discovery by Professor Gras.[9] Nearly all histories still refer to the act of 1689 as inaugurating the bounty policy, but clearly that of 1673 takes precedence.

Under the terms of this law exportation of grain was permitted from any port where the price of wheat did not exceed 40s. a quarter ; of rye, 32s. ; and of malt or barley, 24s. A bounty of 5s. on wheat, 3s. on rye, and 2s. 6d. on barley and malt was granted on all such grain exported to a foreign country in a ship in which the master and at least two-thirds of the crew were English. Every person shipping grain in this manner was to bring a certificate to the customs officials of the port where exported, specifying the quality and quan-tity shipped, which must be sworn to by one or more credible persons. Furthermore, the exporter was compelled to give a bond of £200 for every hundred tons shipped. He was released from this bond only when he presented trustworthy evidence to the customs commissioner that the grain in question had been landed in a foreign country, taken by the enemy, or lost at sea. The customs commissioner at the port where the grain was shipped was to pay the exporter from the receipts of the customs as soon as the corn was loaded and the certificate and bond received. Evidently it was deemed unnecessary to secure proof of the delivery of the corn to a foreign port before paying the bounty since the bond protected the commissioner against fraud in that direction.[10]

This act of 1673 was to remain in operation until May 13th, 1678, but the debentures show the actual enforcement lay between the years 1674-5 and 1680-1, Michaelmas to Michaelmas in each case.[11] During these years about £150,000 were paid out in bounties and, combined with the expenses of war, this expenditure proved too great a drain on the treasury. As a result the act was not renewed, but it served as an admirable precedent in 1689 when the low price of grain again caused distress among the landowners.[12]

Nothing in the entire history of the Corn Laws aroused a greater controversy than the act of 1689 which re-established the bounty on grain exported. This applies to both causes and results, but particularly to results. Contemporary evidence on the reasons for passing the law is rather meagre. It seems to have been one of the measures of minor significance which was lost sight of in the stirring events following the " Glorious Revolution." Most of the explanations offered for the granting of the bounty came in the second half of the eighteenth century when the effect of the measure on English agriculture was warmly debated. Arthur Young maintained that it was a reward to the landed interest for their efforts in placing the crown on the head of William III.[13] Dalrymple stated that it was given to the Tories " in return for their consenting to a land tax."[14] Comber held that " In the most favourable view of the origin of the measure, we cannot but regard it as the result of a convention between the government and the landed interest, to which the commercial body, though materially affected by it, were not parties."[15] Among modern writers Cunningham has taken the position that it was a Whig measure passed to foster agriculture so that the landed interest would be able to contribute to the expenses of the local and national government.[16] Gras has pointed out that the low price of grain and the precedent of 1673 offers the most plausible explanation for the renewal of the bounty.[17] The price of wheat had fallen to 21s. 11d. at Michaelmas of 1688 in Oxford, and to 23s. for the year in Windsor. This fall in price combined with the frank statement in the preamble of the act that experience had justified the bounty when prices were low, seems to substantiate the conclusion of Gras.

The act of 1689 was clearly based on that of 1673. Even the phraseology in the sections following the preamble are almost identical. Briefly stated, a bounty of 5s. on wheat, 3s. 6d. on rye, and 2s. 6d. on barley or malt, was to be paid by the commissioner to the exporter for every quarter of grain shipped, if the price at the port did not exceed 48s. for wheat, 32s. for rye, and 24s. for barley or malt.[18]

Although this act aroused little comment at the time it was passed, or even for a great many years thereafter, nevertheless, after 1750 it was continually either praised as evidence of the highest statesmenship or derided as a bit of stupid governmental interference. Because of this difference of opinion it is necessary to examine carefully the development of the production and exportation of grain during the period that this act was in operation. After 1765 the period from 1689 to 1765 came to be represented as the golden age of English agriculture, particularly for the wheat grower.

Probably the most important factor in determining the price of grain during these years was the size of the crop in each district. The means of communication were so poor before the age of canals and turnpikes, which began about the middle of the eighteenth century, that it was almost impossible to ship grain from a locality where the crops were plentiful to one less favoured. As a result there was a wide variation in the price of grain. Even in the metropolitan market, which had developed earlier to supply London, this same rule applied. The districts which furnished her with grain were restricted principally to the eastern and southern coasts, and to the upper Thames Valley.

Since the importation of foreign grain was almost negligible, the quantity and quality of the crops in this region played a large part in fixing the price in the London Market.

Unfortunately there are no national averages dealing with the price of grain before 1771. Figures used before that date are taken from records of Eton College in the Windsor Market and from Lloyd's *Prices of Corn in Oxford*. The Windsor table is merely an average of the price of wheat for the two market days before March 25th and September 29th ; and the Oxford table of the price at Michaelmas. Such averages seem, at first sight, inadequate for making generalizations on the price of grain for England as a whole. But recent and more extensive investigations by Sir William Beveridge have shown that the average price for wheat of middling quality over a considerable part of England between the years 1660 and 1770 was practically the same as the average for Windsor and Oxford. In order to get middling quality prices he has reduced the Oxford rent prices from Lloyd by eight per cent. and the Windsor rent prices from Tooke by nine per cent. The variation in price for single years between his figures and those of Windsor and Oxford is, in some instances, unusually great ; and in every case, apparently, this difference cannot be explained away entirely by local harvesting conditions. The results of his researches, however, clearly justify the use made of the Windsor and Oxford tables both by pamphleteers of the eighteenth and nineteenth centuries and in the present study.[19] It is well known that a slight deficit or surplus advances or lowers the price of a commodity a great deal more than the actual per cent. of the deficit or surplus. To-day with a world market a deficit in one place is filled by a surplus from another ; but in the England of the Restoration period, owing to the poor system of communications, this was impossible.

Thus in estimating the increase in the production of grain down to 1750, due consideration must be given both to the size and quality of the crops year by year, and to the amount exported. A collection of reports on weather conditions during these years throws considerable light on the variations in price and exportation figures.[20] On this basis the years from 1689 to 1750 can be divided into two periods : 1689-1714 and 1715-1750. Down to 1714 prices tended to be high and exports low, due, in all probability, to the unusual number of defective harvests. The act of 1689 had been passed, judging by the rather scanty evidence available, to find a market for a surplus created by a series of good crops. But soon after the law went into effect, a succession of bad harvests tended, to a considerable extent, to render it inoperative. After 1715, however, a period characterized by steadily-increasing exports and few short crops set in. Only in the years 1727-29 and 1739-40 were serious complaints made about the high prices and scarcity of grain, and they evidently were due to rainy summers[21] and a cold winter.[22] With the exception of these two brief periods exports increased steadily during the years following 1715 and reached their highest point in 1750.

But despite the steady increase in the export figures from 1715 to 1750 the period was not one of quiet and complacent contentment as

it has been pictured so often by later writers. The old fear of starvation, with its centuries of tradition, was aroused in many parts of
the country by this very exportation. Such fears were generally
stronger in the northern and western sections of the country than in
the wheat districts of the east and south coasts. In 1727 the tinners
in Cornwall plundered the granaries on the ground that the scarcity
was due to exportation.[13] Even in the period of unusually low prices
from 1730–39 there are many instances cited in the *Gentleman's
Magazine* in which mobs plundered corn dealers or prevented exportation. By an act which went into operation on June 24th,
1738, heavy penalties were inflicted upon anyone who used violence
in hindering another person from buying grain, or prevented the
transportation of grain to a market or seaport.[14] But this feeling of
discontent was not confined to the consumers. Whenever the price
of wheat fell, as in the years 1731–33 and 1743–45, serious complaints
arose from the landed interest. Thus the increased production of the
period, accompanied by lower prices and additional exportation, did
not bring entire satisfaction to either producer or consumer.

So far, stress has been laid on the quality and quantity of the crops
in determining the price of grain and amount exported. Other
factors that have to be reckoned with are wars, the value of money,
and the improvement in agriculture. It is usually argued that war
raises the price of grain, as well as of other commodities, both by
causing the levying of taxes which enhance the cost of production, and
by the extraordinary demands of the army and navy which raise the
price of provisions. These two factors may have kept the price of
grain higher during the war years from 1688 to 1713 ; but it is doubtful if they had any influence on prices in the Wars of Jenkins' Ear
and of the Austrian Succession from 1739 to 1748, since England had
become an exporter of grain. Any increase in the cost of production
and in price of grain because of the extraordinary demands of the
army and navy were more than offset by the cutting off of the continental markets to which the English were accustomed to send their
surplus. Dividing the years from 1688 to 1750 into alternate war and
peace periods we find that the price of wheat was actually higher in
times of peace than of war.[15] These figures, however, must not be
accepted as absolute proof, since they represent only the prices at
Eton for two market days during the year and do not take into account
the good and bad harvests.

It is not easy to estimate the effect of the value of money on the
price of grain during the period covered by this chapter because the
statistics of the amount in circulation, which make such a study much
easier at a later time, are not available. Probably the reform of the
coinage in the sixteen-nineties,[16] which naturally caused a temporary
scarcity in money, prevented the price of grain from rising higher at
the time. It is now commonly held that prices in general were rising
in England from the sixteenth century, when the precious metals
from Spanish-America began to affect the price level, down to the
Peel Bill of 1819. This contention is contrary to the opinion of
Adam Smith who ascribed the fall in price of grain in the first half of
the eighteenth century to an appreciation in the value of silver, on

the ground that the influence of the American mines in depreciating the value of silver had ended by 1636.[27]   If prices were rising in the first half of the eighteenth century, then the fall in the price of grain during that period must be accounted for in some other way.   It may also be concluded that rising prices prevented a greater fall in the price of grain.

The effect of improvements in agriculture during the first half of the eighteenth century on the increased production and exportation of grain may be overestimated.   The significance of these improvements on the future of British agriculture is difficult to exaggerate, but the effect was not, as a rule, felt until after 1760.   Probably the individual who made the greatest contributions was Jethro Tull, yet his own experiences show how firm was the resistence to improvement from both farmers and agriculture labourers.   As one writer states, " the chief legacies which Jethro Tull left to his successors were clean farming, economy in seedings, drilling, and the maxim that the more the irons are among the roots the better for the crop.   It was along these lines that agriculture advanced.   On open-field farmers who sowed their seed broadcast, thickly and at varying depths, Tull's experiments were lost.   Equally fruitless, so far as his immediate neighbours were concerned, was his demonstration of the value of sainfoin and turnips, or the drilling of wheat and roots.   Even his system of drilling roots was neglected in England, till it had been tested and adopted in Scotland."[28]

It was only when large landlords, of whom Lord Townshend of Raynham in Norfolk was the best known, threw themselves enthusiastically into the task of improving their estates that real progress was made.   Townshend was especially interested in improvements in the rotation of crops, and in the field cultivation of turnips.[29]   So successful was he in improving his estates that his methods were adopted by other landlords and farmers.   But even the fame of Townshend, as well as the financial rewards which he and other landlords reaped, was not sufficient to produce an immediate and widespread adoption of these changes in the technique of farming.   " Outside Norfolk, the landlords and farmers still classed turnips with rats as Hanoverian innovations, and refused their assistance with Jacobite indignation.   Even in Townshend's own county, it was not till the close of the century that the practice was at all universally adopted ; still later was it before the improved methods were accepted which converted Lincolnshire from a rabbit-warren or a swamp into cornfields and pasture."[30]   Clearly it is a mistake to place too much emphasis on the improvements in agriculture, in trying to account for the increased production and exportation of grain, simply because the work of the pioneers was so noteworthy.

Having estimated the effect of good and bad crops, wars, value of money and improvements in agriculture on prices and exports of grain, the question of the part played by the acts of 1670 and 1689 must be considered.   We have seen that the size and quality of the crops were the most important factors in determining both the price and surplus for export, but that war might prevent exportation and by causing a fall in price discourage increased production.   Also, that the fall in the value of money may have prevented the further fall in the price of grain, but in all probability had little influence on production. Improvements in agriculture were more significant for the second half of the eighteenth century than for the first half, and hence the effect on the increased production of wheat is apt to be exaggerated. The act of 1670 limited the importation of grain, but during most of this period England was exporting and not importing and hence this regulation played an unimportant part in increasing production. The same, however, cannot be said for the bounty act of 1689. Disregarding the question of the wisdom of the bounty, which will be dealt with at greater length in the next chapter, there is no doubt that the policy did increase the production of wheat and other grain by widening the market. That the amount of wheat grown increased enormously in the first half of the eighteenth century cannot be denied. The increase seems to have been absorbed by the rapidly-developing export trade and by the greater use of white bread by the lower classes. As Lord Ernle states, " Under the spur of the bounty, land which had been converted to pasture was again ploughed for corn, and proved by its yield to have profited by the prolonged rest. . . . Wheaten bread ceased to be a luxury of the wealthy, and, at the accession of George III. had become the bread-stuff of half the population."[31] No attempt can be made to estimate the proportionate influence of the bounty act of 1689 on this increased production, but certainly it was very significant.

Thus far, continual reference has been made to the increased exportation of grain in the first half of the eighteenth century, and the figures themselves show this increase to have been of great importance. Until after 1711 the annual average exportation of wheat did not reach 100,000 quarters, and only in 1703, 1706 and 1707 were the figures that high for a single year. For the years 1712–15 the yearly average mounted to 170,000 quarters, but fell again from 1716–21 to about 80,000. During the next five years the average rose to nearly 190,000, but the bad harvests of 1727 and 1728 practically stopped exportation. In 1733 over 400,000 and in 1738 over 500,000 quarters were shipped out of the country. The decade of the seventeen-thirties was one of large exports, the average for the years 1731–39 being well over 300,000. The bad harvest of 1740 and the War of Austrian Succession, however, caused a slump which did not end until 1748. One writer insists that the War did not seriously interfere with exportation because of a system already in existence. By this system the English exporter contracted to deliver to the French, on the one side, certain quantities of wheat at a fixed price, and to purchase from the English farmers, on the other, certain amounts at a stipulated price regardless of the market price of wheat. This practice was not, according to the writer, interrupted by the War of Austrian Succession, in which the English and French were on opposite sides, for in 1747 the French contracted for 400,000 quarters.[32] Most of this wheat seems to have gone to the manufacturing cities of northern France. But whether or not the War was responsible, the exportation of wheat declined during the years 1742–47 to an average of 270,000 quarters.

The four years beginning with 1748 were unquestionably the

banner years with an average of practically 700,000 quarters ; and
the highest point was reached in 1750 when 950,000 quarters were
exported.   After this year the figures steadily declined except
during the years 1759 to 1764 which will be taken up later.   The
export of rye, barley, or oatmeal did not attain important dimensions at any time from 1689 to 1750 ; but that of malt reached
practically the same figures as wheat.   Malt was made from both
wheat and rye, but by all odds the greatest part was made from
barley.   However, the figures are open to suspicion because of the
frauds practised in exportation.   Malt was said in some cases to have
been steeped until swollen to ten times its original bulk in order to
secure the bounty.   These fraudulent practices will be dealt with
more fully in the next chapter.   From 1697 to 1750 roughly 10,000,000
quarters of wheat, 2,000,000 of rye, 90,000 of oatmeal, 2,000,000
barley, and 10,000,000 of malt were exported.

Despite the great amount of grain exported nothing could be more
erroneous than the idea that the Corn Laws of 1663, 1670, or even
1689, were of primary national interest down to 1750.   Almost no
mention is made of them during the reign of Charles II., or at the time
of the Revolution of 1689.   The period from 1660 to 1750 abounds in
economic tracts and pamphlets, and yet not one, apparently, is
devoted entirely to the Corn Laws.[33]   There are scores dealing
with commerce, manufacturing, and improvement in agriculture, but
none exclusively with the corn bounty or the restriction on importation.

Interest in the Corn Laws seems to have been aroused only in times
of scarcity when the consumers in London and in the mining and
manufacturing districts of the north and west rioted.   The government, evidently, was sensitive to public opinion as expressed in food
riots and was careful to stop the exportation of grain whenever prices
rose to a point indicating scarcity.   In 1698 exportation was prohibited for a year ;[34] in 1709, until September 29th, 1710 ;[35] and in
1740, until December 25th, 1741.[36]   In addition, the bounty paid on
the exportation of grain was suspended from February 9th, 1699,
until September 29th, 1700.[37]   But the government took action only
when forced to do so by an alarming advance in price.

Another proof of the inaction of the government and of the absence
of any widespread interest in the Corn Laws is the fact that no
machinery was provided for the administration of the acts of 1670
and 1689.   The law of 1670 levied duties of 16s., 8s. and 5s. 4d. when
the price of a quarter of wheat at the place of importation was less
than 53s. 4d., between 53s. 4d. and 80s., and above 80s. respectively.
However, no means were provided by the act for determining the
price at the port of entry.   No attempt was made to remedy this
omission until 1685 when an act was passed to provide such machinery
on the grounds that its absence had resulted in the importation of
great quantities of grain without the duty being paid.   This situation,
the preamble stated, was " contrary to the true intent and meaning
of the said act."[38]   By this law of 1685, Justices of the Peace in every
county where corn was or might be imported were required, beginning
September 29th of that year, to determine at their respective Quarter
Sessions after Michaelmas and Easter the common market prices of

middling English corn and to send a copy of such prices to the chief officer or collector of customs in each port, where it was to be posted in some public place in the customs house. The Justices of Peace were to determine these prices by the oath of " two or more Honest and Substantial persons of the respective Counties being neither Merchants nor Factors for Improving of Corn nor any ways concerned nor interested in the Corn so Imported," and who had either a £20 freehold or a £50 leasehold and were " skilful in the Prices of Corn." Some freedom of action was left to the Justices for they were permitted to use " such other ways and means as to them shall seem fit." London was excepted from this general rule and prices were to be fixed there by the Mayor, aldermen and Justices of the Peace in the months of April and October. Here, likewise, it was to be done on the oaths of substantial housekeepers living in Middlesex or Surrey and not on those of corn chandlers, mealmen, factors and merchants.[39] Both in London and in other ports the prices so fixed were to continue for six months. This act, as will be subsequently shown, was never actually carried out.[40]

The same absence of machinery characterizes the act of 1689, whereby a bounty was to be paid on wheat, rye, barley or malt, when the prices were at or above 48s., 32s. and 24s. respectively. Despite the fixing of this price level the law contained no regulation for determining the price at the port of exportation. Furthermore, no machinery for determining the price was in existence at the time. The act of 1685, even if it had been enforced, applied only to foreign grain imported and not to British grain exported. Article VI of the Act of Union between England and Scotland in 1707 gave a bounty of 2s. 6d. on beer or bigg,[41] and on oatmeal when the price at the time of its exportation from Scotland was at or under 15s. In the same year the bounty was extended in England to include beer or bigg, and malt made from wheat. But in neither of these two instances was any regulation made for determining the prices at the ports of exportation.

No attempt was made to remedy the non-enforcement of the law of 1685 until 1729. The necessity for some new enactment was ascribed to the fact that many Justices of the Peace had neglected to fix the price of corn at the quarter sessions and to return certificates for the customs officers. Failure to do so had caused great loss " to the revenue, and detriment to the farmer and fair trader."[42] The act directed that all Justices of the Peace who neglected to fix the price at the first quarter sessions after Michaelmas should, at the following sessions, determine what the price had been at that time. The customs officers were to act as though the price had been actually set at the proper time, and all grain imported since the first day of the Michaelmas quarter sessions, upon which the duty was not paid, was to be forfeited. If in the future Justices of the Peace neglected to certify the prices, customs officers were to allow the importation of foreign grain upon payment of the lowest scale of duties fixed by the act of 1670.

This act of 1729 also dealt with the exportation of grain. It provided that, in the future, any grain exported according to the

c

act of 1689 should be measured by the customs officers. Furthermore, going on the erroneous assumption that the means of determining the prices of imported grain applied to prices of grain exported, this act of 1729 extended the application of the law of 1685 to ascertain the prices at which beer or bigg, oatmeal, and malt made of wheat, could be exported. Thus there was a method, though an ineffectual one, of determining the prices in accordance with which the duties on imported corn, and the bounty on beer or bigg, oatmeal and malt made of wheat, should be paid.[43] But this method did not extend to wheat, rye, barley and malt exported under the terms of the bounty act of 1689.

Evidently the supplementary act of 1729 proved as ineffective as that of 1685, for three years later a further change was made in the mode of ascertaining the prices governing the importation of foreign grain. After June 1st, 1732, the Justices of the Peace in quarter sessions were to charge the grand jury to determine by inquiry the common market prices of middling corn according to the act of 1670.[44] This law of 1732 expressly stated that the change was made to prevent fraudulent importation, and hence it did not extend to any of the bounty acts.

Thus there was no legal means of determining the prices of grain exported under the terms bounty act of 1689. Accordingly, the customs officers adopted a rule of their own, whereby they obliged the exporter to swear that the corn entered for exportation did not exceed the bounty price on the last market day. Since this was not sufficient authorization for a bounty debenture, or even for allowing exportation, the officers fell back on the formula in *Crouch's Compleat Guide to the Officers of his Majesty's Customs*, which directed that, " if the officers are satisfied that the respective prices of corn do not exceed the limitations for the bounty (which they are careful to inform themselves of from market day to market day, remembering that they must be accounted for as at the time of shipping and not of entry) and the exporter has given the collector a certificate under his hand, containing the quantities and qualities of the corn so shipped."[45] This procedure was not only unauthorized but was actually contrary to the laws governing duties on importation, for the act of 1685 stated that the persons taking oaths respecting the price of corn must not be, in any way, concerned or interested.

Clearly the administration of the Corn Laws down to 1750 left much to be desired. There were no laws for determining the price of grain at ports of exportation, and those for regulating importation were ineffective. The methods pursued in both were unsatisfactory and open to frauds.

In summarizing the period from 1660 to 1750 we find that the government by passing the laws of 1670 and 1689 sought to help the producer ; and that these acts, particularly that of 1689, were one of the factors in the improvement of agriculture and the increased exportation of grain. On the other hand, we also find that these Corn Laws did not arouse any great interest either in Parliament or in the pamphlet and periodical literature of the period ; that Parliament did not provide any effective machinery for determining the price of grain exported and imported ; that the local officials made no attempt to properly administer these laws ; and that they did not prevent fluctuations in price and hence did not do away with the alternate complaints of the producer and consumer.

Is it possible to reconcile these two groups of conclusions ? Clearly these laws were passed for a certain purpose, and the results by 1750 had been, by no means, a failure. Why, then, was no further interest shown in Parliament or current literature ? It may be argued that the Corn Laws were functioning in a satisfactory manner, and their acceptance was so general that there was no object in discussing them. But this conclusion implies that effective machinery for its enforcement was provided and that local officials were conscientious in discharging their duties. Yet, as we have seen, only three attempts were made to provide this machinery, and forty-four years elapsed between the first and second. All three of these laws failed because the unpaid Justices of the Peace were neither competent nor willing to administer them properly. It is impossible to blame the Whigs, whose interests were more commercial than agricultural, for this neglect. The gentry were well represented in the unreformed House of Commons, and undoubtedly a vigorous protest against the failure to provide machinery would have resulted in speedy action by the government. Also the gentry when acting as Justices of the Peace neglected to enforce the laws which, apparently, had been passed in their interest. Failure to enforce the laws that sought to regulate the importation of grain is easy to understand since the amount was negligible, but failure to administer vigorously the laws that provided a bounty on exportation is more puzzling.

Perhaps the most plausible explanation is that the laws regulating the importation and exportation of corn were accepted, as a matter of course, by both the landed and commercial interests as a part of the mercantile system. In all probability the Corn Laws were administered in much the same fashion as other parts of the system. In the same manner the fluctuation in the price of grain from year to year seems to have been looked upon as the normal condition. The variation in the quality and quantity of the crops from season to season, along with the poor system of communications before the construction of the turnpikes and canals of the second half of the eighteenth century, made alternate high and low prices inevitable.

The question naturally arises why the Corn Laws, which were so little discussed before 1750 and whose shortcomings were accepted as a matter of course, sprang into prominence as a public question after that date. This will be dealt with in the next chapter.

CHAPTER II

NOTES

¹ Gras, *Evolution of the English Corn Market*, p. 250.
² Cunningham, *The Growth of English Industry and Commerce*, vol. 2, p. 540.
³ 4s. for rye, peas and beans ; 2s. 8d. for barley and malt ; 2s. for buck-wheat;
and 1s. 4d. for oats.
⁴ Adam Smith, *The Wealth of Nations*, I., p. 34.
⁵ 5th and 6th Edward VI., c. 14.
⁶ Gras, *Evolution of the English Corn Market*, p. 153.
⁷ 22nd Car. II., c. 13, sect. 1 and 2.   ⁸ 25th Car. II., c. 1, sect. 31.
⁹ *Quarterly Journal of Economics*, XXIV, pp. 419–22.
¹⁰ 25th Car. II., c. 1, sect. 31.
¹¹ Gras, *Evolution of the English Corn Market*, p. 145 and Appendix G.
¹² *Ibid.*, p. 253.
¹³ Arthur Young, *Political Arithmetic*, edition 1774, p. 29.
¹⁴ Sir John Dalrymple, *Memoirs*, vol. 1, p. 372.
¹⁵ Comber, *An Inquiry into the State of National Subsistence*, edition 1808, p. 133
¹⁶ Cunningham, *The Growth of English Industry and Commerce*, vol. 2, pp.
541–2.
¹⁷ Gras, *Evolution of the English Corn Market*, p. 253, and note 254.
¹⁸ 1 W. and M., C. 12.   An Act for the encouraging the Exportation of Corn.
" Forasmuch as it hath been found by Experience, That the Exportation of
Corn and Grain into foreign parts, when the price thereof is at a low rate in this
Kingdom, hath been a great advantage not only to the Owners of Land, but to
the Trade of this Kingdom in General :
" Be it :—enacted by . . . That when Malt or Barley Winchester Measure, is,
or shall be at 4 & 20s. per quarter, or under ; Rye at 2 & 30s. per quarter, or
under ; & Wheat at 8 & 40s. a quarter, or under ; in any part or parts of this
Kingdom, or Dominion of Wales : Every Merchant or other Person, Who shall
put on Shipboard in English Shipping, the Master, & Two Thirds of his Mariners
at least, being Their Majestie's Subjects, any Sorts of the Corn aforesaid, from
any such Posts where the Rates shall not then be higher than as aforesaid, with
Intent to Export the said Corn to Parts beyond the Seas : Every such Merchant
or other Person shall bring a certificate in Writing under his or their hand, containing the Quantity & Quality of Corn so Shipped, to the Farmers, Commissioners, Collectors, or other Persons appointed, or to be appointed, for the time
being, to collect the Duties & Rates arising by Customs within any such Post, &
upon proof made of any such Certificate by one or more credible Person or Persons
upon their Oaths, Which Oaths the said Commissioners, or other Persons are
hereby Authorized & Required to Administer, & upon Bond given by every such
Merchant or other Person, in the Sum of Two hundred pounds at the least for
every hundred Tuns of Corn so Shipped, & so proportionably that the said Corn
(Danger of the Seas excepted) shall be Exported into Parts beyond the Seas, &
not be again Landed in the Kingdom of England, Dominion of Wales, the Islands
of Guernsey and Jersey, or Town of Berwick upon Tweed : Every such Merchant
so Shipping off any of the aforesaid Corn, & giving Certificate & Bond as aforesaid,
shall have & receive from such farmers, Commissioners, Collectors, or other
Persons in any Post respectively, where the same Corn shall be so shipped, for
every quarter of Barley or Malt ground or unground 2s. 6d. ; for every quarter
of Rye ground or unground 3s. 6d. ; for every quarter of Wheat ground or unground, 5s. ; Which Sum or Sums, every such Commissioner, Farmer, or other
Person, are hereby Authorized & Required upon Demand by such Exporter, to
make present payment of accordingly, Without taking or requiring anything for
Custom, or any Fee or Reward for Corn so Laden to be Exported, or for so much
Grain as shall be exported in any Ship wherein any other goods shall be Shipped ;

Any Law, Statute, or Usage in any wise to the contrary notwithstanding : & upon Certificate returned under the Common Seal of the Chief Magistrate in any Place, or Places beyond the Seas, or under the Hands & Seals of Two known English Merchants upon the Place, that such Corn was there Landed, or upon Proof by Credible Persons, that such Corn was taken by Enemies, or perished in the Seas, the Examination & Proof thereof being left to the Judgment of such Commissioners, Farmers, Collectors, or other Persons ; which Proof being made, or Certificate Delivered to such Person or Persons respectively, as took Bond as aforesaid, the said Bond shall be delivered up to such Importer or his Order, to be Cancelled, without any fee for the same ; And the Moneys by any such Commissioners, Farmers, Collectors, or other Person, so paid in Obedience to this Act, shall be accepted of in his or their Accompts, as so much paid to Their Majesties and he and they is and shall be Discharged therefore accordingly."

[19] The averages of Sir William Beveridge, unpublished at this time (June, 1929), are based mainly on the prices of corn of middling quality in Exeter, Winchester College, Oxford, Windsor, London, Cambridge, Nottingham, Shrewsbury, York, Portsmouth, Canterbury and Maidstone. The measure used in computing these averages is the Winchester quarter of eight bushels.

In the narrative, through the year 1770, the prices of wheat cited in Oxford and Windsor tables will, likewise, be those of the Winchester quarter of eight bushels. The Oxford prices are taken from Lloyd, *Prices of Corn in Oxford*, and the Windsor ones from Appendix C of the *Speech of George Rose in the House of Commons, May 5th*, 1814. Consequently these prices will not coincide with those for the imperial quarter cited in Appendix B.

[20] The following table is a collection of odd bits of testimony on the weather and nature of the crops from 1689 to 1750. It is based on narrative found in Tooke's *History of Prices*, vol. 1 :

1680–92.	" Twelve years of favourable seasons and low prices, with the exception only of one year, viz., 1684, in which, judging by a reference to the price, there seems to have been a somewhat deficient crop." Pages 25-6.
1692.	" Great rains in autumn ; an earthquake was felt in England, and in most parts of Europe."
1693.	" A very wet summer ; . . . "
1694.	" A very wet summer."
1695.	" Many of the Scotch are driven into Ireland by the excessive price of corn."
1696.	" A very wet summer . . . "
1698.	" A very wet summer. Great complaints are made of the dearness of provisions and the decay of trade."
	" These cold and wet seasons lasted more than seven years ; the dismal effects of famine were felt in most parts of Europe." Pages 30-1. Quoted from *An Inquiry into the Prices of Wheat, Malt, and occasionally of other Provisions, as Sold in England from the Year 1000 to the Year 1765*.
1699.	" Now begins the first of several hot summers." Page 31.
1700–08.	" Plentiful crops, low prices, and farmers at times unable to pay rent. Abundance of provisions made people willing to contribute to the expense of the war." Pages 34-5.
1708.	" A hard frost, which brought on a prodigious scarcity of provisions, more in France than in England. In general the summer was cold and wet."
1709.	" The Queen, in her speech in parliament, complains of corn being exported at such high prices as distressed the poor. . . . There fell this year rain to the depth of 26¼ inches. I think the mean depth of rain falling in England is 19½ inches." Pages 35-6.
1715–50.	In this interval there appear to have been only three seasons " which, whether by inference from prices, or by historical notice, could be considered as of a marked deficiency of produce, or in any way approaching to what could be designated as seasons of scarcity." These were 1727, 1728 and 1740 (pp. 39–40).

The following table is a similar collection of bits of testimony based on Comber, *An Inquiry into the State of National Subsistence*.

1689–99. " The years 1689, 1690 and 1691 were plentiful years, the average of which was only 26s. But there was an uninterrupted succession of wet summers and cold and ungenial harvests from this time to the year 1699, the average price of which period was 50s." Page 135.

1708. " A very hard frost happening in 1708, occasioned wheat to rise to 50s. the next year." Page 137.

1714–29. " The price of grain does not appear to have been such as to cause any complaints in the reign of George I. But in the first year of that of his successor, though the general price appears to have been only 32s. 8d., the tinners in Cornwall rose and plundered the granaries. . . . We learn, in fact, from contemporary authority, that the scarcity was owing to much rain, which had fallen that year, and that the months of March, April, May, June, and part of August of the following year were also rainy." Pages 141–2.

[21] Comber, *An Inquiry into the State of National Subsistence*, p. 142.
[22] Tooke, *History of Prices*, vol. 1, p. 43.
[23] Comber, *An Inquiry into the State of National Subsistence*, pp. 141–2.
[24] 11th George II., c. 22.
[25] War   1688–97   50s. 8d.
    Peace   1698–1701   52s. 6d.
    War   1702–12   44s. 11d.
    Peace   1713–39   40s. 4d.
    War   1740–48   35s. 5d.
    Peace   1749–54   38s. 2d.

Brand, *A Determination of the Average Depression of the Price of Wheat in War, below that of the Preceding Peace; and its Re-advance in War Following,* pp. 10–11.
[26] Tooke, *History of Prices*, vol. 1, pp. 33–4.
[27] Adam Smith, *The Wealth of Nations*, vol. 1, pp. 175–6.
[28] Lord Ernle, *English Farming Past and Present*, p. 172. For an account of the shortcomings of Tull, without, however, questioning his real contributions, see an article by T. H. Marshall in *The Economic History Review*, January, 1929, pp. 41–60.
[29] Curtler, *A Short History of English Agriculture*, p. 183.
[30] Lord Ernle, *English Farming Past and Present*, p. 175.
[31] *Ibid.*, pp. 148–9.
[32] Comber, *An Inquiry into the State of National Subsistence*, p. 144–5.
[33] I found no pamphlet of this description either in the British Museum, the Bodleian Library, the University of Cambridge Library, or the Goldsmith Collection, or in any book store dealing in pamphlets on this period.
[34] 10th William III., c. 3. [35] 8th Anne, c. 2. [36] 14th George II., c. 3. [37] 11th William III., c. 1. [38] 1st James II., c. 19, sect. 2. [39] *Ibid.*, sects. 3–5.
[40] See 2nd George II., c. 18, for the failure of the act of 1685.
[41] Bigg is Scotch four-rowed barley. [42] 2nd George II., c. 18.
[43] Pownall, *Memoir for Lords of Treasury*, p. 306.
[44] 5th George II., c. 12.
[45] Pownall, *Memoir Drawn up, and laid Before the Lords Commissioners of the Treasury, Containing an Historical Review of the Statutes that Have Been Made Relative to the Corn Trade*, p. 308.

CHAPTER III

THE REVOLT AGAINST THE RESTORATION CORN LAWS

Corn Laws come into prominence in 1750 as result of enormous expenditures in bounties on exported corn—Pamphlet war over the merits of the bounty system—Arguments of Arthur Young in favour of the bounty on corn—Of Adam Smith against—Estimate of the effects of the bounty—Reasons for the decline in the exportation of grain—Large number of deficient crops from 1756 to 1773—Food riots particularly from 1756 to 1758 and 1766 to 1767—Immense pamphlet literature explaining the causes of scarcity and suggesting remedies—Attitude of government toward the rising prices of grain and the food riots—Attempts to relieve distress by temporary acts, orders in council, committee reports, and enforcing the laws against engrossing, forestalling and regrating in 1766—Acts of 1770 and 1772—Agitation for a new permanent law—Failure of bill of 1772—Act of 1773—Opinions of contemporary and modern writers on this law—Its significance in the history of the Corn Laws.

THE wisdom of the bounty act of 1689 seems to have been first seriously questioned about 1750. This critical attitude made the Corn Laws a question of public interest, a position that they maintained almost continuously until after their repeal in 1846. The increased interest came not because of the bad crops of 1756 and 1757, or on account of the frequent suspensions of the bounty and right of exportation of grain from 1756 to 1773, as some writers represent, but because the amount of money expended on the bounty was making serious demands on the treasury.

In the previous chapter it was shown that an enormous increase in the exportation of grain, and hence in the amount of money expended on the bounty, took place between 1748 and 1751. It was typical of the lack of machinery for regulating the acts of 1670 and 1689 that no appropriation or subsidy had ever been passed to cover the bounty on grain exported. According to the law of 1689, the customs officer, at the port where the corn was shipped, was to pay the bounty to the exporter out of the money which had been collected on imports. A receipt for sums expended in this manner was accepted in his accounts as the equivalent of that amount paid to the Crown.[1] But since it often happened that the customs officers at outports lacked the money to pay the corn debentures, they were instructed, under these circumstances, to certify the debentures and the commissioners were to order that they be paid in three months' time by the receiver general in London from the customs of that port.[2]

These debentures were paid out of the customs called tunnage and poundage granted to Charles II. in 1660. The grant was originally for one year only, but it was continued by subsequent acts and eventually made permanent.[3] Half the net produce from this so-called old customs, after deducting salaries, corn debentures and other bounties and drawbacks, was set aside in 1708[4] for a period of ninety-six years in order to secure to public creditors an annuity of eighty thousand pounds. In 1720, £69,819 was subscribed to the stock of the South Sea Company, but even after this deduction the income from the half subsidy was sufficient to meet all charges until the enormous increase in the exportation of grain from 1748 to 1751. As a result, by Christmas of 1749 there was not enough surplus to meet the claims of the South Sea Company's annuity.[5] When the case was laid before the Attorney-General he gave the following opinion : " This half Subsidy is an added Duty granted by 6th Anne and never was a Fund for the Corn Bounty granted by I W. & M., C. 12. That Act could not charge it as this Duty was not then existing and the Act of the 6th of Anne instead of charging it, expressly appropriates it to another purpose and directs it to be brought into and paid separately into the Exchequer for that purpose. And I think that the South Sea Company have a right to receive their annuity preferably to the Corn Bounty out of this half subsidy. As to the other Bounties, such of them as are given subsequent to the South Sea Company's Fund and out of all the Customs generally, will take the place of the Company's Annuity. But the others will not unless there is something particular to distinguish them."[6] Thus it was the unpaid debentures that brought the Corn Laws into prominence.

When the government took up the perplexing problem of dealing with the unpaid debentures it was clear that no legal claim could be made on the old customs. The only justification for the procedure described in the preceding paragraph was that usage and tradition had sanctioned this method, and that the acts of 1701[7] and 1707[8] referred to this manner of paying the debentures.[9] But even the slight legal claim based on these two acts was weakened by the act of 1708[10] which set aside the half subsidy for a specific purpose. In spite of this no act was passed appropriating money to settle the outstanding debentures. A law was passed to take effect March 25th, 1753,[11] which allowed three per cent. on all unredeemed debentures beginning six months after the day they were presented to the commissioners of customs at London. The acts of 1689, 1701 and 1707 were referred to as a sufficient excuse for continuing the system. The policy of allowing interest on outstanding debentures was, evidently, only a makeshift. The rapid decline in exports after 1752 relieved the government of an embarrassing problem.

In the midst of this difficulty over making payments on outstanding corn debentures, some vigorous attacks on the bounty system as a whole began. Nicholson, in his *History of the Corn Laws*, states that a violent controversy over the bounty on corn raged through the entire eighteenth century.[12] While there may have been isolated attacks on the bounty before 1750, the real controversy did not begin until after that date.

In 1751 Charles Townshend enunciated a doctrine in direct opposition to the one upon which the laws of 1670 and 1689 were based.[13] He laid down the following maxims which, in his opinion, were incontrovertible. " That the wealth of any nation is in proportion to its quantity of trade and the number of manufacturies. That the value of the produce of such a nation is likewise in the same proportion. That the continuance of its manufacturies trade and wealth depends solely on the degree of vent its manufactures have in foreign markets. That good regulations for promoting universal industry are necessary among the people of such a nation. That it is the interest of such a nation to suffer its ports to be opened for the admission of every kind of foreign produce, or manufacture whatsoever, to which any degree of labour can be added : And that labour is distant wealth. That contradicting this maxim, by laying duties, or prohibitions, on any kind, or all kinds of foreign produce, or on foreign goods imperfectly manufactured, forces such foreign nation, or nations, to set up new manufactures, and to improve their old, to the detriment of the country, where such prohibitions are established. That consequently, by the known rule of contraries, sending out any commodities unmanufactured, or which are not fully manufactured, must be detrimental to any country. That it must still be more detrimental to any country to grant a bounty for exportation of its commodities of this sort. That Corn, as it is capable of being manufactured, is unquestionably a commodity of this sort."[14] Turning to the historical side, Townshend denied that the fall in the price of grain and the rise in rents were due to the bounty, but insisted that they were due to the peace which England had enjoyed in contrast to the wars of the continent.[15] His argument is based on the assumption that the price of labour varies directly with the price of grain. Hence both the bounty on exportation and the restrictions on importation placed the English manufacturers at a disadvantage in competing with foreigners. The bounty gave foreign manufacturers cheaper grain, and, consequently, lower labour costs in production ;[16] and the restrictions on importation made these same costs higher for the English manufacturer in case the price of grain in England was higher than on the continent.[17] Clearly, Townshend's position shows a strong commercial bias. His objection to the bounty is not directed against its effect on English agriculture, but rather against its hampering influence on trade and manufacturing. He is not a free trader because he believes in protection for fully manufactured articles. The interests of the producers of food and raw materials, and even of partially manufactured goods, were to be subordinated to those of the manufacturers of finished articles.

Immediately a protest went up from the landed interest and the exporters of grain. *The Gentlemen's Magazine* for 1752 printed several articles from country newspapers on the subject. It is clear that the interests attacked were alarmed at the prospect of losing the bounty. They argued that England would export little corn without the bounty, since the countries which were buying English grain would either secure it from the Baltic countries or raise it themselves. Then they attempted to show that the bounty benefited every class in the community. The farmers knowing that they were assured a market, raised larger crops and kept more cattle ; the landlord received larger rents ; provisions were cheaper for the poor, a situation which was a righteous thing in itself and which was also a great boon to the manufacturers, since cheap food meant cheap labour. Furthermore, as a national policy advocates of the bounty held that it was beneficial because it employed vast numbers of people, brought in immense sums of money, and increased the merchant marine.[18] Some urged that the bounty and the exportation could not be injurious to manufacturers, because most of the manufacturing districts were inland.[19]   Others glorified the legislators of 1689 and gave them credit for a foresight which, doubtless, would have astonished them. One writer, in *The Stamford Mercury*, stated that, " our wise ancestors when they gave the bounty, expected it would make us a corn nation, which we were not at that time.   Experience hath convinced us of the rectitude of the measure."[20]   The fear of losing the bounty became so widespread among the landowners and farmers that Henry Pelham, the Prime Minister, felt that it was necessary to reassure them.   On August 29th, 1753, in addressing the gentlemen, clergy and freeholders of Sussex at Lewes, he eulogized the bounty act and denied that there was any intention of repealing it.[20a]

Thus the chief arguments on both sides were based on economic generalizations.   Those who opposed the bounty held that English manufacturers were injured because their continental rivals were thus able to secure cheaper grain, and hence cheaper labour.   Those who favoured the bounty held that each class and the nation as a whole shared in its benefits.   However, the attacks on the bounty were not confined to abstract economic principles, but extended to the actual operation of the machinery of the bounty act.   It was charged that great frauds were practised to secure the bounty.   These included the giving of false weights and prices by the exporters,[21] as well as shipping inferior grain.   Unsaleable barley, it was alleged, was made into malt to gain bulk, shipped to get the bounty, and then thrown overboard.[22]   Still another abuse which was reputed to be practised was the steeping of grain made into malt until it was ten times its original size.   The defenders of the bounty maintained that the charge of giving false weights was exaggerated.   They based their argument on the fact that the most valuable part of the corn trade under the bounty act was the exportation of wheat to Spain, Portugal and the Straits.   Here the freight was as high as, or higher than, the bounty.   Thus the exporter, unless he owned the ship, would have to pay as much or more in freight as he had secured by fraud. These frauds, then, would have to be practised on grain sent to France and Holland where the freights were low.   But this practice in turn would be checked by the fact that it was chiefly rye, barley and malt upon which the bounties were much lower than on wheat, that were sent to Holland.   Thus in order to work these fraudulent practices successfully, it would be necessary for the ship officers, the exporter, and his employees, to agree in deceiving the government. The very numbers concerned furnished, in the opinion of the advocates of the bounty, an ample defence against such a danger.[24]

The system of determining the prices at which grain could be exported has been described in Chapter II.   There is no doubt that the method was open to fraud by its very looseness, but to what extent fraudulent practices occurred is difficult to say.   The impression was widespread at the time that the exporters of grain were not averse to depressing the market if it were necessary to lower the price before the corn could be shipped and the bounty collected.

From arguments based on economic principles and on the actual working of the bounty act, both sides turned to an historical survey of the production and exportation of grain under the laws of 1670 and 1689. During this period, especially between the years 1765 and 1773, the Eton Tables of the Windsor Market were quoted extensively by both sides. Advocates of the bounty triumphantly pointed out that wheat was cheaper during the seventy-five years following 1689 than during the seventy-five years preceding. The fact that these Windsor prices were merely the average of two market days during each year in a single place detracts somewhat from their value.

The third quarter of the eighteenth century saw a large output, both of periodicals and pamphlets, on the merits of the bounty on the exportation of corn. It is unnecessary to examine in detail these various publications since several of the pamphlets summed up all arguments advanced on both sides of the question. Arthur Young was one of the most vigorous defenders of the bounty policy and hence a survey of his principal arguments may be taken as typical of that of its advocates. Young maintained : that the bounty since 1689 had caused a regular decline of prices and hence could not have injured manufacturers ; that the price fell at home in proportion to the quantity sent abroad ; that all important articles except corn had risen in price ; that the fall in the price of wheat prevented other provisions from rising higher ; that the bounty encouraged and improved agriculture in England not by high but by regular prices ; that in his travels through Wales and the North of England, he found no proportion between the rates of wages and of provisions ; that corn growing did not affect the price of butcher's meat, since summer grazing took place on rich meadow and pasture which rented higher than arable land, and hence would not be ploughed, and winter grazing on turnips, etc. ; that manufacturers with whom he had spoken denied that the English were undersold ; that the poor were worse off when provisions were cheap than when they were dear, because when provisions were cheap they wasted their substance and time in idleness ; and that grain should be kept at a regular price, the higher the better.[25] In taking this position he laid himself open to the charge of committing the *post hoc* fallacy in his first, second and fourth points.[26] Furthermore, several of his points are inconsistent. He argues that since food has declined in price since 1689 the manufacturer could not have injured by having to pay higher wages. Later he says that he has found no connection between wages and provisions, a point, if true, which would make his first assertion not wrong but useless, since the rise or fall in prices would not affect wages. Finally, he maintains that cheap food is bad for the poor since they waste their time and substance in idleness. In this case the poor and the manufacturers were both injured by the cheapness of food since 1689 : the former for the reason he has given, and the latter because the poor would not work.

Most of the arguments given by Young were used frequently in the

twenty years preceding his pamphlet of 1770.[27] These arguments
are ascribed to him merely because he summed up nearly all the
important ones, and because he is the best known of the pamphleteers
who favoured the bounty. For the same reasons Adam Smith's
arguments against the bounty will be cited as typical of the opponents
of this policy. He had the benefit of all that was written in the
previous twenty-five years and, after the publication of *The Wealth of
Nations* in 1776, he was recognized as the foremost opponent of
artificial stimulation of trade. On the effects of the bounty since
1689, he held : that while the price of corn did fall in England during
the years 1689 to 1764, that it also fell during the same period in
France where exportation was subject to a general prohibition ; that
the fall in the price of grain was due to a " gradual and insensible rise
in the real value of silver,"[28] and not to the bounty or prohibition of
exportation ; that the bounty by increasing production made prices
higher both in years of plenty and scarcity—in the former by preventing the natural fall, and in the latter by denuding the country
of the surplus from the years of plenty ; that the bounty did not
encourage tillage by opening up more extensive foreign markets,
which, it was claimed, would in the long run assure lower prices in
the home market ; that every bushel of grain exported by means of
the bounty, which could have been exported without it, imposed
two different taxes upon the people—the actual money to pay the
bounty, and the difference between the price in the home market
and what the price would have been if it had not been artificially
raised ; that the enhancement of the value of corn, through the
stimulation of the bounty, could raise the nominal but not the real
price ; that the real effect of the bounty was " not so much to raise
the real value of corn as to degrade the real value of silver or to make
an equal quantity of it exchange for a smaller quantity " of other
commodities;[29] that the only ones in the community who profited
by the bounty were the exporters and importers of grain ; that the
increase in the nominal or money price of corn through the bounty
did not increase the real wealth of the landed interest, nor did it
encourage the growth of corn, since it did not enable the farmer to
employ more labourers ; that, in this respect, corn differed from
almost all other sorts of goods, for monopolies and bounties in the
case of manufactured goods raised the real as well as the nominal
price ; that the real value of every commodity was " finally measured
and determined by the proportion which its average money price "[30]
bore to the average money price of corn ; and that the improvement
and prosperity ascribed to the corn bounty were due to the " security
which the laws in Great Britain give to every man that he shall
enjoy the fruits of his own labour," which was " alone sufficient
to make any country flourish, notwithstanding these and twenty
other absurd regulations of commerce."[31]

Adam Smith's position contains no such glaring inconsistencies as
Arthur Young's, and hence is not open to attack from within. However, many of his points may be attacked on their historical side.
His contention that prices fell from 1689 to 1764, owing to the appreciation of silver, is not substantiated by later investigations.[32] Even

more difficult to accept is his insistence that the bounty did not encourage the growth of corn. It was a well recognized fact in the first half of the eighteenth century that many farmers were producing grain for exporters, who, taking advantage of the bounty, made long-time contracts both with the farmer for supplying it, and with the French and Dutch for purchasing it.[13] Smith himself, in his dissert-ation on the inland dealer, alludes to the practice of contracting for a fixed price, usually 28s. a quarter, over a long period of years,[14] but he says nothing of this same practice being used in exportation. Furthermore, his differentiation between the effect of a bounty on grain and on other commodities is a difficult one to maintain.

A comparison of the arguments of Young and Smith shows many points of similarity in method. Each, seemingly, combed the period from 1689 to 1764 for evidence to support his point of view. The only obvious bit of empirical work was done by Young when he examined the relation between wages and provisions during his tours in Wales and in the north of England. But his conclusions in this instance conflicted with certain of his other points. Both Smith and Young believed that the improvement in tillage was due to an event in 1689 ; the former ascribed it to security perfected by the revolution, and the latter to the bounty act of that date. Smith pointed out that the advocates of the bounty were guilty of the *post hoc* fallacy in insisting that, because the improvement in cultivation followed the bounty act, the law was responsible for the change. Yet he, himself, is guilty of the same fallacy when he holds that this improvement came as a result of the security perfected by the revolu-tion of 1689. Both believed in fixed economic principles applicable to all times. Young held that the bounty was the key to the econ-omic prosperity of all classes, and especially to that of the landed interest, which was ten times as important as all other interests.[15] Smith, on the other hand, held that it was simply an obstacle to econ-omic progress. Neither showed the slightest inclination to treat the bounty as a policy whose value depended upon conditions at the time of its application.

A less biased judgment of the effects of the bounty after 1689 would indicate that it had neither the beneficial nor pernicious effects ascribed to it by the supporters and opponents. The only incontro-vertible fact is that between 1689 and 1765 English agriculture under-went a vast improvement. Undoubtedly, many causes contributed to this change, but exactly what proportion should be attributed to the bounty is difficult to say. The first half of the eighteenth century is well known for its improvements in stock breeding, rotation of crops, manuring, and draining. Much of the advance must be ascribed to pioneers in these fields. Probably the " security perfected by the Revolution " of 1689 had less to do with it than the bounty. However, the only way to judge the merits of the bounty is to study the conditions under which it was passed and under which it operated. This method explains how it could be beneficial at one time and harmful at another. In 1689 England was a country of primitive farming and poor internal communications. There were no large inland cities, because such cities could not have been fed. The agricultural sections of the east and south coasts, and the upper Thames valley, which until 1660 had merely supplied London and other seaports, were now raising a surplus. By 1689 it had become necessary to find a market for this surplus, and the bounty unquestionably aided in finding one. It may have been a bad economic policy to subsidize the exportation of grain, but it is useless to deny that it stimulated the growth of grain in the first half of the eighteenth century. Perhaps it overstimulated it at the expense of meat and dairy products, as its opponents claimed ; but even this is difficult to prove.

The amount of grain exported before 1713, or even before 1732, was not large, but the next twenty years saw an enormous increase in this direction. In spite of the increase, the percentage of grain exported remained a small part of that produced. Charles Smith, in his *Tracts on the Corn Trade and Corn Laws*, has estimated the proportion that the average yearly importation and exportation of wheat, rye, barley and oats during the years 1697 to 1765 bore to the amount grown. After elaborate computations[34] he concluded that " The export is bare *one thirty-second* part of the consumption, *one thirty-third* part of the growth exclusive of the seed, *one thirty-sixth* part of the growth, including the seed, and not near *one-third* of the seed itself, supposing it only one-tenth of the growth ; . . . and yet what prodigious benefit hath the nation reaped from the exportation ! The import hath been about a *five hundred and seventy-first* part of the consumption and *one eighteenth* of the export, and never equalled but a small part of the growth."[37] These figures, however, are misleading, since they are based on the assumption that the population of England and Wales remained practically stationary between the years 1689 and 1765. Charles Smith estimates this population at about six million.[38] Although no statistics as reliable as those of the national census, beginning in 1801, are available for these years, still fairly reliable ones are to be found in *An Abstract of the Population and Parish Returns for* 1821.[39] According to the estimates made in this abstract, the population in 1700 was 5,475,000 ; in 1760 it was 6,736,000, and in 1770 it was 7,428,000. Roughly, the population increased by a million and a half between the years 1689 and 1765. Furthermore, the figures on the annual consumption are simply estimates of what an average person should consume during the year, and are not as reliable as are the statistics on exportation and importation. In addition, his taking the yearly average of the amount of grain exported between 1689 and 1765 is manifestly unfair. We have already seen that the exportation of grain, and especially wheat, did not attain great dimensions until after 1730, and hence the average is weighed down by the low yearly average between 1689 and 1732. In 1750 the exportation of wheat was nearly a quarter of the annual consumption, and the average of the five years ending in 1764 was about a tenth. Thus it would appear that the annual exportation of grain from 1748 to 1764 was nearer one-fifteenth or one-twentieth than one thirty-third.

From the facts offered in the preceding paragraph, it is evident that under ordinary circumstances a good sized and increasing surplus of grain was exported annually until 1750. Between 1750 and 1765, although there is no evidence that the crops were bad, except in 1757 and 1758, the amount declined. After 1765 the exports became negligible, in spite of the fact that enclosures and improvements in agricultural methods provided a steadily increasing supply of grain. Clearly the period was over in which the bounty was needed to stimulate the production of grain. After 1660 a surplus was produced beyond the needs of London and other sea ports. The bounty helped to find a market for this surplus, and in addition it increased the production of wheat by opening up a new market on the continent. After 1745 the turnpikes and, after 1760, the canals revolutionized the internal communications of England. The transportation of food and raw materials made possible the growth of the industrial cities of the midland and north. These cities, particularly after 1780, offered an expanding market to the corn-growers which supplanted the export trade to Holland, France and the south of Europe. This new market was a sufficient incentive to cultivation in itself, and hence the bounty was no longer needed. English agriculture from 1660 to 1760 may have been in the " infant industry " stage, but after 1760, evidently, it needed no artificial stimulation.

Nevertheless, the landowners after enjoying the benefits of the bounty for three-quarters of a century were loath to give up a vested interest of such an advantageous nature. A west country maltster, writing in 1764, stated that since the purpose of the bounty of 1689 had been fulfilled it should now be repealed.[40] Perhaps the greatest benefit that resulted from the development of wheat-growing in the first half of the eighteenth century was the rise in the standard of living of the common people, who were, in many instances, able to substitute white for black bread.[41]

In addition to the inability of the Treasury to pay the corn debentures and to the controversy over the bounty, the Corn Laws also came into prominence because of the unusual number of deficient crops beginning in 1756. In the first half of the eighteenth century poor harvests came only in the years 1709, 1727, 1728 and 1740 ; but a startling reversal of this succession of good years set in between 1756 and 1773. The crop of 1756 was deficient because of rains and winds in the spring, summer and harvest ;[42] and that of 1757 was also deficient, " although not in the same degree."[43] From 1758 to 1763, inclusive, the seasons appear to have been favourable, and the next two crops were only slightly deficient.[44] However, from 1766 to 1774 there were bad crops every year except 1768 and 1769, which appear to have been of normal size.[45] The price of grain and the annual import and export figures were influenced to a considerable extent by the variations in the seasons.[46]

As usual deficient crops produced scarcity and high prices. These, we have seen, were generally accompanied by suffering and rioting among the classes most affected. Even during the years of plenty in the first half of the century there was considerable feeling in the west and north against the exportation of grain lest it produce scarcity and high prices. But down to 1756 there seem to have been no such extensive riots as broke out in August of that year in the midlands and north. Mobs attacked millers, farmers and corn dealers. A mill between Wakall and Wednesday was sacked and the flour carried away or destroyed. At Nuneaton, Atherstone, Polesworth and Tamworth, much damage was done to the mills, farmhouses and houses of the dealers. Many of the latter were Quakers, and in three instances their meeting houses were nearly destroyed.⁴⁷ Rioting continued all during the autumn. At Kidderminster the poor manufacturing people, and at Ludlow the colliers sacked the market place.⁴⁸ In fact, cases of plundering mills, markets and farmhouses became common.⁴⁹ Still, all this had been done in previous years of scarcity, although, perhaps, not on such a large scale. On the whole the most puzzling thing about this outburst beginning in 1756 is the amazing output of pamphlets dealing with the causes of and remedies for the scarcity and high prices of grain. If deficient harvests in 1709, 1727–28 and 1740 produced riots as in 1756–58 why did not these same deficiencies produce a voluminous pamphlet literature ? Clearly the absence of the latter cannot be ascribed to greater facility of publication in 1756 because pamphlets on other subjects are fairly common in these earlier years. Nor does the bounty controversy in the years preceding 1756 explain this output, for in that case the attack would have been made on the bounty and not on the corn dealers.

While rioting occurred in all the years of scarcity between 1756 and 1773, only in 1766–67 was it comparable to that of 1756–58. In 1767, for example, the poor people in various cities and towns, assembled in mobs and took charge of the markets. Their first intentions were to see what they considered justice done by setting a moderate price on provisions offered for sale. Their next step was to handle roughly those whom they considered guilty of raising prices. The intentions of the people making up these mobs may have been reasonable, according to their own standards, when they first assembled ; but, as a rule, mob action ended in riots in which property was destroyed and blood shed. In many cases it was necessary to call out the military forces to disperse the rioters. Consequently the jails were filled with these unfortunate wretches, and judges with special commissions were sent to try the prisoners at once. Many of the leaders were condemned to death, but " most of these were, however, afterwards reprieved, several were transported, some got a free pardon, and of some examples were made."⁵⁰

The unusual number of bad crops between 1756 and 1773 accompanied by riots in the years of highest prices made the question of scarcity a very important one during this period. An attempt will now be made to trace in the pamphlet and periodical literature of the time the explanations offered for scarcity and high prices, and the remedies, in addition to the repeal of the bounty paid on the exportation of grain, suggested to alleviate these conditions. To a considerable extent the explanations and remedies will be treated chronologically. Nearly every conceivable explanation was offered every year, but in some years much greater emphasis would be placed on a particular cause or remedy than in others.

Most of the writers in 1756 blamed the corn middlemen for the scarcity. These middlemen included not only the corn buyers—badgers, kidders, laders, broggers and carriers,[51] but assemblers and speculators, such as factors, jobbers, merchants, corn chandlers, millers, maltsters, mealmen, flourmen, bakers, brewers, distillers and taverners.[52] One writer argued that, " If there is a real scarcity of corn in the land, it must be owing either to the shortness of the last year's crop ; or to the greatness of the exportation ; or to the increase of the consumption, which has been made by our good allies the mercenaries, or by our good brethren the malt-distillers. But if there is no real want of corn among us, then it is certain, the present dearness must be owing to the wicked combination of the forestallers, factors, engrossers, badgers, farmers or maltsters."[53]

The solution most commonly suggested was to enforce the statutes of Edward VI. and Elizabeth against forestallers, engrossers and regrators. Another writer suggested that the best way to break the power of the middlemen was to follow the example of the Scotch magistrates, and order every farmer to bring to market all the surplus corn in his possession beyond that necessary to keep his family until the next harvest.[54] Other improvements on the existing laws which it was believed would curb the middlemen were to stop exportation and distillation of wheat when it reached a certain price ; to forbid the same person grinding and dealing in grain ; and to make illegal the sale of corn by any weight except the statute measure.[55] Revival of old practices and schemes was frequently advised. In 1758 the *Book of Orders*, which embodied the government policy in dealing with corn middlemen between 1586 and 1630, was reprinted and dedicated to William Pitt and Legge, the Chancellor of the Exchequer, with the recommendation that the government once more enforce its provisions.[56] In the same year Pitt's sister proposed the revival of the old scheme of erecting public granaries or magazines. Her plan was to build one in every county and to fill them each year " in such proportions as shall by the government be judged convenient."[57] When corn rose above a fixed price the magistrates were to sell it at a rate settled by Parliament in an act passed each year. If the fixed price was not reached, the grain was to be disposed of at harvest before any of the new crop was permitted to be marketed. In order to facilitate the sale, this corn was to be sent to the different markets of the country at the expense of the government.[58] Neither of these two plans were acted upon, for eighteenth-century political ideas did not look with favour upon a revival of the bureaucratic system of the crown.

The attacks on the middlemen did not go unchallenged. A corn factor answering the charges against factors, badgers and distillers, blamed the farmers for holding back grain. He upheld the distillers for using corn at reasonable prices, scored the mob for attacking badgers and denied that factors ever met to settle prices. In his defence of the middlemen, one which was by no means new and was later popularized by Adam Smith, he showed the utility of middlemen in diverting provisions to places where they were most needed. He believed the remedy for scarcity was, first, to allow a bounty on importation when exportation and distillation were prohibited ;

D

second, to enforce a standard measure of eight gallons ; third, to prevent fraud in sales ; and fourth, to punish all mobs which obstructed the carrying on of the corn trade.[59]

An even more vigorous defence of the farmers and middlemen was made by the author of the *Corn Tracts and Corn Laws.* He denied that any considerable number of farmers had sufficient capital to hold back their wheat, since the poor ones were forced to thresh and sell at once in order to meet their obligations, and even those in moderate circumstances were seldom able to keep it beyond May. Only a few rich farmers could afford to keep back all or a greater part of their crops for a year and thus speculate on the rise or fall of the market.[60] The grinding of corn and the baking of bread were already carefully regulated by law ; and if mal-practices existed in either trade, the solution lay not in slander and mob violence against those engaged in these businesses, but in providing laws to cover the defects.[61] He insisted that the corn trade policy as a whole coulu not be improved upon, although small flaws might be numerous. The existing policy, he maintained, encouraged the farmer to till the soil ; insured the people corn at a moderate price ; and enabled the corn middlemen to transport the surplus of one part of the country to meet the demands of another. He conceded that the outlines of this general plan might be improved by including in one act of Parliament all laws relating to the corn trade except the baking act.[62]

Next to the wickedness of the middlemen, the most common explanation of the high prices of the years 1756 to 1758 was the adulteration of bread by the bakers. The complaints were directed against the so-called Assize of Bread. This system of periodically fixing the price of wheaten bread probably extended back to Anglo-Saxon times. Under the Tudors and Stuarts the Privy Council frequently issued the *Book of the Assize of Bread* prescribing the proportion of white, wheaten and household bread to be made from each batch of flour and the relative weight that the loaves of these different calibres should bear to each other.[63] After the Restoration this practice fell into disuse along with the rest of the bureaucratic system directed by the Privy Council. In 1710 the assize was revived, and the Lord Mayor and aldermen or other chief magistrates in the various cities, towns and corporations were ordered to set the assize and weight of all bread sold within their jurisdiction. In so doing they were to take into consideration the price in the public markets of grain, meal and flour from which the bread was made.[64] Having determined the local price of wheat, they were to add to it the baker's allowance of 12s. and to compute the exact weight which a penny loaf should contain in order that four hundred and seventeen pounds of bread should sell for precisely the sum so determined.[65] This temporary law of 1710 was made permanent in 1714 by 1st George I., c. 26, which authorized the well-known quartern loaf. Nevertheless, the laws of 1710 and 1714 were not successful. The lack of success was evidently due in great measure to the change in the status of the corn middlemen in the seventeenth and eighteenth centuries. The early assize assumed that the baker would buy his encourage commerce in such a way as to stimulate employment, were accepting a measure that exposed the British agriculturist to foreign competition. The Tory, who had advocated foreign commerce in the interest of the consumer, looked askance at it, when it threatened to under-sell his tenants in the home market. Like other compromises, the measure failed to satisfy anyone, and it did not even answer the expectations of its author."[145] Nicholson admitted that, " Compared with the subsequent statutes, this Act seems to be altogether in favour of the consumer, but probably it was passed under the impression that there would be very little import except in years of scarcity ; and the nominal duty would take the place of temporary suspensions."[146] Morley stated that, " This was the most liberal piece of legislation until the Act of Repeal in 1846."[147]

If the interpretation previously given of the act of 1773 is a correct one, then many of the conclusions just cited must be erroneous. McCulloch's position that the act was a material improvement on the preceding system can be considered only after the years following 1773 have been studied. Cunningham's point of view is, in some respects, difficult to reconcile with the facts. The act of 1773 may have been a reversal of that of 1689, but not of the policy actually pursued from 1689 to 1773. Furthermore, his contention that the measure was a compromise is not convincing. It is true that the landed interest on the one hand would have preferred a much higher import and bounty price level, and that the commercial and manufacturing interests, on the other, would have enjoyed having the bounty and restrictions on importation abolished entirely. But the measure of 1773 came less as a result of conscious negotiations between the two interests, than as a mutual agreement to make the laws regulating the importation and exportation of grain conform with the actual practices. It was really a case of making the *status quo* permanent, and thereby relieving both sides of the uncertainty and annoyance of temporary measures after it was recognized that the old system had collapsed. Nicholson was doubtless right in saying that the landed interest acquiesced because they believed importation would take place only in years of scarcity. Disillusionment upon this point, in the years following 1773, had much to do with the passing of a new law in 1791. In short, the landed interest approved the act of 1773 because they merely gave up something which was not at that time and never had been of any value to them. But later, when the concessions that they had made at this time became valuable, they regretted having surrendered them.

CHAPTER III

NOTES

[1] 1st William and Mary, c. 12.

[2] Townshend Papers : Letter of December 18th, 1751. These papers will be referred to as the Townshend Papers in the footnotes of this Chapter. They are some miscellaneous letters, papers and memoranda belonging to different members of the Townshend family. I was permitted to use them through the courtesy of Mr. Kashnor of the Museum Book Store, London, in whose possession they were in 1921.

[3] Townshend Papers, 1751.   [4] 6th Anne, c. 48.

[5] Townshend Papers, 1751.

[6] Ibid. See also Treasury Out Letters, T. 27, vol. 27, pp. 2–3.

[7] 12th and 13th William III.

[8] Act of Union with Scotland. 5th Anne, c. 29.

[9] Townshend Papers, 1751.   [10] 6th Anne, c. 48.   [11] 26th George II., c. 15.

[12] Nicholson, The History of the English Corn Laws, p. 27.

[13] National Thoughts Recommended to the Serious Attention of the Public, by a Landowner.

[14] Ibid., pp. 26–7.   [15] Ibid., p. 34.   [16] Ibid., p. 31.   [17] Ibid., pp. 35–6.

[18] The State of the Corn Trade Considered, etc. (1753), pp. 29–30.

[19] The Gentleman's Magazine, XXII, p. 411.

[20] Ibid., p. 605. Quoted from The Stamford Mercury, of January 4th, 1753.

[20a] In the course of Pelham's speech, which was made following his nomination to represent Sussex in the next Parliament, he declared : " Gentlemen, the honour you have done me for many years in intrusting me with being your representative has dignified me to an advanced age in life, so that I may now sincerely say that I am grown old in your service, but I hope that, now no other consideration will divert me from prosecuting every scheme to promote the trade of the County of Sussex which is a maritime and corn country : and the bounty for debenture to encourage the exportation of corn having been falsely reported to be taken off, I must beg leave to assure that no such thing was intended.   Well must I consider what the consequence of such an act would be which must reduce the rent of lands a third in value, greatly lessening the estates of all landed gentlemen, impoverish gentlemen and yeomen of small fortunes, and farmers of long leases must be inevitably ruin'd.   As trade and particularly the corn trade is the chiefe concern of the County of Sussex, it shall be my constant care to encourage and support the same by encouraging our farmers in their agriculture and extending our commerce abroad we have no reason to fear being what we ever have been, a rich and powerful people."   British Museum Additional Manuscripts, 32,732, f. 570.

[21] Townshend Papers. Letter from the Hague, April 2nd, 1751.

[22] Considerations on the Present High Prices of Provisions and the Necessaries of Life, by a West Country Maltster, 1764, p. 4.

[23] Comber, An Inquiry into the State of National Subsistence, pp. 142–3.

[24] Townshend Papers, April 2nd, 1751. " Holland is supplied with one-third of its imported Wheat and Rye, with one half its Barley & with almost all its Malt from England & here it may be proper to observe that three fourths of the Rye and Malt brought hither is used in the Distillery."

[25] Arthur Young, The Expediency of a Free Exportation of Corn at this Time, 1770, pp. 5–30.

[26] Joseph Wimpey, Thoughts upon Several Interesting Subjects, 1770, pp. 18–19.

[27] The Expediency of a Free Exportation of Corn at this Time.

[28] Adam Smith, The Wealth of Nations, vol. 2, Everyman's edn., p. 8. This paragraph is a summary of pp. 6–42.

[29] Ibid., p. 10.   [30] Ibid., p. 16.   [31] Ibid., p. 40.

[32] Palgrave's Dictionary of Political Economy, 1926, vol. 3, p. 192.

[33] Comber, An Inquiry into the State of National Subsistence, pp. 145–6.

cottager were allotted a few acres, each small farmer "such proportion as he can conveniently add to his farm," and the rest divided into lots of one hundred acres for sale or lease, then provisions would be made for both large and small scale farming.[80]

From the preceding pages it is clear that explanations for scarcity and high prices, and suggestions for remedying both, were not lacking during the years 1756 to 1773.   Clearly, the most popular explanation was the wickedness of the middlemen.   Adulteration of bread by the bakers, war taxes, national debt, corruption in the court, luxury of all classes, payment of tithe in kind, enclosure and engrossing of farms, and bad harvests, all had their advocates.   The remedies suggested, naturally, depended upon the explanation offered.   To curb the middlemen the most popular suggestions were to enforce the laws against forestallers, engrossers and regrators ; to forbid the exportation of grain ; to prevent the use of grain in the distilleries ; to erect public granaries ; and to place restrictions on combinations of corn dealers.   Those who defended the middlemen insisted that the best way to secure relief was by protecting the latter from mobs. Pamphleteers who held bakers responsible believed the best remedy was a new law regulating the assize of bread.   Advocates of enclosure were convinced that the solution lay in extending the area of cultivation and in improving farming methods.   It is obvious that some of these suggestions were meant as advice to the government, and some to the general public.   In the case of the latter it is more difficult to estimate the effect of pamphleteers, because there is no record of the policy of the public at large comparable to the speeches made and laws passed by Parliament, and the orders in council issued by the Privy Council.   Of course the mere fact that the government adopted a certain policy which several pamphleteers were advocating vigorously is not positive proof that the government either got the idea from this source or felt compelled to take action in accordance with the line suggested.   Nevertheless, it is worth while tracing the policy of the government during these years of intermittent scarcity and high prices between 1756 and 1773.   It will be seen that the measures adopted during these years did coincide to a considerable extent with public opinion as expressed in pamphlets and periodicals, but to what extent the government was influenced from this direction cannot be definitely determined.

When Parliament met late in 1756, the rising price of grain and the protracted rioting led to the immediate passage of an act prohibiting the exportation of corn, malt, meal, flour, bread, biscuit and starch until after December 25th, 1757.[81]   Early in 1757, upon the recommendation of a committee appointed to find means of relieving the high prices, three additional acts were passed.   The first discontinued the duties on corn and flour imported before August 24th, 1757 ; this provision also applied to all grain, flour and bread captured from the enemy and brought into Great Britain.[82]   When enforced, this act nearly starved the Isle of Man, and hence an exception was made permitting 2,500 quarters to be sent there from Southampton and Exeter.[83]   The second act prohibited, during the remainder of the existing war, the exportation of grain from the American colonies to any part of Europe south of Cape Finisterre.   All grain exported must be sent to Great Britain, Ireland or other colonies.[84]   The third prohibited the making of low wines and spirits from wheat, barley, malt, or any other sorts of grain, meal or flour, between March 11th and May 11th, 1757.[85]   Both the first and third acts were renewed before they expired.   The discontinuation of duties on imported grain, flour, etc., was extended to November 15th,[86] and the prohibition against the use of grain in the distillery until December 11th, 1757.[87]

When Parliament assembled in December of 1757 the prices of grain were still high, and it was deemed expedient to continue until December 24th, 1758, all acts passed during the preceding year to regulate the use of, and trade in, corn.[88]   When Parliament again met late in 1758 it was felt, evidently, that the period of scarcity was not over, and hence these acts were again renewed until December 24th, 1759.[89]   However, on the strength of the fall in the prices of grain the prohibition against exportation was removed after March 25th of that year.[90]   At the opening of the session of 1759–60 Parliament cautiously renewed until December 24th, 1760, the act prohibiting the use of corn and flour in the distillery.[91]   But shortly after the renewal a new act reduced the limit to April 21st of that year.[92]

The rise in the price of grain after the harvest of 1764 again placed the burden of action upon Parliament.   Consequently, influenced by the clamour which almost invariably followed such a rise, Parliament discontinued the duties on wheat and flour imported, and the bounty on wheat exported until August 24th, 1765.[93]   A further precaution was taken by giving the King discretionary power, on the advice of the Privy Council, to prohibit the exportation of wheat, meal, flour, bread, biscuit, or starch, during the next recess of Parliament when wheat reached the price of 6s. a bushel at Bear Key.[94]   Prices continued on about the same level during the next year, but since the riots and complaints increased three new acts were passed early in 1766 in an attempt to relieve the situation.   First, grain could be imported, duty free, from the American colonies until September 29th.[95]   Second, the duty on oats was suspended for the same period.[96]   Third, exportation of grain and flour was forbidden until after August 26th, 1766.[97]

After adopting these conventional methods of securing relief, the House of Commons evidently feeling that some additional light on the state of the corn trade was necessary, appointed a committee to consider the laws regulating this trade.   The report of the committee was given on April 25th by Sir Joseph Mawbey, and consisted mainly of the testimony of a Surrey farmer who complained that the factors, jobbers and other middlemen controlled the London oat market for their own profit.   The remedy suggested was to open the port of London four times a year, on the grounds that such an action would prevent the buying of grain for speculation and would enable the farmer to sell directly to the consumer instead of to the middlemen.[98]   How the opening of the port would accomplish this was not explained.   The other point which the committee emphasized was that the scarcity was due to the middlemen hoarding vast quantities of grain in one place.[99]

Whether it was this report or the effect of the riots and pamphlets that was responsible for a most amazing action on the part of the new Chatham-Grafton government is not clear. This action was the putting into execution of the laws against forestalling, engrossing and regrating by a proclamation of September 10th, 1766.[100] The acts of 1552 and 1563 were referred to especially. The folly of such an action was soon evident. To attempt to replace the marketing conditions of the latter half of the eighteenth century with those of the sixteenth century, or even earlier, was manifestly absurd. Furthermore, it showed an utter lack of comprehension of the functions of the middlemen, as well as an utter incompetence in determining the real cause of the scarcity. Perhaps the worst side of the blunder was the fact that it seemed to justify the mobs in their attacks on the corn dealers, since it implied that the latter were responsible for the high prices. The wisdom of this measure was seriously questioned by many persons. One writer stated that " many doubted whether this proclamation was well conceived, or well timed. It was, in some sort, prejudging the question, and declaring the scarcity to be artificial, which experience has since shown to have been but too natural. . . . It was apprehended that this measure would have an effect contrary to the intentions of the council, and by frightening dealers from the markets, would increase the scarcity it was designed to remedy. This was so well felt, that little was done towards enforcing that proclamation, and it soon fell to the ground."[101]

The new government encountered additional difficulty when the law forbidding the exportation of grain expired on August 26th. Parliament was not sitting at the time and had neglected to provide for such a situation before summer recess. As a result prices of grain rose because exportation was now possible. The Lord Mayor and aldermen of London, the cities of Bristol and Norwich and other corporations and bodies of men, sent addresses to the government complaining that the present crop was short, and that the country would be denuded of wheat unless exportation was prohibited. The situation was aggravated by the fact that certain continental countries whose crops had failed were endeavouring to make up their deficit by purchases in London. As a result of these complaints the government issued two orders in council on September 26th. The first suspended the exportation of wheat and wheat flour until November 14th, which was three days after the time set for the first meeting of Parliament.[102] The second prohibited the distillation of wheat in any form during the same period.[103]

When Parliament assembled in November both the House of Commons and the House of Lords petitioned for an extension of the prohibition on the exportation of wheat. Consequently an additional order in council, issued on November 12th, continued indefinitely the order of September 26th and extended its application to the exportation of barley and malt.[104] A series of acts were then passed to continue by law what had been done by order in council. The exportation of grain, meal, malt, flour, bread, biscuit and starch ; and the use of wheat or wheat flour in the distillery was forbidden from November 14th, 1766, to September 10th, 1767. A clause was added, to prevent a repetition of the distress caused by the expiration of the prohibition to export in the midst of the last recess, which gave the King the right by order in council to prohibit exportation from September 10th until twenty days after the opening of the next session of Parliament.[105] Permission was given to import wheat and wheat flour, duty free, from any part of Europe until March 1st, 1767,[106] and from the American colonies until August 1st.[107] Later the act applying to Europe was extended to June 1st.[108] Oats, oatmeal, rye and rye meal were admitted under the same conditions until September 29th, 1767.[109] Finally the free importation of wheat, wheat flour, barley and barley meal, and pulse, was extended until September 10th.[110]

Scarcity and high prices were still problems after the harvest of 1767, as shown by the fact that the distress which they created was the principal point recommended to Parliament, in the speech from the Throne on November 24th. In spite of this, the government took no steps to relieve the distress on the ground that while relief was greatly desired, it was not obtainable at the time. In the debate that followed, the wisdom of such a recommendation was seriously questioned because it implied that relief was within the power of Parliament, and would encourage riots and lawlessness.[111] The best Parliament could do in the way of solving the perplexing problem of scarcity was merely to continue the acts of the last session. The acts prohibiting the exportation of grain and the use of wheat in the distillery,[112] and those allowing free importation of foreign grain and flour were continued until twenty days after the commencement of the next session of Parliament.[113] An additional act was passed permitting the free importation of Indian corn from the American colonies until February 1st, 1769.[114] Having done this, Parliament turned its attention to other matters and waited until after the general election before giving the subject further consideration.

When the new Parliament met in May of 1768 the acts passed in the last session were once more renewed. The prohibitions against exporting grain and distilling wheat, and permission to import wheat, barley, pulse, oats and rye, free of duty, were all continued until twenty days after the commencement of the next session.[115] When Parliament reassembled in November the act permitting free importation of foreign grain was not renewed, but those prohibiting the exportation of grain and the use of wheat in the distillery were continued.[116] Although the question of high prices and scarcity did not continue to attract the attention in Parliament that it had since 1766, still there was enough pressure from outside to ensure the annual renewal of the law against the exportation of grain and the use of grain in the distillery. It is significant that the first act passed after the opening of each of next three sessions—January[117] and November[118] of 1770, and January,[119] 1772—was one continuing this prohibition against exportation and use of wheat in the distilleries.

In 1770 and 1772 Parliament passed two rather important acts which affected both the internal and external corn trade.   Whether these temporary enactments which have been described in the preceding pages were in any way responsible for these two permanent measures is uncertain.   By the act of 1770,[120] machinery was provided for registering the price at which grain was sold in the various counties, and the quantity exported and imported.   The Justices of the Peace were to appoint persons in each locality to make weekly returns. Such returns were to be sent to the Treasury, which was to publish them weekly and quarterly in *The London Gazette*.   This act was the basis of the first real average prices of grain.   Beginning in 1771 the average annual prices are based on these reports and not on an average of the Lady Day and Michaelmas prices in the Windsor Market.

The act of 1772 repealed all laws against badgers, engrossers, forestallers and regrators.   The reason assigned was that the restraints " by preventing a Free Trade in the said Commodities have a Tendency to discourage the Growth, and to enhance the Price of the same ; which Statutes, if put in Execution, would bring great Distress upon the Inhabitants of many Parts of this Kingdom, and in particular upon those of the Cities of London and Westminster."[121]   The repeal of these acts was undoubtedly a good thing, but the value of the action was somewhat impaired by the fact that these offences were still indictable under the common law as the famous Rusby case in 1800 was to prove.

After the renewal in January of 1772 of the prohibition against the exportation of grain and the use of wheat in the distilleries, there seems to have been a general feeling, in Parliament and outside, that something must be done to stop the uncertainty caused by these yearly suspensions of existing laws.   Prices were beginning to rise and a repetition of the food riots of 1767 was feared.   All interests— consumers, producers and government—evidently preferred that a permanent system should replace the uncertain one then in existence. The people of London, Westminster and other large cities were uneasy, because in periods of scarcity and rising prices they were dependent upon temporary acts of Parliament to prevent exportation of grain. Most members of the landed interest seem to have favoured a permanent settlement on the grounds that anything was preferable to the uncertainty existing.   Besides, they were not reaping the benefits of the high bounty and import price levels of the acts of 1689 and 1670, and they were subjected to opprobrium for their avarice without reaping the benefits which were supposed to accrue.   They were quite willing to compromise and lower these price levels if only the bounty were retained on exports and the duties on imports.   The attacks on the bounty and the popularity of the new free trade doctrines had much to do with this willingness to compromise. Even Charles Smith, the ablest defender of the bounty, advocated lowering both bounty price levels and the amount of the bounty to meet the changed conditions.[122]   Doubtless the government was weary of having the problem of annual suspensions and temporary measures always confronting it, and was quite as willing as the producer and consumer to solve the problem.

Accordingly a series of resolutions were introduced in the House of Commons on April 14th, 1772, by Governor Pownall.[123] The substance of these resolutions was : first, that a duty of 6d. a quarter should be charged on all wheat imported when the price was at or above 48s. ; second, that exportation should be forbidden when wheat was at or above 44s. ; and third, that a bounty of 5s. a quarter should be paid on all wheat exported when the price was less than 44s.[124] In explaining his resolutions Pownall declared that the shortage of recent years was due not to decreased production but to increased consumption. The latter he ascribed to the immense increase in manufactures and shopkeepers, the prodigious extent of commerce, the number of government employees and the growth of manufacturing and seaport towns. He pointed out that no large increase was necessary to absorb the surplus grain which had formerly been exported ; since, according to the estimate of Charles Smith, the average exportation since 1689 was not more than one thirty-sixth of the growth.[125] A temporary act to open the ports for free importation of grain was then proposed by Pownall, and the resolutions offered as a foundation for a permanent law to take effect when the temporary one expired. This proposal was adopted and an act passed allowing the importation, duty free, of wheat, wheat flour, rye, rye meal and Indian corn until December 1st, 1772.[126]

The next day, April 15th, the resolutions were reported and a bill was ordered to be brought in. This bill was passed on May 13th and sent to the House of Lords. On June 3rd it was returned with the amendment " that no bounty should be paid upon exported corn." Pownall and Burke, who were principally responsible for the measure, agreed that the bill as amended must be rejected. Pownall insisted that it " was a flagrant encroachment upon the privileges of the House," and that the Lords, " forgetful of their duty, had interfered in raising money " by this amendment.[127] Burke was even more insistent upon the necessity of rejection. His speech was studded with such impassioned sentences as : " Can liberty exist a moment, if we allow them to lay their sacrilegious hands upon this holy of holies, this palladium of the constitution ? " and " Had gentlemen any feeling for the honour of the House, would they submit to the disgrace of waiting three hours in the lobby of the House of Lords, among their lordships' footmen ? Sir, this has been my fate, when ordered by the House to carry their Bills to the Lords ; and I do not speak of it out of any personal pride, or as an indignity to myself, but as a flagrant disgrace to this House, which I apprehend is not inferior in rank to any other branch of the legislature."[128] After such an appeal there could be no doubt as to the result. The bill was rejected. The speaker then tossed it over the table, and several members on both sides of the question, to symbolize the solidarity of the House in the face of such an indignity, kicked it as they went out.[129]

The fact that no permanent arrangement had been made in the preceding spring, combined with an unsatisfactory harvest, made necessary some measures for temporary relief. Hence when Parliament assembled in November of 1772 three acts were passed to alleviate the usual distress ; first, importation of all grain or flour from Europe or Africa was allowed, duty free, until January 1st, 1774 ;[130] second, this privilege was extended to the American colonies from December 1st, 1772 to January 1st, 1774 ;[131] and third, the exportation of corn and the use of wheat in the distillery were prohibited during the same period.[132]   Evidently, the shortness of the crop justified this action, because early in 1773 the distress became so acute in London that the city offered a bounty of 4s. a quarter for 20,000 quarters of wheat to be imported between March and June of that year.[133]

After passing these temporary measures, the House of Commons next took up the matter of securing a permanent law along the lines of the one lost in the last session.   Although a series of resolutions similar to those of the preceding April were introduced on December 9th,[134] the bill based upon them did not pass the Commons until April 2nd, 1773,[135] and did not receive the royal assent until May 10th.[136]   The terms of the new act, which went into operation on January 1st, 1774, marked a decided change from those of the laws of 1670 and 1689.   Wheat could be imported, when the price at the port of entry was 48s. or above, upon the payment of a nominal duty of 6d. a quarter.   Exportation was forbidden when the price reached 44s., but below that level a bounty of 5s. was to be paid upon wheat exported.   The same principles with lower price levels were applied to rye, peas, beans, barley, beer and oats.[137]

An innovation was introduced in this act, evidently on behalf of the growing manufacturing towns and seaports, which the landed interest complained of bitterly in later times.   This innovation was the warehousing of foreign grain.   Under the arrangement provided in the law, foreign corn might be landed without the payment of duty, when the price was below the low import duty level, provided that the exact amount imported was entered in the book of the customs officer and the grain was immediately lodged in a warehouse under the joint locks of the King and the importer.   Such grain would eventually be removed, and either sold in England or re-exported.   In case it was sold in England it was to pay the duty due at that time on imported corn ; and in case it was re-exported a bond was to be given that it would not be re-landed anywhere in Great Britain.   The purpose of this clause was to permit both Englishmen and foreigners to store up grain when the import duty was high, and hold it on the chance that the price would rise to a point where the duty would be merely nominal.   This part of the act was a distinct concession to the towns which hoped to secure a ready supply against a future scarcity.

The Corn Law of 1773 has been held up as a landmark by both friends and opponents of protection for agriculture.   The former, beginning with Dirom, who wrote in the seventeen-eighties, have always insisted that it was at this time that the wise policy, formulated in the acts of 1670 and 1689, was abandoned.   The latter often refer to it as the only good measure, dealing with the external corn trade, which was passed before 1846.   Upon careful consideration this act does not appear to merit either the excessive criticism or praise to which it was later subjected.   There was no abandonment of the principle of excluding foreign grain by a prohibitive duty, or of paying a bounty on the exportation of English corn.[138] Not a single benefit had been lost to the landed interest which they had actually enjoyed under these acts. Almost invariably, as the preceding pages have shown, the bounty had been suspended and exportation prohibited before the price of wheat had reached 44s., and foreign importation allowed, duty free, before the price had reached 48s. The *actual* protection enjoyed by corn-growers during the previous seventy-five years had been nearer that fixed by the act of 1773, than by those of 1670 and 1689. This situation was especially true of the period from 1765–73, and it was the realization of the fact that made the landed interest acquiesce in the nominal change.

Arthur Young voiced his approval of Governor Pownall's act, as it was commonly designated, and called it a wise measure on the grounds that it was permanent ; that the idea of the bounty was preserved ; that it was equally adapted to encourage husbandry and navigation ; and that it obviated the objection to the old laws whereby the uncertainty whether the prices in England would allow importation, handicapped shipping in foreign countries.[139]

Adam Smith also cordially endorsed the new measure, but not so unreservedly as Young. He approved of lowering the import level at which the low duty came into operation, the lowering of the bounty price level and the warehouse clause. While he opposed bounties, he maintained that since they existed " the sooner they cease, and the lower they are, so much the better."[140] On the other hand, he believed that exportation of all kinds of corn was prohibited at too low a price, and that it was a blunder to forbid exportation at the very point that the bounty, which was given to encourage it, ceased. Either the bounty should have been withdrawn at a lower price or exportation allowed at a higher.[141] He concluded that, " With all its imperfections, we may perhaps say of it what was said of the laws of Solon, that, though not the best in itself, it is the best which the interests, prejudices and the temper of the time would admit of. It may perhaps in due time prepare the way for a better."[142]

Most modern political and even economic historians writing on the eighteenth century are careful to confine themselves strictly to the provisions of the act. McCulloch followed Adam Smith in pointing out the defects, but nevertheless maintained that, " with all these defects, the act of 1773 was a material improvement on the former system and ought not to have been altered unless to give greater freedom to the trade."[143] Cunningham held that this law was a reversal of the policy of 1689, the objects of which were to maintain prices at a steady level and to give a stimulus to English agriculture. In both objects, he believed, it had been successful ; yet the act of 1773 was substituted for the purpose of securing a food supply, either from home production or from abroad, at a steady price.[144] The measure, he held, was in " the nature of a compromise ; in so far as they accepted it, the representatives of each of the historic parties departed from the traditional policy which was associated with Whigs and Tories respectively. The Whigs, who had been eager to

corn and have the miller grind it.   But when the millers began to
buy and grind their own grain and to sell their own flour, they made
the quality of flour which paid them best and not that fixed by the
act of 1710.   One brand of flour was superior and one inferior to that
fixed by the assize.[66]

The operation of the assize in London in 1757 seems to have
artificially increased the scarcity of grain and hence made matters
worse for the populace.   The magistrates, in their endeavour to
reduce prices, had been very prompt in following each fall in the price
of wheat and flour with a new assize of bread, and even to set it lower
than the returned prices would bear.   This produced an artificial
scarcity, for the mealmen, fearing that they would face a loss under
such conditions, cut down on their usual business and sent the corn
and flour to places where the assize was more favourable.   This state
of affairs came to light when some factors and mealmen were examined
before the Privy Council on August 25th, 1757.   After that, consequently, more care was taken in setting the assize and the markets
were once more regularly supplied.[67]

The interest aroused between 1756 and 1758 by the scarcity of
corn and by the bread assize died down with the return of ordinary
harvests in 1758.   The only phase of the Corn Laws that attracted
much attention in the few years following was the bounty : a topic
which seems to have been controversial in good and bad years alike.
But once a series of bad harvests began in 1765 the old interest
revived.   Although prices of provisions in general were rising in the
latter part of that year, few pamphlets appeared until 1766.   Explanations of the high prices were eagerly sought and made.   The
chief cause ascribed, as in 1756–58, was the iniquity of the middlemen,
who, most people believed, made prices high by manipulating the
market and hoarding supplies.   The solution of the pamphleteers was
the time honoured one of " cutting out the middlemen."   One writer
hoped to accomplish this by going back to former marketing conditions
when the farmer sold his butter, corn, cheese, eggs, etc., at the town
market.[68]   New explanations, such as taxes occasioned by the late
war, the taking of tithe in kind,[69] and the great quantity of money
in circulation, were also offered.[70]   One writer thought that the
scarcity was due to the great number of women who flocked to the
cities since innoculation against smallpox had removed the fear that
had previously kept them at home.   He also admitted that the
amazing use of tea was partly responsible, since it caused arable farms
to be turned into dairies to supply milk for this beverage.   This writer
likewise deplored the numbers of drunken men and strumpets at
hangings and would have solved this by reviving the law against
lusty beggars, whereby all found outside their own parishes were to
be whipped and sent back.[71]   Another pamphleteer combining
statistics and religion ascribed the scarcity to the increase in
population and the chastising hand of God.[72]   In very few instances
was it pointed out that the wheat crop in the preceding year had been
deficient.[73]

Occasionally a writer took the pains to refute the conclusions of a
fellow pamphleteer, but as a rule new explanations, or vigorous

reassertions of the old ones, were considered more effective. A good example was the controversy between Soame Jenyns and a writer who called himself *A Gentleman of Cambridge.* Jenyns insisted that the high price of provisions arose from two sources : the increase of national debts or the poverty of the public ; and the increase of riches, or the wealth of the private individuals.[74] From this resulted : first, an increase in the amount of money which meant a depreciation in value and a rise in prices ; second, the impoverishment of those with a fixed income and enrichment of merchants and traders ; and third, the ultimate bankruptcy of the country.[75] *The Gentleman of Cambridge* answered that the solution of the problem was to curtail government and individual expenditure. Most of the tract is filled with a denunciation of the corruption and bribery of the court—a very popular subject at this time—and especially with the part that Jenyns, a placeman, played. He agreed that the country must save itself from ruin, but maintained that the way to do so was to narrow the channels through which the riches of the public flow, " in such torrents into the pockets of those whom, perhaps, Sir, you would call *public* men, I mean ministers, placemen, pensioners, and all the numerous train of court dependents."[76] He proposed to give the King an allowance to pay his own servants, and to give no official, not even the First Lord of the Treasury, more than one thousand pounds per annum.[77] Needless to say his suggestions were not adopted by the government as a remedy for the high price of corn and other provisions.

Between 1768 and 1773 the annual output of pamphlets declined, although, as was shown earlier in the chapter, the crops were not good during this period. Pamphleteers now inveighed less against the bounty and middlemen and more against luxury, taxes, national debt and depopulation resulting from the enclosing and engrossing of farms. One of the chief evidences of luxury was held to be the use in agriculture of the horse instead of the ox. One writer suggested that the best way to remove the existing distress caused by high prices would be by substituting the ox for the horse. He then proceeded to eulogize other animals and to disparage the horse in the ollowing manner : " The ox gives us his labour, the cow gives us milk, affords us butter and cheese, and the sheep yields us a fleece yearly, that furnishes employment and covering to millions. Nor does the value of these animals terminate with their existence ; they are benefactors after death, and in beef, mutton, tallow, suet and hides, they feed, light and chiefly clothe the Public. Can this be said of a horse ? By no means. He presents us, all-admired as he is, with nothing but his labour ; he must be maintained three or four years before this labour can be expected ; and when he dies, his worth dies with him, for he will then scarcely bring five shillings for the hounds."[78] Arbuthnot, whose testimony on the deficient harvests from 1769 to 1773 is quoted by both Tooke and Comber, insisted that the real cause for high prices of grain and provisions was actual scarcity and not one of the many reasons cited above.[79] He suggested that the present unsatisfactory conditions might be improved by enclosing and parcelling out the King's forests and chases. If each

[34] Adam Smith, *The Wealth of Nations*, vol. 2, p. 29.

[35] Arthur Young, *The Expediency of a Free Exportation of Corn at this Time*, p. 41.

[36] The author estimates the amount of grain that each person and animal should consume annually.

[37] Charles Smith, *Tracts on the Corn Trade and Corn Laws*, 1804, pp. 166-7.

[38] *Ibid.*, p. 161.

[39] Ordered printed by the House of Commons, July 2nd, 1822.

[40] *Considerations on the Present High Prices of Provisions and the Necessaries of Life*, by a West Country Maltster, 1764, p. 4.

[41] Lord Ernle, *English Farming Past and Present*, pp. 148-9.

[42] Tooke, *History of Prices*, vol. 1, p. 48.

[43] *Ibid.*, p. 49. [44] *Ibid.*, p. 49. [45] *Ibid.*, pp. 67-9. [46] *Ibid.*, pp. 48-74.

[47] *The Gentleman's Magazine*, XXVI, p. 408. [48] *Ibid.*, p. 544.

[49] *Ibid.*, XXVIII, pp. 191 and 239.
Tuesday, March 28th, " At the York Assizes, which ended the 25th, four persons were found guilty of high treason in obstructing the militia act, and received sentence of death accordingly ; two of the Wesleydale rioters were likewise capitally convicted for violently taking away meal on the highway in returning from market ; above twenty prisoners more were tried for riots, some of whom were continued, others fined and imprisoned, and others admitted to bail. Great lenity was shown by the judges and jury, where the prisoners did not appear to act with premeditation."
Tuesday, April 25th, " The judges' report of the seven rioters convicted at the late assizes at York was laid before his Majesty, when two of the ringleaders, namely, Robert Cole, for obstructing the militia act ; and George Berry for violently taking away corn, were ordered for execution ; Four of them to be transported for life, and one pardoned."

[50] The Annual Register, 1767, pp. 39-40.

[51] Westerfield, *Middlemen in English Business*, pp. 134-7.

[52] *Ibid.*, pp. 152-182. A full account of the corn middlemen is also given in Gras, *Evolution of the English Corn Market*, c. 6 and 7.

[53] *Considerations on the Present Dearness of Corn*, 1757, pp. 4-5.

[54] *A Compendium of the Corn Trade*, 1757.

[55] *The Causes of the Present High Price of Corn and Grain*, etc., 1757.

[56] Gras, *The Evolution of the English Corn Market*, p. 207.

[57] Miss Clara Pitt, *Scheme for Erecting Public Magazines, to Supply England with Corn*, 1758, p. 5-6.

[58] *Ibid.*

[59] *Sentiments of a Corn Factor on the Present Situation of the Corn Trade*, 1758, pp. 9-31.

[60] Charles Smith, *Tracts on the Corn Trade and Corn Laws*, 1804, pp. 32-6.

[61] *Ibid.*, p. 37. [62] *Ibid.*, pp. 56-9.

[63] Sidney and Beatrice Webb, *Economic Journal*, June, 1904, p. 198.

[64] 8th Anne, c. 19.

[65] S. and B. Webb, *Economic Journal*, June, 1904, p. 199.

[66] *Ibid.*, p. 201.

[67] Charles Smith, *Tracts on the Corn Trade and Corn Laws*, 1804, pp. 51-3.

[68] *The Causes of the Dearness of Provisions Assigned*, 1766, p. 32.

[69] *Three Letters to a Member of the Honourable House of Commons*, from a Country Farmer, 1766, p. 31.

[70] N. Forster, *An Inquiry into the Causes of the Present High Price of Provisions*, 1767, pp. 1 and 49.

[71] *Considerations on the Dearness of Corn and Provisions*, etc., 1767, pp. 7-32.

[72] *Popular Considerations on the Dearness of Provisions in General and Particularly of Corn Bread*, c. 1767, pp. 4-8.

[73] *An Appeal to the Public; or, Considerations on the Dearness of Corn*, 1767, p. 15.

[74] Soame Jenyns, *Thoughts on the Causes of the Present High Prices of Provisions*, 1767, p. 3.

[75] *Ibid.*, pp. 9-22.

[76] *An Answer to a Pamphlet Entitled " Thoughts on the Causes and Consequences of the Present High Price of Provisions,"* by a Gentleman of Cambridge, 1768, p. 24.

[77] *Ibid.*, p. 25.

[78] Francis Moore, *Considerations on the Exorbitant Price of Provisions*, 1773, p. 96.

[79] Arbuthnot, *An Inquiry into the Connection Between the Present Price of Provisions, and the Size of Farms*, 1773, p. 67.

[80] *Ibid.*, p. 73.

[81] 30th George II., c. 1. [82] 30th George II., c. 7. [83] 30th George II., c. 9. [84] *Ibid.* [85] 30th George II., c. 10. [86] 30th George II., c. 14. [87] 30th George II., c. 15. [88] 31st George II., c. 1. [89] 32nd George II., c. 2. [90] 32nd George II., c. 8. [91] 33rd George II., c. 4. [92] 33rd George III., c. 9. [93] 5th George III., c. 31. [94] 5th George III., c. 32. [95] 6th George III., c. 3. [96] 6th George III., c. 4. [97] 6th George III., c. 5.

[98] *Journal of the House of Commons*, vol. 30, p. 763.

[99] *Ibid.* The committee arrived at this conclusion from the testimony of a lighterman who declared that some factors had as much as 5,000 quarters of corn in one place. On the whole the most valuable part of the report was the appendix containing the prices of wheat and malt on Lady Day and Michaelmas at Oxford from 1733 to 1765, at Cambridge from 1677 to 1765, and at Winchester from 1661 to 1765.

[100] *The Annual Register*, 1766, pp. 224–6.

[101] *Ibid.*, 1767, p. 40. [102] *Ibid.*, 1766, pp. 226–7. [103] *Ibid.*, 1766, pp. 227–8. [104] *Ibid.*, 1766, pp. 228–9.

[105] 7th George III., c. 3. [106] 7th George III., c. 5. [107] 7th George III., c. 4. [108] 7th George III., c. 11. [109] 7th George III., c. 8. [110] 7th George III., c. 22.

[111] *The Annual Register*, 1768, p. 76.

[112] 8th George III., c. 1. [113] 8th George III., c. 2. [114] 8th George III., c. 3. [115] 8th George III., c. 1. First Session of new Parliament.

[116] 9th George III., c. 1. Second Session.

[117] 10th George III., c. 1. [118] 11th George III., c. 1. [119] 12th George III., c. 1.

[120] 10th George III., c. 39.

[121] 12th George III., c. 71. The acts especially referred to were the 3rd, 4th, 5th and 6th of Edward VI. ; the 3rd of Philip and Mary ; the 5th of Elizabeth ; the 15th of Charles II. ; and the 5th of Anne.

[122] Charles Smith, *Tracts on the Corn Trade and Corn Laws*, 1804, p. 108.

[123] Thomas Pownall, 1722–1805, usually called Governor Pownall, was Governor of Massachusetts from 1757 to 1759 and of South Carolina from 1759–60.

[124] Following the same principle, import duty of only threepence was charged on rye when the price was at or above twenty-eight shillings, and exportation was forbidden when the same figures were reached.

[125] *Parliamentary History*, vol. 17, pp. 475–482.

[126] 12th George III., c. 33.

[127] *Parliamentary History*, vol. 17, pp. 512.

[128] *Ibid.*, pp. 513–4. [129] *Ibid.*, pp. 515.

[130] 13th George III., c. 1. [131] 13th George III., c. 2. [132] 13th George III., c. 3.

[133] Tooke, *History of Prices*, vol. 1, p. 69.

[134] *Journal of the House of Commons*, vol. 34, p. 30.

[135] *Ibid.*, p. 245. [136] *Ibid.*, p. 307.

[137] 13th George III., c. 43.

[138] The duties on wheat by the act of 1670 were as follows :

Not exceeding 53s. 4d. a quarter	16s.
Exceeding 53s. 4d. but not exceeding 80s. ...	8s.
Exceeding 80s.	4d.

The duties on wheat by the act of 1773 were :

Not exceeding 44s. a quarter...................	22s.
Exceeding 44s. but under 48s.	17s.
At or above 48s.	6d.

[139] Arthur Young, *Political Arithmetic*, pp. 41–2.

[140] Adam Smith, *The Wealth of Nations*, Everyman's edn., vol. 2, p. 42.

[141] *Ibid.* [142] *Ibid.*

[143] J. R. McCulloch, *Dictionary of Commerce*, p. 430.

[144] Cunningham, *The Growth of English Industry and Commerce*, vol. 3, fifth edn., pp. 723–4.

[145] *Ibid.*, 724–5.

[146] Nicholson, *The History of the English Corn Laws*, 1904, p. 71.

[147] Morley, *The Life of Richard Cobden*, 1903, p. 167, note.

CHAPTER IV

THE FAILURE OF THE LAW OF 1773

Flaws in act of 1773 necessitate supplementary measures—Inadequate machinery for its enforcement—Frauds practised—Attempts to improve administration of this law by the acts of 1781 and 1789—Sketch of the quality and quantity of the crops from 1773 to 1791—Recommendations of the Committee of the Privy Council on Trade and Plantations—Reasons landed interest agitated for additional protection—Arguments of Dirom—Vigorous opposition to any change in the law of 1773 from the growing industrial and commercial cities—The act of 1791—Significance of the clash between the landed and commercial interests —Opinions of contemporary and modern writers—Reasons act of 1773 disappointed expectations.

THE law of 1773 went into operation on January 1st, 1774, and was repealed by the act of 1791. This period of over seventeen years may be divided into two parts. Down to 1790 the chief interest lies in the administration of the new law and particularly in the efforts to improve its machinery. After 1790 the interest shifts to the agitation for a new law. Everyone interested in the corn bill of 1773 hoped evidently, when it became a law, that the perplexing problems of the preceding years would be solved and that the question would fall into the background. This hope was not to be realized for, in some form or another, the law of 1773 was to be in the foreground in nearly every year from 1773 to 1791.

Soon after the law went into operation it was discovered that certain of its provisions prevented the exportation of grain to the colonies. Hence a series of acts had to be passed to allow the exportation of a limited amount to the places which were suffering. In 1774 relief was given to the sugar colonies in America [1] and to Hudson Bay,[2] and in 1777 similar relief was extended to St. Helena, East India, Newfoundland, Nova Scotia, Bay Chaleur and Labrador.[3]

Other ambiguities and flaws in the act of 1773 soon demanded attention. The method of ascertaining the price of grain exported was unsatisfactory. Consequently it was decreed that the average price of the grain sold in the public market or nearest port on the last market day preceding the shipping should determine the export price.[4] In addition it was found that Indian corn had been omitted in the act of 1773, but this oversight was remedied when Parliament assembled late in 1774.[5] Also from time to time it was necessary to add to the list of ports which were permitted to import grain. In 1776 this privilege was extended to Preston ;[6] in 1778 to Portsmouth, Sandwich, Chichester and Chester ;[7] and in 1779 to Cowes on the Isle of Wight.[8]

But even after these flaws had been removed the law of 1773 did not function in a satisfactory manner because the machinery for regulating the importation and exportation of grain, especially in the

London and Home Counties markets, was inadequate. An act in 1732 gave the Mayor and aldermen of London the power to fix the import prices in the months of April and October. Another act in 1766 extended this power to the months of January and July. A great improvement was made in 1770 when it was enacted that a weekly return should be made of the prices of grain, based on from two to six markets, in every county in Great Britain. These returns, while giving the Justices of the Peace at the Quarter Sessions material on which to base the import prices they fixed for the next three months and furnishing the first national annual price of grain, did not eliminate fraud. Until after the act of 1781 went into operation the Mayor and aldermen of London, at the Quarter Sessions, certified the prices of " middling " corn to the collector of customs. These prices were determined by the oath of two persons who fulfilled the property qualifications specified in the law of 1685. In general, these persons did not govern themselves either by the spirit or letter of the law,[9] for they often bought the best grain at an extra high price and took oath that it was the common market price of the middling quality and thereby allowed importation to take place.[10]

In the outports manipulation of the market by the corn middlemen to secure importation was equally flagrant. The most common practice was to pay a high price just before the Quarter Sessions and, by giving oath that this was the price, to secure the opening of the port for three months. This practice was very distressing to the farmers who supplied markets near a seaport, for under such circumstances the price of grain was apt to be greatly lowered. Perhaps nothing indicates how poorly the whole system was administered as the fact that Justices of the Peace in one district of the country would permit importation when it was forbidden in an adjoining district, and allow exportation and importation of the same kind of grain at the same time from a single port.[11]

Similar frauds were practised in determining the prices regulating the bounty on corn, but they were of longer standing and some of them have already been described. In London until 1781, the oath of the exporter and the average prices returned by the meal weighers on the market day preceding the shipping of the grain, determined whether the bounty should be paid. The exporter might influence the price of any kind of grain which the meal weighers reported by purchasing a small amount of inferior quality at a low price. Furthermore, these imported prices were necessarily incomplete and hence were often misleading.[12] It was possible, by manipulating the prices governing both importation and exportation, to import foreign grain and to re-export it with a bounty.[13]

By 1781 it was clear that the methods prescribed for determining the prices of grain in London, Essex and Kent, according to the acts of 1685, 1732, 1766, 1770, 1773 and 1774, were unsatisfactory. None of these provided the necessary machinery for ascertaining the average price of grain which would regulate exportation and determine whether the bounty should be paid. It was to remedy this state of affairs that the act of 1781 was passed. This law provided that an official, called the Inspector of the Returns of Corn, should be appointed, who was to receive a weekly report from every corn factor in Mark Lane, containing an account of the quantities and prices of all grain sold, and the names of the purchasers. The inspector was to make an average of each kind of grain, keep a record, and publish weekly prices in *The London Gazette*. These prices were to determine whether the bounty was payable on the different kinds of grain shipped during that week. The weekly averages were to be presented to the Mayor and aldermen on the first day of each Quarter Sessions in July, October, January and April ; and the averages for the past three months were to determine what kinds of corn might be imported during the next three months. These prices were to be published in the Gazette once in the four weeks immediately after the Quarter Sessions. In order to avoid the usual fraud in swearing, the two corn factors, who were selected to verify the average prices, were to be chosen by lot. The corn factors of Mark Lane were to appoint the Inspector of Corn Returns, and his salary and other expenses incurred in the enforcement of the act were to be met by an assessment of a halfpenny per last on all grain appearing in the weekly returns.[14]

On the whole, the law of 1781 seems to have been an improvement upon the system which existed down to that time. Like many preceding laws it would have been more effective if it had been well administered. In 1783 Claude Scott, a great London corn factor, testified that the new law was working well except for a serious inconvenience caused apparently by a mistake in the wording of the act. The bounty was made payable according to the average price of the week in which the entry for exportation was made. Since this was not known until Saturday night of the week following, an exporter often had to ship without knowing whether or not he would receive the bounty, or would be obliged to wait and remove his grain from the ship if the average was beyond the export limit. This defect, Scott suggested, could be remedied by making the exportation and bounty depend upon the average prices of the preceding week.[15] In spite of this constructive criticism no immediate effort was made to remove the flaw in the administration of the measure. Furthermore, there seems to have been no widespread complaint against this defect. Whether this evident lack of interest was due to the fact that Scott exaggerated the uncertainty created, or that the law was so laxly administered that it did not seriously inconvenience the corn factors, is not clear.

In 1789 the part of the act of 1781, which required two corn factors, chosen by lot, to give oath at the Quarter Sessions, was repealed. Instead, each corn factor was required to swear that the weekly returns which he made, were accurate.[16] The regulations of 1781 which dealt with exportation and the bounty were left unchanged, but those on importation were slightly altered. The average taken of each kind of grain to determine whether the ports should be opened was to be reckoned on the six weeks preceding the Quarter Sessions, instead of the entire three months.[17] The principles of the act of 1781, which had applied only to London, Essex and Kent, were now extended to the maritime counties. In each of the eleven districts, into which these maritime counties were divided, the Justices of

Peace at the next Quarter Sessions were to select not more than twelve nor less than eight markets from which the price of corn was to be taken. In counties where there were less than four market towns, prices were to be taken from all that had markets. In each town an inspector of the prices of grain was to be appointed by the Justices of the Peace. These inspectors were to make a return of the weekly prices to the receiver of corn returns, appointed by the act of 1770, and were to send a duplicate list to the collector of customs in each port in the district. The receiver was to make an average of the six weekly price averages preceding February 1st, May 1st, August 1st and November 1st, and was to send a copy to each collector of customs where foreign grain might be imported. These averages were to regulate importation. Exportation and the bounty were to be regulated by the weekly averages which the receiver of corn returns sent to the various customs collectors. The corn buyers in the markets of these out-districts were to take an oath, similar to the one administered to the corn factors in London, that the returns they made were accurate.[18] This law of 1789 marked the last attempt to supply a better system of administration before the passing of a new corn law in 1791.

The preceding paragraphs have shown how hard the government tried to improve the machinery for administering the Corn Law of 1773. But in addition to having this problem on its hands during the years following 1773, the government discovered that the permanent measure of that year did not do away with the necessity for temporary measures. All interests concerned had hoped that the law of 1773 would do away with these frequent suspensions of the bounty and laws against importation ; and while it did materially reduce them, war and poor crops prevented their absolute discontinuance.

The crops from the harvest of 1773 to that of 1790 were variable. Both 1773 and 1774 were years of scarcity, judging by contemporary testimony and the size of the imports in the following twelve months.[19] On the other hand, the harvests of 1775 and 1778 were plentiful, those of 1776 and 1777 were at least normal and that of 1779 was reputed to have been a fourth above the average.[20] The crops during the seventeen-eighties showed the same variations. That of 1780 was slightly deficient ; those of 1781, 1785 and 1786 were average ; and those of 1782, 1783, 1784 and 1789 were very unfavourable.[21] In fact, the deficient harvest of 1789, which was caused by a severe winter and a backward spring, combined with the unsatisfactory crop of 1790 to bring the question of a new law once more into prominence. Tooke, generalizing on these years, states that " although not marked by any extraordinary inclemency of weather, or by a considerable degree of scarcity, so far at least as regards wheat, excepting from 1782 to 1784, the seasons were irregular, and a large proportion of them were attended with harvests of scanty produce ; not scanty merely with reference to an increasing rate of consumption, but scanty relatively to the average produce of a given extent of cultivation."[22]

The action of the government, as earlier chapters have shown, was influenced to a great extent by the quality and quantity of the crops. Since the harvests were plentiful and prices low from 1775 to 1780 the complaints came not from the inhabitants of London and the growing manufacturing cities, but from the landed interest. Arthur Young, writing in 1780, describes conditions in these years in the following manner : " In the years 1776, 1777, prices fell considerably ; and in 1779, so low, that very general complaints have been heard of ruined farmers and distressed landlords ; and at the time I am now writing, the fact holds that there is a considerable fall in all products, and a great number of farmers ruined."[23] Although the landlords could bring their grievances before the government even more readily than the London, Westminster and provincial mobs, still there was no easy solution for plentiful crops and low prices, as there was for short crops and high prices. The only relief, apparently, that the government felt it could offer was an act allowing half the usual bounty on grain when exported in neutral instead of British vessels. The reason ascribed for passing this act was not the low price of grain, but the fact that so much of the British marine was engaged in war service. The law was to remain in operation until March 25th, 1781,[24] and later it was renewed for an additional year.[25]

In the seventeen-eighties, on the other hand, the number of deficient crops exceeded the good ones. The result was that the government had to fall back on the temporary measures which had been used so often from 1765 to 1773. After the bad harvest of 1782 three acts of this nature were passed. First, corn and flour could be imported in neutral vessels upon the payment of the duties of 1773 and two additional five per cents.[26] Second, importation of Indian corn duty free was permitted until September 30th, 1783,[27] but this concession was only a slight one considering the low duty payable under normal conditions. Third, the bounty on exportation was suspended in England until August 26th, 1783 and in Scotland until September 26th of the same year.[28]

From 1783 until the very deficient harvest of 1789 no further suspensions of any part of the law of 1773 were deemed necessary. Perhaps the extraordinary prosperity which the country enjoyed after 1785 had much to do with the absence of complaints during these years. But when the scanty crop of 1789 was followed by rising prices, the usual riots and violence took place. In addition, the crops on the continent, and particularly in France, were even more deficient, and extensive commissions for purchasing English corn for exportation were constantly being received.[29] To remedy the situation, an order in council was issued on December 23rd, 1789, prohibiting the exportation of grain from any port in England, and permitting the importation upon payment of the low duties.[30] When Parliament met in January of 1790 an act was immediately passed indemnifying all persons concerned in executing this order. Also, the prohibition against exportation and the permission to import were continued until September 29th, 1790.[31] Before the end of the session, when the quality and quantity of the crop of 1790 were still unknown, these provisions were further continued until February 28th, 1791. In addition, the Crown was given the power, through an order in council, to permit exportation and to forbid importation, upon the payment of low duties, in case the harvest was favourable.[32]

Down to the session of Parliament which opened in January of 1790 the attention of the government was clearly centred on improving the administrative machinery of the law of 1773, and on providing relief from too abundant or too scanty crops by temporary measures. It is noteworthy how little unfavourable comment the law aroused down to 1790 and 1791. A glance at the titles of the pamphlets on this period, listed in the bibliography, will show that most of them dealt with enclosure, improved methods in agriculture and suggestions for a more effective administration of the existing law. The demands for a new law, which were so insistent before 1773, were practically non-existent during the years before 1790.

What really paved the way for a new law was a " Representation," dated March 8th, 1790, which was drawn up by the Committee of the Privy Council on Trade and Foreign Plantations. This " Representation," which was presented to the members of both Houses, was not intended as a first step in the direction of a new law, but as an attempt to lay down the principles upon which the corn trade of the kingdom should be governed, to point out the flaws in the existing system, and to offer suggestions for improvements. It opened with a contrast between the nineteen years from 1746 to 1765 and the eighteen from 1770 to 1788 in both exports and imports. It expressed the hope that the change was due to increased population and opulence diffused through the classes, since there were no grounds for the belief that agriculture had declined. The subject, the committee held, was all important because in ordinary years, Europe was barely self-sufficient and a deficit could be supplied only from America.[33] The internal corn trade should be conducted on the assumption that, " The best market for corn in every country is the home market ; and the circulation of it within every kingdom ought to be free, so that the surplus of one part may supply the deficiencies of the other, and that the price throughout the whole country may be brought as near as possible to a level."[34]

The committee next expressed the belief " that the principles on which our corn laws are founded are in general wise ; the two objects they have in view are, first to secure a reasonable price at all times to the farmer, and in the next place to prevent that price being at any time so high as to distress the poor and the manufacturer."[35] In general the laws regulating the internal and external corn trade followed these principles with the possible exception of the act of 1663, which interfered with engrossing corn when above certain prices,[36] and the part of the law of 1773 which stopped exportation at a price which, perhaps, was not sufficiently high to encourage agriculture.[37] The Corn Laws which seemed the most in need of attention were those dealing with the method of ascertaining the price of corn for importation. The act of 1770 was completely executed in all parts of England, but that of 1789 was so imperfectly drawn up that only the district of London, Essex, Sussex and Kent had carried it out, and the other eleven districts had done nothing by December of that year. Since that time, five districts had put it into execution. The attorney and solicitor-general of the Crown gave it as their opinion, " That in those districts where market towns have not been selected and nominated, or inspectors appointed by the justices at the last Michaelmas quarter session, they cannot now be appointed, as no authority is given by the act for that purpose."[38] Since all the powers of former laws were repealed by the act of 1789, which had itself ceased to operate, a new law was an absolute necessity.[39] The committee then offered twelve elaborate suggestions as the basis for a new act.[40]

A committee had been appointed in the House of Commons on February 19th to consider the act of 1789. This committee on March 31st introduced a series of resolutions based on these twelve suggestions of the Committee of the Privy Council on Trade and Foreign Plantations. The first reading of a bill embodying these resolutions came on May 3rd. Immediately petitions began to pour in from manufacturing cities, particularly those of Scotland, either protesting against the bill or asking for certain amendments. Such petitions came from the Lord Provost, magistrates, and Common Council of Glasgow ; the Glasgow Chamber of Commerce and Manufacture ; the Trades House of Glasgow ; Merchants House of Glasgow ; Annual Committee of the Convention of Royal Boroughs of Scotland ; magistrates and town councils of Greenock and Paisley ; Master, wardens and merchant venturers of Bristol ; merchants and bus owners of Rothesay ; and many others.[41] The committee struggled manfully with the petitions and tried unavailingly to reconcile them with the bill. On June 1st, the attempt to pass a bill during the session was abandoned and further consideration of the report and bill was put off for three months.[42]

On the strength of a rather inferior harvest in 1790, due to a wet summer, Parliament in December of that year continued the two acts passed in the previous session suspending the exportation of corn and permitting importation, on the payment of the low duties, until June 10th, 1791.[43] Next, the bill which had been abandoned in the last session was taken up on December 15th, resolutions similar to the ones of March 31st were read, agreed to, and a bill based upon them was ordered brought in. The next day the first reading of the bill occurred and on the 17th the second.[44] The bill was then put aside until the following February.

In the early months of 1791 a number of pamphlets appeared attacking both the law of 1773 and the bill under consideration. In general the act of 1773 had been accepted by both sides at the time it was passed and in the years that followed. Now the landed interest changed its attitude and declared that the act had been both a reversal in policy and a mistake. Three of the most vigorous advocates of this point of view were Lord Sheffield, Sir John Sinclair, President of the Board of Agriculture, and William Mitford. Lord Sheffield held that there was no need of England being dependent on foreign countries for corn as long as the vast wastes were uncultivated ;[45] that all alterations in the act of 1773 were objectionable except the one regulating the opening of the ports ; that the great and leading principle of not tolerating importation, except in case of great emer-

gency, had been abandoned ;[46] that the only means of rendering
Great Britain independent of foreign corn was to give a monopoly
of the home market to the farmers, " not merely for their emolument,
but for our own safety."[47] At the same time he did not abandon
the old argument of the bounty supporters, for he insisted that " it
is a steady price that is to be wished for, not a low price ; and that
regular price can be obtained by our growing more corn than we can
consume and by encouraging the exports of the surplus."[48] He
especially objected to the clause in the proposed measure which
provided for public magazines for foreign corn.   Besides discouraging
tillage by being a sword of Damocles over the head of the farmer, it
would simply enhance the frauds already prevalent in the corn trade
whereby the granaries as well as the ports would be opened by the
price juggling of the corn middlemen.[49] Once the magazines were
opened by this fraudulent manipulation, corn would penetrate every
part of the country through the elaborate system of canals.[50] He
also objected to the clause allowing warehoused corn to be ground
and re-exported, because he feared that bad corn might be introduced
and good corn drawn out and shipped from the country.[51] Sheffield
wanted the bounty on wheat continued until the price reached 48s. a
quarter,[52] exportation without the bounty permitted up to 53s. 4d.[53]
and the high duty on importation retained until the same figures
were attained.[54] But above all, he wanted the 8s. duty of 1670
maintained until the price reached 80s.[55] In short he desired a
return to the acts of 1670 and 1689, despite the fact that the years
1765 to 1773 had shown the futility of trying to enforce them.

The point of view of Sinclair was much the same.   Several suggestions and objections of Sinclair, in his *Address to the Landed
Interest*, are worth consideration.   He excelled Sheffield in eulogizing
the bounty and characterized it as " perhaps the happiest idea that
ever entered into the conception of a statesman," and " the only
rational mode of encouraging production."[56] He objected to the
clause in the bill which gave a preference to Irish wheat since, with
the bounty offered by the Irish Parliament, it was highly injurious
to the English farmer.   He further objected to the fact that the
bounty was the same, regardless of the price of grain ; and that the
import duties fell from 24s. 3d. to 6d. without any intervening step.
To remedy these two defects, Sinclair proposed the introduction of
the sliding scale, whereby the bounty would increase as the price
fell and the import duties would decrease as the price rose.[57] This
principle was applied later to the import duties by the acts of 1828
and 1842, but at this time it was not given serious consideration.   He
also wanted a small bounty granted on the coastwise corn trade in
order that the counties of the east and south-east coasts might supply
the manufacturing districts of the north and west with more grain.[58]

Mitford believed that the solution of the problem of feeding Great
Britain by the produce of her own land did not lie in a law regulating
the corn trade, but in the encouragement of corn culture.[59] He was
certain that if the tithes on land were commuted, tillage would improve and production increase to such an extent that Great Britain
would once more become self-sufficient.[60] Under existing conditions

farmers took up stock feeding because the tithe on pasture land was much less than on arable land.[61] In addition, the ten per cent. which went to the tithe-holder often represented the profit of the farmer and so deterred him from breaking up waste land.[62] Mitford also differed from Sheffield and Sinclair on the position of English agriculture, and maintained that the amount of land recently reclaimed was a sufficient refutation of the fear that agriculture was declining.[63] His thesis was not that the production of grain was declining, but that it was not increasing as rapidly as it should because of the handicap of the tithe.

These three writers certainly express the feeling of the landed interest that additional encouragement for agriculture was necessary. All the main arguments advanced by them were to be used extensively in the next half-century, with the possible exception of Mitford's insistence on the tithe. But before turning to the final stages of the corn bill of 1791, the work of the Reverend Alexander Dirom of Aberdeenshire must be considered. Although he wrote his *Inquiry into the Corn Laws and Corn Trade of Great Britain* about 1786, it was not published until 1796 and so cannot be listed with the pamphlets which resulted from the 1790–1791 agitation. Nevertheless, the arguments which he expounded were freely used in the controversy of these years, and although other men advocated these same ideas before Dirom's work was printed, writers and pamphleteers of the first half of the nineteenth century invariably referred to him as the leading and original apostle of this creed.

On the whole it is easier to understand Dirom's position when his sources and methods are appreciated. He relied principally upon acts of Parliament, the import and export figures since 1697, and the Eton and Oxford semi-annual prices to prove his conclusions. He believed implicitly in the wisdom of the men of 1689, in the glories of wheat production in the first half of the eighteenth century, in the golden decade of the seventeen-forties, and in the decadence of agriculture since 1773.[64] His opinion of the act of 1773 is best shown in his insistence that as a result " exportation has been restrained, and agriculture of course repressed ; importation has been facilitated, and the trade laid open to fraud, by permitting the re-exporting, and carrying coastways, from one port to another, grain imported."[65] His partiality for the period before 1773, and particularly for the years from 1741–1750 is even more effectively brought out by his brief statement that " these were our halcyon days, and we have seen the melancholy reverse."[66] Briefly stated, Dirom's thesis is that by the acts of 1670 and 1689 a marvellous system had been reared up under which all classes were happy and prosperous, but that by temporary acts from 1765 to 1773 agriculture had been unnecessarily interfered with, and by the permanent act of 1773 this wonderful system had been completely uprooted.

Having now examined the more prominent pamphlets published in 1791 favouring additional protection to agriculture, as well as the conventional arguments of Dirom, it is easier to understand the point of view of the protagonists of the corn bill which passed its second reading in the House of Commons in December of 1790. On February 8th,

1791, the bill was recommitted.   Immediately petitions poured in from the manufacturing and commercial cities asking for changes in the price level, in the division of districts, in the import conditions from America and Ireland, and in the warehousing clauses.   These petitions continued to arrive until the day of the third reading of the bill.   *The Report of the Committee of the Town Council of Glasgow, Appointed to Consider the Corn Bill* gives the point of view of the new manufacturing cities as the pamphlets examined in the preceding paragraphs gave that of the landed interest.   The position taken in the report is that free importation and exportation of grain at all times, with the exception of stopping exportation altogether in time of extreme scarcity, are beneficial to all interests ; and that bounties on exports and high duties on imports are correspondingly most prejudicial.[67]   The stock arguments for the benefits to be derived from this policy are then enumerated.   The strength and wealth of a nation consist in the number of its inhabitants and of their pro- ductive labour.   The price of labour is regulated by the price of corn, and as the last twenty-five years have shown that the country is not capable of supplying herself, it is absurd to force grain out of the country by bounties.   Furthermore, bounties are unnecessary, first, because the supply of home-grown corn does not equal the demand ; and second, because they are chiefly paid on the grain grown on the richest lands which require no artificial aid.   High duties keep up the price of food for the industrious labouring class and so cause them great hardships.   Free importation and exportation would make Great Britain the granary of Europe and help to increase her trade, shipping and seamen.   In case foreign competition became too severe, the farmers could turn their attention to the production of meat, poultry, milk, grass, hay, etc., the price of which would be greatly enhanced by the increased population.[68]   Some specific objections to the bill were made which chiefly concerned the discrimination against Scotland in ports for warehousing grain and in the price at which oatmeal could be imported.

But despite the fact that most of the petitions sent to the House of Commons were from manufacturing and commercial cities, most of the changes made favoured the landed interest.   The revised resolutions offered to the House of Commons on May 17th had under- gone a tremendous change from the resolutions which the Committee of the Privy Council on Trade and Foreign Plantations had offered in March of 1790.   Foreign corn was to pay three different duties depending on the price at the time of importation.   The really new principle introduced was the colonial preference given to Ireland and the North American colonies, which was to be found in every sub- sequent corn bill until 1846.[69]   This concession seems to have been offered to the consumer partly to compensate for the rise in the im- portation level above that of 1773.   As late as May 25th a resolution was passed permitting corn and flour to be warehoused in certain ports at the expense of the importer and to be sold for home con- sumption on payment of the regular duties plus an additional one of 2s. 6d. a quarter on wheat, and on other grain in proportion.[70]   The bill with this addition was passed in the House of Commons on May

27th, 1791,[71] and a few days later in the Lords.[72] On June 10th, the day Parliament was prorogued, the bill received the royal assent.[73] The act which went into operation on November 15th, 1791, was in its final form, an enormous affair covering eighty-five pages in the *Public General Acts*. The laws of 1685, 1689, 1732, 1770, 1773, 1781, 1789, and as much as that of 1663 as prohibited the engrossing of corn, were repealed. It was permissible to export wheat when the price was less than 46s. a quarter and a bounty of 5s. was paid on all which was exported when the price was less than 44s. The importation of wheat was governed by the following regulations : when under 50s. a quarter a duty of 24s. 3d. was charged ; when at or above 50s. but less than 54s., a duty of 2s. 6d., and when at or above 54s., a duty of 6d.[74] Wheat could be imported from Ireland and the North American colonies under the same duties when the price was 2s. less on each of the three price levels. The machinery for administering the new law was, in its main outlines, based on the act of 1789. Since the act became inoperative so soon, as will be shown in the next chapter, a detailed account of this section will not be given.[75]

The chief interest in the act of 1791 lies not in its effect on British agriculture, as its exponents hoped, but in the fact that it marks the first real clash between the landed interest and the growing commercial and manufacturing cities of the midlands and north. The difference in the spirit in which the acts of 1773 and 1791 were passed is of greater importance than the actual difference in the details of the two. The landed interest acquiesced in the nominal changes made in 1773 because the act of that year merely put in legal form an arrangement which had been in existence for some time. Those interested in greater protection for agriculture would have preferred a higher price level at which the bounty ceased, and a higher one for the application of the nominal duty on importation ; but they realized that the average prices which they had enjoyed between 1689 and 1773 were less than 44s. to 48s.—the limits within which wheat was expected to fluctuate under the act of 1773. Even before this law was passed the landed interest did not reap the benefits of high prices during years of scarcity because Parliament under pressure from London and the manufacturing and mining districts, was forced to allow importation free and prohibit exportation. Hence, those interested in protection for agriculture had agreed to the act of 1773 because they were really giving up nothing that was worth anything at the time ; but they discovered by 1790 that what they had given up was now worth something and they regretted having surrendered it.

There is no doubt that the enormous increase in the demand for agricultural produce in the seventeen-eighties, which was one of the factors which led to a rise in prices, gave the landed interest some grounds for their demand for increased protection. The years following the American Revolution were among the most epoch-making in English industrial and commercial history. The great inventions in the textile industries, which are so heavily emphasized in all histories of the Industrial Revolution, were not widely used until the seventeen-eighties when cotton spinning factories, operated first by water and then by steam, came into prominence.   In addition the great advances in metallurgy and Watt's improvements on his earlier steam engine, made these years as noteworthy as did the rapid expansion of cotton spinning factories.   Just as significant as the advance on the industrial side, was the startling jump in the import and export figures from 1785 to 1800.   Improved roads and new canals were constructed in response to the demand for cheaper means of communications for food, raw materials and manufactured products.   This wonderful burst of prosperity which, incidentally, did so much to make the reputation of William Pitt as a statesman, naturally had its influence on agriculture.   The growth of the industrial cities of the north and midlands, of the ports on the west coast and of the population in the mining districts greatly increased the demand for food.   The demand was partly met by the wholesale enclosure of arable and waste land from 1765 to 1815, a phase of the subject which will be treated in detail in Chapter VI.   But when the demand for food increased and the price of agricultural products began to rise, the landed interest felt that the act of 1773 prevented them from reaping the benefit to whicl. they were entitled.   In short, the acts of 1670 and 1689 were worth no more in 1773 than the act of that year ; but in 1791 they were worth infinitely more.   This feeling is the basis of the statement by Lord Sheffield in the House of Commons, February 28th, 1791, that there had been a revolution eighteen years before.   The old policy, he declared, was to encourage tillage and to get rid of the surplus corn by means of a bounty ; the new one was to keep down prices by facilitating imports and checking exports.[76]

A similar change of mind was evident among the consumers of the growing cities.   They seem to have welcomed the act of 1773 as making permanent lower price levels than those of the laws of 1670 and 1689, instead of having to depend upon temporary suspensions of the bounty and right to export, and prohibitions against importation by act of Parliament and by order in council.   It is true that at the time many writers argued ably on the benefits the working classes and manufacturers would derive from free trade in corn, but these were " theoretical " writers and the classes alluded to rightly felt that the act of 1773 was a distinct gain for them.   By 1791 they were sorry that they had not received more, just as the landed interest regretted having conceded so much.   The arguments of the theorists of 1773 were the substance of the petitions from the great manufacturing cities and seaports against unfavourable changes in 1791.

Opinions of later writers are both divergent and interesting. McCulloch declared that in addition to the clamour of the landholders " a dread of becoming habitually dependent on foreign supplies operated on many, and produced a pretty general acquiescence in the act of 1791."[77]   Tooke ascribed it to the complaints of the landed interest on low prices following the abundant harvest of 1791.[78]   Comber insisted that, " This act in avoiding the extremes both of importation and exportation, left us without any system ; and in professing to consolidate all the laws in relation to this subject, demonstrated the difficulty of forming any.   The evident bias, however, of the legislature, was an hostility to importation, and a jealousy of the competition of the foreign grower ; and at the time that the nation was complaining of the dearness of grain, the prices were kept up by a monopoly of the home market."[79] Cunningham argued that whereas the act of 1773 was intended to secure a food supply either from home or abroad, at a steady price, in that of 1791 Parliament reverted to the principle of promoting native production and, along with the Revolutionary and Napoleonic wars, gave an unhealthy stimulus to tillage for a time.[80] Hunt followed McCulloch in holding that, " Landowners and farmers were dissatisfied, and a general fear lest the country should become dependent on foreign corn led Parliament in 1791 to adopt a policy of encouraging home production."[81] Nicholson in this instance admittedly drew on McCulloch for his conclusions.[82]

McCulloch's conclusions and those of his followers seem to be based entirely on the arguments of Sheffield and Sinclair. A glance at the enormous number of petitions against both the bill of 1790 and of 1791, which are to be found in the *Journal of the House of Commons*, is enough to dispose of his " general acquiescence " theory. In fact the opposition was so severe that the bill of 1790 had to be abandoned, and the one of 1791 was passed under the strongest protests from the growing manufacturing and commercial cities. Tooke's reason for the passing of the bill seems absurd. It must have been at least September before the size of the harvest could be determined, and since the bill had passed the Commons in May and received the royal assent on June 10th, his explanation is unsound. Cunningham's mistake in this case is due, apparently, to his interpretation of the act of 1773. This law, as has been shown in Chapter III, was not revolutionary, and that of 1791 was changed only in detail and not in principle. Changes were made where it was believed that the act of 1773 could be improved : first, a slightly higher level at which grain could be imported upon paying the low duty ; second, a duty of 2s. 6d. part way between the high and low duties ; third, a differentiation between the points at which the bounty stopped and exportation was forbidden ; and fourth, a colonial preference. The " Representation " of the Committee of the Privy Council, upon which the act of 1791 was based, was for the avowed purpose of improving the acts of 1773 and 1789 and there is nothing to show that " Parliament reverted to the principle of promoting native production." The landed interest was in control of Parliament and raised the price levels at which the high and low duties were applied. This action, although it unquestionably increased the protection to agriculture, was in no sense a change in principle.

Nearly all modern writers and some contemporary ones agree that English agriculture did not decline from 1765 to 1791. The increase in the amount of grain grown seems to have been a direct result of the increased demand occasioned by the rapid growth of the manufacturing and commercial cities. Corn, like other commodities, is produced for a market. The bounty in the first half of the eighteenth century had helped in finding one, but after 1765 it was of little use except in years of super-abundance. The new cities of the midlands and north now offered a steadily-growing market, and the demand

for food seems to have increased more rapidly than the supply. Still
the surplus of wheat and other grain exported each year down to
1765 was a comparatively small part of the crop, and hence the
additional demands within the country easily absorbed this surplus.
The act of 1773 was drawn up by able landowners and was, apparently,
acquiesced in by all classes. It has been shown that there was
little complaint against the principles of the act down to 1791, but
that there were a great many attempts to improve its administration.
The avowed intention of the framers of the bill in 1773 was to keep
wheat fluctuating between 44s. and 48s. The surplus was to be
shipped out of the country by the aid of the bounty when the price
fell below 44s., and imports were to be allowed at a nominal duty
when the price rose above 48s. Even in 1790 no criticism was made
of this principle in the " Representation " by the Committee of the
Privy Council.

Why then did the act of 1773 fail to keep the price within the
limits expected ? The answer is apparently to be found in the rise
of the merchant importer. Down to 1765 there was no regular
system for importing wheat, although that of other grain, particularly
oats, seems to have started as early as 1763. In most years before
1765 there was either no wheat or only a negligible quantity imported.
Even in years of scarcity such as 1741 and 1757 the total imports of
all kinds of grain were only a little over one hundred and fifty thousand
quarters. Clearly there was no regular group of importers in England
who could place orders for considerable quantities of grain in other
countries and be certain of their delivery. If such machinery, or
sources of supply, had been in existence in these years of scarcity,
they certainly would have been utilized. No country in Europe
produced grain for the English market in the first half of the eighteenth
century, because England was an exporting and not an importing
grain country. Under these circumstances English importers did not
develop.

But after 1763, in the case of oats, and 1765, in the case of wheat,
such a system did evolve. The relatively high prices of the years
from 1765 to 1773 resulted, as has been shown, in Parliament allowing
importation, duty free, nearly every year. During these years a
regular import traffic in corn developed. Doubtless the new import
merchants joined in the cry with the artisans of the cities for these
annual suspensions of the acts of 1689 and 1670. The landed interest
hoped that all this would be stopped by the act of 1773, but they
reckoned without the new corn importers. The corn exporter had
always juggled the market in order to secure the bounty. Now the
same practice was extended to influencing the price which determined
the importation of grain. By fictitious sales to one another, these
importers were able to raise artificially the price of any kind of grain
to the level at which it could be imported, duty free, for the next
three months. They were able to do this owing to the wretched
system of administering the act of 1773. The constant attempts to
improve it from 1773 to 1791 showed a keen realization of this fact.
Thus inability to supply the machinery by which the act could be
properly administered, along with the clever juggling of the market

by the importers, caused the complete failure of a law which had been carefully framed and received with unusual unanimity. With no apparent chance of any real improvement in the actual administration of the law, even though the machinery was perfected on paper, and with the corn merchants alive to the method of manipulating importation and exportation for their own benefit, there was no hope that the act of 1791 would function any more satisfactorily than its predecessor. But it was never given a real trial, since the French Revolutionary and Napoleonic wars, combined with a series of bad harvests, soon sent the prices of grain above the low duty levels fixed by this law.

CHAPTER IV

NOTES

1 14th George III., c. 5.　2 *Ibid.*, c. 26.
3 17th George III., c. 28.　4 14th George III., c. 64.　5 15th George III., c. 1.
6 16th George III., c. 42.　7 18th George III., c. 25.　8 19th George III., c. 29.
9 Reports of the Select Committees of the House of Commons, vol. 9, p. 32.
10 *Ibid.*　11 *Ibid.*, p. 33.　12 *Ibid.*　13 *Ibid.*, p. 34.
14 21st George III., c. 50.
15 Reports of the Select Committees of the House of Commons, vol. 9, p. 34.
16 29th George III., c. 58.　17 *Ibid.*　18 *Ibid.*
19 Tooke, *History of Prices*, vol. 1, pp. 69–70.　20 *Ibid.*, p. 75.
21 *Ibid.*, pp. 76–80.　Tooke makes no reference to the years 1787 and 1788.
22 *Ibid.*, pp. 81–2.　23 *Ibid.*, p. 76.
24 20th George III., c. 31.　25 21st George III., c. 29.　26 23rd George III., c. 1.
27 *Ibid.*, c. 9.　28 *Ibid.*, c. 81.
29 *London Gazette*, December 23rd, 1789, p. 801.　30 *Ibid.*
31 30th George III., c. 1.　32 *Ibid.*, c. 42.
33 Representation, by the Right Honourable the Lords of the Committee of
Privy Council, appointed for the consideration of all matters relating to Trade
and Foreign Plantations, March 8th, 1790, p. 11.
34 *Ibid.*, p. 12.　35 *Ibid.*, p. 14.　36 *Ibid.*, p. 13.　37 *Ibid.*, p. 16.　38 *Ibid.*,
p. 32.　39 *Ibid.*
40 *Ibid.*, pp. 32–41.
" The Committee therefore humbly offer the following advice :
" First.　That England continue to be divided into districts, according to the
plan of the act of last session ; and that Scotland be divided into districts in like
manner.
" Second.　That whenever the export of any sort of corn is stopped in any one
district, because the price thereof is above the export price, corn of the same sort
should not be allowed to be carried from thence coastwise to any other district,
the ports of which are open for the exportation thereof.
" Third.　That the act of 10th George III., c. 39, for registering the prices of
corn, so far as relates to the appointment of inspectors, be repealed, and that the
registry of corn published weekly in the Gazette, be formed upon averages taken,
according to the prices returned by the inspectors appointed under the act of
last year.
" Fourth.　That a duty of one halfpenny per last be paid on all British corn
imported coastwise, and one penny per last on all corn imported from foreign
countries into all the ports of Great Britain, as is now paid in the port of London ;
and that the money arising from these duties be made a fund for the payment of
inspectors, and defraying the other expenses incurred by this act ; and that the
corn returns sent by the post be not subject to the payment of postage.
" Fifth.　That the inspectors be paid not by salaries, as directed by the act
of last year, but by a certain allowance for each return, certified to have been
properly made, by the receiver of corn returns, according to the act of the 10th
year of Your Majesty's reign, c. 39.
" Sixth.　That in case returns from any district shall be completely made
according to the directions of the act, the importation and exportation of every
sort of corn in that district, shall be governed by the average price of the rest of
the kingdom.
" Seventh.　That a power be lodged in Your Majesty, with the advice of Your
privy council, during the prorogation of parliament, to prohibit generally the
exportation from this kingdom of any sort of corn, and in like manner to permit
generally the importation, on low duties, of any sort of Foreign corn, whenever
the average price thereof, taken from the returns of the whole kingdom, is higher
than the price at or above which Foreign corn is allowed by law to be imported,
if Your Majesty in Your wisdom for the public benefit shall so think fit.

" Eighth. That the collector of the customs at every port in Great Britain, do transmit weekly to the receiver of corn returns, an account of the quantity of the several sorts of corn shipped in such ports to be carried coastwise with the name of the ship or vessel, the name of the master, and the port or place in Great Britain, to which the corn was intended to be carried ; and also an account of the quantities of the several sorts of corn brought coastwise into each respective port, with the name of the ship or vessel, the name of the master, and the name of the port or place from whence it is brought ; and that the said receiver do, at the end of every three months, transmit to the commissioners of His Majesty's customs in England and Scotland, an account, to be formed and made in such manner as the said commissioners shall approve, of the quantity of the several sorts of corn shipped to be carried coastwise into each port respectively.

" Ninth. That the warehouses in which Foreign corn imported is to be lodged, under the joint lock of the King and the proprietor, according to the statute of the 13th of Your Majesty's reign, c. 43, be provided at the public expense ; and that the officers of the customs, whose duty it is to attend those warehouses, be paid by the public, as is now practised with respect to the warehousing of tobacco.

" Tenth. That Foreign corn imported and not warehoused be not allowed again to be exported.

" Eleventh. That corn so warehoused be permitted to be taken out, to be ground by the importer or proprietor, on condition that he give bond, not subject to any stamp duty, in double the value of the said corn, that he will export from the port where it was warehoused, within two calendar months from the time of taking out the said corn, a quantity of flour equal to the corn taken out, reckoning the quantity of wheat meal, or other ground corn, for every bushel of such corn unground, according to the proportion as it is now settled by law ; or that he will pay the duty chargeable on the said corn at the time that it was taken out of the warehouse. And that no importer or proprietor shall be entitled to receipt of any bounty on any corn or flour exported by him, until after he has settled his account of the corn so taken out of the warehouse, and discharged his bond.

" Twelfth. That wheat be permitted to be exported, but without bounty, when the price thereof is between 44s. and 46s. and other corn when the prices thereof shall be in like proportion ; and that wheat be allowed to be imported into this kingdom, from Your Majesty's kingdom of Ireland only, on the low duties, when the price thereof is at or above 46s. and other sorts of corn when the prices shall be in like proportion."

[41] *Journal of the House of Commons*, vol. 45.
[42] *Ibid.*
[43] 31st George III., c. 4.
[44] *Journal of the House of Commons*, vol. 46.
[45] John, Lord Sheffield, *Observations on the Corn Bill*, 1791, p. 13.
[46] *Ibid.*, p. 17. [47] *Ibid.*, p. 20. [48] *Ibid.*, p. 24. [49] *Ibid.*, p. 53. [50] *Ibid.*, p. 54. [51] *Ibid.*, p. 63. [52] *Ibid.*, p. 31. [53] *Ibid.*, p. 34. [54] *Ibid.*, p. 36. [55] *Ibid.*, p. 39.
[56] Sir John Sinclair, *Address to the Landed Interest on the Corn Bill now Depending in Parliament*, 1791, p. 19.
[57] *Ibid.*, p. 26. [58] *Ibid.*, p. 31.
[59] William Mitford, *Considerations on the Opinions Stated by the Lords of the Committee of Council in a Representation to the King*, etc., 1791.
[60] *Ibid.*, p. 29. [61] *Ibid.*, p. 32. [62] *Ibid.*, p. 34. [63] *Ibid.*, p. 54.
[64] A few quotations from Dirom will, perhaps, give a better idea of the intensity of his point of view than a general summary of arguments and position. The three selected offer sharp contrasts on the periods before and after 1773.

" Such was the spirit of our farmers, when they were freed from the trammels of prohibitory and improper laws, that for the ten years, from 1741 to 1750 inclusive, the average yearly amount of our exportation, rose to the amazing quantity of 848,660 quarters ; the importation amounted only to 15,193 quarters ; and the average price of wheat fell to £1 13s. 8d. per quarter." (p. 123).

" But we now come to a law of this year (1773), by which *the venerable old code*, so beneficial to manufactures and industry, and so salutary to the kingdom in general ; *that code*, which had raised the agriculture of Great Britain from the lowest state of depression, to the highest degree of prosperity ; which had produced plenty, at reasonable prices, for so great a number of years, at home ; and had

F

brought such immense sums of money for the excrescent stock of corn, from abroad, was now torn up by the roots, and scattered in the winds." (pp. 90–100).

" The beneficial consequences to the kingdom, which these wise laws brought about, have already appeared ; and it is difficult, even for the imagination, to fancy any reason for reverencing them, except the misrepresentations of interested and designing men." (p. 133).

[65] Dirom, *Inquiry into the Corn Laws and Corn Trade of Great Britain*, 1796, p. 134.

[66] *Ibid.*, p. 135.

[67] *Report of the Committee of the Town Council of Glasgow, appointed to Consider the Corn Bill at Present Pending in Parliament*, 1791, pp. 3–4.

[68] *Ibid.*, pp. 3–8.

[69] *Journal of the House of Commons*, vol. 46, pp. 582–4.

[70] *Ibid.*, p. 639.   [71] *Ibid.*, p. 655.

[72] *Ibid.*, pp. 698–700.   The House of Lords added a long list of amendments which were all grammatical changes and not alterations in principle or price levels.

[73] *Ibid.*, p. 707.

[74] Bounties of 3s., 2s. 6d., and 2s., were paid respectively on rye, barley, beer, or bigg ; and oats when the prices were under 28s., 22s. and 14s. Importation of the different kinds of grain was permitted under the following regulations : Rye, peas and beans when under 34s. paid a duty of 22s. ; when at or above 34s. but under 37s., a duty of 1s. 6d. ; and when at or above 37s., a duty of 3d. Barley, beer or bigg, and Indian corn, when under 25s. paid a duty of 22s. ; when at or above 25s. but under 27s., a duty of 1s. 3d. ; and when at or above 27s., a duty of 3d. Oats when under 17s. paid a duty of 6s. 7d. ; when at or above 17s. but under 18s., a duty of 1s. ; and when at or above 18s., a duty of 2d.   A colonial preference of 2s. a quarter was given for rye, and of 1s. for barley, beer or bigg, and oats.

[75] The care and elaborate detail with which the sections of the act dealing with determination of price levels and machinery for enforcement were drawn up shows a real desire to eliminate the flaws in the acts of 1773 and 1789.

Many of the provisions of former laws were re-enacted.   England was divided into twelve maritime districts much as in the act of 1789, and Scotland was divided into four.   The exportation and importation in London, Kent, Essex and Sussex was to be regulated by the prices taken at the Corn Exchange in Mark Lane.   A Corn Inspector to be appointed by the proprietors of the Exchange was to take oath and discharge his work faithfully.   Every Corn Factor in London or the suburbs was to send the Inspector each Wednesday an account of the quantity and price of the grain he had sold during the previous week.   The Inspector was to send the average of all these to the Receiver of Corn Returns on every Friday, who in turn was to send a copy to each of the collectors of customs in London, Essex, Sussex and Kent.   These figures were to govern exportation and the payment of bounty until new ones arrived.   The Inspector was also to make an average of the last six weekly returns of all grain except oats within seven days after February 15th, May 15th, August 15th and November 15th of each year and transmit it to the customs collectors of the ports in London, Essex, Sussex and Kent.   This average was to govern importation during the next three months.   In the case of oats the average for the entire twelve weeks preceding the dates given was to determine importation during the next three months. To cover these expenses all English corn brought into the Thames east of London was to pay 1d. per last and all foreign corn 2d.   In the other eleven districts of England the Justices for the Maritime Counties were to appoint an Inspector of Corn Returns, a person not dealing in grain for each city or town.   This Inspector was to receive a weekly report from every miller or corn dealer in the city of the quantity and price of all kinds of grain bought during the week, and was to transmit to the Receiver of Corn Returns the average of each.   The latter then averaged the price of each kind of grain for each of the eleven districts and transmitted a certificate of them to every port.   Both inspectors and corn dealers were to take oath that all the returns they made after June 24th, 1791, would be accurate to the best of their knowledge and belief.   In case a city was a county itself the mayor or other chief officer and justices were to appoint the Inspector. The exportation and bounty in the various ports were to be regulated by these weekly averages, and the importation by an average of the last six weekly averages in each district preceding the 15th of February, May, August and November.

In the case of oats, the average was for the entire preceding three months. While Scotland was divided into districts similar to the English ones, the regulations were different. The Sheriff of each county on September 15th, 1791, and on the 15th or within three days of, on every succeeding month, was to convene a jury of five to seven men, none of whom were concerned in the sale of corn, and determine on their oath what the price of middling British corn was in each of the preceding four weeks. These prices, transmitted to the Receiver of Corn Returns at London were to be not only those of the measures and weights used in each respective county, but the prices at the Winchester bushel and oatmeal boll of 128 pounds. The Receiver of Corn Returns was to make an average for each district from these returns and send a certificate thereof to each port in Scotland. The same system that was used in the eleven maritime districts of England so far as sending prices to the Receiver of Corn Returns was extended to the inland counties on the ground that " it will be useful that an account should be obtained." The averages sent to the various ports were to be published in the *London Gazette*. In case Parliament was not sitting and the average price of corn became higher than that at which the same sort of foreign corn was allowed to be permitted at the low duties, the King in Council could prohibit exportation and permit importation at the low duties. In all cases the standard measure was to be the Winchester bushel and quarter.

[76] *Parliamentary History*, vol. 28, pp. 1269–71.
[77] J. R. McCulloch, *Dictionary of Commerce*, 1850, p. 430.
[78] Tooke, *History of Prices*, vol. 1, p. 81.
[79] Comber, *An Inquiry into the State of National Subsistence*, 1808, pp. 177–8.
[80] Cunningham, *Growth of English Industry and Commerce*, vol. 3, 1917, pp. 725–7.
[81] Hunt, *Political History of England*, vol. 10, p. 274.
[82] Nicholson, *The History of the English Corn Laws*, 1904, p. 33.

CHAPTER V

THE CORN LAWS AND THE WARS, 1791 TO 1813

Reasons why years from 1791 to 1813 can be treated as a unit in a study of the Corn Laws—Wars during these years affected the external corn trade more than previous wars had done—Section I, 1791 to 1801—French Revolution at first hailed with enthusiasm in Great Britain—Reasons for reaction against it—War against France badly managed—Success of British Fleet—Failures of the first and second coalitions—Quality and quantity of the crops during these years—Scarcity, high prices and distress in crisis of 1795 and 1796—Causes assigned and remedies suggested by select committees and pamphleteers—Attempts of the government to improve conditions by passing usual scarcity laws, paying bounties on imported grain, endorsing the "voluntary pledge" system, adopting Speenhamland system of poor relief, and using questionable tactics in dealing with corn importers—Crisis of 1799 to 1801 more severe than one of 1795 and 1796—Causes assigned and remedies suggested by select committees and pamphleteers—The Rusby Trial—New attempts by the government to relieve suffering—Return of normal prices—Section II, 1801 to 1813—Effect of the war on the external corn trade—Reasons for the new law of 1804—Its significance—High prices of grain from 1805 to 1813 due to poor crops and Continental System—Measures taken by government to secure relief—Corn Laws fall into the background from 1805 to 1813—Conclusion.

THE years covered by this chapter, 1791 to 1813, do not coincide with the usual divisions in political histories of 1789 and 1815 for Europe as a whole, or 1793 to 1815 for Great Britain alone. In treating the Corn Laws during these years it is impossible either to ignore the great upheaval caused by the French Revolution and Napoleonic wars, or to follow them with chronological exactness. In addition, the plan followed in the preceding chapter of tracing the law of 1773 from the time it was passed until it was repealed, cannot be followed in this instance because the law of 1804, which repealed that of 1791, was not of sufficient importance to receive much attention. Nor is it possible to continue the narrative down to the passing of the law of 1815 ; because the year 1813 saw a revival of the interest in the Corn Laws, which had lapsed after 1805, and the beginning of the agitation for a new act. As a result, this chapter, although in the main following the war period from 1793 to 1815, also includes the months from November of 1791 to the outbreak of the war in February of 1793 and excludes the years 1813–15.

The French Revolutionary and Napoleonic wars influenced the external corn trade more than previous wars had done. The War of the League of Augsburg and the War of the Spanish Succession had made little difference in this respect, because England, during those years, was neither an importing nor an exporting grain nation. The War of the Austrian Succession affected the foreign grain trade only in so far as it interfered with exportation to France. The Seven Years War was even less significant because England had ceased to export grain in large quantities, and had not yet begun to import to any considerable extent.   Lastly, at the time of the American Revolution, England was still either exporting or importing a small amount of grain.   Whether it was importation or exportation, and the size of either, depended largely upon the size of the crops.   Even in the closing years of the war neither trade seems to have been interfered with sufficiently to warrant any action being taken by government. After the great crop of 1779 a law was passed giving neutral ships half the bounty on grain normally paid to English shippers.   This concession, it was explained, was made because so much of the British marine was occupied elsewhere.

But by 1793 conditions had changed to such an extent that the country might be seriously inconvenienced by war.   After the American Revolutionary War, England underwent a rapid development in industry and foreign trade, and as a consequence the export of grain became less, and the import more significant.   Thus deficient crops were a source of greater danger than earlier because the city population of the country had increased so enormously that, in spite of the improved methods in agriculture, a considerable importation was necessary to offset the shortage.   During the first war, 1793-1802, the danger was due to the fact that no part of Europe was accustomed to produce wheat on the chance that there might be a shortage in England or some part of the continent.   During the wars with Napoleon, especially from 1806 to 1813, this danger was increased by the Continental System.

Because the years covered by this chapter are so lacking in unity, except that which the wars provide, it is hoped that the organization will be rendered less cumbersome by dividing it in two sections at 1801.   This division will coincide roughly with the two great wars, 1793 to 1802 and 1803 to 1815, and will distinguish on the one hand the period of bad crops ending in 1801 from the period of low prices culminating in the new law of 1804 and of the Continental System, 1806-13, on the other.   Such an arrangement, although it has its disadvantages, seems to present less difficulties than the treatment of the years covered in this chapter as a unit.

SECTION I, 1791-1801

In treating the regulation of the external corn during these years it is impossible to ignore the effects on England of the French Revolution and of the manner in which the war against France was conducted.   The first reactions of the British to the French Revolution were decidedly favourable.   The reformers, particularly the ones who wanted to make the House of Commons more representative, were encouraged to redouble their efforts by the great successes which they saw won across the channel.   Even more remarkable was the influence of such young poets as Wordsworth, Coleridge, Southey, Landor and Burns.   Men as temperamentally different as Charles James Fox and Horace Walpole hailed the early events with enthusiasm.   William Pitt appears to have looked upon

the first three years of the Revolution with mild approval. He
lacked the fervour and enthusiasm of his early years in Parliament,
and he had not yet become the official spokesman of unchanging
Toryism that he was to become after 1794. Looking at the events
in France from the point of view of a British Prime Minister, he seems
to have been even more satisfied because it seemed certain that Great
Britain's rival must emerge from such an internal conflict in a
weakened condition. The reaction against the French Revolution
in England came not as a result of Burke's *Reflections*, but from a
growing suspicion of French ideas and reforms in practically all
classes. It is questionable whether the masses were ever enthusiastic
about revolutionary ideas, but it is certain that by 1791 they were
violently opposed in most English cities. By 1792 whatever
hesitation was felt by most classes of the community in condemning
these ideas was dissipated by the September Massacres, and by the
events following which culminated in the execution of Louis XVI.
In spite of this obvious shift in public opinion, the government was
convinced that a real revolutionary conspiracy was widespread in
Great Britain and that it must be rigorously repressed. The pro-
secutions in both England and Scotland are generally admitted to be a
blot on this period. Although the government, fortunately, was
unsuccessful in 1794 in the attempt to convict of high treason the
members of the Society for Constitutional Information and the
London Corresponding Society, it found other means of stopping
reform movements. By a series of laws passed from 1795 to 1800
the penalties for treason were applied to spoken or written words,
the right to hold public meetings was greatly curtailed, existing
reform societies were suppressed and combinations among workmen
forbidden. Thus the immediate result of the French Revolution in
Great Britain was to ruin a promising reform movement, and to
diminish the rights of freedom of speech and of the Press.[1]

Despite this shift in public opinion during the year 1792, Pitt was
very reluctant about going to war with France. He even reduced the
military and naval estimates for the year. Although the French government declared the River Scheldt open to trade, threatened to declare
war on Holland, issued the proclamation of November, 1792, against
kings, and finally executed Louis XVI., Pitt continued to hold back.
Finally the French declared war on February 1st, 1793. Pitt's record
as a war minister is an almost unbroken series of blunders and failures.
Both the army and navy were in bad shape when the war started and
Pitt showed little ability either to improve them himself or to select
competent men to do so. The army was badly handled during this
period and the navy was a disappointment until the great victories
of Jervis and Duncan in 1797. Even in the field of finance, where
Pitt had made a great reputation in the previous ten years, he made
the disastrous mistake of financing the war to a large extent by loans
instead of by taxation. Perhaps the greatest defect of Pitt as a war
minister was " his failure to form and carry out a consistent and
coherent plan of campaign."[2]

The war falls into three periods : the first coalition, 1793-95 ; the
isolation of Great Britain, 1795-99 ; and the second coalition, 1799-

1802. In the first period the allies made up of Great Britain, Austria, Prussia, Holland, Spain, Portugal and Sardinia, expected an easy victory over the disorganized French. But by the end of 1795, owing to the tremendous enthusiasm of the revolutionary soldiers and the jealousy and incompetence of the allies, the French were completely victorious. Holland and Spain became allies of France, and Prussia made peace. Of the greater powers only Austria and Great Britain were left. Austria was eliminated early in 1797, owing chiefly to the brilliant feats of Napoleon Bonaparte in northern Italy. The years of 1795–99 were dark years for the British, in other respects than the collapse of the coalition and the defeat of Austria. The threatened invasion both of England and Ireland, along with the mutiny of the Channel Fleet at Spithead and the North Sea Fleet at the Nore early in 1797, had a most depressing influence on the country. The tide of reverses began to turn in 1797 with the victory of Jervis over the Spanish Fleet at St. Vincent, of Duncan over the Dutch at Camperdown, and of Nelson over the French at the Nile in 1798. Thus Great Britain was once more supreme on the seas. Partly on the strength of these victories the second coalition of Russia, Austria and Great Britain was formed. But this promising beginning was soon shattered by the withdrawal of Russia and the defeats administered to Austria by Napoleon in northern Italy. Napoleon in turn was disappointed in his plan for a Franco-Russian alliance and the exclusion of English trade from the continent by the assassination of the Czar Paul and Nelson's seizure of the Danish Fleet. As a result, both the French and British were willing to end the war. The peace preliminaries were signed in October, 1801, and the permanent treaty followed in March of 1802.

Clearly the Corn Law of 1791 did not have a fair chance of operating under the conditions expected at the time it was passed. Not only did war break out a little more than a year after the act went into operation, but the ten years following 1791 saw an unusual number of bad crops and years of scarcity. In studying these ten years the plan adopted in earlier chapters will be followed. The causes for years of scarcity, remedies suggested both in and out of Parliament, and policies adopted by the government to alleviate and offset the effects of the shortage will, as a rule, be taken up in order.

Within a year after the law of 1791 went into operation the government was called upon to resort to the familiar temporary measures. The harvest of 1792 was so inferior that an order in council was issued on November 9th prohibiting the exportation of grain until the following spring.[3] It was evident that the act of 1791 was to be no improvement over its predecessors in doing away with temporary laws and orders in council. Early in 1793 it was also found that the machinery for determining the prices regulating importation and exportation was not functioning properly, despite the care taken in drawing up that part of the law of 1791. Since this act was not meeting expectations either in avoiding the temporary measures in time of distress or in providing workable machinery for determining prices, it is unfair to blame the war entirely for its failure. The war, undoubtedly, caused the act to become inoperative, but evidence of the flaws in the measure were already appearing before the outbreak. The changes in the method of determining the prices of grain, which were introduced by the supplementary act of 1793, are not of great importance in themselves because the rise in prices soon made any machinery of this sort unnecessary.[4]

The disappointments of war in the years 1793-96 were accompanied by a critical condition in Great Britain which resulted from a series of poor crops. In 1794 a hot, dry summer caused a deficiency which, however, was not felt until early in 1795, because the harvest was much earlier than usual and the condition of the grain, particularly the wheat, was splendid.[5] Then, when it was realized that the wheat crop of the preceding year was short in spite of its excellent condition, and that there was no surplus from earlier years because there had been no good harvest since 1791, prices began to rise rapidly. As usual authority was given the Crown to prohibit exportation and allow importation, duty free, by order in council, if such a step seemed advisable.[6] In addition, corn bound for France in neutral ships was seized. This action served the double purpose of relieving distress at home and of increasing it in France. Care was taken to pay for the cargoes in order that neutral shippers would not be alienated. The government even went so far as to make purchases of grain in the Baltic.[7] The next year, when the government continued this policy, it had disastrous results. A final precaution was taken by Parliament just before the end of the session in an act prohibiting the use of grain or flour in the distillery from July 10th, 1795, to February 1st, 1796.[8]

Had the harvest of 1795 been good, or even moderate, the scarcity and high prices of the first part of the year would have been of comparatively little importance. Unfortunately the winter of 1794-5 was one of the three memorable cold ones of the eighteenth century, and a very meagre crop was the result. In 1709 and 1740, however, deficient crops had been preceded by many abundant ones, and the industrial population of the midlands and north was much smaller. In addition, a greater per cent. of the population were consuming wheat bread in 1795 than during the first forty years of the century. Consequently, the scanty harvest of 1795 was attended by more momentous social and economic results than those of 1709 and 1740.

The hope of the farmers of the law of 1791 had been that the price of wheat would fluctuate between 44s. and 54s. After the harvest of 1795 the price shot up above 100s., and the suffering experienced by the lower classes was almost unprecedented. The cost of wheat was the highest ever recorded in the Eton Tables since 1595, and in the Oxford prices since 1583.[9] Riots in all parts of England followed this rise in the price of grain. The populace of London and Westminster held the war responsible for the distress and attacked the carriage of the King as he was on his way to deliver his speech at the opening of Parliament on October 29th, 1795. A shot, probably from an air-gun, was fired into the carriage of the King and the mob shouted " Peace ! Peace ! "[10]

The threatening populace and starvation prices made it necessary for the government to take some action. Two acts were passed in the hope that some measure of relief might be afforded. The first one prohibited, until six weeks after the commencement of the next session of Parliament, the exportation of corn, meal, flour and potatoes, and permitted their importation, duty free, in any ship whatsoever.[11] The second one prohibited the making of starch and hair powder from wheat or other food articles. This act was to remain in force until February 1st, 1797, and an elaborate machinery for administering it was provided.[12]

But the situation was so serious that Pitt felt, evidently, that the usual measures taken to afford relief would be inadequate. A few days after the opening of Parliament he moved that a select committee be appointed to collect evidence on the high price of corn. The motion was readily agreed to and the committee appointed. Beginning with November 16th, this committee presented a series of five reports which show both how desperate the situation appeared and how perplexing a satisfactory solution seemed to the members. The first report recommended that the government " desist from making any further purchases of corn ; and that a bounty should be granted upon the importation of certain sorts of grain into this country for the encouragement of private speculation."[13] The committee went into elaborate details over the maximum number of quarters and the amount of the bounty to be paid on wheat and Indian corn imported under these conditions.[14] The second report recommended the extension of this bounty on importation to rye.[15] The third report, which was made after an attempt to estimate the deficiency of the crops of 1795, stated that wheat and rye were about a fifth or sixth below average, but that rye and oats were nearly double those of 1794 and at least a fifth above normal. The solution, therefore, seemed to lie in economical use of wheat and in a more extensive consumption of barley, oats and potatoes. In order to economize on wheat, the committee recommended a voluntary pledge by individuals to reduce their consumption by a third. This reduction could be accomplished either by eating mixed bread, in which one-third of the flour used was not wheaten, or by consuming a third less bread than usual.[16]

In addition to the reports of this committee, the government, during the latter part of 1795 and early part of 1796, received a great deal of unofficial advice from pamphleteers. The number of pamphlets that appeared during these months far exceeded the number published in either 1757 or 1767. Many old explanations for scarcity and high prices, which seemed decently buried, were now disinterred. The usual outcry was raised against corn dealers, and many a pamphleteer insisted that the laws against forestallers, engrossers and regrators should be enforced.[17] All these laws had been repealed in 1772 and 1791, but unfortunately the practices were still punishable under the common law. Some of the causes assigned were semi-humorous ones, such as excessive use of hair powder,[18] and the number of dogs in the country.[19] Davies, who was probably the ablest of these writers, gave, in his *Case of Labourers in Husbandry*, four principal reasons for the enhanced prices : new taxes, luxury, depreciation of money, and bounties on exportation of grain. Under luxury he included increased consumption of meat and wheaten bread, decreased tillage, distillation of wheat and increased number of horses.[20]   Some writers, however, appreciated that the chief difficulty was due to the deficiency in the crops and hence that most of the causes assigned were only minor ones which tended to aggravate the main one.

The distress felt in 1795 and 1796 gave a tremendous impetus to the arguments of the landed interest that England should be self-sufficient. Such men as Sinclair and Sheffield were certain that the best way of making the country self-supporting was by bringing all waste, uninclosed and unproductive land under cultivation.   The Board of Agriculture felt that the best way to accomplish this would be to pass a law facilitating the enclosure of wastes and commons.[21]

With all the advice showered on both the ministers and the members of Parliament by the committee and pamphleteers, some attempts to relieve the widespread distress by legislative action was inevitable. Following the line adopted immediately after Parliament was opened when acts had been passed prohibiting exportation or use of grain in making starch and hair powder, two additional bills were passed in December.   One made it a criminal offence to hinder the transportation of grain ;[22] the other extended the prohibition against the use of grain and flour in distillery until February 1st, 1797.[23]   The House of Commons next took up the reports of the committee appointed to collect evidence on the high price of corn.   Following the recommendation of the committee, a law was passed ordering the payment of bounties on wheat, wheat flour, Indian corn, Indian meal and rye imported into Great Britain in British or neutral vessels. A bounty of 20s. a quarter was to be paid on all wheat up to 400,000 quarters which was imported from south of Cape Finisterre, the Mediterranean or Africa, before September 30th, 1796, and under similar conditions 500 quarters could be imported from the American colonies.   Likewise, bounties of 15s. on heavy wheat, 12s. on light wheat and 4s. 6d. per hundred on wheat flour up to 500,000 quarters were offered on importations from Europe.   If wheat in excess of this amount arrived before September 30th all over 500,000 quarters was to be paid a bounty of 10s. a quarter.   In order to secure the bounty, it was necessary for the importation to take place at one of the sixty enumerated ports.[24]

Next the House of Commons took up the plan to secure a voluntary pledge to decrease the consumption of wheaten bread.   A resolution was agreed upon by the Commons which stated " that the persons subscribing to this Engagement do also engage to recommend the same in the most earnest manner to be adopted in their respective neighbourhoods."[25]   Those urging the agreement pledged themselves to reduce the normal consumption of wheat in their families by at least a third : either by cutting down the amount of wheaten bread used, or by eating bread containing substitutes.   The House of Lords agreed to both the resolution and agreement.[26]   In an attempt to facilitate the plan of making bread of mixed flour, an act was passed permitting the bakers to make and sell certain kinds of mixed bread which was to be marked with the letter M.[27]   But any attempt to get the poor to use such bread was a dismal failure.   They flatly refused to buy or eat it, being actuated partly by prejudice and suspicion, and partly by an instinctive clinging to their standard of living.[28]

In general, the attempts to remedy the scarcity by the use of mixed flour and substitute bread failed not only because of the opposition of the poor, but of the baker and miller as well.   One member of the House of Commons, who was sceptical about the success of such a measure as this agreement, called attention to the failure of a similar one the summer before.   He insisted that it was difficult to secure substitute bread from the baker or mixed flour from the miller.   In wealthy families more was wasted through unpalatable bread being thrown away than was saved by the reduction in the use of wheaten flour.[29]   When this member took up the attitude of the poor he was even more emphatic.   " But did they follow our example ? " he asked. " Did they eat the same household bread that we did ?   No such thing.   In spite of all our remonstrances, the poor in my neighbourhood (and I have no doubt that it was pretty much the same in all the populous villages round us), would eat nothing but the finest and whitest wheaten bread.   If one baker refused to supply them with it, they went to another.   In the end, the bakers, though they gained by it, assured us, that by our contributions we were defeating our own purposes ; for that in fact they had never, in any equal period, sold so much white bread to the poor, as while we were eating a coarser sort ourselves, and doing everything we could to lessen the consumption of wheat."[30]

Thus the attempt to solve the question of scarcity by finding substitutes for wheat failed largely because the poor resisted the plan as an attack upon their standard of living.[31]   Perhaps the most unfortunate result of the scarcity of 1795 was the part played in the introduction of the famous Speenhamland policy for poor relief. Whitbread's attempt in the Commons, to secure a minimum wage, failed.   It was believed at the time that the prices of grain would fall back to the former levels as soon as the crops were of normal quantity and quality.   For this reason both the landed and industrial interests opposed the increase of wages lest they be difficult to lower when prices of grain fell.   The Speenhamland plan, so called from the fact that the Berkshire Justices of the Peace and other " discreet " persons formulated this policy for that county when they met in the Pelican Inn at Speenhamland on May 6th, 1795, fixed the amount of bread each man, woman and child was to be allowed a week.   If the family wages were insufficient to purchase this amount the necessary deficit was to be paid out of the poor rates.   As a temporary scheme to tide over the effects of a bad harvest there was nothing particularly pernicious in this plan ; but when the price of grain continued at a fabulous price during the greater part of the next twenty years, the landed interest found it profitable to support the labouring classes in this fashion, and to absorb all the surplus themselves.

Actual relief from the high prices caused by the scarcity of grain and foodstuffs came neither from legislative measures adopted by the government nor from the harvest of 1796, but from, what seems to have been, a rather discreditable performance on the part of the government.   When the war broke out in February of 1793 the government took over the foreign corn trade with the avowed intention of starving France. Apparently this policy came nearer to starving England than France. The merchants who were engaged in the foreign corn trade became alarmed by the uncertainties created by governmental interference and either abandoned the trade or bought cautiously.[32] When Parliament met in October of 1795, the government signified its intention of abandoning the corn trade and of requesting the merchants to resume importation. The latter consented on condition that the government should agree, first, not to interfere any longer in the grain trade ; second, to declare the stock on hand and on the way ; third, to sell this stock in limited quantities ; and fourth, to sell it at the market price.[33] The promises and agreement of the government are on record in the transactions of Parliament for November 13th and November 16th and in the first three reports of the Select Committee of the House of Commons on the High Price of Corn.

Either the merchants were more capable purchasers than the government, or corn was easier to acquire in 1796 than in 1795, for the importation of wheat rose from 313,793 quarters to 879,200, and other kinds of grain in about the same proportion. Nevertheless, the government broke at least four of its promises. First, on January 6th, 1796, the Victualling Board secretly contracted with Mr. Claude Scott, a prominent corn merchant, to import 50,000 quarters of Polish wheat. Second, the government never declared the quantity of grain on hand. Third, instead of selling the stock on hand in limited quantities from December of 1795 to March of 1796, or supplying the Victualling Board during this interval, the government held its corn and permitted the Board to purchase supplies in the open market. This practice tended to further enhance prices and to encourage merchants to import excessive quantities. Fourth, the government waited until the grain purchased by the merchants had arrived or was on the way, and then threw their stock on the market. At the same time the Victualling Board began to use the government stock which lightened the demand on the market. The fact that the merchants' and the government's stocks of grain were thrown on the market at once, combined with the lighter purchases of the Board, caused the price of wheat to fall from 124s. a quarter, on March 7th, to 70s. on April 11th. This action of the government was repeated in May when prices rose again. As a result the merchants lost from thirty to seventy per cent. on their investment.[34]

A group of merchants from Liverpool, Hull, Newcastle, Lynn, Bristol, Bridgport and various parts of Scotland determined to seek compensation. After endless petitions and committee reports, the matter was finally brought before the House of Commons on May 10th, 1798. Although Pitt had promised the merchants his support, it was largely through his opposition that the proposed indemnity was defeated.[35] Whatever the motives of Pitt and his government may have been in both 1796 and 1798, the results seem to have been disastrous. Unless the government had experts to handle the corn trade, the effect of interfering with the merchants was bound to prove harmful. In addition the government did not actually purchase the grain directly, but employed a large scale corn importer. In viewing this affair as a whole, it seems impossible to escape the conclusion that Pitt and the other ministers appear in the light of a group of well-meaning but blundering amateurs. There is little doubt that their actions made the corn importers cautious and in the famine year of 1800 were one of the causes assigned for scarcity.

Having forced down prices early in 1796 by the methods just described, the government had comparatively little additional trouble either with high prices of grain or the external corn trade until 1799. The harvest of 1796 was abundant, while those of 1797 and 1798 were moderate.[36] But even with fair crops, large importations and comparatively low prices of grain, the prohibition against exportation was continued. Parliament, on November 11th, 1796, extended until six weeks after the opening of the next session all the temporary acts passed in the previous year prohibiting the exportation of corn, meal, flour and potatoes, and the importation duty free in any ships.[37] On the strength of falling prices, the parts of these acts which related to barley, beans, peas and oats, or flour made from any of them, were repealed on June 19th, 1797.[38] Even after the harvest of 1797 the prohibition of the exportation of wheat was continued.[39]

These three years of ordinary crops and normal conditions in the corn trade ended even before the harvest of 1799. As early as May, certain knowledge that the coming crop was deficient started prices rising and resulted in Parliament passing an act to enable the Crown, by order in council, to prohibit exportation and allow importation, duty free, during the summer recess if such action seemed necessary.[40] After the harvest, which was even worse than had been expected, the price of wheat rose steadily until in December it was above 90s. a quarter. Once more Parliament fell back on temporary acts. The use of flour or corn in the distillery was forbidden in Scotland until March 1st, 1800,[41] and in England until September 20th, 1800.[42]

But the prices of grain continued to rise, and by January of 1800 wheat was above 100s. a quarter. A committee in the House of Commons was then appointed to consider the Assize of Bread Act of 1773 and other effectual means of remedying the deficiency in the last crop. The first report of this committee clearly showed that the failure of certain recommendations in 1795 and 1796 had not been lost on them. It was strongly recommended that no attempt be made either to force bread made of a coarser flour upon the people of the metropolis or to manufacture a standard flour. In view of the disastrous results from governmental interference in the corn trade in 1796, the committee vigorously opposed any renewal of such a policy. A final recommendation was a warning to certain individuals who, with a mistaken idea of charity, delivered flour and bread to the poor at reduced rates. The committee deemed it advisable " that all charity and parochial relief should be given, as far as is practicable, in any other articles except bread, flour and money, and that the part of it which is necessary for the sustenance of the poor, should be distributed in soups, rice, potatoes or other substitutes."[43] The second report of this committee, which was given on March 6th, 1800, stated first, the expediency of giving a bounty to encourage the

importation of corn from the Mediterranean and America, of procuring
a considerable supply of food from the fisheries, and of stopping the
distilleries ; second, the propriety of subjecting millers to some new
regulations, of individuals reducing the consumption of flour, and of
the adoption of a new table of assize ; and third, the advisability of
encouraging the use of rice and Indian corn, and the growth of potatoes
and other vegetables.[44]

The action taken on these recommendations in the House of
Commons indicated a rather foggy state of mind. Some members
believed that the scarcity was exaggerated and that the government
should not interfere. Others thought the solution lay in a standard
flour or bread or in " healthful " substitutes.[45] But in the end, the
measures adopted were essentially those recommended by the committee. First, the use of wheat in making starch was prohibited until
October 1st, 1800,[46] and, second, the act forbidding the use of corn
and flour in the Scottish distilleries was continued.[47] Next a series
of acts was passed offering bounties on grain imported. These
bounties, unlike those of 1795 and 1796, did not take the form of the
payment of a lump sum per quarter, but guaranteed a certain price.
Wheat, for example, was to be paid a bounty equal to the difference
between the amount actually received and 90s. a quarter.[48] The
bounties were to be regulated by the average prices published in *The
Gazette* the second week after importation. An elaborate system was
arranged to carry out these regulations.

In addition to the recommendations of the committee, both the
ministers and Parliament had additional advice showered upon them
by a vast number of pamphleteers. These pamphlets, which appeared
both before and after the harvest of 1800, attempted as pamphleteers
had in previous periods of scarcity to determine the causes and
remedies for the high price of grain. The reasons most commonly
assigned were bad crops, increasing population, heavy burdens on
agricultural produce, speculation of corn dealers—forestalling, engrossing and regrating—incompetent tillage, insufficient protection
for agriculture, engrossing of small farms, war, increased consumption
of the army and navy, monopoly of grain in the hands of the farmers,
increase in the size of the national debt and of the amount of taxes,
paper money, vermin, withdrawal of the importers from the external
corn trade and greater parish allowances for poor relief.

A great many remedies were suggested for scarcity and high prices.
The most important of these were to make peace, to extend governmental control, to render the country self-sufficient as she had been
before 1765, to pass temporary measures to tide over the crisis until
a good harvest came, and to enforce the common law against forestallers, engrossers and regrators. These five remedies will be taken
up in order.

Advocates of peace held that the war was responsible for the
increase of taxes, the public debt, paper money, the amount expended
in poor relief, the vast consumption by the army and navy, and for
the difficulties of importation. These pamphleteers insisted that the
cessation of war would remove the taxes which increased the cost of
production on so many articles, stop the excessive issue of paper

money by the Bank of England and the country banks, halt the further
increase in the public debt, reduce consumption by turning capital
into productive channels, do away with government contractors who
raised the market price of certain articles, increase production through
the return of the agricultural labourers in the army and navy, and
stop the influx of foreigners who consumed but did not produce anything.   The weapon which peace advocates hoped to wield was the
pressure of public opinion.   They advised the people to meet in
counties, cities and boroughs, and to petition the throne and
Parliament to end the cruel and merciless war.[49]

The second remedy suggested for reducing the high prices was to
extend government control in several directions, despite the unfortunate experience of 1796.   Writers who advocated this policy
were not in agreement in regard to the spheres over which the government should extend this control.   One pamphleteer advised that the
farmer and dealer should be compelled " by force of law to sell their
corn at a price that may enable the poor to purchase a sufficient
quantity for their own and their families' subsistence by the produce
of their daily labour."[50]   He was certain that this could be adjusted
by a maximum price fixed by the government.   Another writer, with
equal lucidity, stated that " the price of corn in a common year
multiplied by its quantity should be estimated ; and, according to
the crops of other years, the price should be so regulated as not to
make the farmers any losers by short crops, but not to allow them to
double the price because there may occasionally happen to be a
deficiency of a tenth."[51]

Against this view may be placed Burke's letter to Pitt in 1795,
entitled *Thoughts on Scarcity*.   It was now published as a warning
against further state supervision.   Two sentences sum up his attitude :
" Of all things, an indiscreet tampering with the trade of provisions
is the most dangerous, and it is always worst in the time when men
are most disposed to it—that is, in time of scarcity."[52]   And, " The
state ought to confine itself to what regards the state or the creatures
of the state, namely, the exterior establishments of its religion ; its
magistracy ; its revenue ; its military force by sea and land ; the
corporations that owe their existence to its fiat ; in a word, to everything that is truly and properly public, to the public peace, to the
public safety, to the public order, to the public prosperity."[53]

Other writers believed that the government should stop the consolidation of farms ;[54] and still others that the issue of notes by the
country banks and Bank of England should be stopped, limited or
regulated in some way.[55]

The third remedy suggested for scarcity and high prices was to
make the country self-sufficient as she had been before 1765.   Advocates of this solution held that if the farmer were given a monopoly
of the home market, improved methods in agriculture and rapid
enclosure of the arable and waste lands would soon bring about the
desired result.   Nearly every writer agreed that a general enclosure
act was desirable, but opinions differed widely on the disposal of the
enclosed lands.   Some wanted large farms in order to insure a larger
food supply, while others favoured smallholdings for the benefit of

the dispossessed cottager. One of the most enthusiastic of the latter suggested that, " It would be conducive to the general welfare, if cottages were erected at the expense of the parish, whenever a man requires it for establishing a family, and a bit of ground for a garden should be allotted to each cottage."[56]

Perhaps the most prominent advocates of enclosure were James Anderson and Lord Sheffield. The former's explanation of the scarcity of 1800 was simple, mathematical and mechanical. He showed that in 1750 England exported 1,667,140 quarters of grain, and in 1800 imported 3,938,829, making a deficit of 5,605,969 quarters. Hence, he concluded, " nor is it, I think, possible for any candid mind, from this view of facts, to entertain a doubt that the change is to be attributed solely and entirely to the variations that have been made in the corn laws, though the amount of the deficiency, as I have repeatedly stated, has doubtless been augmented by the agency of other causes co-operating with it."[57] On the historical side he followed Dirom in lauding the period from 1689 to 1773 as the golden age of English agriculture, and the period since 1773 as one of decline. He repeated that the spirit of the law of 1689 was to promote exportation and prevent importation, and that the intention of the act of 1773 was the opposite. Each, he believed, had succeeded in its purpose.[58] Further, the only effect of the present law was to enrich a few too opulent corn dealers, to comply with the popular clamours, and to prevent the extensive cultivation which the country demanded and the untilled soil would permit.[59] Thus Anderson stressed the necessity of a new corn law to bring waste lands under cultivation. Lord Sheffield, while holding substantially the same views, dwelt less on the wonders of the act of 1689, and more on the possibilities of the vast uncultivated wastes. In addition, he held a higher opinion of those engaged in the corn traffic than did Anderson, and he deprecated the attacks made upon them. Further, Anderson believed a corn law offering greater protection, and hence more incentive to produce and export, would suffice ; but Sheffield maintained that a general enclosure act and commutation of tithes were necessary as well.[60]

Arthur Young stood midway between the defenders of the smallholder and cottager and the advocates of the large scientific farmer. Earlier he had been a vigorous propagandist for the elimination of the smallholder and the substitution of the large farmer on the grounds of efficiency. But by 1795 the evils of dispossessing the smallholder and the cottager, and the demoralizing effect of the Speenhamland system on the new proletariat seem to have modified his views. He was still a believer in the large farm and the improvement of culture by enclosing the wastes and commons, but now he wished to have the agricultural labourers and cottagers retain an interest in the soil. He advised giving a plot of land and a cow to labourers where there were commons, and to cottagers where there were no commons.[61] His idea was, in his own words, to " secure to the poor cottagers their fair share, without expense, forever and inalienably annexed to the cottage which gives the right."[62]

A so-called Society of Practical Farmers administered a severe rebuke to Young for expounding such ideas. After pointing out the stock arguments in favour of large holdings, they insisted that it would be much better if the farmers, out of their hearts, would give their labourers cottages with pieces of ground attached on which to raise potatoes and other vegetables after the working day was over. In addition, the landlords should introduce into the farmers' leases compulsory clauses forcing the latter to supply their labourers with milk the year round at a reasonable rate.   This, they insisted, would lift the labourer above risk and also preserve his proper respect for his employer. [63]

The fourth remedy suggested for solving the problem of scarcity was temporary measures.   Most of these were the same as the ones put forward by the committees on scarcity in 1795, 1796 and 1800, and some of them had been acted upon already.   The chief recommendation was to reduce consumption.   Another was the growth of potatoes, which, it was held, might stave off starvation among the poor during the period immediately preceding the grain harvest, since potatoes were harvested two months earlier than wheat. [64]   A third suggestion was to give poor relief in the form of soup, rice, etc., so as to husband the corn supply.

The fifth, and easily the most popular, remedy suggested was the punishment under the common law of the practices of forestalling, engrossing and regrating.   The actual pamphlets ascribing the scarcity and high prices to the activities of the corn dealers are few in number, but the arguments in favour of this point of view appear to have been on everybody's lips, since so many pamphleteers took the pains to defend the middlemen.   Riots of greater violence than usual took place in most of the larger cities of England, and were directed against bakers as well as corn dealers.   The inflamed state of public opinion in London was given an abundance of fuel by the famous Rusby trial.   This affair is significant both because it represented the culmination of mob violence, and the attitude of so important a Justice as Lord Kenyon of the King's Bench, and because it gave a practical demonstration of the danger of the courts interfering with the internal corn trade, as the affair of 1796 had shown the danger of the government taking a hand in the foreign grain trade.

Mr. John Rusby, a jobber dealing in the Mark Lane Exchange, was indicted for regrating or re-selling in the same market on the same day.   The offence took place November 8th, 1799, when he was alleged to have bought from the factors Joseph Shrimpton, John Greenside and John Sharwood, ninety quarters of oats at 41s. a quarter and to have sold thirty quarters of the same oats, through the factors Prest and Nattrass, to William Hardy at 43s.   The trial was held on July 4th, 1800, in the court of the King's Bench before Lord Kenyon and a special jury.   The arguments advanced by the prosecution were to have particularly unfortunate results, because of their influence on the London mob. [65]   Even more disastrous was Lord Kenyon's summing up for the jury.   He dwelt eloquently on the damage done to the poor and starving, and expressed the pious wish that Adam Smith could have been alive and present at the trial because he was certain that the learned gentleman might revise his

G

opinion that forestalling, engrossing and regrating were as imaginary as witchcraft. He concluded : " Gentlemen, a precedent made in a court of justice that will stem the torrent of such affliction to the poor is certainly useful to the public."[66] The jury took the hint and rendered a verdict of " guilty."

The results of the verdict were scarcely what was expected by the prosecution and Kenyon. The ignorant populace, which had always felt that the corn dealers were responsible for the high prices, now started a series of riots over all England. The decision of Kenyon gave them the excuse they desired. A London mob tore down Rusby's house and would, in all probability, have lynched him had he not been fortunate in fleeing before their arrival. *The Annual Register* put the case rather cautiously in stating that by the prosecution of Rusby " the discontents of the people were not sufficiently allayed."[67] The mobs throughout the country, as a rule, first attempted a forcible reduction of the prices of grain and foodstuffs, but this procedure was usually accompanied by violence and plundering. In many places the militia had to be called out to put down the riots. The greatest disturbance in London came on December 15th, several weeks after the destruction of Rusby's house. On the night before, inflammatory notices were posted on the Monument urging people to take vengeance on the monopolists and forestallers. In the morning a mob proceeded to Mark Lane and demanded a lowering of the price of corn. Alderman Combe addressed the mob, but " finding his persuasions fruitless," he ordered the riot act to be read and order was restored without the calling of the militia. Mobs assembled on several days following " but the ready attendance of the volunteers, and the firmness of their countenance, alarmed the populace, and, without the actual use of firearms, repressed the commotions."[68]

The effect of the riots in which Rusby's house was destroyed and the influence of his conviction nearly caused another disaster. Many factors, jobbers and importers, alarmed by the double danger of conviction and mobbing, ceased doing their customary business with the result that prices were further enhanced. It is possible that the suffering would have been really acute had not ten thousand barrels of flour arrived in the midst of this uncertainty and relieved the threatened famine.[69]

Rusby, who had been sentenced to pay a heavy fine, appealed the case. On the appeal the Court was equally divided over the question whether or not regrating, engrossing and forestalling were still offences at common law.[70] At all events Rusby was never sentenced and no more attempts seem to have been made to punish these practices.

Another result of the Rusby trial and the mob violence that followed, was the publication of a considerable number of pamphlets defending the functions of the middlemen. Practically all of these pamphleteers bewailed the useless outcry and violence against the corn dealers. Adam Smith's account of the services rendered by these middlemen were quoted over and over again, particularly the paragraph beginning : " The interest of the inland dealer, and that of the great body of the people, how opposite soever they may at first appear, are, even in years of the greatest scarcity, exactly the same."[71] Morris' *A Short Enquiry into the Nature of Monopoly and Forestalling*, was likewise republished. He followed Adam Smith in holding that the interest of the corn dealer in the distribution of his stock was the same as that of the public, and that a combination to raise prices was impossible. He further held that corn middlemen supplied the public more judiciously and at less expense than would otherwise have been the case.

Perhaps the ablest of the pamphlets defending these dealers was one by Sir Thomas Turton. He deals specifically with each kind of middlemen engaged in both the internal and external corn trade. In this he differs from both Smith and Morris, who group all those interested in the internal trade as inland dealers. First Turton dealt with the millers, factors and bakers in order. From an investigation of the one hundred and fifty mills around London he showed that not only were they not hoarding grain and flour, but that most of them had scarcely a week's supply in advance and that some were idle from lack of corn.[72] In this case the factors in turn could not be supplied with the material to create a monopoly or secure excessive profits.[73] The baker, who was more often subject to rough treatment by the mob than the other two because he sold the article directly to the consumer, was even less liable to make excessive charges because his profits were regulated by the Assize of Bread. The one true charge against him was that his bread often fell short of its assized weight. But this offence, though serious, was not always intentional, and since it was punishable by law there was no excuse for the frequent plundering of the shops and the physical injuries to the baker.[74] Turton next took up the middlemen who dealt with external corn trade. An inquiry into the disposal of imported grain showed that the rumours of merchant importers hoarding vast quantities of wheat in Thames warehouses were false, because practically all of it was sold, on arrival, to millers. In fact he had been assured that not a single quarter of English wheat had been warehoused in the preceding eight months.[75] The corn factor, like the flour factor, merely sold on commission and seldom speculated on his own account.[76] It might be argued that the jobber, who usually bought the corn imported by the merchant through a factor and sold it either to the retailers or direct to the consumers, was enhancing the price by taking a profit. But if the merchant had to perform this function himself, he would be obliged to charge a higher price in order to make up for the time his vessel was detained and for the slower turning of his capital.[77] Thus it was difficult, in the opinion of Turton, to prove that high prices were due to the machinations of either the internal or external corn dealers.

The unfortunate results of the Rusby trial, combined with this series of pamphlets on the functions of the middlemen, seem to have driven home the futility of blaming forestalling, engrossing and regrating for rising prices. In future times the starving poor doubtless blamed the corn dealers, but no serious attempt seems to have been made by any writer to explain high prices in this way.

A good harvest in 1800 would have brought the relief which so many acts of Parliament, schemes for improving production and distribution, and able pamphlets explaining the causes of scarcity, failed to do. But the harvest brought no relief. It is true that the wheat crop was not as deficient as that of 1799, but it was sufficiently short to make certain a continuation of high prices and distress for another year.[78] The significance which the government attached to the existing condition is shown by the fact that the speech of the King at the opening of the session on November 11th, 1800, was almost entirely devoted to this topic. The stress laid upon three points showed that the government had followed closely the pamphlet warfare of the preceding months. These three points were : first, the necessity of an extension of tillage and an improvement in agricultural methods ; second, the desirability of getting some measure of immediate relief by encouraging importation ; and third, the necessity of distinguishing fraudulent practices to enhance prices from the regular and long-established course of trade which was so indispensable for supplying the market in the present state of society.

Although the King's speech showed familiarity with the recent suggestions for solving the problems of scarcity and high prices, the actual steps taken were precisely those of the preceding year. The customary scarcity acts were renewed and a committee appointed to consider the high prices of provisions. The Crown was given the right to prohibit the exportation of any article used as food.[79] The use of corn in distilling or making starch was forbidden until January 1st, 1802 ;[80] and the former acts prohibiting exportation and permitting importation duty free were continued until forty days after the commencement of the next session of Parliament.[81] Bounties were to be paid on all wheat, barley, rye, oats, peas, beans, Indian corn, rice and flour or meal made from grain, which was imported between December 1st, 1800, and October 1st, 1801, in British vessels or those of a friendly nation. Following the precedent of the previous year, a fixed price was assured and the bounty was to make up the difference between the actual price received and the guaranteed one. Prices of 100s., 65s., 50s., 40s., 75s. and 50s. a quarter were guaranteed respectively for wheat, rye, barley, oats, peas and beans.[82] In order to husband the scanty supply of wheat, an act was passed directing the Justices of the Peace to consider what articles of food could best be substituted for bread, and to order overseers to provide provisions for parochial relief along these lines.[83] Lastly, despite the unfortunate experience in 1795-6, another attempt was made to secure the sale of mixed bread. The manufacture of fine flour, or the making of bread solely from fine flour, was prohibited until November 6th, 1801 ; and from thence to the end of six weeks after the opening of the session of Parliament. The exact size of the sieve, through which the flour was to be passed, was carefully defined. Only one kind of bread was to be assized, and that was to be made from the finest flour permitted by this act. Bakers were permitted to make mixed bread, provided that it was marked and the price charged did not exceed that of the assized bread.[84] This act was as complete a fiasco as the brown bread experiment of 1796. Within a short time its repeal was recommended ;[85] and although the suggestion was not carried

out in this session of Parliament, there was, evidently, no further
attempt to enforce it.

The committee appointed to consider high prices of provisions
rendered six reports before the end of 1800, and seven in the first half
of 1801. The recommendations made were in most cases the ones
suggested by the pamphleteers, or by the committee appointed a year
earlier to investigate scarcity. Some of these were carried out in the
acts enumerated in the previous paragraph. About the only new
suggestions were those of the seventh and last report which dealt with
improving conditions at Mark Lane in London. But since the government had had its fingers burned too often in the last six years by
striving to extend its control with insufficient machinery, nothing was
done about it.[86]

Despite the advice of pamphleteers and committees, and the laws
passed by Parliament, prices of grain continued extremely high. In
February of 1800 the average monthly price of wheat had been over
100s. a quarter. In July this average price had risen to 134s. 8d.,
and in December had fallen only to 130s. 8d. The early months of
1801 saw the price of wheat soar even higher. The average for March
was 154s. 2d., and single days saw it much higher. With prices at
this level suffering and distress among the poor was inevitable.
Naturally there were even more riots than in the previous year. The
fears of the propertied classes, which had been aroused by the excesses
of the French Revolution, were greatly increased by these riots. Some
insisted that it was high time for men of property to look to their own
interests, and that it was as important to keep numerous bodies of
volunteers in arms to prevent internal insurrection as it was to repulse
foreign invasions. This tendency to widen the chasm between propertied and proletarian classes was accentuated by the manner in
which mobs were put down in many places. On the other hand, there
were many indications that this cleavage was not complete. In
several places the city magistrates were able to quell riots without
resorting to force. Another favourable sign was the solicitude shown
by wealthy individuals for the suffering of the poor, and the genuine,
though inefficient, attempts of the government to relieve the
scarcity.[87] One writer frankly admits that, " The privations and
sufferings of the lower orders . . . were so great, that every candid
mind was less offended at the commotions of the populace, than struck
with their forbearance and patience."[88]

Relief from this state of scarcity and high prices came not from any
action of the government, but from a moderately abundant harvest in
1801.[89] Despite the rapid fall in the price of wheat, the government
was still reluctant about sweeping away the scarcity measures.
Hence, when Parliament assembled in November of 1801, the acts
forbidding exportation and permitting importation of grain, duty free,
were renewed until January 1st, 1803.[90]

With the return of something like normal conditions in the production and distribution of grain, following the harvest and peace
preliminaries of 1801, a period of nearly nine years of dreary war and
intermittent crop failures ended. During these years, the government
had displayed the same hopeful inefficiency in dealing with the pro-

blems of the internal and external corn trade that it had shown in
conducting the war.   The nation as a whole seems to have faced the
problems of peace with a sigh of relief.   But after a brief period of
cessation of hostilities, the struggle was to be renewed with even
greater military, social and economic problems.

SECTION II, 1801–1813

The Peace of Amiens which was concluded in March of 1802, and
from which so much was expected, lasted only until May of 1803.
When the war was resumed, internal conditions in both France and
Great Britain were far more favourable than they had been during the
last war.   Napoleon, after making himself ruler of France by his
coup d'état of November, 1799, established a most efficient despotism.
The censorship of the Press, the control of education, the bureaucratic
system, and the elaborately-organized secret police were all carried
to a higher degree of perfection than under the Bourbons.   France
" accepted the result because she was sick of anarchy, and the new
regime gave her, at the least, order, stability and internal peace."[91]
The plebiscite of 1802, in which the nation approved of his assumption
of the Consulship for life, and of 1804, in which his adoption of the
title of Emperor was ratified, showed that this despotism rested upon
national consent.
    Great Britain, although entering the war with France without allies,
was really in much better condition for carrying on the struggle than
she had been during the years of 1793–1801.   There was no longer
any question of sympathy with the revolutionary cause, but a well-
nigh universal feeling that the country was fighting for her very
existence.   Perhaps the most favourable sign was the condition of
the navy which was vastly improved over that of the late war.   With
the great victories gained from 1797 to 1801, with the incomparable
Nelson as leader, and with such able administrators as Lord St.
Vincent and Lord Barham in charge of the Admiralty, the nation
could look forward with confidence to a continued control of the seas.
The army was by no means in as good condition, but the enthusiastic
drilling of companies of volunteers gave promise for the future.   This
national feeling even extended to the political leaders of the country,
and when Pitt returned to office in 1804 only the stubbornness of
George III., and the lack of insistence by Pitt, prevented Fox and his
followers from joining the government.   Upon the death of Pitt in
1806 a ministry made up of Whigs and Tories was formed, but it
broke down in 1807 over the question of Catholic Emancipation.
Consequently, from 1807 the conduct of the war was entirely in the
hands of the Tories.[92]
    The war between the years 1803 and 1813 may be divided into three
phases : first, the establishment of British supremacy on the seas from
1803 to 1805 ; second, the formation and collapse of the third coalition
against Napoleon from 1805 to 1807 ; and third, the war of commerce
from the time the Berlin decree was issued in November of 1806, to the
collapse of the Continental System with the failure of Napoleon's

Russian campaign of 1812, his defeat at Leipsic in October of 1813, and the expulsion of the French from Spain by Wellington in the same year.

The first period ended with the overwhelming victory of Nelson over the French Fleet at Trafalgar on October 21st, 1805. Before this blow, the third coalition of Great Britain, Russia, Austria and Sweden had been formed. It proved even more futile than the two preceding ones. Austria was driven to make peace by the overwhelming defeat at Austerlitz in December of 1805. Prussia, which had declined to join the coalition, was goaded into declaring war and was quickly overwhelmed by Napoleon at the battles of Jena and Auerstadt in October of 1806. Next Russia was decisively beaten at Friedland and the Czar Alexander made peace with Napoleon at Tilsit in July of 1807. By a secret supplementary treaty Alexander not only agreed to declare war on Great Britain, but also to aid Napoleon in coercing the remaining independent nations of Europe to do likewise.

Napoleon was now free to give his undivided attention to the British : and although he did not give up hopes of invading the island until 1809, he concentrated most of his efforts on his Continental System. In November of 1806 he had issued the Berlin Decree declaring the British Isles to be in a state of blockade. The British Government had countered with an order in council in January of 1807 forbidding all trade between any two ports from which British ships were excluded. After Tilsit this blockade was extended to all ports from which British goods were barred. Napoleon replied with his Milan Decree of 1807 which threatened with seizure any neutral vessels which called at a British port. The chief neutral sufferer from these regulations was the United States. In 1809 Great Britain limited her blockade to the coasts of Holland, France and Italy. Napoleon, on the other hand, took even more drastic measures. · He discovered that both tropical produce and manufactured goods were coming into Europe from Great Britain in large quantities. Consequently in 1810 he imposed high duties on the chief colonial and tropical products by the Trianon Tariff, and ordered the seizure and destruction of British manufactured goods by the Decrees of Fontainbleu. The British undertook to offset the effects of the Continental System in three ways : first, by encouraging both direct trade with vassal states of Napoleon which disapproved of the system and smuggling through such bases as Heligoland in the North Sea and Gibraltar, Malta, Sicily and the Ionian Island in the Mediterranean ; second, by conquering the colonial possessions of France and her allies, an achievement which gave the British a monopoly of the colonial products, and furnished a wider market for British manufactured goods ; and third, by encouraging and helping Europe and nations to resist or revolt against Napoleon. British forces were landed in Calabria and Sicily in 1806, in Sweden in 1808, and on the island of Walcheren in the Netherlands in 1809. In addition, the Peninsular War was waged by the British from 1808 to 1814. In the main the policy followed by the British government was successful, since the overthrow of Napoleon eventually came as a result of the rising tide of national feeling, and both the Continental System and the aid and encouragement of the British were contributing factors.[93]

In the remainder of this chapter and in chapter VI the effect of the war and the Continental System on the internal and external corn trade will be dealt with. From 1802 to 1804, the Corn Laws once more occupied a prominent place, but from 1804 until after the harvest of 1813, poor crops and the Continental System kept prices of grain so high that these laws were inoperative.

After the terrible years of scarcity from 1799 to 1801 a rapid fall in the price of grain set in which brought considerable distress to the landed interest. The harvests of 1802 and 1803 were of ordinary, but not superabundant quantity.[94] The prices of wheat, barley and oats all dropped steadily during the year 1802, especially after the harvest of that year, and in December wheat was worth only 68s. 3d.   The decline continued during 1803 and the early part of 1804, wheat finally fell below 50s. a quarter, and barley and oats even more in proportion,[95] so that the average price of grain was not far from its pre-war level.   This fall in price produced the customary cry of agricultural distress, and brought on an agitation for a new corn bill. Yet despite this rapid decline, Parliament continued to renew the act allowing free importation and prohibiting exportation of grain. On December 29th, 1802, it was continued until January 1st, 1804,[96] and on December 15th, 1803, until March 25th, 1805.[97] A series of petitions was presented to the House of Commons early in 1804 from the landowners, barley-growers, maltsters and others in the counties of Norfolk, Suffolk, Stafford, Warwick, Essex and Lincoln asking that the act of 1791 should be revised.

The Commons were sufficiently impressed by these petitions to appoint a committee to investigate the law of 1791.   The report of this committee, which was given on May 14th, commenced with the time-honoured and self-evident hypothesis that the farmer must have a price which would induce him to grow enough grain to meet the demand ; and that the best method of providing this incentive was to insure him a fair and reasonable price.   The committee deemed that the act of 1791 did not assure the farmer " a fair and reasonable " price, and hence recommended increased protection.   In the case of imported wheat the price levels per quarter were raised from 50s. and 54s., to 63s. and 66s.   The high duty of 24s. 3d. was to apply below 63s. ; the first low duty of 2s. 6d., from 63s. to 66s. ; and the second low duty of 6d., at and above 66s.   The protection given other kinds of grain was also increased, and the colonial preference of the law of 1791 was retained.

A bill based on this report was finally drawn up and, after several amendments were added and changes made, was finally passed on July 7th.   The Lords, in turn, passed the measure on July 19th with a long series of amendments.[98]   One in particular, which changed the method by which the prices of Irish grain were to be determined, was declared by the Speaker to be inconsistent with the privileges of the House of Commons.   A motion by Mr. Western that the amendments should be considered three months from this day was passed, and consequently the measure was lost.   Mr. Western immediately announced his intention of bringing forward another bill, based on the same principles, despite the protests against such a step being taken so late in the session.[99] Western's new bill was rushed through in an astonishingly short time. On June 23rd the resolutions were read and accepted in the Commons, and a bill based upon them was ordered brought in. The bill passed the third reading on June 26th ; was agreed to by the Lords on the 28th ; and received the royal assent on the 30th.[100]

In comparison with 1790 and 1791, there were relatively few petitions against either bill introduced in 1804. In the case of the second one, the explanation, doubtless, was the short time which elapsed between the time it was introduced and passed. Most of the complaints came from cities on the east coast of Ireland. Petitions from Dublin, Limerick, Youghall and Drogheda pointed out that this measure would ruin their grain trade with Great Britain.[101]

The act which went into effect on November 15th, 1804, really introduced no new principles. All wheat exported when the price was less than 48s. was to receive a bounty of 5s. a quarter. Foreign wheat, when the price was less than 63s. a quarter, was to pay a duty of 24s. 3d. ; when at or above 63s., but under 66s., 2s. 6d. ; and when at or above 66s., 6d. Wheat from the North American colonies was admitted under the same scale of duties, but the price levels were ten shillings lower in all three instances. Higher protection was given to rye, peas, beans, barley, beer and oats.[102] The existing method of computing quarterly, monthly and weekly prices was retained.

The act of 1804 is, on the whole, unimportant because it was almost entirely inoperative until after the huge harvest of 1813. Its chief interest lies in the state of mind it disclosed in the landed interest. Undoubtedly the high prices of 1799–1801 stimulated wheat growing and were partially responsible for the fall from 1802 to 1804 ; but this did not excuse the landlords for attempting to use their political power to raise prices again. Supporters of the law claimed that it would do what the acts of 1670 and 1689 were supposed to have done : render prices steady and encourage agriculture. This same excuse had been offered for passing the laws of 1773 and 1791, and was to be used often in the next forty years. In reality the act of 1804 was merely a link between that of 1791, which marked the first decided use of political power by the landed interest to secure class legislation, and that of 1815, which marked the most extreme use of this power. In the previous chapter it was pointed out that the rise in prices offered some justification for increasing the protection on grain in 1791, but the additional rise since the act of that year did not offer an adequate excuse for securing further protection. The high prices of grain from 1793 to 1801, in the main, were due to unusually deficient crops and were rendered worse by the fact that the war interfered with making up the deficit from abroad. Thus in 1804 the landlords and farmers were deliberately trying to secure for themselves permanently a range of prices which had been produced by extraordinary circumstances. The law of 1804 was a piece of class legislation, and was harmless in the end only because even more unusual circumstances rendered inoperative the price levels fixed.

Most of the complaints against the act came from the new industrial cities of northern England and western Scotland. Petitions from numerous places[103] chiefly objected to the increased protection, to the additional warehousing charges, and to certain details in the method of taking the averages. Outside these petitions it is amazing how little comment the act caused even when the speed with which it was rushed through Parliament is considered. No pamphlet of any note seems to have appeared except a brilliant one by James Mill, entitled, *An Essay on the Impolicy of a Bounty on Exports of Corn*. It is probably the ablest pamphlet against the bounty which was produced during the entire controversy over the merits of that system, but it is an attack on the principle of the bounty rather than on the increased protection offered under the act of 1804. Mill advocated a free importation and exportation of grain on the ground that it would reduce the medium price but little, and that this slight disadvantage to the farmer would be more than offset by preserving him from fluctuating prices. In addition, he believed that this freedom in the corn trade would be of incalculable value to the foreign commerce of the country.[104]

Cobbett entered a very vigorous protest in his *Register* against the new act. He pointed out the absurdity of paying out great sums of money in bounties to encourage importation in 1800 and 1801, and of passing laws to keep out imports and encourage exports in 1804. He believed that the measure was passed for the benefit of certain classes, and insisted that Pitt " should have listened with great caution to the advice of contractors and corn merchants or to that other race of beings who have sprung from the dunghill of paper money and who are called speculating farmers ; yes, he should have listened to these persons with great caution, and even with distrust, when their object was to obtain a law evidently for the sole purpose of advancing their own interests, though the well-being of the whole nation should thereby be hazarded."[105] Cobbett next called attention to the rise in the price of wheat in the interval when the bill lay before the Lords and he maintained that this advance was a purely speculative one. Pitt, he declared, was insincere and inconsistent in saying that the rise was due to news of a scanty harvest, and at the same time insisting that the bill was necessary to prevent the prices of grain from sinking lower.[106]

The attacks on the law might have increased in volume had prices continued to be low ; but a very deficient harvest in 1804, particularly in wheat, brought on such high prices[107] that the interest shifted to plans for relieving the distress among the lower classes. Apparently the rioting, which invariably accompanied high prices, took place on a smaller scale than usual. *The Annual Register*, for example, makes no mention of the customary violence. But the distress, evidently, was great enough to bring about the suspension of the law of 1804, and the substitution of permission to import foreign grain, duty free, and of prohibition to export until March 25th, 1806.[108]

The poor crop of 1804 marked the beginning of another long period of scarcity and high prices. In the spring of 1805 the price of wheat rose above 100s. a quarter ; and, when the summer turned out to be a cold one another deficient crop was expected.   The deficit was not as great as was anticipated, and by the spring of 1806 the price of wheat had fallen under 75s.[109]   The act which gave the Crown permission to forbid exportation and allow importation of grain, duty free, was extended to March 25th, 1809, presumably to save the trouble of annual renewal.   In March of 1806 the Prussian Government added to the difficulties by prohibiting the entrance of British ships into any of its ports or rivers.   This exclusion from Prussian ports, which affected the grain supply from the Baltic region, was further extended by Napoleon's Berlin Decree.   Combined with a slightly deficient wheat crop in 1806[110] and a very deficient one in Scotland in 1807, which offset the average yield in England,[111] this shutting off of one of the chief sources of foreign grain kept the price of wheat above the 66s. fixed by the law of 1804.   The chances of supplying the existing and future deficiencies in grain received additional blows when the Danes closed the Sound to the British in the fall of 1807 following the bombardment of Copenhagen, and when the Russians placed an embargo on British shipping following the Treaty of Tilsit.   The harvest of 1808 brought little relief because most kinds of grain were even more deficient than in the preceding year.   Wheat especially was damaged by wet and stormy weather at harvest time.[112]   The tightening in the operation of the Continental System and the American Embargo kept the price of wheat fluctuating between 80s and 100s.   The harvest of 1809 was eagerly awaited, both because of the dire necessity of the country and of the favourable prospects. But these hopes were dashed by continuous rains during the harvest which caused much of the wheat to mildew and sprout.   Some of the grain was said to be unfit for anything but distilling[113] and that was forbidden.

The government was somewhat handicapped in attempting to relieve the situation by legislative enactments, such as had been tried so often in the past, because suspending laws against importation was useless.   But late in 1809, and during 1810, relief came from an un-expected source.   France in 1809 had an enormous crop of wheat which sank the price so low that it caused much dissatisfaction among the peasants.   Napoleon then decided to permit exportation to Great Britain under a system of export licences.   There is a decided lack of agreement among modern historians over Napoleon's reasons for taking such an action.   Some believe it was fear of an uprising in France ; others, that Napoleon wished to squeeze as much revenue from export licences as possible in order to injure Great Britain. Muir holds that Napoleon had convinced himself that he could ruin Great Britain more readily by encouraging her to buy and preventing her from selling.[114]   Another writer insists that Napoleon had no chance of starving Britain and that the allowing of this exportation of grain merely showed his realization of the fact.[115]   In any case the two million quarters, principally wheat, which were obtained from France were a welcome addition, whether or not the country would have starved without it.

The harvest of 1810 was only fair in quantity ; but it was secured in excellent condition which, along with the enormous imports, caused a fall of 25s. to 30s. in the price of wheat between August of 1810 and June of 1811.[116] This fall did not produce universal relief, since it resulted in the ruin of a great number of corn dealers who had speculated on a further advance in prices. The harvests of 1811 and 1812 were both greatly deficient,[117] and in neither year was relief secured by foreign imports as in 1809 and 1810. As a consequence the prices of wheat reached a level as high as those of 1800 and 1801. The actual deficiency of the crops in 1811 and 1812 was, in all probability, not as great as in 1794, 1799 and 1800, but the virtual exclusion of foreign corn made conditions as bad or worse as in those years.[118]

The action taken by the government in the years from 1810 to 1813 was, as nearly as circumstances permitted, almost a duplication of that adopted in previous periods of scarcity. The act which gave the Crown the right to suspend exportation and to permit importation duty free was renewed for a year, evidently as a matter of course, in both 1809[119] and 1810.[120] Parliament had continued the prohibition against the use of grain in the distillery until December 31st, 1810,[121] but had not renewed it upon expiration. This measure was again re-enacted on February 7th, 1812, to remain in force until the end of the year,[122] and it was then once more continued until December 31st, 1813.[123] In addition, Parliament forbade the use of wheat and articles of food in the manufacture of starch or hair powder. This law which was to remain in force until November 1st, 1812,[124] was later continued until October 1st, 1813 ;[125] but, owing to improved conditions, it was repealed on March 23rd.[126] All such temporary measures ended with the enormous harvest of 1813 which started wheat prices falling at a terrific rate, and which played an important part in bringing about the agitation for a new corn law.

On the whole, the most amazing feature of the years from 1805 to 1813 is, on first thought, the manner in which the question of the Corn Laws falls into the background. From the protests against the act of 1804, which were referred to a committee, until the agitation following the harvest of 1813 the number of pamphlets, speeches in Parliament, and references in *The Annual Register* are remarkably few in number. But when the workings of the Continental System are taken into consideration, the neglect of this subject becomes intelligible. During these years very little grain was imported into Great Britain, except in 1809 and 1810 ; this situation was due to Napoleon's decision, and not to any action which the British government or individuals in the country took. The Embargo and Non-Intercourse policy of the United States added to the difficulties of importation. The actual imports from America, although not large, were increasing, and the loss of any amount was felt during these years. To make up for the decline of imports, a great extension in the area of cultivation and a marked improvement in farming methods were made.[127] But this was a process which was going on outside Parliament. On the economic side the attention of the government was largely centred on financing the war and on the currency problem. Such questions as the bullion report were of greater interest than the Corn Laws. Still another reason for the apparent lack of interest in this question was the fact that the majority of the members of Parliament represented the landed interest, and the landlords were quite satisfied with the rapidly-increasing rents and the farmers with the large profits. The fact that both were rendering inestimable services to the country by increasing the production of grain does not obscure the fact that they were well paid for their efforts.

CONCLUSION

The conclusion of Tooke that the Corn Laws were practically inoperative from 1792 to 1813 is undeniable. From 1792 until the failure of the harvest of 1794, wheat was above 54s. as often as it was below. During the two starvation years from the harvest of 1794 to the fall in prices in the spring of 1796, prices of all kinds of grain were far above the low import duty level. The exportation of wheat was forbidden, and importation, duty free, was permitted during the years 1796 to 1801. The price of wheat did not fall below the 54s. maximum fixed by the act of 1791 until late in 1803 or early in the following spring ; then the act of 1804 raised this maximum to 66s. From the time the first three months averages were taken under this law until 1813 the price of wheat was never below 66s. and consequently it was inoperative practically from the beginning.

The chief interest in the period from the passing of the law of 1791 down to the harvest of 1813, lies in the changed attitude of the government and Parliament toward the functions and purpose of the Corn Laws. Down to the Restoration in 1660 these laws were passed almost entirely in the interests of the consumer, and not until after that date was the producer considered of equal importance. Despite the enormously high import, export and bounty levels of the acts of 1670 and 1689, the eighteenth century legislation was not class-conscious. These price levels were nominal and not real, owing to the suspension of exportation and importation in periods of scarcity long before they were reached. The eighteenth century Parliament was, in the main, a group of landlords who, except where their own interests were affected, passed laws for the benefit of an active commercial class. They even suspended the Corn Laws, in which they were vitally interested, when the pressure of public opinion made itself felt through petitions from and riots in London and the growing commercial and industrial cities. After 1760 this pressure increased with the development of the midlands and north. The act of 1773, as was shown in Chapter III, merely reduced the nominal price levels of the acts of 1670 and 1689 to points consistent with the actual prices of the eighteenth century. The landed, commercial and industrial groups all, seemingly, agreed upon the desirability of taking such a step. Thus down to 1791 the landowners in Parliament appear to have made no real effort to use their political power for their economic benefit at the expense of other interests. Even the Representation of the Privy Council in March of 1790 was untinged by class-consciousness. The raising of the maximum price level of wheat in the act of 1791 from 48s. to 54s. seems to have been the first use of political power by the landlords to enhance the price of their agricultural products in the face of the opposition of other classes. Perhaps they were perfectly justified in taking such an action, because the law of 1773 was preventing them from securing the benefit of the rise in prices to which they felt they were entitled through the increased demand for food. But whether or not the use of their political power was justified in this particular instance, it started a precedent for doing so when circumstances did not warrant it.

Another change in attitude came as a result of the French Revolution. Previously the upper classes in Great Britain did not look upon the lower ones as their natural enemies. There was no question of intimate relation between classes and masses, but the feeling was more one of caste than of antagonism. In addition there was a real liberal and reforming spirit in the ruling class beginning in the seventeen-sixties. Nearly all the great reforms of the years from 1823 to 1850 were proposed during this period and would, doubtless, have been carried out much sooner but for the French Revolution and Napoleonic wars. This desire of the upper classes to reform from above was characteristic of the enlightened despotism of the time. Some were sincerely interested in reform, while others were mere dabblers.

The French Revolution changed all this feeling. P. A. Brown, in *The French Revolution in English History*, has described how this hot house reform plant was frozen by the wintry blasts of French excesses. The magnificent condescension with which the upper classes talked of improving conditions for the masses changed to class hatred and suspicion, and to opposition to any change. This fear was increased by the riots which took place in the years of scarcity. Members of the propertied classes openly declared that it was time for them to band together against the lower classes, and that a large body of volunteers to protect property was as essential as defending the country against Bonaparte.

As a result of this change in attitude, the spirit in which the landed interest conducted the fight for a new Corn Law in 1814–15 was in marked contrast to that of 1790–1. A combination of the rise in the standard of living of the landlords and farmers, which neither were willing to surrender, with this new feeling of suspicion against the lower classes, made the landed interest willing to use its political power to secure what was almost entirely a piece of class legislation.

CHAPTER V

NOTES

[1] It is difficult to deny the conclusion of Muir that : " Whatever may be the case in other countries, the British Commonwealth owes very little—directly, at all events—to the inspiration of the French Revolution. The revolution brought to Britain not advance but reaction, not amendment but bitter suffering. And when the period of reconstruction began, it was not from the vague and abstract speculations of revolutionary philosophy that the guidance was drawn, but from British sources ; from the work and schemes of the pre-revolutionary reformers, from the teaching of Adam Smith and Jeremy Bentham, from the practical experiments of trade unionists and co-operators." *A Short History of the British Commonwealth*, vol. 2, p. 148.

[2] *Ibid.*, p. 171.

[3] Tooke, *History of Prices*, vol. 1, p. 81.

[4] The principal change introduced in this supplementary act dealt with the method of determining the averages. The weekly average price was to be determined in each of the towns of England designated in the act of 1791, but the receiver of corn returns was to make an average of the prices of all the cities instead of merely those in each district. 33rd George III., c. 65.

[5] Tooke, *History of Prices*, vol. 1, p. 181.

[6] 35th George III., c. 4.

[7] Tooke, *History of Prices*, vol. 1, p. 181–2.

[8] 35th George III., c. 119.

[9] The years in which both sets of prices were first recorded.

[10] *Parliamentary History*, vol. 32, p. 153.

[11] 36th George III., c. 3.   [12] *Ibid.*, c. 6.

[13] *Reports from the Committees of the House of Commons*, vol. 9, p. 45.

[14] *Ibid.*, p. 46. The recommendations made were : first, that a bounty of 29s. be paid on wheat imported from any port south of Cape Finisterre, in the Mediterranean, or in Africa before August 31st, 1796, up to 300,000 quarters ; second, that a bounty of 15s. a quarter be paid on all wheat from other ports of Europe and America imported before August 31st, 1796, up to 500,000 quarters, and all imported beyond that amount to receive a bounty of 10s. ; and third, that a bounty of 5s. a quarter be paid on Indian corn imported before August 31st, 1796, up to 500,000 quarters.

[15] *Ibid.*, pp. 46–50. It was proposed to grant a bounty of 10s. on all rye arriving in Great Britain before September 30th, 1796, up to 300,000 quarters, and 6s. for any exceeding that amount.

[16] *Ibid.*, pp. 53–4.

[17] *The Crying Frauds of the London Market*, 1795, takes this point of view.

[18] Mr. Donaldson, *A Letter to the Right Honourable Mr. Pitt on the Use of Hair Powder*, 1795.

[19] The Rev. Edward Barry, *On the Necessity of Adopting Some Measures to Reduce the Present Number of Dogs*, 1795.

[20] David Davies, *The Case of Labourers in Husbandry Stated and Considered*, 1796.

[21] *The First Report from the Select Committee of the House of Commons on Cultivation and Improvement of the Waste, Uninclosed, and Unproductive Lands of the Kingdom*, 1796.

[22] 36th George III., c. 9.   [23] *Ibid.*, c. 20.

[24] *Ibid.*, c. 21. In addition a bounty of 5s. a quarter was offered on all Indian corn up to 500,000 quarters, and 3s. for all above that amount ; and 10s. up to 100,000 quarters and 6s. above.

[25] *Parliamentary History*, vol. 32, p. 694.   [26] *Ibid.*, pp. 695–6.

[27] 36th George III., c. 32.

[28] Sidney and Beatrice Webb, *The Assize of Bread*, *Economic Journal*, June, 1904, p. 210.

[29] The man testifying about the lack of success with bread made from this mixed flour maintained that it was " heavy and ill-made, perhaps for want of use, and still more, I suspect for want of inclination. Nothing is well done, if it be done against the grain. This bread, however, I persisted to eat for several days with the hope at least that, as far as the use of my family went, there would be a saving in the consumption of wheat. . . . I found that, in this period of economy, there had been more bread consumed or destroyed in my house, than at any other equal period. Why ? Because the bread was ill-made and un-pleasant, and for that reason wasted. None but the best bread is fairly eaten in families, where the servants and other inmates are numerous. What they do not like, they throw away." See *Parliamentary History*, vol. 32, pp. 697–8.

[30] *Ibid.*

[31] An excellent account of this resistance is given in J. L. and Barbara Ham-monds' *The Village Labourer*.

[32] Francis Chalmer, *An Appeal to the County of Lancaster on the Present Scarcity*, 1800.

[33] *Ibid.*, pp. 19–20.   [34] *Ibid.*, pp. 27–32.

[35] On May 4th a deputation interviewed Pitt and pointed out the losses they had sustained as a result of the action of the government. Pitt replied, according to these merchants, " possibly equity, but certainly Policy required that some Relief should be granted to Parties suffering so severely from such a cause ; but as it was very early in the year in point of time of sale of foreign corn, it was too soon to enter upon the business ; but after the losses were ascertained, he should be glad to see the Parties ; and begged leave to assure them that he was well inclined to favour their application." Consequently on February 22nd, 1797, many petitions were presented to the House of Commons asking relief for those suffering the losses, on the grounds that they had performed a function of great benefit to the public and would be discouraged from again providing a foreign supply if no recompense was made. On June 20th a Report by a com-mittee of the House of Commons concluded that charges of importers against the government were true (*Journal of the House of Commons*, vol. 52, p. 685). On August 2nd, Mr. Chalmer on behalf of the sufferers interviewed Pitt. When the latter asked what per cent. of loss the merchants were willing to accept, Mr. Chalmer informed him that since the government had allowed neutral ships seized a profit of ten per cent., that he felt the corn merchants would cheerfully accept a loss of ten per cent. Pitt then closed the interview by saying, " The Corn Merchants may if they please apply again for relief in the next Sessions, and I will give them some Support." In consequence of this promise and others the merchants did apply to Parliament for mitigation of their losses. But when the matter came up in the House of Commons on May 10th, 1798, Pitt, instead of supporting the measure, denounced and abused the merchants in such a way that the proposed indemnity was defeated by sixty-three to twenty-four (*Journal of the House of Commons*, vol. 53, p. 562). Chalmer sums up this part : " Thus the sufferers by importation of foreign corn in 1796 had, in addition to their original losses, to deplore a very considerable loss of time, an expense of £2,500, paid in charges of Journeys, Solicitors' bills, fees, etc., and a severe disappointment rendered doubly mortifying from their having been two years buoyed up with hopes of compensation ; they were beyond measure galled to find that they had been lured up by deceitful promises to pernicious hopes only with a view to be treated with public insult and public indignity ; and that even falsehood was not spared to render them odious to the public, for no reason they could ever divine but because the exertions of private individuals had proved superior in a ratio of five to two to those of government in the Corn Trade for the supply of the Kingdom." *Ibid.*, pp. 45–61.

[36] Tooke, *History of Prices*, vol. 1, pp. 187–8.

[37] 37th George III., c. 7.   [38] *Ibid.*, c. 83.

[39] 38th George III., c. 10.   [40] 39th George III., c. 87.

[41] 39th and 40th George III., c. 7.   [42] *Ibid.*, c. 8.

[43] *The Annual Register for* 1800, p. 97.

[44] *Reports from the Committees of the House of Commons*, vol. 9, p. 84.

[45] *Parliamentary History*, vol. 34, pp. 1489–96.

46 39th and 40th George III., c. 25.　**47** *Ibid.*, c. 21.

48 *Ibid.*, c. 29.

49 Robert Waithman, *War Proved to be the Real Cause of the Present Scarcity, and the Enormous High Price of Provisions,* 1800 ; and John Duthy, *Observations on the Present High Price of Provisions,* 1800.

50 *Thoughts on the Dearness of Provisions,* etc., p. 4.

51 *Letter to the Right Hon. Lord Kenyon—on the Present High Price of Corn and Other Provisions,* p. 14.

52 Edmund Burke, *Thoughts and Details on Scarcity Originally Presented to the Right Hon. William Pitt, in the month of November,* 1795, p. 1.

53 *Ibid.*, pp. 45–6.

54 William Brooks, *The True Causes of Our Present Distress for Provisions* (n.d.).

55 *Letter to the Right Hon. Lord Kenyon,* p. 15.

56 *Thoughts of an Old Man of Independent Mind, though Dependent Fortune, on the Present High Price of Corn,* 1800, p. 32.

57 James Anderson, *A Calm Investigation of the Circumstances that have led to the Present Scarcity of Grain in Britain,* 1801, p. 30.

58 *Ibid.*, p. 89.　**59** *Ibid.*, p. 90.

60 John, Lord Sheffield, *Remarks on the Deficiency of Grain,* etc., 1801, p. 246.

61 Arthur Young, *The Question of Scarcity Plainly Stated, and Remedies Considered,* 1800, p. 78.

62 Arthur Young, in *The Annals of Agriculture,* vol. 25, p. 456.

63 *A Letter to the Right Honourable Lord Somerville,* by a Society of Practical Farmers, 1800, pp. 59–60.

64 Major-General J. Money, *A Letter to the Norfolk Farmers, on the Present High Price of Corn,* 1800, p. 59.　Also Arthur Young, *The Question of Scarcity,* etc., p. 65.

65 The Crown based its case upon the testimony of a corn chandler, Richard Snell ; of William Hardy, who purchased the thirty quarters ; and of the corn factors concerned, John Sharwood and Nattrass. Snell swore that he tried to buy the ninety quarters from the sample exhibited on the stand of Shrimpton, Greenside, and Sharwood, but that he was willing to pay only 40s., whereas Sharwood asked 44s. Later he saw Mr. Rusby purchase it and carry the sample to his own stand, and a few moments later he saw the same sample exhibited by Prest and Nattrass. He ascertained that they were the same by an examination of the sample and an inquiry concerning the craft on which the oats were to be found. John Sharwood testified that he had sold the ninety quarters to Rusby at 41s. a quarter on November 8th. Nattrass swore that he had sold thirty quarters at 43s. for Smith, Rusby and Smith on the same day, but was unable to remember which member of the firm delivered the sample to him. The defence undertook to prove that Mr. Rusby had had nothing to do with the re-sale. His partners had strongly disapproved of the purchase and despite his protests Mr. Thomas Smith had taken the sample to Prest and Nattrass to be re-sold. As a result of the altercation between Rusby and Smith following the re-sale, the latter, on the next market day asked Nattrass to transfer the sale from the firm to his own personal account. This defence was weakened by the fact that Nattrass brought a copy instead of the book of original entry. When he did bring the original it showed that the name of Thomas Smith had been substituted for that of the firm, but he could not swear when the change had been made except that it was before he heard of the prosecution of Mr. Rusby. The prosecution made much of the changed entry. Mr. Erskine in closing the case for the Crown dwelt ironically on the sentimental jobber who was unwilling to distress a corn factor, and yet had not ventured to swear that such transactions were not the practice of his firm daily.

66 *Trial of John Rusby, in the Court of King's Bench—for Regrating Corn in the Corn Exchange, Mark Lane,* 1800, p. 37.

67 *The Annual Register,* 1800, vol. 42, p. 212.　**68** *Ibid.*

69 Sir Thomas Turton, *An Address to the Good Sense and Candour of the People on Behalf of the Dealers in Corn,* 1800, p. 7.

70 *The Encyclopædia Britannica,* 11th edn., vol. 9, p. 646.

71 Adam Smith, *The Wealth of Nations,* Everyman's edn., vol. 2, p. 24.

72 Sir Thomas Turton, *An Address,* etc., 1800, p. 51.

73 *Ibid.*, p. 75　**74** *Ibid.*, pp. 80–81.　**75** *Ibid.*, p. 97.　**76** *Ibid.*, p. 10

H

[77] *Ibid.*, p. 120.

[78] Charles Long, *A Temperate Discussion of the Causes Which Have Led to the Present High Price of Bread*, 1800, p. 17.

[79] 41st George III., c. 2.   [80] *Ibid.*, c. 3.   [81] *Ibid.*, c. 5.   [82] *Ibid.*, c. 10.

[83] *Ibid.*, c. 12.   [84] *Ibid.*, c. 16.

[85] *Seven Reports from the Lords' Select Committee to whom it was referred to consider so much of His Majesty's Speech as relates to the high price of Provisions,* 1801, p. 131.

[86] *Ibid.*, p. 145.

[87] *The Annual Register*, vol. 42, 1801, p. 2.   [88] *Ibid.*, p. 1.

[89] Tooke, *History of Prices*, vol. 1, p. 237.

[90] 42nd George III., c. 13.

[91] Muir, *A Short History of the British Commonwealth*, vol. 2, p. 227.

[92] *Ibid.*, Book VIII, chaps. 7 and 8.   [93] *Ibid.*, chaps. 8 and 10.

[94] Tooke, *History of Prices*, vol. 1, p. 238.

[95] *Ibid.*, p. 239.

[96] 43rd George III., c. 12.   [97] 44th George III., c. 4.

[98] *Journal of the House of Commons*, vol. 59.

[99] *Hansard*, vol. 2, pp. 1072–3.

[100] *Journal of the House of Commons*, vol. 59.   [101] *Ibid.*

[102] A bounty of 3s. a quarter was paid upon all rye exported when the price was less than 32s. ; of 2s. 6d. on barley, when less than 28s. ; and of 2s. on oats when less than 16s. The high duty was enforced when rye was under 42s. a quarter, barley under 31s. 6d., and oats under 21s. The first low duty was applied when rye was at or above 42s. but under 44s., when barley was at or above 31s. 6d. but under 33s., and when oats were at or above 21s. but under 23s.

[103] Petitions were sent from Lanark, Paisley, Port Glasgow, Renfrew, Lochwinnoch, Beith, Glasgow, Dumbarton, Rutherglen, Perth, Hamilton, Stirling, Falkirk, Dunfermline and Renton.

[104] James Mill, *An Essay on the Impolicy of a Bounty on the Exportation of Grain and on the Principles which ought to Regulate the Commerce of Grain*, 1804, p. 67.

[105] *Political Works of Cobbett*, vol. 1, p. 519.   [106] *Ibid.*

[107] Tooke, *History of Prices*, vol. 1, p. 259.

[108] 45th George III., c. 26.

[109] Tooke, *History of Prices*, vol. 1, p. 266.

[110] *Ibid.*   [111] *Ibid.*, p. 267.   [112] *Ibid.*, p. 271.

[113] *The Farmer's Magazine*, vol. 11, p. 100.

[114] Muir, *A Short History of the British Commonwealth*, vol. 2, p. 260.

[115] Galpin, *The Grain Supply of England during the Napoleonic Period*, 1925, p. 200.

[116] Tooke, *History of Prices*, vol. 1, p. 298.

[117] *Ibid.*, p. 319.   [118] *Ibid.*, p. 325.

[119] 49th George III., c. 23.   [120] 50th George III., c. 19.   [121] 50th George III., c. 5.   [122] 52nd George III., c. 3.   [123] 53rd George III., c. 7.   [124] 52nd George III., c. 127.   [125] 53rd George III., c. 2.   [126] 53rd George III., c. 23.

[127] The Enclosure movement will be treated in Chapter VI.

CHAPTER VI

THE ENCLOSURE MOVEMENT AND THE CORN LAWS

Phases of the enclosure movement that will be treated—Land and classes in a typical eighteenth century village—Brief sketch of enclosure to 1765—Points of view of Lord Ernle, Curtler, Gonner, Johnson, Levy, Slater, Hasbach and the Hammonds on the five points which follow—Causes—Methods employed—Distinction between enclosure of common arable fields and commons or wastes—Influence upon the production of grain—Effect upon the different classes engaged in agriculture—Relation of enclosure to the Corn Laws—Effect upon the position of the landowners as spokesmen for other classes.

No attempt will be made in this chapter to present even a brief, well-rounded sketch of enclosure in Great Britain, for only enough of the movement before the eighteenth century will be given to make intelligible the rapid enclosure from 1765 to 1815. The phases that will be treated are : the land and classes in a typical eighteenth-century agricultural village ; the characteristics of enclosure down to 1765 ; the great enclosure movement from 1765 to 1815 ; and the relation of enclosure to the Corn Laws.

No account will be given of the development of the English village from the Old English period to the eighteenth century, although survivals of various phases of the earlier centuries were still very much in evidence in 1750.[1] A typical eighteenth-century village was divided into arable fields, common meadow land and common or waste land. The arable land was divided into strips, which belonged to many different owners, and these strips were scattered among the fields and cultivated on a uniform system by agreement. The common meadow land was divided up by lot among the owners of the strips. After the harvest was gathered on the arable fields and the hay carried on the meadows, both lands were used for pasture. The waste, which might be woodland, roadside strips, or commons in the modern sense, was used as a common pasture during the entire year.

The classes that lived in a normal village were, considering its size, astonishingly numerous. There was usually a lord of the manor, although the rights of a lord might belong to the Crown, a university, the church, or to a nobleman or commoner who owned many villages. The classes that actually tilled the soil were the freeholders, large and small, who owned their land ; the copyholders, who held land by various forms of customary tenure ; the tenant farmers or leaseholders, whose tenure varied from tenants-at-will to leases for three lives ; the cottagers and squatters ; and the farm servants who lived in their employers' homes.[2] In some instances the lord of the manor still owned demesne land and in others he had sold it. In any case he owned the waste land, but his rights were limited by those of the freeholders, copyholders and cottagers. The holdings of the freeholders, copyholders and tenant farmers varied so much in size that none of the three formed a distinct class. In fact, a small freeholder, copyholder or tenant farmer might be almost indistinguishable from a cottager who owned or rented a few strips. The cultivation of strips in the arable field carried with it the rights known as *common appendant*, which gave owners or occupiers of these strips a share in the common meadow land, and rights of pasture on the waste, and on the arable and meadow after the crops had been gathered. The cottagers owned or rented cottages with a little land attached and had rights of common on the wastes and sometimes on the common fields. The squatters were usually settlers who built themselves huts and cleared a piece of land in the wastes. Such encroachments were generally sanctioned by varying local customs. The farm servants were, as a rule, children of small farmers or cottagers earning enough money to marry and secure a cottage of their own.[3] Hasbach was especially impressed by the completeness of gradation, both social and economic, in this system, because " The smaller gentry connected the great landlord with the wealthy yeomen ; and the yeomanry were intermediate between the gentry and the large copyholders and farmers. These again shaded into the little men, whether yeomen, copyholders or leaseholders. And as yet there was no proletarian class, solely dependent on wages and in particular on money-wages, and expecting to leave its children in the same position."[4]

Until the effects of the Industrial Revolution and of the great enclosure movement from about 1765 to 1815 were appreciably felt, the village was the home of the overwhelming majority of the English people. In fact, from before the Norman Conquest to the beginning of the nineteenth century, it was easily the most important part of the social structure. Within the village, particularly from the so-called breakup of the manor in the fourteenth century, a movement had been under way which affected to a considerable extent the farming methods employed on the arable land. This movement is called by the somewhat general term of enclosure, which came to denote several processes. Primarily enclosure meant surrounding a piece of land with hedges or other barriers to prevent the passage of men or animals. Whether or not the hedge was intended to keep a pasture separate from the surrounding unenclosed arable land, or a piece of arable land separate from the adjoining common, it was a sign of exclusive ownership of the part enclosed as opposed to community owner-ship.[5]

Although consolidation of strips in the common arable fields, followed by enclosure, and the extension of cultivation into the waste lands was going on before the fourteenth century,[6] both practices received a great impetus in the years following the Black Death of 1348–49. This plague had considerable influence in bringing about the development of sheep farming, which was one of the main factors in the substitution of enclosed for open fields. The change was due partly to the scarcity of labour and partly to the simultaneous develop-ment of the cloth-making industry in England.[7] Enclosure was really rendered inevitable, according to Curtler, by the progress of agricul-ture. " The old common field system was only suited for a primitive state of society and was bound to disappear with the advance of civilization. It was extremely wasteful ; the scattering of the strips all over the open fields led to an astonishing waste of time, and confusion : the pace of the common work was set by the worst farmer ; therefore, no individual initiative or enterprise was possible ; the crops grown were scanty in the extreme ; much of the land was worn out by constant plowing without manuring ; the live stock on the common pastures was miserably small and continually afflicted by disease."[8]

A study of the records of various manors has shown that both lords and tenants were enclosing land long before complaints were made in Parliament and in contemporary literature.[9] But it was the fashion until the last generation to hold that a great enclosure movement had taken place during the Tudor period, followed by a period of inactivity which lasted until the last half of the eighteenth century, when the process had been resumed on an even larger scale. This misconception of the enclosure movement as a whole seems to have been a result of relying too much upon the testimony of contemporaries, on the laws passed, and on other measures adopted by the government. Only when the opposition of the peasantry and defenders of the existing order was expressed in contemporary literature, or through governmental action, was enclosure considered noteworthy. Now we know not only that the movement started long before the Tudor period, and that, in spite of a relative decline from about 1600 to 1750, it was continuous well into the nineteenth century ; but also that the periods in which few complaints were registered and little action taken by the government were periods of voluntary enclosure.[10] In neither the Tudor period, nor in the years from 1765 to 1815, were the complaints primarily against the substitution of permanent consolidated plots for temporary and scattered strips ; but against joining several of these plots in a larger unit. This process was generally called engrossing as opposed to enclosure. In the Tudor period engrossing took place because the increased demand for wool made it more profitable in many places to turn several arable holdings into one sheep walk. In the years from 1765 to 1815, engrossing occurred because it was more profitable to turn small holdings into large wheat farms.

The government during the Tudor and early Stuart periods took a more hostile attitude toward enclosure and engrossing than it did in the years from 1765 to 1815. Beginning in 1487, the first of a series of twelve depopulation acts was passed by Parliament. In addition, seven royal commissions were appointed to investigate the subject, and numerous proclamations were issued dealing with certain phases during the century and a half following the first act. It is outside the field of this chapter to consider the effect of the sixteenth century enclosure upon the different classes of agricultural society, but the conclusions of two writers of widely-divergent points of view on the effects of the movement as a whole are worth consideration. Curtler concludes : " To sum up the effects of Tudor enclosure we may say that the area and population affected were small ; that there was very little illegal eviction for the purpose of enclosing ; but a considerable

amount of oppression within the law ; that the change in the rural
economy, though it seems small to us, appeared of great import to
contemporaries ; that there was much enclosure and consolidation
by the small man as well as the great ; that the revolution, though
inflicting a certain amount of hardship as was inevitable, was beneficial ; and in the seventeenth century the rural community entered
on a period of revived prosperity."[11]   In opposition to this point of
view is that taken by R. H. Tawney in *The Agrarian Problem in the
Sixteenth Century*, " To the modern economist, who uses an ancient
field map to trace the bewildering confusion of an open field village
beneath the orderly lines of the dignified estate which lies upon it
like a well-written manuscript on the crabbed scrawl of a palimpsest,
the wastefulness of the old regime, compared with the productiveness
of the new, may well seem too obvious to leave room for any accession
of material wealth which followed the first feeble approach towards
the methods of modern agriculture is unquestionable. But the
difference between such a standpoint and that of our peasants is not
one of methods but of objects, not of means but of ends. We can
imagine that to an exposition of the advantages of large-scale farming
and enclosure, such as many stewards must have made to the juries
of many manors, they would have answered something after this
fashion : ' True, our system is wasteful, and fruitful of many small
disputes.   True, a large estate can be managed more economically
than a small one.   True, pasture-farming yields higher profits than
tillage.   Nevertheless, master steward, our wasteful husbandry feeds
many households where your economical methods would feed few.
In our ill-arranged fields and scrubbly commons most families hold a
share, though it be but a few roods.   In our unenclosed village there
are few rich, but there are few destitute, save when God sends a bad
harvest, and we all starve together.   We do not like your improvements which ruin half the honest men affected by them.   We do not
choose that the ancient customs of our village should be changed.'
Such differences lie too deep to be settled by argument, whether they
appear in the sixteenth century or in our day."[12]
    From the end of the sixteenth to the middle of the eighteenth
century enclosure went on steadily.   Until the Civil War broke out
in 1642 the government still opposed the movement by laws, royal
commissions and proclamations ; but after the Restoration in 1660
less opposition came from this direction.   The fifty years preceding
the rapid increase in enclosing and engrossing for the purpose of
making large arable farms which began about 1765, was a period
favourable to the smallholder and labourer.   The big farms of the
east and south coasts supplied London with grain and aided by the
bounty, sent the surplus to the continent.   The small farmer, as a rule,
produced grain for consumption rather than for the market.   In fact,
along with the cottager and squatter, he often purchased the grain
he consumed.   The low price of wheat from 1715 to 1765 was an
important factor in the increased consumption of wheat by the lower
classes.   The smallholder tended to concentrate on dairy products,
poultry and live stock.   These commodities were chiefly produced
for his own consumption, but often there was a surplus for the

market.[13] After 1765 one of the chief complaints directed against
large farms was the failure to supply dairy products and poultry as
small farms had done.[14] Evidently there was no reason why the
small landowner, small tenant farmer, cottager and squatter should
not have been prosperous in the first half of the eighteenth century.
There was a market for their surplus products,[15] and, if they did not
raise their own grain, they could purchase it cheaply from the
relatively high wages which they were paid by large farmers, and
from the money which they and their families earned, in some parts
of the country, from the domestic or putting out industries.

About 1765 the increase in the amount of land enclosed again
brought the question into prominence. The movement from 1765
to 1815 will now be treated under the following heads : causes ;
methods employed ; distinction between enclosure of all the lands
of a village and of the common pasture and waste only ; influence
upon the production of grain ; and effect upon the different classes
engaged in agriculture. In recent years several able works on different
phases of this question have appeared.[16] These writers really fall
into two distinct schools. Prothero (Lord Ernle), Curtler, Gonner,
Johnson and Levy admit that the movement was hard on the smallholder, but hold that it was inevitable, necessary and beneficial. The
Hammonds, Slater and Hasbach agree that it was hard on the smallholder, but question, in various degrees, the inevitability, necessity
and benefits. The point of view of at least one member of each school
will be presented upon each of the five heads just enumerated.

First, the pro-enclosure group are unanimous in the belief that the
cause of enclosure and improved methods in agriculture was the
increased demand for food by the growing manufacturing and commercial cities. Under the existing agricultural system, they maintain
that it was impossible to produce a large surplus for this market. As
a result the unit of holding most suitable for arable farming, the large
farm, became the rule. " On the large farm the methods and technique of wheat-cultivation were perfected to a degree which was the
admiration and astonishment of both English and continental
agricultural experts. But the old agricultural system had to be
broken down before the new could be built up. The small farms and
peasant properties, and the little holdings of the cottager and labourer,
had to be sacrificed. The industrious small agriculturist had to give
way to the large farmer possessed of capital and education."[17]

The anti-enclosure writers, particularly Hasbach and the Hammonds, look upon the movement not as beneficial and inevitable, but
as evidence of the sordid greed of the landowners and farmers which
caused greater evil than good. Hasbach insists that the factors in
the break-up of the eighteenth century village were, " first, the more
luxurious standard of life adopted by the landlord class, and their
consequent need of a larger income ; secondly, the enclosures, for
the most part results of that need ; then the increased price of provisions, to which the enclosures contributed ; next the system of the
large farm, pioneered about this same period ; and finally the new
method of cultivation, which demanded men of a different class and a
larger capital. . . . And there were the indirect taxes, imposed to

pay the interest on the growing national debt rolled up by trade wars and colonial wars, which of course increased the cost of living."[18]

Levy's explanation of the underlying causes for enclosing and engrossing is certainly more convincing than that of Hasbach. The landlords would have been unable to fix higher rents out of sheer greed if there had not been a demand for corn by the growing commercial and industrial cities, which made large scale corn production more profitable than small scale subsistence farming. If greed or desire to keep rents high were the determining factor, the landlords would have not failed as signally as they did when they attempted to maintain rents at a high level after 1815.

Second, the actual methods employed in enclosing both arable and waste during these years are worthy of consideration. In the centuries before 1765 land had been enclosed by common agreement, by one person purchasing all conflicting rights, by force and fraud, by special licence of the monarch as in Tudor times, and by private acts of Parliament. But during the half-century following—in fact until the law of 1845 was passed—the private act seems to have supplanted all other methods. This means of enclosure started in the early years of the eighteenth century. In the reign of Queen Anne only two acts were passed; under George I., 16; under George II., 226; but under George III. the number rose to 3,554.[19] The first ones were usually short and varied a great deal in form. Some of them merely recognized agreements which had been carried out without dispute or had been registered in Chancery.[20] As the number of acts passed increased, uniformity in certain points developed. " Those points related to the appointment of commissioners, the method of procedure of these commissioners, the making of roads, the mode of allotment, rules as to hedging and ditching, the apportionment of expenses, the enrolment and custody of the award."[21] The law of 1801 provided that certain clauses usually found in these private acts should in the future be incorporated in all private bills.[22] Outside of standardizing the acts this law seems to have had less influence on enclosure than was anticipated.

The usual procedure for getting an act passed and having the actual enclosure made was as follows. A public meeting of the interested members of the village was called by posting notice, usually on the church door, and a petition to Parliament was considered. This petition had to be signed by those who favoured enclosure. A majority of the persons interested was not required, but at least a majority of the value of the property was necessary. In some instances this requirement was as high as three-fourths or four-fifths. This value, according to the Parliamentary committee of 1800 on enclosures, was " calculated sometimes in acres, sometimes in annual value, sometimes in assessment to the land tax, sometimes in assessment to the poor rate."[23] The petition was then presented to Parliament, where by permission of the House a bill was introduced and after the second reading was referred to a committee. Having heard the evidence, the committee reported to the House, and its report determined whether the bill was rejected or read a third time and passed. If it were passed, commissioners numbering from one to seven were generally named in the act and went to the village to undertake the rather arduous task of carrying out the actual enclosure. First the common fields and rights were evaluated, and then a survey was made of the size and value of the land of each proprietor. This required the services of an expert surveyor. The commissioners then had to decide upon the claims of the lord of manor, the tithe owner, and all inhabitants of the village who had legal claims in the common fields, meadows or wastes. This was a task of extraordinary difficulty, since it involved the entire re-distribution of the land of the village. The expenses of enclosure were usually met either by levying an assessment on the interested persons in proportion to the value of their property, or by selling parts of the land to defray a fraction or all the costs.[24]

Most of the pro-enclosure writers either state or assume that the poor people had a fair chance to oppose the petitions to Parliament ; that, as a rule, justice was secured in both the committee and both Houses of Parliament ; and that the commissioners, in most instances, carried out the actual enclosure in an efficient and impartial manner. The Hammonds, on the other hand, dissent on all three points. They call attention to the fact that the poorer members of the village had no effective way of making their opposition felt. The majority, three-fourths, or four-fifths, rule was not as great a protection as it seemed, since the rule for valuing property varied so much. Neither in the committee nor in the House of Commons were the interests of the small proprietors considered. The only possible obstacle, according to the Hammonds, to a group of interested landowners having their friends push through an enclosure bill, would come from a powerful individual who felt that his or his friend's interests had not been duly consulted. The arbitrary power of the commissioners left the poor with very little protection against injustice. In most instances there was no appeal if an individual was given land of inferior quality or in an inconvenient location.[25] In discussing these three points, Curtler admits that the methods used by the large proprietors were often high-handed, but excuses them on the grounds, that such proceedings were quite possible without inflicting great hardships on anyone with a legal claim under an enclosure Act ;[26] and that " the large proprietors and farmers were perfectly convinced that enclosure was indispensable to agricultural progress, and knew well, too, that there was a strong, and for the most part factious and ignorant, opposition to this desired improvement."[27] He is inclined to allow the Hammonds' charges against discrimination in Parliament to go unanswered although he cautiously quotes the report of 1825, that " under the present system it has been found that the members to whom the bills have been committed have been generally those who have been most interested in the result."[28] On the third point, that of the fairness of the commissioners, Curtler points out the difficulties confronting these men were very great, because the innumerable claims " opened up an immense field for individual dissatisfaction and grumbling, of which we may be certain full use was made by all those who fancied themselves wronged. No doubt some were wronged, but we may be quite certain that a far greater number falsely imagined they were."[29] His conclusion is that " in spite of some blundering and favouritism there is no reason to think that the commissioners behaved with the gross partiality often attributed to them, and on the whole they did their work honestly and impartially."[30]

The third point of significance during the fifty years following 1765 is the distinction between the enclosure of the common arable fields and of the common waste lands. Slater defines acts for enclosing this waste as *acts for extending cultivation*, and those for enclosing all lands, common arable as well as waste, as *acts for extinguishing village communities*.[31] In the sixteenth and seventeenth centuries both arable and waste had been enclosed, but the former predominated. In the eighteenth century, particularly after 1765, about two-thirds of the land enclosed was waste.[32] Johnson has estimated that about twenty per cent. of the total acreage of England was enclosed during the eighteenth and nineteenth centuries.[33] However, the significance of enclosure during these years would be missed if it were treated merely as a process already four-fifths accomplished.[34] Enclosures down to the eighteenth century consisted, as a rule, of a part or all of the lord's demesne and common arable land. The Hammonds point out that " the life of the common-field system was still the normal village life of England, and that the land which was already enclosed consisted largely of old enclosures or the lord's demesne land lying side by side with the open fields. . . . If a village living on the common-field system contained old enclosures, effected some time or other without Act of Parliament, it suffered just as violent a catastrophe when the common-fields or the waste were enclosed, as if there had been no previous enclosure in the parish."[35] In addition to the actual percentage of land enclosed and the importance of the increase in the proportion of waste, the geographical area which was most affected after 1765 is not without significance. In the main, it was a wedge-shaped triangle extending from East Riding to Bristol to Dorset on one side, and from Dorset to Norfolk on the other.[36] Thus the south-east, south-west, north and part of the west seem to have been quietly enclosed before the middle of the eighteenth century without the troublesome procedure of an act of Parliament. Slater offers as a possible explanation that in the fifteenth and sixteenth centuries enclosure was gradually spreading over the southern and midland counties ; and that the counties of Oxford, Buckingham, Wiltshire and others, where the complaints were made in the sixteenth century, were successful in resisting this non-Parliamentary enclosure and hence had to wait for the more expensive procedure of the eighteenth century.

The actual acreage of common arable, pasture and waste, as distinct from common pasture and waste alone, throws a great deal of light upon the effects of the rising prices of food on enclosures. According to Slater the amount of common pasture and waste land enclosed by act of Parliament from 1727 to 1845 was as follows : from 1727 to 1760, a total of 74,518 acres or 2,192 annually ; from 1761 to 1792, a total of 478,259 acres or 14,946 annually ; from 1793 to 1801, a total of 273,891 acres or 30,432 annually ; from 1802 to 1815, a total of 739,743 acres or 52,838 annually ; and from 1816 to 1845, a total of 199,300 acres or 6,643 annually. On the other hand the enclosure of all the lands of a village, or, as Slater terms it, the extinguishing of village communities, tells another story. The actual number of acres enclosed under this classification was 2,101,380 from 1724 to 1801 and 627,816 from 1802 to 1815.[37] When allowance is made for the negligible enclosure before 1760 and for the heavy enclosure during the ten years preceding 1802, it becomes evident that the number of acres of arable, pasture and waste annually enclosed did not increase greatly after 1802. When combined with the statistics cited above, it becomes equally clear that the enormous amount of land enclosed during the Napoleonic War was largely common pasture and waste. The latter were broken up, especially from 1806 to 1813, in an attempt to raise enough wheat to offset the loss of the imports from the continent.

The fourth point to be considered during the half-century following 1765 is the influence of enclosure upon the production of grain. With the exception of the controversy over the part played by the movement in causing the disappearance of the small landowner, no phase of the question has been so earnestly contested. Some of the critics of enclosure do not deny that it increased the production of grain. Slater admits this point, and the Hammonds go on that assumption in making their case against enclosure. Prothero, Curtler, Gonner and Levy all stress this increase as the greatest justification for the movement, although they do not agree on the degree of benefits conferred. Only Hasbach argues that the net produce and not the gross was increased by enclosure. Johnson, it is true, concedes this point, but with the reservation that, since many more labourers were employed, it was an uneconomical method.[38] Since Levy makes the ablest case for the increase of the output, an examination of his position along with that of Hasbach will show the two points of view.

Levy's argument is as follows. From 1715 to 1765 the small farmer was prosperous because there was a market for his meat, butter, eggs and poultry ; while the large farmer, whose chief business was the sale of corn, was often in distress because of its low price.[39] But from 1765 to 1815 a great rise in the price of wheat occurred owing to bad seasons, inadequate imports and rapidly-growing population.[40] The improvement in the standard of living which had taken place among the poorer classes as a result of low prices from 1715 to 1765 was now lost. Nevertheless, although high prices meant misery for the lower classes, they made the raising of wheat profitable for the large farmer. On the other hand, the small farmer was injured because the great mass of people were less able to buy meat, butter, cheese, poultry and eggs.[41] Even pasture farming, judging by the writings of contemporaries, was given up wherever it was possible from 1760 to 1813. Furthermore, the small farmer found it difficult to compete in corn growing with the large one even where he survived enclosure.[42] In the main, enclosures were not followed by an extension of pasture-farming except in a few midland counties, such as Leicestershire, Northampton, Warwickshire and Huntingdonshire. The overwhelming testimony of contemporaries shows that this did

not occur as a rule.[43]   Also, Arthur Young's calculation that profit
was greater on an acre of pasture than on an acre of arable, was an
attempt to divert part of the corn-growing area to pasture, since he
did not share the passion for corn-growing.[44]   Consequently, though
enclosure and engrossing may have caused individuals great suffering,
they also made possible corn-growing with high profits, because
improved methods of cultivation produced increasing quantities.[45]

The point of view of Hasbach is almost exactly the opposite.   He
holds that until the decade from 1730 to 1740 the English policy
made for an extension of corn-growing ; but that after those years
there was a widespread transition to cattle-breeding and laying down
of arable to pasture.   This change was due to the fall in the price of
grain, to the rise in the price of animal products, to the fact that
pasture-farming required less labour and fewer persons chargeable
on the poor rate, and to the discovery that certain soils were better
suited for pasture than for arable.   This transition was especially
true of the midlands, rather than of the eastern and southern counties.
The bad seasons after 1765 and the change in the Corn Laws in 1773,
also tended to make farmers substitute pasture for arable.[46]   Thus it
became customary to use the worst land for wheat and the best for
pasture.   This practice was followed even during the Napoleonic
wars when commons and wastes were broken up to supply the
increased demand for wheat.[47]   The enclosure movement, then, was
caused not by an increased demand for wheat, but by the high
standard of living of the landowning classes which made it necessary
to appropriate the commons and raise rent.[48]   This movement sometimes meant economic progress ; but it was often transformed into a
curse by introducing large farms where small ones would have
functioned, and by the fact that improvements were not unfrequently
badly carried out.[49]   Because of these drawbacks, " one is hardly
inclined to suppose that the production of corn increased between
1700 and say 1793."[50]

Hasbach's concludes that it is improbable that the area under corn
was extended after 1730 to 1740, and that the gross and net production
was affected by the fact that corn tended to be grown on the worst
soils, and that an increased number of horses consumed more of it ;
that the mismanagement of enclosures sent up the prices of all the
necessaries of life ; that the price of the products of the small farmer
such as poultry, eggs and butter was immoderately raised ; and that
the numbers of small farmers and their necessitous circumstances
made them supply the market cheaper than larger farmers who were
able to hold back their products, and thus enhance the price enough
to cover both their own profits and increased rents.[51]

Although it is possible to make a case for the diminution, or at
least for the failure to increase, of the products of the small farms
during the eighteenth century, it seems difficult to establish such a
conclusion for grain.   Hasbach's position that the production of corn
did not increase from 1700 to 1793 appears untenable even when his
admission that more wheat and oats and less of other kinds of grain
were grown is taken into consideration.   In reality, the growth of
wheat must have shown a marked increase during these years.

Practically all contemporary writers agree that until about 1765 the consumption of wheat by the lower classes increased amazingly, and that wheat bread was substituted for black. Furthermore, it was shown in Chapter V how tenaciously the poor clung to wheaten bread during the starvation periods of 1795–6 and 1800–1. Although in some other respects they lost much of the advance in their standard of living made in the first half of the eighteenth century, they resolutely refused to allow other kinds of bread to be substituted for the white. The statistics on population from 1700 to 1800, naturally, are not as reliable as the census which began in 1801, but those figures available give a fair idea of the increase during the eighteenth century.[52] According to the estimates based upon the birth and burial records of the parish registers, the population was 5,475,000 in 1700 and 8,675,000 in 1790. The first official census of 1801 showed a total of 9,168,000. Contemporary writers estimated that the average annual consumption of wheat per person was one quarter. The actual increase in population alone would indicate a great increase in the consumption of wheat from 1700 to 1790, without taking into consideration the fact that a higher percentage of people ate wheat bread at the end of the century than at the beginning. The growth of oats by agreement of practically all writers increased rapidly during the same period because of the vast number of horses which supplanted oxen as beasts of labour. It seems scarcely possible that the production of barley and rye could have declined to such an extent as to have equalized the increase in the production of wheat and oats. It may be argued that the decline of exports, and the increase of imports, during the eighteenth century would enable the additional population to be fed ; but an examination of the statistics shows how impossible such an explanation actually is. In 1700 the exports of wheat, barley, oats and rye were 49,057, 63,468, 391 and 27,231 quarters respectively. It is true that in 1700 the bounty was suspended during part of the year, but even in 1701 the export figures were only 98,324 quarters of wheat, 72,400 of barley, 286 of oats and 43,917 of rye. In 1793, which was a year of exceptionally high importation because of the bad wheat crop of 1792, the balance of imports over exports was 421,783 quarters of wheat, 143,722 of barley, 704,147 of oats and 55,080 of rye.[53] The difference is about 800,000 quarters in wheat, barley and rye which, allowing a quarter per person, would account only for a relatively small part of the increased population. Oats are eliminated since they were used almost exclusively for horse feed and not for human consumption.

Some additional light is thrown on the question of the increase or decrease of the acreage of wheat through enclosure during the second part of the eighteenth century by the statistics given in the report of the Committee on High Prices for 1800. According to these figures, which included enclosure both of common fields and waste, the acreage had increased from 155,572 acres in 1755 to 165,837 in 1800. A similar estimate for the years 1761 to 1799, based on the enclosure of open arable fields only, showed a decrease of 16,387 acres in the area of wheat under cultivation.[54] Still the production of barley, oats, cattle, dairy products and sheep had been increased where the results of enclosures had been investigated.[55]   But whether or not the acreage of corn was increased or decreased it does not alter the fact that the population of England increased by about 3,200,000, and that the increase in imports and the decrease in exports accounted for only 800,000.   Thus the question whether or not the increased grain supply came from extended acreage or improved methods of cultivation is debatable, but the fact that it nearly kept pace with the increase of population is not.   After 1800 practically all writers agree that both the acreage and production were greatly increased by breaking up the wastes.

The fifth and last point to consider on the enclosure movement from 1765 to 1815 is the effect which it had on the different classes engaged in agriculture.   It is generally conceded that the landowners, tithe-owners and large farmers profited, while the small farmers, cottagers, squatters and farm servants lost.   The controversy comes over the disappearance of the yeomen or freeholders.

The landowners undoubtedly profited the most and their greatest gain came from increased rents.   This increase usually followed the consolidation of several small farms into a few large ones.   But there were two additional advantages to the landlord in engrossing farms : the saving in the cost of repairs, and the greater ease with which rent was collected from fewer tenants.[56]

The tithe-holder also gained from enclosure since the value of the tithe increased when common arable fields and wastes were turned into large wheat farms.   In some instances the tithe-owner's claim was satisfied either by estimating the share of tithe at one-seventh of the land to be allotted,[57] or by allotting to tithe " an amount equal to its former value, together with an increase proportionate to the general increase over the whole enclosure, subject to a deduction of its proper share of the expenses."[58]   As a rule tithe-holders backed the landowners in the fight for enclosure, but there were instances, as in the case of their opposition to a general enclosure bill in 1797,[59] in which this was not the case.

The large-scale farmers profited by rising prices and improved methods in agriculture, because a large farm was necessary for the wholesale production of wheat.   The numbers of these large-scale farmers were considerably increased by enclosure and engrossing ; and they were generally recruited from small farmers who rose, or from small landowners who sold their land and devoted the capital to improvements on rented farms.   As far as these two classes are concerned, a real struggle to determine the survival of the fittest ensued.   Those who won became large farmers and those who lost often sank to the position of agricultural labourers.   But whatever his origin may have been, enclosure was usually beneficial to the large farmer.

On the other hand, the small farmer, regardless of the tenure under which he held land, was almost invariably injured.   The tenant-at-will was often deprived of his land for the purpose of consolidating it in a larger farm.   Tenants holding for a longer time might share the same fate, if the terms of their tenure permitted their ejection. Sometimes tenants who were not deprived of their land outright were forced to relinquish it because the landlord raised the rent to a price which they could not pay. The copyholder shared many of the disabilities of the tenant, but it was more difficult to eject him or raise the rent at any time. In addition to the uncertainty of tenure and rent, it was difficult for a small farmer, regardless of his legal status, to survive the loss of the commons. He no longer had a place to pasture his stock, to allow his poultry to run, or to gather his fuel. Advocates of enclosure frankly admit this difficulty, but justify the disappearance of the small farmer on the ground that the stock and poultry were half starving, and that the man himself was better off working for wages.

The cottagers disappeared even more rapidly than the small tenant farmers. They were usually given compensation for the loss of their rights of common in the shape of a small allotment of land ; but as it was insufficient to keep a cow, they were generally forced to sell out.[60] In many cases the cottagers received nothing for the rights they lost, as compensation was often given to the owner of the cottage.[61]

The squatters, on the whole, suffered relatively more than the cottagers, because their status was more uncertain. There seems to have been no settled rule to deal with them, but in general none of less than twenty years standing received any consideration except the privilege of buying their encroachment. Squatters of more than twenty or forty years standing were often treated as cottagers.[62]

But the question which has involved by all odds the greatest controversy in recent years is the relation of enclosure to the disappearance of the yeomen or freeholders. The modern discussion began with Dr. Rae's article in *The Contemporary Review* of 1883. He ascribes the disappearance of the yeomanry to their loss of the carrying trade and income from domestic industries, to the fluctuating prices after 1815, and to the land speculation previous to that year. Taylor, in *The Decline of the Landowning Farmers in England*, also emphasizes their disappearance after 1815. However, other writers are inclined to stress the importance of enclosure. Hasbach believes that the larger yeomen profited by it, after recovering from the heavy expenses entailed by the process, but that the smaller ones were injured. The expenses of enclosure were very high, the loss of the commons was irreparable and, he alleges, the smallholder was generally cheated and discriminated against in the process.[63] The Hammonds take much the same point of view in regard to the unfair execution of the enclosure acts and its influence in facilitating the disappearance of the small owner, as well as the small tenant farmer, cottager and squatter.[64] Levy holds that it was the change from the small to the large farm that resulted in the disappearance of the yeomanry, and points out that this process was " the clearest illustration of the irresistible force of the economic conditions which were sweeping away the old system of agricultural holdings . . . even those members of the class who had not suffered and could not suffer by the enclosures disappeared in the course of the period 1760–1815."[65] This interpretation makes the yeoman class voluntarily assisting, instead of being the victims of enclosure.

The writers cited in the preceding paragraph relied to a considerable extent upon pamphlet material covering the entire field. But three other writers have approached the subject from a somewhat different angle. Johnson has examined the Land Tax returns of about five hundred of the fifteen thousand odd parishes in England, H. L. Gray has made a careful calculation of the yeomen in Oxfordshire in the last half of the eighteenth and the first half of the nineteenth century, and E. Davies has studied the small landowner from 1780 to 1832 in the light of the land tax assessments of approximately two thousand parishes. As a result of his investigations Johnson concludes that the closing years of the seventeenth century, and the first fifty years of the eighteenth century, were fatal to the small landowner.[66]

Gray's researches indicate that Johnson rather than Rae, Taylor, Levy or Hasbach is correct. In recapitulating, Gray states : " There was in Oxfordshire no decline in the area of yeomen farmers between 1814 and 1832, as Rae and Taylor would lead us to think, and scarcely any falling off in the number of yeomen farmers from 1785 to 1832. The temporary increase in the ranks of the latter during the period of the French war does not well accord with Levy's contention that misfortune came to them with the advancing price of grain. Enclosure after 1785 did not fatally affect yeomen with holdings of from two acres to three hundred acres, and did not to any great extent during the preceding thirty years. In this respect, the views of Miss Leonard, Hasbach, Mantoux and Slater do not receive confirmation. Toynbee, in saying that the disappearance of small freeholders has been continuous, was better advised than when he added, ' it was not until about 1760 that the process of extinction became rapid.' Mr. Johnson, alone, reasoning from the Land Tax Returns and other data, reaches conclusions about the period when the yeomanry disappeared more in accord with those which seem to hold for Oxfordshire."[67] This estimate, however, is only for Oxfordshire and may not be typical of the remainder of England.

Davies' study covers the years 1780–1802 and 1802–32 in which the returns of some 2,000 parishes in Cheshire, Derbyshire, Leicestershire, Lincolnshire, Northamptonshire, Oxfordshire and Warwickshire are analysed. The conclusions reached as a result of this survey are : " By 1780 the occupying owners, including the freeholders, copyholders and lessees for lives, had ceased to be an outstanding feature of English rural economy. In 1,395 parishes situated in Derbyshire, Leicestershire, Lindsey, Northamptonshire, Nottinghamshire and Warwickshire, they contributed only 10.4 per cent. of the land tax, so that already nearly 90 per cent. of the land was in the occupation of tenant farmers. . . . The direct effect of the industrial changes on the fate of the occupying owners before 1832 appears to have been greatly exaggerated. Their disappearance was largely accomplished by 1780–86, since nearly 90 per cent. of the land was in the occupation of tenants-at-will or tenants on short lease. If industrial changes had been a potent factor in bringing about this result, then they must have been in operation prior to 1780. But it is difficult to believe that the industrial revolution had gathered sufficient momentum before 1780 to cause such far-reaching changes.

From 1780–1815 the movement appeared to have favoured rather than harmed the occupying owner, since it provided him with a growing and lucrative market. His old markets also remained, as there was no evidence to indicate that domestic industries in the counties studied were in any way adversely affected previous to 1814 ; indeed, most of them flourished as late as 1832."[68]

After considering all the testimony and facts presented upon these different points, what conclusions may be drawn, and what light do these conclusions throw upon the question of the Corn Laws before and after 1815 ? The evidence available to-day on enclosure from 1765 to 1815 appears to justify the following conclusions : that the movement was almost inevitable in view of improved communications and the necessity of producing corn for the rapidly-expanding market ; that enclosures need not necessarily have been followed by the extinction of the cottagers, although engrossing of farms sealed the fate of the tenant farmer ; that the small landowner, evidently, had chiefly disappeared by 1780–86, and hence enclosure after 1765 cannot be held primarily responsible for their disappearance ; and that no adequate attempt was made to prevent the absolute divorce from the land of the cottagers, squatters and very small owners. Arthur Young's scheme for giving to this class small plots of land, which would be inalienable and vested in the parish, might have done much to prevent the formation of a landless proletariat. Throwing the cost of enclosure on the big landowners and tithe owners, who profited most by the change, would also have saved many small owners. Thus enclosure, which really meant a necessary advance in agricultural technique, was badly marred by the ruthless methods used, and by the unnecessary and unfortunate social results.

We now come to the last and, from the standpoint of this study, the most important point to be decided : namely, the relation of enclosure from 1765 to 1815 to the Corn Laws. Unquestionably, the improvement in agricultural technique, toward which enclosure contributed materially during those years, played some part in the passage of the law of 1791 ; but both that act and the one of 1804 were practically inoperative because of high prices from the time they went into force. Although these tremendous changes in the English village had little influence on the Corn Laws until 1815, they were to have an enormous effect after that date. The remaining chapters will show how the very uprooting of so large a part of the agricultural population from the soil, in the end proved the undoing of those who profited most by enclosure.

During the greater part of the eighteenth century the landed gentry in Parliament could at least pose as the representatives of the great mass of the English population, the agrarian class ; but after 1815 this was no longer possible. It is true that the smallholder was little interested in corn culture, but the gentry could assume the role of spokesmen of the agricultural interests in supporting the Corn Laws. The factory system was getting under way only in cotton spinning at the outbreak of the French Revolutionary and Napoleonic Wars, so that the manufacturing and commercial cities were then greatly inferior in numbers to the agricultural interest. By 1815 all this had

I

changed. Agricultural society was now divided into three main classes : the landlord, the large farmer and the agricultural labourer who was subsisting in part on poor rates.   A much smaller percentage of the population were now engaged in agriculture.   Many tenant farmers, cottagers and squatters, when they were not among the fortunate few who became large farmers, or started factories in the north, were reduced to the position of Speenhamland agricultural labourers, or helped to swell the ranks of the proletariat in the new industrial cities.   Thus after 1815 the landlords had no class backing them except their own tenant farmers.   The agricultural labourer had no cause to love the existing regime ; and the commercial and industrial population of the cities, both capitalists and labourers, wanted cheap bread.   Consequently the landlords found themselves represented, or perhaps misrepresented, as a small minority levying toll on the vast majority of the people.   By enclosure and improved methods in farming they increased their rents and probably the output of the land ; and by increasing the production of grain, they could claim to be public benefactors during the Napoleonic wars. But when they tried to keep up prices by Corn Laws the commercial and industrial capitalists threw their weight on the side of the city proletariat, many of whom had been driven to the cities by agrarian changes, and ultimately overthrew the system of agricultural protection.   This repudiation of protection was made easier by the landlord's loss of the support of the lower agricultural classes.   Thus the only class upon whom the landlords could rely for support was the large farmers, and the confidence even of this group in protection wavered at times between 1815 and 1846.

CHAPTER VI

NOTES

[1] Surveys of this subject may be found in any text book on English economic history. Vinogradoff's *The Growth of the Manor*, 1911, gives perhaps the best account of the earlier stages. A good chapter on the period down to the sixteenth century is available in Lipson's *Economic History of England*. Practically all works on the enclosure movement referred to later in the chapter deal with this early period in some measure.

[2] The description given in this and in the preceding paragraph is taken from *The Village Labourer*, 1911, p. 4, by J. L. and Barbara Hammond.

[3] *Ibid.*, pp. 5–8. Also Hasbach, *The History of the English Agricultural Labourer*, 1920, pp. 71–8.

[4] Hasbach, *op. cit.*, p. 103.

[5] Slater, *The English Peasantry and the Enclosure of Common Fields*, 1907, p. 2. Enclosure as a sign of private ownership must not be confused either with enclosure as a part of the common field system or from the wild state as an inevitable result of the growth of population.

[6] The Statute of Merton in 1235 and of Winchester in 1285 gave lords of the manor the right of enclosing the commonable waste provided that proof was given that the tenants were left sufficient for pasture. Slater, *op. cit.*, p. 6.

[7] Curtler, *The Enclosure and Re-distribution of our Land*, 1920, pp. 63–4.

[8] *Ibid.*, p. 63.

[9] During the several centuries in which enclosure was going on, that of the common arable fields, meadows and waste usually took place in one of the following ways : " (1) By act of Parliament, viz., (*a*) by private Act, (*b*) under the authority of the General Enclosure Acts of 1830 and 1836, (*c*) by the Enclosure Commissioners and their successors, the Board of Agriculture, under the General Enclosure Act of 1845 and its amending Acts.

" (2) By common agreement of all the collective owners.

" (3) By the purchase of the part of one owner of all conflicting rights.

" (4) By special licence of the Tudor monarchs.

" (5) By various forms of force and fraud." (Slater, *op. cit.*, p. 6.)

In addition the waste might be enclosed as described in note 6.

[10] See Curtler, *The Enclosure and Re-distribution of our Land*, chaps. 11 and 12 ; and Johnson, *The Disappearance of the Small Landowner*, 1909, chap. 3.

[11] Curtler, *op. cit.*, p. 122.

[12] Tawney, *The Agrarian Problem in the Sixteenth Century*, 1912, p. 409.

[13] Levy, *Large and Small Holdings*, 1911, p. 5.

[14] Girdler, *Observations on Forestalling, Regrating and Ingrossing*, 1800, p. 29.

[15] Levy, *op. cit.*, p. 7.

[16] In addition to the works of the Hammonds, Hasbach, Slater, Johnson, Curtler and Levy, which have already been referred to, the chapters on this subject in Lord Ernle's *English Farming Past and Present*, and in Curtler's *A Short History of English Agriculture*, are very helpful. In many respects the ablest work on enclosure is Gonner's *Common Land and Enclosure*.

[17] Levy, *op. cit.*, p. 44.

[18] Hasbach, *op. cit.*, pp. 103–4.

[19] Curtler, *The Enclosure and Re-distribution of our Land*, p. 148.

[20] *Ibid.*, pp. 149–150. [21] *Ibid.*, p. 150.

[22] 41st George III., c. 109.

[23] Curtler, *The Enclosure and Re-distribution of our Land*, p. 153.

[24] *Ibid.*, chap. 14.

[25] Hammond, *op. cit.*, chap. 2.

[26] Curtler, *op. cit.*, p. 155. [27] *Ibid.* [28] *Ibid.*, p. 156. [29] *Ibid.*, p. 158.

[30] *Ibid.*, p. 159.
[31] Slater, *op. cit.*, p. 7.
[32] Johnson, *op. cit.*, p. 86.   [33] *Ibid.*, p. 91.
[34] Hammond, *op. cit.*, p. 18.   [35] *Ibid.*
[36] See maps in Slater opposite p. 73, and in Gonner and Johnson at the end of the volumes.
[37] Slater, *op. cit.*, Appendix A and Appendix B.
[38] Johnson, *op. cit.*, p. 87.
[39] Levy, *op. cit.*, p. 9.   [40] *Ibid.*, p. 11.   [41] *Ibid.*, p. 13.   [42] *Ibid.*, p. 21.
[42] *Ibid.*, p. 28.   [44] *Ibid.*, note pp. 27–8.   [45] *Ibid.*, p. 27.
[46] Hasbach, *op. cit.*, pp. 55–6.   [47] *Ibid.*, p. 56.   [48] *Ibid.*, p. 61.   [49] *Ibid.*, pp. 60–1.   [50] *Ibid.*, p. 376.   [51] *Ibid.*, p. 383.
[52] For a discussion of the statistics on population in eighteenth-century England see G. Talbot Griffith, *Population Problems of the Age of Malthus*, chap. 1, and M. C. Buer, *Health, Wealth and Population in the Early Days of the Industrial Revolution*, chaps. 2 and 3. In this chapter I have used the Rickman estimates, which are based on the 1801 census and the parish birth and burial records before that date. In addition there are the Finlaison estimates and these of Rickman corrected in order to make allowances for the births and deaths not registered. The differences in the estimates for 1700 and 1790 are shown by the following column :

					1700	1790
Rickman ...	...	...	...	...	5,475,000	8,675,000
Finlaison ...	...	...	...	...	5,134,000	8,541,000
Rickman corrected		...	...	...	5,835,000	8,216,000

The Finlaison estimate shows a greater and the Rickman corrected a smaller ncrease in population than the one followed in the narrative ; but all substantiate the contention that the production of grain must also have increased during this period.
[53] Smith, *Tracts on the Corn-Trade and Corn-Laws*, 1804, pp. 305 and 318.
[54] *Report of the Board of Agriculture on Enclosures*, 1808, pp. 232–252. The area examined was in the midlands.
[55] *Ibid.*, p. 254.
[56] Levy, *op. cit*, p. 23.
[57] Curtler, *The Enclosure and Re-distribution of our Land*, p. 163.
[58] *Ibid.*   [59] *Ibid.*, p. 152.
[60] Levy, *op. cit.*, p. 24.
[61] Hammond, *op. cit.*, p. 77.   [62] *Ibid.*, p. 79.
[63] Hasbach, *op. cit.*, pp. 109–11.
[64] Hammond, *op. cit.*, p. 73.
[65] Levy, *op. cit.*, pp. 28–9.
[66] Johnson, *op. cit.*, p. 136.
[67] *Quarterly Journal of Economics*, 1910, p. 325–6.
[68] E. Davies, " The Small Landowner, 1780–1832, in the Light of the Land Tax Assessments," in *The Economic History Review*, January, 1927, pp. 110–12.
J. H. Clapham, in *An Economic History of Modern Britain*, vol. 1, argues against the disappearance of small farmers : " There are figures in the census of 1831 which illustrate, with some precision, the extent to which really small farming had survived in Britain. They are entirely destructive of the view that, as the result of agrarian change and class legislation, an army of labourers toiled for a relatively small farming class. Of 961,000 families engaged in agriculture, 144,600 were those of occupiers—owners or farmers—who hired labour ; 130,500 were those of occupiers who hired no labour ; and 686,000 were labouring families " (p. 113). This evidence was not introduced into the narrative because the statistics cited apply to both owners and tenants, apparently, and not merely to owners.

CHAPTER VII

THE CORN LAW OF 1815

Agitation for a new corn law in 1813—Reasons for the appointment of a select committee—Report of the committee—Ingenious speech by Parnell in support of these recommendations—Opposition in the Commons of Hamilton, Rose and Horner—Reasons for the withdrawal of the bill—An examination of the motives underlying the work of the committee—Renewal of the agitation in 1814—Change in the attitude of the English landed interest—New resolutions introduced by Parnell—Speech of Rose and answer of Parnell—Discussion of the resolutions in the Commons and the introduction of a bill based upon them—Reasons for failure to pass this bill—Law of 1814 abolishing restrictions on the exportation of grain—Agitation again renewed in 1815—New light thrown on the question by the reports of the select committees of the Commons and Lords, and by able pamphlets on many phases of the subject—Critical condition of agriculture—Nine resolutions introduced by Robinson—Speeches for and against the new bill in the Commons—Opposition to the bill outside Parliament shown by the number of petitions against it and by the actions of mobs—Discussion of the bill by the Lords—Provisions of the new law—Consideration of the different policies which could have been adopted at this time—Acts of 1814 and 1815 meant the abandonment of principles upon which the acts of 1670 and 1689 were based—Change in spirit even more important—Effect of the law of 1815 upon public opinion—Attitude of the different classes in the community toward the law—What should have been done in 1815 ?

In Chapter V it was shown not only that the Corn Laws of 1791 and 1804 were practically inoperative from 1793 to 1813, but also that from 1805 to 1813 there was little discussion of the subject in Parliament, periodicals or pamphlets. During these latter years the high price of grain was caused partly by the Continental System, which in the main cut off supplies from the continent ; and partly by four successive bad harvests from 1809 to 1812. The enormous harvest of 1813, which sent prices down to the lowest point in years, was to play a very important part in the agitation for a new corn law in 1814 and in 1815 ; but the first move in this direction took place before the harvest of 1813.

On March 22nd, 1813, a select committee was appointed to inquire into the corn trade of the United Kingdom. The original proposal had been for Ireland only, but an amendment substituting the words United Kingdom was carried.[1] Although the object in appointing this committee was not perfectly clear at the time, later developments indicated that the original purpose was to secure the right of free exportation of grain. Sir Henry Parnell, an Irish landlord, was appointed chairman of the committee and evidently it was planned in the interests of Ireland. Judging from Parnell's speech in 1814, the Irish felt it a grievance that they were not free to export corn to the West Indies, Brazil and other places, instead of merely to Great Britain.[2]

The report of this committee, which was ordered to be printed on

May 11th, was not presented to the House of Commons until June 15th.   The justification offered for changing the existing system was as follows.   Great Britain was becoming increasingly dependent upon foreign grain, as imports in the previous twenty-one years amounting to £58,634,135 clearly showed.   Although there had been a great increase in the number of acres tilled, and a considerable improvement in the methods of cultivation during the preceding ten years, there was room for further advance in both Great Britain and Ireland. Down to 1765, when the system of restraining imports and encouraging exports had been enforced, Great Britain not only supplied herself with grain but also exported a considerable amount.   In addition the prices during those years were both steady and moderate.   When this system was abandoned after 1765, the country not only was unable to supply itself, but it was also forced to import vast quantities. Only when the Continental System cut off the foreign supply did the United Kingdom in 1812 export more corn than she imported. These facts seem to establish the superiority of restricted over free importation of grain.

The committee then offered the following six resolutions : first, that the import prices, duties and bounties payable on corn by the act of 1804 be repealed ;   second, that Ireland be divided into four maritime and four inland districts, where the prices of corn should be taken and returned to the Receiver of Corn Returns as in England ; third, that import and export prices be regulated by the aggregate average price of corn in the twelve maritime districts of England, the four maritime ones of Scotland, and the four maritime ones of Ireland ; fourth, that when wheat was above 90s. 2d. a quarter none was to be exported ;   fifth, that when wheat was under 105s. 2d., a duty of 24s. 3d. was to be charged, if above that amount but under 135s. 2d., a duty of 2s. 6d., and if at or above 135s. 2d., a duty of 6d. ;   and sixth, that no foreign flour or meal be imported into Great Britain. However, that the prices fixed in the fourth and fifth resolutions were not to be permanent.   The export price level was to be readjusted on February 1st of each year and was to be determined by adding one-seventh to the average of the previous twenty years.   The import price level was likewise to be replaced on February 1st of each year by a new list prepared by the Receiver of Corn Returns.[3]

This report with its rather sweeping recommendations was backed by only fourteen pages of evidence which dealt exclusively with Ireland.   It included a set of five questions sent to the Board of Agriculture and to the Farming Society of Ireland, and the testimony of five witnesses.[4]   Decidedly it was scanty and one-sided evidence upon which to advise the changes suggested in the six resolutions, especially when the price of corn at the time is taken into consideration.   As Smart remarks, " The most charitable judgment that could be passed on such a Report is that it was disingenuous."[5]

The case for additional protection was given by Sir Henry Parnell, chairman of the committee, in a speech delivered in the House of Commons on June 15th, 1813.[6]   He began with the statement that the object of the report was to show the evils of the present system of protecting agriculture, and to secure the growth of more corn at

steady and moderate prices. The alterations suggested, he was careful to point out, were not made to increase the profits of farmers and
landlords, since both of them had been extremely prosperous in
recent years. Furthermore, the landed interest had not asked for
any change in the Corn Laws, either by petition from outside
Parliament, or by a bill introduced by a member. The changes
suggested by the committee were made in an effort to protect the
nation from the dangers of the importation of foreign corn. One of
the obvious results of this importation was the enormous price of
grain in recent years. Parnell admitted that both depreciation of
money and manipulation of the market by the corn importers influenced prices, but insisted that much of the rise was the result of
foreign importation. In the long run this practice diminished the
production of British corn, but of even greater significance was the
danger of becoming dependent on enemies or potential enemies for
subsistence. The classic example of such a danger, which Parnell
cited, was the importation of 334,887 quarters of wheat and 202,922
quarters of flour from France in 1810. By this means, it was alleged,
Napoleon had been able to quell an insurrection in southern France
caused by low prices, as well as to collect heavy export duties at the
expense of England. Such a state of affairs was one to cause alarm,
since supplies might be cut off by war at any time. There was the
additional risk that an enemy might increase its naval strength by
sending corn to Great Britain in its own vessels.

The next point in favour of greater protection was, according to
Parnell, the necessity of counteracting the influence of the existing
system of bounties, monopolies and protective duties whereby capital
was actually being diverted from agriculture. He held that agriculture would need no protection if all trade were free, and he boldly
stated that, " If all those who are concerned in manufactures and
commerce will consent to adopt the system of a perfect free trade,
those who are now advocates for restraints on the importation of corn
will willingly abandon on their part all claim to any such protection."[7]

Parnell now turned aside to examine the arguments of Adam Smith
on free trade, and concluded that the authority of the great economist
could not be used against the resolutions of the committee. First,
Adam Smith recommended free trade only on the " supposition that
all the nations of Europe should adopt the same common policy."
Second, Adam Smith's chief objection to government interference was
that it " diverted capital from its natural into less productive,
channels." But such an objection could not be made to a proposal
which encourages the investment of capital in land, especially since
Great Britain did not supply herself with grain. Third, Adam Smith
had stated that " defence is, however, of more importance than
opulence,"[8] and Parnell held that raising enough corn to prevent the
country from starving came under the classification of defence.

Although great pains were taken to explain in detail the necessity
for making each change suggested in the six resolutions that dealt
with importation, the same cannot be said for those concerned with
exportation. The whole system of restrictions and bounties on the
exportation of corn was to be abolished and the trade made absolutely

free at all times.   The principal reason given for making so drastic a change was Adam Smith's statement that prohibition of exportation prevented the extension of cultivation, and freedom of exportation facilitated it.

In conclusion Parnell prophesied that if the proposals were adopted the consequences were certain to be beneficial.   The farmers would be able to increase production, and hence supply not only the home market but also the colonies and foreign countries as well.   Even, " If steadiness of price shall be alone the result, a most valuable object will be acquired, because it is not a high price which injures the poor man, but a price that fluctuates...."[9]   But the most substantial benefit would be the economic independence secured by doing away with dependence on foreign corn.

Turning from the general effects, Parnell showed how the proposed measure would affect each class and interest.   The landlords, farmers, agricultural labourers, manufacturers, town labourers and Irish landlords and farmers were all shown that the change would benefit them ; but the result promised one class was often the opposite of that promised another.   The landlords and farmers of both Great Britain and Ireland were offered a monopoly of the home market presumably with high prices.   The labourers, both agricultural and town, were offered steady and moderate prices and were told correctly enough that fluctuating prices were worse for them than high ones.   The manufacturers who feared high prices because of the effect on wages, and hence on the cost of production, were assured that the changes suggested would reduce prices without lessening the prosperity of " their best customers, the agricultural classes."[10]   Those who dreaded dependence on foreign countries, and that element must have been strong after twenty years of war and four consecutive bad harvests, were shown that the new policy would avoid this danger. In short, the landlords and farmers were assured that the monopoly of the home market would give them high rents and profits by keeping prices at a high level ; and labourers and manufacturers were assured that it would result in moderate and steady prices such as prevailed before 1765.[11]

Taken as a whole, this speech is remarkable for its inconsistencies and inaccurate statements, and yet it is amazingly clever in that it appealed to every interest in turn.[12]   But the manner in which it was immediately assailed in Parliament and outside proved that each interest did not necessarily accept Parnell's point of view of the benefits it would confer.   The inconsistencies and flaws in the report and speech were immediately exposed by various speakers in Parliament.   Opposition to the proposed measure was expressed on the grounds both of expediency and of principle.   The chief objections were the lateness of the session, the insignificant reasons offered for making such a significant change,[13] the fact that in allowing exportation without restrictions a principle of five hundred years' standing was overthrown without an adequate investigation, the cumbersome and unfair method of determining the price level for importation,[14] and the futility of taking any action when such freedom in the corn trade and prosperity among agriculturists prevailed.[15]   But all things considered, the most significant protest came from " Squire " Western. He was the author of the act of 1804, and from the spring of 1814 until the repeal in 1846 he was, in all probability, the most stalwart defender of the landed interest in Parliament. He objected to the proposed measure because of the pernicious influence it would have on public opinion. At that time, he pointed out, corn was so high that thousands were scarcely able to buy bread ; and if by this bill all hope of cheaper bread was permanently shattered, the popular clamour was bound to be great.[16]

Despite opposition, Parnell's motion for the House to go into committee was passed, but on June 29th Parnell withdrew the bill because of the lateness of the session.[17]

In view of the circumstances under which these proposals for increased protection were made, some explanation of the motive is necessary. Clearly, as Western pointed out, the demand did not come from the landed interest, since the landlords were enjoying unprecedented rents and the farmers huge profits. Furthermore, nothing could be more ill timed than the attempt to make permanent a famine which had resulted from four successive bad harvests and an almost total exclusion of foreign corn. If the British landlords were satisfied with the existing system, it would appear at first sight as if the Irish ones should also have been, since they profited more, relatively, from the exclusion of continental corn than the British. A possible explanation is that, although they found supplying England very profitable, they believed that selling to the colonies would be even more so.[18] But the act of 1804 forbade the exportation of grain when above, what was in 1813, a very low price. The original object of Parnell seems to have been freedom of export, and judging by the ease with which it was secured the next year, there was no serious obstacle in the way of its attainment. But just before the committee was formally appointed, a much more ambitious idea seems to have struck the Irish members : namely, the prospects of securing a monopoly of the English market at famine prices. If England could be persuaded to shut out foreign corn altogether, then the prospects of a golden harvest for Irish landlords was dazzling.[19] Evidently this interpretation of the motives of the committee was rather widespread at the time, because Parnell in a speech delivered in the House of Commons in 1814 felt it necessary to defend the recommendations of both 1813 and 1814. He began his defence with, " So many persons have called the whole proceeding, both in Parliament and out of it, an ' Irish job,' that it is necessary to make a few observations, to show how far such a character can be justly given to it."[20] But despite the adroit speech of Parnell in June of 1813, his resolutions, as it has been shown, were coldly received even by the English landed interest. In spite of this reception, it is highly probable that the alluring prospects dangled before the eyes of the English farmers had considerable influence on the future agitation for protection for English agriculture. But, it is even more probable that Parnell's attempt to secure higher protection would have sunk into obscurity, if the tremendous harvest of 1813 had not sent prices falling so rapidly. Further, the arguments used in favour of giving the British producers a monopoly of the home market were in common use before 1813, and Parnell can lay no claim to originating them.

Although the next session of Parliament was opened in November of 1813, owing to a series of delays and a long adjournment from January until March 21st, 1814, the debates on the proposed changes in the Corn Laws were not resumed until May 5th.   At the time of the resumption, conditions in agriculture were vastly different from those in June of 1813.   Instead of high prices, war, four successive deficient harvests, suffering in the labouring classes, and prosperity among the landlords and farmers, there were now low prices, peace, the most abundant harvest in years, a plentiful supply of grain, and distress among the farmers.   If it were hard to persuade an unwilling country, which had known only high prices for years, to accept an alteration in the Corn Laws for the reasons that Parnell had assigned in his famous speech, it was even more difficult to convince a country now enjoying the delights of cheap bread, that the importation of corn should be stopped.   As Smart phrases it, " The argument for ' independence of the foreigner,' too, seemed to lose its force when three of the great powers of Europe were our close allies, and when our great enemy had, with some appearance of relief, got rid of the chief troubler of the peace, and accepted a new king who had long enjoyed our hospitality."[21]   But this feeling was characteristic of the labouring classes, and possibly of the manufacturers, rather than of either the landlords or farmers ;   and it was the landowners who controlled Parliament.

The fall in the price of wheat had been enormous.   The average for June, 1813, was 117s. 10d. ;   that of April, 1814, 75s. 8d. ;   and that of May, 69s. 7d.[22]   Naturally the attitude of the landed interest was very different from what it had been in June of 1813.   At that time they had shown themselves totally indifferent to any further protection because wheat was high and there was little prospect of peace or importation ;   but now an enormous harvest, followed by peace and considerable importations, spread dismay in their ranks.   Farmers in recent years had made enormous profits and, presuming on the indefinite continuance of high prices, they had sunk a vast amount of capital in improvements and had renewed their leases, in many instances at rents proportionate to prices.   Both farmers and landlords had raised their standard of living during the period, and both were loath to submit to any lowering at this time.   Consequently the landed interest as a whole succumbed to the arguments of Parnell in 1814, although indifferent to them a year earlier.

Some apprehension was felt in the growing cities of the North and Scotland that the measure of the previous year would be revived. On April 6th, 1814, Lord Archibald Hamilton presented a petition from Lanark, and on April 25th one from Glasgow, asking that no alteration be made in the Corn Laws.[23]   After presenting the second one, Lord Archibald asked Parnell what he intended to do about the matter.   The latter replied that if the House agreed to his motion to go into committee to consider the Corn Laws, he would move a series of resolutions containing some alterations in those of the preceding year. If these resolutions were passed, he would bring in a bill founded on them.[24]

Accordingly on May 5th Parnell introduced a new set of resolutions. The principal recommendations were that the exportation of grain and flour " should be permitted at all times, without payment of any duty, and without receiving any bounty whatever ; "[25] and that for the existing duties on imported grain and flour the following should be substituted. Wheat from foreign countries was to pay duties of 24s. 3d., 2s. 6d., and 6d. respectively when the price was under 84s., above 84s. but under 87s., and at or above 87s. Wheat from the North American Colonies was to pay the same schedule of duties when the price in each of the three levels was 10s. less. The duties on rye, beans, peas, barley, beer and oats were also raised.[26]

These new recommendations along with the report and resolutions of 1813, were severely attacked by Mr. George Rose. He objected to the first of the new resolutions on the grounds that it meant abandoning a principle which had been on the statute books for over five hundred years, without a syllable in the report to indicate why it was given up. The report itself, in his opinion, was filled with inaccuracies and indicated superficial views of the whole matter. He prefaced his attack on the report with the statement that, " It hardly is necessary for me to premise that I should hold myself inexcusable if I were to convey an insinuation that the Hon. Baronet meant to mislead the House by any mis-statement, a certainty of detection must have prevented such an intention, even if he had not been restrained by better motives, which I am persuaded invariably govern his conduct. He must, however, permit me say, that he did not apply such a degree of industry to the occasion as is required from the chairman of every committee to which an inquiry is referred."[27] The secrecy with which the committee appointed to inquire into the internal regulations of the Irish corn trade was transformed into one to revise the Corn Laws of Great Britain was amazing, and the haste shown in rushing bills through the sessions of 1813 and the present one was in marked contrast to the time given the acts of 1773, 1791 and 1804. Rose then cited many instances of flimsy evidence such as presenting only seven statutes to prove all the committee's points, erroneous use of the Eton prices of wheat, and the statement that a new policy was inaugurated in 1765. Especially did he object to the statement that Great Britain became an exporting country in 1812. " Wheat was that year 128s. ; to what part of the world (except to Iceland and Norway in small quantities) could it be sent at that price ? in truth little or none was exported anywhere, with that exception, but for our armies in the Peninsula, as will be seen in the separate account for that year presented from the Customs."[28]

After exposing the fallacies and inconsistencies in the report and resolutions, Rose turned to his own views of the subject. He held " that the grower of corn should be very effectually protected, to the extent of the price being high enough to ensure his being able to pay a fair rent, and to have a reasonable profit to himself ; but when that object shall be secured, the consumer should have every possible facility of supply at a price not exceeding the protecting one."[29] The application of this principle demanded that exportation as well as importation should be regulated, since he took it for granted that no one entertained " the remotest idea of an entirely free trade in corn, which would be equally mischievous to the grower and consumer."[30]

In conclusion, Rose pointed out that the committee held out " to captivate one description of people, an expectation that by increased cultivation bread will become cheap ; and to another, that by raising the prices of importation and lessening those for exportation, corn will be dearer ; the attempts made to reconcile these two objects can hardly mislead anyone, notwithstanding the very ingenious arguments used."[31]

Parnell immediately answered Rose in an equally long speech. Most of the accusations about the inaccuracies and careless work of the committee he met by a polite denial. He then took up the most important free trade arguments, but made no attempt to refute the previous speech point by point. First, he maintained that artificial conditions created by the war made it impossible for agriculture to withstand the influx of foreign corn which would result from a policy of having other nations pay for manufactured goods with grain. Second, to the argument that it was possible to obtain a sufficient supply abroad, he replied that, even if this were true, in the long run it would make prices higher. Third, he pointed out to free-traders that unrestrained importation would lessen the purchasing power of the landed interest, and hence deprive manufacturers of their best customers. Finally, the argument, that the proposed measure would, by making grain higher, raise the price of manufacturing labour, and hence deprive the British manufacturers of their superiority over foreigners, was, in his opinion, the easiest to refute. Granting for sake of argument that these regulations would raise the price of corn, it did not follow that wages would also rise, since the latter were determined by supply and demand. But even if it were true that wages were determined by the price of corn, British manufacturers would not be undersold in foreign markets because their superiority lay, not in cheaper labour, but in greater skill, better machinery and more extended capital. Adam Smith had made three exceptions to the general rule of complete freedom of trade. First, if a particular industry was essential to the defence of the country, protective duties might be imposed; second, if a tax were placed on an article produced at home, one of an equal amount should be placed on the importation of the same article from abroad ; and third, where any commodity had been encouraged by high duties, it was unjust and attended by injurious consequences suddenly to restore free importation in that article. Clearly the changes proposed in the corn importation regulations were justified by all three of these exceptions.

In concluding his speech Parnell maintained that the authors of the Corn Bills, " so far from intending to sustain high rents, rather look forward to a reduction of all those which have been calculated on the prices of the last few years ; so far from intending to raise the price of corn or bread, they are altogether influenced by a desire to secure plenty and low prices, by averting that sudden stop to cultivation, which will certainly take place, if no protection is given to the farmer, and which must be followed by high prices and scarcity. And, finally, so far from wishing to benefit only the grower of corn, they seek to protect and promote the interests of the consumers, which when well understood, differ in no kind of degree from those of the growers. These are the real motives which have influenced their conduct. To attribute any other to them, is to do that which is an unwarrantable misrepresentation, and that which no argument or fact that they have ever advanced will at all justify."[32]

Huskisson now moved an amendment to the second resolution which really altered the nature of the protection offered. His objection was not to the giving of additional protection to agriculture, in which he thoroughly believed, but to the fact that the proposed plan tended to confer a monopoly of the home market upon the British producer. He therefore proposed that the prohibitive duty of 24s. 3d. should be kept on at 63s., and that for every rise in price of a shilling the same amount should be taken from the duty. In order to preserve the colonial preference he suggested that the duty on colonial grain should be half the amount on foreign.

Despite the really great difference in the amendment and the original resolution, Parnell accepted it for the sake of unanimity. But unanimity was not secured by this acquiescence. Some members, it is true, were mollified by the amendment ; but others either objected to the change, or found both the original resolution and the amendment equally obnoxious. The view of the landlords was presented on May 16th in a vigorous speech by Western. The first part was confined to an historical survey of the Corn Laws since 1670. There was nothing new in his exposition, for he simply followed Dirom and Anderson in eulogizing the acts of 1670 and 1689, and in denouncing those of 1773 and 1791. The moral drawn was obvious : " we should revert to the policy of the Revolutionary laws, we should give our farmers that confidence which they inspired, and thus again throw off all dependence upon foreign countries."[33] The measure proposed seemed too inadequate to accomplish this for it afforded " no certainty of market to the British grower, and no security against an influx of foreign corn."[34] He readily admitted that variations in seasons made the quantity of corn uncertain ; but he believed the only way to reduce this variation to a minimum was to create a demand beyond actual necessity, and this should be " effected by bounties on exportation, and still more by an extended home consumption."[35] He strongly endorsed the part of the report which stressed the importance of steady prices as opposed to fluctuating ones, and concluded with a warning against the idea that any permanent advantage could come from encouraging the importation of foreign corn,[36] and against the danger of sacrificing political independence by depending on such grain.[37]

The next day, Foster, after arguing along the same lines as Western, moved as an amendment to the second resolution, that foreign corn be excluded until the price reached 100s.[38] Vansittart, Chancellor of the Exchequer, replied that, rather than consent to this amendment, he would postpone consideration of the resolutions until next session. After some rather acrimonious speeches on both sides the amendment was defeated by 81 to 60.[39]

On May 18th the House of Commons voted to have a bill brought in based on the resolutions. Petitions now began to pour in from all parts of Great Britain. " For the early part of the year, the Journals of the House of Commons record about 130 petitions ' respecting the Corn Laws,' and over 170 ' against the Bill '."[40] When Prothero presented one from the inhabitants of Bristol, both Western and Parnell sarcastically complimented him on the superb manner in which he handled his constituents.[41] On June 6th Canning advised against proceeding in face of such opposition. Vansittart thought it wise under the circumstances to show some consideration for the number of petitions and the sentiments of the petitioners, and consequently moved that a committee be appointed to report to what extent the law of 1804 was a protection to the corn-growers. Canning proposed as an amendment that this committee consider the petitions against the proposed alterations in the Corn Laws. Vansittart consented and the motion passed by 173 to 67. He next moved that the report be considered in three weeks. General Gascoigne then moved that it be amended so as to read in six months instead of three weeks. The amendment passed by 116 to 106.[42] As a result all hope of passing a bill in the present session was lost.

The failure of this measure did not prevent the original purpose of the Irish landowners—freedom of export—from being secured. On May 16th Vansittart introduced a bill in the Commons to permit the exportation of grain and flour from any part of the United Kingdom at all times without duty or bounty.[43] This bill aroused little opposition. It passed the Commons on May 23rd, the Lords on June 13th, and received the royal assent on June 27th.[44]

Despite the opposition aroused against any change in the Corn Laws and the enormous number of petitions setting forth reasons why no alteration should take place, astonishingly few pamphlets appeared in opposition to the new measures proposed. This fact is even more striking when the large number of pamphlets which were published during the next year opposing the bill of 1815, and the several able ones which appeared in 1814 advocating further protection for home corn are taken into consideration. So great was the difference in the numbers and quality of the pamphlets on the opposite sides of the controversy in 1814 that Jacob declared : " It is to be lamented that, though Lord Lauderdale, Sir H. Parnell, Mr. Western and some others, have addressed the public on the subject of the Corn Laws, and though the petitions presented to Parliament last year were so numerous, no authors have appeared to oppose the views of those writers, except some anonymous ones in periodical publications ; so it is difficult to guess what objections can be made to such regulations as we have endeavoured to show to be necessary for the good of the community."[45] In addition to Rose's speech, which he published in pamphlet form, and which was more an attack on the poor calibre of the report and the free exportation of grain than on the additional protection proposed, only three opposition pamphlets of any importance seem to have appeared. These were: J. Broadhurst, *Substance of a Speech Against the Proposed Alteration of the Corn Laws, Intended to Have Been Spoken in the House of Commons on June 6th, 1814*; John Naismith, *An Inquiry Concerning the Propriety of Increasing the Import Duty on Foreign Corn;* and an anonymous author, *An Inquiry into the Policy, Efficiency and Consistency of the Alterations in Our Corn Laws; in a Letter to Sir Henry Parnell.*

The chief arguments advanced in these pamphlets against greater protection to agriculture were that it was unnecessary to keep up the existing prices to insure high rents because the landlords could afford to accept lower rents when the war taxes were taken off and currency became thirty per cent. more valuable ;[46] that a higher price of corn did not serve as a stimulus either to the tenant or to the cultivating proprietor, since the landlord absorbed the surplus of the one by advancing the rent and the other was certain to cultivate his land so as to secure a net profit ;[47] that although some protection might be necessary to offset the burden of the enormous taxes borne by the landowners, the amount could be fixed only after information was obtained on the price of raising corn in the exporting countries ;[48] that past experiences showed that raising the import price level higher did not give the landed interest the advantages expected ; and that cutting off the supply of foreign grain by a high tariff might ruin the industrial and commercial prosperity of Great Britain.[49]

The anonymous author of the letter to Parnell divided his time between a merciless arraignment of the vacillating nature of the proposals of the committee in 1813 and 1814, and a bold argument for complete free trade. He pointed out that Parnell had introduced a set of resolutions in 1814 which were decidedly different from those of the previous year, and then had readily acquiesced in the change in principle which Huskisson had suggested in his amendment. Vansittart had complimented Parnell on the " candour " of his ready compliance. In commenting on these words of approbation, the author stated " if candour means a facility of adopting and rejecting without inquiry, the praise was certainly merited."[50] In advocating free trade in corn he was quite willing to admit that the immediate results might be as disastrous as the committee feared. " Our markets will be glutted, our farmers will be impoverished, our poor lands will cease to be cultivated, and the capital invested in agriculture will seek some more profitable employment." But even this price was worth paying for the new order which would arise. Freed from the enormous rents and high prices of labour the cultivator would enter upon a period of prosperity, since he would have the advantages accruing to the home producer without the handicap under which he laboured at present. Thus trade would rapidly increase, manufacturers would be under no high labour handicap, and the taxes, though remaining the same, would be divided among greater numbers and would be drawn from greater accumulations of wealth. Then, he concluded, " our prosperity will be permanent : for there will be no germ of corruption within and no cause to apprehend any destructive tempest from without."[51]

But if the advocates of additional protection could complain that there were no outstanding pamphlets opposing higher duties on corn, the opponents of the bill of 1814 could not counter with a similar complaint. The most notable pamphlets defending the bill or advocating additional protection of some sort were those by Baron Hepburn, Jacob, Lauderdale, Campbell and Huskisson.[52] In the main they put forward the same arguments that Parnell had used in two speeches.[53]

The only avowed non-partisan pamphlet was published by Malthus.[54] At this time he had not made up his mind upon the question of the revision of the Corn Laws, and consequently he contented himself with summarizing the arguments of both sides and suggesting a temporary or permanent fixed duty. To him the question seemed to depend upon three points : " First, Whether, upon the supposition of the most perfect freedom of importation and exportation, it is probable that Great Britain and Ireland would grow an independent supply of corn. Secondly, Whether an independent supply, if it do not come naturally, is an object really desirable, and one which justifies the interference of the legislature. And, Thirdly, If an independent supply be considered as such an object, how far, and by what sacrifice, are restrictions upon importation adapted to attain the end in view."[55]

On the first point he was convinced that, owing to the expenses of enclosure, taxes and labour, as compared with the rest of Europe, nothing was more unlikely.[56] On the second, after weighing the advantage of buying in the cheapest market against the four disadvantages of dependence on foreign supply, an excessive proportion of manufacturing population, the loss of the benefits to the wage-earners of a high nominal price of corn and labour, and the danger of a sudden exposure to unlimited importation, Malthus conceded that it might be impolitic to check agriculture.[57] On the third point, he admitted that the sacrifices necessary to attain an independent supply were a certain waste of national resources in growing corn, a relative disadvantage in foreign commercial transactions, some check to population, and the necessity of constant revision and interference.[58] He then came to the rather cautious conclusion that, " Should it however be determined to proceed *immediately* to a revision of the present laws, in order to render them more efficacious, there would be some obvious advantages, both as temporary and permanent measure, in giving to the restrictions the form of a constant duty upon foreign corn, not to act as a prohibition, but as a protecting, and at the same time, profitable tax."[59] Despite the endorsement of Malthus, the idea of placing a moderate fixed duty on imported corn seems to have gained few friends at this time.

Perhaps the best summary of the conflicting arguments and opinions, cited from speeches in Parliament and from petitions and pamphlets outside, was given by a writer in *The Annual Register*. He stated that, " Without presuming to give any opinion respecting the general justice or policy of the proposed alterations in the system of the Corn Laws, we may venture to observe, respecting the parliamentary proceedings on the subject, 1, that the very high standard fixed in the first set of resolutions for the points at which exportation was to cease, and importation to be allowed, did certainly indicate in the proposers a design of keeping up a price of corn adequate to the support of that extraordinary rise of rents which has taken place of late years : 2, that the great majorities in the House of Commons in favour of the mitigated resolutions cannot in fairness be attributed to any other cause, than a conviction of the public utility of the measures proposed : and 3, that the number of petitions against any change in the existing laws can afford no rule to judge of the merits of the case, when it is considered with what ease a ferment is excited among the people, especially in a matter apparently connected with their subsistence. The question, as a subject of sound and sober policy, cannot be said yet to have received a satisfactory discussion."[60]

Thus by February 17th, 1815, when Parliament again took the question under consideration, it had been subjected to a much more satisfactory discussion. Not only did the additional months give time for a more careful and thorough examination of the arguments already advanced, but also the reports of the committees of the Lords and Commons, and new pamphlets, threw additional light upon the subject.

The reports of the committee of the House of Lords, which was appointed to inquire into the petitions presented in the session of 1814, will be considered first. They were two in number, and were backed by about two hundred and fifty pages of testimony and about a hundred pages of accounts. The first report merely stated that no petitioners had appeared to substantiate or support any of the allegations made in the petitions.[61] The second report made no definite recommendations, but confined itself to a statement that the evidence taken appeared to divide itself into four main heads of inquiry : first, the means the United Kingdom actually possessed of raising an adequate corn supply of its own growth ; second, the probability of securing a corn supply from the continent ; third, the price at which the British farmer would be able to raise wheat if a free importation were allowed at all times ; and fourth, the effect which the price of corn would have upon manufacturing and agricultural labour.[62] However, the committee examined witnesses, not under these headings, but upon the comparative quality and value of foreign and home-grown grain, the state of agriculture in the United Kingdom, the connection between wages and the price of grain, the profits of millers, and the comparative advantage of conveying wheat and flour by sea. The witnesses examined included corn merchants, farmers, landowners and manufacturers. Since this mass of testimony led to no other conclusion by the committee than that the subject needed further investigation,[63] it is scarcely worth while examining the material in greater detail.

On the other hand the committee of the House of Commons in their report of July 26th, 1814, although using practically the same methods and examining a great many of the same witnesses as the other committee, came to very definite conclusions. They investigated, " 1st, The recent Extension and Improvement of the Agriculture of the United Kingdom ; 2nd, The present Expense of

K

Cultivation, including Rent ; 3rd, The Price necessary to remunerate the Grower."[64]

On the first point, the committee heaped up unquestionable evidence of the additional capital applied to land already under cultivation, and of the reclamation and enclosure of fens, commons and wastes.[65] On the second point, they found that both the general expenses of cultivation and the money rent of land, upon the average, had doubled in the past twenty years. At the same time, the landlord's share of the gross proceeds appeared to have decreased from about a third to about a fourth or fifth.[66] On the third point, " the Price necessary to remunerate the Grower of Corn," the committee frankly admitted the difficulties of arriving at any definite conclusion. They pointed out that the cost must fluctuate " according to the variations of soil, markets, skill and industry in the occupier, and many other circumstances affecting differently not only different districts, but different farms in the same district."[67] Having considered all these points, along with the testimony of thirty-six witnesses, mostly surveyors, land agents, farmers and corn factors or importers, the conclusion reached was that 80s. a quarter represented the lowest price which would afford an adequate return.[68]

In the end the committee offered two recommendations as a basis for Parliamentary legislation. First, that the importation of foreign corn should be prohibited until a fixed price was reached in order to protect the British producer and to enable him to extend cultivation as he had done in recent years. In the case of wheat this fixed price was 80s. Second, to avoid the dangers of famine in case of a deficient crop in Great Britain, the bonded warehouse system should be used to make the country a depot for foreign grain, thus insuring a ready supply in case of need.[69] Clearly this second recommendation was made in an attempt to offset the impression given by the first one, that the change in the existing system was entirely for the benefit of the landed interest.

In addition to these reports a considerable number of important pamphlets, both for and against additional protection to agriculture, appeared in the early months of 1815. On the side of greater protection, Malthus, Spence, Jacob, Sheffield and Hall were outstanding ; and on the other side, which included both out and out free-traders and men who merely opposed a change in the existing laws, Ricardo, Torrens, John Price Smith, J. D. Hume and Robert Wilson[70] were equally representative. Since an analysis of each of these pamphlets would involve needless repetition, a representative one will be taken from each of the two groups and treated in detail. Malthus' *The Grounds of an Opinion on the Policy of Restricting the Importation of Foreign Corn* is selected as representative of those advocating additional protection because it is, on the whole, the ablest pamphlet on the subject, and because it gives the reasons for his conversion to this point of view since the preceding year. On the other side, Ricardo's *An Essay on the Influence of a low Price of Corn on the Profits of Stock; showing the Inexpediency of Restrictions on Importation* is chosen both because of the merit of the work and because it was written as an answer to Malthus.

It is interesting to note the change in the point of view of Malthus since his " balanced " pamphlet of 1814. He stated that additional facts gave a decisive weight to the side of restricting importation which were lacking when he wrote his *Observations*. These were " 1st, The evidence, which had been laid before Parliament, relating to the effects of the present prices of corn, together with the experience of the present year. 2ndly, The improved state of our exchanges, and the fall in the price of bullion. And 3rdly, and mainly, the actual laws respecting the exportation of corn lately passed in France."[71] The evidence of the enormous losses resulting from the rapid fall of corn and the scanty crop of 1814, left no further room to doubt the actual distress of the agricultural class or the fact that " the immediate evils which are capable of being remedied by a system of restrictions, are of no inconsiderable magnitude."[72] The uncertain state of the currency in 1814 had made a permanent measure inadvisable at that time ; but this uncertainty existed no longer, and hence the reason for inaction no longer applied.[73] But by all odds the most important reason for not relying on a supply of foreign corn, was the French law forbidding the exportation of wheat after it reached 49s. a quarter. France possessed the largest and finest corn country in Europe and England must expect to secure her main imports from that source. The results of the year 1814 had proved conclusively that although the corn of the Baltic could not seriously depress the British market, that of France, combined with a bad crop at home, could make the price fall below a remunerative one.[74]

Malthus then took up the effect which the opening of the ports to foreign corn would have on each class in the community. He held that the agricultural labourers would be thrown out of work when low prices forced the farmers to give up their leases ; that the town and city labourers would suffer from lower wages and greater fluctuations in food prices ; that the farmers would suffer as they had since 1813 ; and that even the great majority of the commercial and manufacturing classes would feel the effects of the shrunken purchasing power of their usual customers. The only classes which would really profit by free importation were the stockholders and those living on fixed salaries, whose purchasing power would be enormously increased,[75] and those engaged in foreign trade.

Malthus concluded his pamphlet with the statement : " I firmly believe that in the actual state of Europe, and under the actual circumstances of our present situation, it is our wisest policy to grow our own average supply of corn ; and, in so doing, I feel persuaded that the country has ample resources for a great and continued increase of population, of power, of wealth, and of happiness."[76]

In the main the other pamphleteers reiterated either the arguments of Malthus or those of other writers and speakers which have already been given. Not all advocates of restriction treated the question with the studied moderation of Malthus. The introductory paragraph of Spence shows quite a different spirit. " Though from the outset of the discussion convinced of the futility of the arguments of those who opposed the Corn Bill, and disgusted with the selfishness of many of the petitioners against it, who, though entrenched in monopoly on every side, and ready to set the kingdom in a flame, at the slightest intimation of anything like foreign competition with their manufactures, could oppose, as the very height of injustice, the slightest approximation to similar privileges on the part of their agricultural brethren, I thought it needless to add to the publications . . ."[77] Nevertheless, he did add to the list.   Sheffield showed this same dissatisfaction with the political economists and petitioners in his complaint that, " Nothing can be more unreasonable than to apply general principles and theories to the political economy of this country in its actual predicament of taxation and price of labour ; and nothing, surely, is more disgusting, than the new system of being instructed and governed by petitions from those, who from their stations in life are least informed, and perfectly incapable of judging the real, permanent interest."[78]   Two points, which Malthus did not take up, were stressed by other writers : that it was uncertain whether France, Spain, Austria and Prussia would open their markets to English-manufactured goods even though the price of these commodities was reduced by cheap labour made possible by cheap foreign corn ;[79] and that the warehousing of foreign corn would permit a huge supply to be collected which could be thrown upon the market when the price reached a certain level, and which would go a great way toward nullifying the protection given by the new measure.   Sheffield prophesied correctly when he declared that the grain dealers who possessed warehoused corn would juggle the market prices in order to get the ports opened for importation.[80]

Ricardo took the stand that out and out free trade in corn would be beneficial not only to the country as a whole but also to every class except the landlords.   " If the legislature," he insisted, " were at once to adopt a decisive policy with regard to the trade in corn—if it were to allow a permanently free trade, and did not with every variation of price, alternately restrict and encourage importation, we should undoubtedly be a regularly importing country.   We should be so in consequence of the superiority of our wealth and population compared to the fertility of our soil over our neighbours."[81]   He admitted that the most serious objection to cheap corn came from the danger of relying on a foreign supply which might either be cut off by war, or by the refusal of exporting nations to allow their corn to leave the country during bad seasons.   In answer to this argument, he pointed out that very little corn could be secured from abroad at this time, but that more grain would be grown on the continent if there was a steady demand for it in Great Britain.   In case large numbers in foreign countries became interested in raising and shipping corn, no sovereign or combination of sovereigns would risk interfering with this traffic.   It was also unlikely that any people would submit to such interference.   The example cited by Ricardo to prove his point was the revolt of Russia against the Continental System,[82] and he might have added England in the War of the Austrian Succession, and France in 1810.   The experience of Great Britain during the Napoleonic Wars showed that high prices had a prodigious influence in bringing about increased production in time of need. Thus the country could in a crisis subsist by an economical use of the home produce and of the warehoused grain until enough capital and labour could be diverted into land to make up the deficiency.[83]

Ricardo was also firmly opposed to the stand taken by Malthus and other protectionists that unrestricted importation would be unfair to those who had invested capital in agriculture. He pointed out that owners of antiquated machinery experienced a similar loss when Arkwright's water frame and Watt's steam engine were perfected. The most he was willing to concede was temporary protection during the transition period largely because he felt it might " be desirable, that the farmers, during their current leases, should be protected against the losses which they would undoubtedly suffer from the new value of money, which would result from a cheap price of corn, under their existing money engagements with their landlords."[84] Restrictive duties for three or four years should enable the farmer to adjust himself to changed conditions, and after that no duty ought to be imposed on imported corn which was not charged on corn of home growth.[85]

Ricardo also differed radically from Malthus on the effect which free importation of grain would have on the different classes of the community. Whereas Malthus believed that all except the stock-holders, annuitants and merchants engaged in foreign trade would be injured, Ricardo held that only the landlords would suffer.[86] They agreed that the annuitants and stockholders would benefit, but Ricardo felt that at best it would be only a partial recompense for the losses which they had suffered through the depreciation of currency in the previous twenty years.[87] He closed his pamphlet with an expression of regret that considerations for a particular class should check the progress of the wealth and population of the country. " If the interests of the landlord," he concluded, " be of sufficient consequence, to determine us not to avail ourselves of all the benefits which would follow from importing corn at a cheap price, they should also influence us in rejecting all improvements in agriculture, and in the implements of husbandry ; for it is as certain that corn is rendered cheap, rents are lowered, and the ability of the landlord to pay taxes, is for a time, at least, as much impaired by such improvements, as by the importation of corn. To be consistent then, let us by the same act arrest improvement and prohibit importation."[88]

In general, the pamphleteers who opposed further protection to agriculture followed Ricardo both in repudiating the vested interest argument of those who had sunk capital in inferior lands,[89] and in refusing to admit the necessity of anything but temporary protection during a transition period. Only Hume seems to have argued for a fixed duty.[90] Torrens in the conclusion of The External Corn Trade is particularly clear on the second point : " When, in order to give time for a reduction of rents, for a withdrawing of capital from very inferior soils, and for the increased quantity of commodities to make good the financial deficit occasioned by a rise in the value of money, a temporary protection shall have been afforded to agriculture, the legislature may proceed to regulate tithes, to repeal whatever taxes may fall with disproportioned weight upon tillage, and to provide for an equalization of all rates and assessments."[91]

In addition to the new light which the reports of the committees and the pamphlets on both sides of the question threw on this perplexing problem of restricting the importation of corn, the harvest of 1814 also helped to clarify the issues. The crops were, on the whole, unfavourable, but prices did not rise as a result as they had from 1805 to 1812. Wheat, owing to the cold winter and rainy harvest weather, was considerably affected with blight and mildew, and consequently was inferior both in quality and quantity. But the immense surplus from 1813 and the importation of 800,000 quarters not only prevented a rise in price but led to a slight fall.[92]

On February 17th, 1815, the question was reopened in the House of Commons by the introduction of a series of nine resolutions which were based on the recommendations of the committee of the House of Commons. These resolutions were introduced by Robinson, the Vice-President of the Board of Trade. At the outset he admitted the difficulties involved in the proposed measure, but he felt that the former prejudices and misrepresentations had now been done away with as a result of the extensive investigations since the preceding year. Before long he was to find that the prejudices against additional protection had not died down. He was firmly convinced that a law based upon these resolutions would benefit all classes, and denied that the plan was in any sense a class measure. He went into elaborate details to prove the advantages of the home market, the evils of throwing inferior land out of cultivation, and the danger of depending on foreigners for the national food supply. He even reiterated the cheerful prophecy that in the end the measure would make corn cheaper than free importation.

The substance of these nine resolutions was as follows : first, foreign corn and flour might, at all times, be imported and warehoused duty free ; second, both might be exported duty free at any time ; third, when the price fixed for allowing imports was reached any kind of grain might be taken out of the warehouses and sold in Great Britain ; fourth, this price was to be 80s. for wheat, 55s. for rye, peas and beans, 40s. for barley, beer or bigg, and 26s. for oats ; fifth, if the average price for the six weeks preceding February 15th, May 15th, August 15th and November 15th should fall below these prices, no importation was to be permitted from the Eider to the Garonne until a new average was taken ; sixth, corn from the North American colonies was to be admitted at 67s. for wheat instead of 80s., and the price levels of other grain were lowered proportionately ; seventh, this corn might be warehoused free ; eighth, it might be exported duty free at any time ; and ninth, it might be sold when the corn from the colonies was admitted for consumption.[93]

From the time the resolutions were introduced until March 10th, the House of Commons dealt almost exclusively with this problem. Able speeches against the resolutions were made by Philips, Baring, General Gascoyne, Horner and Whitbread. The attacks were usually along the following lines : that no matter how skilfully the fact was disguised, the object was to raise the price of corn for the benefit of the landed interest ; that the exclusion of foreign corn would discourage production in European countries and make it impossible for Great Britain to secure a supply in case of a deficiency at home ; that the effect on manufacturing would be disastrous both by raising the labour costs and by artificially diverting capital from more to less productive channels ;[94] that the danger of foreign dependence was not great as the experience of Holland and Venice, and of Great Britain in 1810, showed ;[95] and that the innumerable petitions which crowded the table showed that a clear majority of the people were in favour of leaving the Corn Laws as they were.[96]

On February 22nd, the first three resolutions were agreed to by the House ; but on the fourth one Baring, after pointing out that the distress was only temporary, moved as an amendment the addition of the words " for a time to be limited." The sum, he stated, could afterwards be arranged, although he intimated that 75s. would be the amount fixed.[97] The next day this amendment was negatived without a division.

The debates of the next few days were fiercely waged, but little progress was made. A description given by one writer of those of the night of February 23rd to 24th may be taken as typical. " The debate although protracted until four o'clock this morning was not distinguished for any new or interesting topics. It may be very justly observed, upon an impartial review of the arguments employed in the recent debates, that no great question has ever elicited less ability and less knowledge ; and when the historian shall have occasion to record the whole proceedings, he will, we fear, have little cause to compliment one single member of the House of Commons for his masterly consideration of the subject in a comprehensive national point of view, embracing at once the agricultural, commercial and manufacturing interests of the Empire."[98]

In the end all the resolutions were passed and leave was given to bring in a bill based on them. Calcraft's amendment which substituted 82s. for 80s. was defeated by 154 to 35,[99] and Atkin's, which substituted 76s. for 80s., by 109 to 30.[100] On March 1st the bill was read a first time, and it seemed that the struggle was over. But on this very day petitions began to pour in and continued to do so until the bill was passed. Practically every manufacturing and commercial city in the country sent one signed by thousands of names. This effectively refuted Robinson's statement that there was less opposition throughout the country than in the previous year, a fact which was eagerly seized upon by various speakers opposing the bill.[101]

Despite protests inside and outside the House of Commons, the bill was read a second time on March 3rd. But the opposition fought every step. Amendments to postpone consideration of the measure for various periods of time were continually proposed although voted down by substantial majorities. The debates on the night of March 6th were particularly bitter. Supporters of the bill were taunted with its increasing unpopularity among the people, with the fact that it was the work entirely of the landlords and of no interest to the tenants and agricultural labourers, and that it was a bait held out to the landed interest by the government to induce them to vote the twenty million pounds necessary to wind up the war.[102]

On this same day, March 6th, the London mob which had such a glorious eighteenth-century tradition of influencing Parliament, began to take a hand in the matter.   Huge crowds gathered at the Mansion House to sign the city petitions against the corn bill, but so many people assembled that many were unable to sign.   *The Advertiser* expressed the pious wish, which was not to be gratified, that the mob would not riot lest it might frustrate the constitutional right of petition.[103]   More direct action was taken by the mob against members of Parliament in its attempt to influence the vote on the bill. Some members were treated roughly.   " They were stopped, questioned as to their votes, maltreated and bandied about like shuttlecocks between battle-dores."[104]   In the evening the mob assembled near the House of Commons and blocked the avenues. They broke the windows of the house of Lord Darnley in Berkeley Square and those of the Lord Chancellor in Bedford Square.   The next night they began action by breaking those in the home of Castlereagh in St. James' ; then moved on to the house of Robinson, who had introduced the bill in the House of Commons.   Here three soldiers and the butler fired on the crowd and killed several members, including a woman.   The mob also broke the windows of *The Morning Herald* in Catherine Street, and then proceeded to the office of *The Morning Post* in the Strand and gave three cheers.[105]   Evidently members of Parliament were not maltreated as on the previous day for, although a large crowd gathered in the Palace yard, " yet they heard with complacency Sir Francis Burdett declare himself friendly to the principle of the Corn Bill, on the footing of protection having been given to every species of industry."   On Wednesday the home of Ponsonby at 19, Curzon Street, and of Sir Joseph Bankes in Soho Square were both ransacked ; although the latter was not a member of Parliament.   According to *The Morning Post*, " The mob usually begins to assemble about Whitehall and Charing Cross, from whence they proceed through St. Giles, where they gather many recruits ; after which they go along Oxford Street into the squares westward. The mob is particularly enraged against the three great parishes of St. Mary-le-bone, St. George, Hanover Square, and St. James, which comprehend the town houses of nearly all the great families of the United Kingdom.   They complain of these parishes for not having called a Vestry, that is not having called a meeting of the Vestry to Petition against the Corn Bill ; and hence it is that they direct their course up among the great squares, after Parliament rises, or when driven away from the vicinity of the Houses of Parliament."[106]

The subsequent debates in the Commons could not fail to be influenced by the actions of the mobs.   The opposition, however, continued to denounce the unseemly haste with which the bill was being rushed through the Commons and it proposed amendment after amendment to postpone further consideration of the bill.   Baring in particular moved several to this effect.   At the same time he deplored the riots and violence in connection with the Westminster petition, but pointed out that most meetings to draw up petitions in other parts of the kingdom had been orderly.   Despite the attempts of the opposition to deprecate the actions of the Westminster and London mobs, the affair gave the advocates of the corn bill and the government the chance to pose as defenders of " law and order." Western was cheered when he strongly insisted upon the propriety of calling out military forces if the civil power was insufficient to repress a mob which was trying by violence to influence the action of the House. Castlereagh declared that the executive would stand by the legislature firmly and would protect its members along with the laws and liberties of the country. He felt certain, he added, that his feelings were in unison with those " of every man in that House, and with those of every man out of it who knew how to value the British constitution, and the blessings which he enjoyed in this free and happy country."[107]

The newspapers which were opposing the bill, like the members in Parliament, were thrown on the defensive by the riots ; but in most instances they based their defence on the contention that the vast majority of the public meetings were peaceful and that the great mass of citizens had not forfeited their right of petition. *The Morning Post* spoke of the corn bill as " that most obnoxious and ill-advised measure," and insisted, if it had not been for the outrageous riots, " that Reason, supported by the voice of the country, would long ere this have proudly held her seat in the deliberations upon this subject, and the Bill would have stood no chance of passing in its present shape."[108] *The Morning Chronicle* admitted that the riots must be stopped, but said it was absurd for members of the government to say that without protection government, Parliament, the constitution, and the liberties of the English people would be gone. The country at that very moment was complaining " of partially protecting laws, of unequal and oppressive taxation, of neglected representations, and disregarded prayers."[109] *The Glasgow Chronicle* likewise deplored mob violence and disclaimed any responsibility for such action, but resented Waithman's statement before the merchants of London that the corn bill question was one which the lower classes could not understand. *The Chronicle* answered : " This perhaps may apply to the English, but not certainly to the Scots ; whose judicious resolutions, always, we believe, composed by themselves, prove that they are at least as conversant with the subject as the higher classes."[110]

On March 10th the Westminster petition with its 42,473 signatures was presented by Sir Francis Burdett. He stated, in presenting the petition, that he was sorry about the late riots and that he had advised his constituents to give up this crude opposition to the corn bill and to concentrate on an evil which comprised all evils : Parliamentary reform. Under present conditions a man in the position of Castlereagh could carry through, by a large majority, any measure that he saw fit. " Whatever falls from him," Burdett sneered, " is received as if he were clothed with the mantle of the prophet, there he sits as an oracle, and all the people bow obedience to him." Although he himself was a friend of the Corn Laws no one had attacked his house. This speech provoked angry replies from both Robinson and Castlereagh. Robinson in particular was very agitated when he rose to describe how his life was saved by the soldiers when the mob attacked his home. He took occasion to deny that the soldiers were in ambush when they fired from his house, since they even warned the mob before firing. Castlereagh next called attention to the radical change in Burdett's attitude since the time he had so stoutly averred that " every man's house is his castle." Now Burdett justified the lawless mob, and declared that anyone who defended his family and property against such a mob was guilty of murder, and anyone who defied the laws and constitution was a patriot. Castlereagh ended by charging Burdett with attempting to subvert the constitution. The latter replied that his object was to restore and not to overthrow the constitution. Castlereagh, he insisted, would have been impeached and executed for trafficking in seats, in an uncorrupt House.[111]

After the Westminster and other petitions were disposed of, the House took up the question of the third reading of the bill. Amendments to postpone the reading for six months, to substitute 76s. for 80s., and to make the duration of the act co-extensive with the Bank Restriction Act, were all defeated by decisive majorities. Only Baring's motion that the bill might be liable to amendment or repeal during the present session was agreed upon. The bill was then passed.[112]

Now that all attempts to defeat the measure in the Commons had failed, the opposition outside Parliament began to look elsewhere for support. *The Statesman* even hoped that the Prince Regent might refuse assent to the bill or dissolve Parliament.[113] *The Brighton Herald* expressed a similar hope that the House of Lords would pay more attention to the numerous and respectable petitions which covered the table, since it seemed impossible " that so great a portion of the well-informed and well-disposed part of the community can have erred so widely as to have lost all title to the serious consideration and the respectful attention of the Representatives of the people."[114]

On March 13th the corn bill was brought up to the Lords, read the first time, and ordered to be printed. The opposition to the measure was led by Earl Grey and Lord Grenville. In the main the arguments advanced against it were the same as those already given in the Commons: that the petitions against the bill were sufficiently numerous to deserve the consideration of the Lords whether the petitioners were right or wrong in their contentions ; that the committee of the Lords appointed the previous June to investigate the need of further protection had not arrived at any conclusion and had advised that additional inquiries should be made ;[115] that the effect which the measure would have on the wages of labourers should be ascertained before further action was taken ; that nothing could be more absurd than to imagine that a commercial country could keep itself wholly independent of a foreign supply ;[116] and that the aims of the bill were inconsistent since it was argued on the one hand that a cheap, abundant and independent supply of grain would be secured, and on the other hand, that it required a high price to keep the inferior land, in which so much capital had been sunk, under cultivation.[117]

The supporters of the bill had so large a majority in the Lords that they evidently felt safe in confining their arguments principally to showing why additional delay was unnecessary and probably would be disastrous. Sidmouth held that there was no lack of information on the subject since it had been discussed for over twenty years, and that only inconvenience, anxiety and irritation would result from further delay.[118] Liverpool, likewise, was of the opinion that procrastination would be costly to the country and new investigations would throw no new light upon the subject. If Parliament ever intended to give relief to agriculture, now, and not later, was the time to do so.[119]

On March 20th the Lords spent nearly two hours receiving petitions. Lauderdale insisted that he had a letter proving that compulsion was used by mobs to secure signatures. Such a statement aroused the indignation of Grey, who pointed out the absurdity of contending that all names had been secured in this manner. Another evidence of high feeling came when the Lord Chancellor rejected a petition from Forfar because the names and petitions were on separate parchments. Grenville protested unavailingly against rejection on such petty grounds. The bill was finally read a third time and passed. Twenty-one voted in the minority.[120] Eleven of the peers then signed a protest which summed up the reasons for opposing the measure in a much clearer fashion than any of them had done in the course of the debates.[121] The act received the assent of the Prince Regent on March 23rd.[122]

The new law followed in most details the nine resolutions introduced by Robinson on February 17th. It provided that foreign corn could be imported and warehoused at all times, duty free, and taken out for home consumption when the average prices of the various kinds of grain reached the level at which imports were permitted. Foreign corn then could be imported or taken out of the warehouses without paying any duty whatsoever when the prices were at or above the following : wheat, 80s. ; rye, peas and beans, 53s. ; barley, beer or bigg, 40s. ; and oats, 27s. These average prices were to be reckoned quarterly by the method already in operation. The prices of the preceding three months were to determine whether each kind of grain would be admitted during the following three. An exception to this rule was applied to the grain imported from ports between the Eider and Bidassoa. If the average price of any kind of grain for the six weeks immediately following February 15th, May 15th, August 15th or November 15th should fall below the level named above, no more imports were to be permitted from those ports until the new average was taken. The same conditions of admission were to apply to corn from the British North American colonies, except that the average prices were reduced to the following levels : wheat, 67s. ; rye, peas and beans, 44s. ; barley, beer or bigg, 33s. ; and oats, 22s. The act then expressly reserved the rights of London and of any other city or town corporation to retain their local duties, and special exemptions and privileges already guaranteed by law. Further, all acts of Parliament for regulating the importation and exportation of corn, and for ascertaining the average prices, were still to be enforced unless expressly altered by the present act. Lastly, Baring's amendment was tacked on at the end providing that the law might be varied, altered, or repealed during the present session.

Out of all the jumble of conflicting evidence and opinions expressed in reports of select committees, pamphlets, newspapers, periodicals, petitions and speeches in Parliament what conclusions can be drawn ? First, it is necessary to discover, as nearly as possible, what the actual conditions affecting agriculture in the United Kingdom were at this time ; and second, what possible assistance, protection or other, could Parliament give at this time to relieve the landed interest.

The following facts concerning conditions in Great Britain in 1815 seem undeniable. The acts of 1791 and 1804 had been practically inoperative during the years down to 1815, and hence could not be held responsible for the state of agriculture at the end of the Napoleonic Wars. The corn growing area of the United Kingdom had been greatly increased since 1806 by breaking up wastes and improving inferior lands. Both rent and farming expenses had practically doubled during the twenty-two years of war. From 1813 to 1815 agricultural classes, particularly the farmers, suffered severely as a result of the immense crop of 1813, and the poor quality of that of 1814, the return of peace, and the renewed importation of foreign corn. The landlords and farmers had rendered the country a valuable service, especially from 1806 to 1813, in increasing the food supply, and they had been very well paid by high rents and profits. The manufacturing and city population comprised a much greater proportion of the total than they had in 1792. Practically all branches of manufacturing were already protected, as was agriculture by the act of 1804. The state of the currency at the time made a permanent settlement of the problem of protection for agriculture more difficult. Evidence on the remunerative price of wheat was indecisive because of the varying fertility of the soil and the uncertainty of the currency, labour costs and taxation. There was a feeling in Parliament, as Smart has expressed it, that " something must be done for agriculture." Even the opponents of the bill in Parliament had in most instances admitted the necessity of temporary protection while the adjustment to new conditions was made.

What possible choice of policies did Parliament have for regulating the external grain trade ? Actually there were five alternatives for governing both the importation and exportation of grain. On the side of importation these were : first, absolute prohibition ; second, no restrictions ; third, a sliding scale of import duties such as those in the acts of 1670, 1773, 1791 and 1804, and those proposed by Huskisson in 1814 ; fourth, a fixed duty at all times ; and fifth, absolute prohibition up to a fixed price and above that point no restrictions of any kind. On the side of exportation the five possible choices were : first, absolute prohibition ; second, no restrictions ; third, a sliding scale of duties ; fourth, a fixed tax ; and fifth, payment of a bounty when the price was below a certain level. It was possible to combine more than one of these alternatives in the same law. For example, the payment of a bounty, unrestricted exportation between certain price levels and absolute prohibition above a fixed price had all been found in more than one act. But, as a matter of fact, the problem of exportation did not concern the government, or the advocates and opponents of the measure of 1815, since that side of the regulation of the external corn trade had been settled by the law of 1814.

Of the five alternative policies for governing importation the government chose the fifth. The choice was of greater significance than is commonly appreciated. Combined with the act of 1814, it definitely ended the system established by the acts of 1670 and 1689. As it was shown in Chapter III, there was no change of principle in 1765 or 1773 as the corn bill advocates had charged. The principle of the act of 1689, which was to drain off the surplus grain when prices were low by paying a bounty on all which was exported, was destroyed by the act of 1814 ; and the principle of the act of 1670, which was based on three scales of import duties varying with the price of grain, was destroyed by the act of 1815. A comparison of the laws of 1670 and 1804 brings out this point very clearly. The act of 1670 placed a duty of 16s. a quarter on wheat imported when the price was not above 53s. 4d. ; of 8s. when above that amount but not exceeding 80s. ; and of 4d. when above 80s. The act of 1804 placed a duty of 24s. 3d. a quarter on wheat imported when the price was less than 63s. ; of 2s. 6d. when at or above that amount but less than 66s. ; and of 6d. when exceeding 66s.[123] Thus it is evident that the acts of 1814 and 1815 established an entirely new system, on the one hand by abolishing the bounty and, on the other, by substituting a policy of absolute prohibition up to a fixed price level, and freedom of importation, duty free, above that level for one of three scales of duties on importation.

Furthermore, the change was not only one of principle but of spirit as well. Behind the old system lay a definite philosophy of social justice in which the interests of both the producer and consumer were considered. The intention was to keep the price at a level which would be fair to both. Thus up to a certain price the producer was given practically a monopoly of the home market and was assisted in exporting his surplus by a bounty. Beyond certain prices, exportation was forbidden and importation allowed at a nominal duty or free. Those who favoured the acts of 1814 and 1815 claimed that the interests of the consumer were safeguarded by assuring him a certain supply of corn, which could be secured only by giving the producer a monopoly of the home market. Further, it might be argued that although the producers were given additional protection against foreign importation, this was, to a certain extent, offset by the loss of the bounty on exportation in 1814. But both of these arguments fail to take into account that the purpose of the act of 1815 was to keep corn at a high price for the benefit of the producer, and that the bounty would be worthless, since the scale of prices contemplated by the act of 1815 was so much higher than those of surrounding countries that exportation was impossible. The old system allowed for abundant and deficient crops : in the former the surplus would be disposed of with the assistance of the bounty, and in the latter the deficit would be made up allowing importation and by stopping the use of grain in the distillery. Under the new system the fluctuation, up to the point at which foreign grain was admitted duty free, varied directly with the size of the crop at home.   The warehousing scheme, if it functioned as it was expected, would do something to prevent wheat rising much above 80s., but below that the price would have to fall to the level of other countries before much relief could be expected.   Under both the old and new plan the country ran the risk of finding no surplus available for them from the continent, since they wanted imports only in years of scarcity in Great Britain, and grain was not apt to be grown in other countries for exportation except in response to a steady demand.

But in addition to the actual terms of the act of 1815, the debates over the measure make it evident that greater consideration was given the producer than the consumer.   The Parliamentary debates preceding the passing of the acts of 1670 and 1689 are too scanty to give the underlying motives of their advocates ; but those in the sessions of 1773, 1791 and 1804 show that the idea of looking after the interests of both producer and consumer still prevailed.   This statement is not meant to imply that class interests were entirely overlooked by those in favour of additional protection on the three occasions mentioned.   The motives back of the passing of the acts of 1773 and 1791 and 1804 have been dealt with at great length in earlier chapters. It is undeniable that the landed interest used their position in Parliament, both in 1791 and 1804, to raise the import duty level. In each instance, it must be admitted, they had some justice in their claims that advancing prices made greater protection necessary. But at least they clung to the principles of the acts of 1670 and 1689, and attempted to regulate imports and exports according to the quality and quantity of the crops.   It may be argued that the critical condition of agriculture in 1815 justified additional protection much more than in the years 1791 and 1804.   In that case the principles of the act of 1804 should have been retained, and the import duty and the export bounty price levels, and even the amount of the bounty, raised to meet changed conditions.   The abandonment of the whole export side of the policy was due, evidently, to the desire of the Irish landowners to supply the West Indies and other British American colonies with grain.   Yet there was practically no opposition in Parliament to either dropping the bounty or to sweeping away the restrictions on exportation.   Perhaps this was due to the fact that Great Britain had exported very little corn in the past fifty years and practically none in the last twenty-five.   In 1814 Rose made his great fight against the bill of that year on the ground that the old export policy was being dropped.   Yet he received almost no support and the act of 1814 passed with little opposition.   It is still stranger that the landed interest did not see the danger of a one-sided law like that of 1815.   Evidently the only protectionist who protested against it was George Webb Hall, a man who shared with Western the belief in the value of the highest possible protection for agriculture.   He suggested that the bounty be raised from 5s. to 20s.   Of course, he was not taken seriously, but as a matter of fact the policy he suggested was much more logical than the one actually adopted.

Perhaps of greater significance than the changes in principle and spirit in the laws of 1814 and 1815, was the effect of the agitation from 1813 to 1815 upon public opinion.   In Chapters IV and V it was shown that vigorous protests were made against the upward revision of corn duties by the larger cities in both 1791 and 1804. But these protests were negligible in comparison with those of 1814 and 1815. In 1791 the increase in the amount of the duties was a small one, and one which was regarded as fair by many disinterested persons. Furthermore, the manufacturing population was a much smaller proportion of the whole than in 1815. All things considered, the feeling at the time seems to have been that the landed interest had not made undue use of its political power in securing the law of 1791. In 1804 greater resentment was expressed, but two things prevented the affair from stirring up much class hatred against the landlords : first, the measure was rushed through Parliament so rapidly that little time was given to arouse the classes that it affected adversely ; and second, immediately after it was passed, prices rose far above the 63s. limit and remained above that price for so many years that the act was inoperative.

In order to estimate the effect which the agitation from 1813 to 1815 had upon public opinion, it seems best to divide the people into classes and see how each group was affected, or believed it would be affected, by further restrictions on the importation of corn. Although it is impossible to make this division into clear-cut classes, since in many instances the same person might be in two or more of the classes enumerated ; nevertheless, it is the most satisfactory way of considering the influence of this measure upon public opinion. For this purpose the population will be divided into the following classes : landlords, tenants, agricultural labourers, manufacturers, manufacturing and city labourers, annuitants, and stockholders, and the trading class which included all from the great export merchants to the smallest retailers.

The landlords were interested in the bills of 1814 and 1815 because they wanted to keep up the war rents when peace came. For this reason it is unnecessary to inquire further about their attitude, which has been presented over and over again in pamphlets and Parliamentary speeches. The chief point of interest, as far as the landlords are concerned, is that they posed as speaking not only for themselves but for the tenants and agricultural labourers as well.

The attitude of the farmers or tenants is more obscure. The landlords, as spokesmen for all classes engaged in agriculture, always assumed that the tenants were more eager than themselves for additional protection. Unfortunately, there is little direct evidence on the subject because few tenants expressed themselves in pamphlets or in letters to the papers. It is true that many signed petitions to Parliament asking for additional protection, but the small percentage of them who did so makes this test inconclusive. Even the effect of these signatures is partly offset by uncontradicted statements, such as those of the Earls of Carlisle and Grenville, that the tenants were not interested. In the accounts of public meetings in Ireland favouring the corn bill and in the petitions sent to either House, the petitioners are usually described as noblemen, clergy, freeholders and landholders. The word " occupier " in these petitions is the exception and not the rule.

The most striking case of an occupier expressing himself came in the well-advertised affair of a meeting of landholders and occupiers at Warminster. This meeting was called for January 6th, 1815, by John Benett, Esquire, of Pyt-House, for the purpose of drawing up a petition to both Houses on behalf of the proprietors and occupiers of land. When the meeting assembled at the Town Hall, some persons were present who were not owners or occupiers. The petition which Benett presented invited mechanics and tradesmen to sign on the ground that their interests " were blended " with those of the agriculturists. Such a protest rose from the audience after vigorous speeches by Bleeck, an occupier, and Hunt, that Benett drew a pen through the words " tradesman and mechanic." Accounts differ on the vote over the petition which followed. A so-called impartial report by Hunt stated that the chairman declared a majority kept on their hats, which was a sign of opposition. The chairman then announced that the meeting was too tumultous and with Mr. Benett and a few friends retired to the inn. On the other hand, Mr. Benett, in a letter to the *Salisbury and Winchester Journal*, dated January 19th, asserted that the commotion and violent opposition by persons who were neither landowners nor occupiers forced the chairman to remove the meeting to the Arms Inn, where nearly all the landowners and occupiers assembled. It is impossible in this chapter to trace this interesting controversy through all its stages in the provincial and London papers. What is of interest from the point of view of the subject under discussion is the attitude of Bleeck as a tenant. He declared that he was a small proprietor as well as an occupier and hence was, according to the notice calling the meeting, eligible to attend. " Gentlemen," he said, " you may believe me when I tell you that I did not go there to whine and complain ; I did not go there to tell my friends and neighbours that I should ' fly my country ' ; I did not go to petition the Legislature to adopt such measures in my behalf as would have a tendency to raise the price of corn ; I am proud to say, that I did not go with any such feelings, or such intentions : I went to caution the occupiers of lands, and the small proprietors, not to be misled by the fallacious reasonings of the great land-owners,—not to sign any petition for legislative interference, the effect of which must be to keep up the price of corn ; and that such a measure, so far from affording them relief, would tend only to perpetuate their burthens ; I went also to remind some of those who were present, how often they had, in that very room, offered to sacrifice their last guinea, and shed their last drop of blood, in the service of their country ; and though, during the whole progress of the war, they had gone on in an uninterrupted course of prosperity, yet now, as soon as they experienced a little reverse, were the first and loudest to grumble and complain."[124] Even more explicit was his statement that a number of both occupiers and owners were present at the meeting " who were most decidedly opposed to the objects of the petition ; and I can say from my own knowledge that seven-eighths of all the occupiers of lands in this extensive parish, entertain similar opinions."[125]

Whether the attitude of Bleeck is representative of the sentiment of the tenants is difficult to determine. Perhaps the safest conclusion to draw, in view of the meagre evidence, is that the tenants were not the driving power behind the movement which led to the passing of the act of 1815. Clearly the landlords took the initiative in the matter. It is true that the farmers were hit first and hardest by the fall in the price of corn, but no one knew better than the landlords that if it were permanent the fall in rents would ultimately be felt most severely by them. The farmers, although they favoured some sort of relief from the terrible distress which the fall in the price of grain had occasioned, were by no means unanimous in the belief that a new law would alleviate conditions. Many believed with the labouring classes that rent should be reduced, since they feared that rent would be charged on the basis of 80s. wheat. Under this arrangement they would be running the risk that wheat would often fall below 80s., and would seldom rise above that level because of the amount warehoused and waiting to be thrown on the market. Beyond these points it seems impossible to judge the attitude of the tenants.

But if it is difficult to determine the attitude of the tenants toward the corn bill of 1815, it is next to impossible to decide upon that of the agricultural labourers. They had no means of expressing their opinions, if, indeed, they had formulated any. The landlords, however, posed as their protectors and boldly asserted that, unless the price of corn kept up, the labourers would suffer great hardships because they would be thrown out of employment through the inability of the farmer to hire them. As a matter of fact, although the nominal wages of the agricultural labourers had risen from 1792 to 1813, they had not kept pace with the rise in prices ; and hence real wages had actually fallen during these years. This claim of the landlords, that high prices were necessary to afford the labourer employment, did not coincide with the testimony of certain witnesses testifying before the committee of the House of Lords appointed in 1814 to consider the petitions against the corn bill of that year. These witnesses declared that when the price of corn dropped, wages rose because labourers would work only enough to exist ; and when the price of corn rose, wages fell. If this were true, it was necessary for the labourer to work doubly hard when prices were high, and many employers justified high prices on the ground that they kept the working class from idleness. But however much it might be argued that hard work was good for the labourer's soul, the argument that wages were lowest when food was highest could not be reconciled with the contention that high prices were necessary to keep the labourer in employment. Actually, neither position was entirely correct, since, as was stated above, the nominal wages of the agricultural labourer rose, but the real wages fell. Another factor which tended to make this class indifferent to the corn bill was the operation of the Poor Law. In most parts of England, except the north, their wages were supplemented by poor relief and it came to matter very little to them or to the employers whether their means of subsistence came as wages or poor rates. Although the operation of the Poor Law did not do away with the advantages and disadvantages to the

L

labourers of a sudden fall or rise in the price of corn, it did, evidently, produce a fatalistic attitude toward the measures proposed from 1813 to 1815.

The manufacturers were absolutely opposed to the corn bill on the grounds that it would raise the price of corn and with it labour, and thus handicap British manufactures in competing in foreign markets. This argument was used over and over again in speeches and pamphlets, and it is at least as old as Townshend's pamphlet of 1751. But the opposition of the manufacturers was not aggressive and straightforward, as it became after about 1825 and particularly after the organization of the Anti-Corn Law League ; because they were handicapped by the fact that so many manufactured articles were enjoying protection. Wilberforce had pointed out that the importation of about a hundred and fifty articles was prohibited for the purpose of favouring home manufacturers.[126] When this argument was used in favour of the corn bill during the debates in the Lords, Grenville had quoted the resolutions of the Gloucester woollen manufacturers to the effect that, " The principle of exclusion has recently been abduced as a matter of reproach to the commercial interest, and of imitation to the landed ; but a principle so completely exploded and abandoned by the one, is hardly worth the adoption of the other."[127] He further deprecated the benefits accruing to the manufacturers from this policy and declared that if this protection " by the entire prohibition of some articles of commerce and by the imposition of prohibitory duties on others, were considered at the present moment, it would be found that they were almost null."[128] Smart remarked that " the only reasoned answer " he had noticed was that of Grenville.[129] But despite this endorsement, Grenville's answer seems scarcely satisfactory and certainly was not regarded so at the time. The principle may have been abandoned, but the protection that accompanied it had not been. It was not until the manufacturers actually repudiated protection for themselves that they openly dared to attack the landed interest as monopolists. The important fact is that the manufacturers did not offer to give up the protection they were enjoying in 1815 if the landed interest would do likewise. Again and again spokesmen for agricultural protection made this very proposal, doubtless feeling that they were safe in doing so, but the manufacturers and their representatives always remained silent. Grenville's reply then was not a reasoned one. A reasoned reply would have been to offer to give up the protection they enjoyed instead of saying that it was " almost null," or that it was a principle " completely exploded." It would seem that if manufacturers believed what Grenville said, they would have offered to abandon it at once.

Since the manufacturers were unwilling to offer to give up their own protection, they were forced to join with the labouring class and to fight the corn bill with petitions based on the arguments that exclusion of foreign grain would injure the labourers by raising the cost of living and the manufacturer by increasing the cost of production. They had the advantage of such able writers as Ricardo, Torrens, West, Smith and Hume who argued in a conclusive, but polite and academic manner, the advantages of free trade in corn. Torrens even devoted a chapter to prove that it was better for all classes concerned even though manufactured articles were protected. Some of the petitions to Parliament in 1814 and 1815 spoke harshly of the motives of the landlords, but such passages were apt to be found in the parts of the petitions which spoke of robbing the poor classes of the bounty of nature. The bitter personal attacks on the motives and characters of the landlords, which were so characteristic of the anti-Corn Law literature from the eighteen-twenties on, had scarcely begun at this time. Still an occasional flare-up gave promise of what the line of attack was to be. Torrens' work is especially moderate and judicial, yet in one place he says : " To increase the rent roll of proprietors, by compelling all other members of the community to pay more for their corn than they otherwise need to do, would be as gross a violation of natural justice, as it is possible for the mind to conceive. It would be tantamount to laying a tax upon bread, for the purpose of pensioning off the landed aristocracy. It would be nothing better than legalized robbery, taking money out of the pockets of the poor and of the industrious, in order to lavish it on the idle and the rich."[130] Perhaps this reluctance on the part of the manufacturers to oppose the landed interest came as a result of long years of fairly cordial agreement without serious conflict in interests.[131] The clash over the corn bill in 1815 came with too great suddenness for them to attack a class whom they had not previously regarded as rivals. In short, although the manufacturers were opposed to the corn bill on the grounds that it would hurt business, they had not reached the stage where they were willing either to give up their own protection as a price, or to carry on a vigorous campaign against the landowners.

The attitude of the city and manufacturing labourers was unmistakable. Repeatedly in petitions they reiterated the reasons for their opposition. They had a reasonable expectation that with the return of peace, prices of provisions would fall and the more burdensome taxes be removed, thus enabling all classes to " participate in those blessings and advantages to which they had formerly been accustomed in times of tranquility."[132] They expressed themselves not only in public meetings but even more earnestly in riots. Of all classes they expounded their point of view with the least assumption of altruism and the greatest fervour. They were opposed to the corn bill because they believed that it struck a decided blow at their standard of living.

The position of the annuitants and stockholders was one of equally great but less vociferous opposition to the measure. This group was made up largely of owners of stocks and bonds, government employees, and clergy. Relatively they had been hit harder by the rise of prices in the preceding twenty years than the labouring classes, because their purchasing power had been cut practically in half during that period. On the other hand their incomes were larger on the average than those of lower classes and this advantage partly offset the greater relative decline. Naturally, they were anxious to see prices drop to their old level once more so that their incomes would be as valuable as formerly.

Their position was ably stated in several of the pamphlets opposing the bill, and, doubtless, they were solidly back of the petitions sent to Parliament from most of the large cities.

Lastly, the attitude of the commercial and trading class depended more or less on the nature and size of the business of the individual. In reality they should not be listed as a distinct class, but rather should be joined to the particular class or classes whom they served. Thus the large-scale exporter of manufactured goods had precisely the same point of view as the large manufacturer ; the small trades-man or retailer the same as the artisan and mechanic in the vicinity upon whose business he depended ; the importer of corn, the same as the classes who benefited by imported grain ; the tradesman who was dependent on the business of the landlords and farmers, the same as his customers, etc. In the main, however, the commercial and trading classes were opposed to the new law ; the large wholesale and foreign merchant because it interfered with foreign trade, and the small tradesman because it affected his own standard of living and lessened the purchasing power of his customers.

In concluding this phase of the subject it may be wise to repeat the reservation made earlier, that the various classes were not separated by clean-cut divisions. The same man might be a landlord, manufacturer, annuitant and exporter. Nevertheless, the interests of the classes enumerated were largely affected in the manner just described.

Perhaps the most significant phase of this agitation during 1814 and 1815 was the new position in which it placed the landlords. They succeeded, almost as a matter of course, to the position of hatred and opprobrium which the corn dealers and millers had occupied for so many centuries in the eyes of the common people. It has been shown in the earlier chapters that the mediæval city population feared the corn dealers because poor means of com-munication often made grain scarce and monopoly easy and profit-able. Local municipal regulations, which were later expanded into national laws, forbade forestalling, regrating and engrossing. But this feeling against corn dealers did not die out, but continued down to the beginning of the nineteenth century. Even in the first half of the eighteenth century, which was a period of plenty, riots in the few years of deficient harvests were invariably directed against the corn middlemen. From 1757 to 1800, owing to frequent short crops and high prices, the corn trade increased immensely. Even as late as 1800 an enormous number of pamphlets had appeared blaming the corn dealers for the distress. Furthermore, it was at this time that the famous Rusby trial for regrating came up, and at this time that Kenyon delivered his notorious decision denouncing the middle-men as fattening on the distresses of the people. The London mob wrecked Rusby's house and but for his timely escape would probably have lynched him. It is significant that in 1815 it was the houses of the corn bill advocates which were attacked. In 1800 the mob gathered about Mark Lane to " influence " the corn factors and merchants ; in 1815, about the House of Commons to " influence " the landlords. The petitions to Parliament during the eighteenth century usually asked that the wickedness of the corn dealers should be curbed by suspending importation, allowing exportation or some such device. In 1815 the petitioners begged that the proprietors and cultivators should not be allowed to maintain a luxurious standard of living at the expense of the other classes. In short a suspicion and hatred of several centuries' standing was diverted from the corn dealers to the landlords. It may be argued that the analogy between manipulating the grain market for personal profit and passing a protective measure in Parliament, was a slight one. Nevertheless, they had this in common from the point of view of the consumer : both were attempts, by what seemed to the latter wicked means, to profit at their expense. When the manufacturing and commercial classes began in the eighteen-twenties the policy of inciting the lower classes against the landowners, they found it a comparatively easy task, due, in no inconsiderable degree, to the law of 1815.

Only Cobbett of all writers on the subject correctly diagnosed the situation. The law, he prophesied, would not produce the results which the landlords expected, but instead would bring upon them the wrath of the manufacturers and operatives. Briefly, the landed interest would be reviled for their rapacity without securing the benefits which were supposed to accrue to them.

Evidence on both sides of the question and the state of public opinion having been examined, the following questions arise : first, was Parliament justified in passing the act of 1815 ; and second, if not, what action should it have taken ? The answer to these questions depends largely upon a person's opinion of the subsequent economic development of Great Britain. Since the trend of this development has been decidedly industrial and commercial rather than agricultural, the overwhelming majority of economic historians have regarded the law as a tremendous error. But it is interesting to note that, although most of these writers of the past seventy-five years condemn the act severely, few have stated what should have been done at the time. Even the free trade writers who generously recount the difficulties faced and the justification for passing the measure, have, as a rule, refrained from a positive statement of what they believe the proper action at the time would have been. Only List came out bluntly and said that England should have gone over to free trade in 1815.[133]

But since the answers to the questions of the previous paragraph depend on the subsequent economic development of the country, an examination of the possible policies which might have been adopted is necessary. Great Britain was confronted with the option of following one of three policies : first, a continuation of the old protective system with the choice of the possible alternatives on both imported and exported grain, listed earlier in the chapter ; second, an extension of the system of colonial preference ; and third, free trade. In passing the law of 1815 Parliament was merely clinging to the old system, although the principle of the act, as has been shown, was different from that of 1804. Only one writer seems to have suggested the development of an imperial zollverein. On the other hand, several writers suggested the practicability of free trade, but there was no chance of such a policy being put into operation when the landlords controlled Parliament and when the manufacturers declined to give up their protection on manufactured articles.   Great Britain took a few steps in extending colonial preference in the eighteen-twenties and early eighteen-forties, but eventually, in 1846, decided upon free trade.

In deciding which of the three policies Great Britain would have been wisest in selecting in 1815, some consideration must be given to the fact that within thirty-one years of the passing of the law of 1815, both protection and the steps toward colonial preference were discarded and free trade adopted.   If looked at from this point of view, it would seem that thirty-one good years were lost.   However, such a statement can be only an opinion, because it is impossible to tell how free trade would have worked if it had been introduced in 1815 or soon after, and it is equally impossible to tell how it would have been received by the European countries and the United States. Great Britain was at least thirty years ahead of all these countries in manufacturing, especially of textiles and hardware, and perhaps these countries would have put on the same high protective tariffs whether or not the law of 1815 had been passed.   On the other hand, the agricultural interest in these countries might have been strong enough to have brought pressure to bear on their governments not to place too severe restrictions on British textiles and hardware, provided that corn was admitted free into Great Britain.   Another point upon which no decisive evidence can be secured is the ability of the European countries to supply corn to Great Britain in large amounts.   No investigation was made in 1815 of the possibilities of securing the desired surplus from the plains of North Europe, especially Poland, and from America.   It is generally argued that Great Britain adopted free trade at just the right time, on the grounds that previous to 1850 Europe was too impoverished to buy British goods, and that the difficulty of transportation by land or water made it impossible for any country to import a very large percentage of foodstuffs.   But granting that the grain secured under a system of free trade would not have been as great down to 1850, as it was after that date when the gold discoveries and the wonderful expansion of land and water transportation enabled the British foreign trade to make such strides, it does not follow that conditions from 1815 to 1850 would not have been better than under the system actually in operation during those years.

Since nobody in 1815 seriously entertained the idea of free trade, and since there is no really reliable evidence on what the subsequent action of foreign governments would have been, or on the possibility of the importation of a sufficient supply of corn, it may seem useless to speculate on what the result would have been.   Under these circumstances an opinion may be of little value, but all phases of the subject considered, it seems that the wisest policy the country could have adopted would have been free trade, with a transitional period of five years or more of decreasing protection for both manufacturers and corn growers to adjust themselves to the new conditions.

Briefly, the situation after the law of 1815 went into operation was as follows: Parliament had definitely committed the country to a policy of protection against foreign corn in the face of the overwhelming disapproval of the nation. It was done with the hope of keeping up prices of grain and rent. Those who favoured the measure had claimed that it would make prices steady, and those who opposed, that it would make prices fluctuate according to the quality and quantity of the crops in the United Kingdom. Chapters VIII and IX will show which group prophesied correctly. The act, however, left the landlords posing as the protectors of the tenants and agricultural labourers, and facing the hostility of the city labourers, annuitants and manufacturers.

CHAPTER VII

NOTES

[1] *Journals of the House of Commons*, vol. 68.

[2] Smart, *Economic Annals of the Nineteenth Century*, 1801–1820, 1910, p. 373.

[3] The new prices were to be determined as follows : " To the average of the preceding twenty years, of each sort of corn and grain, shall be added one-third part thereof, and the sum shall be the price under which importation may take place at the high duty : to the average price of the preceding twenty years, of each sort of corn and grain, five sevenths parts thereof shall be added, and the sum shall be the price between which, and the price at which importation may take place at the high duty."

[4] These were Mr. Edward Wakefield, who had been to Ireland often but not since Christmas of 1809 ; Mr. John Killaby, who was acquainted with the state tillage in Ireland through his profession as a civil engineer and as owner of a small mill at Tullamore in King's County, Ireland ; Benjamin Shaw, Esquire, who was a member of the House and testified on the expense of bringing grain from Ireland to England ; Mr. Gerald Callaghan who was engaged in the corn trade as a merchant miller and distiller in the house of Daniel Callaghan & Sons of Cork ; and Mr. George Grierson who was owner of about seven hundred acres of land in Ireland and a member of the Farmer Society in Ireland.

[5] Smart, *Economic Annals of the Nineteenth Century*, 1801–1820, 1910, p. 377.

[6] *Hansard*, vol. 26, pp. 644–659.   [7] *Ibid.*, pp. 651–2.

[8] Adam Smith, *The Wealth of Nations*, Everyman's edn., vol. 1, p. 408.

[9] *Hansard*, vol. 26, p. 658.

[10] Smart, *Economic Annals of the Nineteenth Century*, 1801–1820, p. 385.

[11] *Ibid.*   [12] *Ibid.*   [13] *Hansard*, vol. 26, p. 659–62.   [14] *Ibid.*, p. 663.

[15] *Ibid.*, pp. 668–9.   [16] *Ibid.*, p. 667.   [17] *Ibid.*, pp. 986–7.

[18] Smart, *Economic Annals of the Nineteenth Century*, 1801–1820, p. 388.

[9] *Ibid.*, pp. 388–9.

[20] *The Substance of the Speeches of Sir H. Parnell, Bart., in the House of Commons with Additional Observations on the Corn Laws*, p. 167.

[21] Smart, *Economic Annals of the Nineteenth Century*, 1801–1820, p. 407.

[22] Tooke, *History of Prices*, vol. 2, p. 390.

[23] *Hansard*, vol. 27, pp. 417–8 and 523.   [24] *Ibid.*, pp. 523–4.

[25] *Ibid.*, p. 666.   [26] *Ibid.*   [27] *Ibid.*, p. 667.

[28] *The Speech of the Right Hon. George Rose, in the House of Commons, on 5th of May, 1814, on the subject of The Corn Laws*, p. 23.

[29] *Ibid.*, p. 31.   [30] *Ibid.*, p. 33.   [31] *Ibid.*, p. 49.

[32] *The Substance of the Speeches of Sir H. Parnell, Bart., in the House of Commons with Additional Observations on the Corn Laws*, p. 170.

[33] *The Substance of the Speech of Charles C. Western, Esquire, in the House of Commons, May, 1814*, p. 21.

[34] *Ibid.*, p. 22.   [35] *Ibid.*, p. 20.   [36] *Ibid.*, p. 26.   [37] *Ibid.*, p. 27.

[38] *Hansard*, 27, p. 939.   [39] *Ibid.*

[40] Smart, *Economic Annals of the Nineteenth Century*, 1801–1820, p. 414.

[41] *Hansard*, 27, pp. 966–9.   [42] *Ibid.*, pp. 1084–1102.   [43] *Ibid.*, pp. 891–95.

[44] 54th George III., c. 69.

[45] Jacob, *Considerations on the Protection Required by British Agriculture, and on the Influence of the Price of Corn on Exportable Productions*, p. 159.

[46] Broadhurst, *Substance of a Speech against the Proposed Alterations of the Corn Laws*, pp. 27–30.

[47] *Ibid.*, p. 47.   [48] *Ibid.*, p. 50.

[49] Naismith, *An Inquiry Concerning the Proprietory of Increasing the Import Duty on Foreign Corn*, p. 530.

[50] *An Inquiry into the Policy, Efficiency and Consistency of the Alterations in our Corn Laws , in a Letter to Sir Henry Parnell, Bart.*, p. 180.

[51] *Ibid.*, pp. 225–6.

[52] Full titles of these pamphlets are to be found in the bibliography at the end of the volume.

[53] These arguments were : first, the historical one that low prices and abundant quantities before the passing of the act of 1773 and high prices and scarcity since that time ; second, that protection would encourage cultivation and hence insure plenty at moderate and steady prices ; third, that manufactured articles were protected and agriculture was entitled to similar protection ; fourth, that a sudden exposure of English agriculture to the ravages of competition after years of a virtual monopoly was unfair and dangerous ; fifth, that the expense of transportation no longer protected English agriculture owing to great discrepancy in prices between Great Britain and the continent ; sixth, that it was necessary to keep money cheap until retrenchment in the present expenditures was attained and the free import of corn would lower prices and raise the value of money ; seventh, that it was impossible to secure more than a small per cent. of the total consumption abroad so there was a great danger in allowing land to be thrown out of cultivation by admitting even this small per cent. ; and eight, that it was a very dangerous thing to be dependent on foreign nations for subsistence which might at any time use this advantage for political ends : the fate of Rome, ascribed to decay of cultivation in Italy because of tribute corn, was usually cited as a warning example.

[54] *Observations on the Effects of the Corn Laws, and of a Rise or Fall in the Price of Corn on the Agriculture and General Wealth of the Country*, 1815.

[55] Malthus, *Observations*, etc., p. 16.   [56] *Ibid.*, p. 21.   [57] *Ibid.*, pp. 26–33.

[58] *Ibid.*, pp. 34–5.   [59] *Ibid.*, p. 43.

[60] *The Annual Register*, vol. 56, p. 130.

[61] The report gave detailed instructions on how testimony could be given.

[62] *First and Second Reports from the Committee of the House of Lords, appointed to inquire into the State of the Growth, Commerce and Consumption of Grain*, 1814.

[63] *Ibid.*, p. 8.

[64] *Report from the Select Committee of the House of Commons on Petitions relating to the Corn Laws of this Kingdom*, 1814, p. 2.

[65] *Ibid.*   [66] *Ibid.*, p. 4.

[67] *Ibid.*, p. 5. One interesting bi-product of the reports of the Commons and Lords, and the controversy of 1813–1815 was the almost simultaneous explanation by Sir Edward West, writing under the name of " A Fellow of University College, Oxford," and Malthus of the Law of Diminishing Returns and the Law of Rent.

West defined the former as a result of the fact, " that in the progress of improvement of cultivation the raising of rude produce becomes progressively more expensive, or, in other words, the ratio of the net produce of land to its gross produce is continually diminishing," *Essay on the Application of Capital to Land*, 1815, reprinted in 1905, p. 9. He then traced the development of colonists from the pastoral to the agricultural stage where they first cultivate only the most fertile lands. The pressure of population forced them to have recourse to less and less fertile soil, and to a more intensive method of cultivation. The fact that unimproved land was brought into cultivation proved that the additional work was more profitable here than if employed on the old and better lands. This showed conclusively " that in the progress of improvement an equal quantity of work extracts from the soil a gradually diminishing return " (p. 15). The division of labour and application of machinery made labour continually more productive in manufactures, and the same causes although tending to operate in agriculture were more than counteracted by the necessity of having recourse to inferior land, or by more intensive and by expensive cultivation of more fertile parts (p. 24). He then stated that he agreed with Adam Smith's definition of natural rent as a part of the net produce of land remaining after the payment of the common profits of stock on the tenant's capital. The actual amount of the rent of the most fertile land would increase with the bringing into cultivation of less fertile soil, but the ratio of this rent to the gross produce would diminish. This accounted for the unanimous testimony of all witnesses before the Corn Committees " that where lands are in a high state of cultivation the rent bears a less ratio to the gross produce than where they are less expensively tilled " (p. 25).

Malthus, in stating this same law of diminishing returns, spends more space on its application to rent than on an actual exposition. " The rent of land," he defines, " to be that portion of the value of the whole produce which remains to the owner of the land, after all the outgoings belonging to its cultivation, of whatever kind, had been paid, including the profits of the capital employed, estimated according to the usual and ordinary rate of the profits of agricultural stock at the time being " (*An Inquiry into the Nature and Progress of Rent*, 1815, pp. 1–2). The immediate cause of rent is the excess of price over the cost of production of the raw produce. This high price is due to three causes : one, the quality of the earth which produces more necessaries of life than the person employed on the land requires ; second, the qualities these necessaries of life possess of being able to create their own demand ; " and three, the comparative scarcity of the most fertile land " (p. 8). It is the law of diminishing returns which makes it more profitable to employ capital on less fertile soil instead of additional amounts on the most fertile. Since the produce of the less fertile soil covers the labour costs and profits of stock, the more fertile now produces something in excess of these, and this excess is rent (p. 18). Thus with every addition of poor land to the area of cultivation, rent on all more fertile land rises, providing, of course, that the price of produce does not fall (p. 21).

⁶⁸ *Ibid.*, pp. 6–7. Many of the witnesses believed that from 84s. to 96s. was necessary to remunerate the wheat growers, but the committee decided that such witnesses were usually those whose experience had been with cold clay or waste and inferior lands on which the expense of cultivation was, naturally, greater.

⁶⁹ *Ibid.*, pp. 15–16.

⁷⁰ Full titles of these works are given in the bibliography at the end of the volume.

⁷¹ Malthus, *The Grounds of an Opinion on the Policy of Restricting the Importation of Foreign Corn*, 1815, p. 3.

⁷² *Ibid.*, p. 7.   ⁷³ *Ibid.*, p. 8.   ⁷⁴ *Ibid.*, p. 13.   ⁷⁵ *Ibid.*, pp. 23–37.

⁷⁶ *Ibid.*, pp. 47–8.

⁷⁷ Spence, *The Objections against the Corn Bill refuted*, etc., 1815, p. 1.

⁷⁸ Sheffield, *A Letter on the Corn Laws, and on that Means of Obviating the Mischiefs and Distress, which are Rapidly Increasing*, 1815, p. 5.

⁷⁹ Jacob, *A Letter to Samuel Whitbread, Esq., M.P.*, 1815. p. 8.

⁸⁰ Sheffield, *A Letter on the Corn Laws*, etc., p. 33.

⁸¹ Ricardo, *An Essay on the Influence of a low Price of Corn on the Profits of Stock*, 1815, p. 28.

⁸² *Ibid.*, pp. 29–30.   ⁸³ *Ibid.*, p. 31.   ⁸⁴ *Ibid.*, p. 38.   ⁸⁵ *Ibid.*   ⁸⁶ *Ibid.*, p. 48.

⁸⁷ *Ibid.*   ⁸⁸ *Ibid.*, pp. 49–50.

⁸⁹ John Prince Smith, *An Argument and Constitutional Advice for the Petitioners against the Corn Bill*, 1815, pp. 29–31. Smith argued that farmers and landlords should take their chances of land being thrown out of cultivation by low prices, and meet competition as new machinery was met in factories.

⁹⁰ Hume, *Thoughts on the Corn Laws, as connected with Agriculture, Commerce and Finance*, 1815, p. 52.

⁹¹ Torrens, *An Essay on the External Corn Trade*, 1815, pp. 347–8.

⁹² Tooke, *History of Prices*, vol. 2, p. 2.

⁹³ *Hansard*, vol. 29, pp. 806–808.   ⁹⁴ *Ibid.*, pp. 808–18.

⁹⁵ *Ibid.*, p. 831.   ⁹⁶ *Ibid.*, pp. 960–1.   ⁹⁷ *Ibid.*, pp. 978–9.

⁹⁸ The Place Collection, *The Sun*, February 24th, 1815.

⁹⁹ *Hansard*, vol. 29, p. 1117.   ¹⁰⁰ *Ibid.*, p. 1126.

¹⁰¹ Philips and Gascoyne in particular.

¹⁰² *Hansard*, vol. 30, pp. 15–16.

¹⁰³ The Place Collection of Newspaper Clippings, *The Advertiser*, March 7th, 1815.

¹⁰⁴ *Ibid., The Statesman*, March 7th, 1815.

¹⁰⁵ It is interesting to note that *The Morning Post* in 1815 was on the side of the populace and opposed to additional protection.

¹⁰⁶ The Place Collection, *The Morning Post*, March 10th, 1815.

¹⁰⁷ *Hansard*, vol. 30, pp. 78–9.

¹⁰⁸ The Place Collection, *The Morning Post*, March 9th, 1815.

¹⁰⁹ *Ibid., The Morning Chronicle*, March 10th, 1815.

¹¹⁰ *Ibid., Glasgow Chronicle*, March 7th, 1815.

[111] *Hansard*, vol. 30, pp. 107–9.   The Westminster petition was as follows :

" To the Honourable the Commons of the United Kingdom of Great Britain and Ireland in Parliament assembled : The Humble Petition of the Inhabitants Householders of the City and Liberties of Westminster, whose names are hereunto subscribed," Sheweth,

" That your petitioners, fully sensible of the value of our excellent constitution of government, though always lamenting the limitation and abridgment of its blessings by a corrupt system of administration, and the want of an equal representation of the people, have patiently endured the unexampled burthen of taxation, occasioned by the late protracted, calamitous, and, in their judgment, unnecessary war, although they could not but feel that it fell with very unequal severity on the inhabitants of towns, while the owners and occupiers of lands were in general much more than compensated, by the enormous increase of rents, and by the high price of the produce of the earth.

" That on the unexpected and fortunate return of peace, it was reasonable to hope, that this forced and unnatural state of things, would be, in a great degree, corrected ; that the rent of land and prices of provisions would be reduced ; that some of the more grievous and burthensome taxes would cease ; that commerce would flow into its accustomed channels ; that a stimulus would be given to our manufacturing and trading interests, by the freedom of intercourse with foreign nations ; and that all classes of our fellow-subjects would participate in those blessings and advantages to which they had formerly been accustomed in time of tranquillity.

" That your petitioners have, however, noticed with extreme concern and anxiety the introduction into your honourable House of a Bill relative to the importation of Corn, which, if passed into a law, must necessarily and directly produce, and in the judgment of your petitioners is intended to produce, a great permanent increase in the price of one of the first necessaries of life, for the sake of enabling the proprietors and cultivators of land to maintain undiminished a splendid and luxurious style of living, unknown to their fathers, in which they were tempted to indulge during the late war, so highly profitable to them, and so calamitous to most of their fellow-subjects.

" That it appears to your petitioners, that the measure which is the object of this Bill neither has been, nor can be proved to be called for by any necessity ; that, on the contrary, the system of prohibition is injudicious ; and that whenever the produce of all the land which can be cultivated at a moderate expense, is found insufficient for the support of a greatly increased manufacturing population, it is wiser to import, from countries where it can be grown at a low price, the additional quantity of corn required, which the spirit and industry of our merchants would at all times obtain in exchange for manufactures exported, than to diminish the national capital and increase the price of bread, in attempting to force it from barren spots at home by an enormously expensive mode of cultivation.

" That the certain consequences of this prohibitory measure, if persevered in, will be, as your petitioners conceive, considerable inconvenience to the middle orders of society ; great distress to the poorer and more numerous classes ; a most serious injury to the manufactures and commerce of the country ; a great loss of national property ; a powerful inducement to emigration ; and eventually, though not immediately, a bar to the prosperity of the landed interest itself. For these reasons, they are firmly persuaded that it is both impolitic and unjust.

" Your petitioners, therefore, humbly pray that the said Bill may not pass into law, and that the degree of freedom which the corn trade at present enjoys may not be diminished.

" And your petitioners shall ever pray."   *Hansard*, 30, pp. 110–11.

[112] *Hansard*, vol. 30, pp. 115–25.

[113] The Place Collection, *The Statesman*, March 8th, 1815.

[114] *Ibid.*, *Brighton Herald*, March 11th, 1815.

[115] *Hansard*, vol. 30, pp. 125–38.   [116] *Ibid.*, pp. 144–7.   [117] *Ibid.*, p. 197.   [118] *Ibid.*, pp. 140–1.   [119] *Ibid.*, pp. 185–6.   [120] *Ibid.*, pp. 256–63.   [121] *Ibid.*, pp. 263–5.

" 1. Because we are adverse in principle to all new restraints on commerce. We think it certain that public prosperity is best promoted, by leaving uncontrolled the free current of national industry ; and we wish rather, by well-considered steps, to bring back our commercial legislation to the straight and simple line of wisdom, than to increase the deviation, by subjecting additional and extensive branches of the public interest to fresh systems of artificial and injurious restriction.

" 2. Because we think that the great practical rule, of leaving all commerce unfettered, applies more peculiarly, and on still stronger grounds of justice as well as of policy, to the corn trade than to any other. Irresistible indeed must be that necessity which could, in our judgment, authorize the Legislature to tamper with the sustenance of the people, and to impede the free purchase and sale of that article, on which depends the existence of so large a portion of the community.

" 3. Because we think that the expectations of ultimate benefit from this measure are founded on a delusive theory. We cannot persuade ourselves that this law will ever contribute to produce plenty, cheapness or steadiness of price. So long as it operates at all, its effects must be the opposite of these. Monopoly is the parent of scarcity, of dearness, and of uncertainty. To cut off any of the sources of supply can only tend to lessen its abundance ; to close against ourselves the cheapest market for any commodity, must enhance the price at which we purchase it ; and to confine the consumer of corn to the produce of his own country, is to refuse to ourselves the benefit of that provision which Providence itself has made for equalizing to man the variations of season and climate.

" 4. But whatever may be the future consequences of this law, at some distant and uncertain period, we see, with pain, that these hopes must be purchased at the expense of a great and present evil. To compel the consumer to purchase corn dearer at home than it might be imported from abroad, is the immediate practical effect of this law. In this way alone can it operate. Its present protection, its promised extension of agriculture must result (if at all) from the profits which it creates by keeping up the price of corn to an artificial level. These future benefits are the consequences expected, but as we believe erroneously expected, from giving a bounty to the grower of corn, by a tax levied on the consumer.

" 5. Because we think that the adoption of any permanent law, for such a purpose, required the fullest and most laborious investigation. Nor would it have been sufficient for our satisfaction could we have been convinced of the general policy of so hazardous an experiment. A still further inquiry would have been necessary to persuade us that the present moment was fit for its adoption. In such an inquiry we must have had the means of satisfying ourselves what its immediate operation will be as connected with the various and pressing circumstances of public difficulty and distress with which the country is now surrounded ; with the state of our circulation and currency ; of our internal and external commerce ; and above all with the condition and reward of the industrious and labouring classes of our community.

" On all these particulars, as they respect this question, we think that Parliament is almost wholly uninformed ; on all we see the reason for the utmost anxiety and alarm from the operation of this law.

" Lastly, Because if we could approve of the principle and purpose of this law, we think that no sufficient foundation has been laid for its details. The evidence before us, unsatisfactory and imperfect as it is, seems to us rather to disprove than to support the propriety of the high price adopted as the standard of importation, and the fallacious mode by which that price is to be ascertained.

" And on all these grounds we are anxious to record our dissent from a measure so precipitate in its course, and as we fear, so injurious in its consequences."

[122] 55th George III., c. 26.
[123] These duties do not include the 12½ per cent. additional duties by 44th George III., c. 53.
[124] *Corn Laws, Mr. Bleeck's Letter in Reply*, 1815, p. 33.
[125] *Ibid.*, p. 36.
[126] *Hansard*, vol. 29, p. 1029.   [127] *Ibid.*, vol. 30, p. 192.   [128] *Ibid.*, p. 191.
[129] Smart, *Economic Annals of the Nineteenth Century*, 1801-20, note 3, p. 454.
[130] Torrens, *The External Corn Trade*, 1815, p. 317.
[131] Halevy, *A History of the English People in 1815*, 1924, p. 180.
[132] Westminster Petition to House of Commons presented March 10th, 1815.
[133] List, *The National System of Political Economy*, pp. 297-8.

CHAPTER VIII

THE LAW OF 1815 IN OPERATION

Outstanding characteristics of the years from 1815 to 1822—Fluctuation in the prices of grain—Alternate complaints from the agriculturists and consumers —Different causes for agricultural distress assigned from year to year—Low prices in 1815 and 1816—Arguments and proposals of Western—Attitude of the government—Speech of Brougham on behalf of the Whig opposition—Pamphlet and periodical literature during these years—High prices from 1816 to 1819— Enormous increase in importation of grain—Opposition of landed interest to this importation—Little agitation against the Corn Laws during these years—Widespread prosperity in 1818 and reasons for its collapse—Resumption of cash payments—History of suspension of cash payments since 1797—Peel Act of 1819 —Manner it was carried out—Agitation for increased protection on corn from 1820 to 1822—Attitude of the government toward this agitation—Select committee of 1821—Its report and recommendations—Reasons latter not acted upon —Select committee of 1822—The resolutions based on its report—Terms and significance of the law of 1822—Pamphlet and periodical comment in 1821 and 1822—The Merchants' Petition of 1820—Its place in the history of free trade —Conclusion—Years 1815 to 1822 mark the failure of the landed interest to keep up prices of corn by law—Recognition of their failure in the reductions of rent.

THE seven years following the passing of the act of 1815 are marked by the resolute attempts of the landed interest to keep the price of wheat at 80s. Despite these efforts, the price of grain fluctuated violently, and the fluctuation resulted in alternate complaints from the agriculturists and consumers. In fact, the most vigorous demands for a change in the existing system of protection on corn, particularly after 1820, came from the landlords and farmers. Finally, after the new Corn Law of 1822, the landed interest seems to have become resigned to the lower prices and rents. Considering the vigorous opposition in 1814 and 1815 to the bills of those years, the comparative inactivity of the opponents of increased protection is somewhat puzzling. Perhaps the explanation lies in the fact that during over half of these seven years prices were low, and that the lower classes had more pressing grievances to hold their attention. The most significant protest was the Merchants' Petition of 1820 ; but the importance of this document, as will be shown later in the chapter, was due to the fact that it is usually considered to be the first outright challenge of the industrial and commercial classes to the protectionist policy of the landed interest.

The ineffectiveness of the law of 1815 was well demonstrated by the variations in the quantity and quality of each crop in the next seven years. Only in the first few months following March 23rd, 1815, when the act went into operation, did it seem probable that the prediction of its advocates would be fulfilled. The price of wheat rose steadily during the first few weeks that the law was in force, but this rise can

be explained in part at least by the return of Napoleon from Elba and
the uncertainty of the campaign of the Hundred Days.   The quarterly
average for wheat in the period preceding February 15th, 1815, was
59s. 6d., as opposed to 69s. 8d. on May 15th, and 67s. 11d. on August
15th.   But when it became evident that the wheat crop of 1815 was a
good one, and that fair weather had allowed it to be secured in good
condition,[1] the price fell to 57s. 2d. for the quarter ending November
15th, and to 53s. for the one ending February 15th, 1816.

The result of this fall in the price of wheat was the renewal of the
complaints of 1814 and 1815 over the critical condition of agriculture.
Rents had not been reduced, owing to the law of 1815, and now that
prices were even lower than those of the two previous years, the loss
of the capital of the farmers as a result of three successive losing crops
made their condition almost unendurable.   Petitions once more
covered the tables of both Houses of Parliament, not protesting against
additional protection as in 1814 and 1815, but begging for some relief
for the harassed farmers.

The case for the agricultural interest was ably presented in the
Commons on March 7th by Western.   He first cited evidence of the
critical condition of agriculture ; then took up the causes of this state
of affairs ; and lastly, enumerated remedies for the situation. Perhaps
the most vivid illustration given was the Isle of Ely, where, Western
insisted, " In one hundred . . . containing about one-third part of
the island, the number of arrests in 1812 and 1813 were 50, in 1814
and 1815 two hundred and three ; the number of executions, in the
first of these periods, 7 ; in the last, 60 ; amount of executions in the
first period, £765 ; in the last, £18,522.   In addition to the above, the
distresses for rent and drainage taxes, which have been taken within
the last two years, amount to £11,000, and within the same period, in
the vicinity of Ely, several farmers have failed, whose debts altogether
amounted to £72,500, and the creditors, in hardly any instance, have
received a dividend.   It appears also, there are nineteen farms
untenanted in Ely, and the parishes immediately adjoining."[2]

What, Western asked, had caused this ruin and desolation to replace
the flourishing and prosperous condition of agriculture ?   In his
opinion the trouble was not due to any single cause, such as excessive
taxation, the national debt, extensive paper circulation, pressure of
the tithe, or burden of the poor rate.   Although admitting that a
combination of all of these may have had an unfortunate effect, nevertheless, he maintained that agriculture had held its own and had even
made rapid progress until the middle of 1813.   Many people attributed the fall in price to the return of peace, but he did not hold this
opinion because he believed that the loss of the war demand had been
counteracted by the passing of the law of 1815, and because the price
fell in 1813, when there was no expectation of peace.[3]   " The first,
and obvious, cause," he insisted, " has been a redundant supply in the
markets, a supply considerably beyond the demand, and that created
chiefly by the produce of our own agriculture."[4]   He then stressed a
principle which his opponents of the previous year had urged so
vigorously against the law of 1815, namely, " that if there is a small
deficiency of supply, the price will rise in a ratio far beyond any pro-

portion of such deficiency ; the effect indeed is almost incalculable ; so likewise on a surplus of supply beyond demand, the price will fall in a ratio exceeding almost tenfold the amount of such surplus."[5] In addition to the redundant supply, the diminished consumption of the labouring classes, due largely to a decline in their earnings, had done much to reduce the price of grain.   As a result, he pointed out, that " the laborious classes are suffering in a degree quite unexampled— they appear to be starving, as it were, in the midst of plenty : the productive industry of the country is absolutely suspended ; and the sources of future harvests are rapidly falling into decay."[6]

Relief, Western insisted, must come from two sources : from an increased price of grain and other produce as a result of an increased demand ; and from diminished taxation which would reduce the cost of the article and increase consumption.   The second method, although more desirable, was inadequate without the former, because it was impossible to reduce the peace establishment below fifty millions annually, and it was equally impossible for the country to pay this amount at the existing price of grain.   Relief was most needed, from the taxes on barley and agricultural horses, the duty on hops, and the property tax.

Western next made a brief digression to defend the law of the previous year.   He denied that it afforded no relief to agriculture, since without the prohibition more corn would have been imported and the price further depressed.   At this point he injected his argument of 1804, namely, that the way to make corn cheap was to secure a monopoly of the home market to the British producer.   He seems to have been unconscious of the inconsistency of this argument ; for it was against the low price of grain created, as he admitted, by over-production in a monopolized market, that he was at this time inveighing.   His criticism of the warehousing clauses of the act of 1815, however, was more effective.   He objected to the warehousing of foreign grain because it made possible the heaping up of great quantities of wheat which could be dumped on the market as soon as the price reached 80s., and because it prevented speculators from buying up and warehousing home-grown corn when the price was low.

In conclusion, Western proposed his fourteen resolutions, and advised their adoption on the grounds that no harm could result from such an action.[7]

It was not until March 28th that consideration of these resolutions was resumed.   But in the meantime reduction of taxes along the lines suggested by Western had been carried out.   On March 18th the Commons, by a vote of 238 to 201, refused to continue the property tax,[8] and on the 20th the Chancellor of the Exchequer announced that the duty on malt would be discontinued.   Under these circumstances it was natural that the advocates of further relief for agriculture should stress the inadequacy of the price of grain.   Graphic descriptions of the prevailing distress were given.   Perhaps the best known of these was Brand's statement that " Whole parishes had been deserted, and the crowd of paupers increasing in numbers as they went from parish to parish, spread wider and wider this awful desolation."[9] But despite their eloquent and truthful accounts of the suffering of the agricultural classes, the government was opposed to further action on Western's resolutions on the ground, as Robinson expressed it, that the repeal of the malt duty and property tax was sufficient.

When the resolutions were again taken up on April 9th, Brougham distinguished himself by making one of his famous speeches. He held that over-production in agriculture was the chief cause of distress and that rectification of the burdens on land the most important means of relief. The causes for the extraordinary extension of agriculture were numerous; the scarcity of wheat in 1796 and of all grain in 1799–1800; the military and naval operations; the suspension of cash payments in 1797; the great extension of colonial possessions; the completion of the commercial and manufacturing monopoly of the country; and the great improvements in agriculture itself. These improvements, he insisted, were not only proved by statistics, but were evident even to a careless observer. " Not only have wastes disappeared for miles and miles, giving place to houses, fences, and crops; not only have even the most inconsiderable commons, the very village greens, and the little strips of sward by the wayside, been in many places subjected to division and exclusive ownership, and cut up into cornfields in the rage for farming; not only have stubborn soils been forced to bear crops by mere weight of metal, by sinking money in the earth, as it has been called—but the land that formerly grew something has been fatigued with labour, and loaded with capital, until it yielded much more; the work both of man and cattle has been economized, new skill has been applied, and a more dexterous combination of different kinds of husbandry been practised, until, without at all comprehending the waste lands wholly added to the productive territory of the island, it may be safely said, not perhaps that two blades of grass now grow where one only grew before, but I am sure that five grow where four used to be."[10]   The full effects of these improvements, which were not felt until after 1812, combined with unusually good harvests had depressed prices.

Turning to the Corn Law of 1815, Brougham declared that, although he was not in the House when the acts of 1804 or 1815 were passed, he had favoured both measures.   On the other hand, he was greatly opposed to a bounty on export, on the grounds that it would perpetuate over-cultivation; and to Western's proposal to exclude foreign corn from the warehouses of the country, because foreign exporters could as readily pour in corn from the other side of the water as to unload it from warehouses.   He concluded his speech with the reiteration that the burden of taxes on land must be lightened, and suggested that the government should " break into " the sinking fund to the extent of six million pounds.[11]

The government was still unwilling to make greater concessions in the way of the reduction of taxes.   Castlereagh in replying to Brougham blamed the delay in passing the act of 1815 for much of the distress of the farmers, and expressed the opinion that it was only a matter of time until the price of wheat would rise to 80s., and all the difficulties would be solved.   Finally, a select committee was appointed to consider the expediency of additional duties on foreign seeds, wool, and other produce.   However, since nothing touching the Corn Laws resulted from the activities of this committee, its work may be ignored.[12]

Outside Parliament the matter of agricultural distress received considerable publicity. A few able pamphlets were published, which proved conclusively, what no one seriously doubted, that the distress was real. The arguments for protecting agriculture were the same as those used in 1814 and 1815, and the same as those which were to be used during the next thirty years. On the whole, none of them gave as fair and as well-rounded a presentation of the causes as did Western in his speech. Most of the pamphleteers attacked excessive taxation[13] as the chief cause of distress, and advocated the lightening of the burden as the surest means of alleviating the distress. Others followed or preceded Western in his suggestion for government magazines to store the surplus produced at home. Dr. George Skene Keith believed that the present Corn Law was a failure, and that a new one should be passed imposing a duty of 32s. on wheat when the price was under 64s., of 16s. when under 72s., and of 8s. when under 80s. ; and of 1s. when at or above 88s. On the other hand, in order to avoid the fluctuation caused under the existing law by free exportation, he suggested a bounty on exported wheat of 6s. to 8s. when the price was under 54s., and one of 3s. to 4s. when under 72s.[14] None of these suggestions was taken up by the government, or by members who favoured some kind of relief for agriculture.

The results of the agitation of 1816 may be summed up as a repeal of the malt and property tax, but a failure to secure free warehousing and government stores to absorb the surplus home production.

From this time until 1819 no further complaints of agricultural distress are heard. The miraculous disappearance of complaints was due to the rapid rise in the price of wheat even before the harvest of 1816. The monthly price for March was 55s. 4d. ; for May, 73s. 7d. ; and for August, 82s. 1d. This rise previous to the harvest was the result of certain knowledge that the crop would be defective. After a mild winter, severe frosts and heavy snows in February were followed by a cold spring. The weather remained colder and drier than usual until the middle of July, when heavy rains set in and con-continued through the entire progress of the harvest. Such weather resulted in a corn crop of great deficiency in quantity and inferiority in quality. Recognition of the inevitability of such a harvest, combined with rising prices in Germany and France, had caused the advance noted.[15] But despite this rapid upward movement of prices, the quarterly averages of August 15th were not high enough to admit foreign grain. However, by those of November 15th wheat, rye, barley, and Indian corn were all admitted duty free, and by those of February 15th, 1817, beans and peas were added. Yet, in spite of the fact that it had been obvious since the spring of 1816 that the ports would be open before the end of the year to foreign corn, much less grain than would naturally be expected was imported or taken from the warehouses.[16] The explanation of this neglect of the English market is, evidently, to be found in an even greater demand for grain on the continent. In southern Germany, Austria, and France the rise in the price of corn had been earlier and greater than that in

M

Great Britain.   In fact the harvest of 1815 was less abundant on the continent than in England, and hence the rise of prices had begun in the fall of that year.   In August of 1816 the French ports were thrown open to importation, duty free, and in November the government offered a bounty on imported corn.[17]   This, in a large measure, accounted for the small importation to Great Britain after November, 15th, 1816.   In fact, so critical was the situation in France, especially in the spring of 1817, that a considerable quantity of corn was shipped from England to France.[18]   As a result, British exports for this year reached the highest figure since 1792 with 378,431 quarters.

In 1817, fine weather in the summer and during the harvest was responsible for the assumption in September that the crops were better than was later found to be the case.[19]   On the strength of this erroneous assumption the price of wheat for the quarter ending November 15th fell 5d. below 80s., and hence the ports were closed to further importation.   At the same time the ports were closed to oats and rye. This state of affairs lasted only until February 15th, 1818, when the quarterly average once more threw open the ports to wheat and oats. In France, where the rise in prices had been much greater down to the middle of 1817 than in Great Britain, the same good weather was experienced after June.   Here the effect was to send prices much lower than in Great Britain.   Thus while France, because of higher prices, evidently, attracted the foreign corn in 1816 and in the first part of 1817, after that it was diverted to Great Britain, where the prices had not fallen to such an extent as in France.   The result was that an immense amount of grain, especially wheat, was imported into Great Britain during 1817.   No less than 1,780,679 quarters of grain, of which 1,020,949 were wheat, was brought into consumption, not including 699,809 imported from Ireland.   But these figures are small in comparison with those of 1818, when by all odds the greatest importation of grain in any single year of British history up to that time took place.[20]   The total amount of foreign corn entered for consumption was 3,538,564 quarters, of which 1,593,518 were wheat. This amount was exclusive of the 1,207,851 from Ireland, which brought up the total to 4,746,415 quarters.   The previous high mark was in the famine year of 1801, when with the aid of huge bounties 2,406,445 quarters were secured.

The size of these importations was anything but pleasing to the landed interest.   Both landlords and farmers discovered that under the law of 1815 the price of wheat could rise very little above 80s. unless there was a greater demand elsewhere for foreign grain.   Thus, under ordinary circumstances, the surplus of Europe would be thrown on the British market as soon as the price reached 80s.   Under these conditions, the farmer believed that he was denied the advantage of an enormous rise in price to offset the disadvantage of a short crop. It was rumoured that the landlords and tenants would petition for a new corn law or a repeal of the present one,[21] although just what they wished to have substituted was not clear.   On January 22nd, 1819, the first of these petitions from the landholders of Rutland asked for such protection to agriculture as manufacturing and industry enjoyed under the Navigation Laws.[22]   On February 25th a vast number of petitions from landholders in nearly every part of England were read. These petitions, while asking for additional protection, did not state whether or not it was to come by raising the import price level.[23] But despite the petitions the government opposed any change in the Corn Laws. A combination of the flimsiness of the evidence for additional protection, and a memory of the danger from public opinion in 1815, were, doubtless, responsible for this stand. Robinson expressed this point of view in his statement that " His Majesty's ministers were decidedly of the opinion, not only that it would be unadvisable to agitate such a question, but in any case of any substantive proposition being brought forward, would meet it with the most determined resistance. They looked upon the last measure as one of sound legislative policy, and that had produced all the benefits which were expected to be derived from it to the agricultural interests of the country. But they would consider it to be the height of imprudence, amounting almost to insanity, to introduce any new measure ; or to revive discussions, which could have no other effect than that of exciting differences and animosities from one end of the kingdom to the other."[24] Despite the firm stand of the government, petitions continued to arrive from the landed interest, until the effects of the closing of the ports to foreign grain were again felt.[25]

The season of 1818 was a very extraordinary one, and had considerable influence on the size of the importation. After a wet spring, dry weather set in about the middle of May and lasted until the middle of September in the part of the country north of the Trent. This drought aroused expectations of a much greater deficiency in the crops than the harvest subsequently proved, and played an important part in the enormous importation of the year.[26] The crop of 1819, on the other hand, had the benefit of a mild winter and a good spring, so that a full average harvest resulted despite the complaints from southern England of injuries from previous bad weather.[27] Consequently the prospects of a good crop, combined with the unnecessarily large importation of the year before, were enough to close the ports in the first part of 1819.

At first sight it is difficult to understand why there was so little agitation against the Corn Laws in the years immediately following 1815. It is true that until the end of 1816 the trouble did not lie in high, but rather in low, prices. Nevertheless, during the year there was much rioting, barn burning, and other violent actions by the agricultural labourers, but these were directed against unemployment and hard times rather than against the Corn Laws. On the other hand, the distress among the city operatives was extremely severe because of the inability of Europe and the Americas to absorb as much of the British manufactured goods as had been anticipated. There were many bread riots among the unemployed in the industrial classes, but like those indulged in by the agricultural labourers they appear to have been directed against unemployment and starvation conditions rather than against the Corn Laws specifically. There are few pamphlets or articles in periodicals on the Corn Laws, but there are many covering the commercial, industrial, and agricultural distress of the time. Usually the Corn Laws are mentioned, but only as one of the many causes for the maladjustment.   In 1817 agriculture was relieved by the rapid rise in the prices of grain, but commerce and industry were merely further depressed.   Beginning late in the year and lasting until the early part of 1819, a great revival in trade took place.[28]   Castlereagh went so far as to state that 1818 was " the most splendid year ever known in the history of British commerce."[29] The periodicals of the time breathed a spirit of healthy optimism and seemed serenely confident that the prosperity would be one of indefinite length.   Unfortunately it did not last very long.   " Two things evidently were forgotten.   The one was that a nation which depends so much on other nations for its materials and for its market, cannot prosper unless these other nations are prospering also. . . The other was that, in manufacturing industries the tendency of great activity of trade is always to induce employers to sink capital in concrete forms sufficient not only to meet the maximum demand at the time but also to meet the expected greater demand."[30]   Thus the commercial crisis in the United States and the revolutions in Spanish America were to have a calamitous effect upon this British trade boom.   When Parliament rose in July of 1819, the prospect was as dark as it had been bright in January, and unemployment and starvation were widespread. The enormous drop in the foreign trade is shown by the fact that imports for 1819 were over six millions, and exports nine millions, less than those of 1818.

By all odds the most important step in 1819, as far as influence on future corn law agitation is concerned, was the act for the resumption of cash payments, usually called the Peel Bill.   The suspension of cash payments in 1797, the decline of the value of the paper pound from 1797 to 1815, and the discussion of the report made in 1810 by the committee appointed to consider the high price of bullion form the background for a study of resumption.[31]   In this connection it is sufficient to trace the fluctuation in the value of the paper pound from 1815 to 1819.   In 1797, before cash payments were suspended, gold bullion was convertible in coin at the Bullion Office of the Bank of England at 77s. 6d. per ounce, or at the Mint at 77s. 10½d.[32]   But after the suspension of cash payments the price of gold reckoned in paper pounds fluctuated violently.   For example, " In August, 1813, it attained the height of 110s., making the value of £1 in notes only equal to that of 87¼ grains of gold instead of 123¼.   By October, 1814, the divergence had greatly diminished ; the price of gold had sunk to 85s.   In February, 1815, just before the escape of Napoleon from Elba, it was a little higher, at 89s., and that event made it shoot up to 107s.   After Waterloo it fell rapidly, and was only 83s. in October, 1815.   In the next twelve months it fell to 78s. 6d., never again during the suspension to rise above 83s."[33]   With gold only 7½d. above the coinage par, the Bank of England decided to try the experiment of redeeming notes on a small scale.   The directors announced that all one- and two-pound notes issued before 1812 would be redeemed in gold.   Few were presented for redemption.   Emboldened, they offered to redeem after May, 1817, all such notes issued earlier than 1816.   Again comparatively few were presented.   They then undertook to repay in gold notes of all denominations issued before January 1st, 1817. The price of gold had now risen to 80s., and large numbers of notes were presented for redemption. From August of 1817, to February of 1819 the treasure of the Bank fell by $7\frac{1}{2}$ millions, and the notes by only $4\frac{1}{2}$. Thus Cannan concludes that " the Bank must have been counteracting the effect of that action by issuing additional new notes."[34] If such action had not been taken, the process of increasing the gold and decreasing the notes in circulation might have brought the latter to par.

Early in 1819 two secret committees of the Lords and Commons were appointed to consider the resumption of cash payments by the Bank of England. Peel was made chairman of the committee of the Commons. As a result of the recommendations of this committee an act was passed providing for the resumption of cash payments after May 1st, 1823. Until that date payment was to be made only in bullion in the shape of sixty-ounce gold bars. Between February 1st and October 1st, 1820, these bars were to be worth 81s. an ounce in notes ; between October 1st, 1820, and May 1st, 1821, 79s. 6d. ; and between May 1st, 1821, and May 1st, 1823, 77s. $10\frac{1}{2}$d.[35] Despite this arrangement the Bank, by an agreement with the government, resumed payments of note in coin on May 1st, 1821. By that date the landed interest was blaming the Peel Act for the fall in the price of agricultural produce.

It has already been shown that the harvest of 1819 was a fairly good one, except in parts of southern England. Although the ports were closed to wheat as early as February 15th, the price did not fall greatly before the harvest of 1820. In August of 1819 it was 75s., and in August of 1820, 72s. The lowest point was 64s. in January of 1820. Despite the relatively high price of wheat, Parliament was overwhelmed with petitions from agriculturists asking for relief from the distresses they were suffering. The remedy usually suggested was to make it more difficult to import foreign grain either by raising the import price level or by putting on a fixed duty of 30s. a quarter, as George Webb Hall proposed. But because it was recognized that either of these proposals would raise a storm of protest greater than that of 1815, and since the city labourers were suffering severely from the industrial and commercial depression, the attack was made on the system of taking the import price averages. It was charged that so much fraud and inefficiency were prevalent in the operation of the law of 1815 that the actual price received by the farmers was far below that determined by the average. Thus, it was claimed, the ports were thrown open to importation when the farmers were being paid little more than 70s.

In addition to this attack on the mode of taking averages, no striking new arguments were brought forward for increasing the protection on grain, but practically all the ones used in 1815 were reiterated with unusual vigour. Petitioners insisted that agriculture asked only the same protection as was given to manufacturers ; that the burden of the poor rates and other taxes pressed almost exclusively on land ; and that corn could be brought from parts of Europe at half the price which British farmers could afford to sell. The law of 1815, it was pointed out, was clearly a failure, since the enormous imports of 1818 showed that it had failed in its primary purpose of making the country independent of foreign grain.

Those who opposed additional protection to agriculture countered with even more effective arguments. They held that the extent of agricultural distress was exaggerated ; that the agriculturists were relatively better off than the other classes ; that the average price of wheat for the five years following 1815 was only 1s. 2d. a quarter under the 80s., which had been fixed as the " remunerative " price in the act of that year ; and that any additional protection was useless since no foreign wheat had entered the country since February 15th, 1819, and no grain of any variety since August 15th.

The government also had no sympathy with the demands of the agriculturists. Robinson, who had introduced the bill of 1815, opposed any change in that measure in language very unlike that used during the debates of that year. After admitting that any land would produce corn if sufficient capital and labour were expended upon it, he asked, " But would any man say that it was possible the legislature could justly be called upon to adopt such measures as would retain bad land in cultivation, when the circumstances which had originally led to its cultivation were totally changed ? It was not by any act of the legislature that land had been called into cultivation, and it was not, therefore, to be expected that by any act of the legislature it should be continued in cultivation."[36] Liverpool was even more emphatic in his opposition. " I was," he declared, " one of those who, in the year 1815, advocated the Corn Bill. In common with all the supporters of that measure, I believed that it was expedient to grant an additional protection to the agriculturist. I thought that, after the peculiar situation of this country, during a war of twenty years, enjoying a monopoly in some branches of trade, although excluded from others : after the unlimited extent to which speculation in agriculture had been for many years carried, and considering the low comparative price of agriculture produce in most of the countries of Europe ; the landed property of the country would be subjected to very considerable inconvenience and distress, if some further legislative protection were not afforded to it. I thought the Corn Bill was advisable with a view of preventing that convulsion in landed property, which a change from such a war to such a peace might otherwise produce. On that ground I supported the Corn Bill."[37] But the present situation, he held, was entirely different. " Whatever may be the distress under which agriculture labours, I am convinced that there are no such certain means of aggravating that distress as perpetually to tamper with it by the adoption of new measures and new laws. Whatever may be the system adopted, let it be adhered to. Let the farmer and the tenant, let the buyer and seller, know that it will be adhered to ; and they will soon come to some arrangement for their mutual advantage."[38] He then pointed out that the supporters of the bill had said that 80s. would be the maximum price for wheat, and the average of the past five years had proved them correct. Turning to the question of the taking of price averages, he readily admitted that, if the present system did not work properly, it must be amended. " But," he added,

" I must decidedly object to any alteration in the principle of taking averages."[39]

In the end a committee in the House of Commons was appointed at the request of the landed interest, but Robinson managed to have the inquiry limited to the mode of " ascertaining, returning, and calculating " the average prices of grain in the twelve maritime districts, and to any frauds committed in violation of the existing laws. The committee reported in July and made many elaborate suggestions for improving the methods of taking averages and preventing frauds ; but by the time the report was placed before the House, it was too late in the session to take any action. Consequently the problem was postponed until the next year.

When agricultural distress was considered again in February of 1821, the landed interest had a much better case than it had in the two previous years. This change for the worse in agriculture was largely a result of the crop of 1820. The winter had been severe and the spring, although variable, was so cold that the crops were somewhat backward in the middle of June. From that time on through the harvest, the weather was favourable, with the exception of some heavy showers in July. All crops turned out far larger than was expected ;[40] and witnesses before the committees of 1821 and 1822 testified that the crop was at least a fourth above the average. But it was not generally known how large it actually was until wheat of this year continued to appear in the markets during the next two and three years.[41] The natural result was a rapid fall in the price of grain, particularly of wheat, and a tremendous increase in the problems of the farmer. As one writer stated, " Whatever might be the cause of the change, its effect was, to diminish exceedingly the gross returns of the farmer. Some of his outgoings were, no doubt, diminished also ; but the diminution was only partial, and especially in articles of luxury not at all proportional to the fall of the money-value of grain. His receipts were no longer sufficient to replace the funds which had been expended on permanent improvements ; much less to afford a reasonable rent. All his fixed money payments, such as rent, assessed taxes, and the interest of money borrowed, pressed upon him with augmented weight. Thus gloomy and cheerless was the prospect to all who had invested their property in the cultivation of the soil. They flattered themselves, however, that the distress was of a transient nature ; and hoping for the speedy approach of better times, they made shift to pay their rents either by borrowing money, or by taking it from their capitals ; so that the landlords did not yet participate in the existing embarrassments to the extent they were ultimately to feel them."[42]

Under these conditions it was difficult for the government to refuse an inquiry into the possible means of relieving agriculture. Besides, no less than twelve hundred petitions had been sent to Parliament in 1819 and 1820 complaining of the operation of the law of 1815.[43] Accordingly on February 26th, 1821, Robinson introduced a resolution proposing, on the strength of the recommendation made on the previous July by the committee appointed to consider the taking of the price averages, that the maritime towns and counties be substituted for the twelve maritime districts in determining the aggregate prices.   This resolution was agreed to, and a bill based upon it was ordered to be brought in.

But this concession did not satisfy the country gentlemen in Parliament.   They felt that the predicament of the farmer and the number of petitions justified some additional attempts at relief.   As one writer expressed it, " No new causes of embarrassment had sprung up, but the price of corn still continued low, landlords were still reluctant to reduce their rents within natural limits, and farmers still laboured under all the difficulties arising from that diminution or destruction of their capital, which the change in the price of their commodities had occasioned.   Numerous petitions for relief were presented to parliament ; but it was easier to demand than to discover a remedy.   Some wished the government to alter the standard of the currency ; some suggested the propriety of expunging part of the national debt ; some placed their hopes in the removal of taxes ; and some had a perfect faith in the omnipotence of high protecting duties.   All called for inquiry."[44]   The result of this feeling was a motion on March 7th by Gooch, the Member for Suffolk, that a committee be appointed to consider the petitions.   The motion was carried unanimously, and Gooch was appointed chairman of the committee.[45]

On June 18th the committee gave its report, and the 344 pages of evidence which accompanied it showed, at least, that the task had been conscientiously performed.   The first part of the report was devoted to an enumeration of the many causes that had contributed to the low prices of agricultural products, to a sketch of earlier periods of depression, and to an explanation of the maladjustments in manufacturing and agriculture.   The committee assumed that the basis of a wise regulation of the Corn Laws was to maintain " a permanent and adequate supply of corn, at prices as steady as possible," and that this depended upon guarding, as much as legislative interference was able, " against the effects of fluctuations of seasons."   The existing system was unsatisfactory because " It exposes the markets of the country, either to be occasionally overwhelmed with an inundation of foreign corn, altogether disproportionate to its wants ; or, in the event of any considerable deficiency in our own harvest, it creates a sudden competition on the continent, by the effect of which the prices there are rapidly and unnecessarily raised against ourselves."[46]   One of the worst features of the law of 1815 was the tendency it excited among continental nations to exclude British manufactured goods. In this conflict of retaliatory exclusion Great Britain was handicapped, since she absolutely required the corn of other nations when there was a deficiency in her own crops, whereas other nations felt no such overwhelming necessity for securing British manufactured goods.   In addition, such a sudden influx of foreign corn tended to derange the exchanges, and might lead to draining the country of coin and bullion when cash payments by the Bank were resumed.

The committee, going on the natural assumption that Parliament would not wish to abandon entirely the principle of the existing law, suggested that a fixed duty be imposed on imports when the ports were opened to foreign corn.   If this suggestion were followed it would be necessary to fix the imports at a lower level, because otherwise the duty would merely check importation and enhance prices even beyond those of the existing law. The chief benefits of such a change would be to check extravagant speculation and huge imports, and if these were accomplished many evils complained of in the petitions would be remedied. The influence of the members of the landed interest on the committee was clearly shown by the cautious reservations which were added to this suggestion. The committee stated that they wished to have it distinctly understood that they were " not insensible to the importance of securing the country from a state of dependence upon other, and possibly hostile countries, for the subsistence of its population," and " still more anxious to preserve to the landed interest, the weight, station and ascendancy, which it has enjoyed so long, and used so beneficially."[47]

The committee also took up some of the specific complaints of the petitioners. One group of the latter ascribed the distress to the amount of public burdens, combined with diminished incomes with which to meet them. The committee, while admitting that the weight of taxation unquestionably pressed more heavily when prices were low, denied that the existing agricultural distress was due either exclusively or principally to this cause. A second group of petitioners asked protection not only for grain, but also for all agricultural products equal to that given manufactured goods. The committee answered that the phrase " equal to that given manufactures " was a misleading one, since it was doubtful if any manufacture of importance, with the exception of silk, derived any real benefit from protection. Those who suggested that a 40s. duty on wheat would give agriculture this " equal " protection were told that Parliament would not seriously consider such a proposal, since it would be impossible to collect the duty in times of high prices and distress. A third group of petitioners complained of the warehousing clause in the act of 1815 on the ground that it caused dealers to invest their money in foreign corn instead of British ; and that the large stock ready to be brought into consumption when the price reached 80s. depressed the market. To the first objection the committee answered that there was no proof that much capital was invested in corn, or would be invested in British corn, if the warehousing of foreign grain were abolished ; and to the second, that it would be as easy to store this grain in Flanders or Holland as on the Thames.

In conclusion the committee frankly stated that after a long and anxious inquiry they had been unable to discover any means of removing the present pressure. So far as it was " the effect from our own growth, the inconvenience arises from a cause which no legislative provision can alleviate ; so far as it is the result of the increased value of our money, it is one not peculiar to the farmer."[48]

Parliament rose on July 11th, and hence the report was not formally taken up during the session. But the attitude of the landlords and farmers was not difficult to imagine. What they wanted was action and relief, and not a report which told them what they already knew, namely, that their case was desperate. In fact, of all the proposals made for changing the Corn Laws, or alleviating distress, only the bill introduced by Robinson for taking the price averages governing importation by maritime counties and towns, instead of districts, became a law.[49] The result was that the landed interest became more outspoken in their denunciation of the commercial classes than they had been since 1815. On the other hand, the report received warm commendation from some quarters. *The Annual Register* character-ized it as " one of the most valuable documents ever laid before Parliament. It is full of the soundest views ; and, at the same time that it admits abstract principles in all their extent, modifies them by due regard to the circumstances of the times. It is a pleasing monu-ment of the rapid progress, which enlarged notions on a very abstract subject have made, within the last few years, among that class of the community, on whose opinions the improvement of our legislation and the excellency of our internal public economy chiefly depend."[50]

Considering the extent of the distress it is noteworthy how few pamphlets and how little space in newspapers and periodicals were devoted to the subject of agricultural distress during the year 1821. None of the pamphlets of this year added anything to the speeches in Parliament, or to the exhaustive study made by the committee appointed to consider the petitions. Lord Stourton in his two letters to the Earl of Liverpool blamed the disaster on the selfishness of the people and their rulers in not giving some additional protection to agriculture in 1814.[51] Other extreme statements of this sort were made, but specific remedies were few. George Webb Hall, for example, suggested permanent duties of 40s. a quarter on wheat, 26s. 6d. on rye, 13s. 6d. on oats, and 20s. on barley.[52] But, as it has already been pointed out, the committee dismissed this suggestion in a very sum-mary fashion. When the complaints in the petitions, in Parliament-ary speeches, in pamphlets, and in periodicals are examined, the most striking fact is the absence of any general agreement as to the cause of agricultural distress.

From the time Parliament rose in July of 1821 until the question was again taken up in the next session in February of 1822, this distress had become even more severe. The winter of 1820–21 was mild, and the spring until May unusually warm ; but a cold May and June, a showery July, and a very rainy harvest season, ruined this early promise. It was soon found that the quality rather than the quantity of the wheat had suffered.[53] The large surplus from 1820, combined with the large quantity and inferior quality of the crop of 1821, sent the price of wheat down to 48s. 6d. in February of 1822, and to 38s. 10d. by November of the same year.

In February of 1822 the question of agricultural distress was re-opened in Parliament by a new flood of petitions. One from the county of Norfolk, presented on February 7th, complained that all-devouring taxation was the cause of the trouble.[54] This was typical of the line of attack which was to be employed during the year, in and out of Parliament, by the landed interest. During the previous year, it was pointed out, there had been no general agreement among the agriculturists as to the cause of distress, but " excessive taxation " now became the battle cry. At the very opening of the session Hume moved as an amendment to the address following the King's speech that the House represent to His Majesty that excessive expenditure was the chief cause of the distress and should be reduced in every branch of the government. The motion was beaten by 89 to 17.[55]   On February 11th Brougham led an attack on the government, the object of which, seemingly, " was to feel the pulse of the Country Gentlemen, and to ascertain how far they were likely to abandon the government."[56]   He ascribed the distress to excessive taxation, of which an undue share was borne by the agricultural classes.   He proposed reductions in salaries in every department, and the decrease of taxation by four million pounds in order to offset the effect of the resumption of cash payments.[57]

The government did not allow these attacks to pass unnoticed. Castlereagh, now Lord Londonderry, replied to Brougham a few days later in a speech which showed clearly the stand the government intended to take during this session.   First, he pointed out that the solution of the problem of agricultural distress did not lie in taxation. The taxes which the farmers paid were only about one-seventh of their rent ; and hence, if all these taxes were abolished, the distress would not be removed.   Further, the actual reductions in taxes already made by the government amounted to three million pounds, and it was useless to expect any great additional saving beyond this sum.   Second, he stated that he would be glad, if it were possible, to assist the farmers by an advance of four million pounds as the manufacturing and commercial classes had been helped earlier by one of five millions.   The greatest drawback to such an advance was the fact that there were no large and tangible properties in the hands of a few farmers.   Third, he gave notice that he intended to move for a revival of the agricultural committee, although he expected no relief for the farmer from any change in the law of 1815.

On February 18th Londonderry moved that the report of the committee of 1821 and the petitions complaining of agricultural distress be referred to a select committee.   The motion was passed, and the committee appointed after a vigorous debate.[58]   The country gentlemen headed by Benett insisted that rigid economy and retrenchment were needed ; and Ricardo, representing the commercial interests, held that the cause of distress was excess of supply over demand. Peel brought out the only new point of any importance when he emphasized the significance of the enormous imports from Ireland. He held that three successive good harvests combined with these Irish imports were responsible for the existing distress and not foreign imports or changes in the currency.   But the most interesting part of the debates turned on the authorship of the report of 1821.   Gooch, the chairman, said that he had not drawn it up, and that it seemed worse than useless to him.   Without mentioning Huskisson's name he threw out some very obvious hints.   Wodehouse next stated that Huskisson had also drawn up the report of 1814, and proceeded to read contradictory selections from the two.   Huskisson then denied writing the report of 1814, and insisted that it was the work of Parnell. He admitted that he had drawn up the one of 1821 under protest, but pointed out that many alterations were made in his draft of which he did not approve.   He was willing to defend his original draft, but not the report as it was published.   He ended by declaring that after such

unjust accusations he would decline to serve on the new committee.[59]
With few exceptions the committee was a reappointment of the one
of the previous year. Londonderry was made chairman in place of
Gooch.[60]

In the House of Lords the question of agricultural distress was
taken up on February 26th. The immediate occasion was the presentation of the Kent petition complaining, as usual, that taxation
was the cause of the depression. The Earl of Liverpool, speaking on
behalf of the government, took as firm a stand against further reduction in taxes as Londonderry had in the Commons. The remedies
proposed in most petitions, he held, were based on errors. It was
absurd to talk of reducing taxation to the level of 1792 in view of the
enormous increase in population, manufacturing, foreign commerce,
cultivation, and wealth in general. Furthermore, the distress was not
confined to Great Britain but extended over France, the Netherlands,
and northern Europe. As proof he quoted the reply of the King of
France to the French Chamber of Deputies. " I know the difficulties,
which attend the sale of corn. Notwithstanding the recollection of a
recent dearth, I have for the first time restrained the importation of
foreign grain. The laws have been executed ; but no law can prevent
the inconvenience which arises from a superabundant harvest. The
whole of Europe experiences it at this moment." For the same
reason, Liverpool pointed out, the distress could not be due to the
debt and taxation, because countries without any national debt were
suffering as much as Great Britain. He next showed that only during
the present year was taxation blamed for the distress. Since 1815
taxes had been reduced from seventy to fifty millions ; and while
many argued that this merely balanced the fall in the value of the
currency produced by Peel's Act of 1819, it was absurd in view of the
fact that the depreciation in 1819 was only four per cent., and at its
greatest extent never more than twenty-five per cent. Some of
Liverpool's references to the landlords indicated that their savage
attacks on the government had not gone unnoticed. If prices, he
pointed out, had fallen to the level of 1792, rents had not. The fall
in prices had benefited the *great majority* of people, especially the
annuitants and city population. What the agriculturists really
wanted was a market for their produce, and the government was
unable to legislate one into existence.[61]

On April 1st the select committee appointed by the House of Commons gave its first report. The most important recommendations
dealt with draining the surplus grain from the market and with
amending the law of 1815 to prevent the sharp transition from no
importation to unlimited importation. The committee advised that
the excess supply should be deposited in warehouses until the market
price became more favourable. The government, under the proposed
arrangement, would, upon request, make advances on the deposited
grain. The remedy suggested to avoid the transition from no importation when the price of wheat was below 80s. to unlimited importation when at or above that amount, was to impose a duty of 12s. to
15s. on wheat imported when the price ranged from 70s. to 80s., and
one of 5s. when the price was from 80s. to 85s.

The newspaper comments on the report were not very enthusiastic. *The Traveller* of April 2nd compared the recommendations unfavourably with those of the preceding year, and pointed out that they would give satisfaction to nobody, since, " Those who wish for increased restrictions on the commerce in grain, believe that its recommendations are inadequate ; and those who would establish a system of greater freedom consider its principles unsound."[62] *The Morning Chronicle* condemned the report on the grounds that the solution proposed was absurd, and prophesied that " This wretched production merits the execration of the whole country, and will satisfy no class."[63]

On April 29th Londonderry gave the government's proposals. He declared that he was still sceptical about the wisdom of having the government advance a million pounds on the security of warehoused wheats ; but since the committee had advised it he was incorporating the proposal in his ten resolutions. The measures, he pointed out, which deserved the attention of Parliament, were : finance, currency and relief for agriculture. The resolutions which dealt with relief for agriculture were : first, an advance of a million pounds in exchequer bills for wheat in warehouses when the average price was under 60s. ; second, a reduction in taxation by the amount saved in converting naval and military pensions into an annuity of 2,800,000 pounds; third, permission to grind and ship warehoused foreign corn ; and fourth, a new Corn Law based on the recommendations of the committee.[64]

From April 29th to May 13th the debates raged over these resolutions. Western, Ellice, Attwood, Lethbridge, and Burdett, especially, attacked either the resolutions or the government. Some blamed the Peel Act of 1819,[65] and insisted that its repeal was necessary. Others attacked the proposed remedies, particularly the first resolution, because they were of no value to agriculture. Londonderry finally withdrew the proposal to advance a million pounds in exchequer bills on the ground that it was not supported by those who had brought it forward.[66] This action in turn aroused Attwood. He insisted that three sessions had now been wasted on committees whose recommendations were ignored. Lethbridge reproached the government for goading to desperation the loyal agricultural interest, and expressed the hope that the House of Commons would not be led astray by the false speculation and " abominable theories of the political economists." He then moved that a duty of 40s. be imposed upon imported wheat at all times, and a corresponding one on about twenty other articles of agricultural produce. The next day this motion was beaten by 243 to 24.[67] Burdett took advantage of the question under discussion to abuse Londonderry and the government. He expressed great sympathy for the landowners who were in the hands of such a weak and corrupt ministry. Amid loud cheers he declared that such an administration was a national calamity and that there was no hope for agricultural improvement under the existing government.[68]

During the course of these debates Attwood and Ricardo clashed over the Ricardian theory of rent and the effect of the Peel act on prices. But since this ground was covered more thoroughly in the pamphlets of Ricardo and Sinclair, which will be taken up shortly, these speeches will be passed over.

On May 13th, after a long debate, Londonderry's resolutions were adopted.   A bill based on them was then introduced in the Commons, passed, and on June 5th sent to the Lords.   The greatest opposition came from the Earl of Lauderdale.   He vainly attempted to secure the passing of a motion to have the bill read a third time in three months.   After the bill was passed on June 10th[69] he entered a protest on the Journal which summed up the point of view of the more extreme members of the landed interest.[70]

Under the provisions of this act, foreign wheat was to be entirely excluded until the price reached 70s.   But at this point importation was not permitted duty free, as it was under the act of 1815 ; for when the price was between 70s. and 80s., a duty of 12s. was levied ; when between 80s. and 85s., one of 5s. ; and when above 85s., only 1s. Corresponding scales of duties were fixed for other kinds of grain. The colonial preference was retained and the price level on wheat lowered from 67s. to 59s.   However, this scale of duties did not go into operation until the price of wheat reached 80s., because that part of the act of 1815 which forbade the opening of the ports until that price was reached was not repealed by the new law.   It will be shown in the next chapter that the price of wheat never reached 80s. as long as the act of 1822 remained in force.   Still another obstacle was an additional duty of 5s. during the first three months that the ports were open.   Thus the duty on wheat for these three months was not 12s., but 17s.   Special arrangements were made to cover the grain warehoused before May 13th in order that persons who owned this wheat could not accuse the government of bad faith.   The owners were given the option either of taking out their wheat for home consumption when the price reached 70s., upon the payment of a duty of 17s. during the first three months, and of 12s. after that time ; or when the price reached 80s., duty free.   All grain warehoused after May 13th was subject to all the regulations of the new act.[71]

When the extent of the depression in agriculture and the time devoted to the subject in Parliament is taken into consideration, it is surprising that a greater number of pamphlets was not published in 1822.   Perhaps those who were most interested in securing relief for agriculture devoted their time to drawing up the petitions which were sent to Parliament.   Those who were opposed to any additional protection for agriculture used the same arguments as the speakers in Parliament.   They ascribed the distress to an over supply produced by too abundant harvests in Great Britain and Ireland.   Western, as usual, represented the point of view of the landed interest, not only by his speeches in the Commons but in his two addresses to the landowners of the United Kingdom.   His attitude in the second is worth noting, because it indicates the line of attack which the landlords were to follow in the next few years.   In 1822, we have seen that the distress was almost universally ascribed by agriculturists to excessive taxation ; but now the resumption of cash payments was to supplant this explanation.   Western, in his second address, placed all of the blame on resumption.   " Peel's Bill, I say, is the *sole* cause of our *excessive* and unparalleled distress.   It is not that abundant harvests may not lower the price of corn occasionally to some degree of temporary injury to the growers ; but no human being ever heard before of their being *ruined* by the blessing of Providence on their labours. . . . It is not a *ruinous* abundance of corn, but a destructive famine of money that is the bane of the country ; let us have plenty of corn and plenty of money."[72]

By all odds the best pamphlet published was Ricardo's *On Protection to Agriculture.* It was a systematic treatise on the fragmentary ideas expressed in his speeches in the Commons. Its significance lies in the influence that it had on future anti-Corn Law agitation. He considered, in turn, remunerating prices ; the effects of taxes imposed on a particular commodity, of abundant crops on the price of corn, of Peel's Bill on prices, of a low value of corn on the rate of profits ; how a system of protection like that established by the act of 1815 was certain to produce fluctuating prices ; and whether the present state of agricultural distress could be attributed to taxation. He held that the present low range of prices was due more to over supply than to the Peel Act ; and that the fall in prices had been increased by the operation of the Corn Law of 1815 which made the average price in England higher than in other countries. To obviate the difficulties he proposed to have foreign wheat excluded until the price reached 70s. and then admitted on a payment of a duty of 20s. This duty was to be reduced by 1s. a year until it reached 10s. To prevent a glut following an abundant harvest, he suggested that a drawback of 7s. a quarter should be allowed on all wheat exported.

Ricardo concluded his pamphlet with a detailed argument against the alleged danger of dependence upon foreign grain. In the first place he maintained that no great quantity could be obtained from abroad without increasing the remunerative price and thus obliging those countries to have recourse to inferior lands. " In proportion as the price rose abroad, it would become advantageous to cultivate poorer lands at home ; and, therefore, there is every probability that, under the freest state of demand, we should not be importers of any very large quantity."[73] But granting that England should become dependent on foreign countries for a large supply, then such a quantity would be constantly and uniformly grown expressly for that purpose. Thus it would be as much to the interest of the producing, as to the purchasing country to see that friendly relations were maintained.

Sinclair in *An Answer to a Tract recently Published by David Ricardo, On Protection to Agriculture,* undertook to refute the conclusions of this pamphlet. It betrays all the impatience of a practical agriculturist with a despised " theorist." Sinclair found that nearly all the general principles laid down by Ricardo did not coincide with his own experience. He denied that the value of wheat was regulated by that grown upon marginal land : first, because other articles grown, and not corn alone, determined profits ; second, because the better wheat came to market first and set the standard ; and third, because in speaking of soils the influence of climate was neglected. He also declared that Ricardo in his rage for throwing out of cultivation the inferior soils overlooked the following points in their favour : 1. That inferior soils pay less rent to the landlord, and less local taxes ; 2. That a large portion of them are usually kept in grass, and only a moderate portion of them cultivated ; 3. That they are in general sufficiently fertile for the production of green crops and the inferior sorts of grain ; 4. That by skilful management they occasionally yield grain of superior quality ; and 5. That by constant culture, skilfully managed, they may become ultimately fertile."[74]

Perhaps the most regrettable part of the whole agitation to relieve agriculture was the fairly widespread opinion among the landed interest that a reduction should be made in the interest on the national debt. This feeling increased when it became obvious that Parliament was not going to enact any extreme measures to relieve the distress. A rather angry debate occurred in the Commons on June 14th over the matter. It came as a result of a petition from Kent, complaining of agricultural distress and asking for Parliamentary reform, to which a rider was tacked requesting that the interest on the national debt be reduced. Knatchbull, the member from Kent, presented the petition, but insisted that the rider did not represent the point of view of the Kentish landowners. He blamed the Whig leaders who had called the meeting and had expressed no opinion upon the proposal. Lord John Russell defended his actions at the Kent meeting, and asked Knatchbull why, if a majority opposed, they had not introduced resolutions expressing their true opinions. He insisted that Parliamentary reform was not to be associated with the reduction of the interest on the national debt, which he would consent to only in case of overwhelming necessity.[75] Londonderry protested even against this phrase as giving "too much countenance to the spoilation of property." Brougham boldly answered that the rider was not worse than the actions of Londonderry in the resumption of cash payments. Others went further and declared that it was equally dishonest to contract a national debt which could not be paid, and suggested that it would be better to follow the French example in dealing with assignats and adjust the debts contracted in depreciated currency to the new standard.[76]

The Annual Register bore witness to how widespread the feeling for partial repudiation was among the gentry. After dealing with the country meetings in which the chief panacea proposed was the reduction of taxes, one writer stated that " These measures, however, were paltry and insignificant, when compared with three topics, which formed the darling themes of the meetings which arrogantly presumed to speak the sense of the people of England. These three topics were, parliamentary reform—the abolition of tithes—and a forcible reduction of the interest of the national debt. The last of these was spoken of with complacency, and listened to with a toleration, which a few years ago would have been incredible. Country gentlemen of moderate politics and of consequence in their own districts, were not ashamed to allude to this wild and wicked dream of rapine, as a menace which might soon turn out to be most necessary and most prudent, and to hear with approving silence, or at the most with faint and hesitating dissent, the virulent rhapsodies of political bigots or incendiaries, who recommended its immediate adoption. It was a melancholy thing to see how effectual pecuniary embarrassments had been to delude many of that class, in whose soundness of principle and understanding

England had long reposed confidence, into a forgetfulness of justice
and policy. Beginning to feel the temporary pressure of distress,
they dared to raise, or foster the cry, ' Plunder all, in order that we
may live more at our ease.' . . . It was most fortunate for the
country, and most creditable to our nobility, that, although many of
our country gentlemen (more especially of the secondary class) were
seduced by circumstances into notions quite irreconcilable with justice
our high aristocracy remained true to old English maxims. The
representatives of all our great families, whether ministerial or anti-
ministerial, with scarcely a single exception, opposed and reprobated
every proposal tending to recommend a breach of faith with the public
creditor ; and their unanimity and firm adherence to sound principles
tended, no doubt, to arrest the progress of the pernicious doctrines
with respect to national bankruptcy, which were beginning to have
some currency."[77]

Practically all of this chapter has been devoted to questions of
agricultural distress ; and, as far as the Corn Laws are concerned, to
the attempts of the landed interest to secure greater protection. Such
emphasis may seem unjustifiable since the opposition to the Corn Law
of 1815 came from the industrial and commercial classes of the cities,
both capitalists and labourers, who suffered a great deal during the
years from 1815 to 1822. Although both factory workers and agricultural labourers strove to improve their critical condition during
these years, in the main, their complaints were not directed against
the law of 1815. Since protection on grain played a comparatively
small part in their distress, as this chapter has shown, and since they
themselves blamed the Corn Laws only during the brief periods when
wheat was high ; the vicissitudes of the agricultural labourers and city
operatives do not fall within the scope of this chapter.[78]

The period from 1815 to 1822 was also something of a surprise
because of the failure of the industrial and commercial groups to make
a continuous fight against the law of 1815. Like the labouring classes
they seem to have neglected the question because the price of grain
was low during most of the period and because other problems pressed
more severely. But the significance of one step taken by this interest
is, in view of the free movement of the next twenty-six years, difficult
to over-estimate. This was the famous Petition of the Merchants of
London presented to the House of Commons on May 8th, 1820, by
Baring.[79] This petition has been described as the " originating
impulse " of the free trade movement. When combined with the
elaborate discussion which followed its introduction in the Commons,
with the proposal to relax the terms of the Navigation Laws, and with
the resolutions of the government to gradually take off the existing Irish
duties, " it seems clear that 1820 may be taken as the year in which Free
Trade began to be looked upon as a practical as well as an ideal policy."[80]
The spirit of the petition is, perhaps, portrayed most clearly in its
third paragraph, " That the maxim of buying in the cheapest market
and selling in the dearest, which regulates every merchant in his
individual dealings, is strictly applicable as the best rule for the trade
of the whole nation."[81] Its real significance, as far as the Corn Laws
were concerned, was the more favoured position in which it placed

N

the merchants and manufacturers in dealing with the landed interest. In Chapter VII it was pointed out that although the commercial and industrial groups presented good academic treatises in 1815 on the advantages of free trade in corn, they did not offer to give up their own protection on manufactured articles if the landed interest would surrender theirs on grain. It was not until such a movement as the one started by this petition was under way that the fight against the Corn Laws could be carried into the enemies' country. An offer of this kind deprived the landed interest of the argument that they asked only the same protection as that granted to manufacturers, and forced them back on the position that it was not safe to depend upon foreign countries for the means of subsistence. Had the free trade movement of the next quarter of a century failed, the Merchants' Petition would have occupied a less important position in history ; but since it was the initial blow against the old system which was to crumble in 1846, it is, unquestionably, one of the most important points taken up in the present chapter.

The seven years from the passing the Corn Law of 1815 to the one of 1822 were not marked by uniformity either in agriculture or in industry. Agriculture was in a critical condition when the law of 1815 was passed, and continued in this state until after the harvest of 1816. Then came nearly three years of high prices, to be followed in turn by a severe slump which lasted until the harvest of 1823. Thus 1815 did not begin and 1822 did not end a period of agricultural depression. Furthermore the act of 1822 did not usher in a new policy of protection for agriculture because, owing to certain provisions already described, it never actually came into operation down to the time that it was repealed by the act of 1828.

In spite of all this apparently contradictory evidence these seven years are a unit as far as the Corn Laws are concerned. They mark the definite failure of the landed interest to keep up by legislation the price of grain and hence of rent. They made the fullest use of their political power to keep the price of wheat at 80s. a quarter, and yet during nearly five of these seven years Parliament was deluged with petitions complaining of distress and asking for further concessions to agriculture. Only in the latter part of 1816 and in 1817 and 1819 were there many protests against the law of 1815 by the industrial and commercial classes, and these were years of industrial depression. In 1818, a year of great prosperity, complaints from both sides ceased. Yet it is noticeable that appeals came more readily from the farmers when agricultural prices were low than from the consumers when the prices were high. This can be explained on the fact that rents were fixed after 1815 on the basis of 80s. wheat. Also complaints from the farmer were bound to be given more careful consideration since the landowners were more heavily represented in Parliament than the commercial and industrial interests ; and landlords knew that continued low prices meant arrears, and eventually reduction in rent.

But even though these seven years do mark the failure of the landed interest to keep up the price of wheat by means of their votes in Parliament, the law of 1822 does not give any indication of a change in attitude. What really marked the end of the period under discussion, was not the passing of the act itself, but the recognition by the landlords that prices and rents could not be kept up by law even when a monopoly of the home market up to 80s. was given to wheat. From 1813 until the act of 1815 was passed, the excuse given for low prices was inadequate protection.   Another excuse would have been necessary in 1816 if the bad crop had not sent up the price of wheat. From 1819 to 1822 a multitude of explanations was offered.   It was finally driven home to most of the landed interest, with the exception of George Webb Hall and his followers, that the solution did not lie in additional protection, since after 1819 the existing law had done all that could be done in keeping out foreign corn.   All but the most extreme representatives of this group, at least in Parliament, shrunk from imposing a fixed duty of 40s. a quarter on wheat, reducing the interest on the national debt, or again depreciating the currency.   So the obvious flaws in the law of 1815 were remedied, but nothing further was done.   Clearly there was no justification for the landlords keeping up rents on the basis of 80s. wheat when it was obvious that prices would not be maintained at that level.   As a result there seems to have been a general reduction in rent at this time, as well as an adjustment of wages and general expenses to new conditions.   Smart quotes as typical of the early part of 1823 the following statement : " Something like a new era has begun in agriculture ; rents have been reduced and leases renewed ; things, in short, are getting into something like their old train—the effects of the revulsion from war to peace are beginning to disappear."[82]   Thus landlords appear to have become resigned to a return to normal conditions.   This does not mean that all complaints of distress or suggestions for remedies stopped, for, as it will be shown in the next chapter, they continued, though with diminishing volume, during the first months of 1823.   But the great mass of landlords and tenants seem to have realized, after the matter was thrashed out in the session of 1822, that Corn Laws could not keep wheat at 80s.

Thus the important factor in the period from 1815 to 1822 was the opposition to the law of 1815 by the landed interest because it did not give adequate protection to agriculture.[83] But no sooner were the landlords and tenants reconciled or resigned to the existing system than the manufacturers, foreign traders, and town labourers started a determined drive for reducing or sweeping away protection on agricultural products.

CHAPTER VIII

NOTES

[1] Tooke, *History of Prices*, vol. 2, p. 3.

[2] *Hansard*, vol. 33, p. 33-4.   [3] *Ibid.*, pp. 34-6.   [4] *Ibid.*, p. 36.   [5] *Ibid.*

[6] *Ibid.*, p. 41.

[7] *Ibid.*, pp. 55-6. These resolutions were :

"1. That the portion of the community, whose capitals are engaged in agriculture, as well as those numerous classes whose employment depends thereon, are at present suffering under the pressure of unexampled distress.

"2. That the continuance of such distress is fraught with extreme danger to the most important interests of the country.

"3. That the demand for the extended produce of our agriculture is, at this time, insufficient to produce that price, which is necessary to cover the heavy charges and burthens upon it.

"4. That the demand for barley has been very materially reduced, by the excessive duties to which it is subjected in the course of the various operations which adapt it to the use of the consumer.

"5. That the continuance of those duties, during peace, when the facility of smuggling is so much increased, cannot fail to injure the home manufacture of spirits, which must still farther diminish the demand for barley.

"6. That it is therefore necessary to reduce the duties on malt, beer and spirits.

"7. That in order to equalize the supply of grain and promote its cultivation, it is desirable that an appropriation should be made from the extra produce of abundant harvests, to supply the deficiency of seasons less favourable.

"8. That the admission of foreign corn to be warehoused, prevents such applications to our own occasional abundance, and assigns to foreign agriculture the formation of those stores, which might otherwise be created from the produce of our own.

"9. That it is therefore expedient, to repeal so much of an act of last session for the regulation of the corn trade, as permits the warehousing of foreign corn, at all times, duty free.

"10. That in order further to promote the appropriation of a part of our present abundance, and reserve it for further consumption, it is expedient to aid the means of those individuals who may be disposed so to employ their capitals, by an advance of exchequer bills, to a limited amount.

"11. That excessive taxation renders it necessary to give protection to all articles, the produce of our own soil against similar articles, the growth of foreign countries, not subject to the same burthens, and, in conformity with that policy which has been uniformly observed, of protecting by duties and encouraging by bounties or drawbacks, all our other manufactures.

"12. That it is therefore expedient to impose additional duties and restrictions on the importations of all articles, the produce of foreign agriculture.

"13. That it is expedient, under due limitation, to encourage, by bounty, or drawback, the exportation of the redundant produce of the agriculture of the United Kingdom.

"14. That the tithe and the poor rates to the payment of which those whose capitals are engaged in agriculture are almost exclusively subjected, have recently been felt to press with increasing unexampled severity, and that it is therefore necessary to relieve them, as far as possible from the operation of other burthens."

[8] *Ibid.*, p. 451.   [9] *Ibid.*, p. 671.   [10] *Ibid.*, p. 1094.   [11] *Ibid.*, p. 1116.

[12] For an account of the recommendations of this committee, see Smart, vol. 1, pp. 534-8.

[13] Especially Jacob, *An Inquiry into Agricultural Distress.* Keith, *Statement of Facts*, etc.; *Observations on the State of the Country since the Peace.*

[14] Keith, *Statement of Facts*, etc., pp. 20 and 23.

[15] Tooke, *History of Prices*, vol. 2, p. 14.

[16] Even the usual import figures are misleading because they include the amount warehoused rather than that actually brought into immediate consumption.

[17] Tooke, *History of Prices*, vol. 2, p. 16.

[18] *Ibid.*, p. 17. [19] *Ibid.*, pp. 19–20.

[20] The ports were open after February 15th to oats, all year to barley and Indian corn, from May 15th to August 15th (to June 20th only from ports between the Eider and the Bidassoa), after November 15th to rye, and after February 15th to wheat, except from September 26th to November 15th between the Eider and Bidassoa.

[21] Smart, vol. 1, p. 654.

[22] *Hansard*, vol. 39, pp. 67–9. [23] *Ibid.*, pp. 256–60.

[24] The Place Collection, January 24th, 1819, p. 87.

[25] On February 15th the ports were closed to wheat; on May 15th to rye and beans; and on August 15th to barley, Indian corn, oats and peas, with the exception of grain from ports between the Eider and Bidassoa, to which the ports were closed by the six weeks average of June 26th.

[26] Tooke, *History of Prices*, vol. 2, pp. 21–2. [27] *Ibid.*, p. 80.

[28] Smart, vol. 1, p. 610. [29] *Hansard*, vol. 39, p. 366. [30] Smart, vol. 1, p. 671.

[31] Cannan, *The Paper Pound* of 1797–1821, gives an excellent survey of this subject.

[32] *Ibid.*, p. 7.

[33] *Ibid.*, p. xxvii. Quoted from *Lords' Committee on Resumption of Cash Payments*, 1819. [34] *Ibid.*, p. xxxi.

[35] Smart, vol. 1, p. 679.

[36] *Hansard*, vol. 1, Second Series, p. 643.

[37] *The Speech of the Right Honourable The Earl of Liverpool*, May 26th, 1820, pp. 21–2.

[38] *Ibid.*, pp. 23–4. [39] *Ibid.*, p. 28.

[40] Tooke, *History of Prices*, vol. 2, p. 82. [41] *Ibid.*, pp. 82–3.

[42] *The Annual Register*, 1820, p. 5.

[43] Smart, *Economic Annals of the Nineteenth Century*, vol. 2, p. 3.

[44] *The Annual Register*, 1821, p. 66.

[45] The other members of the committee were Castlereagh, Robinson, Althorpe, Bankes, Brougham, Huskisson, Knatchbull, Wortley, Baring, Parnell, Wodehouse, Western, Holme, Sumner, Escourt, Bourne, Tremayne, Rowley, Calthorpe, Hunter, Blair, Irving, Lethbridge, Littleton, Bridges, Calvert, Ricardo, Curwen, Denis Browne, Williams, Wynn and Foster.

[46] *Report from the Select Committee, to whom the several Petitions Complaining of the Depressed State of the Agriculture of the United Kingdom were referred*, 1821, p. 22.

[47] *Ibid.*, p. 36. [48] *Ibid.*, p. 54.

[49] 1st and 2nd George IV., c. 87.

[50] *The Annual Register*, 1821, p. 68.

[51] Stourton, *Two Letters to the Right Hon. The Earl of Liverpool*, 1821, p. 26.

[52] This suggestion was taken up by a committee of agriculturists who presented a petition to the Commons asking for protection of this nature.

[53] Tooke, *History of Prices*, vol. 2, p. 83.

[54] *Hansard*, N.S., vol. 6, pp. 96–101. [55] *Ibid.*, p. 47.

[56] Smart, vol. 2, footnote p. 61. [57] *Ibid.*, p. 98.

[58] *Hansard*, vol. 6, p. 509. [59] Smart, vol. 2, p. 68.

[60] *Hansard*, vol. 6, p. 509. [61] *Ibid.*, pp. 681–717.

[62] The Place Collection, 1822, p. 111. [63] *Ibid.*

[64] The other six resolutions were: first, a vote of credit placed at the disposal of the Lord Lieutenant to alleviate distress in Ireland; second, a million applied to public works in the same country; third, to take from the Bank an advance of four million pounds on exchequer bills to pay off the Navy five per cents. and to inflate the currency; fourth, to renew for ten years the act permitting country banks to issue notes under five pounds; fifth, to convert naval and military pensions into an annuity of two million eight hundred thousand pounds running

for forty-five years ; and sixth, to tie up the five million pounds clear surplus to accumulate at compound interest.

[65] Especially Western, Lethbridge and Burdett.

[66] *Hansard*, vol. 7, pp. 365. Subsequently, the resolution permitting the grinding of foreign corn in bond for exportation was also withdrawn.

[67] *Ibid.*, p 453. [68] *Ibid.*, pp. 413–14. [69] *Ibid.*, pp. 1556–57.

[70] *Ibid.*, pp. 1557–58. The protest read as follows :

" Dissentient : Because this bill repeals the regulations as enacted by the 55th of George III., c. 26, whereby, the state of the agriculture of the United Kingdom, it was by Parliament provided, as necessary to afford to agriculture a degree of protection equal to what the law gives to other branches of industry, that wheat from abroad should not be exposed to sale until the price in our markets amounted to 80s. ; and at a time when it is admitted to a competition with our farmers when wheat is at 70s. a quarter, on paying a duty of 17s. for the first three months, and afterwards of 12s. till it rises to 80s.

" Under this bill, therefore, the farmer will not only be deprived of the monopoly he enjoyed in the home market, till wheat attained the price of 80s. a quarter, but he will be exposed when it is at 70s. to a competition with the foreign grower, whose wheat, value 35s. may, on payment the duty of 17s. be brought into our market at 52s. per quarter, and after the ports have been open for three months may be sold at 47s. as it will then only bear a duty of 12s.

" That these regulations are ruinous to the agricultural interest cannot be doubted. The petitions on the table of this House, in the strongest terms of deprecating the proposed alteration in the law, sufficiently display the opinion of those whose habits give them practical knowledge on the subject ; whilst the Committee themselves, from whom the proposal emanated, by disclaiming all intention of rendering worse the present condition of the British cultivation, and proposing, as the bill enacts, that the 55th of the late king should remain in force till wheat rises to 80s. a quarter, have clearly avowed their opinion that the bill, when it takes effect, must prove injurious to the agricultural interest.

" It is to me, therefore, a subject of deep regret, when the distress of the British cultivation is so feelingly described in the numerous petitions on our table, that this House should enact a regulation which, though it is only to take place at a future period, cannot but produce immediate discontent : for to me it appears that every sense of political discretion, and every feeling that actuates a generous mind, must unite in pointing out, that the moment in which the legislature is unwillingly compelled to avow its incapacity to devise any means of present relief for the distressed farmer, is the time of all others in which it ought to avoid announcing a future injury to his despairing mind," Lauderdale.

[71] 3rd George IV., c 60.

[72] Western, *Second Address to the Landowners of the United Empire*, 1822, pp. 6–7.

[73] Ricardo, *On Protection to Agriculture*, 1822, p. 85.

[74] Sinclair, *An Answer to a Tract recently Published by David Ricardo*, 1822, p. 12.

[75] *Hansard*, vol. 7, pp. 1080–81.

[76] Smart, vol. 2, pp. 119–120.

[77] *The Annual Register*, 1822, p. 2–3.

[78] For a full account of this subject, see Hammond's *The Village Labourer, The Town Labourer and The Skilled Labourer*.

[79] The petition was drawn up by Thomas Tooke, author of *The History of Prices*.

[80] Smart, vol. 1, p. 759.

[81] The full petition reads as follows:

" That foreign commerce is eminently conducive to the wealth and prosperity of a country, by enabling it to import the commodities for the production of which the soil, climate, capital and industry of other countries are best calculated, and to export in payment those articles for which its own situation is better adapted.

" That freedom from restraint is calculated to give the utmost extension to foreign trade, and the best direction to the capital and industry of the country.

" That the maxim of buying in the cheapest market and selling in the dearest, which regulates every merchant in his individual dealings, is strictly applicable as the best rule for the trade of the whole nation.

" That a policy founded on these principles would render the commerce of the world an interchange of mutual advantages, and diffuse an increase of wealth and enjoyments among the inhabitants of each state.

" That, unfortunately, a policy the very reverse of this has been, and is, more or less, adopted and acted upon by the government of this and of every other country, each trying to exclude the productions of other countries, with the specious and well-meant design of encouraging its own productions ; thus inflicting on the bulk of its subjects, who are consumers, the necessity of submitting to privations in the quantity or quality of commodities ; and thus rendering what ought to be the source of mutual benefit and harmony among states, a constantly-recurring occasion of jealousy and hostility.

" That the prevailing prejudices in favour of the protective or restrictive system may be traced to the erroneous supposition that every importation of foreign commodities occasions a diminution of our own productions to the same extent : whereas it may be clearly shown that, although the particular description of production which could not stand against unrestrained foreign competition would be discouraged, yet as no importation could be continued for any length of time without a corresponding exportation, direct or indirect, there would be an encouragement, for the purpose of that exportation, of some other production to which our situation might be better suited ; thus affording at least an equal, and probably a greater, and certainly a more beneficial employment to our own capital and labour.

" That, of the numerous protective and prohibitory duties of our commercial code, it may be proved, that, while all operate as a very heavy tax on the community at large, very few are of any ultimate benefit to the classes in whose favour they were originally instituted, and none to the extent of the loss occasioned by them to other classes.

" That, among the other evils of the restrictive or protective system, not the least is, that the artificial protection of one branch of industry, or source of production, against foreign competition, is set up as a ground of claim by other branches for similar protection ; so that, if the reasoning upon which these restrictive or prohibitory regulations are founded were followed out consistently, it would not stop short of excluding us from all foreign commerce whatsoever. And the same train of argument, which with corresponding prohibitions and protective duties should exclude us from foreign trade, might be brought forward to justify the re-enactment of restrictions upon the interchange of productions (unconnected with public revenue) among the kingdoms composing the union, or among the counties of the same kingdom.

" That an investigation of the effects of the restrictive system, at this time, is peculiarly called for, as it may, in the opinion of your petitioners, lead to a strong presumption that the distress which now so generally prevails is considerably aggravated by that system, and that some relief may be obtained by the earliest practicable removal of such of the restraints as may be shown to be the most injurious to the capital and industry of the community, and to be attended with no compensating benefit to the public revenue.

" That a declaration against the anti-commercial principles of our restrictive system is of the more importance at the present juncture, inasmuch as, in several instances, of recent occurrence, the merchants and manufacturers in foreign states have assailed their respective governments with applications for further protective or prohibitory duties and regulations, urging the example and authority of this country, against which they are almost exclusively directed, as a sanction for the policy of such measures. And certainly, if the reasoning upon which our restrictions have been defended is worth anything, it will apply in behalf of the regulations of foreign states against us. They insist upon our superiority in capital and machinery, as we do upon their comparative exemption from taxation, and with equal foundation.

" That nothing would more tend to counteract the commercial hostility of foreign states than the adoption of a more enlightened and more conciliatory policy on the part of this country.

" That, although, as a matter of mere diplomacy, it may sometimes answer to hold out the removal of particular prohibitions or high duties, as depending upon corresponding concessions by other states in our favour, it does not follow that we should maintain our restrictions, in cases where the desired concessions on their part cannot be obtained. Our restrictions would not be the less prejudicial to our own capital and industry, because other governments persisted in preserving impolitic regulations.

" That, upon the whole, the most liberal would prove to be the most politic course on such occasions.

" That, independent of the direct benefit to be derived by this country on every occasion of such concession or relaxation, a great incidental object would be gained by the recognition of a sound principle or standard, to which all subsequent arrangement might be referred, and by the salutary influence which a promulgation of such just views by the legislature, and by the nation at large, could not fail to have on the policy of other states.

" That in thus declaring, as your petitioners do, their conviction of the impolicy and injustice of the restrictive system, and in desiring every practicable relaxation of it, they have in view only such parts of it as are not connected, or are only subordinately so, with the public revenue. As long as the necessity for the present amount of revenue subsists, your petitioners cannot expect so important a branch of it as the customs to be given up, nor to be materially diminished, unless some substitute, less objectionable, be suggested. But it is against every restrictive regulation of trade not essential to the revenue—against all duties merely protective from foreign competition—and against the excess of such duties as are partly for the purpose of revenue, and partly for that of protection —that the prayer of the present petition is respectfully submitted to the wisdom of parliament.

" The petitioners therefore humbly pray that the House will be pleased to take the subject into consideration, and to adopt such measures as may be calculated to give greater freedom to foreign commerce, and thereby to increase the resources of the state." *Hansard*, N.S., vol. 1, p. 179.

[82] Smart, vol. 2, p. 143.

[83] Byron has satirized the dissatisfaction of the landed interest, during the years following 1815, in canto XIV of *The Age of Bronze*, Everyman's edn., vol. 1, pp. 470-2 :—

Alas, the country ! how shall tongue or pen
Bewail her now *uncountry* gentlemen ?
The last to bid the cry of warfare cease,
The first to make a malady of peace.
For what were all these country patriots born ?
To hunt, and vote, and raise the price of corn ?
But corn, like every mortal thing, must fall,
Kings, conquerors, and markets most of all.
And must ye fall with every ear of grain ?
Why would you trouble Buonaparte's reign ?
He was your great Triptolemus ; his vices
Destroy'd but realms, and still maintain'd
        your prices ;
He amplified to every lord's content
The grand agrarian alchymy, hight *rent*.
Why did the tyrant stumble on the Tartars,
And lower wheat to such desponding quarters ?
Why did you chain him on yon isle so lone ?
The man was worth much more upon his throne.
True, blood and treasure boundlessly were spilt,
But what of that ? the Gaul may bear the
        guilt ;
But bread was high, the farmer paid his way,
And acres told upon the appointed day.
But where is now the goodly audit ale ?
The purse-proud tenant, never known to fail ?
The farm which never yet was left on hand ?
The marsh reclaim'd to most improving land ?
The impatient hope of the expiring lease ?
The doubling rental ?   What an evil's peace !
In vain the prize excites the ploughman's skill,
In vain the Commons pass their patriot bill ;
The *landed interest*—(you may understand
The phrase much better leaving out the *land*)—
The land self-interest groans from shore to shore,
For fear that plenty should attain the poor.

Up, up again, ye rents ! exalt your notes,
Or else the ministry will lose their votes,
And patriotism, so delicately nice,
Her loaves will lower to the market price ;
For ah ! " the loaves and fishes," once so high,
Are gone—their oven closed, their ocean dry,
And nought remains of all the millions spent,
Excepting to grow moderate and content.
They who are not so, *had* their turn—and turn
About still flows from Fortune's equal urn ;
Now let their virtue be its own reward.
And share the blessings which themselves prepared
See these inglorious Cincinnati swarm,
Farmers of war, dictators of the farm ;
Their ploughshare was the sword in hireling hands,
Their fields manured by gore of other lands ;
Safe in their barns, these Sabine tillers sent
Their brethren out to battle—why ? for rent !
Year after year they voted cent. per cent.,
Blood, sweat, and tear-wrung millions,—why ? for
        rent !
They roar'd, they dined, they drank, they swore
        they meant
To die for England—why then live ?—for rent !
The peace has made one general malcontent
Of these high-market patriots ; war was rent !
Their love of country, millions all misspent,
How reconcile ? by reconciling rent !
And will they not repay the treasures lent ?
No : down with everything, and up with rent !
Their good, ill, health, wealth, joy, or discontent,
Being, end, aim, religion—rent, rent, rent !
Thou sold'st thy birthright, Esau ! for a **mess** ;
Thou shouldst have gotten more, or eaten less ;
Now thou hast swill'd thy pottage, thy demands
Are idle ; Israel says the bargain stands.

CHAPTER IX

THE AGITATION OF THE EIGHTEEN-TWENTIES

Significance of the years from 1825 to 1828 in the agitation against the Corn Laws—Acquiescence of the landowners in lower prices and rents—New methods of securing information on the possibilities of procuring foreign corn—Marked difference in the agitation against the Corn Laws in Parliament and outside— I, The question in Parliament from 1823 to 1828—Reasons for lull until January of 1825—Causes for the revival in interest—Cautious attitude of the government —Two temporary measures at the end of the session of 1825—Effect of the panic of December, 1825, upon the attitude of the government early in the session of 1826—Attacks of Whitmore, Philips and Lord King on the existing laws— Influence of Jacob's report—Government again passes temporary measures at the end of the session—New corn bill promised by the government in the session of 1827—Introduction of measure delayed when Liverpool was stricken with apoplexy—Terms of the new bill explained by Canning—Lost in the Lords through Wellington's amendment—The Wellington-Huskisson controversy—For the third successive time the government has recourse to temporary measures at the end of the session—Wellington ministry formed at the beginning of 1828, the third since the retirement of Liverpool—Difficulties of framing a new bill in 1828— Terms of the new law—Significance of the change in principle—II, Agitation against the Corn Laws outside Parliament—Emphasis placed on the relation of corn and currency—Pamphlets of Joplin, Graham, Rooke, Fletcher and Tooke— Conclusions of Jevons—Significance of the second report of Jacob—Violent attacks upon the social and political position of the landlords—Thompson's *Catechism*—*The Iniquity of the Landholders*—*The Morning Chronicle*—The reactions of the landlords—Indignation of the Die Hards—Expediency arguments of the liberal ones—Conclusion—Reasons for decline in agitation after passing of the law of 1828—Place of the agitation of the eighteen-twenties in the history of the Corn Laws.

In the last chapter it was shown that the years between the passing of the laws of 1815 and 1822 were given unity, not by the introduction of a new policy in 1822 nor by uniform economic conditions during those seven years, but by the acknowledgment of the landed interest that the attempt to keep up rents through the act of 1815 was a failure. Here it will be shown that the years from 1822 to 1828 are a unit, not because of the epoch-making nature of either the law of 1822 or 1828, but because they marked the first attempt of the industrial and commercial classes to unite against the landowners. The significance of this attack, especially after 1825, has been generally overlooked because it declined during the ten years following 1828 and was then renewed by the Anti-Corn Law League with greater volume and success. The reduction of duties on both manufactured articles and raw materials, which Huskisson made in the years following 1823, enabled the manufacturing and commercial classes to attack protection on grain without provoking, as it did in 1815, a reference to the high protection which they themselves enjoyed.

Freed from this handicap of earlier years, writers in newspapers and periodicals, pamphleteers and representatives in Parliament were less hampered in the use of certain arguments and in the flood of personal abuse which they directed against the landowners.   Practically every argument against protection to agriculture and nearly every epithet hurled against the landed interest by Cobden and the Anti-Corn Law League from 1839 to 1846 was anticipated at this time.   The League and its henchmen increased the output rather than the number of arguments, and the volume rather than the intensity of the vituperation.

The change during these years in the attitude of the landowners is also noteworthy.   After 1822, as was shown at the end of Chapter VIII, they reduced rents and, apparently, resigned themselves to lower prices.   In addition their expressions on the subject of protection, whether in Parliament, pamphlets, newspapers or periodicals, became more moderate and impersonal than those of their opponents. It is true that they expressed considerable indignation at the campaign carried on against them, and that they were apt to become self-righteous when contrasting themselves with their opponents ; but certainly they were more sparing of abuse.

Almost as notable as the change in the attitude of the industrial and commercial classes and of the landed interest was the new method employed by the government to secure information on the possibility of obtaining a supply of grain from abroad.   During the agitation of 1814 and 1815 the wildest statements circulated about the amount of corn available for exportation on the continent were given credence, both in and outside Parliament.   The select committees of both the Commons and Lords had attempted in 1814, with indifferent success, to extract trustworthy statistics from importers.   In 1825 when the question again arose, the government sent William Jacob on a tour through Northern Europe to find exactly what the possibilities were of securing grain from each country ; and required British consuls, in any place where there was a chance that corn would be exported to Great Britain, to make reports on the subject.

Another characteristic of the years covered by this chapter is the marked difference between the substance of the Parliamentary debates and that of the newspapers, periodicals and pamphlets. During the years from 1814 to 1822 there was little variation between the two, and a detailed study of the material outside Parliament was valuable as a substantiation of the views expressed in the speeches rather than as a new source of information.   From 1825 to 1828, in particular, the proposals of the government and the speeches on both sides only faintly reflect the turbulence of opinion as expressed in pamphlets and newspapers.   During the four sessions preceding the passing of a new law in 1828 the discussions were largely concerned with the details of a new measure to take the place of the act of 1822. It was outside Parliament, in the main, that the bitter and determined attack on the political and social position of the landed interest was made.   Because of the marked difference in the corn law agitation in and outside Parliament, the two will be treated separately throughout the remainder of this chapter.

THE CORN LAWS IN PARLIAMENT, 1823-28

The period of low prices of grain which began in 1819 did not end with the passing of the law of 1822 and hence the fight for the relief of agriculture continued, although on a smaller scale, in the session of 1823. The harvest of 1822 brought no relief, for " a mild winter, a genial spring and a hot summer "[1] produced wheat of good quality and average yield. In November and December the price of wheat fell to 38s. 10d. and 38s. 11d. respectively—the lowest level in over thirty years. In the first half of 1823, owing to a backward spring and cold weather, the price rose rapidly and reached 61s. 4d. by June.[2] Despite this improvement, the " Die-Hards " among the agriculturists in the House of Commons determined to bring up the question of relief once more. Their battle cry of the session was the " equitable adjustment of contracts,"[3] which was a demand to revise all contracts made from 1797 until cash payments were resumed. Although it was presented in many different ways throughout the session, it secured less and less support as prices rose. On June 11th Western boldly advocated its adoption, but so crushing were the replies of Peel and Huskisson that only twenty-seven members supported him. Peel remarked that, " It really was a pretty summer amusement which the member had cut out for them, when he proposed to them, on the 11th of June, to revise all contracts that had taken place since 1793."[4] Lethbridge, on June 2nd, with less pugnacity but better judgment, withdrew his motion to inquire into the causes for the distressed state of agriculture. The rise in the price of wheat obviously explains the progressive weakening of the demand for alleviation. Doubtless, *The Annual Register* was correct in stating that " These complaints of the agriculturists, though uttered so incessantly, and with so much confidence, were rather the result of recollection of what was passed than of observation of present circumstances."[5]

Even a fall of prices in October, due to a large amount of old wheat being thrown on the market, combined with a deficient wheat crop[6] did not cause a revival of the cry of agricultural distress. The explanation, evidently, is the one given in Chapter VIII : the reduction in rents and the adjustment in labour and expenses of cultivation to new conditions had been made. During the greater part of 1824 the price of wheat was above 60s. and, on the whole, the year was the quietest since the beginning of the agitation for a new law in 1813. There was neither a cry for more protection, nor for repeal or downward revision. Even Huskisson's bill, which permitted the substitution of flour for foreign wheat in warehouses,[7] aroused little comment. On the whole the year was one of widespread content. One writer testified that, " There was . . . no diminution of that prosperity, which the country had enjoyed throughout the whole of 1823. Even country gentlemen—the most querulous of all classes, the least accustomed to suffer, and the most incapable of struggling with difficulties, when difficulties present themselves—could no longer complain."[8]

But this period of contentment, or at least of acquiescence, barely survived the year, for in January of 1825 an agitation was started for a repeal or downward revision of the duties of the Corn Laws. *The Morning Chronicle*, in particular, contained many letters advocating action along these lines. Rumours were circulated, which pleased some and alarmed others, that the government intended to make a change in the existing law. Under the circumstances, petitions began to pour into both Houses. Some asked for a revision and others implored that no change be made. Both the number of petitions and the rumours of change increased during the session of 1825. Finally, on April 25th, the Earl of Lauderdale, in the House of Lords, bluntly asked the Prime Minister if any change was contemplated. Liverpool replied that he believed a change was necessary but not in the present session. When made, it would be upon one of the three following principles : first, an alteration of the price at which importation took place while retaining the existing system ; second, an alteration in the system and imposition of protecting duties with a maximum beyond which import should be free and a minimum below which it should not be allowed ; and third, a general import duty fixed without averages.[9]

Despite Liverpool's insistence that the question would not be taken up in the present session, petitions continued to pour into the House of Commons. Perhaps it was due to this encouragement that Whitmore, who was a landowner, moved on April 28th that the House go into committee to consider the Corn Laws. He began his speech by expressing the conviction that it was " time to make the laws regulating the Corn Trade square a little better with those principles of free trade, which have, so much to the credit of His Majesty's ministers, been not only promulgated, but largely acted upon."[10] The Corn Laws, he insisted, had deranged the trade of the world, reduced the consumption of British manufactures and colonial products, and diminished the surplus of grain on the continent. In case of a short crop in Great Britain the country would not be able to secure the necessary stock from abroad because the land which had been the source of such a supply had now gone out of cultivation. The best change in the Corn Laws, in his opinion, would be to abolish the existing system and to substitute duties of 10s., 15s., 20s. and 25s. respectively when the price of wheat was 55s., 55s. to 50s., 50s. to 45s. and 45s. to 40s. He closed the speech with an appeal to the agriculturists to join in securing a settlement before the causes in operation produced their full effects, and warned them if they did not that they might be compelled by popular opinion " to relinquish all claims, even the fairest and most legitimate, to protection and security."[11] In view of the attitude of the government it is not surprising that nothing came of this motion and speech. Even the forty-seven who voted in favour of it seemed to have done so " merely as a protest against the inaction of the Government."[12]

Although the government declined to take any action toward a permanent alteration in the Corn Laws, it was forced, only four days after Whitmore's motion, to introduce two temporary measures. The price of wheat had remained steadily around 66s., but since the

winter and spring had not been particularly favourable it was feared
that a poor crop might result which would send the price above 80s.
and open the ports to foreign corn. To prevent this from occurring
Huskisson moved two resolutions on May 2nd. The first provided
that owners of foreign corn in bond might, upon the payment of a
10s. duty, bring into consumption in each of the three months preceding August 15th, a third of the amount warehoused. If owners
did not take advantage of this opportunity by that date, the bonded
wheat was to remain subject to the present law. There were at the
time 394,000 quarters of wheat and a small amount of other kinds of
grain in bond. The second resolution provided that Canadian wheat
might be admitted upon payment of a duty of 5s. a quarter. Both
resolutions were subjected to severe handling, especially in the Lords,
but were eventually passed and became laws on June 22nd.[13] A few
slight changes were made in the first resolution such as admitting the
warehoused grain in two instead of three instalments.[14] These acts
had the desired effect, since the ports were not opened on August
15th as the government had feared. The next year Huskisson
announced that about a half-million quarters were taken out of bond
during this period and, in his opinion, this action prevented the ports
from being thrown open to foreign grain in August.[15]

When Parliament met on February 2nd, 1826, the Corn Law
question had been forced into the background by the financial panic
of December, 1825. The commercial and manufacturing interests
were especially anxious to secure substantial relief from the government, and hence were very much disappointed when the King's speech
cautiously announced that a repetition of the present disaster would
be avoided in the future by placing the currency on a firmer foundation. The principal action taken by Parliament was to put an
end to the issue of all one-pound notes except those of the Bank of
England. This action was not enough to prevent stagnation in
manufacturing, with its accompanying distress for the operatives,
during the greater part of the year. Yet despite the number of
riots of the unemployed, the working class do not seem to have
suffered from the crisis as much as might have been expected.[16]

Although the government was determined not to have the Corn
Laws brought up in this session, the manufacturers and working class
of the cities were of another mind. The price of wheat was not
especially high, but to the labourer who was out of work it offered a
tangible explanation for his distress. Petitions calling for the repeal
of the law of 1822 again covered the tables of both houses. In the
Lords, Lord King made himself particularly obnoxious to his fellow
peers by the flippant remarks with which he introduced petitions.
On March 21st, when introducing one of these, he admitted that he
had been requested to desist. Some persons had hinted that his
speeches were like sermons in Lent and repeated as often ; that he
had a vicious propensity for making corn cheap ; and that he called
the Corn Laws names like a prisoner at Old Bailey. He gave the
greatest offence when he labelled the Law of 1822 the " job of
jobs."[17]

The question was brought up in the Commons on April 18th

precisely as it had been in the previous year, by Whitmore moving that the House go into committee to consider the state of the Corn Laws.[18] His speech was much the same as that of April, 1825, with the added authority of Jacob's report on the possibilities of securing wheat from the Baltic countries.[19] He quoted Jacob to prove that everywhere both the landowners and corn merchants were in deepest distress as a result of the Corn Law of 1815 ; and contrasted the condition of Great Britain from 1793 to 1815, a period of virtual free trade, with the years since 1815. The real danger to the country was not that land would be driven out of cultivation, as the amount of poor soil and wastes that were annually brought under cultivation showed ; but that the source of supply abroad, which would be needed in case of a deficit at home, was being dried up. Whitmore ended by proposing the same duties that he had suggested on April 28th of the previous year.

Philips,[20] in seconding the motion of Whitmore, made, on behalf of the manufacturers, the very significant statement that they expected free trade in manufactures if free trade in corn were introduced. He then showed his industrial bias by expressing the opinion that the latter was more important than the former, since an increased demand caused a rise in the price of grain because of the expense of bringing inferior land into cultivation ; whereas manufactures became cheaper with increased demand and production. In return for the taxes that the landlords paid he proposed that a protecting duty equal to the amount of this burden should be levied on foreign corn. When the country gentlemen laughed he reminded them that " laughter was not argument, any more than contradiction was refutation."[21]

Huskisson, who replied for the government, reiterated the decision announced on the first day of the session : namely, that more pressing problems, especially currency, would demand the consideration of the House and that sufficient time would not be left to give the Corn Laws the attention they deserved. Therefore this question would be postponed until another session. He admitted that the present system was a bad one, but insisted that it was impossible to remedy it at the present time. If he thought that the existing distress could really be alleviated by prompt action, he would favour it. Huskisson also took advantage of the opportunity to clarify his position on free trade. One industry, he held, was as much entitled to protection as another, and the amount of protection given should be sufficient to enable each industry to compete on fair terms with the same industry in other countries.[22] In the end the opposition of the government was effective and Whitmore's motion was beaten by 250 to 81.[23]

On April 20th, William Jacob's *Report on the Trade in Corn and on the Agriculture of Northern Europe*, which Whitmore had used in a speech two days earlier, was delivered to the members of the House of Commons. It is an amazingly interesting document[24] and of unusual significance in the history of the Corn Laws during the next few years, because of the numerous references to it both in and out of Parliament. His descriptions of social and economic conditions in Eastern Europe must be passed over at this time but his conclusions on the possibilities of that part of the continent supplying Great Britain with grain will be considered. He held that the fear of Baltic wheat on the part of the British landowners was largely a result of the enormous exportation from that region during the years from 1801 to 1805. This exportation was due to conditions both unusual and unlikely to be repeated. From 1791 on, British ports were almost continuously open to foreign wheat, while during the same period France and Sweden drew on the Vistula region for unusual amounts of grain. "These combined circumstances gave to the agriculture of Poland and Prussia, a portion of capital and motives to exertion, which produced the vast surplus that was exported from 1801 to 1805. Ten years of unexampled prosperity were, however, needed, to reach the point which those years exhibit, and it was only by gradual steps that it was attained."[25] Yet this enormous stimulus lasting for ten years was only able to produce an annual surplus of 550,000 quarters, or the equivalent of about twelve days consumption for Great Britain. The circumstances that produced this surplus were unlikely to be repeated, because wars of the length and intensity of those from 1792 to 1815 were not apt to recur. Furthermore, Ireland had not been opened up at that time as it was after 1806. Jacob concluded, therefore, that, " If a duty in this country of 10s. or 12s. per quarter was imposed, it would not allow of such a profit, on the supposition of the price being from 60s. to 64s., as to induce any great exertions to increase cultivation in the bordering districts on the Vistula."[26]

Although Jacob's report might have been enlightening and valuable for the future, it did not satisfy the hungry operatives of the manufacturing districts. It is true that wheat averaged under 60s. a quarter ; but despite this fact, there were fearful riots in Lancashire during April which the government could not afford to ignore. As one writer stated, " The working classes universally looked on the Corn Laws as the first and great source of their distress, for they could comprehend this position that, the cheaper the corn the cheaper the loaf ; they knew that they could live more comfortably, if they obtained a certain quantity of bread for threepence, than if it cost them sixpence, and further they went not."[27] Perhaps it was this state of mind in the working class that caused the government to reverse its decision not to consider the Corn Laws during the present session. On May 1st, Canning stated in the Commons that the government had decided to introduce a bill to permit the bonded corn in the various ports of the kingdom to be thrown on the market. The number of quarters warehoused was estimated at 250,000 t' 300,000, and Canning was confident that such an amount would relievₓ the distress in the places where the grain was stored, without seriously affecting the agricultural interests.[28] The second proposal of the government was to permit the admission of additional foreign corn, by order in council, if it were deemed necessary during the period between the closing of the present session and for a limited time after the opening of the next one.[29]

These proposals were immediately attacked by the country gentlemen, by those who had favoured action earlier in the session, and by

the opposition. Sir Thomas Lethbridge, on behalf of the landed
interest, denounced them as an attempt to undermine the Corn Laws
in a manner neither fair nor manly. If aid was really needed for
starving operatives, the Commons should assist the parishes which
were unable to support their own poor. He also begged the House
to remember that the distress of the manufacturing labourer was not
due entirely to the price of grain for, " They were bred in habits of
luxury, and had acquired wants which they found it difficult to divest
themselves of."[30] Therefore he moved that a select committee
should be appointed to inquire into the causes of distress in the manufacturing districts and the best means of remedying it. This motion
was beaten by 214 to 82. Whitmore inquired caustically why May
5th was a proper time to consider the Corn Laws when April 18th
was not.[31] The opposition charged the ministry with vacillation,
incompetence and insincerity. Lord John Russell stated that after
passing over the opportunity of doing something early in the session
the government now asked dictatorial powers over that most important of subjects—the food supply.[32]

Despite this flood of criticism, the government stuck resolutely to
its proposals. Huskisson in defending the two measures insisted,
that since the time was too limited to permit change in the Corn Laws
in the present session, they offered the best prospect of alleviating
temporary distress. He called attention to the fact that the 500,000
quarters of foreign corn admitted between June and August of 1825
had prevented the ports from being thrown open on August 15th. If
the first of the two measures now proposed was rejected, the ports
would certainly be opened on August 15th. The alternative to the
second proposal would be to have the government open the ports on
its own responsibility, if conditions warranted such an action between
sessions ; and to ask indemnity from Parliament at the next session.
This plan seemed inferior to Huskisson because it could not specify
the conditions upon which the ports could be opened.[33] In the end,
after several bitter speeches and many amendments, both measures
were passed and received the royal assent on May 31st. The one[34]
permitted all corn warehoused on or before May 2nd to be sold for
home consumption, on condition that no more than half of it was
taken out by July 1st. Wheat was to pay a duty of 12s. a quarter
and other grains a smaller one. The second[35] empowered His
Majesty by order in council to admit foreign corn for home consumption until January 1st, 1827, or until six weeks after the opening of
the next session of Parliament. Such an order was not to continue
for more than two months, was not to extend to wheat warehoused
before May 2nd, and was not to permit more than 500,000 quarters
to come into consumption.

The occasion came for using the latter measure before the summer
was over. The winter of 1825–6 was ordinary and the spring rather
cold and dry until late in May when heavy rains fell. Early in June
an almost unprecedented spell of brilliantly warm weather set in,
which became a veritable drought before it ended after the first week
in September.[36] For a while a great deficiency in all crops was
feared. During July the prices of all kinds of grain were rising rapidly

with the exception of wheat which remained remarkably steady during the entire year. In fact, from June to December the monthly prices of wheat varied less than 3s. On September 1st, in the midst of the most critical period of the drought, the government issued an order in council throwing open the ports to oats, oatmeal, beans, peas and rye. The harvest, which was early because of the drought, showed a deficiency in oats, peas, beans and rye, although wheat was average in both quality and quantity.[37]

The existing House of Commons, which had sat since 1819, was dissolved in June and a general election took place in July. The new Parliament met on November 14th and ten days later Huskisson moved,[38] first, " That all persons concerned in issuing, or advising the issue, or acting in execution of, an Order in Council of September 1st, 1826, for allowing importation of certain sorts of foreign corn, shall be indemnified " ; and second, that the duties specified in the order be continued until February 15th, 1827. After a series of warm but ineffectual attacks, both were approved.[39]

On February 8th the Earl of Liverpool announced that he would shortly take up the question of the Corn Laws, but on the 17th he was struck with apoplexy and the ministry left without a head. As a result of this stroke and of the illness of Huskisson, Canning was called upon to explain the proposed measure. On March 1st he made a long speech and introduced the proposition. Although admitting that they were the product of the government at large and not of a single department, still he emphasized the fact that Liverpool was anxious to assume responsibility for the measure and was " resolved to stake . . . that eminent reputation, which is naturally most dear, as well as most honourable to an individual in his exalted station, and if necessary, that station itself."[40] Since Liverpool's illness made it impossible to introduce the proposals he hoped that he would not prove an altogether unworthy expositor of them. His chief qualification, he claimed, was that he had not taken part in the discussions of 1815 and 1822, and hence was in a position to realize that the hostile feeling on both sides of the question was greater than it should be : first, because the differences were infinitely less than were usually stated in arguments ; and second, because the extreme opinion on either side was seldom unequivocally and unconditionally supported. The necessity of a change in the present system was justified on the grounds that the law of 1815 was full of defects, and the law of 1822 had " never come into operation at all."[41]

Canning next discussed the amount of protection necessary for agriculture and the manner in which it should be given. Liverpool, " whose researches and opportunities of inquiring into this subject " had been so much more laborious than his own, had decided that the landed interest was entitled to protection on wheat up to 60s.[42] It was impossible to provide this protection by a fixed permanent duty, since in time of scarcity such a duty could not be retained ; or by a fixed import level, because that had been attempted unsuccessfully by the law of 1815. The arrangement which seemed to have the best chance of success was " a scale of duties, which should vary inversely as the price of Corn, correcting the excess, and making up

o

the deficiency, and tending by this alternate aid to their general equalization."[43]   Liverpool had decided that 20s. was a fair and reasonable duty when the price of wheat was 60s. and hence these two amounts were used as starting points.   For every shilling that the price advanced above 60s. the duty was to decrease two ; and for every shilling that it fell below 60s. the duty was to increase two. Thus at 70s. the duty ceased.   Under this plan prices would be equalized and fluctuations avoided, and normally the price of wheat would oscillate between 55s. and 65s.   The method of obtaining the averages was also to undergo a great change.   Instead of having a three months' average decide whether the ports should be opened during the next three months, a weekly average would now determine the duty of the following week.[44]

Canning pointed out in conclusion that this plan would have the double advantage of vindicating the respectability of the corn trade and of doing away with the necessity of interference by the executive government.   The resolutions had been framed to allay jealousies and to terminate disputes and he hoped that they would be accepted in that spirit.

Canning was doomed to disappointment in this hope, as the savage attacks of the next two months were to prove.   Opposition came from both the landed interest and the free-traders.   The most vigorous spokesmen for the former were Western, Knatchbull, Lethbridge and Gooch.   Western deplored the departure in 1773 from that policy which had been the admiration of the ages, and he expressed the fear that the measure now proposed would prove worse than any previous one.[45]   Knatchbull taunted Liverpool and Robinson on their change since 1815 ; and, after expressing his disapproval of the resolutions, appealed to the country gentlemen to do their duty by killing the new proposals.[46]   Lethbridge repeated his speech of the previous session and reviewed all the old arguments for protection to agriculture.[47]   Gooch deplored the amount of gold that would leave the country in payment for foreign corn when the import level was so low.[48]   In a later speech after noting the concern of some of his friends over the fact that foreign ships brought corn and took away ballast, he expressed the wish, with some asperity, that such ships would take away cargoes of political economists.[49]

On the whole, the advocates of free trade seemed to have accepted the new plan because, as Lord Milton stated, it was not as bad as the existing system.   Whitmore, however, declared that it was not such a measure as the country had a right to expect.   The most interesting speech on this side of the question was made by Sir Henry Parnell, who had played the leading rôle for the protectionists during the agitation from 1813 to 1815.   He frankly admitted that he had changed his mind on the subject because many puzzling points had been satisfactorily explained since 1813.   Ricardo had promulgated his theory of rent and had published his doctrines on wages and profits since that date.   In addition, Jacob's report had shown that the fear of Polish wheat was exaggerated.   Parnell concluded by affirming that the proposed measure was superior to the existing law ; although Whitmore's proposal of a duty of 20s. when the price of wheat was

50s. and of 10s. when the price was from 55s. to 65s. was preferable to either.[50]

The ministers took a smaller part in the discussions than might have been expected under the circumstances. Robinson, as Chancellor of the Exchequer and sponsor of the Law of 1815, felt that he must answer Knatchbull's charge of inconsistency. He cheerfully admitted that he concurred heartily in the new plan and had no false delicacy in confessing that he had changed his mind since he introduced the resolutions in 1815. His justification was that a minister must grow ; and that while the measure which he had planned in 1815 was a good one, he honestly felt that the one of this session was an improvement.[51] Occasionally other ministers intervened in the debates, as when Peel pointed out to Gooch that if the exportation of gold was dangerous when wheat was 60s. a quarter it would be much more so when the price reached 80s.[52]

The resolutions were debated one by one during the month of March and many amendments proposed. On March 8th Bankes moved that the duty of 20s. should apply when the price of wheat was 64s. but under 65s. The motion was rejected by 229 to 160.[53] The next day Whitmore moved that the 20s. duty start when the price was 50s. instead of 60s. and be lowered with the rise in price until 55s. was reached. Between 55s. and 65s. the duty was to remain at 10s. This motion was beaten by a vote of 335 to 50.[54] On March 27th Hume moved that from July 5th, 1827, to July 5th, 1828, a duty of 15s. be imposed. This duty was to be reduced 1s. a year until 1833 when it would become permanent at 10s. The amendment was defeated by 140 to 16.[55] Several attempts were also made to amend the price levels of other grain than wheat, but all such suggestions of any significance were beaten. The only change of any importance made in the original resolutions was the adjustment of the duty and price levels to the imperial measure. Both the duty and the price levels were figured on the basis of the Winchester measure ; but on March 26th Grant announced that, at the request of the House, the change would be made to the imperial. Thus the 60s. price level became 61s. $10\frac{1}{2}$d., and the 20s. duty, 20s. $7\frac{1}{2}$d. For sake of convenience the former was fixed at 62s. and the latter at 20s. 8d.[57]

On March 29th the bill based on the resolutions was read for the first time.[58] On April 2nd, when the second reading was moved, Lethbridge proposed an amendment that the reading be postponed six months. After an acrimonious debate the vote stood 243 for the second reading and 78 for the amendment.[59] On May 1st the bill was read a third time and passed.[60]

In the Lords the attack on the resolutions was begun on March 8th by the Earl of Lauderdale. He denounced the proposed measure because it was new and unheard of. No greater proof of the worthlessness of the sliding scale could be cited than the fact their ancestors had not introduced it, for if it had had any merit they would certainly have done so. The theorists who declared that the landed interest enjoyed a monopoly in corn likewise aroused his ire. How, he demanded, could 560,000 landowners, almost entirely unconnected and with varying interests, combine to regulate the price of corn? The proposed plan was alleged to have been drawn up by Liverpool, but he would not believe it unless the Prime Minister personally assured him that this was true.   Liverpool, in his opinion, was not the man to upset the country for the sake of some wild theories ; the person who would be apt to do so was Huskisson, whose project this doubtless was.   The best way to regulate the corn trade was to prohibit importation entirely, and leave the opening of the ports to the discretion of Parliament during sessions and to the Privy Council between sessions.   If the legislature actually wished to determine the amount of protection that British agriculture needed, the reasonable procedure would be to determine the remunerative price for growing corn in Great Britain and abroad, and to impose a duty amounting to the difference.   Therefore, he proposed that a select committee be appointed to find at what prices foreign corn could be shipped from different ports, distinguishing in each case the quality and kind of corn.   The motion was agreed to and a committee appointed.[61]

The ultra-Tory point of view which characterized the utterances of Lauderdale was also evident in the famous twenty-six resolutions of Lord Redesdale.[62]   He introduced them on March 29th but did not explain them in detail to the Lords until May 15th.   Briefly his position was that the wealth and strength of the country originated in and must always depend on the cultivation of its soil ; and since this cultivation was by far the most important trade and manufacture in the country, every other trade and manufacture must depend upon it.   The system of free trade, which opponents of protection to agriculture advocated, would be possible only upon the establishment of a universal and constant peace which was utterly inconsistent with existing conditions.   He concluded his speech explaining the resolutions by moving that the House consider them and decide whether to agree to or reject the corn bill which the Commons had passed.[63]

A new ministry had come into existence since this bill had passed its second reading in the Commons ; for when it became evident that Liverpool would be unable to resume his position as Prime Minister, the King, after some hesitation, offered the position to Canning.   On April 10th the latter kissed hands as First Lord of the Treasury and set about forming a government.   Of the late cabinet, the Duke of Wellington, Peel, Eldon and three others refused to serve under Canning.   As a result of this defection some Whigs were taken into the cabinet, and Robinson, raised to the peerage as Lord Goderich, became Colonial Secretary and leader of the government in the House of Lords.   Thus Goderich, who as Robinson had played an important part in pushing the bill through the Commons in March, was now called upon to pilot it through the Lords.   The resolutions of Redesdale, he pointed out, were like a series of essays in political economy ; and although the truth of certain parts could not be denied, they were, as a whole, too all-inclusive for the present circumstances and did nothing to help solve the problem of the new bill.   While he did not spend much time in refuting the resolutions, he did give an admirable answer to those who eulogized the Corn Laws of 1660 to 1773 by pointing out that the system was found so inadequate to meet the needs of the times that eighteen or twenty temporary acts had to be passed in the years immediately preceding 1773.[64]

On June 1st the new bill encountered unexpected difficulties in the Lords. The Duke of Wellington moved that "foreign corn in bond should not be taken out of bond until the average price of corn shall have reached 66s." To the dismay of the government the motion was passed by 78 to 74.[65] All things considered, the failure of Goderich to protest against the Lords amending a money bill from the Commons is puzzling. Perhaps in the excitement of the debate he overlooked the point, but this does not explain why he did not insist upon it twelve days later when the measure was again considered and he expatiated on the difficulty of getting the House of Commons to accept Wellington's amendment. The Duke, as a result of mis-interpreting a letter which Huskisson had written him, evidently felt that the government would not be averse to his amendment. Huskisson in stating the concessions that the government might be willing to make, referred only to the corn in bond at that time, but Wellington had interpreted it to mean all corn bonded in the future. Moreover Huskisson had added, "I am afraid that even this amendment would prove fatal to the bill in our House." Wellington now offered to withdraw his amendment if some pledge was given to return to the principle of the law of 1791. Evidently this was not forthcoming, for after the subject had been once more debated thoroughly, Wellington's amendment was again passed by 133 to 122.[66]

Newspapers which were friendly to the corn bill denounced the Duke's action in no uncertain terms. Typical of these comments was : " That abortion of a Corn Bill which was introduced into Parliament by Mr. Canning and Lord Bathurst, and which they fathered on the politically defunct Premier, has been strangled in its birth ! The long-promised free trade in Corn has been knocked on the head by the renowned hero of Waterloo—and the people in con-sequence must, in the future, square their appetites to the superficies of British soil—or failing the possibility of doing this, remove to climes where nature's gifts are not exclusively confined to the enjoy-ment of the wealthy, but as freely diffused among all classes as they are freely yielded by our mother earth."[67] Even more caustic was the observation that, " The man who, while he had command of the British Army, cared little about what sufferings the soldiery might undergo, or what privations they might endure, provided there was bread enough for his hounds, could not be expected to care much for the sufferings which the distressed operatives might be obliged to endure if his pensions remained untouched."[68]

As a result of the re-passing of the amendment, Goderich announced that he had no intention of bringing up the bill for a third reading.[69] This action made it imperative for the Commons to take some new action, and Western strove manfully to direct it, in what he believed to be the proper channels. He proposed that the suspensive clause in the act of 1822 be removed and all of its provisions be allowed to come into full operation. He admitted that he had opposed the act of 1822, because he believed that it was inferior to the one of 1815 ; but since it had been passed he felt that it should be given a fair trial before it was discarded.[70] Canning objected that such a proposal did not meet the needs of the time. What was needed was a bill as much as possible like the one rejected by the Lords, which would escape the fate of that measure. The principles which must regulate the new measure were : first, that it should be temporary ; and second, that it should be along lines concurred in during the present session. Therefore, he proposed to let out 560,000 quarters of foreign wheat, not by order of the government, since that aroused opposition, but by act of Parliament. In conclusion he moved that all foreign corn and flour, warehoused by July 1st, should be subject to admission for home use up to May 1st, 1828. under the schedule provided in the late bill.[71] After a debate Canning's amendment prevailed over Western's motion by 238 to 52.[72]

In the course of the discussion over the proposals of Western and Canning, it was impossible to avoid considering the action of the Duke of Wellington. Baring affirmed that he had great respect for Wellington but not for his amendment. He expressed astonishment that the Duke was unable to see that the result would be to take the carrying trade out of British hands when prices were low, and to have corn stored just outside the country in periods of distress. Peel resented the attack and declared that it was difficult to see any evidence of the reverence which Baring professed. He believed that it was imperative for Huskisson to explain his part in order that the Glorious Duke might be vindicated. Huskisson then read the exchange of letters between himself and Wellington. On May 24th the Duke had written asking if he objected to the amendment. He answered that he did object, but if the amendment had read " that no corn bonded *after the passing of the present Bill* should be allowed to be entered for home consumption till the average price had reached 66s., and that henceforward all corn so bonded, or thereafter imported should come under the regulations of the Bill, individually I should not object to such a proviso. It would ensure that *no quantity beyond that now in bond* should be thrown upon the market, unless, in spite of that quantity, the price reached a level which might fairly be taken as an indication of our being in want of a further supply from abroad. *But I am afraid that even this amendment would prove fatal to the bill in our House.*" Huskisson insisted that all he meant was " that up to the price 66s., the corn now actually locked up should have a priority, and that thenceforth that and all other corn should be under the regulations of the bill."[73] But Wellington's amendment had made the enactment a permanent and not a temporary one.

This warehoused corn bill was hurried through the Commons and on June 25th the second reading was moved in the Lords by Goderich.[74] He stressed the fact that something had to be done in this session and showed how this temporary measure would at least ease the rush of foreign barley on the abundant crop which was coming. Wellington graciously declared that he was quite prepared to support this bill, since he appreciated the disappointment the government felt at not carrying the permanent measure. Under these circumstances it passed without serious opposition and became a law on July 2nd. It was merely a stop-gap arrangement to apply until the next session of Parliament and was based upon the principle of the sliding scale. It permitted foreign wheat warehoused on or before July 1st, 1827, to be entered for home consumption upon the payment of a duty of 20s. 8d. when the price was 62s. but under 63s. For every shilling that the price rose above 62s. the duty was reduced by two ; and for every shilling that the price dropped below 62s. the duty was increased by two. At 72s. and above the duty was to remain fixed at 1s. Other kinds of grain were to pay proportionate duties ; and wheat from British possessions outside Europe was to be admitted up to May 1st, 1828, upon payment of a duty of 5s. when the price was below 67s., and of 6d. when it was above.[75]

On the same day that this act received the royal assent another bill making some changes in the method of securing the average prices of the different kinds of grain also became a law.[76] In the course of the debates on this measure in the Lords on June 22nd an interesting incident occurred. Lord Farnham moved that, in the sentence preceding the list of the names of cities and towns from which weekly returns were to be made, the words " England and Wales " should be omitted and " Great Britain and Ireland " inserted. The motion to leave the words " England and Wales " was defeated by 45 to 44, and that to insert " Great Britain and Ireland " by 43 to 37. The effect of these divisions was to exclude every part of the United Kingdom from the clause.[77] These two measures ended the Corn Law agitation for the session.

Before Parliament met again in January of 1828 two ministries had come to an end. Canning's death on August 8th put an end to his brief and troubled ministry. Goderich next undertook to form an administration, but a few months at the head of a cabinet filled with jealous individuals and two distinct factions was too much for him, and on January 8th he resigned. Wellington next formed a ministry with Peel as Home Secretary and leader in the Commons, and with Huskisson as Colonial Secretary. The presence of the latter in the cabinet was of decided interest for the future of the Corn Laws in view of the misunderstanding in the last session of Parliament. The uncertainty over the action that would be taken was removed by the statement in the opening address that the government would introduce a bill founded on the principles of the one lost in the last session. But such a bill, coming from a cabinet in which both Wellington and Huskisson were members, was bound to be a compromise. " All March, it was the subject of constant and heated discussion and more than once it threatened to break up the newly-made Cabinet."[78]

When the measure representing the cabinet compromise was presented to the House of Commons at the end of March the prices and prospects of grain were not in the least critical. The crops of 1827 were average in quantity although wheat was somewhat inferior in quality. Thus as events proved, the temporary act passed at the end of the session was unnecessary. However, wheat and flour to the amount of 572,738 quarters were entered for consumption at a

duty exceeding 20s., since the monthly price never reached 62s.
But the fact that there was no apparent danger of the ports being
thrown open to unrestricted importation, as in three previous sessions,
did not lessen the interest in the problem of the Corn Laws. On
March 31st Grant, the President of the Board of Trade, introduced
the long expected bill in the Commons.[79] The intention of the
measure, he stated, was to repeal the acts of 1815 and 1822 ; and to
establish a sounder principle of legislation. This principle was to
be the same as the one in the bill which was lost in the last session,
namely : the sliding scale. A duty of 34s. 8d. was to start when the
price of wheat was 52s., and to decrease to 1s. when the price was
73s.

Since much of the discussion which followed the introduction of the
new bill was based on a comparison with the one rejected the year
before, the following table, which shows exactly how they differed,
may be of more value than mere assertions by speakers on opposite
sides of the question :[80]

When the home price was	the duty was	duty of bill of 1827
52s.	34s. 8d.	40s. 8d.
53s.	33s. 8d.	38s. 8d.
54s.	32s. 8d.	36s. 8d.
55s.	31s. 8d.	34s. 8d.
56s.	30s. 8d.	32s. 8d.
57s.	29s. 8d.	30s. 8d.
58s.	28s. 8d.	28s. 8d.
59s.	27s. 8d.	26s. 8d.
60s.	26s. 8d.	24s. 8d.
61s.	26s. 8d.	22s. 8d.
62s.	24s. 8d.	20s. 8d.
63s.	23s. 8d.	18s. 8d.
64s.	22s. 8d.	16s. 8d.
65s.	21s. 8d.	14s. 8d.
66s.	20s. 8d.	12s. 8d.
67s.	18s. 8d.	10s. 8d.
68s.	16s. 8d.	6s. 8d.
69s.	13s. 8d.	4s. 8d.
70s.	10s. 8d.	2s. 8d.
71s.	6s. 8d.	1s. 0d.
72s.	2s. 8d.	1s. 0d.
73s.	1s. 0d.	1s. 0d.

Huskisson was lukewarm in his defence of the measure, and justified
it largely as a means to abate the present angry squabbles over the
question. He was placed in the uncomfortable position of attempting
to show why this bill, of which he did not heartily approve, was not
inferior to the one of 1827 which he had drawn up himself. He did
insist that the pivot point had not been changed and that additional
protection between 60s. and 65s. was due to the fact that experience
with bonded corn since the last session indicated that it was needed.

Peel and Wellington, however, defended the bill with greater
warmth and colour. Peel termed the measure both just and equitable. Wellington, on the other hand, spent considerable time in
denouncing the temporary act of the last session. He considered it
bad because it brought corn out of bond when the country did not
need it. This action resulted from the owners of bonded grain

becoming panicky over the increased duty proposed by the rejected measure of the last session and the likelihood of one, at least as high, being fixed permanently and hence throwing on the market at a loss a large proportion of what they held.[81]

Representatives of both the landed and manufacturing interests joined in denouncing the proposed measure as worse than the one of 1827. Both sides moved numerous amendments to increase or decrease the amount of protection given under the sliding scale, but all were rejected by monotonously large majorities. Both Hume and Whitmore took advantage of the opportunity to make their sessional speeches. Hume once more proved that the landed interest over-rated their importance and that without foreign commerce the country would never have been rich and powerful.[82] Whitmore presented his plan of previous sessions with slight variations.[83] Both, however, were unavailing in the face of the government's majority.

The last protest of the landed interest came from Western on May 23rd when the third reading of the bill was moved. Although realizing that the majority of the members would be opposed, he was anxious to have his views recorded upon the journals, and he therefore moved a series of resolutions as an amendment. Most of these resolutions were taken up with a history of the Corn Laws in the two preceding centuries and an account of the present critical state of English agriculture. Finally he prophesied that, if the present measure passed, the consequences would be disastrous, because the countries supplying Great Britain with grain would collect heavy export duties. Next, these countries would increase their merchant marines by confining the corn trade to their own ships ; and lastly, " they might in time of war force us to submit to any terms by closing their markets to our manufactures, and withdrawing from our unoccupied and famishing artisans that food which from them alone could then be supplied."[84] Despite the warning of Western, the amendment was negatived and the bill read a third time and passed.[85]

In the House of Lords less opposition to the measure was en-countered than in the Commons. Only on the occasions of the second and third readings was there any lengthy discussion. Lauderdale once more expressed his " Die-Hard " principles when he denounced any attempt to tamper with the existing system. What, he demanded, was wrong with the law of 1815 ? Had the agriculturists asked for its repeal ? Certainly not. It was clear that the measure emanated from the philosophical spirit of discontent that was absurd ; and that it had been forced on the ministers against their wills.[86] Despite this appeal, he received little support in his opposition to the second reading. Numerous amendments were moved on June 26th, when the bill was read a third time and passed ; but all were rejected decisively.

The new law repealed those of 1815, 1822 and 1827. The same principle of the " pivot " point and sliding scale of duties on wheat, which has been described fully in the preceding pages, was applied to other kinds of grain.[87] The colonial preference was considerably increased over that of the acts repealed.[88] The price averages were reckoned by practically the same system as provided in the law of 1827. Weekly returns by inspectors were to be made of the purchases and sales of corn in places named in the act. A comptroller of corn returns was to be appointed by the government to take charge of the reports sent from these places, and to reckon the grand averages. In London the inspector was to be appointed by the Lord Mayor and aldermen ; and in other places, by the Justices of the Peace. The corn dealers were to make weekly returns to the local inspector who, in turn, transmitted to the comptroller the totals of these returns. From these statistics the comptroller, every Thursday morning, computed the average weekly price of each kind of grain. He then published these in *The Gazette* and transmitted a copy to each collector of customs along with the rate and amount of duty to be paid.[89]

The passing of the act of 1828 marked the abandonment of the principle of protection by absolute exclusion up to a certain price, which had been introduced in 1815, and a return to the principle of the sliding scale of duties.

THE AGITATION AGAINST THE CORN LAWS OUTSIDE PARLIAMENT

At the beginning of this chapter the necessity of treating separately the revision of the Corn Laws in Parliament and the agitation against them outside was stressed. As the first section has shown, the government was able to restrain the violence of the controversy within Parliament by a series of temporary measures and promises of future action ; and by changing the law in 1828 in such a manner as to leave both sides somewhat disappointed, but not furious. There were practically no restraints of this sort on the newspapers, periodicals and pamphleteers who made such bitter and determined attacks upon the political position of the landlords. Outside Parliament the question of the Corn Laws was linked up with other questions to a greater extent than within. It is true that it has been impossible to isolate the Corn Laws from other problems at any time during the course of this study. Just as they were complicated by agricultural distress, taxation and resumption of cash payments during the years from 1815 to 1822 ; so in the years following 1822 they were a part both of the free trade movement led by Huskisson, and of the agitation for Parliamentary reform which was to culminate in the act of 1832. The fact that the Corn Law agitation of the eighteen-twenties was simply part of the general free trade movement of the decade has been recognized, especially by free trade writers. On the other hand, the effect of this agitation upon the success of Parliamentary reform has not been sufficiently emphasized. The political power of the landowners prevented the commercial and manufacturing interests from securing greater freedom of trade. The latter appealed to the labouring classes to join in the attack on the grounds that the landlords were taxing their bread. When the Corn Law of 1828 gave no relief, it was natural for the middle class to tell the labouring class that there was no hope for cheap bread until a reform of Parliament took the power out of the hands of the landlords.

The agitation against the Corn Laws outside Parliament, as distinct from that within, was characterized by the emphasis placed on the relation of corn and currency ; by the great significance attached to the conclusions in the second report of Jacob ; and by the intense personal attacks on the landlords.

The currency problem was seldom brought up in Parliament in connection with the Corn Laws even by Western ; but several well-known pamphlets, some of which ran into several editions, were published on the subject. With one notable exception all of these pamphleteers held the quantity theory of money. In Graham's phraseology, " The value of money is in the inverse ratio of its quantity ; the supply of commodities remaining the same. Increase the quantity of money, prices rise. Decrease the quantity of money, prices fall. On the other hand, the quantity of money remaining the same. Increase the quantity of commodities, prices fall. Decrease the quantity of commodities, prices rise."[90] Probably the other writers on this subject, with the exception of Tooke, would have endorsed this definition.

However, when it came to explaining the reasons for the great fluctuation in prices since 1819, a greater diversity of opinion is to be found among these " quantity theory " writers. Joplin blamed the contraction in the issues of the country banks, when the exchanges turned against Great Britain at the end of 1818, for the fall in prices since 1819. Graham held the Peel act of 1819 responsible for this fall. The depreciation before this year was not marked by the difference in the price of paper and gold alone, because the latter itself was depreciated in consequence of the unlimited issue of paper which had forced the precious metal from England into the market of the world. The enhanced value of money was not 3 per cent. or 10 per cent. as Ricardo estimated at different times ; but more like 25 per cent. or 30 per cent. as Baring said, or even 50 per cent. as Attwood claimed.[91] Rooke believed that the fall in prices after 1819 was in great measure due to the accumulation of gold in the coffers of the Bank of England, which not only withdrew the precious metal from circulation but also a large amount of notes. The basic reason for the frequent fluctuations in prices before and after the years from 1819 to 1822, and for the derangements in the currency and exchanges was, in his opinion, the restrictions on what he termed reciprocal barter with other nations. It was impossible to maintain high prices in the home market in the face of low ones abroad, because the foreign exchanges were certain to turn against Great Britain, and to cause either an exportation of precious metals, or to force a reduction in the amount of paper money in circulation.[92] Fletcher pointed out that the recent fluctuation in the price of grain in England was due to the bad state of the currency, the monopoly preserved to the landowners and taxation ; and that the variations in prices throughout the world were due to the alternate increase and decrease in the production of precious metals.[93]

There was a similar lack of unanimity among these writers upon the

relation between the Corn Laws and the price of grain.   Joplin stated
that the existing Corn Laws were founded upon the error that high
prices must be the result of scarcity ; whereas if high prices were
really necessary, and a sufficient tax on foreign corn could not be
imposed to secure them, then the amount of money in circulation
should be increased.   Graham throughout his pamphlet went on the
assumption that the Corn Laws made the price of grain higher ; and
took for granted the impolicy of the law of 1822 and the injurious
effects of paper money.   Rooke held that the Corn Laws were the
greatest of the restrictions on reciprocal barter, and thus contributed
to the violent fluctuations which followed the derangements in the
currency and in the exchanges.   Fletcher insisted that the monopoly
of the landowners under the Corn Laws was a benefit only when the
crops were deficient, for it caused great fluctuations by producing
a greater fall in the case of good crops, and a greater rise in the case
of deficient ones, than would otherwise have occurred.[94]

The solutions that these four writers proposed for the unsatisfactory
Corn Laws and currency, likewise, varied.   Joplin believed that these
conditions would be satisfactorily adjusted if the paper money were
so regulated as to be of the same value as the metallic currency which
would circulate if there were no paper money.[95]   Graham admitted
that the natural and obvious train of his own reasoning would seem
to lead to a repeal of the Peel act.   But realizing the dangers of an
inconvertible paper currency and the impossibility of an " equitable
adjustment of contracts," he proposed that a fixed duty of 15s.
should be substituted for the present Corn Laws ; and that the
monopoly of the Bank of England should be abolished and the issue
of notes of £5 and above be left to private banking companies.[96]
Rooke was convinced that free trade in corn was needed to stop the
fluctuation in prices, because such a policy would raise the price of
grain abroad and thereby enable high prices to be maintained in the
home market.[97]   Fletcher concluded that, " The only mode of bringing prices in this country to the level of the rest of the world, without
disturbing the engagements of the farmers, is by lessening taxation,
which, with the large debt, is only very slowly practicable ; and the
increase of the produce of the mines, which, at present, is an operation
which a few years may bring about."[98]   Tooke, in *The Currency in
Connexion with the Corn Trade and on the Corn Laws*, took a position
diametrically opposed to the four writers whose opinions have just
been considered, on the effect of the quantity of money in circulation.
Further, he held that Peel's Bill had been without effect upon prices
because it had been without effect on the amount of the circulation.
Even granting that a contraction of the currency did take place in
order to prepare for resumption of cash payments, it did not occur
at such a time as to justify assigning it as the cause of the fall in prices.
On the other hand, that fall could be explained by circumstances
affecting the supply and demand of the commodities in question.[99]
In considering the fall in prices from 1819 to 1822 and the rise in
1823, Tooke reversed the cause and effect argument of the inflation
school, and insisted that the fall in prices was the cause of the contraction of the currency ; and the rise, that of the increase.[100]   In

short, his attitude is that almost everything except the amount of the currency in circulation affects prices, and that the amount of money varies according to the demand. Since the Corn Laws interfered with the operation of the law of supply and demand, Tooke, naturally, was opposed to them. However, he objected to them on other grounds as his authorship of the Merchants' Petition showed.

Events since 1828 and the research of modern scholars has corroborated some of the views expressed and discredited others. The influence of the precious metals on international prices was completely established, if indeed it needed to be, by the rise in prices following the discoveries of gold in California and Australia from 1848 to 1851, and in South Africa and the Klondike in the eighteen-eighties and nineties. Likewise, the effect of a depreciated currency on the exchange has .been established beyond dispute by the fluctuations of European exchanges since the war. Tooke has few modern followers who deny the effect of currency on prices. His attempt to refute the inflation theory by showing that an expansion of the circulation was often followed by a fall in commodities showed that he missed the spirit of this theory. What Cannan says of the Bullion Report applies perfectly to Tooke's reasoning : " It certainly does not ask us to believe that each sharp fluctuation of the comparative value of notes and gold shown either by the price of gold or the foreign exchanges was caused by alterations in the circulation of notes."[101] Similarly the quantity theory of money does not exclude the fact that other factors, such as supply and demand, may affect prices.

Probably the most careful work on the variations in prices during this period is to be found in Jevons' *Investigations of Currency and Finance*. He has used Tooke's table of prices in making a rather ingenious calculation. Since these prices start in the year 1782, he has taken the prices of that year as the standard or 100 in his calculations.. He chose forty standard commodities and the yearly variation in the aggregate average of the forty indicates the variation in the gold standard. From 1801 to 1820, by making allowance for the actual depreciation of paper as compared with gold, this variation is reckoned in the paper standard as well. In addition, each of the forty commodities is treated in two separate columns : the one shows the actual variation in the yearly gold price in comparison with 1782 ; the other, the comparative variation or the ratio in which the prices of each commodity or group of commodities have risen or fallen more than the entire forty combined. The group and single commodity, which interest us in this study, are corn—which includes wheat, barley, oats, rye, beans and peas—and wheat. Because of its significance for this phase of the Corn Laws, Jevons' table is given for the years from 1782 to 1850.

Year	General variation of all 40 commodities		Corn		Wheat	
	Gold Standard	Paper Standard	Actual	Comparative	Actual	Comparative
1782	100		100	100	100	100
3	100		127	126	110	110
4	93		116	126	102	110
5	90		104	115	88	97
6	85		105	124	81	96
7	87		102	117	86	99
8	87		99	114	94	108
9	85		105	123	107	126
90	87		117	136	111	129
1	89		112	126	99	111
2	93		110	118	87	94
3	99		129	131	100	101
4	98		140	144	106	109
5	117		168	144	152	131
6	125		153	123	160	128
7	110		112	101	109	99
8	118		116	99	105	90
9	136		159	122	140	108
1800	141		252	179	231	164
1	140	153	232	164	222	159
2	110	119	130	118	131	119
3	125	128	123	98	116	93
4	119	122	134	113	123	104
5	132	136	177	134	177	134
6	130	133	158	122	156	120
7	129	132	168	131	149	115
8	145	149	195	135	160	111
9	157	161	205	131	192	123
10	142	164	175	124	187	132
11	136	147	167	123	178	131
12	121	148	221	183	209	173
13	115	149	197	172	172	150
14	114	153	123	108	113	99
15	109	132	114	104	111	101
16	91	109	123	135	132	146
17	117	120	192	165	191	164
18	132	135	203	155	170	129
19	112	117	177	159	144	129
20	103	106	148	144	134	130
21	94		116	123	114	121
22	88		92	105	90	102
23	89		125	140	108	122
24	88		147	167	130	147
25	103		157	152	139	135
26	90		152	169	119	132
27	90		155	171	119	131
28	81		136	168	123	151
29	79		135	171	134	169
30	81		138	171	130	162
31	82		150	182	135	164

Year	General variation of all 40 commodities		Corn		Wheat	
	Gold Standard	Paper Standard	Actual	Comparative	Actual	Comparative
32	78		130	166	119	152
33	75		119	158	107	143
34	78		123	158	94	121
35	80		119	148	80	99
36	86		131	152	98	114
37	84		132	158	113	136
38	84		134	160	131	156
39	92		155	168	143	155
40	87		150	173	135	155
41	85		140	166	131	154
42	75		120	160	116	155
43	71		113	159	102	143
44	69		125	180	104	150
45	74		130	176	103	140
46	74		140	188	111	149
47	78		176	224	142	181
48	68		125	184	103	151
49	64		106	166	90	140
50	64		94	146	82	127

The figures in the column of the general variation of all forty commodities, gold standard, show a fall from 112 in 1819 to 88 in 1822 and 1824. This, apparently, substantiates the contention of Baring and others who claimed that the currency was raised 25 per cent. in value by the Peel Bill and proves that Ricardo, who claimed the advance no more than 3 per cent. and later 10 per cent., was wrong in both instances. In justice to Ricardo it must be said that he opposed the arrangement made for resumption by the Peel Bill. He wanted the Bank to reduce its issues until the paper pound and the gold one were worth the same. But instead, the Bank began to buy gold, in order to prepare for resumption of cash payments, and hence enhanced the value of gold. Jevons believed with Baring that Ricardo failed to take into consideration that gold itself was depreciated from 1797 to 1819. This lowering of the value came when it was forced out of circulation in England and dumped on the European market.

The "comparative" columns of corn and wheat reveal some interesting facts. Both commodities were very cheap at times, especially from 1819 to 1823, but corn never, in a single year from 1804 to 1850, fell as low as the average of the forty commodities, and wheat only twice—in 1814 and 1835 it touched 99. Both fell below the 1782 price level in 1822, but neither fell as much as the average of the forty commodities. If 1782 is a fair year to take as "100" for these forty articles, the obvious conclusion to draw from this table is that the decline in the price of agricultural products during these sixty-nine years was not as great as that of prices in general. Perhaps the enormous cheapening of the means of production in industry would offset or more than offset this apparent advantage of agriculture. If it does not, the case of the landed interest during these years is greatly weakened.

With contemporary opinion, the researches of Jevons, and the experience of a century to draw upon, what verdict should be passed upon the Peel Bill ? A fair estimate of its effect on prices is that it lowered them about 25 per cent. Unquestionably, it wrought great hardships on more than one class in the community, but it was a better solution than any alternative suggested at the time. An inflated currency such as had existed in the last years of the Napoleonic Wars and such as Cobbett and Western wished to re-establish, would have produced much greater evils by over-issue and derangement of the foreign exchange. Graham's plan for free trade in money would have removed even the insufficient obstacles to over-issue which existed at that time. Apparently the only possible relief to these low prices came, about 1850, with the discovery of gold. It was possible to raise the price of corn by a bad harvest or an inflation of the currency, but neither was permanent nor sure, and either was apt to prove a curse rather than a blessing in the long run. Thus without agreeing with Tooke that the Peel Bill did not affect prices at all, it is possible to admit that it lowered them about 25 per cent. and to still insist that it was preferable to any other policy offered at the time.

The second phase of the agitation outside Parliament against the Corn Laws is the new light thrown on the causes for the depression in the price of corn and the probability of an increased production in European countries by the second report of Jacob. This must not be confused with his first report, which was published in 1826 and which simply gave an account of the conditions under which grain was grown in northern Europe. His conclusion, based on this tour, was that Europe would not be able to supply Great Britain with any considerable amount of grain. The reasons for treating the second report in this part of the chapter, instead of under the discussions in Parliament on the Corn Laws, are that it was not published until 1828 and hence did not influence the deliberations in the way that the first report had done ; and that his explanation of the causes for the depression in the price of corn is one of the notable contributions made on the subject of the Corn Laws during these years and therefore too important to be omitted.

In his first report Jacob showed that there was no prospect of northern Europe sending any great amount of grain to Great Britain. In his second report he showed that the stock of wheat on hand at harvest time in the country had been steadily declining each year since 1823.[102] In view of the slight prospects of getting supplies from abroad and the decreasing surplus at home how was it possible to explain the depressed prices of corn ? Jacob held the novel view that public opinion was largely to blame for the price of wheat continuing low under these circumstances. Without questioning that supply and demand in the long run regulate prices, he insisted " that opinion, whether rightly or erroneously formed, exercises a much more powerful influence for a time."[103] For several years the opinion had been propagated, though in opposition to the doctrines of Malthus, that all over Europe production was increasing faster than population. It was asserted that cultivation had been carried too far and that it would be well to throw inferior land out of cultivation. Such statements, "confidently asserted, scarcely denied, but never investigated," obtained extensive credence by virtue of the high persons associated with them. The opinion that there was a great surplus of grain on the continent was not confined to Great Britain, for Jacob states that, " In the year 1825, I found, in all the corn countries in the north-east of Europe, this view of the matter to prevail universally among the growers of and dealers in corn ; and it would have been like combating the winds to have contended against the prevalent belief. Every grower of corn, whether on a large or small scale, affirmed that there was on hand sufficient for several years' consumption. I saw that their barns and granaries on many of the farms were empty, or very nearly so ; and the owners, still convinced of the truth of the general opinion, assured me, that though the necessary calls for money had compelled them to sell at however low a price they could obtain, I should find, on proceeding farther, such vast abundance in store, as would convince me that they were right in their representations. I did proceed ; I found no stocks anywhere, but everywhere I found the assurance, that farther on I should encounter a superabundant quantity. The farther I advanced from the seashore, the more scanty did I find the provision of bread corn, but especially of rye, which is the chief food of the country I then visited."[104]

The consequences of this error, Jacob pointed out, were of more importance than the causes. The prevailing view naturally influenced the conduct of speculators in corn. The extinction of speculation in corn and the small stocks kept by corn chandlers, mealmen and other dealers, was mainly due to the exaggerated representation of the vast stocks accumulated in Europe which were ready to be poured into this country. In concluding this phase of the subject, he protested vigorously against those, who either through malice or ignorance, led the public to believe that ten million quarters might be imported annually at forty shillings below the English price, and represented that twenty million pounds was thus extorted from the consumer for the benefit of the landlord and farmer ; whereas a twentieth of this amount could not be extracted from the whole continent without bringing the price there up to the level of the English one.[105]

But although many Corn Law advocates were willing to admit the scantiness of the European surplus, they would not admit that the surplus could not be enormously increased if stimulated by a greater demand. Furthermore, many who favoured free trade in grain, as Ricardo, held the same opinion. It is this view that Jacob next turned to combat. Admitting that in new countries like America, Canada or Australia an indefinite increase in production was possible, any attempt to raise successive corn crops in old and long cultivated countries, such as those of northern Europe, would soon exhaust the soil. Only in Holstein and Mecklenburg did he find advanced husbandry. " The greater part of France, a still much greater portion of Germany, and nearly the whole of Prussia, Austria, Poland and Russia, present a wretched uniformity of system. It is called three-course husbandry, consisting of, 1st, one year's clean fallow ; 2nd, winter corn, chiefly rye, with a proportion of wheat commensurate to

P

the manure that can be applied ; 3rd, summer corn, or barley and oats."[106] Such a system barely produced four times the quantity of the seed, and the work done on the land was usually performed in a most negligent manner. No cultivators from the lords to the peasantry had any capital, and most of the latter were content to live on their own produce.

The next question to be answered was whether eastern Europe could produce a surplus if the system of farming were improved. Jacob was of the opinion that even a radical change in the agrarian system could not be expected to yield any great immediate increase in the supply of corn. The change in the method of holding land would be an economic and social revolution which no government would voluntarily attempt. The attempt of Prussia was unlikely to induce other powers to follow her example. But even if the change were made and each tenant or copyholder became a freeholder, he would find himself in possession of an unenclosed compact piece of land, without capital, stock or machinery. Many of these small freeholders would fail financially and fall to the status of day labourers. The land would then be sold to the only person with money, some rich capitalist who would form a large estate and lease it to tenants. The latter would, in all probability, farm it more poorly than did the original holder.[107]

Finally, Jacob had still another reason for believing that Europe could not be counted upon to send a surplus of grain to Great Britain in the future, namely, that the population was increasing more rapidly than the food supply. By a long and careful calculation, based on the best statistics available in each country, he concluded that the population of Europe had increased by 28 or 29 million since 1815. Although admitting that it was more difficult to estimate the increase in production, he felt that it had not kept pace with population and that it was only a question of time until the population would actually press on the food supply.[108]

This second report of Jacob seems to have had little effect upon those who drew up the act of 1828, but it did have a great deal of influence on free trade writers in the years that followed. These writers especially stressed the part that was best for their case : the fact that the amount Europe could send was limited rather than that she might not be able to send any within a few years.

The third and most important phase of the agitation against the Corn Laws outside Parliament deals with the intense personal attacks on the landlords. These attacks on their social and political position were most virulent in Thompson's *Catechism on the Corn Laws* and in an anonymous pamphlet entitled *The Iniquity of the Landlords*. Many newspapers, especially the *Morning Chronicle*, directed a fierce attack along the same lines.

The Catechism, as the title suggests, was a series of questions and theses from the point of view of the landowners, with answers, usually unduly offensive, from that of the manufacturers and labourers. A few selections from the questions and answers in the fourth edition will give a fair idea of the tactics employed. " What is meant by Corn Laws ? Laws which enact that the labourer shall not exchange his produce for food, except at certain shops, namely, the shops of the landowners. For whose benefit are these laws? Manifestly, of those who support them—the landowners. What are the effects of these laws? The same in kind, as would arise from limiting the food consumed in the United Kingdom, to what could be produced in the Isle of Wight."[109]

The greater part of *The Catechism* was devoted to statements by defenders of the Corn Laws and answers similar to those just cited. The following are fairly typical: " That operatives are a lazy race, and seldom go to work before Wednesday. Answer—The landlords never go to work at all.[110] That the excess of population should be relieved by emigration. A.—Every English manufacturer, therefore, who is driven to emigrate, is an innocent man condemned to transportation in the interest of the landlords.[111] That we must reconcile conflicting interests. A.—There can be no conflict on a wrong. When the question is of a purse unjustly taken, it is a fallacy to say we must reconcile conflicting interests, and give the taker half.[112] That, however large and important our foreign commerce may appear, when examined by itself, it must sink infinitely in our estimation when contrasted with our domestic trade. A.—If the commercial interest is small, it is because it is robbed. The highwayman says to the man he has stripped, ' Which of us has the heaviest purse?' And which, do you think, should be attended to by a sagacious government?[113] That this is the true reason of the declension of Venice, Pisa, Florence and the Hanseatic towns, in wealth and population. These *were* the workshops into which the surplus corn of Europe was poured to be consumed in manufactures. A.—It is something to have been Venice instead of a group of muddy islands in the mouth of the Brenta. It is better to *have been* Venice than to have been always mud.[114] That the relation between the landlords and others, arising out of the Corn Laws is a source of kindly feelings and mutual virtues. A.—Exactly the same was said of slavery.[115] That it has become the fashion to represent the landowners themselves as a set of useless, selfish and greedy drones, whose only service to the state is the consumption of a large and increasing revenue, which would otherwise be added to the earnings of the industrious classes. A.—Possibly the drone may have been injured in the comparison. It would have been more exact, if the drone had been in the habit of preventing the entrance of honey into the hive, as the means of enforcing a provision for himself."[116]

All these illustrations dealt with the landlords as defenders of the Corn Laws, but others were merely attacks on their social and political position. Examples of this attitude are: " That the race of English gentlemen, English farmers and English yeomen, is worth preserving. A.—Not if they are kept at the public expense. As long as they keep themselves, everybody is glad to see them.[117] That they are a source of light and knowledge to the lower orders. A.—They teach them what they are anxious they should learn ; and others do the same. That they have sound political principles. A.—They take the side which they think best for themselves ; and others do so, too. That they fought the battle against the Jacobins. A.—Which other people are to pay for. That they keep up rural sports. A.—Men have no claim to be paid for amusing themselves as they like best. That they kill foxes and others. A.—The mole-catcher would do it better. That they sit at quarter sessions. A.—And strange things they sometimes do there. For instance, in Buckinghamshire, they sentenced John Doe to five months' imprisonment for intending to assault the lord's hen pheasant, and Richard Roe to three, for assaulting the serf's daughter.[118] That they are the unpaid magistracy. A.—If they demand to be kept, they are not. That they are generous, brave and human. A.—All Englishmen from time immemorial by their own account have been so too."[119]

Next to *The Catechism* the pamphlet which was most popular with and most often quoted by opponents of the Corn Laws was *The Iniquity of the Landholders*. It began with the bold thesis that the landowners, at the time when they had imposed a tax on the community for the benefit of the state and the defence of the country, had without any shadow or pretence of right imposed a second for their benefit in the shape of the Corn Laws. But there was nothing inconsistent with their previous record in such an action for " the landholders have been at all times the great oppressors of the country. It will be clearly proved, by their own admissions, as well as by records of undoubted authority, that their power has been uniformly employed in enriching themselves at the expense of the other classes of the community."[120] Originally all lands were granted merely as benefices resumable at the pleasure of the sovereign, and in return the holders of land were obliged to defend the country and defray the expenses of government. But step by step they freed themselves from the original conditions upon which they held the land, until by an act, in the twelfth year of the reign of Charles II., the last were abolished. Thus they now held the land and no longer discharged their original compact of defraying the government expenses and defending the country.[121]

Turning from the historical to the contemporary iniquities of the landholders, this anonymous author denied, what even the majority of writers who opposed the Corn Laws admitted, that the burdens on agriculture were greater in Great Britain than in other countries. In America the wages were at least 20s. an acre higher than in Great Britain, which more than compensated for the rates and tithes in the latter. In addition manufactured articles were 25 to 100 per cent. dearer in America. In continental countries, agricultural products were far from being exempted from taxes and formed the chief source of revenue.[122]

All things considered, it was impossible to regard the Corn Laws in any other light than as an unjust and oppressive tax. But, heavy " as these burdens undoubtedly are, their actual weight is but a very trivial evil, compared with the dangerous and degrading principles on which the Corn Laws are found ; viz., that of the right of the landholders, who are in possession of the legislative power, to tax their fellow-subjects for their own personal advantage."[123] As long as such a right existed other classes were no better off than the Christians and Jews who paid for permission to live under the Turkish government. Whether the tribute was exacted as a capitation tax or one on corn really mattered very little. The mass of people now stood in relation to the landlords as the tenants had to their lords under the feudal system. In conclusion this writer held that " it has now been fully proved that these laws are not only unjust, and most highly oppressive, especially to the poorer classes, but also that they are wholly unnecessary for effecting any useful purposes, and I therefore earnestly call upon all men who have any regard to the principles either of religion or morality, or to their own personal liberty or independence, cordially to unite in the most strenuous endeavours to put an end to a system, which is directly opposed to every principle of justice, of prudence and of humanity."[124]

During the three years ending with the Corn Law of 1828, many newspapers, especially the *Morning Chronicle*, kept up an incessant attack on the Corn Laws and landlords. Ridicule, irony and sarcasm were used unsparingly. Some of the attacks were obviously unfair ; others were very effective. Perhaps the wittiest single attack was a parody on the position of the Tories of the extreme right which appeared in the *Kent Herald*. This article referred feelingly to the immense services rendered by the great landlords and asked, " Did they not form troops of yeomanry cavalry and intimidate, by the scythe-like flourish of their broad swords and the trampling of their heavy chargers, the puny dwellers in factious cities who were hatching treason and the abolition of the aristocracy ? Did they not encourage the ' Immortal William Pitt ' in those measures which kept up high prices, and kept out Revolution ? Did they not support ' a just and necessary war ' which destroyed millions of human beings and trebled the amount of the rent rolls of England ? Did they not, in later times, when Bread and Luddites rose together, rally round the Great Castlereagh in his spirited suspensions of the Habeas Corpus and the Constitution ? And have they not prevented, at sundry times, that Reform in Parliament, about which other classes of the community have clamoured so much and so ignorantly ? Did they not back up the Ministry that passed the Corn Bill with troops of soldiers drawn up round the House, lest the hungry and disaffected multitude should prevent a measure then deemed so requisite for the support of the ' social order ' ? Can they, speaking generally, in the memory of any of us, be accused of ever showing symptoms of insubordination or opposition to a system which worked well for them ? If we except some talk of reducing Taxation, abolishing Tithes, cutting of sinecures, paring down the Civil List, Reforming Parliament, and annihilating the National Debt, in the years of 1821 and 1822 when wheat was 38s. a quarter, did they ever lend themselves to the ' wild and visionary ' schemes of Radicals, Liberals and Reformers ? "[125]

If the material cited from *The Catechism, The Iniquity of the Land-holders* and the *Kent Herald* indicates the spirit of the attacks upon the landed interest, it is equally interesting to discover in what spirit it was received by the aristocracy and country gentlemen. Some were filled with rage and some with pompous indignation ; others, recognizing the rising feeling, suggested that some concessions would be wise ; and still others frankly advocated free trade.

Lauderdale, Stanhope and Redesdale express very vividly the anger of the outraged aristocracy. Lauderdale's views have already been sufficiently expressed when the bills of 1827 and 1828 were under discussion in the House of Lords, and those of the other two are no less colourful. Stanhope, in expressing his disgust with these attacks, unblushingly declared : " I am, as you well know, one of those old-fashioned Tories, who wish that Rights may be respected, all Property may be secured, and that ancient Institutions may be preserved."[126] Redesdale was even more belligerent and called attention to the fact that the political ascendancy of the landowners was being challenged. He claimed that the cry had gone forth that, " The landed interest must be put down," and that revolutionists of all kinds joined in the cry because they realized that the ruin of the landholders was the first step toward the overthrow of the ancient constitution.[127] The revolutionists, principally to blame, were the ones who had assumed the appellation of political economists. To effect the destruction of the landed interest, they knew that they must first reduce the profits of the landlords ; and hence they represented that these profits were all that prevented an immense expansion of manufacture and trade. The Corn Laws stood in the way of this nefarious plot ; but-the revolutionists hoped by their repeal to throw out of cultivation all except the most fertile land, and thus to drive out of the country most of the agricultural population and to render the remainder dependent upon trade and manufactures.[128] Redesdale also observed with concern that the constitution was changing in the past half-century through the decline of the influence of the landed interest. In the Commons this was due to the increase of the manufacturers and traders, and to the fact that many of the large landed proprietors were themselves traders ; and in the Lords, to the loss of the ancient influence which this House had possessed. Clearly the trend of measures passed and proposed lately was to destroy the old balance, and " finally to place the government (even if it should retain its ancient form) under the predominant control of a Commercial Republic."[129]

Sir John Sinclair spoke sincerely in the pompous vein which the *Kent Herald* had parodied so admirably. He declared that there was a design afloat to punish the landed interest for its manly stand against French Republicanism ; for its preservation of the constitution under which more people enjoy the blessings of liberty than under any ever in existence ; for its having filled the world with amazement at the naval and military achievements of the country ; for its having elevated the nation to a height of power beyond any ever recorded ; and finally for its having persevered in the struggle against the idol of Radicalism until he surrendered and was safely immured on the rock of St. Helena. He felt that the landed interest should repel this attack and declared that, " As the proprietor of an estate which I am bound to protect from foreign aggression, I am not disposed to yield to the attacks of this domestic invader."[130]

Sir James Graham represented the group of landlords who believed in placating public opinion by some concessions. He held that it was absurd for the landed proprietors to waste their strength in fruitless party struggle, when, by acting with unity of purpose, it would be possible to utilize their vast majority in both Houses in such a manner that nothing except public opinion could limit their power. The seat of this public opinion, he believed, was in the middle ranks of life. This middle class was removed from the wants of the labouring class and from the craving of ambition, and possessed sufficient intelligence to form a sound judgment, neither warped by interest nor obscured by passion.[131] Hence the landed interest should frame its measures in order to secure the support of this class. He implored the landowners to abandon the futile attempt to keep the price of corn artificially high, and to make a timely compromise with the public by accepting a fixed duty equal to the burdens imposed on the British producer, on the importation of foreign grain. Having won the kindly feeling of the people by this concession, the landowners should insist on the revision of the Peel Act of 1819.[132]

Some well-known landholders, notably John Rooke, Lord Milton and Sir Henry Parnell, admitted their conversion to free trade. Rooke begged the landowners to avoid the hostility of public opinion, not as Graham had suggested by merely making concessions, but by accepting free trade. He insisted that they had nothing to fear either politically or financially from the abolition of the Corn Laws ; since the more prosperous the towns were, the heavier the rent rolls of the landlords would be. There was actually a greater danger to their political ascendancy from the attacks of the manufacturers and labourers on the Corn Laws than would result from their actual abolition.[133]

Lord Milton's conversion furnished a notable addition to the free trade camp, because he was the heir to one of the largest landed estates in the country. In 1822 he had strongly favoured protection for agriculture, but a study of conditions in the years that followed had caused him to change his views. In the ten years following 1828 he was to be one of the outstanding advocates of free trade.

But unquestionably the most significant convert was Sir Henry Parnell, who had been the leading advocate of additional protection to agriculture from 1813 to 1815 and who had spoken strongly for free trade in the discussion in the Commons on Canning's resolution during March of 1827. He frankly admitted that information recently obtained from Jacob and the reports of British consuls on the ability of foreign countries to grow corn for the British market had done more than anything else to bring about this change in his point of view.

CONCLUSION

The question naturally arises why, in view of the vigorous campaign carried on against the Corn Laws from 1825 to 1828 and of the conversion to free trade of a number of advocates of protection, the subject should have been relegated to the background after the law of 1828 was passed ? The decline in interest cannot be accounted for by a series of good harvests, as frequently happened in the previous century, because bad or mediocre ones continued until 1832. It is

equally unsatisfactory to account for this decline on the grounds that
the law of 1828 satisfied the complaints made against the existing
system.   If the debates in Parliament and the comments in pamphlets, periodicals and newspapers are a fair criterion, the measure
aroused little enthusiasm outside the government.   The country
gentlemen protested vigorously and the free traders accepted it as
less objectionable than the acts of 1815 and 1822.   When the bill
was passed, the spirit on both sides was one of reluctant acquiescence
rather than of satisfaction or even of relief.   Perhaps the interest
in the Corn Laws was supplanted by that in Catholic Emancipation,
foreign policy and the overthrow of the Tories in 1830.   But the
explanation that seems most plausible is that the manufacturers,
traders and labourers all came to the conclusion that nothing better
than the act of 1828 could be expected under the unreformed House
of Commons.   Consequently, they turned their attention to
Parliamentary reform as a necessary preliminary to the repeal of the
Corn Laws.

The years covered by this chapter, 1822 to 1828, are significant
ones in the history of the Corn Laws principally because they serve as
a link between the years from 1813 to 1822 on the one hand and
1838 to 1846 on the other.   Down to 1822, the landed interest, as
was shown in Chapters VII and VIII, tried to use their political power
to insure war prices in grain.   After that year, apparently, they
resigned themselves to lower prices.   A lull of over two years was
ended in January of 1825 when the attack described in this chapter
was begun by the manufacturing and trading interests against
agricultural protection.   Ten years of comparative inactivity followed
1828 before the intense agitation of the Anti-Corn Law League,
beginning in 1838, helped to bring about the repeal in 1846.   The
agitation carried on against the Corn Laws from 1825 to 1828 is
significant largely because it anticipated the activities of the League
in so many ways.   The whole question was thrashed out in these
years and practically every argument used for and against Corn Laws
later was put forward at this time.   The League simply carried on a
more intensive, better organized and more widely-distributed propaganda than did the opposition in the eighteen-twenties.   Hence the
activities of the League will be interesting more from the point of
view of methods employed than for new and original arguments.

CHAPTER IX

NOTES

[1] Tooke, *History of Prices*, vol. 2, p. 84. [2] *Ibid.*, p. 122.
[3] Smart, *Economic Annals of the Nineteenth Century*, 1821–1830, p. 136.
[4] *Hansard*, vol. 9, 933.
[5] *The Annual Register*, vol. 65, pp. 99–100.
[6] Tooke, *op. cit.*, p. 122. [7] 5th George IV., c. 70.
[8] *The Annual Register*, vol. 66, pp. 1–2. [9] *Hansard*, vol. 13, pp. 142–9.
[10] Whitmore, *Substance of a Speech delivered in the House of Commons on April 28th*, 1825, p. 2.
[11] *Ibid.*, p. 31. [12] Smart, *op. cit.*, p. 303. [13] 6th George IV., c. 64 and 65.
[14] 6th George IV., c. 65. [15] *Hansard*, vol. 13, p. 337. [16] Smart, *op. cit.*, p. 331.
[17] *Hansard*, vol. 15, pp. 36–40. [18] *Ibid.*, p. 318.
[19] This Jacob is the same person who wrote tracts, of which a detailed account was given in Chapter VII, favouring the corn bills of 1814 and 1815. He was sent by the government, in June of 1825, to see what supplies of wheat could be drawn from the Baltic countries in case the Corn Laws were altered. The report referred to is the one he drew up on his return from Eastern Europe.
[20] Member for Wotton Basset.
[21] *Hansard*, vol. 15, p. 338. [22] *Ibid.*, p. 349. [23] *Ibid.*, p. 370. [24] *Ibid.*, pp. 400–89. [25] *Ibid.*, p. 486. [26] *Ibid.*, p. 488.
[27] *The Annual Register*, vol. 68, p. 44.
[28] *Hansard*, vol. 15, pp. 764–65. [29] *Ibid.*, p. 748. [30] *Ibid.*, p. 791.
[31] *Ibid.*, p. 951. [32] *Ibid.*, pp. 814–15. [33] *Ibid.*, pp. 816–26.
[34] 7th George IV., c. 70. [35] 7th George IV., c. 71. [36] Tooke, *op. cit.*, p. 137.
[37] Smart, *op. cit.*, p. 391. [38] *Hansard*, vol. 16, pp. 130–1.
[39] 7th George IV., Session 2, c. 3.
[40] *Corrected Report of the Speech delivered by George Canning in the House of Commons, March 1st*, 1827, p. 4.
[41] *Ibid.*, p. 19. [42] *Ibid.*, pp. 22–3. [43] *Ibid.*, p. 23. [44] *Ibid.*, p. 28.
[45] *Hansard*, vol. 16, pp. 775–6. [46] *Ibid.*, pp. 1041–5. [47] *Ibid.*, vol. 17, pp. 174–8. [48] *Ibid.*, vol. 16, p. 1062. [49] *Ibid.*, vol. 17, p. 198. [50] *Ibid.*, vol. 16, pp. 1101–6. [51] *Ibid.*, pp. 1046–7. [52] *Ibid.*, p. 1066. [53] *Ibid.*, p. 1082. [54] *Ibid.*, p. 1122. [55] *Ibid.*, vol. 17, p. 105.
[56] Grant was President of the Board of Trade.
[57] *Hansard*, vol. 17, pp. 78–9. [58] *Ibid.*, p. 132. [59] *Ibid.*, p. 198. [60] *Ibid.*, p. 392. [61] *Ibid.*, vol. 16, pp. 1020–93. [62] *Ibid.*, vol. 17, pp. 120–8. [63] *Ibid.*, pp. 789–802. [64] *Ibid.*, pp. 803–9. [65] *Ibid.*, p. 1098. [66] *Ibid.*, p. 1238.
[67] *The Trades' Newspaper*, June 17th, 1827 (Place Collection).
[68] *Aberdeen Star* (Place Collection).
[69] *Hansard*, vol. 17, p. 1258. [70] *Ibid.*, pp. 1303–4. [71] *Ibid.*, p. 1305.
[72] *Ibid.*, p. 1339. [73] *Ibid.*, p. 1326–7. [74] *Ibid.*, p. 1380.
[75] 7th and 8th George IV., c. 57. [76] *Ibid.*, c. 58.
[77] *Hansard*, vol. 17, pp. 1372–5.
[78] Smart, *op. cit.*, p. 439.
[79] *Hansard*, vol. 18, p. 1379.
[80] Smart, *op. cit.*, p. 439.
[81] *Hansard*, vol. 18, 1364–70. [82] *Ibid.*, vol. 19, 208–17. [83] *Ibid.*, pp. 843–6.
[84] *Ibid.*, p. 902. [85] *Ibid.*, p. 903. [86] *Ibid.*, pp. 1334–42.
[87] In the case of barley the " pivot " point was 33s. with a duty of 12s. 4d. which increased or decreased 1s. 6d. for every increase or decrease in the price ; in the case of oats it was 25s. with a duty of 9s. 3d., and an increase or decrease of 1s. 6d. ; and in rye, peas and beans it was 36s. with a duty of 15s. 6d. and an increase or decrease of 1s. 6d. The nominal duty of 1s. became operative at 41s.

in the case of barley; 31s. in that of oats; and 46s. in that of rye, peas and beans.

[88] Wheat could be imported up to 67s. upon payment of a duty of 5s. and above that price upon one of 6d.   Barley was to pay 2s. 6d. up to 34s. and 6d. above that amount; oats, 2s. up to 25s. and 6d. above; and rye, peas and beans 3s. up to 41s. and 6d. above.

[89] 9th George IV., c. 60.

[90] Graham, *Corn and Currency*, in an Address to the Landowners, 1828, p. 18.

[91] *Ibid.*, p. 43.

[92] *Free Trade in Corn the real Interest of the Landlord, and the true Policy of the State*, 1828, p. 52.

[93] Fletcher, *Reflexions on the Causes which Influence the Price of Corn*, 1827, pp. 9. and 52.

[94] *Ibid.*, p. 33.

[95] Joplin, *Views on the Currency*, 1826, p. 63.

[96] Graham, *op. cit.*, pp. 197–200.

[97] *Free Trade in Corn and the real Interest of the Landlord and the true Policy of the State*, 1827, pp. 68–9.

[98] Fletcher, *op. cit.*, p. 76.

[99] Tooke, *On the Currency in Connexion with the Corn Trade and on the Corn Laws*, 1829, pp. 1–2.

[100] *Ibid.*, p. 53.

[101] Cannan, *The Paper Pound of 1797–1821*, p. xxix.

[102] Jacob, *Tracts Relating to the Corn Trade and Corn Laws*, 1828, pp. 89–91.

[103] *Ibid.*, p. 108.   [104] *Ibid.*, p. 109.   [105] *Ibid.*, p. 129.   [106] *Ibid.*, p. 140.

[107] *Ibid.*, p. 144.   [108] *Ibid.*, p. 148.

[109] Thompson, *Catechism on the Corn Laws*, 1828, 4th edn., p. 23.

[110] *Ibid.*, p. 37.   [111] *Ibid.*, p. 49.   [112] *Ibid.*, p. 86.   [113] *Ibid.*, pp. 103–4.
[114] *Ibid.*, p. 108.   [115] *Ibid.*, p. 118.   [116] *Ibid.*, p. 94.   [117] *Ibid.*, p. 118.   [118] *Ibid.*, p. 119.   [119] *Ibid.*, p. 120.

[120] *The Iniquity of the Landholders, the Mistakes of the Farmers and the Folly and Mischievous Consequences . . . in regard to the Corn Laws*, 1826, p. 6.

[121] *Ibid.*, p. 7.   [122] *Ibid.*, pp. 31–33.   [123] *Ibid.*, p. 46.   [124] *Ibid.*, p. 48.

[125] *Kent Herald*, September 28th, 1827 (Place Collection).

[126] Stanhope, *Letter on the proposed Alteration of the Corn Laws*, 1827, p. 29.

[127] Redesdale, *Observations upon the Importation of foreign Corn; with the Resolutions moved by Lord Redesdale in House of Lords, March 29th*, 1827, p. 1.

[128] *Ibid.*, pp. 2–4.   [129] *Ibid.*, pp. 136–7.

[130] *The Morning Chronicle*, September 26th, 1826 (Place Collection).

[131] Graham, *op. cit.*, p. 9.   [132] *Ibid.*, p. 64.

[133] *Free Trade in Corn*, etc., pp. 61–2.

CHAPTER X

THE DECLINE IN INTEREST IN THE CORN LAWS FROM 1828 TO 1838

Reasons for immediate decline in interest in the Corn Laws after the law of 1828 was passed—Ten years from 1828 to 1838 falls into three periods—I, 1828 to 1832—Indifferent or deficient crops—Large imports of grain—Slight interest in the subject in Parliament—Negligible output of pamphlets and periodical literature—The labourers' revolt—II, 1832 to 1836—Expectations of a change in the Corn Laws after the Reform Act of 1832—Good crops, low prices and few imports—Agricultural distress—Agitation for relief—Report of committee of 1833—Evidence presented by the committee of 1836—Agriculture relieved of " special burdens " by new poor law, abolition of statute labour for maintaining minor roads, and the Tithe Act—Interest in the Corn Laws in Parliament and outside was slight during these years—III, 1836 to 1838—Deficient crops in 1836 and 1837—Revival of agitation—Status of the Corn Laws in 1838 in comparison with that of 1828.

THE principal reason for the decline in interest in the Corn Laws during the years immediately following 1828 was, as stated at the end of last chapter, that the interests agitating for repeal came to the conclusion that nothing more favourable than the law of 1828 could be expected until the House of Commons was reformed. An additional reason may have been the enormous importations of grain which proved that the new law did not prevent the bringing in of foreign grain to the extent that those of 1815 and 1822 had done.

The ten years covered by this chapter can be divided into three periods. The first, from 1828 to 1832, is characterized by subordination of the agitation for the repeal of the Corn Laws to that of reforming the House of Commons, by poor or indifferent crops, high prices of grain and enormous importations. The second, from 1832 to 1836, is characterized by a continuation of the decline in the agitation for repeal, in spite of a reformed House of Commons, excellent crops, low prices and distress in agriculture. The third period, from 1836 to 1838, is characterized by a renewal of the agitation for repeal, poor crops, high prices, distress in industry and commerce and unemployment.

The general rule laid down in an earlier chapter (that when the price of grain rose, agitation against the Corn Laws followed ; and when the price fell, complaints against agricultural distress ensued) does not apply to the years from 1828 to 1832. Had this rule operated, the agitation against the Corn Laws would have continued down to the good crop of 1832. Four bad or indifferent crops[1] kept the prices high, and as a result foreign grain began to come in upon the payment of a low duty as soon as the law of 1828 went into operation on July 15th.   Between July 15th and the end of the year, 760,479 quarters of wheat and wheat flour were entered for consumption, of which only 20,021 came from the colonies.   During the next four years these imports totalled 1,442,701, 1,727,847, 1,506,740 and 376,755 quarters respectively.   The total imports of all kinds of grain[2] from 1828 to 1832, inclusive, were 1,011,836, 2,025,156, 2,763,217, 2,508,700 and 481,919 quarters respectively.   These huge amounts were exclusive of the imports of all kinds of grain from Ireland which varied from 2,215,521 quarters in 1830 to 2,990,767 in 1832.   Thus the total importation of all kinds of grain amounted to almost exactly five million quarters in both 1830 and 1831.   Clearly the sliding scale principle of the act of 1828 did not exclude foreign grain, when the price was moderately high, in the effective manner that absolute prohibition up to 80s. had done.

In Parliament the Corn Laws aroused so little attention that formal consideration of the question seems to have been given on only three occasions between the passing of the act of 1828 and the Reform Bill of 1832.   On May 19th, 1829, the irrepressible Deacon Hume moved the substitution of a fixed duty and a bounty for the sliding scale of the law of 1828.   Many of his arguments were shrewd and timely, but the House showed its indifference in rejecting the proposal by 154 to 12.[3]

On March 29th, 1830, Lord King moved a series of resolutions on the Corn Laws in the House of Lords.   In the speech explaining these resolutions, he devoted considerable time to the self-sufficient nation argument.   Carried to its logical conclusion, he maintained that it would divert America from agriculture to manufacturing, France from making wine to manufacturing iron, and England from manufacturing to digging on heaths.   The Earl of Malmesbury and the Duke of Wellington replied and especially emphasized the importance of the home market.   In the end the Lords showed so little interest that Lord King's resolutions were negatived without a division.[4]

On September 15th, 1831, Hunt,[5] adhering to the promise made on the first day that he entered the Commons, proposed that the House go into Committee to consider "the said Acts."   He especially stressed the inadequacy of the pay of labourers.   James, in seconding the motion, gave the typical point of view of those who wanted repeal. He stated that, in his opinion, it would have been wiser to have waited until the Reform Bill was passed before introducing the motion ; but that once it was passed, the repeal of the Corn Laws should be the first work of a reformed House of Commons.   The motion was beaten by 194 to 6.[6]

It is true that isolated petitions calling for repeal continued to find their way to the tables of both houses, but in the main the question was a dead one in Parliament during these years.   The three instances cited are the only ones in which much time was given to a discussion of the matter.   The crushing defeat of each proposal merely to consider the existing laws shows the utter lack of interest in Parliament during these years.

The pamphlet literature during these four years is negligible.[7]   The greater part even of this scanty output is either a rather weak continuation of the controversy taken up in the last chapter or printed copies of speeches delivered on some phase of the subject. The outstanding pamphlet was, unquestionably, Milton's *Address to the Landowners of England*, yet his attitude was not new, but merely that of the liberal landlords described in Chapter IX. It was a moderate and conciliatory appeal to the landowners, and lacked the bitter personal denunciation of the average anti-Corn Law pamphlet of the eighteen-twenties. He held that the Corn Laws helped the landlords much less than they believed ; and that they injured the agricultural labourers, tenants, manufacturers and city operatives. By a comparison of wages and prices over a series of years, he showed that the labourers were better off in years when the price of corn was low. This argument, however, did not disprove the contention of landowners who claimed that in time of low prices unemployment was more disastrous to the labourers than high prices. The number of bankruptcies among farmers and the constant remissions of rent in recent years showed that the tenants were not prospering. At this point Milton asked, " Has it never struck you, fellow citizens, that this proceeding is no evidence of liberality, but rather of extortion ; that the return of part of the rent may be proper, when called for by temporary calamity, by the effects of flood, or storm, or by some accidental misfortune overwhelming a particular tenant, or class of tenants ; but that, when resorted to habitually, it is not to be justified ; that it convicts those who have recourse to it of continued attempts to extract from their tenantry a rent not warranted by the value of agricultural produce ; and that, so far from proving the liberality of the landlord, it affords testimony of a very different quality ? "[8]

But Milton's appeal to the landowners failed, for it provoked either a renewed statement of their cause or a patronizing and lofty answer that he was well-meaning but misguided. Typical of the answers to Milton was : " Abolish the Corn Law and you ruin every landlord and farmer, and bring every farming labourer in Britain to the parish ; and with the ruin of these, you produce the ruin of the manufacturers, because they are beyond all comparison the greatest and best customers whom the manufacturers have."[9]

But if comparatively little interest was shown in the Corn Laws on either side of the question, during these years, the amazing revolt of the agricultural labourers in the South of England was not without significance on the future of agricultural protection. Strictly speaking this labourers' revolt is not a part of the history of the Corn Laws, since it was not directed against these laws, but it is important in this study as throwing some light on the point of view of that portion of the agricultural population which normally had no means of expressing itself. As one writer expresses it, " The voice of the poor themselves does not come to our ears. . . . This world has no member of Parliament, no press, it does not make literature or write history ; no diary or memoirs have kept alive for us the thoughts and cares of the passing day. It is for this reason that the events of the winter of 1830 have so profound an interest, for in the scenes now to be described we have the mind of this class hidden from us through all this period of pain, bursting the silence by the only power at its command."[10] Thus the revolt of these few months gives us a momentary glimpse of the mind of the agricultural labourer like a flash of lightning which for a second breaks the monotony of a dark night.

The first riot took place at Hardres in Kent on August 29th. Accounts differ as to the actual cause of the outbreak, which soon spread over the county, but the prominent feature of this social war was the destruction of machinery.[11] The anger of the labourers was especially directed against the threshing machine which threw out of work so many of their number. Along with the destruction of the hated machinery went the burning of ricks. Throughout September and October both practices increased in Kent.[12] During the first part of November they spread to Sussex and parts of Surrey, and after the middle of the month to Berkshire, Hampshire and Wiltshire.[13] In Sussex the movement developed into " an organized demand for a living wage." Demands for higher wages were made upon farmers who were in no position to refuse. Often the latter would add that it would be impossible to continue to pay such high wages unless tithes and rents were reduced. The labourers then added the reduction of these two to their programme of higher wages, and forced a lowering, particularly of tithes, in many places. In Kent and Sussex the sympathy of the farmers and some of the landowners seems to have been with the labourers.[14] If this spirit had lasted and had been more widely spread there was a strong possibility that " the winter of 1830 might have ended in an improvement of wages and a reduction of rents and tithes throughout the South of England."[15] In many places the uprisings had resulted in magistrates calling meetings to consider means of alleviating the wretched condition of the poor.

A settlement along these lines was prevented because the upper classes became frightened by the spread of the movement and by the scarcity of troops. Even landowners who had been sympathetic and had felt that something should be done to improve the life of the labourers, now felt that drastic action was necessary. " Conciliatory methods consequently ceased ; the upper classes substituted action for diplomacy, and the movement rapidly collapsed. Little resistance was offered, and the terrible hosts of armed and desperate men melted down into groups of weak and ill-fed labourers, armed with sticks and stones."[16]

The details of the suppression of the disorders and the trials of the culprits are outside the scope of this study.[17] The significance of the labourers' revolt, as far as the Corn Laws are concerned, lies in the light that it throws upon the life of the lower strata of agricultural society under the system of protection, and upon the justice of the claim of the landowners that they were the natural spokesmen for the agricultural labourers.

The lower classes found a poetical spokesman for their miseries at this time, when Ebenezer Elliott, in 1831, published the first edition of his Corn Law Rhymes. Without a doubt they are too highly coloured and place too much responsibility on the Corn Laws for the sufferings of the poor. Nevertheless, he did paint conditions that actually existed, and by blaming the Corn Laws for this state of affairs he inflamed public opinion in the lower walks of life. The following poem is typical :[18]

> Child, is thy father dead ?
> Father is gone !
> Why did they tax his bread ?
> God's will be done !
> Mother has sold her bed ;
> Better to die than wed !
> Where shall she lay her head ?
> Home we have none.
>
> Father clamm'd thrice a week,
> God's will be done !
> Long for work he did seek,
> Work he found none :
> Tears on his hollow cheek,
> Told what no tongue could speak ;
> Why did his master break ?
> God's will be done !

The years from 1832 to 1836 are in marked contrast to those just described. The poor or mediocre crops of the years 1828 to 1831 inclusive, the enormous imports and high prices of grain, the lack of interest in the Corn Laws in Parliament, the small output of pamphlet and periodical literature on the subject, and the flurry and tragedy of the labourers' revolt give way to something entirely different. The passing of the Reform Bill brought in a reformed House of Commons in which many members were eager to repeal the Corn Laws, and soon after the first of four good or average crops brought in low prices of grain and complaints of agricultural distress from landowners and farmers. Thus at the very moment when circumstances seemed propitious for a revival of the agitation against the Corn Laws, abundant crops and low prices destroyed the most effective argument of the free-traders ; and on the other hand, at the very moment when the landed interest were expecting a renewed attack on their protection, low prices of grain caused them to start agitating for some relief measures from the government.

The fall in the price of wheat, from the harvest of 1832 to the beginning of 1836, was notable ; and in the main it seems to have been due to the abundant crops mentioned in the previous paragraph. In 1832, unusually fine weather from the end of July to the last week in August, especially south of Yorkshire, resulted in a more abundant wheat crop *than* had been expected. In 1833, unusually hot weather in May and June, combined with showers in the latter part of June and all of July, aroused fears of both a thin yield and a wet harvest ; but wheat in particular yielded more and was secured in better condition than had been anticipated. In 1834, weather conditions similar to those of 1833 prevailed except that the showers came at an earlier and more opportune time. The result was one of the most productive wheat harvests on record. In 1835, the most favourable weather conditions lasted until the end of June. At this time some very heavy rains, accompanied by hard winds, levelled the crops in such a manner that they did not recover and the ears tended to ripen near the ground. As a result, although the bulk of the straw was beyond precedent, neither the quality nor the quantity of the wheat

crop equalled that of the previous year.[19]   The effect of these good
crops of wheat can be traced in the table of monthly prices.   The
price was 60s. 4d. in August of 1832, fell to 52s. 6d. in December,
to 47s. 10d. in December of 1833, to 39s. 6d. in December of 1834,
and to 35s. 4d. in December of 1835.[20]   The consumption of wheat
was increased in 1835 because the manufacturing population found it
relatively cheap in comparison with potatoes, meat and other grain ;
and because more was used as cattle and pig feed, and for malting
and distilling.   This increased consumption, combined with a
diminished sowing at the close of 1835, started the advance in the
price of wheat early in 1836.[21]

Either because the government felt the justice of the demands of
the landed interest for relief of some sort, or because they deemed it
expedient to listen respectfully to so formidable a group, the question
was given immediate attention.   The speech from the Throne at the
opening of the session of 1833 recommended that Parliament give the
matter careful consideration.   As a result a select committee of the
House of Commons was soon appointed to inquire into the state of
agriculture.

The report of this committee of 1833 is both interesting and significant.   The members arrived at their conclusions by weighing the
evidence extracted from a large number of witnesses, who were, with
few exceptions, connected with the land as tenants, agents, surveyors
and owners.   The findings of the committee covered such points as
the relation of the supply of wheat in England to the demand, the
inadequacy of present returns and possible remedies, the effect of low
prices on agricultural labourers, and of improved farming methods in
counterbalancing the fall in prices.

On the first point the committee concluded that the produce of
Great Britain on the average of a term of years was not equal to the
consumption and that even the enormous increase of imports from
Ireland did not cover the deficiency.   Therefore, the country, except
in years of extraordinary crops, would be partially dependent upon
foreign countries for her supply of wheat.

On the second point the committee pointed out that, although the
existing prices were inadequate, it was impossible for the government
to give relief by regulating rent and wages.   The only sort of relief
that seemed feasible to offset low prices was the lightening of the
burdens on agriculture such as a commutation of tithes or a revision
of the Poor Law.

But it is on the third point that the most surprising evidence was
cited.   For years the landowners had insisted that the agricultural
labourers were better off when the price of grain was high, because
low prices caused unemployment.   The light thrown on living conditions among these labourers by the revolt of 1830 had done something to shake this thesis, and the report of 1833 now completely
dissipated it.   The committee affirmed that " it is a consolation to
find that the general condition of the agricultural labourer in full
employment is better than at any former period, his money wages
giving him a greater command over the necessaries and conveniences
of life."   In parts of England where the labour supply did exceed

the demand because of the inability of the farmers to employ as many labourers as usual, the alarming increase in the poor rate made it necessary to resort to such devices as granting land attached to cottages and distributing these labourers more judiciously throughout the parish.

On the fourth and last point the committee found that improved farming methods had done much to counterbalance the fall in the price of grain.   The spread of the drill system, a more judicious use of manure, a better rotation of crops, draining and improved methods in breeding sheep and cattle had all contributed in this direction.

The committee strongly advised against tampering with either the Corn Laws or the coinage.   The continuation of the Corn Laws was justified on the ground that prices had been steady under the Law of 1828, despite considerable variation in the seasons ; and a change in the coinage was opposed on the grounds that rents were approximating prices and any new arrangement was certain to be a great grievance. In conclusion, the committee advised a do-nothing policy on the part of the government ; because its members felt " that hopes of melioration in the condition of the Landed Interest rest rather on cautious forbearance than on the active interposition of Parliament."[22]

Clearly it was not a particularly satisfying report from the point of view of the landowners.   The only parts that they really enjoyed were the recommendations to lighten the burdens of agriculture and not to tamper with the Corn Laws.   Some of them wished to push the first point at once, and on February 21st, 1834, the Marquess of Chandos moved in the House of Commons, " That, in any reduction of the burthens of the country, which it may be practical to effect by a remission of taxes, due regard should be had to the necessity of relieving, at the present period, the distressed condition of the agricultural interest."[23] The strength of this sentiment is shown by the fact that the motion was beaten by only 206 to 202.

Relief did come in the matter of poor rates as a result of the new Poor Law of 1834, although that was by no means the primary intention of the act.   The system of poor relief in existence before the passing of the new act, including the Gilbert Act of 1782 and the Speenhamland plan of 1795, has already been described in an earlier chapter.   Under the Speenhamland system, the scale of allowances varied with the price of bread and the size of families.   This arrangement, it was held, threw able-bodied men, whether with or without work, upon the rates ; and the allowances delayed the natural rise of wages, lowered earnings, and encouraged improvident marriages.[24] The war, however, kept these evils in check until 1813, but from then until 1834 they spread rapidly.   A reduction followed both in the demand for permanent labour and in the wages paid.   The Poor Law now enabled the farmer to reduce wages to the lowest point, because allowances from the rates made good the deficiency in the labourers' wages, and provided a cheap and inexhaustible supply of labour.   Against this mass of subsidized labour the free labourer stood no chance.   The ones who had any property could secure no employment or poor relief until they became paupers.   " The demoralization gradually extended from the southern counties to

Q

the North.   In the most practical fashion, labourers were taught the lessons that improvidence paid better than thrift ; that sobriety and efficiency had no special value above indolence and vice. . . . The careful were unemployed, the careless supported by the parish ; the more recklessly a man married and begot children, the greater his share of the comforts of life.   The effect was seen in the rapid growth of population."[25]   Recent investigations, however, have shown that, although conditions may have been as bad as this description indicates, an important factor in the increase in population was the declining death-rate.[25a]

The Poor Law of 1834 which ended this state of affairs was based upon the recommendations of a commission appointed in 1832 to consider the problem.   The best known figures on this commission were Nassau Senior and Edwin Chadwick.   The new law was notable both for the organization provided and the principles of relief that were applied.   Central control was vested in the Poor Law Commissioners, and a board of three men, who had immense discretionary powers for the regulation of local administration.   The regulation for which they were most praised and cursed at that time and since, was the abolition of outdoor relief for the able-bodied, and the imposition of the workhouse test.   The principle upon which relief was given was to make it so distasteful that no one, who was not in dire need, would apply for it.   Perhaps nothing aroused the antipathy of the working classes more in the years that followed, or did as much more to swell the ranks of the Chartists than the workhouse test and the new poor houses or " bastilles."   Certainly the Poor Law of 1834 did not " relieve " the labouring class.   On the other hand, the landowners and farmers could survey the decline in rates with great satisfaction.   In 1783 to 1785 poor relief had cost £1,912,214 ; in 1818, £7,870,801 ; in 1832, £7,036,968 ; and in 1837, £4,044,741.[26] This was certainly no small " lightening of the burdens " of agriculture if the landed interest paid as high a percentage of the poor rates as they claimed when refuting Deacon Hume.

When low prices of grain, particularly of wheat, continued in 1835, the landed interest was not satisfied with the reduction in the poor rates as a sufficient remedy for its ills.   One of the many solutions suggested to further alleviate agricultural distress was proposed in the House of Commons on June 1st, 1835, by E. S. Cayley.   It was inflation in a new disguise.   He culled ancient and modern history for examples of the evils that followed the successive depreciation and appreciation of the currency.   He declared that the success of the Americans and defeat of the English in the War of Independence was due to the fact that the former depreciated and the latter appreciated their currency.   Likewise, the success of the English in the war with Napoleon was due to the policy of depreciation.   All his arguments pointed in the direction of inflation as a remedy for the existing ills ; but he stoutly denied that he desired a return to an inconvertible paper currency, and insisted that all he advocated was a palliation of the mischief done by the Peel Act of 1819.   He indicated what this palliation would be by moving, " That a Select Committee be appointed to inquire if there be not effectual means within reach of Parliament to afford substantial relief to the agriculture of the United Kingdom, and especially to recommend to its attention the subject of a silver, or a conjoined standard of silver and gold."[27]   Sir Robert Peel declared that the motion was merely an attempt to depreciate the currency under the guise of agricultural distress.   The arguments of those who favoured the motion clearly pointed to depreciation even though they denied it.   Nevertheless, this extraordinary motion, though defeated, received 126 votes,[28] which indicates that the Inflationists were not as negligible a quantity as their relative silence in the preceding years would seem to prove.

The depression in the price of wheat reached its lowest point at the end of 1835 and at the beginning of 1836.   Since agriculture had been in a distressed condition for over three years, the government felt that a further attempt should be made to alleviate this state.   Accordingly, on February 8th, 1836, Lord John Russell proposed in the Commons, " That a Select Committee be appointed to inquire into the State of agriculture and into the cause and extent of distress which exists in some important branches thereof."   But before making the motion, Russell showed clearly that the government wished to disassociate itself from any inflation programme, such as Cayley had proposed in the previous year, by having the clerk read the resolution of the House passed on April 24th, 1833, that it was the opinion of the House that any change in the monetary system of the country which would tend to lower the standard of value would be highly inexpedient and dangerous.   The motion was agreed to by the Commons and the committee appointed.[29]   On February 18th a similar committee was appointed in the House of Lords.[30]

The committee of the Commons prepared three volumes of evidence; but, owing to the failure of the members to agree in their conclusions, no actual report was published.   When the conflicting opinions of the men comprising the committee are considered, the difficulties of arriving at an agreement become obvious.   However, the opinions of the two groups were given publicity by two open letters.   The chairman, Charles Shaw Lefevre, addressed a letter to his constituents which gave his personal views and which was rumoured to reflect those of the anti-inflationist wing of the committee ; and E. S. Cayley addressed one to H. Handley, M.P., which was an answer to Lefevre and expressed the views of the inflationists.

It is not the intention at this time to examine the 1,281 pages of evidence comprising the answers to nearly 18,000 questions which were put to seventy-seven witnesses.   These answers throw light on almost every imaginable phase of agriculture, while some are only remotely connected with the Corn Laws.   The evidence has been boiled down to 133 pages and arranged topically by James Carmichael, The section devoted to the Corn Laws has more of Carmichael's own opinions than it has testimony of the witnesses.   He claimed to have been one of the first, if " not the very first to suggest," the sliding scale of duties on the importation of grain.   He still believed in the system and blamed the mode of taking the averages for the disastrous results which had followed its adoption.   He insisted that there was reason to believe that the low duty paid on wheat entered for consumption after July 15th, 1828, was " in some measure effected by a deliberate and widespread combination among the leading speculators and certain corn-dealers of that period, who, by a succession of fictitious sales and falsified returns, succeeded in running up the average price of wheat on the 7th of November, 1828, to 72s. 2d. which thus admitted their own stores at 2s. 8d. per quarter, a mere fraction of the duty which otherwise would have been exigible."[31] It reflected the inefficiency of the corn-return office, he held, that no example of fraudulent practices had ever been discovered or any corn dealer ever prosecuted under the law. Carmichael may have been entirely correct in his suspicion of the corn-dealers, but even he cites no examples of actual malpractices.

Turning to the actual corn returns, however, he has more exact evidence of their notorious inaccuracy. By the direct testimony of the dealers he showed that, in periods of low prices when the duty was too high to admit foreign corn, the law virtually became a dead letter, since the returns were of no interest to either agriculturists or merchants. According to one witness, of all the 149 corn markets " scarcely one approximates to the truth, or even maintains consistency of quantity one season with another, nor contains one-fourth of the corn annually sold in England."[32]

Lefevre's letter was regarded at the time as the report which he, as chairman, had drawn up and which had failed to meet with the approval of the committee as a whole. He took up the complaints of the petitions on agricultural distress which were referred to the committee for consideration. Many of these petitions stressed the burden that agriculture bore in the tithe, county rate and highway rate. Now, as Lefevre pointed out, laws lightening the burden of the tithe and highway rate had been passed ; and there was every prospect for one which would reduce the pressure of the county rates being passed in the near future.[33] Most of the other suggestions of petitioners he rejected as showing a lack of understanding of the difficulties involved, or as being too unimportant to warrant adoption.

In discussing the Corn Laws, Lefevre frankly admitted that he favoured a fixed duty, but conceded that the two objections usually urged against it should have considerable weight : first, that a constant demand would expose British farmers to an inundation of foreign corn far below the present prices on the continent ; and second, that in seasons of scarcity it would be difficult to levy a duty. But, he added somewhat ambiguously, if a fixed duty was found to be unacceptable, he preferred the nearest approximation to one.[34]

It was impossible for Lefevre to ignore the currency problem, since it was rumoured that it was upon this point that the two groups in the committee had failed to agree. He insisted that the question to be decided was not the consequences of the Peel Act since 1819, but whether inflation would improve the condition of the agricultural classes. In his opinion, the effect would be either harmful or of only temporary benefit : it would be decidedly harmful to the landlord unless his rents were raised as much as the prices of all articles of consumption ; it would insure the tenant nothing except at the expense of the landlord under a lease at a fixed money rent ; and it would cause wages to rise eventually in the proportion to the increase in the circulating medium—and if it did not do so, it would mean that the entire burden of the change would fall on the shoulders of the agricultural labourer.[35]

Cayley's pamphlet in answer to Lefevre was a vigorous presentation of the case for an increased supply of money. In referring to Lefevre he admitted that " on his excellence as a chairman, on his patience, impartiality and gentlemanly bearing in conducting the inquiry, there was not, I am confident, a dissentient voice in the committee."[36] However, he implied that this was as far as his recommendation could go. He then attacked the thesis of over-production from three directions. First, the wheat crops of 1833, 1834 and 1835 were not as large as commonly represented. The extremely hot summers were favourable to wheat on the lowland soils, but not on the upland. Hence the large crops on the lowlands were offset by deficient ones on the uplands. Second, there was no real statistical proof that the acreage of wheat had been increased at the expense of other grain, or that much land had been enclosed or reclaimed for the purpose of raising wheat. Third, the testimony before the committees of both 1833 and 1836 showed that over-cropping had rendered the soil less productive and thus had offset the improvements in farming methods.[37]

When the attempt to prove superabundance and over-supply as the cause of the great fall in prices failed, Cayley declares that the committee next took up the position : first, that the distress was confined to the clays, and resulted from a good machine (the uplands) beating a bad machine (the lowlands) ; and second, that while agriculturists might have suffered, or be suffering, agriculture itself had not retrograded. The first was pure assumption and unbacked by evidence ; and the second did not give the reason for the suffering. The farmer was in distress under the present prices when he was prosperous under the same ones in 1790 because expenses had increased. Labour was 62 per cent., household expenses 57 per cent. and local taxes 391 per cent. higher according to the testimony of Mr. Evan David. Clearly, Cayley insisted, " *It is bad prices and heavy expenses, not a good or bad machine, which has distressed the farmer.*"[38]

In the end Cayley was not as frank as Lefevre in stating his remedy. Clearly he believed in some form of inflation as his elaborate arguments showing the correlation between the price of corn and the amount of money in circulation indicated. Doubtless, what he wanted was the adoption of the double gold and silver standard which he had proposed in the previous session of Parliament.

Despite the fact that the committee made no official report, the disguised reports of Lefevre and Cayley brought out many important facts. First in significance, unquestionably, was the reduction in the extraordinary burdens of agriculture through the new poor law, the abolition of statute labour for maintaing minor roads and the tithes act. The details of the poor law have been given, but evidence of its successful working (from the point of view of the tax-payer) was not available at once.

Statute labour on roads had a long history in England. From early times the duty of maintaining communication between market towns had devolved on the inhabitants of the parishes through which the roads passed. Within towns it fell on the townsmen, and within the boundaries of manors upon the tenants. Later, acts of Parliament, beginning with bridges, enforced these local regulations. However, long before 1835 Justices in Quarter Sessions had been empowered to levy a rate to maintain the highways when statute labour proved insufficient. Such a rate was assessed on the principle of the poor-rate. Also it was impossible to escape the liability of such labour by the payment of a money equivalent.[39]   The act of 1835 substituted highway rates in place of statute labour for the maintenance of all minor roads.[40]

Of far greater importance to the agriculturist was the Tithes Commutation act of 1836. The demand for such a reform had been made at least as early as 1750. The tithes were originally a freewill offering, later made compulsory by law, of a tenth of the yearly produce of land, stock and clear profits from personal industry. Lawyers distinguished them by their sources as predial, mixed and personal. The first were derived directly from the soil ; the second arose from the increase or produce of the animals ; and the third, from the clear gain of the labour of men. The usual division, however, was into great or rectorial tithes ; and small or vicarial ones. The great included corn, beans, peas, hay and wood ; and the small, the remainder of the predial and all of the mixed tithes.[41] The tithe, as explained in earlier chapters, was a great obstacle to improving land, or to the introduction of progressive methods in agriculture. Further, the collection in kind provoked endless disputes and litigation. It was commonly admitted that a reform should have been carried out long before. The aim of the act was to commute the tithe of produce in kind into a variable money payment, charge-able on the land, which would preserve the existing relation between the value of the produce and the cost of living. It accomplished this by " converting tithes into a corn rent, fluctuating in value according to the septennial average of the prices of wheat, barley and oats."[42]

Relief finally came to the agriculturists, as it usually did, through the rise in the price of grain rather than from any action of the government. The price of wheat fell to its lowest point in the last week of December, 1835, and the first week of January, 1836, but after that it rose steadily until it reached 48s. 11d. for the month of June.[43] This advance was due to extra consumption, to the knowledge that less wheat than usual had been sown in the fall of 1835, and to the unfavourable appearance of the crops.[44] Thus, before the harvest of 1836 complaints of agricultural distress had declined if they had not entirely disappeared.

These years of low prices and agricultural distress naturally did not furnish a very good background for those who had waited until the Reform Bill was passed before renewing the agitation for a repeal of the Corn Laws. Still they had waited so long for the opportunity that they were resolved to revive the question even though the time was not propitious. Accordingly, on May 17th, 1833, Whitmore moved that a fixed duty, which should be suspended in time of dearth, be substituted for the existing sliding scale of duties. He declared that he had abstained from bringing up the Corn Laws in recent years because he wanted to see how the Law of 1828 would work, and because he believed it was useless to expect anything from the un-reformed House of Commons. Deacon Hume followed with an amendment, which he withdrew before a vote was taken, to admit foreign corn at all times upon the payment of a fixed duty. He pointed out with great glee that during all the years in which he had advocated a fixed duty he had never proposed one lower than 10s. a quarter, whereas the average duty on the 4,795,000 quarters imported since 1827 was 6s. 8d. In the course of the speech he brought in his two favourite arguments : that the landed interest had no " peculiar burden " of taxation ; and that without manufacturing England would be a second Poland. Lord Althorp, answering on behalf of the government, took the stand that was to be expected, namely, that this was " not the time " to agitate such an important question when the amount of business already before the House was so great. After the usual debate the motion was beaten by 305 to 106.[45]

The interest expressed in Parliament was not great and the result seems to have been expected by advocates of repeal. But outside Parliament the disappointment and indignation were widespread. Perhaps nothing except the Poor Law of 1834 did more to disillusion the labouring class of the cities about the beneficial results of the reform of the House of Commons than the refusal of the Whig govern-ment to take any action on the Corn Laws.   One member in present-ing a petition from Wolverhampton to the Commons expressed this disappointed rage in a graphic if slightly discourteous fashion when he denounced " bastard Tories, born on a dunghill. . . . Degenerate apostate Whigs, possessed of no statesmanlike principles ; who, having been borne into office on the shoulders of the people, had since deserted the popular cause ; ingrates, who kicked down the ladder by which they had mounted to power, alike dishonest to their friends and enemies to themselves."[46]   *The Annual Register* also testified to the disappointment which the lower classes felt when the Corn Laws remained untouched.   " They had been taught to consider them as unjust monopolies which enriched the landowner, by depriving the poor of ' cheap bread,' and they firmly expected, that reforming ministers, and a reformed Parliament would forthwith abolish the monopoly and lower prices."[47]

Undiscouraged by his failure of the previous year and by the depressed condition of agriculture, Deacon Hume, on March 6th, 1834, again brought forward his motion for a fixed duty.   The dis-cussion lasted two nights, but little that was new or valuable was brought out.   The only noteworthy speech was made by Mr. Poulett Thompson, member for Worcester and Vice-President of the Board of Trade, who gave what was, perhaps, the first clear cut expression of the point of view, later popularized by List, on the mistake of the Corn Law of 1815.[48]   He declared that, " He meant to consider the question of the restrictions on the importation of foreign corn as a general one, and to show how it had operated in depressing our manu-

factures and commerce. What were its effects in 1815, when,
though peace was declared in Europe, the different states, harassed
by a long war, were distracted in their internal arrangements, and
when the United States were still engaged in war ?   What were its
effects then, when, from one end of England to another, the powers
of steam were developed—when spinning jennies and flax-frames
were in active motion—when, in short, all those different arts for
which this country had been so much distinguished, and which we
had then carried far towards perfection, were utterly unknown to
the greater portion of the natives of both hemispheres ?   Above all,
there were few restrictive laws in the different States—none of those
prohibitory tariffs which now encircled every frontier.   We had then
a field for our industry and enterprise.   The advantage we had
maintained in Europe was entirely owing to our success in manufactures, and that might have been preserved.   We were at least
fifty years in advance in all that could render manufactures successful ; but we neglected the opportunity ; we failed to seize this
advantage, and in lieu of it imposed the Corn Laws ; and continuing
in this course of policy, we obliged the other nations of Europe, in
self-defence, to manufacture for themselves—to turn their ingenuity
and skill, rude as it was, to the cultivation of mechanical arts, in
which we then alone excelled.   To turn their ingenuity and skill, did
he say ?   To form those qualities newly, for previously they possessed
none.''[49]   On the second night of the debates, Hume's motion was
beaten by 312 to 155, but the length of the speeches and the size of
the minority vote indicated that interest in the subject had risen
considerably since the previous year, despite conditions adverse to a
change in agricultural protection.

But even this renewed interest was unable to withstand the increase
in agricultural distress, the not-the-time-plea of the government, and
the indifference of the consumer in a period of easy employment and
low prices.   As a result no motion against or even to consider the
Corn Laws was made in Parliament either in 1835 or 1836.   The
agitation against them was continued in newspapers, periodicals and
pamphlets, but with little effect.   Probably the most striking example
was the theatrical appeal of Ebenezer Elliott in Tait's Magazine.
" How many more sessions of your reform Parliament can you afford
to throw away ?   Think not, then, of his Majesty's renegade ministers.
False to themselves, can they be true to you ? . . . Haste, then, and
destroy these deadly Corn Laws, ere they subvert the empire.   Let
every trade, from every town, one by one, and again, and again, send
petitions to Parliament.   Let brave and enlightened Glasgow speak
again to timid and besotted Liverpool.   Let awakened Liverpool
shout to cowardly and goose-ridden Manchester ; Manchester to
London—and all together to England and the world. . . . Repudiate
at once, and for ever, the idea of a fixed duty. . . . Treat not, then,
for graduated iniquity ; put not in the banns for a new marriage of
reptile-spawning fraud and time ; but with the word Restitution,
pronounced in thunder, startle your oppressors from their hideous
dream of injustice and ruin made permanent.''[50]   But, as Prentice
remarked bitterly, " The call was unheeded ; trade was moderately

prosperous, employment easy to be had, and provisions at a moderate price ; and so the year 1834 drifted on quietly, men thinking it would be time enough to complain of their liability to famine when the famine came."[51]

Attacks on the landowners are comparatively rare at this time in comparison with those before 1828 and after 1838. Still, something of the spirit of *The Catechism* lasted during these years, a good illustration being an ironical *Form of a Petition to the Upper House against any Alterations of the Corn Laws*. In this case it was the Lords rather than the landowners who were attacked, but the technique was the same. This petition contained eighty insulting statements about the motives of the House of Lords in supporting the Corn Laws " by sundry malignant, discontented, innovating and evil disposed persons," and each of the eighty was followed by a defence of Lords which was even more damaging than the original statement. The first two of these affirmations and answers are typical of the whole petition : 1. That (*i.e.*, according to said malignants) the Corn Laws were originated in fraud and ignorance. Whereas it is well known that they were originated by your lordships. 2. That . . . fraud is committed whenever the real motives for any act are withheld, and base motives are advanced instead. Whereas your lordships have always deemed such a course the perfection of political wisdom.[52]

In Earl Fitzwilliam's *Second Address to the Landowners of England on the Corn Laws*, an entirely different spirit is shown than in the articles and poems of Elliott or in the petition to the Upper House. In his first address, Fitzwilliam, then Lord Milton, had stressed the injustice done by the Corn Laws to both the agricultural labourers and the tenants. In this second address he assumed that the report of the committee of 1833 had proved conclusively that the Corn Laws were not advantageous to the labourers, and hence he concentrated on the effect on the tenants. The existing system, he maintained, was unfair to the tenant because his rent was fixed on the basis of the " pivot " point in the law of 1828, and when the price fell below that point he was forced to pay the rent out of his capital. In conclusion he appealed to the landowners to give up the Corn Laws and argued that the alteration in the value of land which would follow the repeal would be exceedingly trifling, and the fall of rents small except where the rapacity or the imprudence of the landlord had induced him to keep up a nominal rent above what he had been able to realize.[53] The pamphlet was marked by an evenness in temper and a moderation of tone, but even these qualities were insufficient to impress landowners when the price of wheat was 37s. 10d. It is regretable that the controversy over the Corn Laws could not have been conducted in this spirit rather than that of the *Catechism* and *Iniquity of the Landholders* in the eighteen-twenties and of the Anti-Corn Law League after 1839 ; but considering what the free traders and protectionists had at stake such an attitude was impossible.

The rise in the price of grain, particularly of wheat, in the first half of 1836, which had caused a decline in the agitation for relief to agriculture, also brought about a revival of interest in the repeal of the Corn Laws. The crops of 1836 were not as deficient as the bad weather of the first half of the year had led experts to believe ; and hence the price of wheat did not advance beyond 48s. for some months. Late in the autumn heavy demands for wheat from the North of England, where the harvest had been attended with heavy rains, and news that the crops had failed in the United States, sent up the price of wheat to 57s. 9d. in December. The winter of 1836–37 was very cold and was accompanied by an unusual fall of snow. The spring weather was unfavourable and crops, generally, were decidedly backward. But after June the weather became very propitious and, despite heavy rains in August and in early September, the wheat was secured in good condition even in the north. As a result the price of wheat fell to 51s. 3d. in December.[54] But this comparatively favourable condition soon changed for the worse. In January of 1838, a severe frost began which lasted through February. The spring weather was unfavourable and the summer rainy. To make matters worse the harvest was late and the stock from 1837 was low. Consequently the averages of September 15th showed that the price of wheat had reached 73s. which permitted the 1,500,000 quarters in bond to be thrown on the market at the nominal duty. This enormous amount caused the market to sag temporarily, but when it was ascertained that the harvest was the worst since 1816 the upward movement of prices began again.[55]

Yet even these higher prices after January of 1836 did not bring any decided agitation for repeal until September of 1838, when the Manchester Anti-Corn Law Association was organized. In 1835 and 1836, as was pointed out earlier in this chapter, no motion was made in Parliament to repeal or change the existing law. On March 16th, 1837, Mr. Clay, in the House of Commons, moved the adoption of a fixed duty of 10s. a quarter on wheat. But this motion secured only 89 votes in its favour as opposed to the 155 that Hume's had mustered three years earlier.[56] Among the 89 were ten members of the government.

A year later, on March 16th, 1838, Mr. Villiers moved that the House consider the operation of the act of 1828. In the course of the debate, Mr. Clay expressed regret that no more than 24,000 had petitioned for repeal of the Corn Laws as opposed to 190,000 for the Poor Law ; and pointed out, prophetically, that there was no hope of getting rid of the Corn Laws unless pressure was exerted from outside Parliament. Mr. Villiers made the somewhat lame defence that people did not petition for repeal of the Corn Laws because they realized the futility of such an action. The motion was finally rejected by 300 to 95.[57] Five days later a motion for leave to bring in a bill to permit foreign bonded corn to be ground for exportation only, was passed ; but on May 9th the second reading of the bill was defeated by 220 to 150.[58] When the question of the Corn Laws was next brought up in Parliament, the circumstances were to be far more dramatic.

The period from the passing of the law of 1828 to the organization of the Manchester Anti-Corn Law Association, though one of relative calm and unimportance in comparison with the ones immediately preceding and following it, was not devoid of significance. On first appearance it may seem that the status of the Corn Laws had changed very little between 1828 and 1838, despite the remarkable variations in the prosperity of different classes. The years from 1828 to 1832, we have seen, were characterized by poor crops, high prices and enormous importations ; those from 1832 to 1836, by excellent crops, low prices and agricultural distress ; and those from 1836 to 1838, by poor and deficient crops, high prices and distress in commerce and industry. The agitation for repeal was weak in the first four years because it was subordinated to that of Parliamentary reform ; in the second four years because of low prices of food and of fairly good conditions in industry ; and in the last two years because of the lack of organization after years of comparative indifference.

Notwithstanding the weakness of the agitation for repeal, at least four points of considerable significance were established. First, the sliding scale of the law of 1828 proved infinitely superior to the total exclusion below 80s. of the law of 1815, despite the fact that importers were able to juggle prices in such a manner as to admit corn under conditions most favourable to themselves. Second, conditions brought out by the labourers' revolt and the report of the select committee of 1833 proved conclusively that the agricultural labourers were better off when prices were low than when they were high. Third, the evidence of the committee of 1836 and of Earl Fitzwilliam established a strong degree of probability that the tenants were paying a higher rent than they should because this rent was too often based on the pivot point of the law of 1828. Fourth, the Poor Law of 1834, Tithe Act, Highway Rate Act and revision of county rates did much to relieve agriculture of the burdens of taxation, and hence to invalidate the claim of the landed interest to protection on the grounds of " special burdens." Thus when hostilities were resumed in 1838, after a semi-truce of ten years, the landlords could no longer pose as spokesmen for the tenants and agricultural labours or advance the " special burdens " plea with the same effect as they had earlier.

CHAPTER X

NOTES

[1] The winter of 1827–8 was mild, and the spring following was not remarkably cold, but heavy rains in July and August inflicted severe damage on the wheat crop. So deficient was the harvest that the monthly average price for November rose to 73s., the highest since August of 1819. The winter of 1828–9 was fairly cold and the spring backward, but the summer and autumn were even wetter than during the preceding harvest. As a result the wheat was deficient in quantity and inferior in quality. The fall in price late in 1829 and early in 1830 was the result of this inferior produce being thrown upon the market. The winter of 1829–30 was severe, and the weather during harvest was unsettled, although not as wet as in the two preceding ones. The crops of 1831 were greatly damaged by a heavy frost in May and by wet weather during the harvest. In 1832, after an ordinary winter and spring, a favourable harvest, the first abundant and well-secured wheat crop in several years, was the result. Tooke, *History of Prices*, vol. 2, pp. 194–203.

[2] Wheat, barley, oats and oatmeal, rye, peas and beans.

[3] *Hansard*, vol. 21, pp. 1464–87. [4] *Ibid.*, vol. 23, pp. 966–85.

[5] Henry Hunt, elected member for Preston in December of 1830.

[6] *Hansard* (New Series), vol. 7, pp. 67–78.

[7] See bibliography at the end of the volume.

[8] Milton, *Address to the Landowners of England on the Corn Laws*, fifth edn., 1832, pp. 24–5.

[9] G. Higgins, *Address, December*, 3rd 1832, p. 11.

[10] J. L. and Barbara Hammond, *The Village Labourer*, 1920, pp. 218–19.

[11] *Ibid.*, p. 220. [12] *Ibid.*, p. 221. [13] *Ibid.*, p. 234. [14] *Ibid.*, p. 229.

[15] *Ibid.*, p. 242. [16] *Ibid.*, pp. 242–3.

[17] The best account of the labourers' revolt is *The Village Labourer*, Chapters X and XI, pp. 216–300.

[18] In *The Black Hole of Calcutta*, Elliott paints the mournful results which the Corn Laws will eventually have on all classes :

> What for Saxon, Frank and Hun,
> What hath England's bread-tax done ?
> Ask the ruin it hath made,
> Ask of bread-tax-ruin'd trade ;
> Ask the struggle and the groan,
> For the shadow of a bone,
> Like a strife for life, for life,
> Hand to hand, and knife to knife.
>
> Hopeless trader, answer me !
> What hath bread-tax done for thee ?
> Ask thy lost and owing debts,
> Ask our bankrupt-throng'd Gazettes.
> Clothier, proud of Peterloo !
> Ironmaster, loyal, too !
> What hath bread-tax done for you ?
> Let the Yankee tariff tell,
> None to buy, and all to sell ;
> Useless buildings, castle strong,
> Hundred thousands, worth a song ;
> Starving workmen, warehouse full,
> Saxon web, from Polish wool,

Grown where grew the wanted wheat,
Which we might not buy and eat.
Merchants, bread-tax'd trade won't pay,
Profits lessen every day ;
Sell thy stock and realize,
Let thy streeted chimneys rise ;
And when bread-tax'd ten are two,
Learn what bread-tax'd rents can do.

What hath bread-tax done for me ?
Farmer, what for thine and thee ?
Ask of those who toil to live,
And the price they cannot give ;
Ask our hearths, our gainless marts,
Ask thy children's broken hearts,
Ask their mother, sad and grey,
Destined yet to parish pay.
Bread-tax'd weaver, all can see
What that tax hath done for thee,
And thy children, vilely led,
Singing hymns for shameful bread,
Till the stores of every street,
Know their little naked feet.

Bread-tax-eating absentee,
What hath bread-tax done for thee ?—
Cramm'd thee, from our children's plates,
Made thee all that nature hates,
Fill'd thy skin with untaxed wine,
Fill'd thy breast with hellish schemes,
Fill'd thy head with fatal dreams—
Of potatoes, basely sold
At the price of wheat in gold,
And of Britons sty'd to eat
Wheat-priced roots, instead of wheat.

Man of Consols, hark to me !
What shall bread-tax do for thee ?
Rob thee for the dead-alive,
Pawn thy thousands ten for five,
And, ere yet its work be done,
Pawn thy thousands five for one.

What shall bread-tax yet for thee,
Palaced pauper ?   We shall see
It shall tame thee, and thy heirs,
Beggar them, and beggar theirs,
Melt thy plate, for which we paid,
Buy ye breeches ready made,
Sell my lady's tax-bought gown,
And the lands thou call'st thy own.

(Corn Law Rhymes, pp. 70–4.)

[19] Tooke, *History of Prices*, vol. 2, pp. 202–3 and 229–33.
[20] *Ibid.*, p. 390.   [21] *Ibid.*, pp. 238–9.
[22] *Report from the Select Committee Appointed to Inquire into the Present State of Agriculture, and Persons Employed in Agriculture, in the United Kingdom*, 1833.
[23] *Hansard*, vol. 21, p. 659.
[24] Ernle, *English Farming, Past and Present*, 1920, p. 327.
[25] *Ibid.*, p. 329.   Since this chapter was written two articles by J. S. Blackmore and F. C. Mellonie have appeared in the Economic History Supplement of *The Economic Journal* (No. 2, May, 1927, and No. 3, January, 1928) in which the view that the Speenhamland system of poor relief resulted in an increasing birth-rate is seriously questioned.   These conclusions were in turn severely criticized by T. H. Marshall in a later number of the same periodical (No. 4, January, 1929).

[25a] G. Talbot Griffith, *Population Problems of the Age of Malthus*, Chap. VI.
[26] *Ibid.*, p. 331.
[27] *Hansard*, vol. 28, p. 244.   [28] *Ibid.*, pp. 337–8.
[29] *Ibid.*, vol. 31, pp. 147–64.   [30] *Ibid.*, pp. 520–30.
[31] James Carmichael, *Review of the Evidence Taken before the Select Committee of the House of Commons on Agricultural Distress*, 1836, p. 35.
[32] *Ibid.*, p. 44.
[33] Charles S. Lefevre, *Remarks on the Present State of Agriculture*, 1836, p. 4.
[34] *Ibid.*, p. 29.   [35] *Ibid.*, pp. 35–6.
[36] E. S. Cayley, *A Letter to H. Handley, Esq., M.P.*, 1836, p. 3.
[37] *Ibid.*, pp. 7–8.   [38] *Ibid.*, p. 9.
[39] Ernle, *English Farming, Past and Present*, 1920, p. 288.
[40] 5th and 6th William IV., c. 50.
[41] Ernle, *op. cit.*, p. 333.   [42] *Ibid.*, p. 344.
[43] Tooke, *History of Prices*, vol. 2, p. 390.   [44] *Ibid.*, pp. 257–8.
[45] *Hansard*, vol. 17, pp. 1349–79.   [46] *Ibid.*, vol. 18, pp. 964–77.
[47] *The Annual Register*, 1833, p. 210.
[48] I have found no previous statement of this sort.
[49] *Hansard*, vol. 21, pp. 1285–6.
[50] Prentice, *History of the Anti-Corn Law League*, 1853, vol. 1, pp. 38–9.
[51] *Ibid.*, p. 39.
[52] *A Form of Petition to the Upper House*, etc., 1834, second edn., p. 3.
[53] Earl Fitzwilliam, *A Second Address to the Landowners of England on the Corn Laws*, 1835, second edn., p. 35.
[54] Tooke, *History of Prices*, vol. 2, pp. 258–63 and 390.
[55] *Ibid.*, vol. 3, pp. 8–11.
[56] *Hansard*, vol. 37, pp. 562–619.
[57] *Ibid.*, vol. 41, pp. 909–46.   [58] *Ibid.*, vol. 42, pp. 1029–45.

CHAPTER XI

COBDEN AND THE ANTI-CORN LAW LEAGUE, 1838 TO 1845

THE history of the Corn Laws from 1838 to 1845 differs from that before 1838 in several important aspects. In the first place, no organization comparable to the Anti-Corn Law League had to be reckoned with before this time. In the second place, no individual ever played as outstanding a rôle as Cobden did. No particular names are associated with the acts of 1670, 1689, 1791 and 1822. The law of 1773 was sponsored by Pownall and Burke, and that of 1804 by Western. In the agitation leading to the law of 1815, Parnell was probably most prominent ; and in that of 1828, Huskisson because of his tariff reforms. Yet none of these men dominated their period as Cobden dominated the years preceding the repeal in 1846. In the third place, the sources have been well worked over, and as a result there are numerous able secondary works which cover practically every phase of the subject.[1]

Because of these differences and because practically all important questions were thoroughly threshed out by 1838, the emphasis in this chapter will be placed on the activities of the League, with Cobden as the leading spirit, in utilizing and spreading the old arguments in such a fashion as to aid materially in the repeal of the Corn Laws. At the same time an attempt will be made to portray the point of view, and describe the activities, of the two other groups or organizations with axes to grind—the landlords and the Chartists—and to place the agitation for repeal in its proper setting. In reality the question of continuing or removing the protection to agriculture was only one phase, although easily the most important single one, of the future commercial policy of Great Britain. Three policies were open to her at the time : continuation of protection, and adoption of free trade or imperial preference. There was a possibility of the latter being adopted during these years and the free-traders were, if anything, more afraid of imperial preference than of protection.

The period from 1838 to 1845 falls naturally into two parts. The years from 1838 to 1842 were characterized by bad crops, stagnation in industry and terrible suffering among the lower classes. The League offered free trade in corn as a solution for the difficulties ; the Whig government timidly suggested a mild lessening of protection and was overthrown. The years from 1842 to 1845 were characterized by good crops, improved conditions in trade and industry, and the fiscal reforms of Peel. The League continued to agitate for repeal, but directed their attention to the tenant farmers rather than to the middle and lower classes of the cities. The result was an intensification of the bitterness between the forces back of the League and the landlords.

The renewed agitation against the Corn Laws, which began in 1838 after ten years of comparative quiet, can, as it was pointed out at the end of the last chapter, be traced to a bad harvest. The price of wheat had reached 73s. by September 15th, which had permitted the million and a half quarters in bond to be thrown on the market at the nominal duty of 1s. Despite this enormous addition to the available stock of wheat the price continued to rise rapidly. The most important result of this short crop, which sent the prices soaring, was the organization of the Anti-Corn Law Association at Manchester which was soon to be transformed into the Anti-Corn Law League. In 1836 a similar association had been organized at London, but, as the historian of the League remarked, " Little else, therefore, came of it than to keep notice directed to the subject of the Corn Law, which, in two years more, with the sterner teacher in its train, was to force itself upon the attention of the sufferers ; and to bring new men, with better organization into the field of contest."[2]

The first meeting to form the Association at Manchester was held on September 24th and was attended by only seven men. But " with that manly determination which characterizes the Anglo-Saxon race, they resolved to overturn every monopoly by legal means, and accomplish without disturbance, without effusion of blood, with the power only of opinion,"[3] a profound revolution. According to Prentice there was no reason why the names of these seven men should not be known. They were Edward Baxter, W. A. Cunningham, Andrew Dalziel, James Howie, James Leslie, *Archibald Prentice* and Philip Thomson.[4]

At subsequent meetings many others, mostly manufacturers, swelled the numbers in the Association. The first of eleven resolutions adopted on January 28th, 1839, gives a very clear idea of its purpose : " 1. That the association be called ' The Manchester Anti-Corn Law Association,' and its object is hereby declared to be, to obtain by all legal and constitutional means, such as the formation of local Anti-Corn Law Associations, the delivery of lectures, the distribution of tracts, the insertion of articles in the public papers, and forwarding petitions to Parliament, the total and immediate repeal of the corn and provision laws."[5]   Every person who paid a subscription of at least five shillings a year was considered a member of the Association. The management was vested in a council, consisting of a president, vice-president, treasurer, and not less than a hundred members. This council was to select from its own numbers an executive committee of twelve members and a finance committee of eight.[6]

The Association at once began a vigorous campaign, as the resolution called for, delivering lectures, distributing pamphlets, and forwarding petitions to Parliament. In February, however, the interest of the Association shifted to Parliament at the opening of the session of 1839. Delegates were appointed from various manufacturing towns to meet in London in order to present their case, and to suggest means of alleviating the existing distress. In the Queen's speech no allusion was made to the Corn Laws ; but the delegates resolved to have it brought up in the speech of the seconder of the address, Mr. George Wood, president of the Manchester Chamber of Commerce and member for Kendal. He was instructed to stress the injurious effects of the Corn Laws on manufacturers and labourers alike. He fulfilled these instructions, but immediately ruined the impression by dilating on the prosperity of the country. As *The London Examiner* pointed out, " There was something at once painful and ludicrous in the effect which this part of Mr. Wood's speech produced. The astonishment of the advocates of free trade in the house—the nervous anxiety of the delegates under the gallery—the whispered assurances of the sagacious that ' Wood was a deep fellow, and would wind it all round before he sat down '—the respectful attention of Sir Robert Peel—the startling applause of the country gentlemen—and the unconscious, earnest and solemn complacency with which the orator himself continued, brick by brick, to demolish the foundations of the castle he was commissioned to garrison—what play writers call ' a situation,' that would have been irresistibly droll, if the House of Commons were the Adelphi Theatre, and the Corn Laws a farce, instead of a question involving the interests of millions, and, perhaps, fraught with a fearful tragedy."[7]   It was Sir Robert Peel, head of the Tory Party, and not a member of the government, who took advantage of the opportunity. With great adroitness he pointed out that the Corn Laws were essential to the landed interest, and that commerce and industry were in such a stable and secure position, as the statistics of Wood proved, that they required no relief.

The delegates were both stunned and enraged at the unexpected turn of events, and tried in vain to recover lost ground. A motion

R

by Mr. Charles Villiers,[8] member for Wolverhampton, " That J. B. Smith, Robert Hyde Greg, and others be heard at the Bar of this House, by their witnesses, agents, or counsel, in support of the allegations of their petition, presented to the House of the 15th instant, complaining of the operation of the Corn Laws,"[9] was beaten by 361 to 172.[10] A few days later Villiers' second motion to consider the act of 1828 was rejected by 342 to 195.[11]

In the Lords, Fitzwilliam's motion of March 14th, that the act of 1828 had failed to secure steadiness in the price of grain so essential to the best interests of the country, merely provoked the reply of Lord Melbourne that, " To leave the whole agricultural interest without protection, I declare before God that I think it the wildest and maddest scheme that has ever entered into the imagination of man to conceive."[12]

The immediate result of this failure in Parliament was the formation of the Anti-Corn Law League. It was to be a permanent organization made up of the cities and districts which had sent representatives to this delegation, and of any others that wished to organize local associations and federate with the League. In order to secure unity of action, the central office was to be established at Manchester. This body was to be entrusted with the duties of engaging competent lecturers, securing the co-operation of the public Press, and establishing a stamped circular for the purpose of insuring a constant correspondence with the local associations.[13]

The policy that was formulated for the League at the time of its organization in March of 1839 was carried out faithfully. From the headquarters at Manchester an enormous mass of pamphlets was systematically scattered throughout the country, and in April *The Anti-Corn Law Circular* made its appearance and within a few weeks had attained a circulation of 15,000. Prentice boasted that, " Numerous pamphlets, ten thousand of each, sent everywhere—a free-trade newspaper with a circulation of fifteen thousand, probably read every week by two hundred thousand persons— there needed only the vocal denunciation of the Corn Laws in the strongholds of the protectionists to increase the alarm. The lecturers soon followed the tracts and the free-trade newspaper."[14] But these paid lecturers, or economic missionaries, as Morley termed them, were not always favourably received. In many places they were refused lodgings in the inns lest their presence offend the regular patrons. In other places they were refused the use of the town hall, and in one instance the lecturer was arrested and fined for obstructing a thoroughfare when the meeting was held in the market place. At Worksop the speaker was not only unable to find a printer who dared print a placard, but was also assaulted by hired bullies.[15] The incident, however, which provoked the greatest indignation from the historian of the League was the riot at Cambridge. Here the students with the sound of " trumpets and other discordant noises " prevented the speaker from being heard. A fierce battle then took place between " town " and " gown," and it required the police to put an end to the riot. In addition to this form of hostile reception, the lecturers had to face the unfavourable comments of the local papers.

But the attacks on the League were not confined to those on their lecturers or in provincial newspapers. Many of the London newspapers, in fact, were rather sarcastic at the expense of the League and its activities. The following attack made by *The Morning Post*, which Morley termed the journal of London idleness, was widely quoted at the time and has been used frequently since in secondary works : " But the manufacturing people exclaim, ' why should we not be permitted to exchange the produce of our industry for the greatest quantity of food which the industry will anywhere command ? ' To which we answer, why not, indeed ? Who hinders you ? Take your manufactures away with you by all means, and exchange them anywhere you will, from Tobolsk to Timbuctoo ; but do not insist on bringing your foreign corn here untaxed, to the ruin of your countrymen engaged in the production of corn. If nothing will serve you but to eat foreign corn, *away with you, you and your goods, and let me never see you more*. We do not want to drive you away. You are welcome to stay if you will ; but remember, if you do, that ' live and let live ' is a fair, and honest, and English mode of proceeding."[16]

Even allowing for the exaggeration which free-trade writers of that time and since have indulged in, there is no questioning the fact that the propaganda of the League had a tremendous effect upon the middle and lower classes in the cities during the years from 1838 to 1842. Part of this success was due to the high price of wheat and the stagnation in industry, but a great deal of it was due to the unusually fine organization which the League had built up. In the years following 1839 the same sort of publicity work was continued. But more lecturers were sent out, more pamphlets circulated, and more copies of *The Circular* distributed. Each year there was a possibility of a decline in the effectiveness of their propaganda if a good crop came, but that possibility did not materialize until 1842. The wheat crops of 1839, 1840 and 1841 were all deficient in either quality or quantity, and some in both.[17]

The progress that the movement to repeal the Corn Laws was making outside Parliament and the lack of success which they had in Parliament in the session of 1839 did not deter the League from continuing to agitate the question in the sessions of 1840 and 1841. Repeating the plan of the year before, when the League was not yet organized, delegates were sent from each locality represented in the League to London in March of 1840. Villiers had agreed to bring forward his annual motion to consider the act of 1828 on March 26th, and it was planned to have these delegates paint the actual conditions in their respective communities and stress the overwhelming necessity for the immediate repeal of the Corn Laws. When the delegates assembled in London they arranged for deputations to be sent to Lord Melbourne, Lord John Russell, Sir Robert Peel, Sir James Graham, and Mr. Labouchere, the President of the Board of Trade. None of the interviews satisfied the delegates. In the one with Lord Melbourne, they were indignant not only at his astonishing ignorance of the question, but with his manner which " excited a feeling little short of disgust, especially, when with a smiling and incredulous air, he listened to the plain and straightforward, but feeling and pathetic description which Mr. Dixon gave of the distress prevailing in Carlisle."[18]   Mr. Baring, Chancellor of the Exchequer, met the delegation instead of Lord John Russell, who was indisposed, and stated that his lordship was favourable to " a moderate fixed duty up to the famine point."   But Prentice adds : " He must have seen, from the countenances of his auditors, what impression this had made ; for, with a good deal of hesitation and stammering, he corrected himself, by substituting the phrase, ' a vanishing point,' when the price of wheat reached seventy shillings."[19]   Mr. Labouchere also made a bad impression because he failed to be moved by a very touching description which one of the delegates gave of the poverty of a working class family in Manchester.   The spokesman himself was so overpowered by his own account that " convulsive sobs choked his utterance, and he was obliged to pause till he recovered from his deep emotion.   The tears rolled down the cheeks of Joseph Sturge ; John Benjamin Smith strove in vain to conceal his feelings."[20]   In addition to his lack of sympathy, Mr. Labouchere declared that he would not go as far as to withdraw all protection to agriculture, which caused Prentice to remark that this statement " was not of a kind to elevate his reputation as a statesman."[21]

Mr. Villiers had no better fortune with his motion to consider the act of 1828 than the delegates had with the prominent statesmen whom they interviewed.   On April 3rd, an attempt to adjourn the debate on this motion was beaten and an ordinary adjournment passed.   Hence the original motion became a dropped order.[22]   On May 26th Villiers, after expatiating on the unsportsmanlike conduct of his opponents, renewed his motion.   But the supporters of the Corn Laws made such a clamour that neither he nor his friends could be heard.   Recognizing the futility of continuing a discussion under such circumstances, those favourable to the motion agreed to the incessant demands for a division.   The only noteworthy comment, during the course of the debates on Villiers' motions, was made by Mr. Clay.   He declared that it was with great reluctance that he troubled the House with a repetition of arguments formerly used. But the subject was exhausted and if the old fallacies were repeated they must be met by the old refutations.[23]

In the first session of 1841 the activities of the free-traders were naturally obscured by the unsuccessful attempt of the Whig government to reduce the amount of protection on certain articles which resulted in its overthrow.   The weakening of the Whigs on the question of protection seems to have been less a matter of conversion than a realization that something had to be done to cover the ever-increasing deficit of the preceding years.   In 1839 a feeble and futile attempt had been made to wipe out the deficiency by a five per cent. increase in all taxes ; but, as generally happens in such instances, decreased consumption prevented much of an increase in revenue. In 1840, a committee on import duties had recommended a simplification of the tariff by substituting duties on a few productive articles, in which the amount was to be regulated with a view to securing the greatest consumption, for those on the enormous number under the existing system.   But, as Morley remarked, " Lord Melbourne's Cabinet had no member of sufficient grasp and audacity in finance to accept boldly and comprehensively, as Peel afterwards did, the maxim that reduction of duties is one way to increase of revenue."[24]

Instead of lowering duties on a great number of small articles, the Whigs chose to attack the giant monopolies of sugar, timber and corn.   They hoped to win over the manufacturing interests by Russell's motion of May 7th to replace the Corn Law of 1828 by a fixed duty of 8s. on wheat.   The attempt failed, both because the menaced corn and timber interests opposed the proposed change, and because no other group, not even the one favouring a repeal of the Corn Laws, was won over.   But it was over the clause in the budget which provided for a reduction of the duty on sugar from 63s. per hundredweight to 36s. that the government was beaten.   When after a debate of eight nights the measure was lost on May 7th by a vote of 317 to 281, the ministers did not resign, but announced that they would continue the old sugar duties.   Peel, on May 27th, brought forward a vote of no confidence in the government and, on June 4th, carried it by 312 to 311.   The Whigs now dissolved Parliament and appealed to the country.   When the new Parliament met, Peel, on August 28th, proposed an amendment to the Queen's address which was passed by a majority of 91.   The Melbourne ministry then resigned.

The usual opinion expressed on the failure of the Whig budget is that it deserved its fate.   It was felt at the time, and historians, later, have usually endorsed this view, that the conversion of the Whigs was not sincere but merely a desperate attempt to keep the reins of government from slipping from them.   On the other hand, Holland makes a very strong case for the disastrous results of this failure upon the cause of protection and the fortunes of the Conservative Party.   He feels that Peel should have allowed the budget to pass before turning out the Whigs.   In that case Peel would have had the support of Russell, and his followers, " in defending, with occasional modifications, this offspring of the Whig genius against the assaults of Radicals of the Manchester school, who were never very numerous in Parliament ; nor would these last have possessed so potent a means of appealing to the reason of the middle classes and the passions of the people.   Sir Robert Peel, personally, would have had a happier Administration.   He would not have had to act like a hero, and suffer like a martyr, in order to overthrow a system which he had pledged himself to defend without sincerely believing in it."[25]

The repealers, who had failed to rally to the support of Russell took advantage of the general election to put more candidates in the field, especially in the industrial centres of the north.   Many seats were won from both Whigs and Tories, and the strength of the League in Parliament, both in numbers and ability, was considerably enhanced.   The most important addition was Cobden, who was returned by Stockport.   The activities of Cobden and other repealers in the short session from August 19th to October 7th indicated that their agitation in Parliament from this time on would be on a larger scale than hitherto.

The attitude of the League toward the overthrow of the Whigs and the triumph of the Tories is an interesting one. Logically the repealers should have been disappointed because the Whig budget of 1841 indicated a weakening on protection which might have led further than the fixed duty proposed. On the other hand, they took some comfort in the fact that Peel, before election, refused to state what policy he would adopt toward the Corn Laws, and even in the short period before Parliament was prorogued on October 7th, although pressed by both Russell and Cobden, he declined to give any indication of forthcoming measures. In addition the fear that the fixed duty would prove less objectionable than the sliding scale, and hence more difficult to remove, probably did much to reconcile members of the League to the apparent set-back in their hopes. Prentice insists that, " The change of ministry caused no diminution of the zeal with which the Anti-Corn Law agitation was carried on. Hope, with some, that the Duke and Peel would yield upon an emergency, as they had yielded upon the Catholic question ; indignation with others at the insolent declarations of the Duke of Richmond, and his class ; and old dislike of the Tories, now again in office ; Whiggism roused into action, now that the Whig hitherto *ins* were *out*, and restored to their old functions of opposition—all tended, not merely to aid the movement, but to give it additional activity."[26]

Before taking up the great fiscal reforms of Peel in 1842, including his new Corn Law measure, it may be well to sum up the achievements and failures of the League down to February of 1842. Taking advantage of bad crops and unemployment in industry, the League had, by a marvellously organized system of propaganda (which included the sending of lecturers throughout the country, of delegations to interview ministers, of members to represent it in Parliament, and the distribution of pamphlets and *The Circular*) aroused the middle and part of the lower classes against the Corn Laws. But despite the unquestioned effectiveness of this propaganda the results were meagre. The members in Parliament pledged to repeal were pitifully few, and the people outside who favoured it were unable to bring effective pressure to bear on the government, or on the representatives in any great numbers. The general election of 1841 was clearly a blow to the immediate prospects of repeal, even though members of the League like Prentice managed to extract some comfort from it. The League failed not only to secure definite results in Parliament, but also to get the united support of the labouring classes.

This second failure brings us in touch with Chartism, the great contemporary movement among the working men. The history of the Chartist movement parallels that of the League. Both came into existence during the years of depression from 1836 to 1842, and both showed their greatest strength during the years from 1838 to 1842 when conditions were blackest. Both declined after 1842 with the return of better conditions ; but, as it will be shown later in this chapter, the League retained a much greater portion of its strength. Both in a way were aimed against the political supremacy of the landed interest : the League, because its members believed that this political control had a pernicious effect upon their business; and Chartism, because the labouring men believed that there was no hope of improving their social and economic position until they had political rights. The League demanded absolute repeal of the Corn Laws; the Chartists, the granting of the six points in *The People's Charter*: annual Parliaments; manhood suffrage; vote by ballot; the abolition of the property qualification for members of Parliament; payment for members; and equal electoral districts.

Because of the many points that the two movements had in common, co-operation, or at least benevolent neutrality, might have been expected; but their relations were characterized instead by active hostility and opposition. The Chartists frankly hated the League as an agent of the middle class, whose objects were to hand over the working class to the manufacturers and money-lords, and to divert attention from factory and Poor Law reform. Most of the Chartists strongly believed in protection for agriculture, because they believed that free trade in grain would throw out of cultivation a great deal of land and drive thousands of agricultural labourers to the factories to compete and to reduce wages. Reduction of prices, which had such a strong appeal to the middle classes, aroused the fierce opposition of the Chartists. They held that the persons who lived on fixed incomes benefited by this reduction, but that it was equivalent to an enormous increase in the national debt for which the labourer paid in taxes.

Contemporary Chartist literature is filled with this antipathy and distrust for the League, but two illustrations should suffice to represent this point of view. James Leach, who argued the Chartist side in one of the many debates with free-traders at Manchester, stressed seven points: that the labourers had been duped by the middle class over the Reform Bill and might be again over repeal; that machinery and not agricultural protection was responsible for the evils of which the workers complained; that the labourers would not profit by the increase in trade which the League promised would result from repeal; that England would not be able to compete with foreign countries through the export of manufactures, partly because of the low wages in foreign countries and partly because other countries would put up protective tariffs; that the real object of the free trade agitation was to reduce wages by securing cheap food; that no good could be done until those who monopolized political power were deprived of their favoured position; and that the real solution of the problems of surplus population and unemployment was the land.[27] John Campbell, secretary of the National Chartist Association, was even more bitter in his denunciation of the motives of the Leaguers. At the end of a seventy-page pamphlet, he concluded: " I think I have clearly established the two propositions, namely, ' What are the motives of the parties who are seeking the repeal of the Corn Laws ? ' And the answer is, that they are doing it for pelf, for individual profit, and not for any wish to benefit the working classes. The second question, viz., ' What would be the effects of their repeal, without accompanying measures ? ' And the answer to that must be, wide-spreading ruin, making us far more miserable than we are ; bringing scores of thousands of individuals from the pursuits of agriculture to the unhealthy occupations afforded in the pestilential cotton and woollen mills, to give birth to a pale, miserable, stunted, decrepit, unhealthy race of human beings ; to extend wider and wider, and farther and farther, the curse of the factory system, a system the most enslaving and degrading, the most revolting and accursed, that ever existed.   I think, my friends, I have clearly proved that such would be the result ; it is for this purpose the repeal is sought, with the additional benefit of *reducing wages*."[28]

The Chartists tried two ways of fighting the League : joint debates ; and breaking up their meetings.   In the former they were almost invariably out-argued by their better educated and informed opponents, " and they often had to beat a ridiculous retreat."[29]   The breaking up of League meetings proved equally unprofitable.   Prentice's *History of the League* is full of what he termed Chartist outrages. Two examples will illustrate this practice.   On February 28th, 1839, at a meeting in Manchester, one of the Chartists, when not recognized by the chairman, " proposed to place in the chair one whom he called ' honest Pat Murphy,' a potato-wheeler in Shudehill, who," according to Prentice, " whatever his honesty might be, was not very cleanly, and very far from sober. . . . The proposer then moved that Pat Murphy take the chair, and cried, ' Come on, Pat.'   The man was then pushed or dragged over the heads of the people, amidst great noise and confusion, and took his place before Mr. Thomas Harbottle, the chairman."[30]   In the riot which followed the " respectable " people departed and left the " vicious " element in control.   The second riot, in June of 1841, turned out more to Prentice's liking. The Chartists surrounded a League platform with banners of their own in order to obstruct the view of the speakers.   When the Chartists declined to remove one particularly large flag, the free-traders undertook to pull it down.   " Sticks had been provided to aid in its defence, and were lustily laid on the heads of those who made the attempt, and the latter being unarmed, it seemed at first as if the bludgeons of the hundreds would prevail over the will of the thousands, but in the short conflict of a minute, the offending flags were seized and torn into ribbons, and the flag staffs, broken into short lengths, became formidable weapons, and in another minute the physical force men fled from the power which they had foolishly roused, each to consider, at the outside of the meeting, on the truth of the saying, that he had tried a game which others could play at."[31]

Three recent works on Chartism have taken up the attitude of the Chartists toward the League.   Hovell, in *The Chartist Movement*, admits that the opposition of the Chartists was futile, especially their practices of joint debates and breaking up League meetings, and yet he believes strongly in extenuating circumstances.   When the two agitations began, there was no reason for thinking that one would be more successful than the other ; and the Chartists had as much right to expect co-operation from the middle class as the League from the working class.   Very soon the Chartists began to hate the Leaguers " for queering their pitch," and their foolish opposition followed.

" But," as Hovell points out, " poor, uneducated men, stirred by passion and resentment, are poor debaters in any case, and the disturbance of opposition meetings was as much a symptom of helplessness as anything else."[32] Beer, in *A History of British Socialism*, is more strongly pro-Chartist and expounds a novel interpretation of the influence of the movement on the repeal of the Corn Laws. He maintains that, despite the hostility of the Chartists, it was their agitation which broke down the opposition of the Whigs and of a group of the Tories to repeal, and paved the way for the victory of Cobden, Bright and the League.[33] The principal evidence cited, a speech of Sir James Graham in February of 1846, does not seem to prove his point. It is true that Sir James gave a vivid account of the strikes and the inflamed state of opinion among the masses during the year 1842, but he did not state that this converted him to free trade. Furthermore, Beer gives no reason why Whigs and Tories waited until 1845–46 before taking action on the conclusion, which he claims they could no longer resist after the failure of the " general strike " of the Chartists in 1842, " that the people must be afforded cheaper means of subsistence in order to render it possible for them to make both ends meet with the low scale of wages."[34] West, in *A History of the Chartist Movement*, devotes little attention to the attitude of the Chartists toward the League. However, he points out a fundamental difference in the point of view of the two organizations. " The Free Traders were conscious and deliberate adherents to the individualist theory of *laissez faire*. The Chartists, permeated with Socialist ideas, were virtually committed to the opposing theory of State interference."[35]

Even Cobden, in 1842, admitted that the hostility of the Chartists had compelled the League to make the agitation a middle class one. And, he added, " we have carried it on by those means by which the middle class usually carries on its movements. We have had our meetings of dissenting ministers ; we have obtained the co-operation of the ladies ; we have resorted to tea parties, and taken those pacific means for carrying out our views, which mark us rather as a middle class set of agitators."[36] This admission, along with the evidence cited on the attitude of the Chartists, proves beyond a shadow of doubt that the League was a middle class organization with the active hostility of a great part of the labouring class.

The League was not in an especially strong position when Parliament opened on February 3rd, 1842. Three years of vigorous agitation had not converted the labouring classes, and owing partly to the existing system of representation, had not prevented the party most opposed to free trade from winning an overwhelming victory at the polls in the previous year. The chief hope of the League was that Peel was unpledged, and that he might be induced to yield in an emergency as he had in the case of Catholic Emancipation. Its members therefore looked forward to an announcement of his policy with great eagerness.

When Peel's corn bill of 1842 is considered, it must be treated as a part of the great fiscal reforms of that year. The new government was confronted with a deficit of about £2,350,000 for the year ending in April ; and if the source of revenue remained the same, it was estimated that the deficit would rise to £4,700,000 in another year. Peel proposed to solve the problem by a series of changes much bolder than those proposed in the Whig budget of the preceding year. First, the income tax, which had been abandoned in 1816, was to be re-introduced. The rate proposed was 7d. upon all incomes above £150. Second, additional revenue was to be raised by extending to coal exported in British ships the duty of 4s. a ton already collected upon coals exported in foreign vessels. The surplus from these two sources, Peel stated, was to be used in " making great improvements in the commercial tariff of England, and, in addition to these improvements, in abating the duties on some great articles of consumption."[37] There were about 1,200 dutiable articles under the existing system and reductions were to be made upon 750 of these under the following plan : duties were not to exceed five per cent. on raw materials ; twelve per cent. on partly manufactured articles ; and twenty per cent. on wholly manufactured articles.[38]

Thus this part of Peel's scheme, a great reduction of protective duties, met with the approval of the free-traders, but the second part, a great extension of the system of colonial or inter-imperial preference, aroused vigorous opposition. Probably Holland was correct in stating that, " It was certainly in order to fortify the old national and imperial system, and to oppose a new bulwark against complete free trade in corn and other things, that Peel and his colleagues extended in 1842 the differential tariff."[39]

On February 9th, Peel stated the principles of his new corn bill and explained them in a long speech in the Commons. He referred in sympathetic terms to the existing commercial distress ; but, he denied that it could be attributed to the Corn Laws, and emphasized the part that the panic in the United States and the war with China had played in the dislocation of industry. He reiterated his opposition to the fixed duty on the ground that it could not be enforced when prices were high, and reaffirmed his confidence in the principle of the existing law. The great objection to the operation of the present act was the temptation to use fraud in raising the price of wheat to 73s. in order to avoid the payment of a large duty. The duty was 26s. 8d. when the price was 60s. ; 20s. 8d. at 66s. ; and 1s. at 73s. Such an arrangement worked a hardship upon producer, consumer and government. The producer was injured by having the bonded wheat swamp the market when the price reached 73s. ; the consumer, by the artificial advance to 73s. ; and the government, by losing the higher duties. The new measure proposed the introduction of " rests " or intervals, in which the same duty applied to several shillings variation in the price. As Peel phrased it, " When corn is at 59s. and under 60s., the duty at present is 27s. 8d. When corn is between those prices, the duty I propose is 13s. When the price of corn is at 50s., the existing duty is 36s. 8d., increasing as the price falls ; instead of which I propose, when corn is at 50s., that the duty shall only be 20s., and that that duty shall in no case be exceeded. . . . At 70s. the existing duty is 10s. 8d. ; the duty I propose is 5s."[40] By this scheme he hoped to do away with any object in holding back wheat after the price reached 60s. When justifying the continuation of protection to agriculture, Peel fell back on the time honoured arguments : it was best to pay a small additional sum for domestic produce as an insurance against the danger of becoming dependent on foreign supplies ; the landed interest had " special burdens " ; and it was best for all classes that the chief supply of corn should be derived from domestic agriculture.[41]

The new measure was attacked by both the Whigs and the League. Lord John Russell spoke at great length on the advantages of a fixed duty, and moved that the House was not prepared to adopt a measure with the sliding scale. This motion was lost by 349 to 226.[42] Villiers, shortly after, moved that the duties on corn cease. After several nights of debating this motion was beaten by 393 to 90.[43] In the course of the debates a clash, showing the mutual feelings of the landowners and the manufacturers, took place between Mr. Ferrand and Mr. Brotherton. The former made a bitter attack on the mill-owners in which he stressed their hypocrisy and the harsh treatment of their labourers. Brotherton defended himself in the following strain : " The honourable Member (Mr. Ferrand) had classed him (Mr. Brotherton) amongst those who make the ledger their prayer-book, the countinghouse their church, and mammon their God. If he had done so, he certainly had not reaped the worldly fruits which the honourable Member supposed to be derived from such a course of life. His riches consisted not so much in the largeness of his means, as in the fewness of his wants. If he had not considered usefulness as superior to wealth he never should have been returned in the manner he had been."[44]

The discussion of Peel's new bill lasted from February 25th to April 7th. Amendment after amendment was proposed, only to be beaten by the invincible majority of the government. On April 7th, the day the measure was passed, Cobden entered a vigorous protest. He denounced the bill as a robbery of the poor without compensation, and predicted that the people would no longer waste their time in petitioning the Commons to repeal the Corn Laws, but would present their petitions, signed by millions, to the Queen, praying to have the House of Commons dismissed and to give the people an opportunity of expressing their opinion of the bread-tax. " A system of promises, of chicanery, of trickery, and delusions, such as were never practised before, had led the electors to return members who would never be returned again ; and he ventured to say, that the premier dared not take the sense of the people on this tax."[45] Doubtless, Cobden meant the sense of the middle class, since we have seen what the attitude of the Chartists was. In reality there was little excuse for such an outburst except his strong feelings on the subject. Peel had come into office by opposing the attempt of the Whig government to lower duties on sugar, and to change those on corn from a sliding scale to a fixed one. Peel had been careful not to pledge himself to any policy, and Cobden had no real reason to expect a more liberal measure at this time.

When the bill was carried up to the Lords, it was attacked vigorously as a betrayal of the country gentlemen. The fight against the measure was led by the Earl of Stanhope, the Duke of Buckingham, Lord Beaumont, the Earl of Malmesbury, and Lord Western. The first three bemoaned the apostacy of the Tories, and Western, who had played so prominent a part in all discussions on the Corn Laws since 1804, bluntly declared that the conservative agriculturists no longer trusted Peel. Personally, he was certain that Peel would sooner or later introduce free trade and he saw no reason why it should be further delayed. On April 22nd the bill was read a third time and passed.[46] Stanhope had his protest against the third reading, which represented the extreme protectionist point of view, entered upon the Journals.[47]

The bill became a law on April 29th and went into effect immediately. The important features, the introduction of the " pauses," and the decrease in the amount of protection, have already been discussed. Equally significant was the extension of the principle of colonial preference. Wheat imported from British colonies was to pay a duty of 5s. when the price was under 55s. ; this duty was to be lowered 1s. for every shilling that the price rose until 58s. was, reached ; the duty was then fixed at 1s.[48] The next year the duty was reduced to 1s. at all times, in consideration of the fact that Canada imposed a duty of 3s. a quarter on wheat from other places than British possessions.[49]

All things considered, Peel's new income tax, reduction in the tariff, and new corn law combined constituted a splendid achievement, and it has generally been recognized as such. It would seem that Cobden with his firm belief in free-trade principles should have recognized the significance of these reforms, yet his speeches in Parliament and his letters to his brother are full of bitter attacks on and sneers at income tax and the tariff changes as well as the new corn law. Morley gives what is certainly the most charitable explanation possible when he says : " We who live a generation after the battle was won, may feel for a moment disappointed that Cobden did not at once judge the Minister's boldness in imposing the income tax as a means of reforming the tariff, in a more appreciative spirit. It is just, however, to remember that in his letters we seize the first impressions of the hour ; that these first impressions were naturally those of chagrin in one who saw that the new scheme, however good in its general bearings, omitted the one particular change that was needful. We must not expect from an energetic and clear-sighted actor, committed to an urgent practical cause, the dispassionateness of a historian whose privilege it is to be wise after the event."[50] However, it was not merely in the " first impressions of the hour " that Cobden expressed this chagrin. A year after Peel had introduced the corn bill, Cobden, in the course of the debates on February 17th, 1843, still insisted that, " It was folly or ignorance to amend our system of duties, and leave out of consideration sugar and corn. The reduction of the duties on drugs and such things was a proper task for some under-Secretary of State, dealing with the sweepings of office ; but it was unworthy of any Minister, and was devoid of any plan."[51] Clearly Morley's apology fails to convince. A more likely explanation of Cobden's conduct is that his whole interest was

so concentrated on the Corn Laws that he was unable to do justice
to such an original and far-reaching plan as Peel put forward ; and
that he was afraid that the reduction in the duties on corn, and the
extension of colonial preference, instead of being a step in the
direction of free trade, would hurt the effectiveness of the agitation
for repeal.

Even after the new law was passed, Cobden and the other League
members in Parliament continued to hector Peel on every conceivable point.   He wrote to his brother that it would not surprise
him if Peel prepared a measure to repeal the Corn Laws before the
next session of Parliament just to stop the mouths of the League men.
In another letter to his brother, written on July 20th, 1842, he states :
" He (Peel) has been excessively worried by *our* clique in the House,
and I have reason to flatter myself with the notion that I have been a
frequent thorn in his side.   If distress should continue to *favour* us,
we shall get something substantial in another twelve months, and I
suspect we may bargain for the continuance of bad trade for that
length of time at least."[52]   Evidently distress among the lower
classes did not grieve Cobden as much as it did the delegates of the
League who had interviewed Lord Melbourne in March of 1840.

The attitude of Peel toward the arguments of the Leaguers and the
distress of the country was one against which even the historian of the
League could muster very little indignation.   In his speech of July
11th, Peel declared, " if I could believe that a material alteration of
the Corn Law would produce any permanent relief, not only I, but
I am sure those who are, like myself, immediately connected with the
land, if they were convinced that the Corn Laws were the main cause
of the distress, and that their repeal would give substantial and
enduring relief, would instantly relax our determination to maintain
them."[53]   When a delegation from the Anti-Corn Law Conference,
which met from July 25th to August 1st, interviewed him, Peel
thanked them for their testimony and expressed deep sympathy for
the distresses of the country, which, he added, " I fear is incon-
testable."[54]

On August 12th Parliament was prorogued and the League was
left free to devote its entire attention to the conversion of the country.
A few weeks later the prospects of the League received an unexpected
blow when the harvest of 1842, despite unfavourable weather down
to the summer, turned out to be the best in years.   From June on
the weather was " almost miraculously fine and warm," and as a
result the crops in all parts of the country were exceptional in both
quality and quantity.   When it was ascertained that the wheat crop
exceeded that of the two preceding years by at least a fourth, and
that the price was certain to fall and the duty to rise, practically
all wheat in bond was entered for consumption at once.[55]   As a result
the price of wheat was about 14s. lower in 1842–3 than in 1841–2.
This decline in price unquestionably weakened the appeal of the
League to those interested in cheap bread.

At the end of 1842 the Council of the League took stock of what had
been accomplished and discussed what their future action should
be.   Thus far the League had been spending about a hundred pounds
a week, and Cobden advised that the expenditure be increased to a

thousand pounds. The Council decided to raise a new fund of fifty thousand pounds for the purpose of continuing on a larger scale the same system of propaganda carried on during the three preceding years. Cobden, in writing to Edward Baines, explained the rôle of the League very clearly : " Recollect that our primary object is to work the printing press, not upon productions of our own, but producing the *essence* of authoritative writers, such as Deacon Hume, Lord Fitzwilliam, etc., and scattering them broadcast over the land."[56] The fact that such a policy was pursued is the chief reason why the organization, rather than the arguments, of the League has been stressed in this chapter. The enlargement of the field of operations was simple : more pamphlets were published, more lecturers sent out, and more local associations formed. Systematization was gained by securing the names of all the registered voters in the country, whether borough or county, and showering them with arguments on the evil effects of the Corn Laws upon both the industrial and agricultural classes.

From 1839 to 1842 the League had, on the whole, worked on the middle and lower classes of the cities, and had found these classes interested either in the revival of trade or in cheap food, and sometimes in both. But when the price of wheat dropped 14s., most members of these two classes, except the manufacturers, either lost interest in, or, as Morley says, were " already convinced " of, the necessity of repealing the Corn Laws. The tenant farmers, on the other hand, were suffering from this fall in the price of wheat and were indignant at the reductions in the duties, particularly on meat, in Peel's 1842 budget ; and consequently they were in a mood to listen to the missionaries sent out by the League. Morley eulogizes this campaign among the farmers as " perhaps the most striking and original feature in the whole agitation. There was true political courage and profound faith, in the idea of awakening the most torpid portion of the community, not by any appeal to passion, but by hard argumentative debate."[57] If one judges by the account which Morley gives in *The Life of Richard Cobden*,[58] this invasion of the country was one long series of triumphs. Usually, this version goes, the reception of Cobden or other free-trade speakers was cold at the beginning and often violence was threatened ; but, as a rule, these meetings of farmers to consider the Corn Laws ended by voting for the abolition of protection. One of the many cases cited was the meeting at Taunton. Here, Morley says, " The farmers listened at first with doubt and suspicion. Gradually their faces cleared, conviction began to warm them, and at last such an impression had been made, that eight hundred farmers out of a meeting of twelve hundred persons, voted in favour of total and immediate repeal."[59]

However, without in the least questioning the marvellous ability of Cobden and other representatives of the League, or the successes that Morley records, an examination of the pamphlets and newspapers of the period does not give the impression either that the campaign among the farmers was such an almost unbroken series of triumphs, or that the tactics employed by the agents of the League were always above reproach. In Huntingdonshire, for example, the League, although represented by Bright and Moore, two of its ablest speakers, failed entirely to convert the audience in the debate on June 17th, 1843. Here Mr. George Game Day attacked the League in its weakest points : the desire to reduce prices in order to reduce wages, and the contradictory statements made on this point by its members. Despite constant interruptions by Moore and Bright, he read quotation after quotation from the speeches of Cobden and other free traders, and from the *Anti-Corn Law Circular*, showing that in one place the statement would be made that the prices of corn and wages would not be reduced by free trade, and in the next place that corn would fall and thus enable the British manufacturer to reduce wages and compete successfully with foreigners. When Day quoted from Almack's pamphlet, *The Character, Motives and Proceedings of the Anti-Corn Law League*, Moore shouted : " That man is paid to tell lies."[60] A subsequent letter by Almack refuting this charge, seems to have remained unanswered. When Day in quoting from the pamphlet of John Campbell, Secretary for National Chartist Association, referred to the author as a poor man, Moore called out : " He is not a poor man. He was paid £1 5s. a week as secretary of the Association, and has since run away to America with all its funds."[61] One of the Council of the Association certified that there was no foundation for such a statement and that Campbell had never dishonestly appropriated any funds. After constant interruptions by Bright and Moore, Day asked : " Why these repeated interruptions ? I heard you state the price of wool incorrectly, and the statistics of crime partially and unfairly. I had these prices and statistics in my hand, but did not interrupt you. . . . Why do you, then, continually interrupt me, and excite others to follow your example ? *Is it in accordance* with your *secret* instructions from the League ? Is it the plan you are ordered to adopt at these meetings for the purpose of stifling opposition ? "[62] In the end the original motion in favour of retaining protection for agriculture was carried by a large majority.[63]

A similar affair took place on March 28th, 1844, when a representative was chosen for the borough of Hastings and St. Leonards. On this occasion Musgrave Brisco, Esq., was returned by a majority of 339 over the nominee of the League, but a speech on his behalf by his friend Dr. Sleigh was subject to constant interruptions. According to the notice at the beginning of the pamphlet edition of this speech, " The unremitting hooting and yelling kept up by a knot of hired persons during Doctor Sleigh's repeated and vain attempts to make himself heard, rendered it utterly impossible for the public reporters to take down even two connected sentences of the speech : the Publisher therefore is indebted to Dr. Sleigh for the following copy of it." These tactics resemble very closely those practised by the protectionists on the " economic missionaries " of the League, of which Prentice justly complained with so much bitterness.

These accounts are interesting for several reasons : first, they throw some light on the tactics adopted by the representatives of the League in these county meetings ; second, they show the landed interest beginning to fight back and to employ the methods of the League ; and third, they indicate that the protectionists had discovered the heel of Achilles of the League in the inconsistent stand on the effects of free trade in corn on wages. Day, later, published a rather ingenious series of selections showing that the *Anti-Corn Law Circular* and Cobden had made contradictory statements on certain very significant points. [64]

ANTI-CORN LAW CIRCULAR

COBDEN

I. " If we have free trade, the landlord's rents will fall 100 per cent." (*League Circular*, No. 15, p. 3, and *Ibid.*, No. 12.)

I. " If we have free trade, the landlords will have as good rents as now." (Speech in House of Commons, May 15th last.)

II. " Provisions will fall one-third." (*League Circular*, No. 34, p. 4.) " The Corn Law makes the labourer pay double the price for his food." (*League Circular*, No. 15.)

II. " Provisions will be no cheaper." (Speech at Bedford, Hartford Reformer, 10th June, 1843.)

III. " The Corn Law compels us to pay *three times the value for a loaf of bread.*" (*League Circular*, No. 13.) " If the Corn Laws were abolished, the working man would save 3½d. upon every loaf of bread." (*League Circular*, No. 75.)

III. " *The argument for cheap bread was never mine.*" (*Morning Chronicle*, 30th June, 1843, speech on Penenden Heath.) " *The idea of low-priced foreign corn is all a delusion.*" (Speech at Winchester, *Salisbury Herald*, July 29th, 1843, p. 3.)

" As a consequence of the repeal of the Corn Laws *we promise cheaper food*, and our hand-loom weavers would get *double* the rate of wages ! " (*League Circular*, No. 7.)

" We shall have *cheap bread*, and its price will be reduced 33 per cent." (*League Circular*, No. 34.)

" The *finest* Georgiana wheat can be laid down at the door of our factories at 30s. a quarter, and we are now (Oct., 1839), paying 70s. or 80s. for the worst." (*League Circular*, No. 13.)

" We are much indebted to Mr. Ibbotson, of Sheffield, Mr. James Wilson, and our esteemed correspondent, for labouring to prove to the Landlords that they may safely do justice to others, without endangering their own interests. And we think very much has been done towards justifying their opinions, *that the money price of grain would not be lowered even by total repeal of the Corn Laws.*" (July, 1839.) (*League Circular*, No. 7, p. 6.)

" Spain could land the very best wheat in England at 40s. for which we are now (Oct., 1839), paying 67s." (*Ibid.*)

" In the American port of Cincinnati alone, there are a million of quarters of wheat which we could purchase at 16s.—or less than one-fourth the price we are now compelled to pay for our home-grown product." (*League Circular*, No. 39.)

IV. Messrs. Villiers, Muntz, Hume, Roche, Thornton, Rawson, Sanders (all avowed Free Traders) say, and the oracle of the League itself has said, that " We want free trade to enable us to *reduce wages*, that we may compete with foreigners." (Speech, pp. 8–10.)

IV. Messrs. Cobden, Bright and Moore, now affirm, " It is a base falsehood to say we want free trade to enable us to reduce the rate of wages." (Mr. Cobden, on Penenden Heath. Messrs. Bright and Moore at Huntingdon.)

V. The League oracle admits that " a repeal would *injure* the farmer, but not so much as he fears." (*League Circular*, No. 58.)

V. Cobden, Moore and Bright, say that it is to the *interest* of the farmer to have a total and *immediate* repeal." (Uxbridge, Bedford, Huntingdon.)

These contradictory statements in parallel columns were published and widely circulated along with Day's speech of June 17th, 1843. Cobden undertook to explain away the seeming inconsistencies in a speech delivered at Covent Garden Theatre in London on March 20th, 1844. He called attention to the fact that the selections cited as contradictory were often made three years apart. Day, in reply, pointed out that *he had* given the dates and numbers of *The Circular* and hence could not be accused of deception. Further, he inquired why dates were of any significance, since Cobden had said that the argument for cheap bread was *never* his.[65] Cobden appears to have dropped the controversy at this point.

The landowners did not confine themselves to attempts to defeat the League in county meetings and to show up the inconsistencies of the free traders, but began the publication of pamphlets on the League and its members which were as insulting and vituperative as any published against them in the eighteen-twenties or by the League. Of all the pamphlets of this nature,[66] Almack's *The Character, Motives and Proceedings of the Anti-Corn Law Leaguers*, is probably the most representative. It opens with two quotations which give a very good idea of what is to follow. " The mean rapacity, and monopolizing spirit of merchants and manufacturers, who neither are, nor ought to be, the rulers of mankind, though it cannot perhaps be corrected, may very easily be prevented from disturbing the tranquillity of any body but themselves."—Adam Smith, *Wealth of Nations*, Book 4, Chap. 3. " Why these individuals, some of them not originally perhaps of the most opulent class of the community, have, during the operation of these laws, amassed enormous fortunes ; yet, during the whole of this period, they have never found an opportunity either of increasing the wages, or diminishing the toil, of their little labourers, to whom they owe every farthing they possess. They have constantly done the reverse. And they talk of Corn Laws as their apology. ' This is too bad.' Can any man be fool enough to suppose, that were the Corn Laws abolished to-morrow, and every grain we consume were grown and ground in foreign parts, that such individuals would cease to ' grind the faces of the poor ' ? "—M. T. Sadler (June 7th, 1832). This second quotation indicates the direction in which a counter-attack on the millowners making up the League was to be delivered.

By a careful combing of the *Circular* of the League, Almack found that the landlords were called " a bread-taxing oligarchy, a handful of swindlers ; despicable, base, sordid, detestable, ruthless, unprincipled, beggarly, cruel, brutal, relentless, tyrannous, reckless, merciless, insatiable, voluptuous, unfeeling, haughty, bold, insolent, flesh-mongering, proud, impudent, scoundrel, law-making landlords ; parliamentary crew, pocket-picking fraternity, monsters, wretches, demons, knaves, thieves, bread-stealers, heartless band, rapacious harpies, labour-plunderers, monsters of impiety, foot-pad aristocracy, power-proud plunderers, putrid and sensual banditti, titled felons, rich robbers, blood-sucking vampires, plunderers of the people, etc."[67] The farmers were let off with such names as " brute drudges, clodpates, hawbucks, bullfrogs, chawbacons, clodpoles, etc."[68]

S

Evidently Almack felt that these epithets justified him in casting aside any restraint that he may originally have felt in speaking of the Leaguers. Regardless of his views on free trade in grain, he showed clearly in the remaining ninety-odd pages of his pamphlet that he believed in reciprocity of abuse. But the core of his work is composed of a vast mass of evidence showing that the repealers advocated abolition of the Corn Laws because they wanted cheap labour in factories. He cited quotations from practically every prominent opponent of the Corn Laws since 1815, including Hume, Rooke, Thornton, Villiers, Colonel Thompson, Whitmore, Burdett, Ricardo, Philips and Baring, to prove this point. Almack was especially aroused at the attempt of Earl Fitzwilliam to prove the advantage of cheap bread and labour to the landowners, and declared that " his lordship proves to us, that low wages mean high wages, and high wages mean low wages, by the self-same process of logic, as that by which it has aforetime been shown, that a horse chestnut is a chestnut horse."[69] His conclusion, which he dramatically italicized, sums up his own view and that of the average landowner on the character, motives and proceedings of the Leaguers : " The party from which the Anti-Corn Law League has been formed, instead of being remarkable for their humane and liberal conduct to the labouring poor, have uniformly been distinguished for their rapacious and brutal cruelty toward them :—That the principal object of the manufacturers in seeking for repeal is, to increase their own gains by reducing the wages of those very men whose privations they already pretend to commiserate. That the dangerous and unconstitutional association called the Anti-Corn Law League was contrived, and is carried on, for the purpose of decoying the labouring poor into the cheap-labour trap, and exciting them to become the willing instruments of their own destruction."[70]

On February 19th, 1844, the protectionists, who had been organizing local associations throughout the country, formed a central society in London. The title chosen was " The Agricultural Protection Society, for the United Kingdom of Great Britain and Ireland," and the following resolutions were the basis on which the organization was founded : " 1. That a Society . . . be now formed for the purpose of upholding, by constitutional means, protection to British agriculture. 2. That the object of this Society is to maintain protection to British agriculture, not less than at present existing. 3. That the Society shall, through the Press, repel the imputations and point out the inconsistencies contained in the statements of those who oppose such protection. 4. That party politics shall not be introduced into the proceedings of this Society, and that the Society shall on no account interfere in any election for a member to serve in Parliament."[71] The Duke of Richmond was made president ; the Duke of Buckingham and Chandos, vice-president ; and the Dukes of Norfolk, Rutland and Cleveland, and the Earl of Yarborough, trustees. To offset this top heavy effect of peers, half of the general committee was made up of tenant farmers. This society has been generally neglected in secondary works on this period. It is true that its activities proved to be something of a disappointment, but they were by no means negligible.   They put out numerous pamphlets, following in the footsteps of the League, and some of them ran into several editions.   Eventually the Society became the nucleus for the opposition to Peel's repeal measure of 1846.

The bitterness of the controversy between the orators and pamphleteers of the League and the landowners declined somewhat at the end of 1844 and in the first part of 1845, if a decrease in the number of pamphlets and articles published is a fair test.   Several factors contributed to this decline, but the most important apparently were the physical impossibility of continuing a campaign of such excessive " mud-slinging " over a period of years ; and the discouragement of the League over two more good wheat crops.   Exceptionally fine weather during the harvest season of 1843 resulted in a wheat crop of practically the same quality and quantity as that of 1842.   The harvest of 1844 was estimated to be the largest in bulk and yield since that of 1834 ; and only 475,000 quarters of foreign and colonial wheat were entered for consumption between August 5th, 1844, and August 5th, 1845.[72]

Although the most novel part of the agitation of the League after the abundant harvest of 1842 was carried on in the country districts and provoked the counter-agitation just described, it would be a mistake to believe that the propaganda in the large cities was abandoned.   At the beginning of 1843, as we have seen, the League raised a £50,000 fund to carry on the agitation.   On January 30th the Great Free Trade Hall was opened in Manchester and was used continuously for large meetings.   By September, although the League was encouraged by their numerous victories in the county meetings of farmers, it was obvious that something had to be done to increase the number of free trade members in Parliament.   During the five years from the establishment of the Manchester Association to 1843, thirty-five members had been added, but that made the total only 125 out of 658 members.   Since the League was already doing its utmost in the way of sending out lecturers and distributing pamphlets, it was resolved to add two additional agencies for propaganda : first, Covent Garden in London was to be engaged for fifty nights to hold Anti-Corn Law meetings ; and second, ten thousand pounds a year were to be expended on a full-sized weekly newspaper which was to be called The League.   This paper was to supplant the small fortnightly publication called the Anti-Bread Tax Circular, and was to be distributed to ten thousand subscribers.[73]

The report of the expenditures during the year 1843 gives a clear idea of the manner in which the League spent its fifty thousand pound fund : 9,026,000 tracts were printed and distributed ; 650 lectures given ; 156 deputations sent to meetings in counties and boroughs ; numerous deputations sent to ˙ boroughs on Parliamentary registration ; 426,000 tracts published in magazines as advertisements ; and vast sums paid for hiring rooms for lectures, printing, placarding, weekly meetings of the League, rent, taxes, wages, stamps, and incidentals.[74]   The next year, despite greater expenditure of money, the League, owing to improvement in trade and the good crops already described, made even less progress in the boroughs and counties than in 1843. The task of securing a majority of the 658 members in the House of Commons seemed more difficult than ever, but at the end of 1844 Cobden set forth a plan whereby he hoped to break the hold of the protectionists on the county seats. This plan was to have persons who believed in free trade qualify for a vote in the counties under the old 40s. freehold clause. As he pointed out, by an expenditure of from £35 to £60 it was possible to secure a freehold that would bring in an income of 40s., which was much easier than taking a £10 house in a borough or city. Clerks and mechanics who were ineligible to vote in the boroughs because they were merely lodgers, and who placed their earnings in savings' banks, were especially urged to take advantage of this opportunity. In this manner Cobden hoped to offset the effect of the Chandos clause in the Reform act, which permitted tenant farmers to vote. The present grip of the monopolists on the county seats came, he held, as a result of the landowners qualifying as voters every brother, son, nephew and uncle who lived on the farm of a tenant. In the last division on the Corn Laws in the Commons, not one of the 152 county members had voted in favour of Mr. Villiers' motion, and it was practically impossible to carry repeal without some of them.[75]

But Cobden seems to have been somewhat sensitive on the comparative lack of success of the agitation during the year 1844, and on the charge that the League was changing its tactics in trying to convert the tenants and to qualify free traders who lived in boroughs for the county franchise. On December 11th, he vigorously denied that these new moves meant a change of policy and insisted that not a single thing had been changed. " I believe," he affirmed, " every step we have taken has been necessary, in order to arrive at the present stage of our movement. We began by lecturing and distributing tracts, in order to create an enlightened public opinion ; we did that for two or three years necessarily. We then commenced operations in the boroughs ; and never at any time was there so much systematic attention, labour and expense devoted to the boroughs in the way of registration as at the present time. As regards our lectures, we continue them still ; only that instead of having small rooms up three pair of stairs back, as we used to have, we have magnificent assemblies, as that now before me. We distribute our tracts, but in another form ; we have our own organ, The League paper, twenty thousand copies of which have gone out every week for the last twelve months. I have no doubt that that Journal penetrates into every parish in the United Kingdom, and goes the round of the district."[76]

Yet despite this spirited declaration, which shows the machinery of the League functioning in such a smooth fashion and the capacity of its leaders to find new fields for effective work, the first part of 1845 proved anything but a propitious period for the activities of the League. Trade was brisk, the manufacturing classes were well employed, and a tremendous interest was being taken in new railways. The expenditure of £1,000 a week by the League could not offset the effects of this widespread prosperity. Even Morley admits that the outlook of the cause was never less hopeful or encouraging.[77]

Thus after six years of agitation, which improved progressively in tactics and effectiveness, the campaign of the League outside Parliament had failed to secure repeal. It is impossible to state exactly how effective the campaign of education and the plan to increase the registration of voters in boroughs and counties, actually was, since only a general election in the first part of 1845 could have determined this point. But lacking these statistics, the fact remains that the agitation did not succeed in causing the people outside Parliament to put enough pressure on their representatives to bring about repeal.

Turning from the campaign of the League throughout the country to that within Parliament, we find that, although at times the outlook was even more discouraging than outside during the years 1843 to 1845, it was ultimately successful. In the session of 1843 the feeling between the free traders and protectionists was extremely bitter and ugly. The fall in the price of wheat after the good crop of 1842 had not put the landowners in a pleasant frame of mind ; and the stagnation in industry, which still persisted, left the millowners exasperated. In addition, the latter part of 1842 had witnessed the most critical part of the Chartist movement, and had left the nerves of the ruling classes everywhere in the country somewhat frayed. All through the session of 1843, which opened on February 2nd, speeches on both sides were unusually stinging. Ferrand's speech in the session of 1842 was exceptional for its indulgence in personalities, but it would not have been considered unusual in 1843. Morley claims that, " This heat in the minds of the ruling class made them anxious at almost any cost to destroy Cobden, who was now openly recognized as the foremost personage in the detested organization."[78] Such a statement requires a careful examination.

The most famous clash of the session was the one between Cobden and Peel on the night of February 17th. It came up, not over the Corn Laws, but in the course of a debate over a reference in the Queen's speech to the prevailing distress. Cobden took advantage of the opportunity to strike at Peel on the Corn Laws. The part of his speech to which Peel took exceptions was : " If you (Peel) try another remedy than ours, what chance have you of mitigating the condition of the country ? You took the Corn Laws into your own hands after a fashion of your own, and amended them according to your own views . . . you acted on your own judgment, and would follow no other, and you are responsible for the consequences of your act. . . . You passed the law, you refused to listen to the manufacturers, and I throw on you all the responsibility of your own measure. . . . It is his duty, he says, to judge independently and act without reference to any pressure ; and I want to tell the right honourable Baronet that it is the duty of every honest and independent member to hold him individually responsible for the present position of the country."

Peel now rose and in a manner " which indicated extreme agitation," declared that " the honourable gentleman has stated here most emphatically, what he has more than once stated at the conference of the Anti-Corn Law League, that he holds me individually "—cheers

from the ministerial benches and confusion in the House and galleries
—" individually responsible for the distress and suffering of the
country ; that he holds me personally responsible. Be the consequences of those insinuations what they may, never will I be
influenced by menaces to consider . . . "[79] The remainder of his
sentence was lost in the shouts from the ministerial bench. Peel's
reply was open to a peculiar interpretation owing to the fact that his
private secretary, Mr. Edward Drummond, had been murdered a few
days earlier by an insane mechanic from Glasgow. The impression
got abroad that the assassin, M'Naghten, thought he was shooting
Peel. This tragic event undoubtedly shook the nerves of the Prime
Minister and may have been responsible for his outburst against
Cobden. The latter immediately answered that he did not say that
he held Peel personally responsible, but responsible by virtue of his
office. Peel and others shouted, " You did, you did." After several
speeches Cobden returned to his explanation and once more insisted
that he merely treated Peel as the government when he used the word
" individually." Peel answered " very stiffly " (according to Morley),
" I am bound to accept the construction which the honourable
member puts upon the language he employed."

This whole affair puzzled people at the time as it has puzzled
historians since. Peel was said by some to have allowed his temper,
usually under excellent control, to run riot, and by others that he
simulated rage in order to damage a dangerous opponent. As it was
natural, enemies of Cobden spoke of him as politically ruined, and his
friends and the public assemblies he addressed hailed him as a hero.
Cobden's own version of the affair, written on February 23rd to his
brother, puts him in a less favourable light than his conduct in the
House. The general verdict, he said, " seems to be a pretty general
notion that Peel has made a great fool of himself, if not something
worse. He is obliged *now* to assume that he was in earnest, for no
man likes to confess himself a hypocrite, and to put up with the
ridicule of his own party in private as a coward. . . . He is looking
twenty per cent. worse since I came into the House, and if I had only
Bright with me, we could worry him out of office before the close of
the session."[80] Upon careful consideration it seems safest to reject
the interpretation of both Cobden and Peel. Cobden, of course, did
not mean to infer that any person should hold Peel responsible in
the M'Naghten manner, but he was adopting an attitude very trying
to a man in Peel's position and nervous state. But it is just as absurd
to believe with Morley that Peel's action was part of a plan of the
ruling classes to discredit Cobden. It is probably safest to regard the
clash as a natural outburst, of which both men should have been
ashamed ; but excusable and explicable on the grounds of the intense
feelings on such a controversial subject at a critical time.

The question of the Corn Laws was brought up three times in the
Commons and once in the Lords during the remainder of the session.
On March 14th, Lord Monteagle moved in the Lords that a select
committee be appointed to inquire into the operation and effect of
the law of 1842. The motion was beaten by 200 to 78. In the
course of Monteagle's speech he quoted a selection from the Report

on Hand-loom Weavers which summed up the political position of the landlords admirably. " The Government of this country resides in a minority—and a narrow minority of the people—the owners of the land. A very small portion of the community constitutes, almost exclusively, one House of Parliament, and forms a very large majority of the other. Such a Government can be safe only so long as it is popular, and popular only while it is believed to be impartial. Its first prudential duty is to avoid the appearance of selfish legislation."[81]

In the Commons, Ward's motion to inquire into the peculiar burdens affecting the landed interest and the peculiar exemptions enjoyed by that interest, was beaten by 232 to 133.[82] Villiers' annual motion, made on May 9th, to consider the immediate abolition of the duty on foreign corn, brought on a debate of five nights but secured only the 125 regular free trade votes in its favour.[83] Lord John Russell's motion, on June 13th, that the House go into committee to consider the Corn Laws, met the same fate as the others.[84]

On the fifth night of the debates on Villiers' motion, Cobden delivered a speech on the Corn Laws. Like the agitation outside Parliament during the year 1843, emphasis was placed not on the hardship inflicted upon the manufacturers and operatives, but on the harm done to the tenant farmers. His argument was merely the conventional one that high rents and expenses under protection more than offset a lower price of grain under free trade.[85]

Just as the speeches and actions in the session of 1843 mirrored the ugly feelings between protectionists and free traders outside Parliament, and the change in the tactics of the League, in the same way those in the sessions of 1844 and 1845 reflected the decline in the influence of the League throughout the country which resulted from improved trade and industrial conditions. Even Morley admits that the Corn Laws fell into the background in the session of 1844, because the revival of trade weakened the strongest argument of the agitators.[86] A writer in *The Annual Register* in commenting on the paucity of discussion on this topic held that the decided stand of Peel at the opening of the session was responsible for the feeble exertions of the free traders.[87]

But the session was not a complete loss to the Leaguers, as events were to prove, because of the influence that Cobden's speech of March 12th had upon Peel. This speech was made when Cobden moved the appointment of a select committee to inquire into the effects of protective duties upon the interests of tenants and agricultural labourers, and it is usually ranked as his second best speech on free trade. He especially stressed three points : the necessity of solving the depression in agriculture by increasing the ability of their customers to buy ; the effect of free trade on rents ; and the harm done agricultural labourers by making food scarce. On the first point he criticized Peel's tariff of 1842 for proposing to degrade prices instead of attempting to sustain them by enlarging the circle of exchanges. On the second point he insisted that he had never said that free trade would deprive landlords of their rents, but he would say, " that if the landowners prefer to draw their rents from the distresses of the country, caused by their restrictive laws to create high prices through scarcity of food, instead of deriving an honourable income of possibly as great, or even greater amount, through the growing prosperity of the people under a free trade, then they have no right, in the face of such facts as I have stated, to attempt to cajole the farmer into the belief that rent forms an insignificant item in the cost of his wheat, or to frighten him into the notion that he could not compete with foreigners if he had his land rent free."[88]   On the third point, which Cobden characterized as a "more important branch of this question," he showed that the agricultural labourer spent a larger proportion of his wages in food than any other class, and therefore could not be benefited by high prices occasioned by scarcity of food.   Turning to the actual condition of the agricultural labourer, Cobden cited statistics and testimony from all parts of Great Britain to prove that their condition was with few exceptions deplorable.   In conclusion he held that the existing system deprived the people of subsistence and the farmers of feelings of honest independence, and robbed the labourer of his hire.[89]

Villiers' annual motion for repeal brought no results, and his opponents complained that his speech introducing it was much too long.   The most significant speech in the debates that followed was that of Lord John Russell who claimed that the Tory government was no wiser than the Whig government which it had supplanted, but had merely enjoyed better crops.   He also prophesied quite accurately that the present Corn Law would not survive two successive bad harvests.[90]

The session of 1844 was notable not only for the feeble offensive of the free traders, but because the League members as representatives of the millowners were forced on the defensive by the agitation for new factory laws.   It gave the country gentlemen great satisfaction to speak of the horrible state of the factories, and to square accounts with the Leaguers who constantly referred to the deplorable social conditions among the agricultural labourers.   This feeling seems to have been so strong that Cobden, in the speech which he made on his motion to inquire into the effects of protection on farmers and agricultural labourers, felt obliged to point out that he was actuated by no invidious feeling toward the agriculturists, since he had served on deputations to the House of Commons to testify on the wretched state of the manufacturing operatives.

Conditions were even less favourable for the free traders when the session of 1845 opened.   Another year of prosperity had further diminished the urgency of repeal.   In spite of the discouraging outlook, representatives of the League brought up the question more frequently than in the last session.   Cobden, on March 13th, moved for the appointment of a select committee.   Like the one of the previous March it was to inquire into the effects of protection upon the interests of tenants and farm labourers, but in addition, into the the effects upon landowners, and into the causes and extent of agricultural distress.   The speech he made upon the proposal of this motion is generally considered to have been his greatest on the subject of free trade.

In discussing the case of the farmers, Cobden showed clearly that he was speaking to a gathering of landlords rather than to a meeting of tenants.   The first great evil that farmers laboured under was want of capital.   He did not mean to speak disparagingly of them, because they were like the rest of Englishmen, and would be just as successful as traders and manufacturers if placed in the same situation. Clearly the country was not lacking in capital as the money invested in France, Pennsylvania and Mexico showed.   The reason capital was not available for the land was because of insecurity of tenure, which was bound up with the protective system.   " Suppose," Cobden suggested, " it could be shown that they are in a vicious circle ; that they have made politics of Corn Laws ; that they wanted votes, to retain Corn Laws ; that they think the Corn Laws a great mine of wealth, and therefore will have dependent tenants, that they may have votes at elections, and so retain those laws. . . . Then their policy reacts upon them ; if they have not men of skill and capital, they cannot have protection and employment for the labourer; and then comes round the vicious termination—pauperism, poor rates, county rates, and all the evils from which they are asking the Prime Minister to relieve them."[91]   Cobden then concluded the section of his speech dealing with tenants by citing case after case to prove that, although the farmers might profit by the enhanced price which they drew from the protection on one or more commodities, they lost even more by the increased cost of the articles which they were obliged to purchase.

Even more impressive than his arguments on the bad effects of protection upon each class in the community were those in which he showed that the benefits of free trade to one group was not secured at the expense of another.   Free trade would help every interest by enlarging the markets both at home and abroad.   The manufacturers would be able to sell more goods abroad ; and hence pay higher wages to the operatives whose improved standard of living would enable them to buy more food, and in turn would raise the price of grain and increase the prosperity of all classes in agriculture—greater profits for the tenants, higher wages for the labourers and increased rents for the landlords.   All classes would have a greater surplus to spend on manufactured goods ; and unemployment and dangers from increasing population would be met by the increase in the demand for labour instead of by poor rates and emigration.   Certainly he placed free trade on a higher level than many members of the League whose object in securing repeal was merely to help business in the manufacturing districts.

But all things considered, the most striking part of Cobden's speech is his closing appeal to the gentry : " You gentlemen of England, the high aristocracy of England, your forefathers led my forefathers ; you may lead us again if you choose ; but though—longer than any other aristocracy—you have kept your power, while the battle-field and the hunting-field were the tests of manly vigour, you have not done as the noblesse of France or the hidalgos of Madrid have done ; you have been Englishmen, not wanting in courage on any call. But this is a new age ; the age of social advancement, not of feudal sports ; you belong to a mercantile age ; you cannot have the advantage of commercial rents and retain your feudal privileges, too. If you identify yourselves with the spirit of the age, you may yet do well ; for I tell you that the people of this country look to their aristocracy with a deep-rooted prejudice—an hereditary prejudice, I may call it—in their favour ; but your power was never got, and you will not keep it by obstructing the spirit of the age in which you live. If you are found obstructing that progressive spirit which is calculated to knit nations more closely together by commercial intercourse ; if you give nothing but opposition to schemes which almost give life and breath to inanimate nature, and which it has been decreed shall go on, then you are not longer a national body."[92]

Peel, who had been very much impressed by the speech of March 12th, 1844, was even more influenced by this one. In the midst of the speech he crumpled up his notes and said to Mr. Sidney Herbert, who was sitting by him, " You must answer this, for I cannot." It was Cobden's arguments, along with Peel's own investigations and a rainy harvest season in Great Britain and Ireland, which were to convert the Prime Minister to repeal before the year was over.

Thus the year 1845 which had opened so brightly for Peel was to end in gloom. After three unusually good wheat crops, the one of this year was deficient in bulk, yield and quality owing to rains in May, July and August. Only the importation of 2,732,000 quarters of foreign and colonial wheat and flour between August 5th, 1845, and August 5th, 1846, kept down the price as low as 54s. 8d. But even more disastrous than the deficiency in wheat was the failure of the potato crop of the United Kingdom, which was due to the first appearance on a large scale of that extraordinary disease or rot.[93] Peel now realized that some drastic action must be taken. By the end of October, reports on the corn and potato crops were so black that Peel decided that the only effective remedy would be the removal of impediments to the importation of grain. At this point the real work of the League was over, because from October 31st, 1845, when Peel consulted his cabinet on this subject, down to June 25th, 1846, when the Lords passed the third reading of the bill to repeal the Corn Laws, he is the centre of the struggle. The League had done its work in converting public opinion to the desirability of repeal, and through its greatest representative, Cobden, had accomplished something fully as significant as far as *immediate* repeal was concerned, in helping to bring about the conversion of Peel.

Since the real work of the League was finished when Peel decided that the impediments to importation must be removed, what verdicts should be passed upon the aims and achievements of the organization ? It is undeniable that the League was an association financed largely by manufacturers from the north of England whose chief aim was to secure the repeal of the Corn Laws because its members believed that protection to agriculture was harmful to their business. Cobden frankly admits that this was the object of the organization when he stated in Manchester on October 18th, 1843, " I am afraid, if we must confess the truth, that most of us entered upon this struggle with the belief that we had some distinct class interest in the question, and that we should carry it by a manifestation of our will in this district against the will and consent of other portions of the community. I believe that was our impression. If there is one thing which more than another has elevated and dignified and ennobled this agitation, it is that, in the progress of the last five years, we have found, gradually but steadily, that every interest and every object which every part of the community can justly seek, harmonizes perfectly with the views of the Anti-Corn Law League."[94] Morley, in referring approvingly to this passage, says, " It was not of himself assuredly that Cobden was speaking." Further, Morley justifies this original attitude by declaring that, " The important fact was that the class interest of the manufacturers and merchants happened to fall in with the good of the rest of the community ; while the class interest against which they were going to do battle was an uncompensated burden on the whole commonwealth."[95]

A careful examination of the evidence seems to indicate that the change in the attitude of the League, which Cobden refers to, was a change in *his* point of view rather than in other members of the organization. Cobden and other manufacturers saw the critical condition of industry in the years following 1839, and realized that, with a population increasing at the rate of a thousand a day, it was necessary to find additional markets in order to employ this growing supply of labour. Manufacturers wanted free importation of corn because they believed that it would stimulate the exportation of British-manufactured goods, and, despite all denials, would offset the advantages of cheap food which rival manufacturing countries enjoyed over Great Britain. As Cobden proved, and Peel worked out for himself, wages do not follow accurately the rise and fall of food prices. Nevertheless, the price of food plays an important part in determining wages, and manufacturers felt that their rivals in other countries should not have too great an advantage in cheap labour based on cheap food. From the middle of the eighteenth century, spokesmen for the commercial and industrial interests had insisted that cheap labour, and hence cheap food, was necessary to compete with foreigners ; but when this was thrown in the teeth of the free traders by both the Chartists and the protectionists a shift in the argument became necessary. What the manufacturers really wanted was not cheap food in Great Britain, but approximately the same priced food as in rival countries. Thus if an international wheat market could be brought into existence by allowing free importation into Great Britain at all times, the price would tend to become the same at home and abroad. In this way the object of the manufacturers would be attained, since it was the relative rather than the actual price of food and labour which caused their concern. Taken from this angle, Cobden was quite truthful in saying that he was not an advocate of the cheap food argument.

In all probability, most members of the League never altered the attitude described by Cobden in the sentence, " I am afraid, if we must confess the truth, that most of us entered upon this struggle with the belief that we had some distinct class interest in it." Cobden himself, however, went far beyond this. He confidently expected free trade to be followed by other nations and early in 1846 made his celebrated but erroneous prophecy : " I believe that if you abolish the Corn Law honestly, and adopt Free Trade in its simplicity, there will not be a tariff in Europe that will not be changed in less than five years to follow your example."[96] Furthermore, he counted on free trade to cure the ills of the world. It was not for him a mere device to help business, but was a complete philosophy which should dictate the policy of all nations. Therefore he treated it with almost religious fervour and felt confident that, if it were only given a fair trial, local differences would be broken down, parts of the world would become inter-dependent economically, and everlasting peace would ensue. Cobden was at his best when he painted the moral results which he felt would follow the spread of free trade throughout the world. " Free Trade ! What is it ? Why, breaking down the barriers that separate nations ; those barriers, behind which nestle the feelings of pride, revenge, hatred and jealousy, which every now and then burst their bounds and deluge whole countries with blood ; those feelings which nourish the poison of war and conquest, which assert that without conquest we can have no trade, which foster that lust for conquest and dominion which sends forth your warrior chiefs to scatter devastation through other lands, and then calls them back that they may be enthroned securely in your passions, but only to harass and oppress you at home. It is because I think I have a full apprehension of the moral bearing of this question, that I take pride and gratification in forming one in the present agitation."[97] This hope, that other countries would follow Great Britain in free trade and break down the dangerous barriers of nationalism, thus far has proved a great disappointment and the tendency of the world to-day is away from rather than toward it. Thus the aim of the manufacturers, which was to improve business, has been more than realized, as the next chapter will prove, but the truly magnificent ideal of Cobden has failed.

The fact that the manufacturers counted upon the repeal of the Corn Laws to help business does not mean that they foresaw the flood of cheap wheat and meat which was to pour into Great Britain after 1875. None of the free traders, including Cobden, expected that a very large part of the population would be dependent upon foreign wheat or meat. Villiers in his speech of February 16th, 1842, declared that even the most sanguine repealer expected scarcely more than four million quarters of wheat to be imported annually under a system of free trade. Porter, in the *Progress of the Nation*, insisted that, " To supply the United Kingdom with the single article of wheat would call for the employment of more than twice the amount of shipping which now annually enters our ports, if, indeed, it would be possible to procure the grain from other countries in sufficient quantity ; and to bring to our shores every article of agricultural produce in the abundance we now enjoy, would probably give constant occupation to the mercantile navy of the whole world." Cobden expected an increase in the amount of grain imported ; but not at a reduced price, since he held that the cost of transportation served as a natural protection to the British corn grower.

The next point to determine is what the League actually achieved by the agitation from 1839 to 1845, which, as has already been shown, was carried on in two fields : among the middle class, operatives and tenant farmers throughout the country ; and in Parliament for the benefit of the members of the government rather than with the idea of converting a majority of representatives. The matchless organization of the League with its lecturers, its distribution of pamphlets, its *Circular*, and then its *League*, its policy of qualifying persons for the franchise in both boroughs and counties, its county meetings, and its monster gatherings in Free Trade Hall, Manchester, and Covent Garden, London, was unable to secure the repeal of the Corn Laws before the harvest of 1845. Several factors explain this apparent lack of success. The very restricted male suffrage—only about one in seven could vote—and the unequal electoral districts made the task of securing the majority of the votes in the House of Commons much more difficult than it would be to-day. The only really effective test of the success of the League in this direction would have been a general election in the first part of 1845. Free traders may argue that the results of the elections of 1847 and 1852 give an approximate idea of the state of public opinion early in 1845. Against this position several objections can be raised. In the spring of 1845 trade and industry were in a prosperous state, whereas from the latter part of the year through 1847 economic conditions were more critical. By 1852 free trade had had a trial and was working satisfactorily. The explanation has sometimes been offered that the agitation outside Parliament had been so successful that Peel dared not risk running counter to it when a deficient crop came. Peel's career down to 1845, and his conduct the next year to an even greater extent, proved that he was not susceptible to pressure of this sort, although he was very apt to be influenced by individuals and by his own investigations.

Apparently the greatest contribution of the League to the repeal *in* 1846 was the part played by Cobden in converting Peel. The agitation outside Parliament may have done more to make free trade inevitable in the long run ; but the influence of Cobden on Peel, along with his own investigations and the poor wheat and potato crops of 1845, was much more significant in bringing about *immediate* repeal. Actually, as Holland has pointed out, Peel stood in the same relation to the Corn Laws as Newman to the Oxford Movement. Cobden had stirred up doubts in the mind of Peel as Cardinal Wiseman had in that of Newman. " Newman and Peel, almost simultaneously crossed the stream upon the shore of which each had stood for the last five years hesitating. Peel could no longer find an honest answer to Richard Cobden, or Newman to Cardinal Wiseman."[98]

But regardless of what opinion is held on the importance of the work of the League and of the influence of Cobden on Peel, it is clear that the repeal of the Corn Laws, without the active support of Peel, was impossible *at this time*.

CHAPTER XI

NOTES

[1] Notably Morley, *Life of Richard Cobden;* Prentice, *History of the League;* and Holland, *The Fall of Protection.*

[2] Prentice, *History of the Anti-Corn Law League*, 1853, voi. I, p. 50.

[3] *Ibid.*, p. 71.

[4] *Ibid.*, p. 72.   The italics are mine.

[5] *Ibid.*, p. 104.   [6] *Ibid.*   [7] *Ibid.*, pp. 108–9.

[8] With the exception of Cobden and Bright, no name is more closely associated with the repeal of the Corn Laws than that of Villiers.   Session after session he moved the repeal and made himself very obnoxious to the country gentlemen, not only by the unpopularity of his motions but by the length of his speeches as well.

[9] Villiers, *Free Trade Speeches*, 1883, vol. I, pp. 80–1.

[10] *Hansard*, vol. 45, p. 695.   [11] *Ibid.*, vol. 46, p. 864.   [12] *Ibid.*, vol. 45, pp. 565–627.

[13] Prentice, *op. cit.*, p. 124.   [14] *Ibid.*, p. 128.

[15] Morley, *Life of Richard Cobden*, 1903, p. 154.

[16] Prentice, *op. cit.*, p. 153.

[17] Tooke, *History of Prices*, vol. 3, pp. 14–18 and vol. 4, pp. 3–10.

[18] Prentice, *op. cit.*, p. 153.   [19] *Ibid.*, pp. 154–5.   [20] *Ibid.*, p. 155.   [21] *Ibid.*, p. 156.

[22] Villiers, *op. cit.*, p. 144.   [23] *Hansard*, vol. 53, pp. 432–78.

[24] Morley, *op. cit.*, p. 169.

[25] Holland, *The Fall of Protection*, 1913, p. 97.

[26] Prentice, *op. cit.*, p. 263.

[27] Hovell, *The Chartist Movement*, 1918, pp. 216–17.

[28] Campbell, *An Examination of the Corn and Provision Laws*, n.d., pp. 70–1.

[29] Hovell, *op. cit.*, p. 218.

[30] Prentice, *op. cit.*, p. 117.   [31] *Ibid.*, p. 215.

[32] Hovell, *op. cit.*, pp. 218–19.

[33] Beer, *A History of British Socialism*, 1921, vol. 2, p. 61.   [34] *Ibid.*, p. 150.

[35] West, *A History of the Chartist Movement*, 1920, p. 176.

[36] Morley, *op. cit.*, p. 249.   [37] Holland, *op. cit.*, p. 101.

[38] *Ibid.*, p. 102.   It is interesting to note the changes Peel made in sugar and lumber, since these interests, along with corn, had been so vitally concerned in the overthrow of the Whig government.   The duty on sugar was not reduced, on the ground that such a reduction would permit competition between the product of the free labour of the British West Indies with that produced by slaves.   On the other hand, the duty on lumber was reduced from 55s. to 25s., whereas the Whigs had proposed to reduce it to 50s.

[39] *Ibid.*, p. 105.

[40] *Hansard*, vol. 60, p. 231.   [41] *Ibid.*, p. 232.   [42] *Ibid.*, p. 620.   [43] *Ibid.*, p. 1082.   [44] *Ibid.*, p. 710.   [45] *Ibid.*, vol. 62, p. 75.   [46] *Ibid.*, p. 995.

[47] *Ibid.*, pp. 995–6.

Following protest *versus* third reading entered on Journals :

" . . . . dissentient—because the new Corn bill, although it was allowed by the Minister who proposed it to cause a very considerable decrease of the protection which the present duties afford to the home grower, is not accompanied, as in justice it ought to have been, by the following measures, namely :—

" 1.   The repeal of all taxes which fall directly upon land—the land tax, the malt tax, and the hop duty.

" 2.   The equalization of all the rates of which the occupiers of land bear at present undue and unfair proportion, poor rates, highway rates and County rates.

" 3. The repeal of the Tithe Commutation Act, which can no longer be just or applicable.

" 4. A legislative enactment, authorizing all persons who hold leases to surrender them on giving six months' notice before Lady-day or Michaelmas.

" 5. A legislative enactment, directing the payment made under every written contract to be reduced according to the proportion which the average prices of wheat, under the new Corn bill, may at the time of making such payments bear to its average price at the time that such contract was formed, so that such payment may be of the same value as was originally intended and agreed to by the parties." " Stanhope."

48 5th and 6th Victoria, c. 14. 49 6th and 7th Victoria, c. 29.

50 Morley, op. cit., pp. 239–40.

51 Bright and Rogers, Speeches of Richard Cobden, 1870, vol. 1, p. 41.

52 Morley, op. cit., p. 243. 53 Hansard, vol. 64, p. 1333.

54 Prentice, op. cit., p. 362.

55 Tooke, History of Price, vol. 3, pp. 10–12.

56 Morley, op. cit., p. 251. 57 Ibid., p. 271. 58 Ibid., pp. 271–280.

59 Ibid., p. 275.

60 Speech of Mr. George Game Day at Huntingdon, June 17th, 1843, p. 9.

61 Ibid., p. 11. 62 Ibid., pp. 17–18. 63 Ibid., p. 24. 64 Ibid., pp. iii, and iv.

65 Mr. George Game Day's Letter to Richard Cobden, Esq., 1844, p. 2.

66 A full list of these pamphlets is given in the bibliography at the end of the volume. The titles in most instances will distinguish the protectionist from the free-trade pamphlets.

67 Almack, The Character, Motives and Proceedings of the Anti-Corn Law League, 1843, pp. 3–4.

68 Ibid., p. 4. 69 Ibid., p. 34. 70 Ibid., pp. 94–5.

71 Cayley, Reasons for the Formation of the Agricultural Protection Society, Addressed to the Industrious Classes of the United Kingdom, 1844, p. 3.

72 Tooke, op. cit., vol. 4, pp. 14–18. 73 Prentice, op. cit., vol. 2, p. 117.

74 Ibid., p. 120.

75 Bright and Rogers, Speeches by Richard Cobden, 1870, vol. 1, pp. 236–40.

76 Ibid., pp. 235–6.

77 Morley, op. cit., p. 313. 78 Ibid., p. 256.

79 Prentice, op. cit., vol. 2, p. 41. 80 Morley, op. cit., pp. 263–4.

81 Hansard, vol. 67, p. 864. 82 Ibid., p. 963. 83 Ibid., vol. 69, p. 407.

84 Ibid., p. 1519.

85 Bright and Rogers, op. cit., pp. 45–63. 86 Morley, op. cit., p. 292.

87 The Annual Register, 1844, p. 134. 88 Bright and Rogers, op. cit., p. 149.

89 Ibid., p. 171. 90 Hansard, vol. 75, pp. 1424–30.

91 Bright and Rogers, op. cit., pp. 263–4. 92 Ibid., pp. 282–3.

93 Tooke, History of Prices, vol. 4, pp. 18–21.

94 Bright and Rogers, op. cit., pp. 97–8. 95 Morley, op. cit., p. 141.

96 Bright and Rogers, op. cit., p. 360. 97 Ibid., p. 79.

98 Holland, op. cit., p. 243.

CHAPTER XII

THE last chapter considered the point of view of the League rather than that of the government or the protectionists, and this chapter will be treated from the standpoint of Sir Robert Peel. At the end of Chapter XI it was pointed out that the deficient wheat crop in England and "rotten potatoes," as Wellington termed them, in Ireland, caused Peel to announce that, in his opinion, the Corn Laws must be altered. But it was recognized, even at the time, that these crop failures merely furnished him with an opportunity of announcing his conversion to the policy of free trade and a repeal of the Corn Laws. Since his fiscal reforms of 1842, friends and foes had watched his slow but certain movement in this direction. His budget of 1845, which followed along the lines laid down by the one of 1842, aroused suspicions on his own side without winning great commendation from the free traders. In 1842 Western had, as we have seen, expressed the opinion that Peel would in time repeal the Corn Laws. In both 1844 and 1845 Peel had announced for the benefit of the sullen protectionists that no change would be made in the existing system of agricultural protection. Yet, in each successive session he relied less upon the main arguments of national welfare and safety, and more upon the minor ones.[1] In 1845 Disraeli delighted the extreme Tories by declaring that, "For my part if we are to have free trade, I, who honour genius, prefer that such measures should be proposed by the honourable member for Stockport, than by one, who through skilful Parliamentary manœuvres has tampered with the generous confidence of a great people and a great party. For myself, I care not what may be the result. Dissolve, if you please, the Parliament you have betrayed, and appeal to the people, who, I believe, mistrust you. For me there remains this at least—the opportunity of expressing my belief that a Conservative government is organized hypocrisy."[2] The impatience and exasperation with which Cobden and other members of the League watched this slow change toward free trade was dealt with in the last chapter.

If then the crop failures merely offered Peel an opportunity of putting into practice a policy to which he had been previously converted, what were the fundamental reasons for his change ? Morley inclines to the view that it was the unanswerable logic of Cobden. Disraeli in his famous description of Peel ascribes it to a " dangerous sympathy with the creations of others," and states that, " There was always some person representing some theory or system exercising an influence over his mind. In his ' sallet-days ' it was Mr. Horner or Sir Samuel Romilly ; in later and more important periods, it was the Duke of Wellington, the King of the French, Mr. Jones Loyd, some others, and finally Mr. Cobden."[3] Lord Dalling and Bulwer explain the gradual conversion and sudden announcement to the peculiar working of Peel's mind. " He had not that order of mind which creates and forces its creations on the minds of others. His mind was, on the contrary, a recipient which opened gradually to growing opinions, and became another mind as these opinions got by degrees possession of it. His changes were thus more sudden in appearance than in reality, because they always went on for a certain time, silently, and to a certain degree unconsciously to himself as well as the world before they were fully felt ; nor were they ever publicly announced till, having passed through a stage of doubt, they arrived at the stage of conviction."[4]

But unquestionably the most important reasons for the conversion of Peel to repeal are those which he himself offers in his *Memoirs*. He states, " I had adopted at an early period of my public life, without, I fear, much serious reflection, the opinions generally prevalent at the time among men of all parties, of the justice and necessity of protection to domestic agriculture. They were the opinions of Sir Henry Parnell and Mr. Ricardo, of Lord John Russell and Lord Melbourne, as well as of the Duke of Wellington, Mr. Canning and Mr. Huskisson."[5] The reasons for changing these objections are given in a clear-cut fashion in a letter to the electors of Tamworth in July of 1847 : " My confidence in the validity of the reasons on which I had myself heretofore relied for the maintenance of restrictions on the import of corn had been materially weakened. It had been weakened by the conflict of arguments on the principle of a restrictive policy ; by many concurring proofs that the wages of labour do not vary with the price of corn ; by the contrast presented in two successive periods of dearth and abundance, in the health, morals and tranquillity and general prosperity of the whole community ; by serious doubts whether, in the present condition of this country, cheapness and plenty are not ensured for the future in a higher degree by the free intercourse in corn, than by restrictions on its importation for the purpose of giving protection to domestic agriculture."[6] After considering several additional points, which, as he says, " were in a great degree new elements in forming a judgment on this vital matter," he concludes : " It was from the combined influence of these various considerations—from diminished confidence in the necessity or advantage of protection—from the increasing difficulty of resisting the application to articles of food of those principles which had been gradually applied to so many other articles —from the result of the experiment made with regard to cattle and meat in 1842—from the evidences of rapidly increasing consumption

T

—from the aggravation of every other difficulty in the maintenance of the Corn Laws, by the fact of their suspension on the first real pressure—it was from the combined influence of such considerations that I came to the conclusion that the attempt to maintain those laws inviolate after their suspension would be impolitic, that the struggle for their maintenance would assume a new character, and that no advantage to be gained by success could counter-balance the consequences of failure, or even the evils attending protracted conflict."[7]

It was in this frame of mind that Peel called his cabinet to meet on October 31st and November 1st, 1845.   At these meetings he laid before the cabinet members the reports of deficiency of food which he had been receiving from Ireland.   On the second day he read a memorandum in which he advised the calling of Parliament before Christmas and declared that the cabinet must decide whether to maintain unaltered, to modify, or to suspend the operation of the Corn Law.[8]   In the conversation which followed the reading of the memorandum, the differences of opinion among the members over the necessity for adopting extraordinary measures, and over the nature of any measures which might be advisable, made a decision impossible at the time.[9]

On November 6th another cabinet meeting took place at which Peel proposed : first, to issue an order in council reducing the duty on grain in bond to one shilling ; second, to call a meeting of Parliament on November 27th, for the purpose of securing indemnity and sanction for the order ; and third, to declare an intention of submitting a modification of the existing Corn Law to Parliament after Christmas.   But the cabinet refused by a large majority to assent to these proposals—in fact only three members supported them.   Peel decided to retain office until an opportunity for reconsideration came up, but under no circumstances to recede from the position he had taken, and to resign ultimately if the cabinet could not be won over.[10]

Before the cabinet met again the situation was further complicated by the publication on November 22nd of Lord John Russell's famous Edinburgh Letter to the Electors of the City of London.   Lord John pointed out that the Queen's ministers had separated without taking any steps to relieve the existing distress.   Two evils, in his opinion, required consideration : one, the potato rot ; the other, the Corn Laws.   The government was not to blame for the rot, but was for the Corn Laws.   After reviewing the history of his own attitude toward protection to agriculture during the past twenty years, he concluded that the time for insisting upon a fixed duty, such as he had advocated since 1841, was now over.   The real Whig point of view and Lord John's reasons for no longer opposing free trade in grain came at the end of the letter : " But the imposition of any duty at present, without a provision for its extinction within a short period, would but prolong a contest already sufficiently fruitful of animosity and discontent.   The struggle to make bread scarce and dear, when it is clear that part at least of the additional price goes to increase rent, is a struggle deeply injurious to an aristocracy which (this quarrel once removed) is strong in property, strong in the construction of our legislature, strong in opinion, strong in ancient associations, and the memory of immortal services. Let us, then, unite to put an end to a system which has proved to be the blight of commerce, the bane of agriculture, the source of bitter divisions among classes, the cause of penury, fever, mortality, and crime among the people. But if this end is to be achieved, it must be gained by the unequivocal expression of the public voice. It is not to be denied that many elections for cities and towns in 1841, and some in 1845, appear to favour the assertion that free trade is not popular with the great mass of the community. The Government appear to be waiting for some excuse to give up the present Corn Law. Let the people by petition, by address, by remonstrance, afford them the excuse they seek."[11]

This letter was very adroit from the point of view of politics, and typical of the Whig attitude toward public questions. Just as a prominent Whig had justified the Reform Bill of 1832 on the ground that it was better to make some concession at the time lest it would be necessary to make greater ones later, so now when it became obvious that public sentiment against landowners and aristocracy was becoming more of a menace than the Corn Laws were a benefit, Russell prudently went over to free trade. The League received the news of the letter jubilantly. Bright declared that it made total and immediate repeal inevitable. Cobden's speech in London on December 17th, 1845, was one of blatant triumph, and his references to Peel somewhat lacking in good taste. One statement was considered somewhat extreme even by his friends : " I have no reason, and I think you will all admit it, to feel any great respect for Sir Robert Peel ; he is the only man in the House of Commons that I can never speak a word to in private without forfeiting my own self-respect, and the respect of all those who sit around me."[12]

The effect of Lord John's letter was a greater bombshell in the government than even he expected. The cabinet reassembled on November 25th and gave the question undivided attention during the next few days. Peel read memoranda to the members of the cabinet on November 26th, 29th and December 2nd. In the third meeting he emphasized the difficulty of replacing duties after a temporary suspension, and reiterated that he could not guarantee permanently any protection offered in a new law. The alternative policy would be to extend the system of inter-imperial preference and admit British colonial grain at a nominal duty ; but he rejected this possibility on the ground that it would be even more unfavourable to foreign countries than the existing law. " Prussia, the United States and other countries, would complain of this," he pointed out, " and with justice : it would be a retrograde policy as to them."[13] Peel still retained his objections to a fixed duty and his faith in the sliding scale as shown by the conclusion of his memorandum of December 2nd : " I should propose that, either by this progressive diminution of duty to be annually continued or at a certain time to be named in the law, all duties on the import of grain, meal and flour should be abolished."[14] By December 5th all members of the cabinet except

Lord Stanley and the Duke of Buccleuch had agreed to support the proposed measure ; but Peel felt that the loss of these two combined with the fact that the assent of many of the others was so reluctant, made it doubtful whether he would be able to carry the measure through Parliament.   As a result of this uncertainty, Peel resigned on December 5th.

Probably even Lord John Russell was astonished when he was asked by the Queen to form a ministry. He really faced a momentous task, since his party had no majority in the Commons ; and he attempted to offset this disadvantage by asking Peel to give assurances which would "amount substantially to a pledge," that he would support the immediate and total repeal of the Corn Laws.   But Peel, as we have seen, believed in immediate temporary suspension and a new permanent law based on a diminishing sliding scale, and hence declined to pledge his support to Lord John.   The latter found an excuse for his failure to form a ministry when Earl Grey (Howick) refused to serve in a cabinet with Palmerston, and, as Disraeli has said, " Availing himself with happy readiness of the distressing incident, he endured the mortification of confessing to his sovereign his inability to serve her, and handed back with courtesy the poisoned chalice to Sir Robert."[15]

During the course of these negotiations Lord John and Lord Lansdowne inquired of the Queen whether the members of Peel's government who disagreed with him on the question of maintaining the Corn Laws were either able or willing to form a new administration, " observing that they might else say at a later period that they were prepared, but they had never been asked."[16]   Peel, after interviewing both Lord Stanley and the Duke of Buccleuch, wrote to the Queen stating that he " feels himself to be fully justified in informing your Majesty that no one of his colleagues who differed from Sir Robert Peel on the subjects which have been under the recent consideration of the Cabinet, is prepared to undertake the formation of a Government, or thinks that it would be for the public advantage that such an attempt should be made by other parties."[17]

Thus when Peel resumed office on December 20th he was in a strong position.   Both Tory protectionists and Whigs had been forced to confess their inability to carry on a government.   The Duke of Buccleuch consented to rejoin the cabinet, but Lord Stanley declined to do so and his place at the Colonial Office was taken by Mr. Gladstone.

On January 27th, Peel presented his proposals to the Commons. The duties on manufactured articles and foreign timber were reduced ; those on foreign meats and vegetables were abolished ; and the preference given to colonial and Indian sugar over foreign sugar was lowered.   In this manner he attempted to make the change in the Corn Laws merely a phase of the wholesale reductions in the duties on all imports.   All existing duties on corn were to terminate February 1st, 1849, and thereafter wheat, oats and barley were to be subject to a nominal duty of 1s. a quarter.   Until this date all grain from British colonies was to be admitted upon the payment of a nominal duty, and foreign wheat was to pay a duty beginning at 10s.

when the price was under 48s. and decreasing with the rise of price until it was fixed at 4s. when 53s. was reached. Peel stated that he could promise no reciprocal treatment by other nations, and even pointed out that other countries had, in some instances, increased duties since the British reductions of 1842 ; but he felt confident that ultimately other nations would follow England's example.

For a time it was questionable whether any organized opposition would be made to Peel's proposals by the protectionists in the Tory Party. The group was lacking at the start in leaders and many of its members recalled the unfortunate consequences which followed the attempt to take revenge on Wellington and Peel after Catholic Emancipation. But in the period from January 27th to February 9th a campaign of definite opposition was formulated. Foremost among the leaders of this protectionist group was Lord George Bentinck, who, though inexperienced in Parliamentary speaking, had as assets the invaluable advice of the astute Disraeli and his own tremendous rancour against the " traitor " who had " sold " the landed interest.

The struggle was waged fiercely in the Commons from January 22nd, when Peel explained why he resumed office, until the third reading of the bill on May 15th. Personal abuse, arguments for protection and colonial preference, and reviews of the inconsistencies in Peel's career were all intermingled during these four months. The free traders for once were able to look on and enjoy the spectacle of their former opponent, Peel, using their arguments against his erstwhile followers. The arguments used on both sides were the time-honoured ones. The protectionists particularly emphasized that the new policy would ruin agriculture ; throw away the advantages of reciprocal bargaining ; wreck the commercial foundations of the Empire; and destroy the territorial constitution of the country. Peel, in addition to the conventional free trade arguments, drew heavily on the results of his experiments since 1842 in lower duties. The protectionists knew that they had no real chance to defeat the corn bill ; but they fought to make as good a showing as possible on all three divisions, and took advantage of the opportunity to express their outraged feelings.

Unquestionably Peel's actions in Catholic Emancipation and in the repeal of the Corn Laws offered an excellent target for hostile darts, and one member of the protectionists made a great Parliamentary reputation by his deadly accuracy at this time. Disraeli, who had been disappointed because Peel had failed to recognize his remarkable talents even after his staunch defence of the latter's budget of 1842, had started his attacks on the Prime Minister in 1845. But in this session of 1846 he threw off whatever restraint he had felt during the previous year, and made full use of his unequalled powers of ridicule, irony and sarcasm. Some of his figures of speech and descriptions are very brilliant, but others " smell of the lamp." Two of his best known attacks on Peel will illustrate his technique. On January 22nd Disraeli compared Peel to the Turkish admiral who, a few years earlier, had been sent from Constantinople with a large fleet to attack Mahemet Ali in Egypt.

" The sultan personally witnessed the departure of the fleet ; all the muftis prayed for the success of the expedition, as the muftis prayed for the success of the last general election. Away went the fleet ; but what was the Sultan's consternation, when the lord high admiral steered at once into the enemy's port ! Now, Sir, the lord high admiral on that occasion was very much misrepresented. He, too, was called a traitor, and he, too, vindicated himself. ' True it is,' he said, ' I did place myself at the head of this valiant armada—true it is that my sovereign embraced me—true it is that all the muftis in the empire offered up prayers for my success ; but I have an objection to war. I see no use in prolonging the struggle, and the only reason I had for accepting the command, was that I might terminate the contest by betraying my master ! ' "[18] On the day of the third reading of the Corn Bill, Disraeli declared, " I find that for between thirty and forty years, from the days of Mr. Horner to the days of the honourable Member for Stockport, that right honourable Gentleman has traded on the ideas and intelligence of others. His life has been one grand appropriation clause. He is burglar of other's intellect."[19] Peel writhed under this attack, but stuck grimly to his task of pushing the bill through the Commons.

After twelve days' debate, Peel's resolutions of January 27th were carried on February 27th by 337 to 240 ; the second reading of the bill, based on these resolutions, was passed on March 23rd by a majority of 88 ; and the third reading, on May 15th, by a vote of 327 to 229.[20] It encountered less opposition in the Lords than had been anticipated owing chiefly to the resolute attitude of the Duke of Wellington. He did not believe in repeal, but he did insist that the Queen's government must be carried on. The bill was read for the third time on June 25th and passed.[21]

On the same evening in the Commons, Peel's Irish " protection of life " bill was beaten by 292 to 219. A combination of Whigs, Radicals, Irish, and Tory protectionists was responsible for the defeat. It was a good example of the effects of blind party rage. The protectionists who, in most instances, believed in the bill, were frankly inspired by motives of revenge. The Whigs, as in 1830, after Catholic Emancipation, were the ones who profited by the revengeful spirit of the country gentlemen ; for, when Peel resigned on June 29th, Lord John Russell became Prime Minister, with a promise of the support of Peel until after the next general election.

The speech in which Peel announced his resignation is characterized by Morley as " remarkable " and by Disraeli as " one of glorification and pique." He paid a generous tribute to Cobden, with whom he was now on good terms,[22] for the part he had taken in the repeal of the Corn Laws. Although admitting that combination of parties had made possible the actual repeal, he insisted that a name would be associated with its success which was neither Lord John's nor his own. "Sir," he said, "the name which ought to be, and which will be associated with the success of these measures is the name of a man who, acting, I believe, from pure and disinterested motives, has advocated their cause with untiring energy, and by appeals to reason, expressed by an eloquence, the more to be admired because it was unaffected and unadorned—the name which ought to be and will be associated with the success of these measures is the name of Richard Cobden. Without scruple, Sir, I attribute the success of these measures to him."[23]

This eulogy gave offence to some of Peel's friends. Gladstone, in particular, objected to it on the grounds that it was too one-sided. " For," he declared, " if his power of discussion has been great and his end good, his tone has been most harsh and his imputations of bad and vile motives to honourable men incessant. I do not think the thing was done in a manner altogether worthy of Peel's mind."[24] Again, in talking with Lord Stanley, Gladstone said : " All that he said was true, but he did not say the whole truth ; and the effect of the whole, as a whole, was therefore untrue. Mr. Cobden had throughout argued the corn question on the principle of holding up the landlords of England to the people, as plunderers and as knaves for maintaining the corn law to save their rents, and as fools because it was not necessary for that purpose. This was passed by, while he was praised for sincerity, eloquence and indefatigable zeal."[25] On the whole this seems a much fairer summary of Cobden's activities than the one given by Peel.

Peel has often been blamed for three things : first, that he repealed the system which he had been chosen to maintain ; second, the mode of proceeding with the repeal of the Corn Laws ; and third, that he did not dissolve Parliament and appeal to the country. However, according to his own testimony he gave all three points mature consideration before acting, and afterwards never felt that he had erred in tactics. When, in his judgment, the time came to abandon protection to agriculture he informed his cabinet of the fact and, upon failing to convince them, resigned. Lord John Russell and Lord Stanley both had chances to form governments and to carry out their respective policies. Peel felt that conditions demanded repeal and he was a big enough man to act even at the risk of wrecking his political career. Peel's reply to the second point can be found in a letter written to Lord Aberdeen, on August 19th, 1847, in answer to the criticism of a certain lord who held that repeal could have been obtained without offending the Conservative Party, if confidential communications to certain peers and party leaders had been made. In this letter he stated : " I am perfectly satisfied that if at any time between the 1st of November and the day on which . . . I announced in the House of Commons the intended repeal of the Corn Laws, I had tried to gain acquiescence, either by belabouring individuals separately, or by summoning the party generally, I should have received scarcely one promise of support. I should have had on the part of the most moderate a formal protest against the course I intended to pursue ; to the most violent I should have given facilities for organized opposition ; I should have appeared to be flying in the face of a whole party, and contumaciously disregarding their opinion and advice after I had professed to consult them ; but (what is of infinitely more importance) *I should have failed in carrying the repeal of the Corn Laws.*"[26] His stand on the third point, refusal to dissolve Parliament and appeal to the country, was based upon the firm belief that the existing Parliament was as competent to act on this question as on any other of public importance.   Still a general election would have delayed repeal only a few weeks, since there is little doubt that the sentiment of the country was strongly free trade in 1846 ; and it would have saved Peel from the somewhat awkward position of passing the repeal with a Parliament elected to maintain protection.

When the conduct of Peel in 1845 and 1846 is compared with that of Bentinck, Disraeli, Russell and Cobden, it will be seen how much he towered above them.   Bentinck was actuated by pique at what he considered to be a class and personal grievance, and even Disraeli's brilliant biography has failed to rescue him from the oblivion that followed his brief career in the limelight.   Disraeli's own conduct has been justified on the grounds of successful opportunism.   He was probably at heart a free trader and merely took advantage of the opportunity to win a place for himself as one of the outstanding Parliamentary speakers and a foremost position in the almost leaderless Conservative Party.   In addition, there was a certain justification for his conduct in attacking Peel, because the latter had consistently failed to make use of his unquestioned talents.   But a clever opportunist, even though he delighted his listeners at the time and countless readers since with his sparkling wit during the debates, cannot be ranked with Peel either in character or achievement.   As far as I know, no one has ever seriously questioned Disraeli's judgment in hounding Peel out of the Party in 1846 ; but it seems that a good case could be made for the harm he did his party and his own career during the next generation.   Protection was soon buried as an issue and there was really no reason why the Peelites, who included most of the able Conservative leaders, should have permanently remained out of the Party.   Yet they refused several offers to return after Peel's death, and the principal reason seems to have been the fact that the leaders never forgave Disraeli's conduct in 1846.   Thus the Conservatives might have been spared some of their twenty-eight years in the wilderness as a minority party and some of their " leaderless " experiences during the same period, if Disraeli had been less brilliant in 1846.

It is strange that the part played by Lord John Russell in 1845 and 1846 has received such slight consideration.   His conduct as a " traitor " resembled that of Peel very closely.   He was *pledged* to the fixed duty from 1841, and Peel, although supported by interests which were alarmed by the Whig reductions of 1841, had *not pledged* himself to adhere to the sliding scale of duties in corn.   Russell declared for repeal in his Edinburgh Letter soon after Peel made his proposals for abrogating the Corn Laws to his cabinet, and yet he was not accused of selling his party.   Further, Russell showed himself to be a trimming politician when he took advantage of the objection of Grey to Palmerston to decline the responsibility of repealing the Corn Laws, and of the " blackguard " combination with Bentinck's " Die-Hards " to oust Peel.   Russell and the Whigs, with the support of Peel and his followers, returned to the status of 1835–41 when they were " in office but not in power."

Cobden's conduct down to his reconciliation with Peel has already been discussed, but the letters which the two exchanged on June 23rd and 24th, 1846, throws additional light on the essential difference between them—the difference between an agitator with high ideals and a statesman. Cobden proposed that Peel dissolve Parliament, place himself at the head of a new middle-class free trade party, and insure his continuance as Prime Minister. Peel answered that he would consider dissolving only if it were necessary to repeal the Corn Laws. Further, if he had merely wished to remain in office, he remarked, " I could perhaps have parried *even your power and carried on the government* in one sense for three or four years longer . . . ''[27] In addition to his desire to retire, he doubtless felt, as Morley noted, that the accepted decencies of party would be outraged if he should lead the Tory country gentlemen in one Parliament and the Manchester manufacturers in the next.

Finally, what results did Peel expect from a repeal of the Corn Laws ? Until 1845 he was not convinced that virtual self-sufficiency was impossible, since the country practically attained this state in the years from 1832 to 1835 and again from 1843 to 1845. But when he took into consideration the enormous growth of industry in Great Britain from 1815 to 1845,[28] he realized both that this development would inevitably continue and that it was impossible for British agriculture to keep pace with the increasing population for any great length of time. In the first years of his ministry Peel favoured reciprocal treaties with other nations, but when these failed to materialize he accepted the point of view of the out and out free traders. By 1845 he had come to the conclusion that Great Britain needed no protection in industry, because she was at least a generation ahead of the rest of the world ; nor in agriculture, because of high freights on grain shipped from foreign countries.

During the course of the debates in 1846, Peel was careful to point out that Great Britain was adopting free trade regardless of the commercial policy of the rest of the world ; but he firmly believed that other countries would be forced to follow her example. Perhaps he was influenced in this opinion by the negotiations that were being conducted with the government of the United States over the Oregon boundary. In America the Democratic Party had triumphed in the election of 1844 on a platform of " fifty-four forty or fight " and a downward revision of the tariff. The practical certainty that the Corn Laws would be repealed after the stand taken by both Peel and Russell in November of 1845 seems to have helped smooth the way for a peaceful settlement of the Oregon question. The Ohio Valley was the section of the United States most concerned with both the boundary and the tariff. The South favoured free trade but not the acquisition of additional free territory. The East favoured a high tariff, but not a war with Great Britain. The Ohio Valley was imperialistic and wanted an outlet for grain. Hence any disappointment which this latter section may have experienced over the failure to secure fifty-four forty was offset by the repeal of the Corn Laws. Probably Peel was encouraged even more by the Walker tariff in the United States than by the conciliatory attitude taken by America on the Oregon question. Down to the present time no record of a bargain between the British and American governments has been unearthed ; but the correspondence of the Earl of Aberdeen, Peel's Foreign Secretary, shows that the British Ambassador in Washington was given a draft of the Walker bill before it was brought up in Congress, and that he sent a copy of it to Aberdeen.[29]   Perhaps this led Peel to feel that repealing the Corn Laws influenced the United States not only in the Oregon question but also in the lowering of the tariff.   On the other hand, Peel says absolutely nothing about the American question affecting his attitude in the elaborate apology and justification for his conduct which he has left us in his *Memoirs*. It seems practically certain that the Corn Laws would have been repealed even if the Walker bill had not been passed ; and that the Walker bill would have been passed even if the Corn Laws had not been repealed.   Nevertheless, it is difficult to believe that Peel was not influenced, in some measure, by the Walker bill.

CHAPTER XII

NOTES

[1] Holland, *The Fall of Protection*, 1913, p. 221.
[2] *Hansard*, vol. 78, p. 1028.
[3] Disraeli, *Lord George Bentinck*, a Political Biography, 1874, p. 221.
[4] Lord Dalling and Bulwer, *Sir Robert Peel*, 1874, pp. 142–3.
[5] *Memoirs by Sir Robert Peel*, 1856, vol. 2, pp. 98–9.
[6] *Ibid.*, p. 102. [7] *Ibid.*, p. 105. [8] *Ibid.*, p. 145. [9] *Ibid.*, p. 148. [10] *Ibid.*,
p. 159. [11] *Ibid.*, pp. 178–9
[12] Bright and Rogers, *Speeches by Richard Cobden*, 1870, p. 341.
[13] *Memoirs by Sir Robert Peel*, op. cit., p. 218.
[14] *Ibid.*, p. 220.
[15] Disraeli, *op. cit.*, p. 23.
[16] *Memoirs by Sir Robert Peel*, op. cit., p. 232.
[17] *Ibid.*, p. 234.
[18] *The Debates upon the Corn Laws*, vol. 1, pp. 56–7.
[19] *Ibid.*, vol. 2, pp. 401–2.
[20] Holland, *op. cit.*, p. 270, gives the final vote as 329 to 229 instead of 327 to 229 as in *Hansard*. According to Holland the vote by parties was as follows: " The ' Ayes ' were composed of 106 Conservatives and 223 Liberals ; the ' Noes ' of 222 Conservatives and 7 Liberals. The 106 Conservatives who followed the Prime Minister were composed of 79 borough members, 2 University members and 25 county members of whom only twelve represented English constituencies."
[21] The terms of the new Corn Law did not remain in force until February 1st, 1849. As a result of scarcity the duties on corn, grain and flour were suspended by the 10th and 11th, Victoria, c. 1, from January 26th until September 1st, 1847. This suspension was continued until March 1st, 1848, for buckwheat and Indian corn by 10th Victoria, c. 3, and for other kinds of grain and flour by 10th and 11th Victoria, c. 64. The duty of 1s. a quarter on grain and $4\frac{1}{2}$d. per cwt. on flour and meal came into operation on February 1st, 1849, as provided in the law of 1846. (*Customs Blue Book*, C.—8706, p. 251.)
[22] Cobden's bitterness against Peel for the 1843 affair had been removed in February. When Disraeli made a reference to that incident, Peel rose at once and stated that his intention at the time had been to relieve Cobden from the imputation which he had placed on him by misapprehension. " If any one present had stated to him that his reparation was not so complete, his avowal of error not so unequivocal, as it ought to have been, he should at once have repeated it more plainly and distinctly. Cobden followed, saying that the Minister's disavowal had not been so distinct as was to have been expected. He was glad that it had now been explicitly made, because it gave him an opportunity of expressing his own regret at the terms in which he had more than once referred to Sir Robert Peel. And so with the expression of a hope that the subject might never be revived, the incident came to an end." (Morley, *Life of Richard Cobden*, p. 354.)
[23] Morley, *The Life of Richard Cobden*, 1903, pp. 388–9.
[24] Morley, *Life of Gladstone*, 1912, vol. 1, p. 216.
[25] *Ibid.* While it is easy to sympathize with Cobden's ideal, it is more difficult to excuse his language about the landlords. As Cunningham said, they angered him not merely because they were selfish, but even more because he thought they were fools to fight against their own interests. Events since 1875 have shown they were not as foolish as he thought. Landlords clearly saw that while free trade might be beneficial to the manufacturers it might not be for them. This point of view is admirably phrased in the following rather lengthy passage in Archibald Allison's *Free Trade and Protection*, 1844, p. 19 : " Those who have the advantage, will always advocate free competition ; those who are labouring under impediments, will always exclaim against them. In some cases the young have the advantage, in others the old ; but in all the free system is applauded by

those in the sunshine, and execrated by those in the shade. The fair debutante of eighteen, basking in the bright light of youth, beauty, birth and connexions, has no sort of objection to the freedom of choice in the ball-room. If the mature spinster of forty would divulge her real opinion, what would it be on the same scene of competition ? Experience proves that she is glad to retire, in the general case, from the unequal struggle, and finds the system of established precedence and fixed rank at dinner parties much more rational. The leaders on the North Circuit, Sir James Scarlett or Lord Brougham, had no objections to the free choice, by solicitors and attorneys, of professional talent ; but their younger brethren of the gown are fain to take shelter from such formidable rivals in the exclusive employment of the Crown, the East India Company, the Bank of England, or some of the numerous chartered companies in the country. England is the old lawyer on the Circuit in manufacturers—but Poland is the young beauty of the ball-room in agriculture. We should like to see what sort of reciprocity could be established between them. Possible the young belle may exchange her beauty for the old lawyer's guineas, but it will prove a bad reciprocity for both."

26 *Memoirs*, by Sir Robert Peel, *op. cit.*, pp. 323–4.

27 Morley, *Life of Richard Cobden*, p. 400.

28 Proof of the industrialization of Great Britain between 1815 and 1845 rests on the testimony of contemporaries and knowledge of the spread of the factory system to specific industries, rather than on statistics. According to Porter, in the *Progress of the Nation*, the census of 1811 showed that 35.2 per cent. of population were engaged in agriculture, 44.4 per cent. in trade and manufacturing, and 20.4 per cent. in other occupations. The census of 1841 showed that 25.93 per cent. of the population were engaged in agriculture, 43.53 per cent. in trade and manufacturing, and 30.54 per cent. in other occupations. The value of these statistics on trade and other occupations is somewhat impaired by the fact that the same rule was not applied for determining the classification in 1811 and 1841 (pp. 53–4). The statistics on exports are equally unconvincing of the development of manufacturing.

Real or Declared Value of British and Irish Produce and Manufactures Exported

1801	39,730,659*	1817	41,761,132	1834	41,649,191
1802	45,102,330*	1818	46,603,249	1835	47,372,270
1803	36,127,787*	1819	35,208,321	1836	53,368,571
1804	37,135,746*	1820	36,424,652	1837	42,069,245
1805	38,077,144	1821	36,659,630	1838	50,060,970
1806	40,874,983	1822	36,968,964	1839	53,233,580
1807	37,245,877	1823	35,458,048	1840	51,406,430
1808	37,275,102	1824	38,396,300	1841	51,634,623
1809	47,371,393	1825	38,877,388	1842	47,381,023
1810	48,438,680	1826	31,536,723	1843	52,278,449
1811	32,890,712	1827	37,181,335	1844	58,584,292
1812	41,716,964	1828	36,812,756	1845	60,111,081
1813	Records destroyed	1829	35,842,623	1846	57,786,875
	by fire.	1830	38,271,597	1847	58,842,377
1814	45,494,219	1831	37,164,372	1848	52,849,445
1815	51,603,028	1832	36,450,594	1849	63,596,025
1816	41,657,873	1833	39,667,347		

* The declared value of British and Irish produce, etc., exported in the years 1801 to 1804 applies to Great Britain only, the real value of exports from Ireland not having been recorded earlier than 1805. The exports from Ireland are, however, inconsiderable (p. 356).

The value of these figures is lessened by the fact that the cost of production of many articles was enormously cheapened during these years by improvements in machinery.

29 In a letter to Aberdeen, written September 13th, 1845, Pakenham, the British Ambassador, reported a conversation which he had with Walker on the terms of the new tariff bill which was to be introduced shortly. (See Foreign Office Papers 5–428.) In a later letter, dated February 26th, 1846, Pakenham even included a schedule of the proposed duties. (See F.O. 5–446.)

CHAPTER XIII

SUMMARY AND CONCLUSION

In conclusion a brief summary will be given of the Corn Law policy from 1660 to 1846, which will be followed by an estimate of the results of free trade in grain since the repeal.

There are three phases in the history of the Corn Laws from 1660 to 1846 : the regulation of the internal trade ; of exportation ; and of importation. The regulation of the internal grain trade has a long history before 1660, but after that date it is of comparatively little significance. By the act of 1663 the mediæval statutes against forestalling, engrossing and regrating were practically abolished, although the actual laws against them were not repealed until 1772, and as late as 1800 a corn dealer was indicted under the common law for regrating. The regulation of the exportation of grain was very important from 1660 to 1814, and during the greater part of this period, along with the regulation of importation, made up a well-defined system for regulating the external corn trade. Before 1660 the chief concern of the government was with the consumer, and exportation was forbidden when the price of different kinds of grain rose above fixed levels ; but after that date the producer became of at least equal importance and was encouraged by a protective duty on importation, by removal of restrictions on exportation, and finally by a bounty on exportation. Importation was regulated by the sliding scale of duties under the act of 1670 and exportation by the bounty act of 1689. This system, which was based on the principle of helping the producer to dispose of his surplus when the price was low, and of keeping out foreign imports until the price was high, lasted until the laws of 1814 and 1815 were passed.

In actual practice this system did not work out very smoothly, because in times of scarcity the government usually suspended the bounty, forbade exportation, and permitted importation duty free. There is no questioning the immense growth of the corn exports down to 1750, and yet the Restoration Corn Law policy was not an important issue down to that date. No machinery was provided for determining the price at which importation or exportation was permitted for many years after the acts themselves were passed ; and when this machinery was provided by law, it was seldom put into operation by the Justices of the Peace. Perhaps the best example of the lack of provisions for carrying out an act is found in the absence of an appropriation for paying the bounty due under the terms of the law of 1689. It was only when the amount paid out became so enormous that the local customs funds were inadequate and the debentures given by customs officers were not honoured by the Treasury in Westminster because of lack of funds, that the merits of the system were considered or questioned.

Beginning with this temporary inability to meet payments due on corn debentures, the Corn Laws became prominent and remained an issue for the next hundred years. From 1689 to 1750 these laws were scarcely disturbed either by criticism or legislative change except when suspended in years of scarcity ; but from 1750 to 1815 constant attacks were directed against them and many changes in details, although not in principle, were made. Owing to a series of bad harvests and the growth of cities the exports of grain dwindled to almost nothing after 1765. As a result a new act was passed in 1773 which reduced the price levels at which the bounty was paid on exportation, and duties collected on importation of grain. Both landowners and consumers readily acquiesced in this revision because it was merely making permanent the new scale of price levels which has been brought into existence by temporary suspensions of the old laws. The consumers were pleased because they no longer had to clamour for the government to suspend the old acts in time of scarcity ; and the landed interests were satisfied because they gave up nothing which they were actually enjoying, and because they believed that except in years of unusual deficiency no great importations would take place.

Nevertheless, this act, which received almost universal commendation at the time it was passed, turned out to be a great disappointment. The landowners, especially, were dissatisfied, because they felt that it had prevented them from taking advantage of the increased demand for corn which had resulted from the rapid expansion of English industry and commerce during the seventeeneighties ; and because regular corn importers had developed contrary to expectations. Thus when the landed interests saw that the concessions made in 1773, although unimportant at the time, were likely to be costly, they used their political position in Parliament to have a new act passed. This law of 1791 and the one of 1804 had much in common : both raised the price levels at which the bounty was paid on exportation and the duties collected on importation ; both became inoperative soon after they went into effect, owing to the enormous rise in prices from 1793 to 1815 ; and both were passed because the landowners, with some justification, used their political position to secure greater protection for agriculture.

During the period from 1793 to 1815 two momentous changes took place which were to have considerable influence on the future of the Corn Laws. The first of these was the development of class consciousness and hatred between the upper and lower classes as a result of the excesses of the French Revolution and of the riots which occurred during the starvation years of 1795-6 and 1799-1801. Landowners frankly said that it was as important to defend their property from the mob as from Napoleon. The second of these great changes was the enormous impetus given to the enclosure movement by bad harvests and the Continental System, which resulted in significant social changes among the agricultural classes. Thus by 1813 the landlords enjoyed enormously increased rents, but they faced a hostile and growing city population with a thinned army of smallholders.

The Corn Laws of 1814 and 1815 definitely ended the Restoration policy. The act of 1814 abolished the bounty and made exportation at all times free ; and the act of 1815 discarded the sliding scale of duties on importation for absolute prohibition up to a certain level —80s. in the case of wheat—and admission duty free above that point. Clearly this second law was a class measure passed to keep up rents, and its effect from almost every angle was disastrous. England should have gone over to free trade in 1815, as List later insisted ; or have approached it gradually over a period of several years, as Ricardo suggested at the time. But neither plan was given serious consideration in 1814–15 because even the manufacturers did not offer to give up their protection if the landlords would do likewise. From the point of view of the landowners the worst feature of the law of 1815 was the fact that it caused them to succeed to the position occupied for centuries by the corn dealers and millers as the object of opprobrium to the consumers. This feeling that the landowners were thieves and enemies of the poor, which was cleverly exploited by the League in the eighteen-forties, was in no small degree a result of the act of 1815.

From 1814 to 1846 only one of the three phases of the Corn Laws, the regulation of importation, is considered, because the regulation of the internal grain trade became a dead letter after the Rusby trial in 1800, and all restrictions on exportation were swept away by the act of 1814. These thirty-two years, like the previous century and a half, were marked by alternate periods of distress among the agriculturists and the consumers. When prices were low, the complaint was of agricultural distress ; and, when high, of scarcity of provisions. From 1815 to 1822 most of these complaints came from the landed interest, and part, at least, of the trouble was due to too high rents based on the expectation that the law of 1815 would keep the price of wheat around 80s. In 1822 a new law was passed, but owing to the terms of one of the clauses it never came into operation. The landlords then seem to have come to the realization that no relief could be expected from legislative enactments, and adjusted rents to the lower price standards. No sooner were the complaints of agricultural distress quieted than a fierce attack was begun in 1825 by the trading and manufacturing classes upon the economic and political position of the landlords. It was principally a pamphlet and newspaper war, and is significant because it laid the foundation for the greater attack of the Anti-Corn Law League after 1839. The situation during the eighteen-twenties was complicated by the tariff reforms of Huskisson and the resumption of cash payments under the terms of the Peel Act. The reductions made in the amount of protection on other articles, the increase in the value of the currency, and Jacob's Report showing the impossibility of securing large quantities of wheat from Eastern Europe, all contributed toward the change in the Corn Laws of 1828. The new act returned to the principle of the sliding scale of duties. Neither the landed nor manufacturing interests were satisfied : the former held that the sliding scale was inferior to the absolute prohibition of the act of 1815, and the latter claimed that no better measure could be expected until the House of Commons was reformed.

The four years following 1828 were notable because of bad crops and high prices, the revolt of the agricultural labourers, and the successful fight to reform the Commons ; and the four years following 1832 were notable because of enormous crops and low prices, the overshadowing of the corn law question by agricultural distress, and the disillusionment of the lower classes with the results of the reform of the House of Commons. In 1836 the pendulum swung back and poor crops, high prices of food and widespread unemployment set in. After two years, these unsatisfactory conditions became even worse and from 1838 to 1842 Great Britain was in a most critical state. During these four years the Anti-Corn Law League, representing the manufacturers, and the Chartists representing the labouring class, took advantage of the bad times to agitate, respectively, for repeal of the Corn Laws and manhood suffrage. After 1842, with the return of good times, the Chartists' movement declined ; but the League continued an effective, although somewhat unscrupulous, campaign until repeal was secured in 1846. The manufacturers wanted free trade in corn both because it would enlarge the market abroad for British-manufactured goods and because it would tend to equalize the cost of food with other countries and thus offset any advantage which rival manufacturers may have possessed through cheap labour based upon cheap food. Yet the manufacturing and trading interests had been unwilling to give up protection in 1815, and they made no widespread expression of a willingness to do so until the presentation to Parliament of the famous Free Trade Petition in 1820. They carried on a fierce but restricted pamphlet war, from 1825 to 1828, and then allowed the question to drag until 1838. Thus the great majority of the individuals who were so anxious for repeal after 1838 were only a few years wiser than Peel and Russell.

The repeal of the Corn Laws resulted from the campaign of the League, in and out of Parliament, and the work in Parliament during 1846 of Peel, Wellington[1] and Russell. The conversion of Peel came from the speeches of Cobden, and from his own investigations on the relation of wages and prices of food and on the effects of his tariff of 1842. From 1842 to 1845 Peel hoped to avoid extreme free trade by an extension of the system of imperial preference, and by keeping the country nearly self sufficient as it was during these three years. By 1845 he had decided that Great Britain's future lay in industry and commerce, and that imperial preference and protection to agriculture would handicap the country in retaining the supreme position she held in both these fields.

The repeal of the Corn Laws in 1846 definitely ended the third phase of the so-called Restoration corn law policy. The regulation of the internal corn trade, which was the most important of the three phases before 1660, was, as has been shown, of little significance after that date. The regulation of exportation, particularly the bounty system, was most important from about 1689 to 1765, and from then until 1814 was about as important or as unimportant as that of importation. From 1689 to 1814 the laws governing exportation and importation were based on a distinct system of social justice. They were intended to keep prices within certain limits considered fair to both producer and consumer. After 1814, when all restrictions and bounties on exportation were abolished, the successive laws of 1815, 1822, 1828 and 1842 represented a one-sided policy of curtailing importation in the interest of the landowners and at the expense of other classes in the country. Before 1814–15 the Corn Laws were merely part of a general national system ; but after that they became obstacles to the country's retention of the industrial supremacy which was attained by the great inventions of the eighteenth century, the backwardness of European nations as a result of the wars from 1792 to 1815, and the amazing spread of factory production to other fields than cotton spinning in the generation following the battle of Waterloo.

The period of the Corn Laws coincides with that of the squirearchy, which came between the strong monarchy of the Tudors and Stuarts and modern capitalism. After the Restoration, and especially after the Revolution of 1689, England was virtually ruled by the gentry and nobles. They controlled both Houses of Parliament, and as Justices of the Peace ruled their own counties and local communities virtually as they pleased. The Reform Bill of 1832 shook their political power in the central government, but it was not until the repeal of the Corn Laws that this power definitely passed to the growing middle class.

In concluding this summary of the Corn Laws down to 1846, it may be well to give my own opinion of each important measure and system adopted during these two centuries. The restrictions on importation were of very little significance during the first century because England was not an importing nation except in years of scarcity when the laws forbidding importation were suspended. The bounty policy on exports down to 1765 was one of the factors contributing to the immense increase in the production of English corn, and as such was decidedly worth while. The act of 1773 was an improvement on the existing laws because it retained the old system but revised the price levels to meet changed conditions. The laws of 1791 and 1804 were mistakes. Owing to the wars they did no real damage, but they were forerunners of the acts of 1814 and 1815 in which the landowners used their political power to further their own economic interests. The law of 1815 was bad from practically every angle : it was drawn so crudely that it could not possibly give the protection that it was expected to afford ; and it was a class measure which cast opprobrium on the landowners. The country should have adopted an out and out free trade policy in 1815, or have arranged to take from five to seven years to do so by a system of decreasing duties. Although conditions abroad after 1815 were not as satisfactory as they were after 1846 for an enormous industrial and commercial expansion by England, still free trade during those thirty-one years would, almost certainly, have proved superior to the shifting systems actually in operation. The law of 1828 was an improvement over those of 1815 and 1822 because the sliding scale is superior to the fixed prohibition ; and the law of 1842 was an improvement over that of 1828 because the amount of pro- tection was materially reduced. The fixed duty would have been

U

superior to any of the laws passed between 1815 and 1846. The machinery of the League was splendidly organized and the aims were admirable ; but the tactics pursued, in many instances, deserve severe criticism. The ideals of Cobden, especially, merit praise, but his conduct often was not above reproach. Peel, in spite of the false position in which he found himself in 1845 and 1846, acted as a statesman should under the circumstances and, in my opinion, established his position as the outstanding Prime Minister of Great Britain in the nineteenth century. Great Britain was wise, considering the existing conditions, in repealing the Corn Laws in 1846. From an industrial point of view she stood head and shoulders above the rest of the world and needed expanding markets to take advantage of this superiority. On the other hand, she had nothing to fear in the home market from the competition of foreign manufacturers and little from foreign wheat-growers under the existing system of land and water transportation.[2]

Turning to the results of free trade in grain after 1846 we find confirmation of both the hopes of Cobden and Peel, and of the fears of the landowners. During the twenty-five and thirty years following the repeal, the predictions of free-traders seemed justified ; for British farming was never more prosperous. The average price of wheat in the generation following 1846 only fell from 57s. to 52s., instead of experiencing the ruinous drop which protectionists feared. Also free trade estimates that not more than four or five million quarters of wheat would be annually imported held good until 1860. Tooke's summary of the years immediately preceding and following repeal bears out this prophecy : " (1) During the eleven years, 1828 to 1838, both inclusive, the total annual importations of wheat and wheat flour, were considerably under 1,000,000 quarters, and of that quantity more than three-fourths were derived from Germany and the North of Europe. (2) During the four years 1839–42, both inclusive, the importations rose to 2,500,000 quarters annually, and a considerable part of these imports were, for the first time, obtained from France, Italy, Canada and the United States. (3) During the three years, 1843, 1844 and 1845, the imports again fell to little more than 1,000,000 quarters, and three-fourths of this import were from Germany and Prussia. (4) During the nine years 1846 to 1854, both inclusive, the annual imports have amounted to the enormous quantity of nearly 5,000,000 quarters, and a very considerable part of that supply has been derived from France, Italy, Turkey, Egypt, Syria, Canada and the United States."[3]

Beginning about 1873, however, a period of depression in British agriculture began which lasted until 1894, and even after that date the recovery was slow. The depression was chiefly due to the deluge of foreign wheat and meat from the United States, Canada, Australia, New Zealand and the Argentine, which was made possible by the tremendous improvements in methods of transportation. The rapid spread of railways into the interior of the different continents, and the improvement in the technique of steamships reduced the freights to a small fraction of what they had been in 1846. Thus from the eighteen-seventies to the present, the worst fears expressed by the landowners during the agitation of the League have been fulfilled. In 1913, for example, the country was importing four-fifths of her wheat. Although some compensations have been found in dairy and truck farming, fruit-growing and specialization in high-class livestock, the British landowners and farmers have not, since the eighteen-seventies, been reconciled to the loss of protection.

The results of free trade were even more satisfactory for the manufacturers and commercial classes than for the landowners and farmers in the thirty years following the repeal of the Corn Laws. A glance at the yearly export figures of practically every commodity will show the tremendous advance made during the third quarter of the nineteenth century. The depression which struck British agriculture in the fourth quarter of the century was shared by industry. The competition of other nations, notably Germany and the United States, the reaction in favour of protection in other countries, and the appreciation in the value of gold all made serious inroads on the supreme position of the British in manufacturing and commerce. Before the outbreak of the War in 1914 the foreign trade of the country was once more in a flourishing state ; but since the War, owing to loss of markets in Europe and Asia and the higher tariffs of the United States and Danubian countries, this trade is once more in a depressed condition.

Protection did not die as a political issue as soon as Corn Laws were repealed, for the protectionists did not give up hope entirely until after two general elections had gone against them. In the Parliament elected in 1847 there were 325 Liberals, 226 Protectionists and 105 Peelites or Conservative free-traders.[4] In the election of 1852 there were 319 Liberals, between 290 and 300 protectionist Conservatives, and between 40 and 50 Peelites.[5] The House of Commons then passed a resolution affirming the principle of free trade.

For about thirty years protection was, as Disraeli said, not only dead but damned. Only after the depression in trade, industry and agriculture had lasted several years, did a serious agitation start in the eighteen-eighties to restore protection. It is not improbable that the Conservative Party might have done something to protect agriculture ; but the Party was not in power until 1885, and after that its leaders feared the loss of the vote of the agricultural labourers if their food was taxed. After the Boer War Joseph Chamberlain revived a plan, which he had formulated as early as 1895, of linking social reform and imperialism. He urged the adoption of a high protective tariff against other nations, combined with a system of preferences to British colonies which were willing to grant similar preferences to Great Britain. In this way he hoped to find new markets for the manufacturers, to protect them and the agriculturists from foreign competition, to strengthen the bonds of the Empire, and to secure revenue to introduce some social reforms. But the labourers would not submit to having their food taxed, the majority of manufacturers did not want protection, and even many landowners did not favour a tariff which admitted colonial wheat and meat free. This feeling played an important part in the overwhelming defeat of the Unionists in the election of January, 1906, when the question of imperial preference was the most important single issue. The question remained an issue in both the elections of 1910, but in neither was the Unionist Party able to secure a majority.

Again in 1923, when Great Britain was suffering from the post-War trade depression, Mr. Stanley Baldwin revived Mr. Chamberlain's plan of a high protective tariff and imperial preferences. In the general election of December, 1923, this question was submitted to the people. A little more than a year earlier and a little less than a year later, general elections were held in which the tariff was not an outstanding issue and in each instance the Conservatives won an overwhelming victory. But in the election of 1923, the Liberal and Labour Parties agreed at least on opposition to protection and together carried 350 seats against 257 for the Conservatives. Apparently the country is still opposed to abandoning free trade. During the War and down to the election of 1923, the various governments introduced tariffs on certain articles on the excuse of war revenues and key-industries, but they were swept away by the MacDonald government in 1924. Since 1924 protection has been restored on certain articles and added on others by the Chancellor of the Exchequer. However, unless the attitude of the country at large undergoes a decided change from that of 1923, free trade cannot be overthrown by such nibbling tactics.

Thus free trade which remained unquestioned for about thirty years after the resolution of 1852 was passed, has survived nearly a half-century longer in the face of the opposition of the landed interest and part of the manufacturers. Have these eighty years since 1846 fulfilled the expectations of the manufacturers who financed the League, of Cobden, and of Peel? The manufacturers wanted to help business and the thirty years following repeal certainly exceeded their fondest expectations. Free trade was only one of the many factors contributing to the amazing prosperity of Great Britain down to 1875, but at least it helped bring about the improvement in the foreign trade of the country. Cobden, as it was shown in Chapter XI, believed that free trade would bring about universal good feeling among the nations of the world by developing a system of economic interdependence. Until about 1870 it seemed that the world was tending in that direction ; but after that time the spirit of nationalism with its big armies and navies, imperialism, and high tariffs reversed the movement. Nationalism and free trade which played so large a part in nineteenth-century history were really mutually incompatible, and it was nationalism which triumphed in the fourth quarter of the century. Thus Cobden's fondest and highest hopes were doomed to defeat less than a generation after his death. Since the Great War the trend of the times almost the world over is toward greater armaments and higher tariffs.

Lastly, why did other nations not follow Great Britain in her free trade policy as Cobden and Peel both expected? The answer is that no other country has ever found herself, nor is likely to find herself, so far ahead of other nations from an industrial point of view that her manufacturers will feel that they can afford to dispense with protection in the home market. Owing to the fact that Great Britain was more than a generation ahead of other nations in 1815, because of the inventions of the eighteenth century and the wars from 1792 to 1815, she really had little to fear from the industries of other nations until about 1875. As a rule manufacturers want protection against foreign articles either because they find difficulty in competing, or because they want even higher profits than they are making. Almost invariably manufacturers are well-organized and are able to force the government to give their interests consideration. The consumers, on the other hand, want lower prices, but they are seldom organized in such a manner as to be able to bring effective pressure to bear upon the government. Thus the interests of the manufacturers, foreign traders and agriculturists are as a rule the opposite of those of the consumers. Only for a brief period in Great Britain were the interests of the manufacturers and consumers identical. Both wanted cheap food, although for different reasons, and hence they united against their temporary common enemy, the agriculturists, and brought in free trade. But in no other country has this union of the trading and manufacturing interests with the consumers taken place, because their interests have never been identical.

To-day Great Britain still clings to free trade in grain, but no other industrial country has consistently followed her example.

CHAPTER XIII

NOTES

[1] The services of Wellington in 1846, as in 1829 at the time of Catholic Emancipation, have been, as a rule, under-estimated because it has been felt that he was a bit ludicrous in pushing through a measure of which he did not approve. Yet in both instances his influence was a powerful factor in putting the bills through the House of Lords. In fact his influence made it much easier for the Tories to pass a revolutionary measure than for the Whigs. The difference in the attitude of the Lords in passing Catholic Emancipation and the repeal of the Corn Laws, and in rejecting the first reform bills and various Irish measures between 1835 and 1841 was due, in part, to Wellington.

[2] It is interesting to note the conclusions drawn by J. S. Nicholson in *The History of the English Corn Laws*: " The general conclusion may be expressed in one proposition—namely, that the history of the Corn Laws strongly supports the negative argument for Free Trade. The history shows, indeed, that in the origins these various regulations were, on the whole, designed to promote the public good ; but some of them became gradually merely useless, and were forgotten before they were formally repealed. Some were practically inoperative for a long period, and as soon as they began to be effective, they began to be hurtful. The evil effects at the time of the repeal were no doubt greatly magnified by popular excitement ; but there was the compensating advantage that the evil was checked before it had become very serious. The history of the Corn Laws has often been perverted, and the actual evils have been much exaggerated ; but when all the rhetoric of exaggeration has been stripped away, and governments and landlords are cleared of iniquity in intention, the record is one of failure in accomplishment. The Corn Laws—even the protective duties—did less harm than was alleged, but fortunately they were repealed when their power for evil was becoming rapidly great." (pp. 185–6.)

[3] Tooke, *History of Prices*, vol. 6, p. 450.

[4] Marriott, *England since Waterloo*, 1923, p. 188.

[5] *Ibid.*, p. 211.

APPENDIX A

A list of the various authorities by which the importation, exportation and consumption of corn have been regulated from the year 1660, stated under the different subjects, taken from the *Customs Tariffs of the United Kingdom from 1800 to 1897* (C.—8706), pp. 251-2.

IMPORTATION REGULATED, AND DUTIES IMPOSED BY :

12th Car. II., c. 4
15th Car. II., c. 7
22nd Car. II., c. 13
9th and 10th William III., c. 23
2nd and 3rd Anne, c. 9
3rd and 4th Anne, c. 5
21st George II., c. 2
13th George III., c. 43
15th George III., c. 1
19th George III., c. 25
22nd George III., c. 66
27th George III., c. 13
31st George III., c. 30
37th George III., c. 15
37th George III., c. 110
43rd George III., c. 70
44th George III., c. 53
44th George III., c. 109
45th George III., c. 29

46th George III., c. 42
49th George III., c. 98
53rd George III., c. 35
55th George III., c. 26
57th George III., c. 27
1st and 2nd George IV., c. 87
3rd George IV., c. 60
4th George IV., c. 69
6th George IV., c. 64 and 65
7th George IV., c. 70 and 71
Order in Council of 1st September, 1826
Treasury Order of 18th November, 1826
7th George IV., s. 2, c. 3
7th and 8th George IV., c. 57
9th George IV., c. 60
5th Victoria, s. 2, c. 14
6th and 7th Victoria, c. 29
9th and 10th Victoria, c. 22 and 23
27th and 28th Victoria, c. 18

IMPORTATION PERMITTED AT THE LOW DUTIES, OR MADE FREE FOR SHORT PERIODS BY :

30th George II., c. 7, 9, 14
31st George II., c. 1
5th George III., c. 31
6th George III., c. 3 and 4
7th George III., c. 4, etc.
8th George III., c. 2 and 3
12th George III., c. 33
13th George III., c. 1 and 2

23rd George III., c. 1, etc.
30th George III., c. 1
33rd George III., c. 3
35th George III., c. 4
36th George III., c. 3
37th George III., c. 7
38th George III., c. 10
10th and 11th Victoria, c. 1, 3 and 64

THE KING AUTHORIZED TO PERMIT IMPORTATION AT THE LOW DUTIES, OR FREE WHEN NECESSARY BY :

31st George III., c. 30
33rd George III., c. 65

39th George III., c. 87, continued by subsequent Acts during the war.

THE LAW OF 1815 SUSPENDED BY :

3rd George IV., c. 60
6th George IV., c. 64 and 65
7th George IV., c. 70 and 71

7th and 8th George IV., c. 57
Order in Council, and 7th George IV., s. 2, c. 3

BOUNTIES ON IMPORTATION ALLOWED BY :

36th George III., c. 21
39th and 40th George III., c. 29, 35 and 53

41st George III., c. 10

CORN INTERCOURSE BETWEEN GREAT BRITAIN AND IRELAND REGULATED BY :

31st George III., c. 30
42nd George III., c. 35, continued by subsequent Acts

46th George III., c. 97

Exportation Regulated by :

12th Car. II., c. 4
15th Car. II., c. 7
22nd Car. II., c. 13
13th George III., c. 43

31st George III., c. 30
33rd George III., c. 65
44th George III., c. 109
45th George III., c. 86

Temporary Prohibitions of Exportation by :

10th William III., c. 3
8th Anne, c. 2
14th George II., c. 3
30th George II., c. 1
31st George II., c. 1
32nd George II., c. 2 and 8
5th George III., c. 32, continued by
    subsequent Acts

29th George III., c. 58
30th George III., c. 1
Order in Council and 33rd George III.,
    c. 3
35th George III., c. 4
36th George III., c. 3
37th George III., c. 7
38th George III., c. 10

The King Authorized to Prohibit Exportation when Necessary by :

31st George III., c. 30
33rd George III., c. 65

39th George III., c. 87, continued by
    subsequent Acts during the war

Bounties on Exportation Allowed by :

1st William and Mary, c. 12
5th Anne, c. 29
13th George III., c. 43
20th George III., c. 31

31st George III., c. 30
33rd George III., c. 65
44th George III., c. 109

Bounties on Exportation Suspended by :

11th William III., c. 1
31st George II., c. 1
32nd George II., c. 2 and 8
5th George III., c. 31

8th George III., c. 1, continued by
    subsequent Acts
23rd George III., c. 81
37th George III., c. 83

Bounties on Exportation Ceased by :

54th George III., c. 69

Duties on Exportation Taken Off by :

11th and 12th William III., c. 20,   54th George III., c. 69
    continued by subsequent Acts

Manner of Ascertaining the Average Prices of Corn Regulated by :

1st Jac. II., c. 19
2nd George II., c. 18
5th George II., c. 12
10th George III., c. 39
21st George III., c. 50
29th George III., c. 58
31st George III., c. 30
33rd George III., c. 65

44th George III., c. 109
45th George III., c. 86
55th George III., c. 26
1st and 2nd George IV., c. 87
7th and 8th George IV., c. 57 and 58
9th George IV., c. 60
5th Victoria, s. 2, c. 14

Flour and Biscuit Allowed to be Substituted for Wheat :

5th George IV., c. 70   5th and 6th Victoria, c. 92

Corn Duties Finally Repealed by :

32nd and 33rd Victoria, c. 14

The larger part of the foregoing statement as to the Corn duties is taken from the *Historical Summary of the Corn Laws*, a little work published in 1841 by Mr. H. Thornton, a clerk in the office of the Inspector-General of Imports and Exports.

APPENDIX B

Below in parallel columns are the annual average prices of wheat for Eton from 1660 to 1770, in both imperial and Winchester quarters, and those of Oxford in the imperial quarter. The columns headed Eton and Oxford represent the prices in imperial quarters, and are taken from the *Customs Tariffs of the United Kingdom from* 1800 *to* 1897 (C.—8706), pp. 253–55. The column headed Tooke represents the prices at Eton in the Winchester quarter, and is taken from Tooke's *History of Prices*, vol. 1, pp. 387–88. In some years the prices in the two Eton columns vary more than the actual difference between the imperial and Winchester quarters warrants. Following these three columns is the annual average price for England and Wales from 1771 to 1850, per imperial quarter. These figures are taken from the pages cited above in C.—8706.

In many cases the price given below does not coincide with the one in the narrative because the latter is often quoted from a contemporary source in which the price may be reckoned either in the Winchester or imperial quarter, in quarters of eight or nine bushels, or in the best or middling quality of wheat.

Years	Eton s. d.	Tooke s. d.	Oxford* s. d.	Years	Eton s. d.	Tooke s. d.	Oxford* s. d.
1660	51 8	51 3	—	1696	65 0	56 0	—
1661	64 1	62 2½	—	1697	55 0	53 4	59 10
1662	67 9	65 9¼	—	1698	62 7	60 8¾	59 10
1663	52 3	50 8	—	1699	58 7	56 0	53 9
1664	37 1	48 0	—	1700	36 7	35 6½	33 0
1665	45 2	43 10¼	—	1701	34 5	31 8¼	25 8
1666	33 0	32 0	—	1702	26 11	26 0¾	25 1
1667	33 0	32 0	—	1703	33 0	32 0	34 2
1668	36 7	35 6½	—	1704	42 7	41 2¼	29 3
1669	40 7	40 0	—	1705	27 6	26 8	24 4
1670	38 1	37 0½	—	1706	23 9	23 1¼	22 0
1671	38 6	37 4	—	1707	26 1	25 2	24 4
1672	37 6	37 0½	—	1708	37 11	36 8¾	44 0
1673	42 8	41 5¾	—	1709	71 11	69 7¼	78 2
1674	62 10	61 0½	—	1710	71 6	69 4	58 8
1675	59 2	52 1¾	—	1711	49 6	48 0	45 2
1676	34 9	33 9½	—	1712	42 5	41 2	33 0
1677	38 6	37 4	—	1713	46 9	45 4	49 6
1678	54 0	52 5¼	—	1714	46 1	44 8¼	33 0
1679	55 0	48 0	—	1715	39 4	38 2¼	44 0
1680	41 3	40 0	—	1716	44 0	42 8	40 3
1681	42 8	41 5¾	—	1717	41 10	40 5¼	39 1
1682	40 3	39 1¼	—	1718	35 6	34 8	29 3
1683	36 7	35 6½	—	1719	32 0	31 0½	31 9
1684	40 3	39 1¼	—	1720	33 10	32 10¼	29 3
1685	42 8	41 5¾	—	1721	34 4	33 4	29 3
1686	31 1	34 2½	—	1722	33 0	32 0	30 7
1687	23 0	31 8¾	—	1723	31 9	30 9¼	29 3
1688	42 1	23 1¼	—	1724	33 10	32 10¼	32 4
1689	27 6	26 8	—	1725	44 5	43 1¼	44 11
1690	31 8	30 9¼	—	1726	42 1	40 10¾	37 10
1691	31 1	29 11	—	1727	38 6	37 4	39 1
1692	42 8	41 9¼	—	1728	49 11	48 3½	51 3
1693	61 11	60 1¾	—	1729	42 10	42 2¼	44 0
1694	58 7	56 10½	—	1730	33 5	32 5¼	31 2
1695	48 6	47 1¼	—	1731	30 0	29 4	25 8

* The Oxford prices are the prices at Michaelmas of each year.

Years	Eton s. d.	Tooke s. d.	Oxford* s. d.	Years	Eton s. d.	Tooke s. d.	Oxford* s. d.
1732	24 4	23 8¼	22 0	1752	38 3	40 8¾	36 8
1733	25 11	25 2¼	22 0	1753	40 10	39 8¼	38 6
1734	35 6	33 5¾	35 4	1754	31 8	30 9¾	30 7
1735	39 4	38 2¾	40 3	1755	31 0	29 11	30 7
1736	36 11	35 10¼	36 9	1756	41 4	40 2½	44 0
1737	34 9	33 6¾	36 9	1757	55 0	53 4	58 8
1738	32 5	31 6¾	20 9	1758	45 9	44 5¼	44 0
1739	35 2	33 2¼	35 4	1759	36 4	35 3	34 9
1740	46 5	48 10½	61 1	1760	33 5	32 5¼	29 3
1741	42 8	41 9¼	36 8	1761	27 7	26 10½	25 8
1742	31 1	28 5¼	27 6	1762	35 9	34 8	31 2
1743	22 9	22 1¾	15 10	1763	37 2	36 1¾	36 8
1744	22 9	22 0¾	22 0	1764	42 8	41 6½	44 0
1745	25 2	24 3½	23 2	1765	49 6	48 0	47 8
1746	35 9	34 8	31 9	1766	44 5	43 1¼	36 8
1747	31 10	30 11½	33 0	1767	59 1	57 4	58 8
1748	33 10	32 10½	31 2	1768	55 5	53 9¼	58 8
1749	33 10	32 10½	30 7	1769	41 10	40 8	45 9
1750	29 8	28 10¾	29 10	1770	44 10	43 6¾	51 3
1751	35 2	34 2½	38 6				

Annual Average Price in England and Wales from 1771 to 1850

	s. d.		s. d.		s. d.
1771 ...	48 7	1798 ...	51 10	1825 ...	68 6
1772 ...	52 3	1799 ...	69 0	1826 ...	58 8
1773 ...	52 7	1800 ...	113 10	1827 ...	58 6
1774 ...	54 3	1801 ...	119 6	1828 ...	60 5
1775 ...	49 10	1802 ...	69 10	1829 ...	66 3
1776 ...	39 4	1803 ...	58 10	1830 ...	64 3
1777 ...	46 11	1804 ...	62 3	1831 ...	66 4
1778 ...	43 3	1805 ...	89 9	1832 ...	58 8
1779 ...	34 8	1806 ...	79 1	1833 ...	52 11
1780 ...	36 9	1807 ...	75 4	1834 ...	46 2
1781 ...	46 0	1808 ...	81 4	1835 ...	39 4
1782 ...	49 3	1809 ...	97 4	1836 ...	48 6
1783 ...	54 3	1810 ...	106 5	1837 ...	55 10
1784 ...	50 4	1811 ...	95 3	1838 ...	64 7
1785 ...	43 1	1812 ...	126 6	1839 ...	70 8
1786 ...	40 0	1813 ...	109 9	1840 ...	66 4
1787 ...	42 5	1814 ...	74 4	1841 ...	64 4
1788 ...	46 4	1815 ...	65 7	1842 ...	57 3
1789 ...	52 9	1816 ...	78 6	1843 ...	50 1
1790 ...	54 9	1817 ...	96 11	1844 ...	51 3
1791 ...	48 7	1818 ...	86 3	1845 ...	50 10
1792 ...	43 0	1819 ...	74 6	1846 ...	54 8
1793 ...	49 3	1820 ...	67 10	1847 ...	69 9
1794 ...	52 3	1821 ...	56 1	1848 ...	50 6
1795 ...	75 2	1822 ...	44 7	1849 ...	44 3
1796 ...	78 7	1823 ...	53 4	1850 ...	40 3
1797 ...	53 9	1824 ...	63 11		

* The Oxford prices are the prices at Michaelmas of each year.

APPENDIX C

Quantities of wheat and wheat flour imported into, and exported from, Great Britain in each year from 1697 to 1850, taken from the *Customs Tariffs of the United Kingdom from* 1800 *to* 1897 (C.—8706), pp. 256–8.

Years	Imported	Exported	Years	Imported	Exported
	Quarters	Quarters		Quarters	Quarters
1697 ...	400 ...	14698	1744 ...	2 ...	234274
1698 ...	1689 ...	6886	1745 ...	8 ...	325340
1699 ...	486 ...	557	1746 ...	– ...	131105
1700 ...	5 ...	49057	1747 ...	– ...	270491
1701 ...	1 ...	98324	1748 ...	6 ...	545240
1702 ...	– ...	90230	1749 ...	382 ...	631007
1703 ...	50 ...	106615	1750 ...	280 ...	950483
1704 ...	2 ...	90314	1751 ...	3 ...	662957
1705 ...	– ...	96185	1752 ...	– ...	430117
1706 ...	77 ...	188332	1753 ...	– ...	300754
1707 ...	– ...	174155	1754 ...	201 ...	356781
1708 ...	86 ...	83969	1755 ...	– ...	237466
1709 ...	1552 ...	71618	1756 ...	5 ...	102752
1710 ...	400 ...	16607	1757 ...	141562 ...	11545
1711 ...	– ...	80941	1758 ...	20353 ...	9234
1712 ...	– ...	148539	1759 ...	162 ...	227641
1713 ...	– ...	179969	1760 ...	3 ...	393614
1714 ...	16 ...	180665	1761 ...	– ...	441956
1715 ...	– ...	173237	1762 ...	56 ...	295385
1716 ...	– ...	75876	1763 ...	72 ...	429538
1717 ...	– ...	25637	1764 ...	1 ...	396857
1718 ...	– ...	74381	1765 ...	104547 ...	167126
1719 ...	20 ...	130533	1766 ...	11020 ...	164939
1720 ...	– ...	84343	1767 ...	497905 ...	5071
1721 ...	– ...	82748	1768 ...	349268 ...	7433
1722 ...	– ...	178915	1769 ...	4378 ...	49892
1723 ...	– ...	158082	1770 ...	34 ...	75449
1724 ...	148 ...	247162	1771 ...	2510 ...	10089
1725 ...	12 ...	211175	1772 ...	25474 ...	6959
1726 ...	– ...	143626	1773 ...	56857 ...	7637
1727 ...	– ...	31030	1774 ...	289149 ...	15928
1728 ...	74574 ...	3935	1775 ...	560988 ...	91037
1729 ...	40315 ...	18993	1776 ...	20578 ...	210664
1730 ...	76 ...	94530	1777 ...	233323 ...	87686
1731 ...	4 ...	130650	1778 ...	106394 ...	141070
1732 ...	– ...	202612	1779 ...	5039 ...	222261
1733 ...	7 ...	427425	1780 ...	3915 ...	224059
1734 ...	7 ...	498747	1781 ...	159866 ...	103021
1735 ...	9 ...	155280	1782 ...	80695 ...	145152
1736 ...	18 ...	118218	1783 ...	584183 ...	51943
1737 ...	32 ...	466071	1784 ...	216947 ...	89288
1738 ...	3 ...	588284	1785 ...	110863 ...	132685
1739 ...	23 ...	285492	1786 ...	51463 ...	205466
1740 ...	5469 ...	54391	1787 ...	59339 ...	120536
1741 ...	7540 ...	45417	1788 ...	148710 ...	82971
1742 ...	1 ...	295698	1789 ...	112656 ...	140014
1743 ...	3 ...	375979	1790 ...	222557 ...	30892

Years		Imported		Exported	Years		Imported		Exported
		Quarters		Quarters			Quarters		Quarters
1791	...	469056	...	70626	1822	...	510602	...	160499
1792	...	22417	...	300278	1823	...	424019	...	145951
1793	...	490398	...	76869	1824	...	441591	...	61680
1794	...	327902	...	155048	1825	...	787606	...	38796
1795	...	313793	...	18839	1826	...	897127	...	20054
1796	...	879200	...	24679	1827	...	711868	...	57323
1797	...	461767	...	54525	1828	...	1410300	...	76489
1798	...	396721	...	59782	1829	...	2190095	...	75097
1799	...	463185	...	39362	1830	...	2205751	...	37149
1800	...	1264520	...	22013	1831	...	2867860	...	65875
1801	...	1424765	...	28406	1832	...	1254351	...	289558
1802	...	647663	...	149304	1833	...	1166457	...	96212
1803	...	373725	...	76580	1834	...	981486	...	159482
1804	...	461140	...	63073	1835	...	750808	...	134076
1805	...	920834	...	77955	1836	...	861156	...	256978
1806	...	310342	...	29566	1837	...	1109492	...	308420
1807	...	404946	...	25113	1838	...	1923400	...	158621
1808	...	84889	...	98005	1839	...	3110729	...	42512
1809	...	455987	...	31278	1840	...	2526645	...	87242
1810	...	1567126	...	75785					
1811	...	336131	...	97765			Cwts.		Cwts.
1812	...	290710	...	46325					
1813	...	559000	...	Records destroyed	1841	...	11705393	...	95329
					1842	...	12905486	...	266907
1814	...	852567	...	111477	1843	...	4510731	...	272948
1815	...	384475	...	227947	1844	...	5743312	...	321884
1816	...	332491	...	121611	1845	...	4723275	...	277944
1817	...	1089855	...	317524	1846	...	9398323	...	592475
1818	...	1694261	...	58668	1847	...	17840363	...	1380981
1819	...	625638	...	44689	1848	...	12938605	...	45945
1820	...	996479	...	94657	1849	...	20013144	...	25872
1821	...	707384	...	199846	1850	...	20021752	...	56050

APPENDIX D

Duties received on corn in the United Kingdom from 1804 to 1850, taken from the *Customs Tariffs of the United Kingdom from 1800 to 1897* (C.—8706), pp. 258-9.

Years Year ending 5th January	£	*Years* Year ending 5th January	£
1804 ...	17692	1828 ...	786097
1805 ...	22736	1829 ...	193250
1806 ...	25958	1830 ...	898793
1807 ...	28541	1831 ...	790109
1808 ...	38693	1832 ...	544792
1809 ...	3519	1833 ...	307987
1810 ...	35980	1834 ...	35234
1811 ...	56268	1835 ...	97984
1812 ...	7814	1836 ...	234576
1813 ...	6980	1837 ...	149661
1814 ...	—	1838 ...	583271
1815 ...	40224	1839 ...	186760
1816 ...	18046	1840 ...	1098780
1817 ...	—	1841 ...	1156639
1818 ...	—	1842 ...	568341
1819 ...	—	1843 ...	1363977
1820 ...	15	1844 ...	758293
1821 ...	—	1845 ...	1098382
1822 ...	—	1846 ...	367031
1823 ...	—	1847 ...	723600
1824 ...	10310	1848 ...	13911
1825 ...	175228	1849 ...	767667
1826 ...	300194	1850 ...	561480
1827 ...	437673		

APPENDIX E

A statement of the quantities of wheat and wheat flour, oats and oatmeal, and the total of all kinds of grain of Irish growth imported into Great Britain from Ireland from 1800 to 1842.

Years	Wheat and Wheat Flour Quarters	Oats and Oatmeal Quarters	Total Quarters
1800	749	2411	3238
1801	150	375	525
1802	108751	341151	461371
1803	61267	266359	343547
1804	70071	240022	316958
1805	84087	203302	306924
1806	102276	357077	466760
1807	44900	389649	463195
1808	43497	579974	656770
1809	66944	845783	932478
1810	126388	492741	631227
1811	147245	275757	429867
1812	158352	390629	597356
1813	217154	691498	977164
1814	225478	564010	812462
1815	189544	597537	821192
1816	121631	683714	873865
1817	55481	611117	695651
1818	105179	1069385	1204733
1819	153850	789613	967680
1820	403307	916251	1415722
1821	569700	1162249	1822816
1822	463004	569237	1063089
1823	400068	1102487	1528153
1824	356384	1225085	1634000
1825	396018	1629856	2203962
1826	314451	1303734	1693392
1827	405255	1343267	1828460
1828	652584	2075631	2826590
1829	519017	1673628	2307244
1830	529717	1471252	2215521
1831	557498	1655701	2429182
1832	790293	2051867	2990767
1833	844211	1762520	2737441
1834	779505	1769503	2792658
1835	661776	1822767	2679438
1836	598757	2132138	2958272
1837	534465	2274675	3030293
1838	542583	2742807	3474302
1839	258331	1904933	2243151
1840	174439	2037835	2327782
1841	218708	2539380	2855525
1842	201998	2261435	2538234

BIBLIOGRAPHY

The following is a list, chronologically arranged, of the pamphlets on the Corn Laws from, roughly, 1750 to 1850. It is a fairly complete one for this period, although, doubtless, some pamphlets have been omitted. Practically every one was examined before this work was written. In addition to the pamphlets the Parliamentary Reports are included in this list.

[Townshend, Lord] : National Thoughts recommended to the serious Attention of the Public, with an Appendix, showing the Damages arising from a Bounty on Corn. (By a landowner.) London, 1751.

Considerations concerning taking off the Bounty on Corn exported ; in some Letters to a Friend. London, 1753.

The State of the Corn Trade considered in Answer to all the Objections against Bounty granted to encourage the Exportation of Corn, and its Influence on the Landed and Navigation Interest clearly and fully explained. London, 1753.

The Manufacturer's Plea for the Bounty on Corn. London, 1754.

An Essay on the Rise of Corn, with some Proposals to reduce the exorbitant Price thereof ; in a Letter from a Gentleman in the Country to an M.P. in London. London, 1756.

Artificial Dearth ; or the Iniquity and Danger of withholding Corn. By a Clergyman in the Country. London, 1756.

Edward, Bishop of Durham : A charge delivered to the Grand Jury concerning Engrossing of Corn and Grain, and the Riots that have been occasioned thereby. London, 1756.

A Compendium of the Corn Trade. The Practice of Ingrossing, Jobbing, etc. The Cause of Plenty and Scarcity ; Constitutional Errors in our Laws and Customs ; a Summary of the Laws ; Assize Tables, etc. London, 1757.

Letter to a Member of Parliament proposing Amendments to the Laws against Forestallers, Ingrossers and Regrators. London, 1757.

Considerations on the present Dearness of Corn. London, 1757.

Seasonable Considerations upon the Corn Trade ; as it respects the Landowner, Tenant or Farmer, the Miller and Baker, and poor and labouring Part of the People. By a Trueborn Englishman and Lover of his Country. London, 1757.

A State of the Corn Trade in London, 1757. (?)

The Causes of the present high Price of Corn and Grain, and a State of the Abuses and Impositions practised upon the Publick in general, and the Poor in particular, by the Millers or Mealmen. With Hints for a Law, for reducing the present Price of Corn, to prevent its ever rising so high for the future, and for correcting and preventing the Abuses and Impositions of the Millers or Mealmen. London, 1758.

Orders appointed by his Majestie (King Charles I.). To be straitly observed, for the preventing and remedying of the Dearth of Graine and Victuals. London, 1630. Reprinted, London, 1758.

Scheme for erecting publick Magazines, to supply England with Corn. (By Miss Clara Pitt, Sister to the Earl of Chatham.) London, 1758.

Sentiments of a Corn Factor on the present Situation of the Corn Trade. London, 1758.

A short Essay on the Corn Trade, and the Corn Laws. London, 1758.

A general Estimate of the Corn Trade. By the Author of the Compendium. London, 1758.

Grove, Mr. : Six Letters upon interesting Subjects. London, 1758.

Manning, James, M.D. : The Nature of Bread. London, 1758 (?).

Jackson, H., Chemist : An Essay on Bread. London, 1758.

Considerations on the present high Prices of Provisions and the Necessaries of
    Life. By a West-Country Maltster. London, 1764.
Report from the Select Committee respecting the high Price of Provisions, 1764.
Means to prevent extravagant high Prices of Corn. 1765.
Smith, Charles : Tracts on the Corn Trade and Corn Laws. London, 1766.
An impartial View of English Agriculture, from permitting the Exportation of
    Corn, in the Year 1663 to the present Time. London, 1766.
Homer, Henry : An Essay on the Nature and Method of ascertaining the specifick
    Shares of Proprietors upon the inclosure of common Fields. Oxford, 1766.
Three Letters to a Member of the Honourable House of Commons, from a Country
    Farmer, concerning the Prices of Provisions ; and pointing out a sure Method
    of preventing future scarcity. London, 1766.
Considerations on public Granaries. Dublin, 1766.
An Essay to state some Arguments relative to public Granaries. Dublin, 1766.
The Causes of the Dearness of Provisions assigned ; with effectual Methods for
    reducing the Prices of them. Glouster, 1766.
A letter from Richard in the Country to Dick in the City. On the Subject of
    public Granaries. Dublin, 1766.
Report from the Select Committee respecting the State of the Corn Trade. 1766.
Letter to a Member of Parliament, on the present Distresses of the Poor ; the
    real Causes of those Distresses, and the most probable means of removing
    them. London, 1767.
An Appeal to the Publick ; or, Considerations on the Dearness of Corn. London,
    1767.
Considerations on the Dearness of Corn and Provisions, and a Proposal to raise
    2,500,000£ per annum, without oppression. London 1767.
[Addington, Stephen] : An Inquiry into the Reasons for and against Inclosing
    the open Fields. Coventry, 1767.
[Lewis, John] : Uniting and monopolizing Farms, plainly proved disadvantageous
    to the Landowners, and highly prejudicial to the Public. By a Gentleman
    in the Country. London, 1767.
Some Observations on the Causes of the Dearness of Provisions in general and Corn
    in particular. By a Country Gentleman. London, 1767.
Forster, N. : An Enquiry into the Causes of the present high Price of Provisions.
    London, 1767.
Jenyns, Soame : Thoughts on the Causes and Consequences of the present high
    Price of Provisions. London, 1767.
Popular Considerations on the Dearness of Provisions in general and particularly
    of Corn Bread, etc. C, 1767.
An Address (to the House of Commons) upon the excessive Price of Corn and
    Provisions. London, 1767.
The Occasion of the Dearness of Provisions and the Distress of the Poor : with
    Proposals for remedying the Calamity. London, 1767.
A seventh Letter to the People of England, London, 1767.
Political Speculations ; or, an Attempt to discover the Causes of the Dearness of
    Provisions, etc. London, 1767.
[Lowe] : Considerations of the Effects which the Bounties granted on exported
    Corn, Malt and Flour, have on the Manufacturers of the Kingdom, and the
    true Interests of the State. London, 1768.
An Answer to a Pamphlet intitled " Thoughts on the Causes and Consequences
    of the present high Price of Provisions." By a Gentleman of Cambridge.
    London, 1768.
An Inquiry into the Prices of Wheat, Malt, and occasionally of other Provisions,
    as sold in England from the Year 1000 to the Year 1765. 1768.
A Defence of the Amendments, proposed in the Corn Laws. Dublin, 1768.
Young, Arthur : A six weeks' Tour through the southern Counties of England and
    Wales, 1768.
Report from the Select Committee on the high Price of Provisions, and on fore-
    stalling Cattle, 1766-8.
Pennington, W. : Reflections on inclosing large Commons and common Fields.
    1769.
Considerations on the Exportation of Corn ; wherein the principal Arguments
    produced in favour of the Bounty are answered ; and the Inferences
    commonly drawn from the Eton Register are disproved. London, 1770.

Young, Arthur : The Expediency of a free Exportation of Corn at this time. London, 1770.

Wimpey, Joseph : Thoughts upon several interesting Subjects, viz. On the Exportation of, and Bounty upon Corn, on the high Price of Provisions, on Manufactures, Commerce, etc. London, 1770.

Young, Arthur : A six months' Tour through the North of England. Four vols., second edition, London, 1770.

Baker, John Wynn : Considerations upon the Exportation of Corn. Dublin, 1771.

Sampson, John : Against withholding of Bread-Corn. London, 1771.

Peters, Matthew : The rational Farmer. Second edition, 1771.

Price, Richard : Observations on reversionary Payments, etc. 1771.

Wimpey, Joseph : An Essay on the present high Price of Provisions. London, 1772.

The Advantages and Disadvantages of inclosing waste lands. By a Country Gentleman. London, 1772.

A Sketch of a Plan for reducing the present high Price of Corn and other Provisions, and for securing Plenty for the Time to come. In a Letter to an M.P. London, 1772.

Elbridge, Thomas Rooke : Considerations on the present Dearness of Provision and Corn in Great Britain ; with Thoughts on a suitable Remedy. London, 1772.

Comber, T. : Real Improvements in Agriculture. 1772.

Young, Arthur : Observations on the present State of the waste Lands of Great Britain. London, 1773.

Moore, Francis : Considerations on the exorbitant Price of Provisions. London, 1773.

Arbuthnot : An Inquiry into the Connection between the present Price of Provisions, and the Size of Farms. By a Farmer. London, 1773.

Dickson, Rev. Adam : An Essay on the Causes of the present high Price of Provisions, as connected with Luxury, Currency, Taxes and National Debt. London, 1773.

Young, Arthur : Political Arithmetic. London, 1774.

Pownall, Governor : Memoir drawn up, and laid before the Lords Commissioners of the Treasury, containing an historical Review of the Statutes that have been made relative to the Corn Trade. London, 1774. (Published with Young's Political Arithmetic.)

Remarks on the late Regulations in the Corn Trade. 1774.

Tucker, Josiah : Four Tracts, together with two Sermons, on political and commercial Subjects. 1774.

An Humble Address to the King concerning the Dearness of Provisions. 1775.

Considerations on the present State of the Poor in Great Britain. 1775.

Anderson, James : Inquiry into the Nature of the Corn Laws ; with a View to the new Corn Bill proposed for Scotland. Edinburgh, 1777.

Kent, Nathaniel : Hints to Gentlemen of landed Property. 1777.

Forbes, Francis : The Improvement of waste Lands. London, 1778.

Remarks and Calculations on the Exportation and Importation of Corn. 1778.

An Enquiry into the Advantages and Disadvantages resulting from Bills of Inclosure. 1780.

Faithful Copies of all the Letters that have appeared in the General Advertiser, under the Signatures of Scourge and W. Bennett, Camberwell ; and relate to the Transactions of the Commissioners of Victualling, and Christopher Atkinson, Esq., their Corn Factor, in the supplying Government with Wheat, Malt, etc. London, 1781.

Observations on a Pamphlet entitled an Enquiry into the Advantages, etc. 1781.

Lamport, W. : Cursory Remarks on the Importance of Agriculture. 1784.

Some Hints in regard to the better Management of the Poor. 1784.

Abstract of Corn Acts ; with Extracts from the Report of the Select Committee. London, 1785.

A Political Enquiry into the Consequences of enclosing waste Lands. Holborn, 1785.

Thoughts upon a Bill lately offered to Parliament, for regulating the Export and Import of Corn. London, 1786.

X

Howlett, John : An Enquiry into the Influences which Enclosures have had upon the Population of England. 1786.

Cursory Remarks on Inclosures. By a Country Farmer. 1786.

Report of a Committee of Directors of the Chamber of Commerce and Manufactures of Glasgow, Relative to the proposed Alteration on the Corn Law. Glasgow, 1787.

Howlett, Rev. J. : Enclosures a Cause of improved Agriculture, of Plenty and Cheapness of Provisions, of Population and of both Private and National Wealth. London, 1787.

Observations on the Corn Bill. London, 1787.

Stone, Thomas : Suggestions for rendering the Inclosure of common Fields and waste Lands a Source of Population and Riches. 1787.

Young, David : Agriculture, the primary Interest of Great Britain. Edinburgh, 1788.

Howlett, John : The Insufficiency of the Causes to which the Increase of our Poor and of the Poor's Rates have been commonly ascribed. 1788.

Applegarth, Robert : A Plea for the Poor ; or, Remarks on the Prices of Provisions and the peasants' Labour, the Bounties allowed on the Exportation of Corn, especially Wheat, etc. London, 1789.

The Corn Trade of Great Britain, for eighteen Years, from 1748–1765 compared with the eighteen Years, from 1771–1788. London, 1790.

Representation of the Lords of the Committee of Council, appointed for the Consideration . . . Upon the present State of the Laws for regulating the Importation and Exportation of Corn. London, 1790.

Report of the Committee of Directors of the Chamber of Commerce and Manufacturers of Glasgow on the Bill brought into the House of Commons last Session of Parliament for regulating the Importation and Exportation of Corn, etc. Glasgow, 1790.

Third Report of a Committee of the Chamber of Commerce and Manufactures in Glasgow, relative to the Corn Laws. Glasgow, 1790.

Mitford, William : Considerations on the Opinion stated by the Lords of the Committee of Council in a Representation to the King, upon the Corn Laws, that Great Britain is unable to produce Corn sufficient for its own Consumption. London, 1791.

Two Letters on the Flour Trade, and Dearness of Corn : Wherein the Former is vindicated and the Cause of the Latter explained ; and the Mistakes and Misrepresentations of ignorant, and merely theoretic Writers, are confuted by a Person in Business. London, 1791. Second edition.

Sheffield, John, Lord: Observations on the Corn Bill, now depending in Parliament. London, 1791. Third edition.

[Corrie, E.] : Considerations on the Corn Laws, with Remarks on the Observations of Lord Sheffield on the Corn Bill. London, 1791.

Sinclair, Sir John : Address to the Landed Interest on the Corn Bill now depending in Parliament. London, 1791.

Report of the Committee of the Town Council of Glasgow, appointed to consider the Corn Bill at present pending in Parliament. Glasgow, 1791.

Free Remarks on the present System of our Corn Laws. Dublin, 1791.

Langrishe, Sir Hercules : Speech in the Irish House of Commons, April 7th, 1791, on the Corn Laws. Dublin, 1791.

Keith, George Skene : Tracts on the Corn Laws of Great Britain. London, 1792.

Phillips, Catherine : Considerations on the Causes of the High Price of Grain, etc. London, 1792.

Observations on the new Corn Bill. By an Essex Farmer. London, 1793.

Two Reports from the Select Committee on the Importation and Exportation of Corn and Grain, and on the Scarcity thereof, 1793.

An Address to the different Classes of Persons in Great Britain, on the present Scarcity and High Price of Provisions. By Rev. Septimius Hodson. London 1795.

McPhail, James : Remarks on the present Times, exhibiting the Causes of the High Price of Provisions, etc. London, 1795.

[Pownall, Governor] : Considerations on the Scarcity and high Prices of Bread-Corn and Bread at the Market ; Suggesting the Remedies in a Series of Letters. Cambridge, 1795.

Donaldson, Mr. : A Letter to the Right Honourable Mr. Pitt on the Use of Hair Powder. 1795.

A Letter to Sir T. C. Bunbury, Bart., on the Poor Rates, and the high Price of Provisions, by a Suffolk Gentleman. 1795.

Thoughts on the most safe and effectual Mode of relieving the Poor during the present Scarcity. London, 1795.

One Cause of the present Scarcity of Corn. By a Physician, 1795.

Wright, Thomas : A short Address to the Public on the Monopoly of small Farms. Mark Lane, 1795.

The crying Frauds of the London Markets : proving their deadly influence upon the two great Pillars of Life, Bread and Porter. By the Author of the Cutting Butchers' Appeal. London, 1795.

Barry, Rev. Edward M. D. : On the Necessity of adopting some Measures to reduce the present Number of Dogs. 1795 (?)

Observations on the present high Price of Corn with Hints on the Cultivation of Waste Lands. By a Farmer. London, 1795.

Wilson, Edward : Observations on the present State of the Poor. Reading, 1795.

The First Report from the Select Committee of the House of Commons on Cultivation and Improvement of the waste, uninclosed, and unproductive Lands of the Kingdom. London, 1796.

Large Farms, recommended in a national View. A Reply to Mr. Wright's Address to the Public on Monopoly of small Farms. London, 1796.

Paul : Observations on a Bill before Parliament, " For Facilitating the Division and Inclosure of waste Lands and Commons, etc." London, 1796.

An Enumeration of the principal Vegetables. . . . That may be substituted, either in part or wholly, in place of Wheat and other Bread-Corn, in Times of Scarcity. Birmingham, 1796.

Davies, David : The Case of Labourers in Husbandry stated and considered. Dublin, 1796.

Hepburn, George Buchan : Observations on the Bill for the Sale of Corn by Weight, etc. Edinburgh, 1796.

Reflections on the Cruelty of inclosing Common-Field Lands, particularly as it affects the Church and Poor ; in a Letter to the Lord Bishop of Lincoln. By a Clergyman of that Diocese. London, 1796.

Lettsom, Dr. : Hints respecting the Distresses of the Poor. Second edition. London, 1796.

Mountmorres, Hervey, Viscount : Impartial Reflections upon the present Crisis. London, 1796.

Gabell, Rev. Henry : On the Expediency of altering and amending the Regulations, recommended by Parliament for reducing the high Price of Corn. London, 1796.

Tapwell, Thomas : A friendly Address to the Poor of Great Britain on the present Scarcity of Wheat, and the Dearness of wheaten Bread. London, 1796.

Wright, Sir James : Observations upon the important Object of preserving Wheat and other Grain from Vermin. London, 1796.

Girdler, J. S. : Observations on Forestalling, Regrating and Ingrossing. 1796.

A Circular Letter to the Diocese of Rochester, on the Scarcity of Corn. 1796.

Vancouver, John : The Causes of Poverty, and the present State of the Poor considered. 1796.

Robertson, Thomas : Outlines of the general Report on the Size of Farms. Edinburgh, 1796.

Five Reports from the Select Committee on the high Price of Corn. 1795–6.

[Brown, Robert] : Letters from a Farmer to a Justice of the Peace . . . on the Bill for regulating the Sale of Corn by Weight. Edinburgh, 1797.

Howlett, Rev. John : Dispersion of the gloomy Apprehensions, of late repeatedly suggested, from the Decline of our Corn Trade. London, 1797.

Eden, Sir Frederick Morton : The State of the Poor. In three vols. London, 1797.

Ingram, Robert A. : An Inquiry into the present Condition of the lower Classes, and the Means of improving it ; . . . in Course of which the Policy of the Corn Laws is examined. London, 1797.

A Proposal for supplying London with Bread, at an uniform Price, from one Year to another, according to an annual Assize. London, 1798.

Heslop, Rev. Luke : Observations on the Statute of 31 George II. C. 29 concerning the Assize of Bread. 1799.

Edward, Morris : A short Enquiry into the Nature of Monopoly and Forestalling, London, 1800.

Arthur Young : The Question of Scarcity plainly stated, and Remedies considered. London, 1800.

Edmund Burke : Thoughts and Details on Scarcity originally presented to the Right Hon. William Pitt, in the Month of November, 1795. London, 1800.

Long, Charles : A temperate Discussion of the Causes which have led to the present high Price of Bread. London, 1800.

Turton, Sir Thos. : An Address to the good Sense and Candour of the People in behalf of the Dealers in Corn : with some few Observations on a late Trial for Regrating. By a Country Gentleman. London, 1800.

Malthus : An Investigation of the Cause of the present high Price of Provisions. London, 1800.

Buxton Lawn : The Corn Trade investigated, and the shocking System exposed which principally causes the amazing Fluctuations in the Prices of Corn and Flour ; and a Proposition most humbly offered for the consideration of the Legislature, which will effectually remedy the alarming fluctuating Price of Bread Corn. Bath, 1800.

Francis Chalmer : An Appeal to the County of Lancaster, on the present Scarcity 1800.

Francis Chalmer : Letters on the Corn Trade ; giving an Account of the Causes of the high Price of Corn. 1800.

Thoughts of an old Man, of independent Mind, though dependent Fortune, on the present high Price of Corn. London, 1800.

Corn Trade. An Examination of certain commercial Principles, in their Application to Agriculture and the Corn Trade, as laid down in the fourth Book of Mr. Adam Smith's Treatise on the Wealth of Nations, with Proposals for revival of the Statutes against Forestalling, etc. London, 1800.

Somerville, John, Lord : The System followed during the two last Years by the Board of Agriculture further illustrated. London, 1800.

[Simmons, Richard] : Thoughts on the present Prices of Provisions, their Causes and Remedies. By an independent Gentleman. London, 1800.

Selections from the Correspondence of General Washington and James Anderson in which the Causes of the present Scarcity are fully investigated. London, 1800.

Money, Major-General J. : A Letter to the Norfolk Farmers, on the present high Price of Corn. Norwich, 1800.

Blane : Inquiry into the Causes and Remedies of the late and present Scarcity and high Prices of Provisions in a Letter to the Right Hon. Earl Spencer London, 1800.

Waithman, Robert : War proved to be the real Cause of the present Scarcity, and enormous high Price of every Article of Consumption, with the only radical Remedies. London, 1800.

Thoughts on the Dearness of Provisions, and the most certain Method to reduce the present high Price of Wheat ; addressed to the principal Inhabitants of Great Britain. Oxford, 1800.

Duthy, John : Observations on the present high Price of Provisions. Winchester, 1800.

Fairburn : Abstract of the Bread Act, Passed Feb. 20th, 1800. London.

Trial of John Rusby, in the Court of King's Bench, Guildhall, London, before Lord Kenyon, and a special Jury, for regrating Corn in the Corn Exchange, Mark Lane, on the 8th of November, 1799. London, 1800.

An Address to the plain Sense of the People, on the present high Price of Bread. London, 1800.

Brewer, Geo. : The Rights of the Poor considered ; with the Causes and Effects of Monopoly. Second edition. London, 1800.

Letter to the Right Hon. Lord Kenyon, Lord Chief Justice of the King's Bench, on the present high Price of Corn and other Provisions. London, 1800.

Brand, J. : A Determination of the average Depression of the Price of Wheat in War, below that of the preceding Peace ; and its Re-advance in the Following. London, 1800.

A Letter to the Right Honourable Lord Somerville. By a Society of Practical Farmers. London, 1800.

Cove, Morgan : An Inquiry into the Necessity, Justice and Policy of a Commutation on Tithes. Hereford, 1800.

Annesley, Alexander : Strictures on the true Cause of the present alarming Scarcity of Grain and other Provisions. London, 1800.

Suggestions offered to the Consideration of the Public, and in particular to the more opulent Classes of the Community, for the purpose of reducing the Consumption of Bread-Corn ; and relieving at the same time the labouring People, by the Substitution of other cheap, wholesome and nourishing Food ; and especially by Means of soup Establishments, etc. Second edition. London, 1800.

Thoughts on the Corn Trade. London, 1800.

Savile, C. : An Address to the Public, on the Scarcity of Corn. London, 1800.

Clapham, Rev. Samuel : The Sinfulness of Withholding Corn : a Sermon. 1800.

The whole Proceedings and Resolutions of the Freeholders of the County of Middlesex at a Meeting publicly convened and held by the High Sheriff, Oct. 29th, 1800. London, 1800.

The Discharge of £37,000,000 of the National Debt, demonstrated to be Part of the Cause of the rapid Dearness of Provisions. London, 1800.

Copper, B. P. : A statistical Account of the Population and Cultivation, Produce and Consumption of England and Wales. London, 1801.

Considerations on the present high Price of Corn with a Proposition for the effectual Regulation of the Prices of all the Requisites of Life. London, 1800.

Gardner, Edward : Reflections upon the evil Effects of an increasing Population on the present high Prices of Provisions, particularly Corn, upon the Bounty Act. London, 1800.

Malham, Rev. J. : The Scarcity of Corn considered. Salisbury, 1800.

Nasmyth, James : An Examination of the Statutes now in force relating to the Assize of Bread. 1800.

Sheffield, John, Lord : Remarks on the Deficiency of Grain, occasioned by the bad Harvest of 1799. London, 1800.

Three Reports from the Select Committee appointed to take into consideration the Means of promoting the Cultivation and Improvement of the waste, uninclosed and unproductive Lands in the Kingdom, 1795–1800.

Six Reports from the Select Committee appointed to consider of the high Price of Provisions, and to whom so much of his Majesty's Speech as relates thereto, and also the several Petitions presented to the House, complaining of the high price of Provisions, were referred, 1801.

Seven Reports from the Lord's Select Committee to whom it was referred to consider so much of his Majesty's Speech as relates to the high Price of Provisions, 1801.

Sheffield, John, Lord : Remarks on the Deficiency of Grain, occasioned by the bad Harvest of 1799 ; on the Means of present Relief, and of future Plenty. Part III. London, 1801.

Anderson, James : A calm Investigation of the Circumstances that have led to the present Scarcity of Grain in Britain. London, 1801.

Walter, Boyd : A Letter to the Right Honourable William Pitt, on the Influence of the Stoppage of Issues in Specie at the Bank of England on the Prices of Provisions, and other Commodities. London, 1801.

Observations of the enormous high Price of Provisions. By a Kentish Clergyman. London, 1801.

Edwards, George : Radical Means of counteracting the present Scarcity and preventing Famine in future. London, 1801.

Frend, William : The Effect of paper Money on the Price of Provisions. London, 1801.

Heron, Robert : Sketch of a Plan for the perpetual Prevention of Dearth and Scarcity of Provisions in Great Britain and Ireland in a Letter to the Right Hon. Henry Addington. London, 1801 (?).

Remarks on the present high Price of Grain, and on the Expediency of further legislative Restriction in order to effect its Reduction. London, 1801.

Duthy, John : The different Effects of Peace and War in the Price of Bread-Corn considered. 1801.

Atwood, G.: Review of the Statutes and Ordinances of Assize, 1202–1797. 1801.

Arthur Young: Inquiry into the Propriety of applying Wastes to the better Maintenance and Support of the Poor. 1801.

Marshall, William: The Appropriation and Enclosure of commonable and inter-mixed Lands. 1801.

Sinclair, Sir John: Essays on miscellaneous Subjects. London, 1802.

Chalmers, George: An Estimate of the comparative Strength of Great Britain. 1802.

Keith, Geo. Skene: General View of the Corn Trade. 1802 (?).

Report from the Select Committee on the State of the Corn Trade between Great Britain and Ireland. 1802.

Chapman, William: Observations on the Prevention of a future Scarcity of Grain, by means contributive to the Benefit of the Landed, Commercial and Manu-facturing Interests. London, 1803.

Mill, James: An Essay on the Impolicy of a Bounty on the Exportation of Grain and on the Principles which ought to regulate the Commerce of Grain. London, 1804.

Curtis, William: Observations on the Operation of the new Corn Bill. 1804.

Report from the Select Committee on Petitions relating to the Importations and Exportation of Corn. 1804.

Report from the Select Committee on re-committed Report respecting the Corn Trade. 1804.

Winter, William Henry: A Defence of the Principle of Monopoly ; of Corn Factors, or Middle-men ; and Arguments to prove that War does not produce a scarcity of Necessaries of Life. London, 1805.

Observations on the Corn Laws. Glasgow, 1805.

Report from the Select Committee on Petitions respecting the Act of last Session regulating the Importation and Exportation of Corn. 1805.

Substance of a Speech delivered in the House of Commons by J. F. Barham, on Monday, May 23rd, 1808, on the Motion for prohibiting Corn, and the Substitution of Sugar, in the Distilleries. London, 1808.

Bell, Archibald: An Inquiry into the Policy and Justice of the Prohibition of the Use of Grain in the Distilleries. Edinburgh, 1808.

Spence, William: Agriculture the Source of the Wealth of Britain. London, 1808.

Mill, James: Commerce Defended. London, 1808.

Spence, William: Britain independent of Commerce ; or Proofs, deduced from an Investigation into the true Causes of the Wealth of Nations, that our Riches, Prosperity and Power, are derived from Sources inherent in ourselves, and would not be affected, even though our Commerce were annihilated. Fifth edition, London, 1808.

Comber, W. T.: An Inquiry into the State of national Subsistence. London, 1808.

Johnson, Samuel Ll. D.: Considerations on the Corn Laws. London, 1808.

Thoughts on Tillage and Corn Laws. By an old tillage Farmer. Exeter, 1808.

Board of Agriculture general Report. 1808.

Flower, Richard: Abolition of Tithes recommended. London, 1809.

Bearblock, Rev. James: Observations on a Pamphlet written by Richard Flower recommending the Abolition of Tithes. London, 1809.

Curwen, J. C.: Hints on agricultural Subjects, and on the best Means of improving the Condition of the labouring Classes. London, 1809.

Parnell, Sir Henry: Treatise on the Corn Trade and Agriculture. 1809.

Dixon, William: An Inquiry into the Impolicy of the Continuance of the Pro-hibition of Distillation from Grain. Liverpool, 1810.

Barham, Joseph Foster: Considerations on the late Act for continuing the Pro-hibition of Corn in the Distillery ; in a Letter addressed to the Right Hon. Lord Holland. London, 1810.

London, John: An immediate and effectual Mode of raising the Rental of the landed Property of England, and rendering Great Britain independent of other Nations, for a Supply of Bread and Corn. London, 1811.

An Appeal to British good Sense on the Occasion of the present Scarcity of Corn. Second edition. London, 1812.

Report from the Select Committee appointed to inquire into the Corn Trade of the United Kingdom, 1813.

Communications to the Board of Agriculture, 1797–1813.

Reports of the Board of Agriculture, 1793–1815.

Preston, Richard : A Review of the present ruined Conditions of the landed and agricultural Interests. London, 1813.

Considerations on the Importation of Foreign Corn. London, 1814.

Booth, George : Observations on lowering the Rent of Land, and on the Corn Laws. Liverpool, 1814.

The Speech of the Hon. Mr. Baron Hepburn of Smeaton, on the Subject of the Corn Laws. Held at Haddington, March 3rd, 1814. Edinburgh, 1814.

The Speech of the Right Hon. George Rose, in the House of Commons, on May 5th, 1814, on the Corn Laws. London, 1814. (Also in Hansard.)

Substance of the Speech of Charles C. Western, Esquire, in the House of Commons, May, 1814. With additional Observations on the Corn Laws. London, 1814.

The Substance of the Speeches of Sir H. Parnell, Bart., in the House of Commons, with additional Observations, on the Corn Laws. London, 1814.

An Inquiry into the Policy, Efficiency and Consistency of the Alterations in our Corn Laws ; in a Letter to Sir Henry Parnell, Bart., 1814.

Lauderdale, The Earl of : Letter on the Corn Laws. London, 1814.

Letter to the Earl of Liverpool, on the probable Effect of a great Reduction of Corn Prices, by Importation ; upon the relative Condition of the State and its Creditors, and of Debtors and Creditors in general. London, 1814.

Jacob, William : Considerations on the Protection required by British Agriculture, and on the Influence of the Price of Corn on exportable Productions. London, 1814.

Brickwood, John, Jr.: Observations on the Corn Laws and the Corn Trade in 1813 and 1814. London, 1814.

Corrie, Edgar : Letters on the Subject of the Corn Laws. Liverpool, 1814.

Western, Chas. C. Letter to his Constituents on the Subject of the foreign Corn Trade, Aug. 5th, 1814. London, 1814.

Report from the Select Committee of the House of Commons on Petitions relating to the Corn Laws of this Kingdom. London, 1814.

First and second Reports from the Committee of the House of Lords, appointed to inquire into the State of the Growth, Commerce and Consumption of Grain. London, 1814.

Edwards : A General Appeal addressed in particular to the Lords, etc. 1814.

Broadhurst, J.: Substance of a Speech against the proposed Alteration of the Corn Laws. London, 1814.

Simpson, Thomas : A Defence of the Landowners and Farmers of Great Britain. In familiar Letters from an agricultural Gentleman in Yorkshire to a Friend in Parliament. London, 1814.

The Corn Laws, a new song, to which is added the Land of the Thistle. Glasgow, 1814.

Huskisson, Right Hon. W. A Letter on the Corn Laws to one of his Constituents, in 1814. London, 1827.

A Letter on the proposed Alteration of the Corn Laws. Addressed to Sir Henry Parnell, Bart., by John Campbell, of Carbrook, Esq. Edinburgh, 1814.

A Letter from the Hon. T. B. Brand, M.P., to W. Wiltshere, Esq., on the Subject of the Corn Laws. London, 1814.

Naismith, John, Esq.: An Inquiry concerning the Propriety of increasing the Import Duty on foreign Corn. 1814.

Culverhouse, C.: An Arrangement of the Bread Laws. Bath, 1814.

Strickland, Thomas : Observations on an intended Proposition to the Legislature in regard to a new Arrangement as to the limiting Price of Corn. 1814.

Keith, Geo. Skene : General Observations on the Corn Trade and Corn Laws. Extracted from Farmer's Magazine, 1814.

Ainslie, Robert : Letters on the Corn Laws. To the Editor of Edinburgh Correspondent, 1814.

Comparative Price of Corn in England and Ireland, 1814.

Jacob, William : A Letter to Samuel Whitbread, Esq., M.P. London, 1815.

Malthus, The Rev. T. R. : Observations on the Effects of the Corn Laws, and of a Rise or Fall in the Price of Corn on the Agriculture and general Wealth of the Country. London, 1814.

Malthus, The Rev. T. R. : The Grounds of an Opinion on the Policy of Restricting the Importation of foreign Corn. London, 1815.

Malthus, The Rev. T. R. : An Inquiry into the Nature and Progress of Rent and the Principles by which it is regulated. London, 1815.

Torrens, R. : An Essay on the external Corn Trade ; containing an Inquiry into the general Principles of that imported Branch of Traffic. London, 1815.

Sheffield, The Right Hon. Lord : A Letter on the Corn Laws, and on that Means of obviating the Mischiefs and Distress, which are rapidly increasing. London 1815.

Broughton, Thomas : A Letter to the Right Hon. Lord Sheffield, in reply to his Observations on the Corn Laws ; showing the Impolicy of the present Bill, and suggesting a Measure calculated to promote general Interest. London, 1815.

Broughton, Thomas : The Question fairly stated relative to the Revision of the Corn Laws, and a permanent Measure suggested, to secure a moderate Price to the Manufacturer, without injury to the Farmer. London, 1815.

Ricardo, David : An Essay on the Influence of a low Price of Corn on the Profits of Stock ; showing the Inexpediency of Restrictions on Importations. London, 1815.

Smith, John Prince : An Argument and constitutional Advice for the Petitioners against the Corn Bill. London, 1815.

Curwen, J. C. : Cursory Observations on the Corn Laws. London, 1815.

Hume, J. D. : Thoughts on the Corn Laws, as connected with Agriculture, Commerce and Finance. London, 1815.

Duppa, R. : Observations on the Price of Corn as connected with the Commerce of the Country and the Public Revenue. London, 1815.

Civis : An Address to the Public on the Impolicy of the new Corn Bill, and on the alarming Tendency of a late Compromise. London, 1815.

Wilson, Robert : An Enquiry into the Causes of the high Prices of Corn and Labour. Edinburgh, 1815.

Observations relative to the Corn Laws, and on the Evidence given before both Houses of Parliament, on that important Subject. (By a Friend to his Country.) London, 1815.

Chapman, William : Observations on the Effects that would be produced by the proposed Corn Laws, on the Agriculture, Commerce and Population of the United Kingdom. London, 1815.

Spence, William : The Objections against the Corn Bill refuted ; and the Necessity of this Measure, to the vital Interests of every Class of the Community, demonstrated. London, 1815.

The Objections against the Corn Bill vindicated. London, 1815.

Considerations upon the Corn Bill. London, 1815.

Observations on Rents and the Price of Corn, and on their Relatives. London, 1815.

Newnham, G. I. : A Review of the Evidence before the Committees of the two Houses of Parliament on the Corn Laws. London, 1815.

Curry, James. A brief Sketch of the Causes which first gave rise to the late high Price of Grain in Great Britain. London, 1815.

Mirabeau, Marquis de : On the Corn Laws ; being a Digest of Extracts from the Economical Table. London, 1815.

Young, Arthur : An Enquiry into the Rise of Prices in Europe, During the last twenty-five Years, etc. London, 1815.

West, Sir Edward : Essay on the Application of Capital to Land. By a Fellow of University College, Oxford. London, 1815. Reprint, 1903.

The Corn Laws. Materials for a Petition to Parliament against the proposed alteration of the Corn Laws. (A Letter signed : Fellow Feeling.) 1815 (?)

Corn Laws. The Evidence of John Benett, Esq. Mr. Benett's Letter. Mr. Bleeck's Letter in Reply. Salisbury, 1815.

Hall, Geo. Webb : Letters on the Importance of encouraging the Growth of Corn and Wool in the United Kingdom. London, 1815.

Simpson, Thomas : Letters to the Honourable and Right Reverend the Lord Bishop of Durham, The Right Honourable Lord Dundas, and the Right Honourable Geo. Rose, Esq., M.P., upon the Subject of the Corn Laws. London, 1815.

Report from the Committee of the House of Commons, on Laws relating to the Manufacture, Sale and Assize of Bread. Ordered to be printed June 6th, 1815.

Observations on the Justice and Policy of regulating the Trade in Corn. Bt. J. D. 1815.

Edye, John : A Letter to William Wilberforce, Esq., M.P., on the Consequences of the unrestrained Importation of foreign corn. London, 1815.

Pettman, William : A Letter to Arthur Young, on the Situation of the Growers of Corn in Great Britain. Canterbury, 1815.

Address to the two Houses of Parliament, on the Importance of the Corn Laws to the national Revenue. London, 1815.

A few Observations on the Corn Law and a short Plan for the better Protection of the Poor. By a Landholder. London, 1815.

Observations and Examples to assist Magistrates in setting the Assize of Bread. 1815.

Speech of Henry Broughman, Esq., M.P., on Tuesday, the 9th of April, 1816 ; in the Committee of the whole House, upon the State of the Agricultural Distresses. London, 1816.

Jacob, W. : An Inquiry into the Causes of agricultural Distress. London, 1816.

The agricultural State of the Kingdom, in February, March and April, 1816. London, 1816.

Crombie, Rev. A. : Letters on the present State of the agricultural Interest, addressed to Charles Forbes, Esq., M.P. London, 1816.

The Speech of Chas. C. Western, Esq., M.P., on . . . The distressed State of the Agriculture of the United Kingdom. March 7th, 1816. London, 1816.

Thoughts upon the Causes of the present Distress of the Country, and upon their Remedy. By a Baronet. London, 1816.

A View of the Causes of our late Prosperity, and of our present Distress ; and of the Means which have been proposed for our Relief. London, 1816.

Simpson, Thomas : A brief Exposition of the actual State of the Landowners and of the Farmers of Great Britain. London, 1816.

Brown, Robert : Letters on the distressed State of Agriculturists. Edinburgh, 1816.

Premiums ordered by the Board of Agriculture for 1815-16.

White, Charles : A short and plain Letter on agricultural Depression, Addressed to the Right Honourable the Earl of Liverpool. London, 1816.

Ainslie, Robert : Practical Observations for the landed and agricultural Interest, on the Question of Corn and Money. Edinburgh, 1816.

Parry, C. H. : The Questions of the Necessity of the existing Corn Laws. London, 1816.

Keith, Dr. George Skene : The Increase and Decrease of the Population of Great Britain as connected with the Increase and Decrease of the Corn Trade. Edinburgh, 1816.

Preston, Richard : An Address to the Fund Holder, the Manufacturer, the Mechanic and the Poor ; on the Subject of the Corn Laws. London, 1817.

Yates, John Ashton : A Letter on the Distresses of the Country. London, 1817.

The Speech of Henry Brougham, Esq., M.P., in the House of Commons, March 13th, 1817, on the State of the Nation. London, 1817.

Observations on the State of the Country since the Peace. London, 1817.

An Address to the Merchants and Manufacturers of Great Britain, on the present State of the Country. London, 1817.

Dissertation on the State of the Nation respecting its Agriculture. London, 1817.

Some Observations on the Report respecting the fair Prices of Corn, struck at Lanark. Glasgow, 1817.

Colebrook, H. T. : On Import of Colonial Corn. London, 1818.

A Letter to the Rt. Hon. F. Robinson on the Policy and Expediency of further Protection to the Corn Trade of Great Britain. By a Corn Factor. 1819.

Clay, John : A Free Trade essential to the Welfare of Great Britain. London, 1819.

The Rights of the Farmer, or, a short view of the Causes which oppress and degrade the Cultivators of the Soil of Great Britain. By a Farmer. London, 1819.

Remarks upon Trade and Commerce as connected with Agriculture. By an Agriculturist. London, 1819.

Complete Refutation of the Arguments used on the Subject of the agricultural Petition. London, 1819.

Chambers, A. H. : Thoughts on the Resumption of Cash Payments by the Bank; and the-Corn Bill. London, 1819.

The Speech of the Right Hon. the Earl of Liverpool in the House of Lords, on Friday, the 26th of May, 1820. London, 1820.

A Letter to the Right Honourable Robert Peel, on the comparative Operation of the Corn Laws, and of public Taxation. By a Briton. London, 1820.

Trenor, Keating : A Letter to the Right Hon. Robert Peel, London, 1820.

Motives for an Enquiry into the present Distresses. London, 1820.

Details of the Combination to raise the Price of Bread. By the Author of " Relief to the Poor." London, 1820.

Report of the Earl of Sheffield, to the Meeting at Lewes, July 26th, 1820, on Wool and Agriculture. London, 1820.

Remarks on the Merchants' Petitions and Publications respecting Restrictions on foreign Commerce ; on the Depression of Agriculture. London, 1820.

Report from the Select Committee to whom the Petitions on the Subject of agricultural Distresses were referred, and who were directed to confine their Inquiries to the Mode of ascertaining, returning and calculating the average Prices of Corn in the Twelve maritime Districts, under the Provisions of the existing Corn Laws, and to Frauds which may be committed in violation of the said Laws, 1820.

Report from the Select Committee, to whom the several Petitions complaining of the depressed State of the Agriculture of the United Kingdom were referred. London, 1821.

Stanhope, Phillip Henry, Earl : Proposed Address to His Majesty on the present Distresses of the Country. London, 1821.

Hall, Geo. Webb : Observations on the Report from the Select Committee of the House of Commons. London, 1821.

Broughton, Capt. Robert E. : A Letter to G. Webb, Esq. London, 1821.

Stourton, Right Hon. Lord : Two Letters to the Right Honourable the Earl of Liverpool, First Lord of the Treasury, on the Distresses of Agriculture. London, 1821.

Stourton, Right Hon. Lord : A Third Letter to the Earl of Liverpool, in which the Justice, Policy and Necessity of legislative Relief to the agricultural Distresses of the Country are considered. London, 1821.

Consideration on the Corn Question, etc. London, 1821.

Further Considerations on the Corn Question, etc. London, 1821.

A Letter to the Right Hon. Frederick J. Robinson, President of the Board of Trade ; on the present depressed State of Agriculture. London, 1821.

Comber, W. T. : The Claims of the Agriculturists, considered, in reference to the recent Development of our Money-System. London, 1822.

Ricardo, David : On Protection to Agriculture. London, 1822.

Bramston, Thomas Gardiner : A practical Inquiry into the Nature and Extent of the present agricultural Distress, and the Means of relieving it. London, 1822. Second edition.

Observations on the present State of Agriculture, Tithes, Poor's Rates, and Taxes in England. Dartmouth, 1822.

The Speech of the Earl of Liverpool, delivered in the House of Lords, on Tuesday, 26th day of February, 1822, on the Subject of the agricultural Distress of the Country, and the financial Measures proposed for its Relief.

Thoughts on the Expediency of a Relaxation of the Corn Laws, as the most effectual Remedy for agricultural Distress. London, 1822.

Western, C. C. : Address to the Landowners of the United Empire. London, 1822. Second edition.

Western, C. C. : Second Address to the Landowners of the United Empire. London, 1822.

Cleghorn, James : On the depressed State of Agriculture. Edinburgh, 1822.

Playfair, William : A Letter on our agricultural Distresses, etc. London, 1822

Sinclair, Sir John : An Answer to a Tract recently published by David Richards, on Protection to Agriculture. Edinburgh, 1822.

Heathfield, Richard : Observations on Trade, considered in Reference particularly to the Public Debt and the Agriculture of the United Kingdom. London, 1822.

Whitmore, W. W. : A Letter on the present State and future Prospects of Agriculture. Addressed to the Agriculturists of the County of Salop. London, 1822.

Richards, James : A Letter to the Earl of Liverpool, on the agricultural Distress of the Country. London, 1822.

Stourton, Right Hon. Lord : Further Considerations, addressed to the Earl of Liverpool, on agricultural Relief, and the Extent of the national Resources. London, 1822.

Inquiry into the Capacity of Government to administer Relief to agricultural Distress. London, 1822.

Substance of the Speech of the Marquis of Londonderry, delivered in the House of Commons, Feb. 15th, 1822, on Subject of the agricultural Distress of the Country. London, 1822.

Substance of a second Speech of the Marquis of Londonderry, delivered in the Committee of the House of Commons on Apr. 29th, 1822, on the Subject of the agricultural Distress of the Country. London, 1822.

A Letter to the Right Hon. the Earl of Eldon, on the present State of agricultural Lessees, and their Right to Relief from the Payment of Rent. By a Barrister. London, 1822.

Sinclair, Sir John, Bart. : Address to the Owners and Occupiers of Land, in Great Britain and Ireland. Edinburgh, 1822.

Observations on the Cause and Cure of the present distressed State of Agriculture. Chester, 1822.

First and Second Reports from the Select Committee to whom the Petitions presented to the House in this Session of Parliament complaining of the depressed State of the Agriculture of the United Kingdom, were referred, 1822.

A Letter to Mr. Canning, on agricultural Distress. By a Country Gentleman. London, 1823.

Erskine, Thos., Lord : A Letter to the Proprietors and Occupiers of Land. London, 1823.

Wright, John : Remarks on the erroneous Opinions which led to the new Corn Law. London, 1823.

Monopoly unmasked, and shown to be the primary Cause of Pauperism and agricultural Distress. London, 1823.

A Postscript to Observations on the present agricultural and national Distress ; addressed to a Noble Lord. By Vindex. London, 1823.

Low, David : Observations on the present State of landed Property, and on the Prospects of the Landholder and the Farmer. Edinburgh, 1823.

Charley, Edwood : A Plan for the Regulation of the Prices of Corn, and for the Prevention of Scarcity. London, 1823.

Hays, John : Observations on the existing Corn Laws. London, 1824.

Rooke, John : An Inquiry into the Principles of national Wealth. Edinburgh, 1824.

An Essay on the Rent of Land. Edinburgh, 1825.

Whitmore, Wolryche : Substance of a Speech delivered in the House of Commons on Apr. 28th, 1825. London, 1825.

The Corn Question ; in a Letter addressed to the Right Hon. W. Huskisson, by one of the proscribed Class. London, 1825.

Letters on the Abuses and Defects of the existing Corn Laws. By a practical Observer. London, 1825.

Low, David : Letter to a Member of Parliament, on the contemplated Changes in the Corn Laws. Edinburgh, 1825.

A Collection of conflicting Opinions upon the Corn Question. London, 1825.

Joplin, T. : Views on the Currency : in which the Connexion between Corn and Currency is shown, etc. London, 1826.

A Compendium of the Laws passed from Time to Time, for regulating and restricting the Importation, Exportation and Consumption of Foreign Corn, from the Year 1660. London, 1826.

Brown, Wm. Keer: A Letter to the Right Honourable George Canning, M.P., relative to a Free Trade in Corn in Great Britain. Second edition. London, 1826.

Higgins, Godfrey: An Address to the Houses of Lords and Commons, in Defence of the Corn Laws. London, 1826.

Whitmore, W. W.: A Letter to the Electors of Bridgenorth upon the Corn Laws. London, 1826.

The Corn Laws considered in their Effect on the Labourer, Tenant, Landlord, etc. London, 1826.

Scott, Sir Claude: Some Brief Observations relative to the practical Effect of the Corn Laws. London, 1826.

Ellman, John: A Letter on the Corn Laws, addressed to the Legislature, showing the Amount of Duty necessary for agricultural Protection; containing also Mr. Huskisson's Letter to his Constituents at Chichester, in 1814. London, 1826.

Thoughts on the Corn Laws and on the novel Doctrines of Free Trade. Northampton, 1826.

M'Donnel, Alexander: Free Trade; or an Inquiry into the Expediency of the present Corn Laws. London, 1826.

Cheap Corn best for Farmers, proved in a Letter to George Holme Summer, Esq., M.P. By one of his Constituents. London, 1826.

Stanhope, Earl: Letter on the Corn Laws. London, 1826.

Wilson, Robert: A Disquisition on the Corn Laws. Hawick, 1826.

An Apology for the Corn Laws; or, high Wages and cheap Bread incompatible By a Country Curate. London, 1826.

Jacob, William: Report on the Trade in foreign Corn, and on the Agriculture of the North of Europe. London, 1826.

West, Sir Edward: Price of Corn and Wages of Labour, etc. London, 1826.

Wyatt, J.: Observations on the Question of the Corn Laws and Free Trade. London, 1826.

A Few Words to the Agricultural Committee of either House on the present Crisis. London, 1826.

A Letter to James John Farquharson, Esq., on the Subject of the late Meeting at Blandford, Dorset, on the Corn Laws. London, 1826.

Letter to a Noble Lord in Administration, on the present distressed State of the Country. By a calm Observer. London, 1826.

Observations addressed to the Shipping, the Agricultural, and the Commercial Interests, on the Impolicy of the Free Trade System pursued by his Majesty's Ministers. Newcastle, 1826.

Protest on the Subject of the Measures now impending in Parliament in Relation to the Corn Laws; entered against the second Reading of a Bill. London, 1826.

Blain, Henry: A Letter to the Earl of Liverpool, on the Revision of the Corn Laws, with a Suggestion for their Modification. London, 1826.

Brown, Wm. Keer: Three Letters to the Editor of the Maidstone Gazette, relative to a Free Trade in Corn. London, 1826.

Atherley, E. G.: A Letter to the Earl of Liverpool, showing that the Objections which are made to the Admission of Foreign Corn, are either totally unsound, or may be easily obviated. London, 1826.

The Iniquity of the Landholders, the Mistakes of the Farmers, and the Folly and mischievous Consequences . . . in Regard to the Corn Laws. London, 1826.

Court, Major M. H.: Illustration of Theory and Facts, giving a Solution of the Intricacies of the Corn Question. London, 1826.

Court, Major M. H.: Theory and Facts in Proof, that the Laws for the Imposition of Tithes are attended with the most calamitous Consequences to the Country, etc. London, 1826.

Cayley, Edward: Corn, Trade, Wages and Rent; or Observations on the leading Circumstances of the present financial Crisis. Second edition. London, 1827.

Stanhope, Earl: Letter on the proposed Alteration of the Corn Laws. London, 1827.

Fletcher, M.: Reflexions on the Causes which influence the Price of Corn. London, 1827.

Corrected Report of the Speech delivered by the Right Hon. George Canning, in the House of Commons, March 1st, 1827, on the Corn Laws. London, 1827.

Bramston, Thomas Gardiner, Esq.: The Principle of the Corn Laws vindicated London, 1827.

Cooke, Layton: Practical Observations on the Importation of Foreign Corn, under a graduated Scale of Duty. London, 1827. Second edition.

Hints to Landlords and Tenants in the Neighbourhood of Doncaster. By a Farmer. Doncaster, 1827.

The Case of the landed Interest fairly stated, in a Letter to the Hon. George Winn, M.P. By a Land Agent. Dec., 1826. London, 1827.

Thoughts on the Policy of the proposed Alteration of the Corn Laws. London, 1827.

Burton, Nathaniel: A Petition with seasonable Advice, to the Members of the new Parliament. London, 1827.

Bennett, John, Esq., M.P.: The national Interest considered ; or, the relative Importance of Agriculture and foreign Trade. London, 1827. Second edition.

The Apology of an English Landowner, addressed to the landed Proprietors in the County of Oxford. Oxford, 1827.

Cedric : The Distribution of the national Wealth ; Corn Laws and Restrictions in General. London, 1827.

The High Price of Bread shown to be the Result of commercial Prosperity, not the Cause of national Distress ; and the Dangers of a Free Trade in Corn pointed out. By a warning Voice. London, 1827.

Second Letter to the Right Hon. William Huskisson, on the Corn Laws. London, 1827.

Observations on the Corn Laws, addressed to W. W. Whitmore, Esq., M.P., in Consequence of his Letter to the Electors of Bridgenorth. London, 1827.

Observations on the Corn Laws. By Atticus. London, 1827.

Wyatt, Harvey : An Address to the Owners and Occupiers of Land on the Importance of an adequate Protection to Agriculture. London, 1827.

Gutteridge, William : The new Tables for the Regulation of the Corn Trade. London, 1827.

The Trial of the English Farmer. By a Farmer. London, 1827.

Remarks on the respective Interests of Land and Trade, as mutually concerned in maintaining Restrictions on the Importation of Foreign Corn. London, 1827.

Report by the Lords' Select Committee appointed to inquire into the Prices at which foreign Corn may be shipped in foreign Ports ; the Quantity of such Corn, and the Price at which such Grain can be imported into this Country. 1827.

Graham, Sir James : Corn and Currency ; in an Address to the Landowners. London, 1828.

Rooke, John : Free Trade in Corn the real Interest of the Landlord, and the true Policy of the State. London, 1828.

Thompson : Catechism on the Corn Laws. London, 1828. Fourth edition.

Redesdale, Lord : Observations upon the Importation of foreign Corn : with the Resolutions moved by Lord Redesdale in the House of Lords, Mar. 29th, 1827, etc. London, 1828.

Jacob, William : Tracts relating to the Corn Trade and Corn Laws. London, 1828.

Sawbridge, H. B. : A Letter on Restrictions and Fetters in Trade. London, 1828.

A Letter to Sir James Graham, Bart., M.P. . . . in Reply to certain Positions contained in a Pamphlet entitled " Free Trade in Corn the real Interest of the Landlord." London, 1828.

An Essay on political Economy : showing in what way Fluctuations in the Price of Corn may be prevented. London, 1828.

A Refutation of a Catechism on the Corn Laws, by a Cumberland Farmer. London, 1829.

Tooke, Thomas : On the Currency in Connexion with the Corn Trade, and on the Corn Laws. Second edition. London, 1829.

An entire new Plan for Corn Laws calculated not only to secure to the People a cheap Loaf, but also to pay a Part of the Taxes of the Empire. London, 1829.

On the distressed State of the Country. By a Merchant. London, 1830.

Scrope, G. Poulett : The common Cause of the Landlord, Tenant and Labourer, and the common Cure of their Complaint in a Letter to the Agriculturists of the South of England.

Speech of C. Poulett Thomson, Esq., in the House of Commons, on March 26th, 1830. London, 1830.

Crewdson, Thomas : An Inquiry into the Effect of the Corn Laws on the Prosperity of Great Britain and Ireland. London, 1830.

Swanwick, Edward : The Doings of the Corn Law. London, 1830.

By Ebenezer Elliot : Corn Law Rhymes. Third edition. London, 1831.

Speech of the late Henry Hunt, Esq., Sept. 15th, 1831. Manchester, 1831.

Torrens, R. Esq., M.P. : Address to the Farmers of the United Kingdom, on the low Rates of Profit in Agriculture and in Trade. London, 1831.

Cayley, E. S. : A Letter to the Right Hon. Lord Viscount Milton. London, 1831.

Davis, Hewitt : On foreign Corn Importation. London, 1831.

Mundell, Alexander, Esq. : The necessary Operations of the Corn Laws. Second edition. London, 1831.

A Letter to the Right Hon. Earl Grey, on his Speech in Favour of the Corn Laws. By an old Farmer. London, 1831.

Hall, Geo. Webb : Letter to the Right Hon. Viscount Milton ; being a Review of the various Sources of National Wealth, and a Reply to the recent Publication of his Lordship against the Corn Laws. London, 1832.

Crombie, The Rev. Alexander : A Letter to Lieut. Col. Torrens, M.P., in answer to his Address to the Farmers of the United Kingdom. London, 1832.

General Remarks of the State of the Poor, and Poor Laws, and the Circumstances affecting their condition. London, 1832.

Milton, Viscount : Address to the Landowners of England, on the Corn Laws. Fifth edition. London, 1832.

Observations on the Corn Laws, addressed to the Agriculturists by one of Themselves, and a sincere Friend to Agriculture. Abingdon, 1832.

Lube, D. G. : Argument against the gold Standard. London, 1832.

On the evil Effects of the Corn Laws ; upon the Labourers, Tradesmen, Merchants, Fundholders and Agriculturists. By a Farmer's Son. London, 1832.

Prentice, D. : Policy of a Free Trade in Corn, accompanied by a Measure for preventing any consequent Change in the Value of the Currency. Glasgow, 1832.

Appeal of the Labourers to the Landowners of England. London, 1832.

Thirlwall, T. W. : The Effect of the Repeal of the Corn Laws. London, 1832.

Barton, John : An Inquiry into the Expediency of the existing Restrictions on the Importation of foreign Corn ; with Observations on the present social and political Prospects of Great Britain. London, 1833.

Higgins, Godfrey : Addresses, etc. Doncaster, 1833.

Monck, Charles Atticus : An Address to the agricultural Classes of Great Britain, on the Evils which are the Consequence of restricting the Importation of foreign Corn. London, 1833.

Oswald, Richard Alexander : Remarks on the Corn Laws. London, 1833.

Parker, George : Letter to Viscount Milton, containing Remarks on his Lordship's Address to the Landowners of England on the Corn Laws. Doncaster, 1833.

Practical Remarks on the Corn Laws as viewed in connexion with the Corn Trade. By a Merchant. London, 1833.

The Reason for protecting home Trade ; or, the Principle of Free Trade refuted. Wm. Atkinson. London, 1833.

Coghlan, Francis : A Letter to the Farmers of England on the Tendency of the Corn Laws. London, 1833.

Tax on Capital, and fixed Duty on Corn. London, 1833.

The Speech of Richard Moorsom, Esq., Dec. 11th, 1832, the Day of the Nomination of a Burgess to represent the Borough of Whitby in Parliament. Whitby, 1833.

Report from the Select Committee appointed to inquire into the present State of Agriculture and Persons employed in Agriculture, in the United Kingdom, 1833.

Wyatt, Harvey : Considerations on the present State of the different Classes of the Landed Interest. London, 1834.

A Form of Petition to the upper House, against any Alteration of the Corn Law, recommended to the general Adoption of the Country at large, but more especially to Agriculturists, Farmers, Labourers, and the common People in General. London, 1834. Second edition.

On the Corn Laws. By an Essex Farmer. London, 1834.

H. B. T. (J. D. Hume) : Letters on the Corn Laws and on the Rights of the working Classes. London, 1834.

A Letter to Earl Fitzwilliam on the Corn Laws. By J. R. T. London, 1834.

A Reply to a Pamphlet lately published by Wm. Cobbett. By Jacobus. London, 1834.

Facts for the Repealers. Dublin, 1834.

Gisborne, T., Esq., M.P. : An Address to the Electors of North Derbyshire. London, 1834.

Bell, David : A Letter to Lord Althorp on the Subjects of a Repeal of the Corn Laws, etc. Second edition. London, 1834.

A Clue to the Cause of dear Bread and fallen Rents. By a landed Proprietor. London, 1834.

Report from the Select Committee appointed to inquire into the present Practices of selling Corn throughout the United Kingdom, with a View to the better Regulation thereof, 1834.

Cheap Corn ; but no Bread ; or, the Results of a free Corn Trade. London, 1835.

The warehousing System. London, 1835.

Fitzwilliam, Earl : A second Address to the Landowners of England on the Corn Laws. Second edition. London, 1835.

Western, Lord : A Letter to the President and Members of the Chelmsford agricultural Society, upon the Causes of the distressed State of the agricultural Classes of the United Kingdom of Great Britain and Ireland. Brighton 1835.

Lord Western's second Letter to the President and Members of the Chelmsford and Essex agricultural Society. Bath, 1835.

A Letter to T. Gisborne, Esq., in reply to his Address to the Electors of North Derbyshire, on the present Crisis. By a Yorkshireman. Uttoxeter, 1835.

Medley, William, Esq. : A Second Address to the Agriculturists of the County of Bucks. London, 1835.

Report from the Select Committee appointed to inquire into the present State of the Trade in Corn between the Channel Islands and the United Kingdom, 1835.

Three Reports from the Select Committee appointed to inquire into the State of Agriculture, and into the Causes and Extent of the Distress which still presses upon some important Branches thereof, 1836.

Lefevre, Charles Shaw : Remarks on the present State of Agriculture. London, 1836.

Cayley, E. S. : A Letter to H. Handley, Esq., M.P.—In answer to Mr. Shaw Lefevre's Pamphlet. London, 1836.

Report by the Lord's Select Committee appointed to inquire into the State of Agriculture, and into the Causes and Extent of the Distress which still presses upon some important Branches thereof, 1837.

Blacker, William : Review of Charles Shaw Lefevre, Esq.'s Letter to his Constituents, as Chairman of the Select Committee appointed to inquire into the present State of Agriculture. London, 1837.

State and Prospects of British Agriculture : being a Compendium of the Evidence given before a Committee of the House of Commons appointed in 1836 to inquire into agricultural Distress. By a Member of Parliament. London, 1837.

Report of the Committee of the Cambridgeshire and Isle of Ely Farmers' Association, upon the State of Agriculture : deduced from the Evidence laid before the two Houses of Parliament, during the Session of 1836. Cambridge, 1837.

Carmichael, James : Review of the Evidence taken before the Select Committee of the House of Commons on agricultural Distress, 1836. Edinburgh and London, 1838.

Mr. Paulton's Lectures on the Corn Laws. London, 1838.

The Injury inflicted upon the People by the Corn Laws. New Brentford, 1838.

The Speeches of Villiers, Molesworth and Chandos on March 15th, 1838. London, 1838.

The Corn Laws. An authentic Report in the Manchester Chamber of Commerce, on the destructive Effects of the Corn Laws upon the Trade and Manufactures of the Country. London, 1839.

Wilson, James : Influences of the Corn Laws, as affecting all Classes of the Community, and particularly the Landed Interests. London, 1839.

Dialogue on the Corn Laws. (The Landlords to the Tradesmen. (An Address.)). Broadway (Worcestershire), 1839.

Whitmore, W. W. : A Letter on the Corn Laws to the Manchester Chamber of Commerce. London, 1839.

Whitmore, W. W. : A second Letter on the Corn Laws, to the Manchester Chamber of Commerce. Second edition. London, 1839.

Speech of the Right Honourable Sir Robert Peel, Bart., on the Corn Laws. London, 1839.

Lord Brougham's Speech in the House of Lords, on Feb. 19th, 1839, on the Corn Laws.

Ashpitol, Arthur : A few Facts on the Corn Laws, defending the agricultural Interest. London, 1839.

Opinions of Sir Robert Peel and Sir James Graham on the Corn Laws in 1839.

Fox, W. J. : Reports of Lectures delivered at the Chapel in South Place, Finsbury. London, 1839.

Fitzwilliam, Earl : Third Address to the Landowners of England, on the Corn Laws. London, 1839.

The Evidence of James Deacon Hume, Esq., upon the Corn Laws, before the Committee of the House of Commons on the import Duties in 1839.

Argument for the general Relief of the Country from Taxation, and eventually from the Corn Laws, by an Assessment on Property. London, 1839.

Lennard, Thomas Barrett : An Address . . . on the Corn Laws. London, 1839.

An Address to the People of the United Kingdom on the Corn Laws. By J. D. C. London, 1839.

Substance of the Speech of Viscount Howick on the Corn Laws. Mar. 13th, 1839.

Porter, G. R. : The Effect of Restrictions on the Importation of Corn, considered with reference to Landowners, Farmers and Labourers. London, 1839.

Monro, David : " Landlords' Rents " and " Tenants' Profits." London, 1839.

Western, Right Hon. Lord : The Maintenance of the Corn Laws essential to the general Prosperity of the Empire. London, 1839.

Westhead, J. P. : A Letter to the Right Honourable Sir Robert Peel, Bart., on the Corn Laws. London, 1839.

Manufacturers and Corn Growers. A Letter to the Public. London, 1839.

Gladstone, John : The Repeal of the Corn Laws, with its probable Consequences. 1839.

Letter to the Duke of Buckingham, on the Corn Laws. By a practical Farmer. London, 1839.

Atkinson, William : The Corn Laws : or, How stands the Question ? London, 1839.

Bell, John : A Vindication of the Rights of British Landowners, Farmers and Labourers, etc. London, 1839.

Torrens, R. Three Letters to the Marquis of Chandos, on the Effects of the Corn Laws. London, 1839.

Thompson, Henry : Free Trade ruinous to England. London, 1839.

The late commercial Crisis ; being a Retrospect of the Years 1836 to 1838 : with Tables . . . for the Abolition of the Corn Laws. Glasgow, 1839.

The Corn Laws considered by " Common-Sense." London, 1839.

Moreton, The Hon. A. H. : Thoughts on the Corn Laws addressed to the working Classes of the County of Gloucester. London, 1839.

Blake, Sir Francis : The House of Lords, the People's Charter, and the Corn Laws. London, 1839.

Thompson, T. P. : Corn-Law Fallacies, with the Answers. Second edition. London, 1839. (From the " Sun.")

Senior's Letters on the Corn Laws. By a Member of the Temple. London, 1839.

Hunter, David : The Corn Law Question shortly investigated. Edinburgh, 1839.

Broadhurst, John, Esq. : Reasons for not repealing the Corn Laws. London, 1839.

Holland, G. Calvert : An Exposition of Corn Law repealing Fallacies and Inconsistencies. London, 1840.

Salomons, David : Reflections on the Operation of the present Scale of Duty for regulating the Importation of foreign Corn. London, 1840.

Jevons, Thomas : The Prosperity of the Landholders not dependent on the Corn Laws. London, 1840.

Pennington, James : A Letter to Kirkman Finlay, Esq., on the Importation of foreign Corn. London, 1840.

The Corn Laws a national evil. . . . By a member of an Anti-Corn Law Association, in the Hundred of Bassetlaw. J. Atkinson. Chesterfield (1840).

Half an ounce of Advice to the labouring Classes on the Repeal of the Corn Laws. By a plain Dealer. Second edition. R. Hatley. Doncaster (1840).

Kell, Rev. Edmund : The injurious Effects of the Corn Laws, on all Classes of the Community, including the Farmer and the Landowner. London, 1840.

Farr, Rev. Thomas : A Remedy for the Distress of the Nation. London, 1840.

Address of the Metropolitan Anti-Corn Law Association. London, 1840.

Tyrconnell, Earl : An Address to the People of the United Kingdom, on the Corn Laws. Richmond, 1840.

The Speeches at a public Meeting held in the Guildhall, Doncaster, on the Corn Laws, on Feb. 22nd, 1840. Leeds, 1840.

Corn Laws. The Nature and Effects of these oppressive Statutes. Edinburgh, 1840.

Thorneycroft, G. B. : The Substance of two Speeches on the Corn Laws. Wolverhampton, 1840.

Thorneycroft, G. B. : Supplementary Facts and Remarks, connected with the Corn Laws. Wolverhampton, 1840.

Atkinson, William : Mr. Huskisson, Free Trade and the Corn Laws. London, 1840.

Rudall, Rev. Edward : The Complaints of the Manufacturers against the Corn Laws considered and answered. Launceston, 1840.

A Letter to the Rev. Edmund Kell, A.M., occasioned by his Lecture advocating the Repeal of the Corn Laws. London, 1840.

Lingard, John : On the Propriety and Justice of the Corn Laws, as now regulated. Second edition. London, 1840.

Hind, Thomas : A Plan for the equitable Adjustment of the Corn Laws. London, 1840.

Boucherett, Ayscoghe, Esq. : A few Observations on Corn, Currency, etc. London, 1840.

Report from the Select Committee appointed to inquire under what restrictions it might be expedient to permit Flour to be manufactured in Bond, 1840.

Renny, James H. : Reflections upon the Corn Laws, etc. London, 1841.

An Essay on Free Trade. By F. C. London, 1841.

McCulloch, J. R. : Statements illustrative of the Policy and probable Consequences of the proposed Repeal of the existing Corn Laws and the Imposition in their Stead of a moderate Fixed Duty on foreign Corn when entered for Consumption. London, 1841.

Thornton, Henry : Historical Summary of the Corn Laws. London, 1841.

Corn and Consols. A Table showing the annual average Prices of Wheat, Barley and Oats, per quarter, and the mean Price of the three per cent. Consols for fifty-one Years (1790–1840). Second edition. London, 1841.

Spencer, Rev. Thomas : The Corn Laws and the national Debt : or, the Parson's dream and the Queen's speech. By a Somerset Clergyman. London, 1841.

A Supplement to Lord Western's Letter to Lord John Russell, upon Corn Laws and commercial Distress, with a brief Review of the Reports of the Manchester Chamber of Commerce, of Dec., 1839, and March, 1841. London, 1841.

Holland, G. Calvert : Letter to J. R. M'Culloch, Esq., in answer to his Statements on the Corn Laws. London, 1841.

Y

Mr. M'Culloch's Pamphlet on the Corn Laws critically Analysed. London, 1841.

Extracts from the Works of Col. T. Perronet Thompson.   1841.

Cheap Bread and its Consequences.   Ninth edition.   London, 1841.

Young, Rev. J. : The Corn Laws, unjust and injurious : an Address to the People of Great Britain.   London, 1841.

Second Report of the Business Committee of the Metropolitan Anti-Corn Law Association.   March 1st, 1841.   London, 1841.

Fernley, J. D. : A Letter to F. A. Phillips, Esq., on his Remarks on the Corn Laws. Stockport, 1841.

The Many sacrificed to the Few ; proved by the Effects. of the food Monopoly. London, 1841.

Address of the Metropolitan Anti-Corn Law Association, to the Public.   London, 1841.

Corn and Cotton : with a Postscript on Distress.   By one of the People.   London, 1841 (?).

The Farmer's Case, shown from the Evidence of the following Agriculturists. London, 1841.

Remarks on the cost Price of producing Wheat in foreign Countries, and matters therewith connected.   By a Merchant.   London, 1841.

Robinson, John : The whole Scheme of the Corn Law Abolitionists unmasked. London, 1841.

Remarks on the Bread Tax.   By anti-Gulliver.   Leeds, 1841.

An Appeal to the Tradesmen of Great Britain on cheap Food and brisk Trade. London, 1841.

A Letter to the Queen in behalf of her suffering People.   By the poor man's Friend.   London, 1841.

Letter to his Grace, the Duke of Wellington, on the Corn Laws.   By a Forfar-shire Merchant.   Edinburgh, 1841.

A religious and moral View of the Corn Laws.   London, 1841.

Ruinous Prices periodically produced by the Sliding Scale.   London, 1841.

Is cheap or dear Bread best for the poor Man ?   London, 1841.

Bermingham, Thomas : A Letter on the Corn Laws.   Dublin, 1841.

Report of the . . . Chamber of Commerce and Manufactures at Manchester, on the injurious Effects of Restrictions on Trade.   March 11th, 1841.   London, 1841.

Kinnear, John : Protection to Landlords : what it has done for their Tenants and what will be done for them by Free Trade.   Edinburgh, 1841.

Appeal to Tradesmen in Town and Country.   By one of themselves.   London, 1841.

Noel, Hon. and Rev. Baptist W. : A plea for the Poor.   London, 1841.

Supplement to the " Plea for the Poor."   London, 1841.

Fifty searching Questions addressed to the Hon. and Rev. Baptist W. Noel, and all other Corn Law Repealers.   By a Clergyman.   London, 1841.

Sulley, R. : The Fallacies of the Protective System exposed.   Manchester, 1841.

The Theory and Practice of the Sliding Scale.   By one of the Corn Trade.   London 1841.

Our daily Bread.   London, 1841.

An historical Examination of the Corn Laws.   London, 1841.

Curtis, John : America and the Corn Laws.   Manchester, 1841.

Daily Bread ; or Taxation without Representation.   By one of the Millions. London, 1841.

The Corn Laws, considered in their Origin, Progress and Results.   London, 1841.

Dalbiac, Sir James Charles : A few Words on the Corn Laws.   London, 1841.

Hall, Geo. Webb : The Connexion between Landlord and Tenant, and Tenant and Labourer.   London, 1841.

Mackenzie, The Right Honourable Holt : Notes addressed to Mr. Pennington, on his Pamphlet on the Importation of foreign Corn.   London, 1841.

Morse, Arthur : A Reply to the Statements of the Society for the Protection of Agriculture.   Swaffham, 1841.

Reply to Tait's Magazine and Mr. Cobden.   Glasgow, 1841.

Thompson, Geo. : Lectures, delivered before the Ladies of Manchester.   Nov. 30th, 1841.   Manchester.

Whitmore, W. W., Esq.: A Letter to the Agriculturists of the County of Salop. June 5th, 1841. Second edition. London.

Whitmore, W. W.: A second Letter to the Agriculturists of the County of Salop. August 5th, 1841. London.

Holland, G. Calvert: Suggestions towards improving the present System of Corn Laws. London, 1841.

Holland, G. Calvert: An Analysis of the Address of F. H. Fawkes, Esq., to the Landowners of England. Second edition. London, 1841 (?).

Thornton, William T.: The True Consequences of the Repeal of the Corn Laws. London, 1841.

James, G. P. R.: Some Remarks on the Corn Laws . . . in a Letter to Col. Charles Wyndham, M.P. London, 1841.

Observations on the Corn Law, by Colonel W. F. P. Napier, addressed to Lord Ashley. Second edition. London, 1841.

Address of George Thompson, Esq., before the Conference of Ministers. August 1841. Manchester.

Morris, A. J.: The moral and religious Bearings on the Corn Law. Lecture, August 22nd, 1841. Manchester, 1841.

Report of the Conference of Ministers of all Denominations on the Corn Laws. Held in Manchester, Aug. 17th, 18th, 19th and 20th, 1841. Manchester and London, 1841.

Farr, Rev. Thomas: The principal Difficulties of the Sliding Scale removed. London, 1841.

Buchanan, James, Esq.: Proposed Measure for Admission of Grain from all Countries into Great Britain, addressed to his Grace the Duke of Wellington. New York, 1841.

Action of the Corn Laws, and of the other Provision Laws, considered on the Principles of a sound political Economy and of common Sense. London, 1841.

Facts for the agricultural and manufacturing Classes in contradistinction to the fallacious Doctrines of " No Corn Laws." By a Tradesman. Manchester, 1841.

A Letter on the Operation of the proposed Reduction of Duty upon imported Wheat. By Candidus. London, 1841.

Blain, Henry: A Letter to Sir Robert Peel, exhibiting the Defects of the present Corn Law. London, 1841.

Thoughts on the Corn Laws. Third edition. London, 1841.

The present and future Prospects of the Country considered. By a Citizen. London, 1841.

Six Anti-Corn Law Fallacies. By a Merchant. 1841 (?).

The Three Prize Essays on Agriculture and the Corn Law. (By G. Hope, A. Morse and W. R. Greg.) Published by the National Anti-Corn Law League Manchester. London, 1842.

O'Connell, Daniel: Observations on Corn Laws, on political Pravity and Ingratitude. . . . A meek and modest Reply to the second Letter of Earl Shrewsbury, Waterford and Wexford, etc. Dublin, 1842.

Neate, Charles: Summary of Debates and Proceedings in Parliament relating to the Corn Laws, from 1812–1840. London, 1842.

Hubbard, John Gellibrand: Vindication of a Fixed Duty on Corn. London, 1842.

Whystock, Richard: An Inquiry into the Cause of the present Depression of Trade and a Remedy proposed. London, 1842.

The Bazaar Gazette. (Published in connexion with the National Anti-Corn Law Bazaar for six Days beginning Jan. 31st, 1842.)

A Reply to the Prize Essays of the Anti-Corn Law League, by a Lincolnshire Landowner. Painter: London 1842 (?).

Authorities against the Corn Laws. Manchester (1842).

Facts for Farmers. (Issued by the National Anti-Corn Law League.) Manchester 1842 (?).

An Address to Farmers, on the Way in which their Families are to be provided for. (Issued by the National Anti-Corn Law League.) Manchester, (1842)

The Anti-Corn Law League to the Duke of Wellington. (A brief Statement of their Case.) Advertiser Officer. Manchester, 1842.

An Argument for Dishonesty, conducted in the Manner of the Corn Law Advocates Manchester, 1842.

Anti-Corn Law Tract : No. 1. A Plea for the total and immediate Repeal of the Corn Laws. Fourth edition. London, 1842.

Anti-Corn Law Tract : No. 2. Sir Robert Peel's " Burdens on Land." London, 1842.

Farewell Address of Geo. Thompson, Esq., to the National Anti-Corn Law League, Delivered Oct. 27th, 1842. Manchester, 1842.

The Anti-Bread Tax Almanack, for 1842. London, 1842.

Nine Letters on the Corn Laws. London, 1842.

Speech of W. Torrens M'Culloch, Esq., to the National Anti-Corn Law League, Dec. 1st, 1842.

Gisborne, Thos., Junior : Letter to the Council of the Anti-Corn Law League. Manchester, 1842.

Murray, John : A Letter to the President and Members of the Birmingham Anti-Corn Law Association on the corn and Provision Laws. Manchester, 1842.

Jenkyn, Rev. T. W. : Corn Laws and Clergy : A Letter to Right Hon. Henry Lord Brougham. Manchester, 1842.

Somerville, Rev. Andrew : Free Trade in Corn and other Commodities. Glasgow, 1842.

Speech of Lord John Russell on the Corn Laws. House of Commons, February 14th, 1842. London, 1842.

The Constitutional Right to a Revision of the Land-Tax. London, 1842.

Greg, W. R. : Dialogue on the Corn Laws between a Gentleman and a Farmer. Lancaster, 1842.

O'Connell, Daniel : Observations on Corn Laws. Dublin, 1842.

The Report of the Statistical Committee appointed by the Anti-Corn Law Conference, held in London on March 8-12th, 1842. London, 1842.

The Speech of W. B. Ferrand, M.P., in the House of Commons, on Feb. 24th, 1842. London, 1842.

Observations on the proposed Measure for the regulation of the Corn Trade. London, 1842.

A Plea for the English Farmer and the English Peasantry. London, 1842.

A Letter addressed to the Lord Bishop of Chester on the Corn Laws. By a Layman. London, 1842.

Corn Law Opposition detected and exposed. By a plain Man. London, 1842.

Massie, Rev. J. W. : Speech, March 22nd, 1842. Manchester.

Giles, Rev. J. E. : The Corn Laws. Speech to the National Anti-Corn Law League. Dec. 1st, 1842.

Thompson, Geo. : Speech at the great Anti-Corn Law Conference, July 6th, 1842. Manchester, 1842.

Campbell, John : An Examination of the Corn and Provision Laws, from their first Enactment to the present Time. Manchester, 1842 (?).

Corn Laws. Selections from Mrs. London's Philanthropic Economy. Manchester, 1842 (?).

Nugent, Lord : A Letter to the Chairman of the Committee of the Anti-Corn Law League of England. London, 1842.

Platt, J. C. : History of the Corn Laws. London, 1842.

The Corn Laws condemned on account of their Injustice and immoral Tendency, by upwards of five hundred Ministers, of different Denominations, resident in Scotland. Edinburgh, 1842.

Greg, Robert Hyde : A Letter to the Right Hon. Henry Labouchere, on the Pressure of the Corn Laws and Sliding Scale. London, 1842.

A Letter intended for the Manchester Guardian, now respectfully recommended to the earnest Perusal of the Ladies of the Anti-Corn Law League. By a Fellow-Townsman. Manchester, 1842.

Bain, Donald : Letter to the Right Honourable Sir Robert Peel, Bart. Edinburgh, 1842.

Nevile, Rev. C. : The Sliding Scale or a Fixed Duty. Second edition. London, 1842.

Cooke, Layton : Observations upon the Construction and Operation of Duties on the Importation of foreign Corn. London, 1842.

Corn Law versus " The Wealth of Nations." Liverpool, 1842.

A Letter to . . . Baron Ashburton . . . on the Importance of the Corn and Flour Trade with England via the River St. Lawrence. New York, 1842.

Anti-Corn Law League ; Aristocracy defended. London, 1842.

A friendly Address to the Operatives of the manufacturing Districts. London, 1842.

Carmichael, James : Remarks on Mr. McCulloch's " Statement " illustrative of the Policy of a Fixed Duty on foreign Corn. Edinburgh and London, 1842.

A few Facts on the Corn Laws. By R.W.S. 1842.

A Letter to his Grace the Duke of Buckingham. By a practical Farmer and Corn Merchant. 1842.

Cory, Isaac Preston : Competition. London, 1842.

Report from the Select Committee appointed to consider the Expediency of renewing any of the Provisions of the Act, commonly called the Grinding Act, 1842.

Six Letters to the Right Hon. Sir Robert Peel, Bart. By a political Economist (T. C. Banfield). London, 1843.

Torrens, R. : A Letter to Nassau William Senior, Esq., in reply to the Article " Free Trade and Retaliation," in the Edinburgh Review, No. CLVII. London, 1843.

Torrens, R. : A Letter to Sir Robert Peel on the Condition of England and on the Means of removing the Causes of Distress. London, 1843.

Monteagle, Lord : The Consequences of the Sliding Scale examined and exposed, being the Substance of a Speech delivered in the House of Lords on Tuesday, March 14th, 1843. London, 1843.

Welford, Richard Griffiths : How will Free Trade in Corn affect the Farmer ? London, 1843.

A Counter-Plea for the Poor ; a Refutation of the Assertions of the Anti-Corn Law League, and the Hon. and Rev. Baptist W. Noel. By the poor man's Friend. London, 1843.

Wilson, James : The Cause of the present commercial Distress, and its Bearings on the Interests of Shipowners. A Speech delivered at the Free Trade Banquet, Liverpool, Jan. 31st, 1843. Liverpool, 1843.

Strictures on the Speech of Lord Ducie, on the Corn Laws, in the Form of a Letter, addressed to the Editor of the Mark Lane Express. London, 1843.

Almack, John, Jr. : Character, Motives and Proceedings of the Anti-Corn Law Leaguers, with a few general Remarks on the Consequences that would result from a Free Trade in Corn. London, 1843.

Things as they are and Things as they ought to be ; being a Report of the Committee, on the Cambridgeshire and Isle of Ely Farmer's Association. London, 1843.

Williams, Albert : The Law or the League ? Which ? A Letter to Robert Palmer, Esq., M.P. London, 1843.

Old England's Commerce. A Story illustrative of the Connexion between the Corn Law and the home and foreign Trade. London, 1843.

Ogle, Nathaniel : Direct or indirect Taxation ? London, 1843.

Hill, James : The Defeater defeated : Being a Refutation of Mr. Day's Pamphlet. London, 1843.

Corn v. Cotton. An Attempt to open the Case between the Manufacturers and the Landlords . . . inscribed to . . . the Duke of Buckingham by The . . . S.S.C. London, 1843.

" The Packet examined," being a Reply to the Publication of the Anti-Corn Law League. . . . By Rurigina. 1843.

Bain, Donald : The egregious and dangerous Fallacies of the Anti-Corn Law League ; or the Protection of Agriculture not a Question with Landlords, but for the whole Kingdom. Edinburgh, 1843.

A Letter intended for the Manchester Guardian, now respectfully recommended to the earnest Perusal of the Ladies of the Anti-Corn Law League. By a Fellow-Townsman. Second edition. Manchester, 1843.

Haughton, William : A Letter to the Right Honourable Sir Robert Peel, Bart., M.P., containing a Plan for a new Corn Law. London, 1843.

Baines, E. J. : Reasons in Favour of Free Trade in Corn and against a Fixed Duty. In three Letters to Lord John Russell. Leeds, 1843.

Harwood, Philip : Six Lectures on the Corn Law Monopoly and Free Trade London, 1843.

The Speech of W. B. Ferrand, Esq., M.P., in the House of Commons, February 13th, 1843, on Lord Howick's Motion upon the Distress of the Country. Second edition. London.

Bright, John, Esq., M.P. : Speech at the Nomination at Durham, July 24th, 1843. Manchester.

Corrected Report of Mr. Bright's Speech at the public Meeting, Wakefield, April 21st, 1843, Manchester.

Easby, John : Repeal ! or Sketches of the League, its Leaders, its Members and its Foes ! London, 1843.

Edwards, Dr. Henry : Address to Agriculturists and Others, in one of the rural Districts. London, 1843.

The West Kent Anti-Corn Law Magazine. January, 1843.

Heyworth, Lawrence : On the Corn Laws and other legislative Restriction. Sixth edition. Manchester, 1843.

On the Corn Laws. London, 1843.

White, John, A.M. : England and Her Interests : The " Times " and the Government and the Anti-Corn Law League considered. London, 1843.

Hubback, Joseph : A Letter on the Corn Laws. Second edition. Liverpool, 1843.

Gladstone, John : A Review of Mr. Cobden's Corn Politics. London, 1843.

Timely Hints addressed to the Landlords and Tenantry . . . by their " Country Cousins." London, 1843.

Reflections on the Designs and possible Consequences of the Anti-Corn Law League. By the Editor of the Circular to Bankers. London, 1843.

An Address to the People of England showing the Fallacy, Impolicy and Self-Interest of the Anti-Corn Law League. By a reflecting Man. London, 1843.

A Free Trade in Corn Ruin to the Citizens as well as the Landed Interest. . . In three Debates as debated between John and James, Citizens of Edinburgh. Second edition. Edinburgh, 1843.

The Speech of Mr. George Game Day at Huntingdon, June 17th, 1843. London, 1844.

The Speech of Mr. George Game Day, of St. Ives, at Huntingdon, Jan. 27th, 1844. London, 1844.

Reasons for supporting the Government and opposing the League ; being a Review of the Necessity for Laws of Protection to our national Industry. By a commercial Man. Hull, 1844.

The Speech of the Right Honourable Lord Monteagle, on moving for the Appointment of a Select Committee on the import Duties. House of Lords, June 13th, 1844. Extracted from Hansard, 1844.

Evans, Edward John : Wages. Observations on the connexion between Corn Law Repeal and the Price of Labour. London, 1844.

Williams, Albert : Great Facts concerning Free Trade and Free Trade Essays. London, 1844.

Smith, Edmund J. : Identity of Interest between Landlord, Tenant-Farmer, and Farm-Labourer as deduced from " Morton on Soils." London, 1844.

Heyworth, Lawrence : On the Corn Laws. Manchester, 1844.

Almack, J. J. : Cheap Bread and low Wages. London, 1844.

Cannon, William J. : The Effect the Repeal of the Corn Laws would have upon Prices and Rents. London and Cambridge, 1844.

Facts and Remarks on the Corn Laws, and the Objects of the Anti-Corn Law League. Newcastle-upon-Tyne, 1844.

An Appeal to Tradesmen in Town and Country. By one of themselves. London, 1844.

Harper, J. : League Fallacies : a Lecture, given at Thirsk, on Feb. 28th, 1844.

The Corn Laws, Free Trade, and Colonization considered : in a Letter to Richard Cobden. By a Manchester Man. London, 1844.

Report of the Speeches delivered at the Meeting of the Landowners and Farmers of the County of Durham, Feb. 20th, 1844. Durham, 1844.

Perversions and Fallacies of the Anti-Corn Law League, as embodied in Mr. Cobden's recent Speech at Jedburgh. Being a Series of three Letters addressed to the Editor of the Kelso Mail, by a border Farmer. Kelso, 1844.

Smith, Thomas Sharpe : On the Source and on the Relief of publick Distress in Great Britain. London, 1844.

Cayley, E. S. : Reasons for the Formation of the Agricultural Protection Society, addressed to the industrious Classes of the United Kingdom. London, 1844.

West, Edward : Second Letter to the Farmers of Dorsetshire on the Cause of Depression in the Prices of agricultural Produce. London, 1844.

Mr. George Game Day's Letter to Richard Cobden, Esq., M.P., March 27th, 1844. London.

Day, William : Incendiarism ! ! ! Who are the Instigators ? London, 1844.

The Speech of W. W. Sleigh, Esq., M.D., March 28th, 1844, exposing the sophisticated Arguments of the Anti-Corn Law League. London, 1844.

The Speech of George Head, Esq., at a Public Meeting held in Carlisle, on Saturday, Feb. 3rd, 1844. Second edition. London, 1844.

Alison, Archibald : Free Trade and Protection. Edinburgh and London, 1844.

Sharp, Joseph Budworth : The Anti-Corn Law League and the cotton Trade London, 1844.

Free Trade with reference to its Effects upon the operative Classes. By Humanitas. London, 1844.

To Artisans and Labourers. London, 1844.

An Essay showing the ruinous Effects which a Free Trade in Corn would have upon the Landlord, the Farmer, the Labourer, the Tradesman, the Fundholder, and the Community at Large. London, 1844.

Barton, John : The Influence of the Price of Corn on the Rate of Mortality. London, 1844 (?)

American Notions of Free Trade. London, 1844.

Substance of a Speech delivered by Mr. Hadden, Jun., at Aberdeen, March 15th, 1844. London.

An Answer from R. Baker of Writtle to Earl Ducie. London, 1844.

The Speech of Augustus Stafford O'Brien, Esq., in the House of Commons, June 26th, 1844. London and Edinburgh, 1844.

How much would the four-pound Loaf be lowered by the Repeal of the Corn Laws? London, 1844.

National Anti-Corn Law League Bazaar Gazette. 17 no J. Gadsby : London, 1845.

Bastiat, M. Fred. : Cobden et La Ligue. Paris, 1845.

Gaussen, Rev. A. : Remarks on improving the Condition of the agricultural Poor. Royston, 1845.

Andrews, H. G. : An Address to the Farmers of Great Britain, on the present State of the Corn Laws, and the Necessity of agricultural Protection. London, 1845.

Edwards, David Owen : A Proposal for an agrarian Endowment of the Population in lieu of the existing Poor Law, and Corn Law. Nov. 14th, 1845.

Speech of the Rev. James Aspinall, at the Great Free Trade Meeting, at Hull, Dec. 15th, 1845.

Lord Grey and Lord Palmerston, A Letter addressed to the Right Hon. T. B. Macaulay on occasion of his Letter to Mr. M'Farlane, from a Free Trader. London, 1846.

Our free trade Policy examined with respect to its real Bearing upon native Industry, our colonial System and the Institutions and ultimate Destinies of the Nation. By a Liverpool merchant. London, Liverpool, 1846.

Brief Considerations with reference to the Corn Laws, and on the Theory of Protection generally. London, 1846.

Drummond, Henry : Letter to the Bishop of Winchester on Free Trade. London, 1846.

Remarks on the Abolition of the protective System. Edinburgh, 1846 (?).

Blake, Barnett : Prize Essay, showing the Advantage of the Corn Law, for the purpose of producing a sufficient Quantity of Food for the Maintenance of the People. Chelmsford, 1846.

Morton, John, and Trimmer, Joshua : An Attempt to estimate the Effects of protecting Duties on the Profits of Agriculture. Sixth edition. London, 18 46

Morton, J., and Trimmer, Joshua : Supplement to an Attempt to estimate the Effects of protecting Duties on the Profits of Agriculture. London, 1846.

A few Words on the Corn Laws. By a Landowner. London, 1846.

Corn and Consistency. London, 1846.

Present Condition and future Prospects of the Country, in reference to Free Trade and its recent Application. By F.C. London, 1846.

Whitmore, W. W. : A third Letter to the Agriculturists of the County of Salop. Jan. 24th, 1846. London.

Hainworth, W. : Remarks on a Pamphlet by Mr. John Morton and Mr. Joshua Trimmer. London, 1846.

God's Laws versus Corn Laws. A Letter to his Grace the Archbishop of Canterbury. From a Dignitary of the English Church. London, 1846.

Corn Laws. Report of a Discussion after Vestry, in a rural Parish of Hampshire. London, 1846.

An Address on the Corn Laws. By a Protectionist. London, 1846.

Sir Robert Peel and the Corn Law Crisis. London, 1846.

Some Account of the Corn Laws and their Operation. Reprinted from " The Daily News " of Jan. 28th, 1846. London, 1846.

The Corn Laws Meeting of agricultural Labourers in North Wilts. From " Times " of Jan. 7th, 1846.

Nevile, Rev. Christopher : Corn and Currency in a Letter to A. Alison, Esq Second edition. London, 1846.

Miller, Hugh : The Tenants' true Quarrel. Edinburgh, 1846.

Butt, Isaac : Protection to home Industry. Dublin, 1846.

A few Words to the agricultural Classes by a Temple Man. London, 1846.

Popkins' Protest : addressed to the House of Lords. London, 1846.

Ward, WM. : Remarks on the Commercial Legislation of 1846. London, 1847.

Williams, Albert, Esq. : A Letter to Lord Geo. Bentinck, M.P. London, 1847.

Reply to the Quarterly Review. By the Author of the " Commercial Policy of Pitt and Peel." London, 1847.

Oastler, Richard : Free Trade " not proven," in seven Letters to the People of England. London, 1849.

Whitmore, W. W. : A few plain Thoughts on Free Trade as affecting Agriculture. Bridgenorth, 1849 (?).

Dunckley, Henry : The Glory and the Shame of Britain. London, 1849.

Blacker, William : Pro Corn Law Tracts. London, 1850.

Bain, Donald : The Use of Protection and the Objects of Protectionists. London, 1851.

Congreve, Richard : No Fixed Duty. London, 1851.

Dunckley, Henry : The Charter of the Nations, or, Free Trade and its Results. London, 1854.

In addition to the Parliamentary Reports which are listed with the pamphlets, he following official publications were used :

1. *The Journals of the House of Commons.*
2. *The Journals of the House of Lords.*
3. *Parliamentary History.*
4. *Parliamentary Debates.* (Referred to in the footnotes as *Hansard.*)
5. *The Public General Acts.*
6. *Reports from Committees of the House of Commons, 1803.*
7. *Historical Manuscripts Commission. Manuscripts of J. B. Fortescue, 9 vols.*

Besides these, numerous Parliamentary Papers and Blue Books, the most important of which was C.—8706, the Customs tariff of the United Kingdom from 1800 to 1897, were used.

In the British Record Office, the Home Office Papers were useful, especially for accounts of riots in different parts of the Kindgom during periods of scarcity.

In the British Museum, collections from the private papers of different statesmen were helpful. The Newcastle Papers, the Hardwicke Papers and the correspondence of Sir Robert Peel were especially full. The following manuscripts threw light on various phases of the Corn Law Question. The numbers after the following items refer to the British Museum Additional Manuscripts.

Papers relating to Corn riots in Penryn Co., Cornwall, 1737. 32,690.

Petitions from Dover to stop exportation, 1740. 32,693.

Proposals for a bill to prohibit export, 1757. 32,875.

Papers relating to the supply of Corn, 1758. 33,053.

Correspondence on the exportation, 1766. 32,977.

Memoir relating to the Corn supplies, 1800. 33,124.

Proposal of Rev. Pool, respecting the scarcity of corn, 1800. 33,124.

Correspondence on the proposed establishment of a grain committee, 1801. 29,234.

Hastings, Warren : Copy of a memorial on the high price of wheat, 1800 ; followed by a second paper on the same subject, 1801. 29,233 and 29,234.

Letters Relative to the Corn Laws, 1810. 35,648.

Letters Relative to the Corn Laws, 1845. 35,653.

Grain and Meal exported from Ireland to Great Britain, 1841-50. 35,653.

Plan for public granaries in 18th and 19th centuries. 29,210.

Correspondence of the Third Earl of Hardwicke on Agriculture and the Corn Laws ; 1795–1829. 35,700.

I was able to use the Townshend Papers, which were invaluable for the period around 1750, through the courtesy of Mr. Kashnor of the Museum Book Store, London.

The more important periodicals used were :

Annals of Agriculture, 1784 to 1815.
The Annual Register.
Anti-Corn Law Circular.
Anti-Bread Tax Circular.
The Banker's Circular.
Blackwood's Magazine.
Cobbett's Political Register.
Edinburgh Review.

Fortnightly Review.
The Gentleman's Magazine.
The League.
Quarterly Review. .
Westminster Review.
The Economic History Review.
The Economic Journal.

The Place Collection of Newspaper Clippings at Hendon, England, which belongs to the British Museum, contains extracts for the period 1813 to 1846, from the following papers :

Morning Chronicle.
Bolton Chronicle.
Leeds Mercury.
Leeds Intelligencer.
Weekly Dispatch.
Mechanics Weekly Journal.
Trades Newspaper.
Morning Herald.
Essex Herald.
Bell's Weekly Messenger.
The Statesmen.
The Sun.

The London Times.
The Glasgow Chronicle.
The Advertiser.
The Courier.
Shrewsbury Chronicle.
Weekly.
The Traveller.
Dublin Morning Post.
The Scotsman.
The New Times.
The Examiner.

SECONDARY AUTHORITIES

The following are the more important secondary works used or referred to in the narrative :

Armitage, Smith, G. : Free Trade and its Results. London, 1903.

Ashley, Sir William : The Economic Organization of England. Fourth impression. London, 1918.

Ashworth, Henry : Recollections of Richard Cobden, M.P., and The Anti-Corn Law League. London, 1876.

Barker, Arthur : The British Corn Trade from the Earliest Times to the Present Day. London, 1920.

Beer, M. : A History of British Socialism. Two vols. London, 1921.

Bland, Brown and Tawney : English Economic History Select Documents. London, 1914.

Bowden, Witt : Industrial Society in England towards the End of the Eighteenth Century. New York, 1925.

Bradley, Harriett : The Enclosures in England. New York, 1918.

Brisco, Norris : The Economic Policy of Robert Walpole. New York, 1907.

Brodrick, G. C. : English Land and Landlords. London, 1881.

Broomhall, George : Corn Trade Year Book, 1897, 1902, 1904, 1910, 1914. Liverpool.

Brown, Philip Anthony : The French Revolution in English History. London, 1918.
Buer, M. C. : Health, Wealth and Population in the Early Days of the Industrial Revolution. London, 1926.
Caird, Sir James : English Agriculture in 1850. London, 1852.
Cannan, Edwin : The Paper Pound of 1797–1821. London, 1919.
Cobden, Richard : Speeches on Questions of Public Policy. Edited by John Bright and J. E. T. Rogers. London, 1870.
Cunningham, W. : The Rise and Decline of the Free Trade Movement. Second edition. Cambridge, 1912.
Cunningham, W. : The Growth of English Industry and Commerce. Vol. 1, fifth edition, 1915 ; vol. 2, 1919 ; vol. 3, 1917. Cambridge.
Curtler, W. H. R. : A Short History of English Agriculture. Oxford, 1909.
Curtler, W. H. R. : The Enclosure and Distribution of our Land. Oxford, 1920.
Dalling and Bulwer, Henry, Lord : Sir Robert Peel. London, 1874.
Disraeli, Right Hon. B. : Lord George Bentinck. Ninth edition. London, 1874.
Ernle, Lord (R. E. Prothero) : English Farming Past and Present. Second edition. London, 1919.
Fay, C. R. : Life and Labour in the Nineteenth Century. 1920.
Fuchs, Carl Johannes : Der englische Getreidenhandel und seine Organisation. Jena, 1890.
Galpin, William F. : The Grain Supply of England during the Napoleonic period. 1925.
Garnier, Russell M. : History of the English Landed Interest. Two vols. London, 1892.
George, M. Dorothy : London Life in the XVIIIth Century. New York, 1925.
Gonner, E. C. K. : Common Land and Inclosure. London, 1912.
Gras, N. S. B. : The Evolution of the English Corn Market. Cambridge, 1915.
Green, F. E. : A History of the English Agricultural Labourer from 1870 to 1920 London, 1920.
Griffith, G. Talbot : Population Problems of the Age of Malthus. Cambridge, 1926.
Hammond, J. L., and Barbara : The Village Labourer, 1760–1832. London, 1920.
Hammond, J. L., and Barbara : The Town Labourer, 1760–1832. London, 1919.
Hammond, J. L., and Barbara : The Skilled Labourer, 1760–1832. London, 1920.
Hasbach, W. : A History of the English Agricultural Labourer. London, 1920.
Hecksher : The Continental System. New York, 1922.
Hertz, G. B. : The Manchester Politician, 1750–1912. London, 1912.
Holland, Bernard : The Fall of Protection, 1840–50. London, 1913.
Hovell, Mark : The Chartist Movement. Manchester, 1918.
Jenks, Leland, H. : The Migration of British Capital to 1875. New York, 1927.
Johnson, Arthur H. : The Disappearance of the Small Landowner. Oxford, 1909.
Kirkland, John : Three Centuries of Prices of Wheat, Flour and Bread.
Knowles, L. C. A. : The Industrial and Commercial Revolutions in Great Britain During the Nineteenth Century. London, 1921.
Lecky, W. E. H. : A History of England in the Eighteenth Century. Seven vols. London, 1919.
Levy, Hermann : Large and Small Holdings. Cambridge, 1911.
List, Friedrich : The National System of Political Economy. Translated by Sampson S. Lloyd. London, 1916.
Malthus, T. R. : On the Principles of Population. Everyman's Edition. Two vols. London.
Marks, Mary A. M. : The Corn Laws : A Popular History. London, 1908.
Marshall, Dorothy : The English Poor in the Eighteenth Century. London, 1926.
McCulloch, J. R. : Dictionary of Commerce. 1850 edition.
Melvin, F. E. : Napoleon's Navigation System. New York, 1919.
Meredith, H. O. : Outlines of the Economic History of England. London.

Moffit, Louis W. : England on the Eve of the Industrial Revolution. London, 1925.

Mongredien, Augustus : History of the Free Trade Movement in England. London, 1897.

Morley, John : The Life of Richard Cobden. London, 1903.

Morley, John : The Life of William Ewart Gladstone. Three vols. London, 1912.

Nicholson, J. S. : The History of the English Corn Laws. London, 1904.

Ogg, Frederic Austin : Economic Development of Modern Europe. New York, 1918.

Parker, Charles Stuart : Sir Robert Peel. Three vols. London, 1892–99.

Peel, Sir Robert : Memoirs. London, 1856.

The Political History of England.

 Vol. VIII, Lodge, 1660–1702. London, 1910.
 Vol. IX, Leadam, 1702–1760. London, 1909.
 Vol. X, Hunt, 1760–1801. London, 1905.
 Vol. XI, Brodrick and Fotheringham, 1801–1837. London, 1919.
 Vol. XII, Low and Sanders, 1837. London, 1913.

Porter, G. R. : The Progress of the Nation. London, 1851.

Prentice, Archibald : History of the Anti-Corn Law League. Two vols. London, 1853.

Ricardo, David : The Principles of Political Economy and Taxation. London, 1917. Everyman's Edition.

Slater, Gilbert : The Making of Modern England. London, 1913.

Slater, Gilbert : The English Peasantry and the Enclosure of Common Fields. London, 1907.

Smart, William : Economic Annals of the Nineteenth Century, 1801–30. London, vol. 1, 1910 ; vol. 2, 1917.

Smith, Adam : An Inquiry into the Nature and Causes of the Wealth of Nations. Two vols. Everyman's Edition. London, 1917.

Stirling, A. M. W. : Coke of Norfolk and His Friends. London, 1912.

Taylor, Charles H. : Decline of the Land-owning Farmers in England. Madison, Wis., 1904.

Tooke, Thomas : A History of Prices and of the State of the Circulation from 1793 to 1847. Four vols. London, 1838–1848.

Toynbee, Arnold : The Industrial Revolution of the Eighteenth Century in England. London, 1908.

Trevelyan, G. M. : Life of John Bright. 1925.

Usher, Abbott Payson : An Introduction to the Industrial History of England. London, 1921.

Veitch, Geo. S. : The Genesis of Parliamentary Reform. London, 1913.

Villiers, Rt. Hon. Charles Pelham : Free Trade Speeches. Two vols. London, 1883.

Walpole, Sir Spencer : A History of England from the Conclusion of the Great War in 1815. Six vols. London, 1913.

Webb, Sidney and Beatrice : The History of Trade Unionism, 1666–1920. London, 1920.

West, Julius : A History of the Chartist Movement. London, 1920.

Westerfield, Ray Bert. : Middlemen in English Business, particularly between 1660 and 1760. New Haven, 1915.

Wood, Sir Henry Trueman : Industrial England in the Middle of the Eighteenth Century. London, 1910.

INDEX

Aberdeen, Lord, 279, 282
Act of Union with Scotland in 1707
17, 24
Agricultural Protection Society, 258
Allison, Archibald, 283
Almack, John, jun., 255, 257, 258
Althorp, Lord, 231
Anderson, James, 80
Anti-Corn-Law League, The, 146, 185,
186, 216, 239, 240, 242, 243, 246, 247,
248, 249, 251, 253, 254, 255, 258, 259,
260, 261, 263, 264, 265, 266, 267, 269,
272, 275, 287, 288, 291, 292
Arbuthnot, 36
Assize of Bread, 2, 34, 35, 37, 77, 78,
83, 84, 96
Attwood, Thomas, 173, 203

Baldwin, Stanley, 292
Baring, Alexander, 135, 198, 207, 244,
258
Beer, M., 249
Benett, Mr., of Pyt House, 144
Bentinck, Lord George, 277, 280
Beveridge, Sir William, 12, 21
Bleeck, Mr., 144
Brand, Thomas, 159
Bright, John, 249, 254, 255, 256, 275
Broadhurst, J., 127
Brougham, Henry, 160, 171, 176
Brown, Philip A., 94
Buccleugh, Duke of, 276
Buckingham, Duke of, 252
Burdett, Sir Francis, 137, 138, 173, 258
Burke, Edmund, 42, 70, 79, 239
Burns, Robert, 69
Byron, Lord, 184

Campbell, John of Carbrook, 128
Campbell, John, 247, 255
Cannan, E., 165, 205
Canning, George, 126, 191, 193, 194,
196, 198, 199, 273
Carmichael, James, 227, 228
Castlereagh, Lord, 137, 138, 160, 164
(Londonderry), 171, 172, 173, 174,
176, 213 (Castlereagh)
Cavalier Parliament, 8
Cayley, E. S., 226, 227, 229
Chadwick, Edwin, 226
Chamberlain, Joseph, 291, 292
Chandos, Marquess of, 225
Charles I., 3, 4

Charles II., 16, 23, 212
Chartism, see Chartists
Chartists, 226, 240, 246, 247, 248, 249,
251, 261, 267, 288
Circular, The Anti-Corn Law to April
of 1841 and *The Anti-Bread Tax* to
1843, 242, 243, 246, 255, 256, 257,
259, 269
Clapham, J. H., 116
Clay, William, 234, 244
Cobbett, William, 90, 149, 208
Cobden, Richard, 186, 239, 245, 246,
249, 251, 252, 253, 254, 255, 256, 257,
260, 261, 262, 263, 264, 265, 266,
267, 268, 269, 270, 272, 273, 275,
278, 279, 280, 281, 283, 288, 290, 292
Coleridge, Samuel, 69
Colonial Preference, 58, 89, 139, 149,
252, 275
Comber, W. T., 11, 60
Continental System, 69, 86, 87, 88, 92,
117, 286
Corn :
Bounties on importation of, 43, 74,
78, 84
Export figures of, 15, 16, 109, see
Appendix C
Frauds to secure bounty on, 16, 26,
27
Government importation of, 76, 77
Import figures of, 109, 118, 119, 120,
162, 220, see Appendix C
Inaccurate returns on price of, 227,
228
Warehousing of, 43, 58, 139, 142, 198
Corn Acts, see Corn Laws
Corn Laws :
See Appendix A
Law of 1361, 3
Law of 1394, 3
Law of 1437, 3
Law of 1463, 4
Law of 1534, 3
Law of 1552, 2, 39
Law of 1555, 3, 9
Law of 1559, 3
Law of 1563, 3, 39
Law of 1571, 3
Law of 1593, 3
Law of 1604, 3
Law of 1624, 3
Law of 1627, 3
Law of 1656, 3
Law of 1660, 3, 10
Law of 1663, 3, 9, 16, 59, 285